D0462004

North Korea
p302

Seoul
p38

Gangwon-do
p118

Gyeonggi-do & Incheon
p92

Chungcheongbuk-do
p288

Chungcheongnam-do
p271

Gyeongsangbuk-do
p143

Jeollabuk-do
p258

Busan & Gyeongsangnam-do
p178

Jeollanam-do
p204

Jeju-do
p226

THIS EDITION WRITTEN AND RESEARCHED BY

Simon Richmond,
Timothy N Hornyak, Shawn Low

welcome to Korea

Yin & Yang

The blue and red circle at the heart of the South Korean flag neatly symbolises not only the divided Korean Peninsula, but also the fluid mix of ancient and modern aspects of the country officially called the Republic of Korea (ROK), where the vast majority of visitors to this part of the world will spend their time. South Korea is a dream destination for the traveller, an engaging, welcoming place where the benefits of a fully industrialised, high-tech nation are balanced alongside a reverence for tradition and the ways of old Asia.

Ancient & Modern

Academics still quibble over whether the Land of the Morning Calm (a term coined by travel writer Percival Lowell in 1885) is an accurate translation of the old Chinese characters by which all of Korea was once known. Dive into Seoul, the powerhouse of Asia's third-largest economy, and calm is the last thing you'll feel. This round-the-clock city is constantly on the move, its 'work hard, play hard' population the epitome of the nation's indefatigable, can-do spirit. Founded on centuries of tradition that manifest in the daily pageantry of the changing of the guard at meticulously reconstructed palaces, or in the chants of a shaman on a hillside, Seoul is nonetheless

Split by a fearsome border, the Korean Peninsula offers the traveller a dazzling range of experiences, beguiling landscapes and 5000 years of culture and history.

(left) Cityscape, Gangnam, Seoul (p82)
(below) Gyeongbokgung Palace, Seoul (p39)

a contemporary urban marvel. You can hardly turn a corner without stumbling across a tourist information booth, a subway station or a taxi that will smooth the way to your next discovery in this multifaceted metropolis.

Contemplation & Celebration

South Korea's compact size and superb transport infrastructure mean that tranquillity is achievable within an hour of the urban sprawl. Hike to the peaks of craggy mountains enclosed by densely forested national parks. Get further off the beaten path than you thought possible by sailing to remote islands, where farming and fishing folk welcome you into their homes and simple seafood cafes. Sample the serenity of a Buddhist temple retreat where the honk of traffic is replaced by the rhythmic pre-dawn chants of shaven-headed monks. If all this sounds a little too peaceful for your travel tastes, rest assured the ROK also knows how to rock. A countrywide itinerary of lively festivals and events means there's almost always a celebration of some sort to attend, and friendly Koreans are happy to share their culture with visitors, regardless of language barriers. If nothing else, your tastebuds will be tingling at the discovery of one of Asia's least known, but most delicious, cuisines.

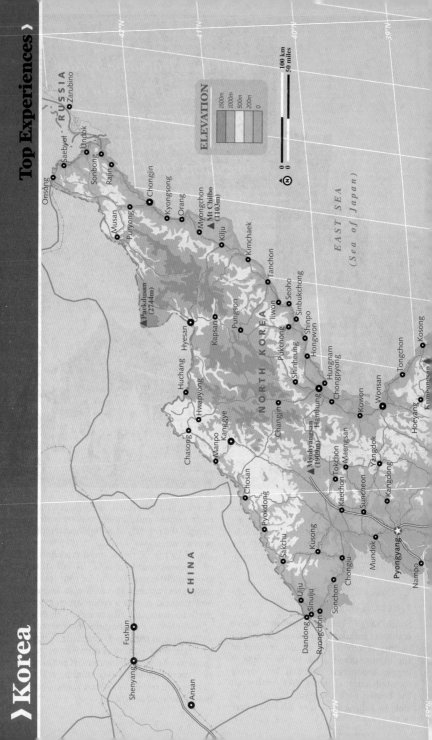

Pyeongchang
Skiing at Alpensia and
Yongpyong resorts (p137)

Sobaeksan National Park
Do a Templestay at
Guin-sa (p300)

Hahoe Folk Village
Charming village of
traditional houses (p175)

Gyeongju
Grand remains of
Bulguk-sa temple (p158)

Busan
Seafood, beaches
and cinemas (p180)

Jeju-do
Natural wonders,
splendid hiking (p226)

The DMZ
Feel the chill of
the Cold War (p93)

Seoul
Historic and contemporary
nonstop metropolis (p38)

Suwon
Walk around
Hwaseong Fortress (p99)

Boryeong
Get dirty at the
mud festival (p285)

Jeonju
Untouched-by-time
hanok village (p260)

JEJU-DO

Jeju-si
Hallim
Hallasan (1950m)
Jungmun
Seogwipo
Hallasan National Park

0   40 km
0   20 miles

Jeju-do

Honshu

Dokdo
Ulleungdo

Sokcho
Pyeongchang
Donghae
Samcheok
Uljin
Yeongdeok
Pohang
Gyeongju
Ulsan
BUSAN

Alpensia
GANGWON-DO
Seoraksan (1708m)
Chuncheon
Hongcheon
Pyeong Lake
Chiaksan (1288m)
Jecheon
Wonju
Sobaeksan (1439m)
Songnisan (1058m)
Huwangsan (721m)
Andong
Hahoe Folk Village
Yeongju
Gimcheon
Deogyusan Yeongcheon
GYEONGSANGBUK-DO

Chungju Lake
CHUNGCHEONGBUK-DO
Cheongju
Gongju
Daejeon
Daegu
Gyeongsan
Geoje
Tongyeong

Cheorwon
Kumchon
Cheongwon
Janggok
Dongducheon
Hwevri
SEOUL
Suwon
Cheonan
CHUNGCHEONGNAM-DO

Panmunjeom
HWANGHAENAM-DO
Kaesong
Ganghwado
Incheon
Incheon International Airport
Anmyeondo
Daecheon Beach
Boryeong
Seocheon
Gunsan
JEOLLABUK-DO
Jeonju
Namwon
Naejangsan (763m)
Jirisan (1915m)
JEOLLANAM-DO
Suncheon
Samcheonpo
Masan
Jinju
Yeosu

Changyon
Haeju
Ongjin
Ryongyon

Taean Haean Maritime National Park

WEST SEA
(Yellow Sea)

Mokpo
Boseong
Gwangju
Gohreung
Dolsando
Yeocheon

Jangheung
Haenam
Wando
Yeondo
Oenarodo
Dodohae Haesang National Park
Geomundo
Cheongsando

Hongdo
Heuksando
Dadohae Haesang National Park
Hajodo
Jindo
Bogildo
Wando

To Jeju-do
(See Enlargement)

Hallyeohaesang National Park

SOUTH SEA
(East China Sea)

JAPAN

Tsushima

SOUTH KOREA

124°E   125°E   126°E   127°E   128°E   129°E   130°E   131°E   132°E

34°N   35°N   36°N   37°N   38°N

13 TOP
EXPERIENCES

Changdeokgung

1 The 'Palace of Illustrious Virtue' (p44) was built in the early 15th century as a secondary palace to Gyeongbukgung; these days this Unesco World Heritage–listed property exceeds Gyeongbukgung in beauty and grace – partly because so many of its buildings were actually lived in by members of royal family well into the 20th century. The most charming section is the Huwon, a 'secret garden' that is a royal horticultural idyll. Book well ahead to snag one of the limited tickets to view this special palace on the moonlight tours held during full-moon nights in the warm months.

Hiking around Jeju-do

2 The frequently dramatic volcanic landscape of Jeju-do, the largest of South Korea's many islands, is best seen on foot. Climbing to the summit of Hallasan (p254), the country's highest peak, is very achievable and, in good weather, provides spectacular views. The Jeju Olle Trail (see boxed text, p244) is a network of 26 half- to one-day hiking routes that meander around the island's coast, part of the hinterland and three other islands. Spending a day following all or part of a trail is a wonderful way to soak up Jeju's unique charms and beautiful surroundings. Hallasan National Park

Boryeong Mud Festival

3 Every July, thousands of people converge upon the unsuspecting (but fully welcoming) town of Boryeong and proceed to jump into gigantic vats of mud. Welcome to the Boryeong Mud Festival (see boxed text, p285). The official line is that the local mud has restorative properties but one look around and it's clear that no one really cares for much except having a slippery sloshin' messy good time. Mud aside, this foreigner-friendly and very high-profile festival also features concerts, raves and fireworks. A tip: don't wear anything you want to keep!

Suwon's Hwaseong Fortress

4 Built as an act of filial devotion and heavily damaged during the early-20th-century colonisation period and then the Korean War, the restoration of this Unesco World Heritage Site (p99) began in the 1970s and is now almost finished. A detailed 1801 record of its construction has allowed the 5.52km-long wall and the Hwaseong Haenggung (a palace for the king to stay in during his visits to Suwon) to be rebuilt with great historical accuracy. A walk around the wall takes you through four grand gates. Fortress observation tower

Cheong-gye-cheon

5 A raised highway was demolished and the dug up ground revealed this long-buried stream (p46). The effort has transformed Seoul's centre, creating a riverside park and walking course that provides a calm respite from the surrounding commercial hubbub. Public art is dotted along the banks of the stream and many events are held here, including a spectacular lantern festival in November, when thousands of giant glowing paper and paint sculptures are floated in the water. There's also a good museum where you can learn about the history of the Cheon-gye-cheon.

Skiing in Pyeongchang County

6 They say the third time's a charm, and so Pyeongchang (p137) won with its third bid to host the Winter Olympics. In 2018 the Games will be held at the Alpensia and Yongpyong ski resorts, as well as the Gang-neung coastal area. Located near each other, Alpensia and Yongpyong have dozens of runs, including slopes for families and beginners, views of the East Sea (Sea of Japan) on clear days, as well as some spanking-new accommodation and leisure facilities. Yongpyong Ski Resort

Jeonju Hanok Maeul

7 Jeonju's version of a traditional village (p260) is arguably more impressive than Seoul's. The slate-roof houses are home to traditional arts: artisans craft fans, hand-make paper and brew *soju* (local vodka). Foodies will be pleased that the birthplace of *bibimbap* (rice, egg, meat and vegies with chilli sauce) offers the definitive version of this dish. If you decide to stay (and you will), you'll find plenty of traditional guesthouses, where visitors sleep on a *yo* (padded quilt) in an *ondol* (underfloor heating) room. In keeping with the theme, there's even one run by the grandson of King Gojong.

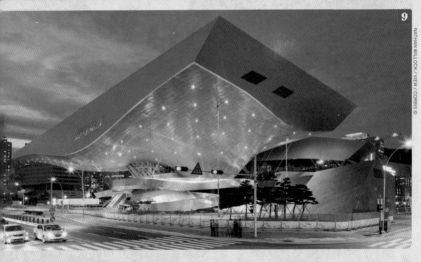

Gwangjang Market

8 During the day it's a known as a place for trading in second-hand clothes and fabrics. But it's by night that Gwangjang (p77) really comes into its own, when some of the market's alleys fill up with vendors selling all manner of street eats. Stewed pigs' trotters and snouts, *gimbap* (rice, vegies and Spam wrapped in rice and rolled in sheets of seaweed) and *bindaettok* (plate-sized crispy pancakes of crushed mung beans and vegies fried on a skillet), are all washed down with copious amounts of *magkeolli* and *soju* (local liquors).

Busan

9 Busan (p180) has everything you could love without Seoul's insane congestion. Mountains, beaches, street food and seafood galore make this one of the most underrated cities in the region. If you like your squid wriggling fresh and your *soju* (local vodka) served up in a tent bar, Busan should be top of your list. The region-leading Busan International Film Festival has a new centrepiece in the Busan Cinema Centre (p190), an architecturally dazzling structure with the biggest screen in the country. It's another example of this southern port's take-no-prisoners pluck. Busan Cinema Centre

Bulguk-sa

10 It's hard to choose just one stand-out treasure in and around magnificent Gyeongju, but this Unesco World Cultural Heritage site (p158) is most likely to take the honour, not least as it contains no fewer than seven Korean 'national treasures' within its walls. The high point of the so-called golden age of Shilla architecture, this incredibly sophisticated yet wonderfully subtle temple complex is a monument to the skill of its carpenters, painters, craftsmen and architects, with its internal pagodas, its external bridges and the gorgeous, undulating scenery surrounding it.

Hahoe Folk Village

11 The closest thing Korea has to a time machine, the charming Hahoe Folk Village (p175), some way from Andong, is a truly wonderful experience for anyone wanting to get a sense of how Korea looked, felt, sounded and smelled before the 20th century rolled over it and changed the country forever. Over two hundred people continue to live here, maintaining traditional ways and customs, and even inviting people to spend the night in their *minbak* (private homes with rooms for rent). For a slice of old Korea, Hahoe should be at the top of your list.

이 곳은 내 땅이오니 출입을 삼가 하십시오

Templestay at Guin-sa

12 A bell rings and you wake at 3.30am to prepare for a morning meditation session. Breakfast is an austere meal, taken in silence so you can contemplate the ache in your bones from bowing 108 times in front of a Buddha image. Later, you'll have more meditation time to contemplate the surrender of your body and mind in the search for inner peace. A Templestay is the perfect antidote to fast-paced modern Korea. While the country is awash with temples, the impressive complex of Guin-sa (p300) is perfect in how it seques-ters you in the fortress-like compound. For more information on Templestays, see p386.

The DMZ

13 It's known as the Demilitarized Zone (DMZ; p93). But this 4km-wide, 250km-long heavily mined and guarded buffer, splitting a hostile North from South Korea, is anything but. An enduring Cold War symbol, the border has become a surreal tourist draw. The tension is most palpable in the Joint Security Area (JSA), the neutral area built after the 1953 Armistice for the holding of peace talks, which can only be visited on an organised tour. Seven observations points along the DMZ allow visitors to peer into the secretive North. United Nations buildings, DMZ

need to know

Currency
» Korean won (₩)

Language
» Korean, English

When to Go

Warm to Hot Summers,
Cold Winters

Warm to Hot Summers,
Mild Winters

Pyongyang
GO Apr–Jun
GO Sep–Oct

Seoul
GO Oct–Jun

Cheongju
GO Oct–Jun

Busan
GO Oct–Jun

Jeju-si
GO Year-round

High Season
(Jun–Sep)

» Be prepared for sweltering heat and a very heavy rainy season through July across the peninsula.

Shoulder
(May, Oct)

» Late spring and early autumn see the country bathed in the fresh greenery or russet shades of the seasons.

Low Season
(Nov–Apr)

» Snow falls and temperatures plummet. Best time for skiing and visiting museums and galleries.

Your Daily Budget

Budget less than ₩100,000

» Dorm bed: ₩20,000

» Street food: ₩1000–5000

» Hiking: free

» Entry to National Museum of Korea: free

» Subway ticket: ₩1150

Midrange ₩100,000–300,000

» *Hanok* guesthouse: ₩70,000

» Entry to Gyeongbokgung (Palace of Shining Happiness): ₩3000

» Barbecued beef meal: ₩40,000

» Theatre ticket: ₩40,000

Top End over ₩300,000

» High-end hotel: ₩200,000

» Royal Korean banquet: ₩70,000

» Scrub and massage at a *jjimjil-bang* (luxury sauna): ₩60,000

» DMZ tour: ₩100,000

Money

» ATMs widely available in South Korea; credit cards accepted at most businesses, but some smaller food places and markets are cash-only.

Visas

» Australian, British, US and most Western European citizens receive a 90-day entry permit on arrival in South Korea; see p391. (For visas to North Korea, see p330.)

Mobile Phones

» South Korea uses the CDMA digital standard; check compatibility with your provider. Mobile phones can be hired at international airports and elsewhere.

Transport

» Trains, buses, ferries and flights service mainland urban centres and the islands scattered around the peninsula. Hiring a car is recommended for touring rural areas.

Websites

» **Lonely Planet** (www .lonelyplanet.com/ south-korea) Best for pre-planning.

» **Korea Tourism Organization** (KTO; www.visitkorea.or.kr) Official government-run site.

» **Korea4Expats** (www.korea4expat .com) Covers many aspects of Korean life.

» **Korea.net** (www .korea.net) A treasure trove of background detail on the ROK.

» **Galbijim** (http:// wiki.galbijim.com) Info on a whole range of Korean topics.

Exchange Rates

Australia	A$1	₩1179
Canada	C$1	₩1148
Europe	€1	₩1420
Japan	¥100	₩1447
UK	UK£1	₩1795
US	US$1	₩1137

For current exchange rates see www.xe.com.

Important Numbers

South Korea country code	☑82
International access code	☑001
Ambulance & Fire	☑119
Police	☑112
Tourist information (English-speaking)	☑1330

Arriving

» **Incheon Airport**
Express train – ₩13,800; 43 minutes to Seoul
Commuter train – ₩3850; 53 minutes
Bus – ₩10,000; one hour
Taxi – around ₩65,000; one hour

» **Gimpo Airport**
Express train – ₩1300; 15 minutes to Seoul
Subway – ₩1250; 35 minutes
Bus – ₩5000-₩7000; 40 minutes to one hour
Taxi – around ₩35,000; 40 minutes to one hour

» **Gimhae Airport**
Limo bus – ₩6000; one hour to Busan
Bus – ₩1400; one hour
Taxi – around ₩20,000; one hour

Advance Planning

In general, a trip to South Korea doesn't require much pre-planning. However, if you are travelling over any of the country's major holidays, you should book all internal transport well ahead of time.

Think about booking ahead if you wish to stay at a *hanok* (traditional house), as these have only three or four guestrooms in total. Top-end international chain hotels can also fill up when conferences are in town.

Hiking on the weekend can be a madhouse – schedule your hikes on a weekday instead. The same goes for skiing trips in the winter.

Call a few days ahead for the best seats at cultural events, and book the USO tour to the DMZ (p93) as soon as you can, as these fill up.

first time

Everyone needs a helping hand when they visit a country for the first time. There are phrases to learn, customs to get used to and etiquette to understand. The following section will help demystify Korea, so your first trip goes as smoothly as your fifth.

Language

Korean is the common language. It's relatively easy to find English speakers in the big cities, but not so easy in smaller towns and the countryside. Learning the writing system, *hangeul*, and a few key phrases will help you enormously in being able to decode street signs, menus and timetables. For more on language, see p398.

Booking Ahead

In general you don't need to worry about where to stay – hotels and motels are so numerous that there is usually little need to book ahead. However, if you want to stay in a *hanok* guesthouse, which often only have a few rooms, advance booking is advised.

Hello.	안녕하세요.	an·nyŏng ha·se·yo
I would like to book a room.	방 예약하려고 하는데요.	pang ye·ya·k'a·ryŏ go ha·nŭn·de·yo
My name is...	제 이름은 ...입니다.	che i·rŭ·mŭn ...·im·ni·da
How much is it per ...?	...에 얼마예요?	...·é ŏl·ma·ye·yo
night	하룻밤	ha·rup·pam
person	한 명	han·myŏng
Thank you (very much).	(정말) 고맙습니다.	(chŏng·mal) ko·map·sŭm·ni·da

What to Wear

The vast majority of Koreans wear Western-style dress these days, although you'll sometimes see people in *hanbok* (Korean clothing). The best version of this type of clothing – in fine silks and organza – are usually worn by women, and sometimes men, for formal occasions. More casual pyjama-style *hanbok* are made from cotton and are very comfortable for everyday wear.

For business, Koreans are quite formal and wear suits and ties. Out on the hiking trails or golf courses you'll see locals kitted out in the latest high-tech performance gear as if they were about to scale Everest or compete in the Masters.

What to Pack

» Passport
» Credit card
» Phrasebook or mini dictionary
» Slip-on shoes
» Travel plug
» Insect repellent
» CDMA enabled phone
» Painkillers (or other hangover cure)
» Padlock
» Medical kit
» Sunscreen
» Penknife
» Torch (flashlight)
» Earplugs
» Eye mask
» Inflatable pillow

Checklist

» Check the validity of your passport

» If you plan to hire a car, bring a current International Driving Permit

» Check airline baggage restrictions

» Check government travel websites (see boxed text, p390)

» Call banks and credit card providers and tell them your travel dates

» Organise travel insurance (see p388)

» Book DMZ trip with USO (see p93)

Etiquette

There are several social rules that Koreans stick to, although they will generally be relaxed about foreigners doing likewise. Follow these tips to avoid faux pas:

» Meetings & Greetings
A quick, short bow is most respectful for meetings and departures. Give or receive any object using both hands – especially name cards (an essential feature of doing business in Korea), money and gifts.

» Shoes
Remove your shoes on entering a Korean home, guesthouse, temple or Korean-style restaurant.

» Eating & Drinking
Pour drinks for others and use both hands when pouring or receiving. Use chopsticks or a spoon to touch food and don't leave either sticking up in a bowl of rice.

» Loss of Face
A mishandled remark or potentially awkward scene should be smoothed over as soon as possible, and if you sense someone actively trying to change the subject, go with the flow. An argument or any situation that could lead to embarrassment should be avoided at all costs.

Tipping

» **When to Tip**
Generally not expected.

» **Restaurants**
No need to tip; only top-end hotel restaurants will add a service charge.

» **Guides**
Not expected; a small gift will be appreciated, though.

» **Taxis**
No need to tip; fares are metered or agreed before you get in.

» **Hotels**
Only in the most luxurious need you tip bellboys etc, and only if service is good.

Money

ATMs are common across South Korea but only ones marked with a 'Global' sign will work with internationally issued cards. Some ATMS have low daily withdrawal limits (under ₩500,000) and very few are open 24 hours; banks typically open from 7am to 11pm.

If you are going to rely on ATMs, make certain you have a few days' supply of cash at hand in case you can't find a machine that accepts your card. Also, inform your bank or credit card provider of the dates you will be travelling in Korea and using your card to avoid the card's use possibly being blocked.

Credit cards are widely accepted, but in places such as country towns and markets, it's cash only.

if you like...

Traditional Architecture

Ornate Buddhist temples and royal palaces hold some of Korea's most impressive traditional architecture. Also see how ordinary folk lived in more modest, but architecturally pleasing, *hanok*.

Changdeokgung The most attractive of Seoul's palaces, this World Heritage–listed site also has a 'secret garden' (p44)

Bukchon Hanok Village Around 900 *hanok* make this Seoul's largest neighbourhood of traditional homes (p45)

Seokbul-sa Hidden in the mountains of Busan, this temple perches daintily among enormous clifflike boulders (p180)

Jeonju Hanok Maeul Jeonju's sprawling *hanok* village is a charming nod to Korea's low-slung architectural style (p260)

Seongeup Folk Village Step back in time in this walled village of thatched-roofed, stone homes on Jeju-do (p244)

Hahoe Folk Village People still live in the rustic homes of this beautiful riverside village complex (p175)

Haein-sa This World Heritage–listed religious complex is home to the Tripitaka Koreana: 81,258 wooden printing blocks containing Buddhist scriptures (p152)

Crafts & Shopping

Markets and mega malls abound across the country, as do places producing attractive handicrafts such as pottery and *hanji* (handmade paper).

Myeong-dong The dazzling neon, the barking street vendors, the sales, the fashions, the K-Pop dance routines – Seoul's premier shopping area is not to be missed (p85)

Shinsegae Centum City Break out your plastic and shop till you drop in Busan at the world's largest department store (p191)

Incheon Ceramic Village See traditional kilns and buy beautiful pots directly from their makers (p104)

Gangjin Celadon Museum Before you buy, you can watch celadon (green-glazed pottery) being crafted and kiln-fired here (p217)

Daegu's Herbal Medicine Market A this fascinating market you can stock up on anything from cheap ginseng to reindeer horns (p145)

Damyang The town is famed for its bamboo products and holds a bamboo crafts festival in May (p210)

Outdoor Activities

Hiking, skiing, cycling, rafting: name the activity and you'll find battalions of Koreans fully kitted out and crazy for it.

Jeju Olle Trail Discover the byways of Jeju-do on this excellent series of hiking routes around the volcanic island (p244)

Cycle along the Han River Hire a bike to pedal the cycle lanes linking up the parks strung along Seoul's major waterway (p28)

Wolchulsan National Park Hike through Korea's smallest national park over a vertigo-inducing 52m-high bridge spanning two ridges (p220)

Seogwipo Korea's best scuba-diving destination, with colourful corals, kelp forests and dolphins (p245)

Chuncheon Cycle, swim, water-ski or row around the tiny island of Jung-do in Uiam Lake (p121)

Muju Check out the Korean ski season at this resort in Deogyusan National Park (p265)

Seoul Fortress Wall Hike beside these ancient walls as they snake over the capital's four guardian mountains (p55)

» Shopping strip, Myeong-dong, Seoul (p85)

World Heritage Sites

South Korea has nine cultural properties and one natural property inscribed on the Unesco World Heritage list (http://whc.Unesco.org/en/stateparties/kr).

Jongmyo The royal ancestral shrine set in peaceful wooded grounds is just one of several World Heritage sites in Seoul (p45)

Hwaseong Suwon's impressive fortress walls have been meticulously reconstructed with great historical accuracy (p99)

Gochang Thousands of bronze-age tombs known as dolmen dot the hills around this small village (p268)

Gyeongju 'The museum without walls' is sprinkled with outstanding examples of Korean Buddhist art in the form of sculptures, reliefs, pagodas and the remains of temples and palaces (p154)

Jeju-do The dormant volcanos Hallasan and Seongsan Ilchulbong and a network of lava-tube caves, including Manjanggul, are all World Heritage worthy (p226)

Seokguram Grotto A superb mid-8th-century stone Buddha resides in the mountains above the temple Bulguk-sa (p159)

Unique Festivals

See p21 for the top five festivals and events in Korea not to miss. Other ones to mark on your travel calendar:

Incheon Bupyeong Pungmul Festival Catch Korean folk music and dance in the historic port (p107)

Chungju World Martial Arts Festival This martial arts bash includes breakdancing and live music (p296)

Dano Festival Connect with your spiritual side at this week-long celebration of shamanistic traditions (p132)

North Korea National Holidays Coordinate your trip to DPRK with a national holiday, as these are taken very seriously, with large and exciting military parades in Pyongyang (p332)

Andong Mask Dance Festival Head to Andong to experience this traditional arts and crafts jamboree (p173)

Taebaeksan Snow Festival Marvel at giant ice sculptures, enjoy sledding and dine inside igloo restaurants at this winter celebration (p141)

Museums & Galleries

South Korea proudly displays its heritage in a vast range of museums across the country, while the fruits of its thriving and creative contemporary art scene can be viewed in hundreds of public and commercial galleries, particularly in Seoul.

National Museum of Korea Packed with national treasures spanning the centuries (p51)

Leeum Samsung Museum of Art Three top architect-designed buildings and a dazzling collection of art from ancient to contemporary (p52)

National Museum of Contemporary Art Make the trek out to Seoul Grand Park to see this classy art museum (p101)

Gwangju Art Museum One of the sites of the popular avant-garde Gwangju Biennale (p206)

Gyeongju National Museum Houses a superb collection of artifacts from the Shilla dynasty and beyond (p155)

Daegu National Museum A refit in 2010 has made this one of Korea's best regional museums (p145)

If you like... spiritual serenity, book an overnight Templestay in one of Korea's many beautiful Buddhist monasteries (p386)

Culinary Experiences

It's not all about *kimchi*! Let your appetite lead you on a merry banquet around Korea and you'll be astounded and sated by the range of culinary offerings, much of it unfamiliar outside of the country.

Namdo Food Festival Tuck into hundreds of different dishes in the fortress-walled Nagan Folk Village (p213)

Busan Sink your teeth into a twitching squid tentacle at Jagalchi fish market (p187), or snack on the nether parts of a chicken in tent bars (p191)

Jeonju Eat *bibimbap*, Korea's most famous culinary export (after *kimchi* of course), at its birthplace (p262)

Boseong The curvaceous rows of tea plants are photogenic but don't forget to try the green-tea ice cream, green-tea noodles and green-tea biscuits here (p216)

Jungmun Resort Sample raw horsemeat at Jeju Mawon, a restaurant in a mock-up of a Joseon Palace (p254)

Chuncheon Famous for its spicy chicken dish *dakgalbi* (p123)

Quirky Encounters

There's no shortage of weird and wonderful things to do and see in South Korea, and when it comes to the bizarre little can compare to North Korea – in short, a trip to the Korean Peninsula can keep you in dinner party stories for life.

Steaming at a jjimjil-bang Strip down for a communal sweat, steam and full body scrub; Seoul's Dragon Hill Spa & Resort is a good one (p58)

Chamsori Gramophone & Edison Museum If you love music and the spirit of invention, don't miss this astounding collection of vintage machines (p132)

Cheorwon March along a North Korean infiltration tunnel under the DMZ and peer into North Korea from the most northern point on the border (p122, p126)

Haesindang Park Admire phallic sculptures in this park in the fishing village of Sinnam (p141)

Sex Museums Gain a very adult education at Jeju-do's trio of nookie-obsessed exhibitions (p248)

Kumsusan Sun Memorial Palace Pay your respects to the embalmed body of Great Leader Kim Il-sung in his former palace (p307)

Scenic Spots

The mountainous Korean Peninsula provides an abundance of ravishing vistas and natural beauty spots. Urban centres have their charms too, but for real serenity head to one of the hundreds of islands.

Namhaedo You'll blink several times and think you've been transported to southern France on this gorgeous island (p199)

Suncheon Bay The bay's rich mud beneath the rustling reeds attracts migratory birds and, in turn, scores of tourists (p212)

Paekdusan A better reason than most to visit the DPRK is this stunningly beautiful and fabled mountain (p319)

Ulleungdo This East Sea island offers mist-shrouded volcanic cliffs, traditional harbour towns and a breathtaking jagged coastline (p168)

Udo Admire the tuff cone volcano Seongsan Ilchulbong from the white coral-sand beach on this lovely island (p241)

Namsan & N Seoul Tower Watch Seoul's nightlights twinkle from the summit of this city-centre mountain (p47)

month by month

Top Events

1 **Yeon Deung Ho (Lotus Lantern Festival)**, May

2 **Jongmyo Daeje**, May

3 **Boryeong Mud Festival**, July

4 **Busan International Film Festival**, September/October

5 **Gwangju Biennale** September to November

January

Come prepared for freezing temperatures and snow across much of the country, particularly in the mountains.

Taebaeksan Snow Festival

Marvel at giant ice sculptures, enjoy sledding fun and dine inside igloo restaurants at this winter celebration in Taebaeksan Provincial Park (p141; http://festival.taebaek.go.kr/part11/home/html/snow.html).

February

Local religious holidays and festivals follow the lunar calendar, while the rest follow the Gregorian (Western) calendar. Therefore, sometimes Seollal will occur in January.

Seollal (Lunar New Year)

Major cities empty out as residents make the trip to visit relatives, honour ancestors and eat traditional foods over this three-day national festival. There are a number of events for travellers in Seoul during this time, held at the major palaces as well as the Korean Folk Village, Namsangol Hanok Village and the National Folk Museum of Korea. For more information visit www.visitseoul.net or www.visitkorea.or.kr. In 2013, Seollal begins 12 February, in 2014 on 31 January and in 2015 on 19 February.

April

It can still be cold and wet in the spring, so it's good to come prepared. Early April is generally when areas of Korea turn pink in a transient flurry of delicate cherry blossoms.

Hangang Yeouido Spring Flower Festival

One of the best places to experience the blossoming springtime trees and flowers is Yeouido. Other good spots include Namsan and Ewha Womens University and Jeongdok Public Library in Samcheong-dong. For more details about the Yeouido event see http://tour.ydp.go.kr.

World Ceramics Biennale

Running into May (and sometimes scheduled for September and October), this bash for people potty about pottery is held in odd-numbered years in Incheon (p103; www.kocef.org).

May

One of the most pleasant months in which to visit Korea, with good weather and less problems finding accommodation than in the busy summer months.

Jongmyo Daeje

Held on the first Sunday of the month, this ceremony honours Korea's royal ancestors and involves a solemn, costumed parade from Gyeongbokgung through downtown Seoul to the royal shrine at Jongmyo, where spectators can enjoy traditional music and an elaborate, all-day ritual. For details see www.jongmyo.net/english_index.asp.

Yeon Deung Ho (Lotus Lantern Festival)

Seoul's Buddhist temples, such as Jogye-sa and Bongeun-sa, are the focus of this celebration of the Buddha's birthday. The weekend preceding the birthday, Seoul celebrates with a huge daytime street festival and evening lantern parade – the largest in South Korea; see www.llf.or.kr for details.

★★ Buddha's Birthday

Brings a kaleidoscope of light and colour, as rows of delicate paper lanterns are strung down the main thoroughfares and in temple courtyards and lit at dusk (celebrated on 17 May in 2013, 6 May in 2014 and 25 May in 2015).

☆ Chuncheon International Mime Festival

The lakeside city hosts street performers, magicians, acrobats and quirky shows such as a soap-bubble opera (p120; www.mimefestival.com).

★★ Dano Festival

Held according to the lunar calendar, this traditional festival features shamanist rituals, mask dances and market stalls (p132; www.gntour.go.kr/eng/sub.jsp?Mcode=404).

July

It can rain – a lot – during this month, so make sure you have appropriate gear and arrange your travel plans accordingly.

🏃 Boryeong Mud Festival

Head to Daecheon Beach to wallow in mud pools and take part in stacks of muddy fun and games (p285; www.boryeongmudfest.com).

September

The end of summer is the busiest time for events and festivals. Book ahead for transport around Chuseok when many Koreans are on the move visiting family and friends.

★★ Chuseok

The Harvest Moon Festival is a major three-day holiday when families gather, eat crescent-shaped rice cakes (get it?) and visit their ancestors' graves to make offerings of food and drink and perform *sebae* (a ritual bow). Begins 19 September in 2013, 8 September in 2014 and 27 September in 2015.

★★ Gwangju Biennale

Held from this month until November in even-numbered years, Korea's leading international art show is a two-month carnival of the avant-garde (p208; http://gb.or.kr/?mid=main_eng).

☆ Mask Dance Festival

This 10-day festival in Andong brings together more than 20 traditional dance troupes (p173; www.maskdance.com).

🏃 Chungju World Martial Arts Festival

Held in the World Martial Arts Park, where you'll see all sorts of unusual martial arts with teams participating from across the world (p296; www.martialarts.or.kr).

★★ Korea International Art Fair

One of the region's top art fairs and a good opportunity to get a jump on the country's hot new artists (p63; www.kiaf.org).

October

Autumn is a great time to visit, particularly if you like hiking as this is the season when the mountains run through a palate of rustic colours.

☆ Busan International Film Festival

Korea's top international film festival attracts stars from across Asia and beyond (p185; www.biff.kr).

★★ Seoul International Fireworks Festival

Best viewed from Yeouido Hangang Park, this festival sees dazzling firework displays staged by both Korean and international teams (www.bulnori.com).

★★ Baekje Cultural Festival

This major festival, packed with events, is held in Buyeo in even-numbered years and in Gongju in odd-numbered years (p279; www.baekje.org/html/en/under/under_06.html)

🍴 Gwangju World Kimchi Culture Festival

Join the celebrations for Korea's most famous contribution to the culinary arts (p208; http://kimchi.gwangju.go.kr).

itineraries

Whether you've got a week or a month, these itineraries provide a starting point for the trip of a lifetime. Want more inspiration? Head online to lonelyplanet.com /thorntree to chat with other travellers.

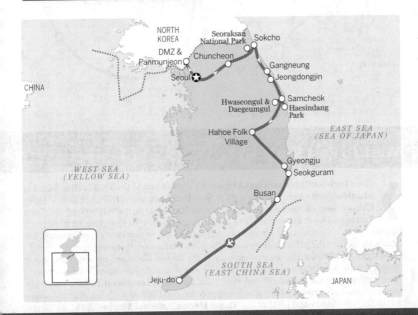

Two weeks
South Korea's Highlights

> Set aside four or five days for **Seoul**, including a day trip north to the **DMZ**. Next head east to **Chuncheon**, where you can cycle around the lake and sample the town's famous chicken dish, *dakgalbi*.

Dine on fresh seafood in **Sokcho**, then hike around the stunning peaks and waterfalls of **Seoraksan National Park**. Follow the coast south to **Gangneung** to view well-preserved Joseon-era buildings, quirky museums and a tiny North Korean spy submarine at Unification Park in **Jeongdongjin**. From **Samcheok** explore the huge caves **Hwanseongul** and **Daegeumgul**, as well as **Haesindang Park**, packed with phallic sculptures.

Travel back to feudal times at **Hahoe Folk Village**. Continue delving into Korea's past at **Gyeongju**, ancient capital of the Shilla kingdom, where you can spend a couple of days exploring royal tombs, the excellent museum and the World Heritage–listed grotto at **Seokguram**.

The dramatically located port of **Busan** with its beaches, fish market and urban buzz is worth a few days. From here you can fly to **Jeju-do**, a beautiful island with amazing volcanic scenery best enjoyed on leisurely hikes.

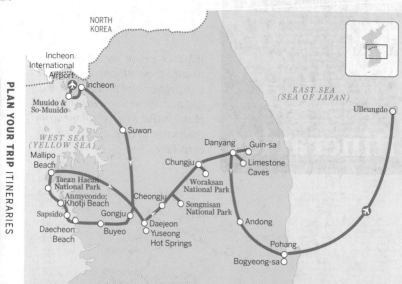

Two weeks
West To East Sea

From **Incheon International Airport** it's a quick hop to the small, idyllic island of **Muuido**, from where you can walk to **So-Muuido** or relax on lovely beaches. Enjoy Chinese food in the historic Chinatown of **Incheon**, then stroll around the Open Port area. Direct buses from here mean there's no need to head into Seoul to reach **Suwon**, where you can stride around the ramparts of the meticulously reconstructed fortress wall, explore the palace and tuck into the town's famous *galbi* (beef ribs).

Gongju and **Buyeo**, the ancient capitals of the Baekje kingdom, are your next stops; hillside tombs, a fortress and museum will give you an insight into Korea's oldest dynasty. After enjoying the sand, seafood and mud skincare spa of **Daecheon Beach**, sail to the serene island of **Sapsido**, where you can spend the night before ferry-hopping through a few of the 130 islands and islets of the **Taean Haean National Marine Park**; the largest island is **Anmyeondo**, where you can continue working on your tan at either **Khotji Beach** or **Mallipo Beach**.

Travel inland to **Daejeon**, where you can soak at **Yuseong Hot Springs**. From here make your way to **Cheongju**, learn about the world's oldest printed book, then move on to **Songnisan National Park**, covering central Korea's finest scenic area and home to a 33m-tall gold-plated Buddha statue.

Chungju, home of the World Martial Arts Festival, is the gateway to the lovely **Woraksan National Park** and for a two-hour scenic ferry trip across Chungju Lake to sleepy **Danyang**, small-town Korea at its most charming. From here explore nearby **limestone caves** and the stately temple complex of **Guin-sa** within Sobaeksan National Park.

Use **Andong** as a base for exploring the surrounding area packed with attractive river and lakeside villages; it's also famous for its *soju* (Korean-style vodka). It's only a couple of hours by bus from here to **Pohang**, where you should ignore the steelworks and focus instead on the temple **Bogyeong-sa** in a gorgeous valley with 12 waterfalls. Afterwards board the ferry to **Ulleungdo** – a sparsely inhabited, ruggedly beautiful volcanic island that is a truly off-the-beaten-track experience.

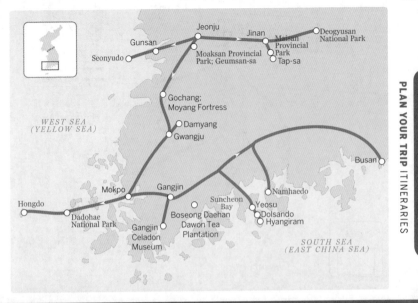

Two weeks

The Deep South Trail

It's less than three hours from Seoul to Jeonju, the start of this 850km route around Korea's greenest and least-developed region, which offers the opportunity to visit hundreds of unspoilt islands, dine in countless seafood restaurants and dig deep into artistic traditions.

Jeonju, provincial capital of Jeollabuk-do, has a fascinating *hanok* village crammed with traditional houses and buildings; it's also the birthplace of the classic rice dish *bibimbap*. Use it as a base for visiting the sixth-century temple Geumsan-sa in **Moaksan Provincial Park**. Don't miss **Maisan Provincial Park**, where you can climb a pair of 'horse ear' mountains and see a sculptural garden of stone pinnacles piled up by a Buddhist mystic at the temple **Tap-sa**. Alternatively, go hiking or skiing in beautiful **Deogyusan National Park**.

The industrial port city of **Gunsan** boasts Korea's largest collection of Japanese colonial period buildings and a well-curated modern history museum; from here hop on a ferry to the relaxing tropical island of **Seonyudo**, situated amid 60 mostly uninhabited small islands. When the tide is in and the sun is out, the views from here are unbelievably beautiful.

Bronze and Iron Age tombs registered with Unesco dot the lush green hills around the small village of **Gochang**, where you can also explore the 15th-century, ivy-covered **Moyang Fortress**.

Further south, **Gwangju** is home to several interesting historical sites, museums and a major arts complex. Shop for bamboo products in **Damyang**, then take the train to **Mokpo** port for boats to the remote havens of **Heuksando** and **Hongdo** in the **Dadohae Haesang National Park**.

Admire Korea's centuries-old tradition of pottery at the **Gangjin Celadon Museum**, and taste food and drinks made from healthy green tea at the beautiful **Boseong Daehan Dawon Tea Plantation**.

Go birdspotting in the Ramsar-listed wetlands of **Suncheon Bay**, then continue to **Yeosu**, site of Expo 2012 and access point for **Dolsando**, where you can hike up to **Hyangiram**, a Buddhist temple perched on a cliff.

For a final island experience, take in terraced rice paddies and misty temples on picturesque **Namhaedo**. The trail finishes at the bustling port of **Busan**.

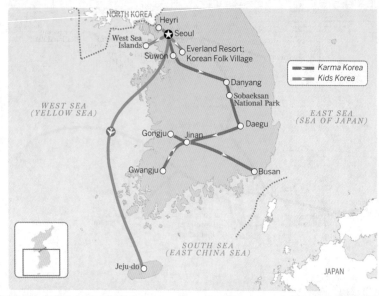

Two weeks
Karma Korea

> Temples feature on this itinerary. In **Seoul** learn about Buddhism during a Templelife program at Seoul's Jogyesa or Bongeun-sa temples.

Danyang is the transit point for **Sobaeksan National Park**, where you'll find highly modern Guin-sa, headquarters of the Cheontae sect. From **Gongju**, one-time capital of Korea's Baekje dynasty, visit Magok-sa, a remote and ancient temple with a hall of 1000 pint-sized disciples that are all slightly different.

Daegu is the base for trips to stunning Haein-sa, housing a World Heritage–listed library of over 80,000 14th-century woodblocks, and Jikji-sa, a magnificent temple dating to the 5th century.

Jinan is the access town for Tap-sa, a tiny temple surrounded by two 'horse ear' mountains and an extraordinary sculptural garden of 80 stone pinnacles (or towers) that were piled up by a Buddhist mystic. From Gwangju, visit Unju-sa, with its fine collection of stone pagodas and unusual twin and reclining Buddhas.

Finish in **Busan**, home to Tongdo-sa, said to be Korea's largest and most important Buddhist temple; it has an excellent Buddhist art museum containing 30,000 artefacts.

Two weeks
Kids Korea

> This two-centre itinerary is ideal for parents looking to balance their own travelling needs with those of their toddlers and teens. **Seoul** has an abundant number of kid-friendly attractions, including parks, aquariums and, in summer, outdoor swimming pools. Older kids will most likely be happy cruising the capital's vast shopping malls and department stores looking for souvenirs of Korea's pervasive pop culture.

Day trips include the beaches of the **West Sea islands**, Korea's biggest amusement park **Everland Resort** and the **Korean Folk Village**. These last two can just as easily be visited from **Suwon**, where everyone will have fun hiking around the walls of an 18th-century fortress. North of Seoul, the modern village of **Heyri** is an opportunity to relax and distract small children with some inventive sculptures and art exhibits.

Hop on a flight to **Jeju-do**, an island blessed with a fascinating volcanic landscape and dozens of sandy beaches. Amusement and water parks, cycle and skate hire, and a whole raft of adventure activities from quad biking to scuba diving are possible on this fun-packed island with plenty of world-class resorts.

Outdoor Activities

Top 5 Outdoor Adventures

Climb Hallasan, Jeju-do

Dive Seogwipo, Jeju-do

Ski at Alpensia, Pyeongchang

Cycle around Seonyudo

Hike through Jirisan National Park

Responsible Outdoors

Pay any entrance fees required by park authorities.

Obtain reliable information about route conditions, and tackle only trails within your realm of experience and fitness level; do not hike closed trails.

Be aware of local laws, regulations and etiquette about wildlife and the environment.

Be aware that the weather can change quickly and seasonal changes will influence how you dress and the equipment you need to carry.

Leave only footprints, take only photographs – don't litter and don't bring back souvenirs such as seashells or flowers.

Korea's countryside, coastline and islands are a year-round outdoor playground with a range of activities, including hiking and cycling. With soaring mountains and a reliable snow record, it's ideal for winter sports and in 2018 it will host the Winter Olympics. Golf is hugely popular, mainly at driving ranges in towns and cities, but there are some gorgeous courses in scenic spots. In the water, you can enjoy diving, surfing, rafting and kayaking.

Hiking & Rock Climbing

Hiking is Korea's number-one leisure activity. There are thousands of trails, with everything from leisurely half-day walks, such as those along the Jeju Olle Trail (p244), to strenuous mountain-ridge treks, most passing through national or provincial parks. Basic shelters are available, but expect a full house during holidays, summer months and autumn weekends. If you're planning a major overnight mountain trek, shelter reservations two weeks in advance are recommended. About one quarter of the trails may be closed at any one time to allow the mountain to regenerate itself.

The country's 20 national parks are beautiful in winter and summer, and snow on trees, and temple roofs provide wonderful photo opps. Keep in mind that appropriate clothing and exposure precautions are a must, as temperatures can reach Siberian levels and whiteout blizzards are possible in the mountains.

Useful websites and resources:

Korea National Park Service (www.knps .or.kr) For trail information and online reservations for park accommodation.

Hike Korea (www.hikekorea.com) Learn about Korean mountain culture as well as many of the country's best trails. The site's author, Roger Shepherd, is one of the authors of *Bakedu-Daegu Trail*, a book that details the 1400km-long 'White Head Great Ridge' down the southern Korean Peninsula.

Adventure Korea (www.adventurekorea. com) Apart from running hiking trips, this expat-focussed operator offers other adventurous activities including biking and rafting trips.

Korea in the Clouds (www.koreaclimbs.blog spot.com) Online guide to hiking Korea's mountains.

Korea on the Rocks (www.koreaontherocks .com) Details on rock and ice climbing across Korea.

Cycling

Almost every city with a waterfront and hordes of tourists has a stand where bikes can be hired from around ₩5000 per day. Most bike paths are geared towards leisure riders, with couples and families in mind, so expect well-marked, paved, flat trails designed for pleasure rather than intense cross-country exhilaration. To hire a bike, some form of ID is usually required; a helmet or lock is almost never included unless you ask.

Filthy (www.mtbk-adventure.com) is a site written by Korea-based expats that details a selection of mountain-biking trails.

Seoul & Incheon

People who value full mobility in their limbs rarely venture onto Seoul's streets with a bike between their legs, but the bicycle trails along the Han River are ideal for a comfortable, car-free family outing. Bikes can be hired on Yeouido, which is a good starting point for a 90-minute, 7km sprint to the World Cup Stadium or a more ambitious 38km ride to Olympic Park. The paved paths are dotted with parks, sports fields, gardens and the occasional snack bar. Further east and north of the river, bikes of similar quality and price can be hired at Ttukseom Resort.

The west coast island of Ganghwado, part of the Incheon municipal area, is also a good place to tour by bike.

Jeju-do

The 200km pedal around Korea's largest island takes from three to five days, depending on your level of fitness and how quickly you wish to take it. Hwy 1132 runs around the entire island and has bicycle lanes on either side. Shore roads also have bike lanes but it's a less-developed system and not always bike friendly. The inland scenery is greener and the roads less busy but they lack bicycle lanes.

Off Jeju-do's eastern coast, Udo offers a short but testing 17km island spin past a lighthouse perched on a 132m-high cliff.

Seonyudo

In the centre of the Gogunsan Archipelago, 50km off the coast of Jeollabuk-do, this pretty, undeveloped island is ideal for a day-trip escape to a picture-postcard setting. Pedal around laid-back fishing villages, cross bridges to neighbouring islands or follow the paved trail alongside a 2km white sandy beach and the ocean. Bring a picnic or enjoy a fresh seafood meal by the ocean.

Chuncheon

Pretty, relaxing Chuncheon is the antithesis of most busy cities. During the day, ferry your bike over to Jungdo for a short island ride amid horse-drawn carriages, while looking out for birds nesting in the reeds. In the late afternoon, cruise on two wheels along the shores of Uiam Lake for a sunset view.

Skiing & Snowboarding

In 2018, Pyeongchang county in Gangwon-do will host the Winter Olympic Games. A giant ski resort, Alpensia, is being built to host the games; when completed it will include a ski jump, a stadium, cross-country and biathlon courses, an ice-ridge climbing centre, golf course, water park and five-star hotels.

Ski season runs from December to March. Lift tickets cost about ₩65,000 and equipment rentals about ₩30,000 per day. Package deals from travel agents include transport to/from Seoul or other major cities, lift tickets, ski and clothing rental and, if required, lessons and accommodation. Overnight packages vary from ₩60,000 for a night in a *minbak* (private home with rooms for rent) or hostel, to over ₩250,000 for flashy condos and stylish hotels. Avoid the overcrowded weekends, especially at resorts near Seoul.

For details of ski resorts within day-trip range of Seoul, see p103.

Gangwon-do

Yongpyong Ski Resort (p137) Korea's oldest and biggest resort, with slopes ranging from bunny options to black diamond runs. It also has cross-country courses and the usual comforts of a ski resort town, but note that international skiers may find the terrain something of a molehill.

» (above) Hikers on Namsan, south of Seoul (p47)
» (left) A cyclist passes bikes for hire at Yeouido Park (p76)

KOREA'S TOP PARKS

National Parks

PARK	AREA	FEATURES & ACTIVITIES
Bukhansan	78 sq km	Great hiking, subway access from Seoul (p97)
Dadohae Haesang	2344 sq km (2004 sq km marine)	A marine park of scattered, unspoilt islands (p225)
Deogyusan	219 sq km	Ski resort, a fortress and a magical valley walk (p265)
Gyeongju	138 sq km	A historic park strewn with ancient Shilla and Buddhist relics (p154)
Hallasan	149 sq km	Extinct volcano; Korea's highest peak (p254)
Jirisan	440 sq km	Straddling two provinces; high peaks are popular with serious hikers (East, p200 and West, p212)
Seoraksan	373 sq km	Korea's most beautiful park (p127)
Sobaeksan	320 sq km	Limestone caves and Guin-sa, an impressive temple complex, to explore (p300)

Provincial Parks

PARK	AREA	FEATURES & ACTIVITIES
Daedunsan	38 sq km	Granite cliffs, great views, hot-spring bath (p264)
Gajisan	104 sq km	Scenic views; famous temple, Tongdo-sa (p194)
Mudeungsan	30 sq km	Near Gwangju, with an art gallery and a green-tea plantation (p206)
Taebaeksan	17 sq km	Visit the Coal Museum, hike to Dangun's altar (p141)

Alpensia (p137) Still-in-the-works mega resort that will host the 2018 Winter Olympics. A good place for family skiing and kids who are learning to ski, and there's an area reserved for snowboarders.

Gangchon Elysian Ski Resort (☑033-260 2000; www.elysian.co.kr/ski/index.asp; Baegyang-ri 29-1, Namsan-myeon, Chuncheon-si) Ten slopes and six lifts. The nearby 50m waterfall is spectacular at any time of year but provides ice-climbers with a challenge when it freezes between December and February. The resort can easily be accessed from Chuncheon or by bus or train from Seoul.

Jeollabuk-do

Muju Ski Resort (p265) The only resort located within a national park, the picturesque Deogyu-San National Park. Opened in 1990, Muju has become one of the country's top winter playgrounds – its 26 slopes have something for everyone, from bunny beginner to mogul-hardened monster. Its après-ski facilities set in an alpine-themed village are the best.

Chungcheongbuk-do

Sajo Ski Resort (p296) Less than 2km from Suanbo Hot Springs, this modest resort has seven slopes and three lifts. Hot springs make for an oh-so-relaxing return after you're done on the slopes.

Ice Skating

Indoor ice skating is available year-round at Seoul's Lotte World (p55). In winter an outdoor rink is set up in Seoul Plaza outside **City Hall** (Map p48; admission W1000; ☉10am-10pm Mon-Thu, until 11pm Fri & Sat, mid-Dec–mid-Feb). There are also temporary outdoor rinks at Grand Hyatt and Sheraton Walkerhill hotels.

Surfing

Haeundae and Songjeong beaches in Busan are among the best places to experience South Korea's surf. However, you'll need to suit up as the best time for surf conditions is in winter, when waves are whipped up by strong winds from the north. Water temperatures at these times dip to 3°C but could be as high as 10°C. If that's too chilly for you, head to balmy Jungmun Beach off Jeju-do's southern coast.

Diving

Korea has an active scuba-diving scene. The top dive site is just off Seogwipo on Jeju-do's southern coast, with walls of colourful soft coral, 18m-high kelp forests (March to May), schools of fish and the occasional inquisitive

» (above) Yongpyong Ski Resort (p137)
» (left) Jack Nicklaus Golf Club, Songdo International City (p105)

RALF DEUTSCH

The owner of Big Blue 33 (p247) in Seogwipo, Ralf Deutsch is originally from Osnabruck, Germany. In 2001, after six years of teaching at Jeju University, he started his dive shop to cater to the growing number of non-Korean-speaking visitors. Since then he's completed over 3200 dives in the waters off the island.

What makes diving in Jeju special? The underwater world of Jeju is a unique combination of cold and warm water. So you will see cold-water-loving kelp forests and flounder right next to warm-water marine life such as soft coral and lionfish. This is due to the *kuroshio*, or black current, that brings warm water from the tropics and mixes with the cold waters, creating an interesting diversity that makes for good diving.

When's best to dive? September and October offer the best conditions, when the water is 27°C and visibility is 20–30m.

Which dive spots do you recommend? Little Munsom and Big Munsom are islands from which you can do a shore dive; the boat here only takes five minutes so it's ideal if you suffer from seasickness and would prefer not to do a boat dive. Among the thousands of fish you might see are mackerel, angel, butterfly, dansel and lion fish, octopus, squid and nudibranch, which are colourful small snails.

dolphin. Diving here is a mixture of tropical and temperate – rather like diving in Norway and the Red Sea at the same time. Visibility is best from September to November but is around 10m at other times, and water temperature varies from 15°C to 28°C.

Other good underwater sites on the east coast are Hongdo, off the south coast; Pohang, Ulleungdo and Dragon Head, off Sokcho; and a wreck off Gangneung. The west coast has some dive operators, for instance at Daecheon beach, but visibility can be poor.

You can go scuba diving with sharks, turtles, rays and giant groupers in **Busan Aquarium** (www.scubainkorea.com; 30min certified/noncertified diver ₩90,000/110,000; ⊙Sat & Sun). Nondivers can do it after a two-hour training session with an English-speaking instructor.

Golf

In 1998, Se Ri Pak put South Korea onto the map by winning the US Women's Open. Today, Korean women dominate the American LPGA Tour and golf is a national pastime with hundreds of courses dotting the country.

The most popular golfing destination is Jeju-do; courses include Jungmun Beach Golf Club (p253) and Pinx Golf Club (p257).

Playing on a course in Korea is not cheap. An average 18-hole round of golf may set you back ₩300,000. But for virtual golf, there are now 3000 golf cafes around the country, so you'll find one in just about any city. A round of virtual golf at chains like **Golfzon** (http://company.golfzon.com) costs about ₩30,000. Also common are golf practice ranges.

Birdwatching

With some of the widest and most extensive tidal flats in the world, the Korean Peninsula is a natural magnet for birds. More than 500 species have been spotted in Korea, including 34 threatened species; most are on their migratory route between Siberia and Manchuria in the north and Southeast Asia and Australia in the south. One of Korea's most famous visitors is the hooded crane, which winters in Suncheon Bay, a wetland park on Jeollanam-do's south coast that is a popular birding spot.

The best areas for birding are on the west coast and islands. The Demilitarized Zone (DMZ) is also a preferred stop for migrating birds because it's been uninhabited for 50 years. In the midst of Seoul, on a pair of islets in the Han River, is the Bamseom Island Bird Sanctuary; it's off-limits to humans but birds – including mandarins, mallards, spotbills and great egrets – can be spotted from an observation platform in Yeouido's Han River Park.

Birds Korea (www.birdskorea.org) has photos of Korean birds and lots of info for bird lovers.

Kayaking, Canoeing & Rafting

Gangwon-do's northwest is the hot spot for kayaking, canoeing and rafting trips from mid-April to October (see p123 for details). **Adventure Korea** (www.adventurekorea.com) and **Koridoor** (www.koridoor.co.kr) also offer white-water rafting trips.

regions at a glance

Seoul

History ✓✓✓
Food ✓✓✓
Shopping ✓✓✓

Historical Landmarks
Given how thoroughly it was trashed during the Korean War, it's no small miracle that so many of Seoul's historical landmarks remain. A number of them are meticulous reconstructions, but that doesn't diminish their significance or impact.

Food & Drink
Seoul is the best place in the country to sample the full range of Korean culinary delights – from hot *kimchi* stews and sizzling street snacks to the delicate and beautifully presented morsels that make up a royal banquet.

Shoppers' Delight
At all times of the day or night there's always somewhere to shop in Seoul. The teeming markets of Dongdaemun and Namdaemun are must-do experiences, as is cruising the boutiques and department stores of Myeong-dong or ritzy Apgu-jeong and Cheongdam.

p38

Gyeonggi-do & Incheon

Islands ✓✓✓
History ✓✓
Art ✓✓

Island Escapes
Scores of islands flaking off like crumbs into the West Sea make for perfect escapes from the Seoul–Icheon urban grip. Try historic Gang-hwado or laid-back Muuido, which has gorgeous beaches.

Historical Sites
The DMZ splitting North and South Korea is a must-see, as are the Unesco World Heritage–listed fortress walls surrounding the inner core of Suwon.

Artistic Places
The pottery town of Icheon draws in ceramics lovers; Heyri near the DMZ border is a serene village packed with small galleries; see something different in the exhibitions at Incheon Art Platform or the sculptures of An-yang Art Park.

p92

Gangwon-do

Hiking ✓✓✓
Skiing ✓✓
Quirky ✓✓

Misty Mountains
Seoraksan National Park abounds with gorgeous vistas of mist-shrouded crags that rarely fail to stun. The valleys are full of quiet temples, hot springs and hiking trails.

Hit the Slopes
Host of the 2018 Winter Olympics, Pyeongchang's Yongpyong and Alpensia ski resorts aren't the biggest in the world but they pack in tonnes of family-friendly options like inner-tube slides.

The Unknown DMZ
Peek into North Korea at the north-ernmost point along the DMZ at the Goseong Unification Observatory, or go deep under the zone itself in the Second Infiltration Tunnel in Cheorwon.

p118

Gyeongsang-buk-do

Temples ✓✓✓
History ✓✓
Food ✓✓

Idyllic Retreats

Topping mist-shrouded mountains throughout the region are mysterious ancient temples, idyllically isolated far from the neon-drenched cities of Gyeongsangbuk-do.

Historical Sites

Head to Gyeongju, the 'museum without walls', for a slice of Shilla history, be it the fabulous finds on display at the excellent National Museum, or the tombs and temples that surround the town.

Delicious Dishes

The island of Ulleungdo offers the best seafood in Korea, or try Andong's famous mackerel. Don't miss Daegu or Gyeongju's innovative and superb eating options, surely some of the best in the country.

p143

Busan & Gyeongsang-nam-do

Food ✓✓
Beaches ✓✓✓
Islands ✓✓

Fresh Fish

You'd have to be swimming in the ocean to get your hands on seafood fresher than produce at Busan's Jagalchi fish market. Pick your creature from a tank and it'll be your next meal within minutes.

Sand Castling

Sure, Haeundae Beach can be overcrowded and overhyped, but it's the nation's most loved for good reason. Kick back in the sand, frolic in the waves, and snack on fresh blowfish, just minutes from downtown Busan.

Island-Hopping

The crumbly coastline has myriad islands to explore but Namhaedo, one of the largest, is stunningly beautiful, with mountaintop temples and terraced rice paddies sloping down to the sea.

p178

Jeollanam-do

Food ✓✓
Islands ✓✓✓
Quirky ✓✓✓

Glorious Food

Kimchi lovers will rejoice at the eponymous annual festival in Gwangju; tea fans can get greentea *everything* in Boseong; and the seafood and much more besides will sate the most finicky of diners.

Islands Galore

The rolling hills lead down to the coastline where one can hop on a boat to explore hundreds of islands. Don't forget to sample the local catch of day: sashimi, abalone and even live octopus.

Eclectic Excursions

From celadon pottery (in Gangjin) to green-tea plantations (in Boseong) to bamboo forests (in Damyang) to F1 motor racing (in Mokpo), Jeollanam-do defies its rural roots with kooky sights and activities.

p204

Jeju-do

Hiking ✓✓✓
Art & Culture ✓✓
Food ✓✓

Hiking Trails

Discover the island the slow way, following one or more of the 26 routes on the Jeju Olle Trail; alternatively, take one of four routes to the top of Hallasan (1950m), South Korea's tallest mountain.

Art & Culture

Jeju-do is packed with all manner of galleries and museums, from the impressive Jeju Stone Park and stunning photos at Kim Young Gap Gallery Dumoak to a trio of quirky sex museums.

Local Delicacies

Jeju's separately developed island culture reveals itself in a distinct cuisine, heavy on seafood but also with cuts of black pig, pheasant and horse on the menu.

p226

Jeollabuk-do

History ✓✓
Hiking ✓✓✓
Temples ✓✓

Go Back in Time

History is celebrated via Jeonju's *hanok* village and its clusters of local artisans. Other equally engaging reminders of the past include the Gochang fortress and the former colonial port of Gunsan.

Green Green Grass

For a small province, Jeollabuk-do packs quite a lot of punch when it comes to national parks. Join droves of outdoor enthusiasts in exploring Korea's natural beauty...but don't forget the *makgeolli*.

A State of Zen

Korean monks have unique ideas when it comes to temple building. Compare the otherworldly stone towers at Tapsa and the camellia-backed Seonun-sa, both vastly different in construction.

p258

Chungche-ongnam-do

Beaches ✓✓
Festivals ✓
History ✓✓✓

Sunbath Fun

There are opportunities galore to work on that tan since Korea's most popular beaches sit in Chungcheongnam-do. Whether you like packed summer scenes or intimate small strips of sand, you'll find it here.

Mud Rollicking

Possibly Korea's most famous (some say infamous) festival, the Boryeong Mud Festival is a messy extravaganza that's hugely popular with foreigners.

Baekje History

The twin sleepy towns of Gongju and Buyeo were once the seat of power of Korea's earliest dynasty, the long-running Baekje kingdom. Festivals, fortresses, tombs and museums pay tribute to its legacy.

p271

Chungche-ongbuk-do

Temples ✓✓✓
Activities ✓✓
History ✓

Find Inner Peace

While Korea may be awash with temples, some of the most grand and glorious ones can be found here. The modern hillside complex of Guin-sa impresses, as does the 33m-high gold Buddha at Beopju-sa.

Slow it Down

This land-locked region, with its quiet towns, offers a chance for leisurely exploration of Korea's heartland. Take a meandering cruise along the Chungju Lake or soak in an *oncheon* (hot-spring spa) at Suanbo.

Footnotes in History

The world's first book printed by movable type was created in Cheongju. Other historical footnotes such as the Cheongnamdae presidential villa will also vie for your attention.

p288

North Korea

Politics ✓✓✓
Quirky ✓✓✓
Scenery ✓

Endless Propaganda

Any trip to North Korea is shot through with politics, from the ubiquitous propaganda to the museums, monuments and art. Coming here is a fascinating chance to see things from a different perspective.

Mind-Bogglers

Whether visiting an exhibit of all Kim Jong-il's gifts housed in a mountainside warehouse or taking a trip on the world's most secretive metro system, there's no possible trip weirder than a tour of the DPRK.

Spectacular Scenery

You may not think of natural beauty when you imagine North Korea, but soaring mountains, sandy beaches and crystal clear lakes make it a great place for nature lovers.

p302

Every listing is recommended by our authors, and their favourite places are listed first

Look out for these icons:

 TOP CHOICE Our author's top recommendation

A green or sustainable option

FREE No payment required

On the Road

Seoul

Includes »

Best Places to Stay

» La Casa (p70)
» Chi-Woon-Jung (p63)
» V Mansion (p68)
» Fraser Suites (p63)
» Park Hyatt Seoul (p70)

Best Places to Eat

» Jung Sikdang (p77)
» Tosokchon (p72)
» Mokmyeoksanbang (p74)
» Samwon Garden (p77)
» Gwangjang Market (p77)

Why Go?

An old Korean proverb goes 'even if you have to crawl on your knees, get yourself to Seoul!' Never has this been more sound advice. Asia's fourth-richest city, Seoul (서울) is a dynamic mash-up of markets and K-Pop, teahouses and temples, palaces and mountains, skyscrapers and pulsing neon. This Unesco City of Design also offers several contemporary architectural marvels, including the Dongdaemun Design Plaza & Park and the giant glass wave of the new City Hall.

Gaze down on this sprawling metropolis of 10.5 million people from atop any of Seoul's four guardian mountains and you will innately sense the powerful *pungsu-jiri* (feng shui) that has long nurtured and protected the city. Public transport is brilliant and whatever you want, at any time of the day or night, Seoul can provide. The joys of eating, drinking, shopping and general merrymaking are all in abundant evidence, from Apgujeong's chic boutiques to Hongdae's bars and restaurants.

When to Go
Seoul

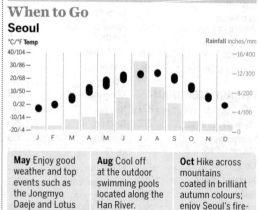

May Enjoy good weather and top events such as the Jongmyo Daeje and Lotus Lantern Festival.

Aug Cool off at the outdoor swimming pools located along the Han River.

Oct Hike across mountains coated in brilliant autumn colours; enjoy Seoul's fireworks festival.

History

When Seoul became the capital of Korea following the establishment of the Joseon dynasty in 1392 its population was around 100,000. Just over 600 years later this has ballooned to 10.5 million (or 24.5 million if you consider the wider metro area), making Seoul one of the world's largest cities.

During the 20th century Seoul suffered first under Japanese colonial rule and then during the Korean War when it was almost entirely destroyed. Rebuilt from the 1960s, Seoul is the country's centre of cultural, economic and political power. Past mayors have gone on to become South Korea's president, including Lee Myung-bak who finished his term of office as president in December 2012.

When Park Won-soon, a former human rights lawyer and independent candidate, was elected Seoul's mayor in October 2011 it was a watershed moment not only for Korean politics but also for the city itself. Under the previous mayors, top of the agenda had been construction-led growth that resulted in flashy, expensive projects such as the reclamation of the Cheong-gye-cheon and the commissioning of Dongdaemun Design Plaza. Park's winning mandate promises to shift the focus to greater welfare spending for Seoul's citizens.

◉ Sights

You'll spend the bulk of your time north of the meandering Han River that splits Seoul into two distinct regions, that are themselves split into 25 *gu* (administrative districts). This is home to historic Seoul, a relatively compact, walkable area.

Seoul's fascinating feudal past can be glimpsed in the palaces around Gwanghwa-mun (the main gate to Gyeongbokgung). Nearby Insa-dong (인사동), Samcheong-dong (삼청동) and Bukchon are all packed with souvenir shops, teahouses, restaurants and small museums, often in converted *hanok* (traditional wooden houses). Note that the narrow streets in these areas can get jammed on weekends and holidays. There are a few other sights of note further north around the remains of the fortress walls that once encircled the city.

Namsan, crowned by N Seoul Tower, the green hill at the heart of the old city, is sandwiched between Myeong-dong shopping district to the north and the foreigner-friendly zone of Itaewon to the south. Not far off to the west are the youthful party districts of Hongdae (the area around Hongik University), Sinchon and Edae.

South of the river, Gangnam's suburbs are thin on major sights but good for shopping and entertainment. Here you'll also find giant complexes such as COEX Mall and Olympic Park.

GWANGHWAMUN & JONGNO-GU
광화문, 종로구

Gyeongbokgung PALACE
(경복궁; Map p42; http://english.cha.go.kr; adult/child ₩3000/1500; ◷9am-5pm Wed-Mon Mar-Oct,

continued on page 44

SEOUL IN...

Two Days

Stroll around **Bukchon Hanok Village**. Grab lunch and go shopping in **Insa-dong**, then attend the changing of the palace guard at **Gyeongbokgung** or join the day's last tour of **Changdeokgung**. Enjoy dinner in **Gwangjang Market**. On day two visit the splendid **Leeum Samsung Museum of Art**. Move on to either the **National Museum of Korea** or the **War Memorial of Korea**. Freshen up at **Dragon Hill Spa**, ride the cable car to **N Seoul Tower** atop Namsan, then return to **Itaewon** for dining and late-night carousing.

Five Days

Follow Seoul Fortress Walls up **Bukaksan** and down to the temple **Gilsang-sa**. In Dongdaemun view the **Dongdaemun Design Plaza & Park**, pick up a new outfit from the market here, then follow the **Cheong-gye-cheon** back to the heart of the city. On day four visit **Seodaemun Prison History Hall** and hike up **Inwangsan**, where you might come across shamans performing ancient ceremonies. End the day with a traditional performing-arts show and royal-cuisine meal at **Korea House**. Cap your Seoul visit off with a meal at the fascinating **Noryangjin Fish Market**, hire a bike in **Yeouido** and cycle along the Han River, and soak up the buzzing nocturnal vibe of **Hongdae**.

Seoul Highlights

1 Soak up the serenity of the Secret Garden at World Heritage–listed **Changdeokgung** (p44)

2 Lose yourself in the picturesque, atmospheric streets of **Bukchon Hanok Village** (p45)

3 Take a break from the city with a stroll beside the **Cheong-gye-cheon** (p46)

4 Hike the ancient fortress walls to the summit of **Bukaksan** (p55) for panoramic views of the city

See Gwanghwamun, Jongno-gu & Daehangno Map (p42)

Korea University

Hoegi

Myeonmok

Jegi-dong

Changdeokgung

Sinseol-dong

Cheongnyangni

Sagajeong

DONGDAEMUN-GU

Dongdaemun & Around Map (p54)

Sindap

Yongmasan

GWANGJIN-GU

Achasan ▲ (278m)

7 Dongdaemun Design Plaza & Park

Dapsimni

Janghanpyeong

Junggok

Sangwangsimni

Majang

Cheonggu

Wangsimni

SEONGDONG-GU

Yongdap

Gunja

Singuemho

Hanyang University

Children's Grand Park

Achasan

Amsa

Haengdang

Yaksu

Geumho

Eung-bong

Ttukseom

Seongsu

Konkuk University

Gwangnaru

Beotigogae

See Itaewon Map (p52)

Oksu

Han River (Hangang)

Guui

Cheonho

See Jamsil Map (p56)

Gangdongdaero

Wiryeseonggil

See Apgujieong, Gangnam & Yongsan-gu Map (p58)

Dogok

Daechi

Daecheong

Munjeong

Naebang

Gaepodong

Nambu Bus Terminal

Maebong

Guryong

Suseo

Munjeong

Bangbae

Yangjae

Irwon

Nambu Ring Road

Jangji

Umyeonsan ▲ (290m)

Daemosan ▲ (293m)

Bokjeong

SEOCHO-GU

Guryongsan ▲ (283m)

SONGPA-GU

Gyeongbu Expwy

GWACHEON-SI

SEONGNAM-SI

Seonbawi

Seoul Racecourse Park

Seoul Grand Park

Gyeogwon University

5 Shop until you drop in Myeong-dong and the all-night **Namdaemun Market** (p85)

6 Party the night away at the bars and clubs of **Hongdae** (p78)

7 Marvel at the space age architecture of **Dongdaemun Design Plaza & Park** (p53)

8 Listen to shamans' chants on the hills of **Inwangsan** (p50)

9 Soak and sweat away your stresses at the **Dragon Hill Spa** (p58)

10 Hire a bicycle and pedal beside the **Han River** (p76)

Gwanghwamun, Jongno-gu & Daehangno

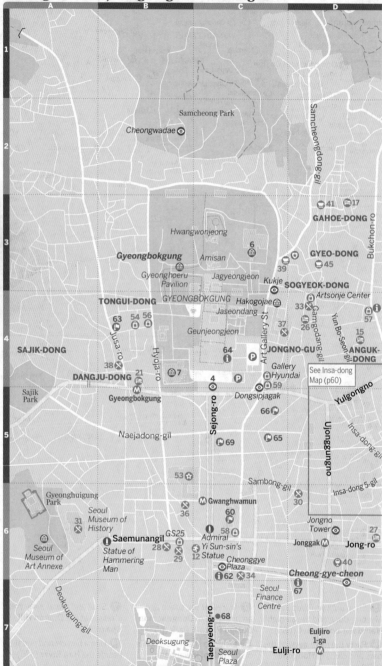

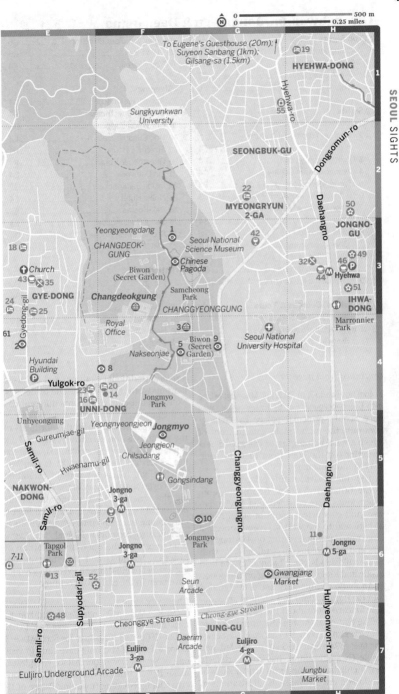

0 — 500 m
0 — 0.25 miles

To Eugene's Guesthouse (20m);
Suyeon Sanbang (1km);
Gilsang-sa (1.5km)

19

HYEHWA-DONG

Sungkyunkwan
University

Hyehwa-ro

SEONGBUK-GU

55

Dongsomun-ro

22

MYEONGRYUN
2-GA

Daehangno

50

JONGNO-
GU

1

Seoul National
Science Museum

42

32

46

49

P

Hyehwa

44

Yeongyeongdang

CHANGDEOK-
GUNG

Chinese
Pagoda

Biwon
(Secret Garden)

51

18

Church

43

35

GYE-DONG

25

Changdeokgung

Samcheong
Park

CHANGGYEONGGUNG

IHWA-
DONG

Marronnier
Park

24

Gyedong-gil

Royal
Office

3

Biwon 9
(Secret
Garden)

Seoul National
University Hospital

61

2

Hyundai
Building

P

Nakseonjae

5

8

Yulgok-ro

23 20

16 14

UNNI-DONG

Jongmyo
Park

Unhyeongung

Gureumjae-gil

Yeongnyeongjeon

Jongmyo

Samil-ro

Hwaehamu-gil

Jeongjeon
Chilsadang

Changgyeonggungno

NAKWON-
DONG

Samil-ro

Gongsindang

Jongno
3-ga

47

10

Jongmyo
Park

11

Jongno
5-ga

Daehangno

Hullyeonwon-ro

7-11

Tapgol
Park

Jongno
3-ga

Supyodari-gil

13

52

Seun
Arcade

Gwangjang
Market

48

Cheonggye Stream

Cheong-gye Stream

Samil-ro

Daerim
Arcade

JUNG-GU

Euljiro
3-ga

Euljiro
4-ga

Jungbu
Market

Euljiro Underground Arcade

E   F   G   H

Gwanghwamun, Jongno-gu & Daehangno

continued from page 39

to 4pm Nov-Feb, to 7pm Sat & Sun May-Aug; Ⓜ Line 3 to Gyeongbokgung, Exit 5) Enter what was once Seoul's principal palace by **Gwanghwamun**, the grand main gate in front of which are held **changing of the guard ceremonies** (on the hour from 10am to 4pm; www.sumunjang.or.kr).

The impressive main palace building is the ornate two-storey **Geunjeongjeon**, where kings were crowned, met foreign envoys and conducted affairs of state. North of here and to the west is **Gyeonghoeru**, a large raised pavilion resting on 48 stone pillars and overlooking an artificial lake with two small islands. State banquets were held inside and kings went boating on the pond.

An audio commentary and a free guided tour (at 11am, 1.30pm and 3.30pm) are available to learn more about the palace.

The **National Palace Museum of Korea** (http://foreign.gogung.go.kr/eng/index.jsp; admission free; ⊙9am-5pm Tue-Sun), to the left just inside Gwanghwamun, has royal artefacts that highlight the wonderful artistic skills of the Joseon era – royal seals, illustrations of court ceremonies, and the gold-embroidered

hanbok (traditional clothing) and exquisite hairpins worn by the queens and princesses. Note this museum closes on a different day to the palace.

In a separate section in the northeast of the grounds is the excellent **National Folk Museum of Korea** (www.nfm.go.kr; admission free; ⊙9am-5pm Wed-Mon Mar-Oct, to 4pm Wed-Mon Nov-Feb). It has three main exhibition halls covering the history of the Korean people, the agricultural way of life and the life of *yangban* (upper class) during the Joseon era. Among the many interesting exhibits is an amazingly colourful funeral bier. Leave time to explore the **open-air exhibition** of historical buildings and structures including a street of buildings styled as they would have been in the early 20th century.

Changdeokgung
PALACE

(창덕궁; Map p42; http://eng.cdg.go.kr/main /main.htm; entry by guided tour adult/child ₩3000/1500; ⊙9.30am-4pm Tue-Sun; Ⓜ Line 3 to Anguk, Exit 3) If you only have time to visit one of Seoul's five major palace complexes, make it this Unesco World Heritage property. Changdeokgung (meaning Palace of Illustrious Virtue) was originally built in the early 15th century as a secondary palace to Gyeongbukgung. Following the destruction of both palaces during the Japanese invasion in the 1590s, Changdeokgung was rebuilt and became the primary royal residence until 1872. It remained in use by members of the royal family well into the 20th century.

You must join a guided tour to see inside the palace compound. English tours run at 10.30am and 2.30pm; if you don't care about the commentary, there are Korean tours hourly from 9.30am. If you wish to gain entry to the Huwon (Secret Garden) – and you do – then join a special tour for an extra ₩5000; these run at 10am, 1pm and 2pm and are restricted to 50 people at a time. Monthly **Moonlight Tours** (₩30,000) limited to 100 people also include the Huwon. Tickets can be bought online from Interpark (http://ticket.interpark.com); look under 'exhibitions and sport' and book well in advance as it's very popular.

Bukchon Hanok Village   NEIGHBOURHOOD
(북촌 한옥마을; Map p42) Meaning 'North Village', Bukchon, between Gyeongbokgung and Changdeokgung, is home to around 900 *hanok*, Seoul's largest concentration of these traditional Korean homes (see p374). It's

an increasingly touristy area, but it's still a pleasure to get lost in the streets here admiring the patterned walls and tiled roofs contrasting with the modern city in the distance.

The **Bukchon Traditional Culture Centre** (Map p42; admission free; ☉9am-6pm Mon-Fri) has a small exhibition about *hanok* and is housed, appropriately enough, in a *hanok*. There are sometimes English-speaking volunteers here and you should be able to pick up the free English booklet *Discovery Buckchon*, which includes a map detailing the top eight photo spots around the area. Digital mobile guide systems can also be rented from the **Bukchon Tourist Information Centre**; rent from 10am to 2pm, return by 5pm.

Jongmyo   SHRINE
(종묘; Map p42; http://jm.cha.go.kr; adult/child ₩1000/500; ☉9am-5pm Wed-Mon Mar-Oct, to 4.30pm Wed-Mon Nov-Feb; Ⓜ Line 1, 3 or 5 to Jongno 3-ga, Exit 11) Surrounded by dense woodland, the impressive buildings of World Heritage–listed Jongmyo house the spirit tablets of the Joseon kings and queens and some of their most loyal government officials. Their spirits are believed to reside in a special hole bored into the wooden tablets.

In the small park at the entrance of the royal shrine, pensioners gather to play *baduk* (go) and *janggi* (a variation of Chinese chess), and to picnic, nap and even dance to *trot* music. A tranquil walk can be had from Jongmyo's grounds through to those of Changgyeonggung via a connecting bridge over Yulgok-ro – if you do this you'll only need to pay entrance to one of the properties.

Jogye-sa
TEMPLE

(조계사; Map p60; ☎732 2115; www.jogyesa.org; ☉4am-9pm; 🅼Line 3 to Anguk, Exit 6) This busy Buddhist temple is the headquarters of the Jogye sect, which emphasises Zen meditation. Its focal point is the shrine **Daeungjeon**, decorated with murals of scenes from Buddha's life, carved floral latticework doors and three giant Buddha statues.

Jogye-sa's **Information Centre for Foreigners** (☎732 5292; ☉10am-5pm) is staffed by English-speaking guides. Ask here about the Temple Life program (₩20,000; from 10am to 2.30pm Saturday) or the mini Temple Life programs featuring two or three activities, generally available daily for a small donation. To find out more about Buddhism or book a Templestay program elsewhere

---

GYEONGBOKGUNG'S TURBULENT HISTORY

Originally built by King Taejo in 1395, Gyeongbokgung served as the principal royal residence until 1592, when it was burnt down during the Japanese invasions. It lay in ruins for nearly 300 years until Heungseon Daewongun, regent and father of King Gojong, started to rebuild it in 1865. Gojong moved in during 1868, but the expensive rebuilding project bankrupted the government.

On 8 October 1895, Japanese assassins broke into the palace and murdered Empress Myeongseong (Queen Min), one of the most powerful figures at that time in Korea. After her body was burnt, it is said only one finger survived the fire. Later 56 individuals were arrested but not one was convicted for the murder. Four months after the assassination of his consort, Gojong fled to the nearby Russian legation building and never returned to Gyeonbukgung. During Japanese colonial rule, most of the palace was destroyed.

---

in Seoul or Korea, the **Templestay Information Centre** (p60; www.templestay.com) is across the street from Jogye-sa.

Changgyeonggung
PALACE

(창경궁; Map p42; http://jikimi.cha.go.kr; adult/youth ₩1000/500; ☉9am-5pm Wed-Mon Mar-Oct, to 4.30pm Wed-Mon Nov-Feb; 🅼Line 4 to Hyehwa, Exit 4) This 'Palace of Flourishing Gladness' suffered the indignity of being turned into a zoo during the colonial period. The oldest surviving structure is the 15th-century stone bridge over the stream by the main gate, while the main hall, **Myeongjeongjeon**, with its latticework and ornately carved and decorated ceiling, dates back to 1616. Stroll to the northern corner of the extensive grounds to discover an impressive **botanical glasshouse**, built in 1909. English-speaking tours (free; one hour) around the palace are offered at 11am and 4pm.

Cheong-gye-cheon
STREAM

(청계천; Map p42; www.cheonggyecheon.or.kr; 🅼Line 5 to Gwanghwamun, Exit 5) A raised highway was torn down and cement roads removed in this US$384-million urban renewal project to 'daylight' this stream. The clear water that now flows for 5.8km down this beautifully landscaped oasis is actually pumped in at great expense for elsewhere, inciting the ire of environmentalists. Despite this, the revitalised stream with its landscaped walkways, footbridges, waterfalls and a variety of public artworks has been a hit with Seoulites who come to escape the urban hubbub and, in summer, dangle their feet in the water.

FREE Seoul Museum of History
MUSEUM

(서울역사박물관; Map p42; www.museum.seoul.kr; ☉9am-9pm Tue-Fri, to 6pm Sat & Sun; 🅼Line 5 to Gwanghwamun, Exit 7) To gain an appreciation of just how much Seoul has changed in the last century visit this fascinating museum that has made a big effort to upgrade its displays, which include a massive scale model of the city. There may be charges for special exhibitions. Classical-music concerts are also sometimes staged here.

FREE Gwanghwamun Square
SQUARE

(광화문; Map p42; Sejong-ro; 🅼Line 5 to Gwanghwamun, Exit 4) At the southern end of this broad elongated square that provides a grand approach to Gwanghwamun is a statue of

Admiral Yi Sun-sin (1545–98), who designed a new type of metal-clad warship called *geobukseon* (turtle boats), and used them to help achieve a series of stunning victories over the much larger Japanese navy that attacked Korea at the end of the 16th century. In the middle of the square stands a statue of King Sejong (r 1418–50). Steps lead down to an **underground exhibition** (admission free; ⊙10.30am-10pm Tue-Sun) with sections on both of these illustrious Korean heroes.

MYEONG-DONG & JUNG-GU
중구

Namsan & N Seoul Tower   VIEWING TOWER
(N서울 타워; Map p48; www.nseoultower.com; adult/youth/child ₩9000/7000/5000; ⊙observatory 10am-11pm; MLine 4 to Myeong-dong, Exit 3) The iconic N Seoul tower, atop the city's guardian mountain Namsan, offers panoramic, if often hazy, views of the immense metropolis. Come at sunset and you can watch the city morph into a galaxy of twinkling stars. The tower has become a hot date spot with the railings around it festooned with locks inscribed with lovers' names.

Walking up Namsan isn't difficult; see p62 for a possible route. Alternatively from Namsan station, ride the **cable car** (one way/return adult ₩6000/8000, child ₩3500/5000; ⊙10am-11pm) or hop on the **shuttle buses 2, 3 and 5** (₩900; ⊙7am-11.30pm) from various subway stations around the mountain.

Deoksugung   PALACE
(덕수궁; Map p48; www.deoksugung.go.kr; adult/youth/child ₩1000/500/free; ⊙9am-9pm Tue-Sun; MLine 1 or 2 to City Hall, Exit 2) Meaning Palace of Virtuous Longevity, Deoksugung is the only one of the four main palaces that you can always visit in the evening to enjoy a quieter atmosphere and see the buildings – both traditional Korean and Western-style neo-classical structures – illuminated.

The palace's main gate is also the scene of a picturesque changing of the guard ceremony (⊙10.30am, 2pm & 3pm Tue-Sun mid-Feb–Dec). Free guided tours of the palace (in English) take place at 10.30am Tuesday to Friday, and at 1.40pm on Saturday in January, March, May, July, September and November, and 1.40pm on Sunday in other months.

Namsangol Hanok Village   ARCHITECTURE
(남산골한옥마을; Map p48; http://hanokmaeul .seoul.go.kr; admission free; ⊙9am-9pm Wed-Mon Apr-Oct, to 8pm Wed-Mon Nov-Mar; MLine 3 or 4 to Chungmuro, Exit 4) Five differing *yangban*

TICKET TO THE PALACES

If you plan to visit Seoul's four main palaces – Gyeonbukgung, Changdeokgung, Changgyeonggung and Deoksugung – you can save some money by buying a combined ticket (₩10,000) valid for up to a month. The ticket is sold at each of the palaces and also covers entry to Huwon at Changdeokgung.

(upper class) houses from the Joseon era have been moved to this park at the foot of Namsan from different parts of Seoul. The architecture and furniture are austere and plain, and conjure up the lost world of Confucian gentleman scholars, who wielded calligraphy brushes rather than swords.

Also in the village you'll find **Seoul Namsan Gugakdang** (Map p48; ☑2261 0512; http:// sngad.sejongpac.or.kr; tickets from ₩20,000), where traditional music and dance concerts are staged most evenings and you can also dress up in *hanbok* (₩10,000 or ₩15,000 with drink at teahouse; from 10am to 11.30am and 1pm to 5.30pm). Displays of the traditional Korean martial art **taekwondo** are staged in the village at 11am, 2pm and 5pm Wednesday and Saturday; to take part make a reservation via www.taekwonseoul.org.

On the right of the entrance gate is an **office** (⊙10.30am-3.30pm) that provides free guided tours around the village and where you can also find out about various cultural programs including calligraphy and making traditional paper *(hanji)*, kites and masks.

Sungnyemun (Namdaemun)   ARCHITECTURE
(남대문; Map p48; www.sungnyemun.or.kr; MLine 4 to Hoehyeon, Exit 5) Seoul's Great South Gate, commonly known as Namdaemun, was destroyed by arson in 2008. Four years of painstaking reconstruction of Korea's No 1 National Treasure are nearing completion and the wraps should now be off the reborn wood and stone gateway, which stands on an island amid major roads; check the website for visiting details.

FREE Seoul Museum of Art   MUSEUM
(서울시립미술관; Map p48; http://seoulmoa .seoul.go.kr; Jeong-dong; ⊙10am-8pm Tue-Sun Mar-Oct, to 7pm Nov-Feb; MLine 1 or 2 to City Hall, Exit 2) Hosting top-notch exhibitions that are

Myeong-dong

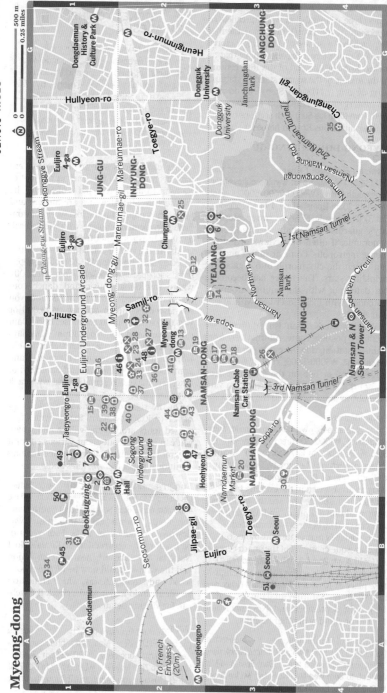

Myeong-dong

always worth a visit, this museum has ultra-modern, bright galleries inside the handsome brick-and-stone facade of the 1927 Supreme Court building. For some special exhibitions an entrance fee is charged.

City Hall   ARCHITECTURE
(Map p48; Ⓜ Line 1 or 2 to City Hall, Exit 5) Looking like a tsunami made of glass and steel, the new City Hall set for completion in early 2013 is a modern reinterpretation of traditional Korean design, the cresting wave providing shade, like eaves found on palaces and temple roofs, over the handsome old City Hall, built from stone in 1926.

Seoul Plaza fronting City Hall is the scene for events and free performances most nights during summer, as well as an outdoor ice-skating rink for a couple of months each winter.

Myeong-dong Catholic Cathedral   CHURCH
(명동 성당; Map p48; www.mdsd.or.kr; Myeong-dong; Ⓜ Line 4 to Myeong-dong, Exit 6) Go inside this elegant, red- and grey-brick Gothic-style cathedral consecrated in 1898 to admire the vaulted ceiling and stained-glass windows. The cathedral provided a sanctuary for student and trade-union protesters during military rule, becoming a national symbol

Hongdae, Sinchon, Edae & Around

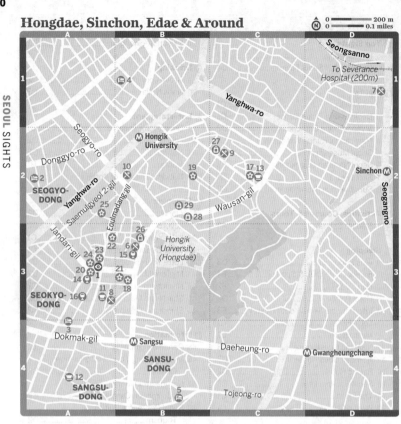

of democracy and human rights. A new entrance plaza is under construction and set for completion in a couple of years.

WESTERN & NORTHERN SEOUL

Seodaemun Prison History Hall   MUSEUM
(독립공원 서대문형무소 역사관; www.sscmc
.or.kr/culture2/foreign/eng/eng01.html;adult/youth/
child ₩1500/1000/500; ⊙9.30am-6pm Tue-Sun
Mar-Oct, to 5pm Tue-Sun Nov-Feb; MLine 3 to Dongnimmun, Exit 5) Chilling tableaux display the
various torture techniques employed by the
colonial Japanese on Korean patriots at this
former prison turned history museum. In the
brick buildings you can walk through night-
marish punishment chambers and claustrophobic cellblocks that were also used by the
Korean authorities after independence.

What you won't see here are details of
how the prison continued to be used by Korea's various dictatorships in the postwar
years right up until its closure in 1987.

Gilsang-sa   TEMPLE
(길상사; off Map p42; ☑3672 5945; www.gilsang
sa.or.kr; Seongbuk-dong; ⊙10am-6pm Mon-Sat;
MLine 4 to Hangsung University, Exit 6) This is
a delightful hillside temple that is beautiful to visit at any time of year, but particularly so in May when the grounds are
festooned with lanterns for the Buddha's
birthday. There's a small teahouse, and the
temple offers an overnight Templestay program on the fourth Saturday and Sunday of
the month. A shuttle bus runs to the temple from near the subway exit at 8.30am,
9.20am, 9.40am, 10am, noon, 1pm, 3pm
and 4.30pm.

Inwangsan Guksadang   SHRINE
(인왕산 국사당; Seodeamun; MLine 3 to Dongnimmun, Exit 2) Originally located on Namsan
and used to make sacrifices and to perform
exorcisms, this is Seoul's most famous shamanist shrine. The Japanese demolished
it in 1925, so Korean shamanists rebuilt it

Hongdae, Sinchon, Edae & Around

here. The shrine is above the temple **Seonamjeong**, marked by a bell pavilion and gates painted with a pair of traditional door guardians.

From the shrine walk left and up some steps to the extraordinary **Seon-bawi**, another sacred Shaminist site. This Dali-esque outcrop of rock provides spectacular views of the city. To the east is part of Seoul's old **fortress wall**, which you can follow back down to the main road and subway.

Jeoldusan Martyrs' Shrine   CHURCH, MUSEUM
(절두산 순교성지; www.jeoldusan.or.kr; admission by donation; ⊙museum 9.30am-5pm Tue-Sun; ⓂLine 2 or 6 to Hapjeong station, Exit 7) Commemorating the hideous torture and murder of thousands of Catholics in 1866, Jeoldusan, meaning 'beheading hill', includes a church, a small museum and a sculpture park. It's a 10-minute walk from the subway exit.

FREE **Ewha Womans University**   ARCHITECTURE, MUSEUM
(off Map p50; www.ewha.ac.kr; ⓂLine 2 to Ewha Womans University, Exit 2) Come here to view Dominique Perrault's stunning main entrance, a building that dives six storeys underground and is split by a broad cascade of steps leading up to the Gothic-style 1935 Pfeiffer Hall. To the left of the entrance is the university **museum** (museum.ewha.ac.kr; admission free; ⊙9.30am-5pm Mon-Sat) dis-

playing gorgeous examples of traditional ceramics, art, furniture and clothing. The campus is a two-minute walk from the station exit.

KT&G SangsangMadang   ARCHITECTURE
(KT&G 상상마당; Map p50; www.sangsangma dang.com; Seogyo-dong, Hongdae; ⊙10am-11pm; ⓂLine 2 to Hongik University, Exit 5) This visually striking building is home to an arthouse cinema, a concert space (hosting top indie bands) and galleries that focus on experimental, fringe exhibitions. There's also a great design shop for gifts on the ground floor.

ITAEWON & YONGSAN-GU
이태원, 용산구

FREE **National Museum of Korea**   MUSEUM
(국립중앙박물관; www.museum.go.kr; ⊙9am-6pm Tue, Thu & Fri, to 9pm Wed & Sat, to 7pm Sun; ⓂLine 1 or Jungang Line to Ichon, Exit 2) Housed in a grand, marble-lined, modernist building, this museum cleverly channels natural light to show off Korea's ancient treasures. Fronting it are picturesque gardens with a reflecting pond, ancient stone pagodas, the original Bosingak bell and the Dragon Falls.

Inside you'll find galleries devoted to the various ruling dynasties, from simple comb-design pots and dolmens to the skillful and imaginative Baekje-era incense holder

Itaewon

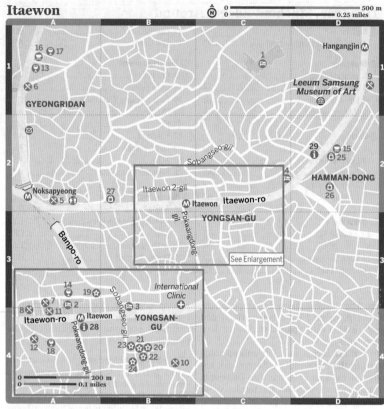

and the intricate goldwork of the Silla dynasty crowns and necklaces. If your time and stamina is limited, head straight to the wonderful ancient ceramics that Korea is famous for (3rd floor). Follow English signs to the museum from the subway exit.

Leeum Samsung Museum of Art MUSEUM
(Map p52; www.leeum.org; admission permanent collection adult/youth ₩10,000/6000, special exhibitions admission varies; ⊙10.30am-6pm Tue-Sun; Ⓜ Line 6 to Hangangjin, Exit 1) If you have time to visit just one art gallery in Seoul, the Leeum – a masterful combination of contemporary architecture and exquisite art – should be your first choice.

The complex is made up of three contrasting buildings designed by leading international architects. **Museum 1**, the work of Mario Botta, houses refined traditional works – beautiful ceramics, metalwork and Buddhist paintings. Modern art, both Korean and international, is the

focus of **Museum 2**, in a building designed by Jean Nouvel. Museum 3, the **Samsung Child Education & Culture Center**, is the vision of Rem Koolhaas, and is used for special exhibitions. Outdoor works include a couple of Louise Bourgeois' giant spider sculptures.

FREE **War Memorial of Korea** MUSEUM
(전쟁 기념관; off Map p52; www.warmemo .co.kr; ⊙9am-6pm Tue-Sun; Ⓜ Line 4 or 6 to Samgakji, Exit 12) This huge museum documents the history of warfare in Korea and has an especially good section on the Korean War (1950–53). Outside there's plenty of large military hardware, including tanks, helicopters, missiles and a B52 bomber, as well as monuments and giant statues. Time your visit to see the **Honour Guard Ceremony** (2pm Friday from early April until the end of June and mid-October to the end of November).

Itaewon

DONGDAEMUN & EASTERN SEOUL

Dongdaemun

Design Plaza & Park   ARCHITECTURE, MUSEUM
(DDP; 동대문; Map p54; http://ddp.seoul.go.kr; Dongdaemun; Ⓜ Line 1 & 4 to Dongdaemun, Exit 7) Set for completion in 2013 is architect Zaha Hadid's sleek concept, a curvaceous concrete structure, its silvery facade partly coated with lawns that rise up on to its roof. The building is planned to be a showcase for Korean and international design.

During the site's excavation major archaeological remains from the Joseon dynasty were uncovered, including original sections of Seoul's fortress wall. The remains have been incorporated into the surrounding park and include the arched floodgate Yigansumun. The **Dongdaemun History Museum** (admission free; ☺10am-9pm) imaginatively displays the pick of the 2575 artefacts from the site and provides the historical background to the ancient foundations preserved outside. Look for the patterned section of pavement made from clay tiles.

The **Dongdaemun Stadium Memorial** (admission free; ☺10am-9pm) relives key moments from the stadium's history and includes video clips. Towering over the park is a pair of the stadium's floodlight towers.

Heunginjimum (Dongdaemun) ARCHITECTURE (Map p54; Dongdaemun; Ⓜ Line 1 or 4 to Dongdaemun, Exit 6) The recently renovated Great East Gate to Seoul's fortress has been rebuilt several times in its 700-year history. Stranded in a traffic island, it's not possible to enter; view it from the remains of the fortress walls that snake uphill towards Naksan Park.

FREE **Seoul Forest**   PARK
(http://parks.seoul.go.kr; ☺24hr; Ⓜ Line 2 to Ttukseom, Exit 8) This big park is a 10-minute walk south towards the river from the subway exit. It provides pleasant, natural surroundings, with lakes, deer enclosures, eco areas, an insect exhibition, a plant nursery and fountains. You can hire a bicycle (₩3000 per hour) or a pair of inline skates (₩4000 per hour) from the **rental stall** (☺9am-10pm) by Gate 1. Cycle paths from here connect to those running along the Han River.

FREE **Children's Grand Park**   PARK
(www.childrenpark.or.kr; ☺5am-10pm; Ⓜ Line 5 & 7 to Children's Grand Park, Exit 1) Let your little ones run wild in this enormous playground, which includes a **zoo** (☺10am-6pm) with

Dongdaemun & Around

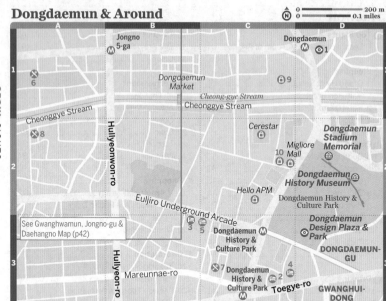

See Gwanghwamun, Jongno-gu & Daehangno Map (p42)

Dongdaemun

pony and camel rides; botanical garden with cacti up one end and a tropical jungle and bonsai trees at the other; wetland eco area; and amusement rides and a giant musical fountain.

SOUTH OF THE HAN RIVER

Olympic Park PARK
(올림픽 공원; Map p56; www.sosfo.or.kr; ☉5.30am-10.30pm; Ⓜ Line 8 to Mongchontoseong, Exit 1) This large and pleasant park, a focus of the 1988 Olympics, also contains the remains of the Mongchon-toseong (Mongchon Fortress), an earth rampart surrounded by a moat, built in the 3rd

century AD during the Baekje dynasty. Walk along the top of the old ramparts and learn more about it at the new **Seoul Baekje Museum** (http://baekjemuseum.seoul .go.kr; admission free; ☉9am-9pm Tue-Fri, to 6pm Sat & Sun).

More than 130 delightfully quirky sculptures that were created for the Olympics are scattered across this park. More art can be viewed inside the **Soma Museum of Art** (www .somamuseum.org; adult/teenager/child ₩3000/ 2000/1000; ☉10am-6pm Tue-Sun), which includes pieces by Nam June Paik and five galleries for special exhibitions.

Bongeun-sa   TEMPLE

(봉은사; Map p56; ☑3218 4801; www.bongeun
sa.org; Jamsil; MLine 2 to Samseong, Exit 6) Just
north of the COEX Mall and Convention
Centre, this Buddhist temple is spread
among a forested hillside and has a quieter,
more secluded atmosphere. Founded in AD
794, its buildings have been rebuilt many
times over the centuries. Entry to the temple is through Jinyeomun (Gate of Truth),
protected by four fierce guardians. On the
left is a small hut where an English-speaking
volunteer guide is usually available.

Lotte World   AMUSEMENT PARK

(롯데월드; Map p56; www.lotteworld.com; Jamsil; ◎9.30am-11pm; MLine 2 or 8 to Jamsil, Exit 3)
Kids and adults alike love this massive entertainment hub, which includes an amusement park, ice-skating rink (B3 fl; per session
adult/child ₩13,000/12,000, skate rental ₩4500;
◎10am-10pm), a theatre, multiplex cinema,
department store, shopping mall, hotel and
restaurants.

The main attraction is Lotte World Adventure & Magic Island (adult/teen/child ₩25,000/
22,000/19,000, passport incl most rides adult/teen/
child ₩40,000/35,000/31,000; ◎9.30am-10pm
Mon-Thu, to 11pm Fri-Sun), a Korean version of
Disneyland with the chipmunk-like Lotty
and Lorry standing in for Mickey and Min-
nie. General admission and ride passport
rates are reduced if you come after 4pm.

On the 3rd floor the Folk Museum (adult/
teenager/child ₩5000/3000/2000; ◎9.30am-
8pm) uses imaginative techniques like dioramas, scale models and moving waxworks
to bring scenes from Korean history to life.
Entrance is included in the day-passport ticket for Lotte World Adventure & Magic Island.

Noryangjin Fish Market   MARKET

(노량진수산시장; www.susansijang.co.kr; ◎24hr;
MLine 1 or 9 to Noryangjin, Exit 1) Every kind of
marine life is swimming around in tanks,
buckets and bowls at Seoul's fascinating
fish market. Giant octopuses, stingray and
lobsters are just some of the vast number
of sea creatures on sale from hundreds of
merchants. You can buy your fish, have it
filleted and then retire to one of several restaurants on the upper floor to eat it; see p77
for a recommendation. Access the market
via the pedestrian bridge that goes across
the train tracks from Exit 1 of Noryangjin
station.

Seonjeongneung   ROYAL TOMBS

(선정릉; Map p56; http://seonjeong.cha.go.kr;
Seonjeongneung Park, Gangnam-gu; adult/teen-
ager ₩1000/500; ◎6am-5.30pm Tue-Sun Mar-
Oct, 6.30am-8pm Tue-Sun Nov-Feb; MLine 2 or
Bundang Line to Seolleung, Exit 8) The tombs of
the Joseon kings and queens are scattered
all around Seoul and the surrounding area.
Thickly wooded Seongjongneung Park contains two main burial areas. The first is for
King Seongjong (r 1469–94) and his second wife, Queen Jeonghyeon Wanghu;
the second for King Seongjong and Queen
Jeonghyeon's second son, King Jeongjong
(r 1506–44). At this tomb you can see the full

SEOUL FORTRESS WALL

By the late 14th century an 18.6km wall encircled Seoul linking up the peaks of Bukaksan (342m), Naksan (125m), Namsan (262m) and Inwangsan (338m). The wall was
punctuated by four major gates facing north, south, east and west, with sub-gates
between them. As Seoul modernised, parts of the wall were demolished and today
only 10.5km of it remains. However, the city has been rebuilding and restoring some of
the missing sections. A hiking route around the original fortress is detailed in the free
English-language booklet *Walking Along the Fortress Wall of Seoul*, available from tourist information offices.

In 1968 North Korean agents launched an assassination attempt on then-president
Park Chung-hee by climbing over Bukaksan and down into the presidential compound
of Cheongwadae. From then until 2006 the mountain was off-limits. Security is still tight
but the 342m peak is now open to the public on a steep hike along the most spectacular
section of Seoul's Fortress Wall, providing amazing views of the city. You need to show
your passport or other photo ID and register when you enter at either Changuimun,
the old sub-gate in Buam-dong, or Sukjeongmun, the main north gate, which can be
accessed from Samcheong Park; there's no need to register in advance as mentioned
on the website (www.bukak.or.kr). Hiking is permitted 9am to 3pm April to October,
10am to 3pm November to March.

Jamsil

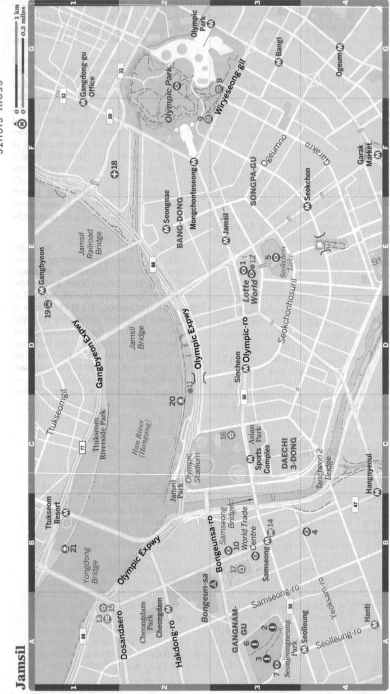

Jamsil

layout – the gateway and the double pathway to the pavilion where memorial rites were carried out.

63 City AQUARIUM, VIEWPOINT
(www.63.co.kr; Ⓜ Line 5 to Yeouinaru, Exit 4) This gold-tinted glass skyscraper, one of Seoul's tallest buildings overlooking the Han River, offers four attractions plus a theatre. The best reason to come here is for the view from **63 Sky Art Gallery** (adult/child ₩12,000/11,000; ◷10am-9.30pm), which combines a 60th-floor observation deck with good changing art exhibitions. In the basement, where you'll find the main ticket hall, is the aquarium **63 Sea World** (adult/child ₩17,000/15,000; ◷10am-9.30pm), with penguin, seal and sea lion shows. If you have more time to kill, there's also **63 Art Hall** (adult/child ₩12,000/11,000; ◷10am-5.30pm), an IMAX theatre showing hourly movies with English-language commentary via an earphone; and the mini Madame Tussaud's–like **63 Wax Museum** (adult/child ₩14,000/13,000; ◷10am-9.30pm). There are discount packages for three and four of the attractions, plus a further small foreigner discount (if you ask).

COEX Aquarium AQUARIUM
(Map p56; www.coexaqua.com; COEX, Yeongdong-daero, Gangnam-gu; adult/teenager/child ₩17,500/14,500/11,000; ◷10am-8pm, last entry 7pm;

Ⓜ Line 2 to Samseong, Exit 6) Seoul's largest aquarium has thousands of fish and other sea creatures from around the world. You can see live coral, sharks, turtles, rays and evil-looking piranhas in their Amazonia World tanks. Exquisite small creatures such as pulsating jellyfish, glass fish and sea horses are also on display as are the ever-popular penguins.

FREE **Bampo Bridge & Floating Island** ARCHITECTURE
(off Map p58; http://hangang.seoul.go.kr/eng; Hanggan Riverside Park; Ⓜ Line 3, 7 or 9 to Express Bus Terminal, Exit 8-1) At 1140m long, the world's longest fountain rains down in graceful arcs from the double-decker **Bampo Bridge** and is best viewed from **Bampo Hangang Park**. The 15-minute show usually happens between April and the end of August at noon, 8pm and 9pm Monday to Friday and noon, 6pm, 8pm, 8.30pm and 9pm on Saturday and Sunday. At night 200 coloured lights turn the water sprays into a rainbow, which explains its official name, **Moonlight Rainbow Fountain**. Shows are cancelled if it's raining.

Just to the west of the bridge are three man-made floating islets, connected by pathways and anchored to the bottom of the river. Crowned by sculptural glass auditoria, the complex is called the **Floating Island** (www.floatingisland.com) and is a pretty sight,

Apgujeong, Gangnam & Yongsan-gu

particularly when illuminated at night. However, not much happens here – there's not even a cafe.

Underneath Bampo Bridge, **Jamsu bridge** has walking and cycling lanes leading across to the Hangang Park on the north side; uphill from here is Itaewon.

🏃 Activities

Bicycles can be rented at several parks along the Han River including on Yeouido and Seoul Forest Park.

Top hotels have attractive sauna and fitness facilities that nonguests can sometimes use for a hefty price. Instead, join locals sweating it out at *jjimjil-bang* (luxury sauna) complexes, some of which have great spa baths, as well as internet, DVD rooms, cafes and sleeping areas. Open round the clock, these places can double up as bargain crash pads. If you use the *jjimjil-bang* as well as the sauna, you'll pay a higher entrance charge.

Dragon Hill Spa & Resort SAUNA
(드래곤힐스파; Map p40; www.dragonhillspa .co.kr; Yongsan; day/night Mon-Fri ₩10,000/12,000, Sat & Sun all day ₩12,000; ⊙24hr; ⓜLine 1 to Yongsan, Exit 1; ⊛) This foreigner-friendly *jjimjil-bang* – a noisy mix of gaudy Las Vegas bling and Asian chic – is one of Seoul's largest, offering enough attractions over its seven floors to keep you entertained for the 12 hours you can stay. In addition to the outdoor unisex pool, all manner of indoor saunas (including one shaped like a pyramid) and ginseng and cedar baths, there is a golf driving range, cinema, PC games room, beauty treatment rooms and multiple dining options.

Silloam Sauna SAUNA
(실로암사우나찜질방; Map p48; www.silloam sauna.com; Jungrim-dong; sauna adult/child before 8pm ₩8000/6000, sauna & jjimjil-bang adult/child before 8pm ₩10,000/7000; ⊙24hr; ⓜLine 1 or 4 to Seoul Station, Exit 1) Across the street from Seoul Station, this spick-and-span foreigner-

Apgujeong, Gangnam & Yongsan-gu

friendly operation (lots of signs in English), with a wide range of baths and sauna rooms, is great if you need to freshen up before or after a trip out to the airport, or get into town late and need a temporary place to stay. Rates for the 8pm to 5am session are slightly higher.

Han River Cruises CRUISE
(www.hcruise.co.kr; Yeouido; adult/child ₩11,000/5500; ⊙11am-8.40pm; Ⓜ Line 5 to Yeouinaru, Exit 3) Take a trip from Yeouido pier to any of the Han River ferry piers or take a one-hour round trip back to Yeouido. You can also board night cruises here and ones on which magic tricks are performed.

Spa Lei SPA
(Map p58; ☑545 4113; www.spalei.co.kr; Cresyn Bldg, Jamwong-dong, Seoch-gu; day/night rate ₩12,000/14,000; ⊙24hr; Ⓜ Line 3 to Sinsa, Exit 5) Luxurious women-only spa providing excellent services in an immaculate, stylish environment. Helpful staff are used to dealing with foreigners.

Olympic Coliseum Golf GOLF
(Map p58; ☑514 7979; Seolleung-ro, Gangnam; ⊙5am-10pm; Ⓜ Line 3 to Apgujeong, Exit 2) Not just for practising your golf swing; at Olympic you can also use the gym and relax in the spa, all for ₩30,000 (70 minutes).

🍜 Courses

O'ngo COOKING
(Map p60; ☑3446 1607; www.ongofood.com; Insa-dong; courses from ₩65,000, tours from ₩57,000; Ⓜ Line 1, 3 or 5 to Jongno 3-ga, Exit 5) Cooking classes and food tours around the city are run by the knowledgeable Dan Grey of Seoul Eats (www.seouleats.com) and his team. The beginners class lasts two hours and covers four dishes; the intermediate course can cover Buddhist temple cuisine.

Hansik Experience Centre COOKING
(Map p42; ☑772 9180; www.korea-food.or.kr; Jonggak; courses from ₩30,000; ⊙courses 10am, 2pm & 5pm Mon-Sat; Ⓜ Line 1 to Jonggak, Exit 5) At the KTO Information Centre is a kitchen where you can get hands-on experience at making Korean foods (hansik), such as kimchi, bulgogi and bibimbap. When cooking classes are not being held it offers free food tasting.

Yoo's Family COOKING
(Map p42; ☑3673 0323; www.yoosfamily.com; Kwonnong-dong; courses ₩20,000-70,000; ⊙Mon-Sat;

Insa-dong

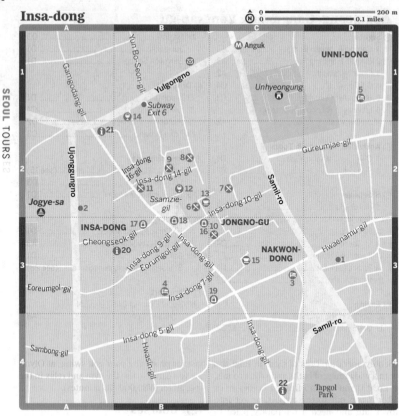

M Line 3 to Anguk, Exit 4) Housed in a *hanok*, Yoo's Family's cooking courses cover making *kimchi* and pancakes as well as various other foods. You can also practise the tea ceremony here, make prints from carved wooden blocks and dress up in *hanbok*. A minimum of two persons is required.

YBM Sisa   LANGUAGE
(Map p42; ☑2278 0509; http://kli.ybmedu.com; Insadong; course from ₩130,000; ⊙6.30am-9pm Mon-Fri, 9am-4pm Sat & Sun; M Line 1, 3 or 5 to Jongno 3-ga, Exit 15) Korean classes (maximum size 10) for all ability levels cover grammar, writing and conversation. Private tuition (₩40,000 per hour for one person) can also be arranged here.

Yonsei University   LANGUAGE
(☑2123 3465; www.yskli.com; Sinchon; M Line 6 to Sinchon, Exit 6) The university runs part-time and full-time Korean-language and culture classes for serious students.

☞ Tours

Seoul City Tour Bus   BUS
(☑777 6090; www.seoulcitybus.com; ⊙Tue-Sun; M Line 5 to Gwangwhamun, Exit 6) If you want to see as much as possible in a short time, this is one way to go. Comfortable and colourful tour buses run between Seoul's top tourist attractions north of the Han River. Hop on and hop off anywhere along the two routes: downtown (adult/child ₩10,000/8000, 9am to 7pm, half-hourly) and around the palaces (adult/child ₩12,000/8000, 10am to 5pm, hourly). Buy tickets on the bus, which can be picked up outside Dongwha Duty Free Shop (Map p42) at Gwanghwamun. Check the website for details of night tours that zigzag across the Han River so you can view the lit-up bridges.

Koridoor Tours   BUS
(☑795 3028; www.koridoor.co.kr) Apart from running the very popular DMZ/JSA tour for the USO (see p96), this company also offers

Insa-dong

city tours; trips to out-of-town destinations such as Suwon and Incheon; paragliding, scuba diving and deep-sea fishing tours; and ski trips to local resorts in the winter.

Royal Asiatic Society WALKING
(www.raskb.com) Organises enlightening tours to all parts of South Korea, usually on weekends; check the website for the schedule. Nonmembers are welcome to join. The reasonably priced tours are led by English speakers who are experts in their field. The society also holds lectures several times a month.

Discover Seoul Desk WALKING
(☑795 0355; www.dragonhilllodge.org/Discover Seoul) Walking tours of Seoul Fortress, led by entertaining guide Jacco Zwetsloot, are offered by the tour desk at the Dragon Hill Lodge on Yongsan Army Base. Join the tours at Gate 1 of the base and make payment over the phone or via email with your credit card.

★★ Festivals & Events

Seoul has a busy calendar of festivals worth watching out for. Visit www.knto.or.kr for locations and dates that vary from year to year.

April
Hangang Yeouido
Spring Flower Festival BOTANICAL
(http://tour.ydp.go.kr) One of the best places to experience the blossoming trees and flowers

is Yeouido. Other good spots include Namsan and Ewha Womans University and Jeongdok Public Library in Samcheong-dong.

May
Jongmyo Daeje CULTURAL
(www.jongmyo.net/english_index.asp) On the first Sunday in May this ceremony honours Korea's royal ancestors, and involves a costumed parade from Gyeongbokgung through central Seoul to the royal shrine at Jongmyo, where spectators can enjoy traditional music and an elaborate ritual.

Lotus Lantern Festival BUDDHIST
(www.llf.or.kr/eng) On the Sunday before Buddha's birthday, a huge parade is held from Dongdaemun to Jogye-sa starting at 7pm.

July
Puchon International
Fantastic Film Festival FILM
(www.pifan.com) Cinema-lovers head out to Bucheon (Puchon), just outside of Seoul, to feast on the best in sci-fi, fantasy and horror. Theatres are within walking distance from Songnae station, Line 1, towards Incheon.

Seoul International
Cartoon & Animation Festival ANIMATION
(www.sicaf.org) Half a million animation fans pack auditoriums in Seoul each year to see why the city is an epicentre of animated craftsmanship.

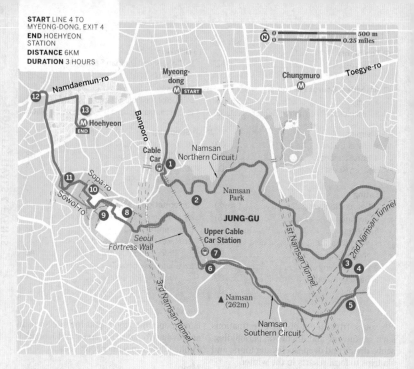

START LINE 4 TO
MYEONG-DONG, EXIT 4
END HOEHYEON
STATION
DISTANCE 6KM
DURATION 3 HOURS

Walking Tour
Namsan Circuit

❯ Following pedestrian pathways and parts
of the Seoul Fortress Wall, this hike takes
you around and over Namsan, providing
sweeping city views along the way and a
chance to enjoy the mountain's greenery and
fresh air. It's best done early in the morning,
but leafy trees do provide some shade most
of the way. From the subway exit walk up to
the ❶ **cable-car station**; just before you
reach here you'll see steps leading up the
mountainside to the pedestrian-only Namsan
Northern Circuit.

Walk left for five minutes, and pause to
look around the shrine ❷ **Waryongmyo**, before following the road as it undulates gently
around the mountain, past routes down to
Namsangol Hanok Village and Dongguk University, until you reach the ❸ **outdoor gym**
uphill from the National Theatre of Korea.

You can cut out the next bit by hopping on
one of the buses that go to the peak from the
❹ **bus stop** near here. Otherwise turn right
at the start of the Namsan Southern Circuit
road and you'll soon see the ❺ **fortress**

walls. A steep set of steps shadows the wall
for part of the way to the summit; at the fork
continue on the steps over the wall and follow the path to ❻ **N Seoul Tower** and the
❼ **Bongoodae** (signal beacons).

Grab some refreshments to enjoy at the
geological centre of Seoul, before picking up
the Fortress Wall trail down to pretty
❽ **Joongang Park**. On the left is ❾ **Ahn
Junggeun Museum** and on the right the
tower block housing Seoul Education Research Institute.

A newly created continuation of the park
over a road tunnel leads via ❿ **Baekboem
Sq** and ⓫ **Adong Sq** down to towards
the Hilton Hotel; along the way you'll see
reconstructed sections of the wall. Finish up
by taking a look at the reconstruction of
⓬ **Sungnyemun (Namdaemun)**, then
browsing ⓭ **Namdaemun Market**.

August

Seoul Fringe Festival
PERFORMING ARTS

(www.seoulfringe.net, in Korean) One of Seoul's best performing-arts festivals, when local and international artists converge on the hipster Hongdae area to flee the mainstream.

September

Korea International Art Fair
ART

(www.kiaf.org) COEX's convention centre is the location for this fair in which hundreds of local and international galleries participate.

Sajik Daeje
CULTURAL

(www.rfo.co.kr) Held at Sajikdan on the third Sunday of the month, the 'Great Rite for the Gods of Earth and Agriculture' is one of Seoul's most important ancestral rituals and designated as an Important Intangible Cultural Property.

Seoul Drum Festival
MUSIC

(www.seouldrum.go.kr) Focusing on Korea's fantastic percussive legacy, this three-day event brings together from around the world all kinds of ways to make a lot of noise.

October

Seoul Performing Arts Festival
PERFORMING ARTS

(www.spaf.or.kr) The city's most prestigious performing-arts fest lasts a month and offers works by Korean and a wide range of international companies and artists in venues across Seoul.

Seoul International Fireworks Festival
FIREWORKS

(www.bulnori.com) Best viewed from Yeouido Hangang Park, this festival sees dazzling fireworks displays staged by both Korean and international teams.

November

Seoul Lantern Festival
CULTURAL

(http://blog.naver.com/seoullantern) Centred along the Cheong-gye-cheon, this festival sees the stream park illuminated by gigantic fantastic lanterns made by master craftsmen.

🛏 Sleeping

Seoul has a good selection of budget accommodation, including several backpacker options, some even in *hanok*. There's also no shortage of top-end places, but in the midrange, if you're looking for somewhere memorable rather than ubiquitously bland, your options will be narrowed to Bukchon's *hanok* guesthouses and a handful of design-conscious operations scattered around the city.

For Seoul, budget places are those that offer double rooms with bathroom facilities for under ₩60,000, midrange places are ₩60,000 to ₩250,000 and top end is over ₩250,000. Prices don't normally change with the seasons, although some hotels and guesthouses may offer special deals online or at quiet times.

GWANGHWAMUN & JONGNO-GU

The neighbourhood between Gyeongbokgung and Changdeokgung used to be home for high-court officials – with tons of atmosphere and close to many sites it's the best place to be based, especially if you stay in one of the many restored *hanok*. Bear in mind that *hanok* rooms are small, bathrooms are cramped (but modern), and you sleep on a thin *yo* (padded quilt) mattress on an *ondol*-heated floor.

TOP CHOICE **Chi-Woon-Jung** HANOK GUESTHOUSE $$$

(취운정; Map p42; 765 7400; www.chiwoonjung.com; 31-53 Gahoe-don; s/d from ₩500,000/1,000,000; Line 3 to Anguk, Exit 2; ❀🛜) The *hanok* as an exclusive luxury experience doesn't get much finer than at this stunning property with four elegant guestrooms, all with beautifully tiled bathrooms and pine-wood tubs. Rooms are decorated with beautiful handicrafts and wrapped around by a Zen-calm garden. Rates include breakfast and dinner, which is a sumptuous royal banquet served by the charming staff dressed in floaty *hanbok*.

TOP CHOICE **Fraser Suites** SERVICED APARTMENT $$$

(Map p60; 6262 8888; www.frasershospitality.com; 272 Nakwon-dong; 1/2/3-bedroom apt ₩330,000/440,000/550,000; Line 1, 3 & 5 to Jongno 3-ga, Exit 5; ❀@🛜⚛) These fully equipped serviced apartments are modern, light and spacious, great for a long-term stay, for which major discounts are available. Its location, steps away from Insadong-gil, can't be beat. A buffet breakfast is included in the rates.

Rak-Ko-Jae
HANOK GUESTHOUSE $$$

(락고재; Map p42; 742 3410; www.rkj.co.kr; 98 Gyeo-dong; s/d ₩198,000/275,000; Line 3 to Anguk, Exit 2; ❀@) This beautifully restored *hanok*, with an enchanting garden and mud-walled sauna, is modelled after Japan's *ryokan*. Rates cover breakfast, dinner, traditional tea ceremony and copious amounts of house-made spirits. Bathrooms are tiny, though.

Hotel Sunbee
HOTEL $$

(썬비호텔; Map p60; ☑730 3451; www.hotel sunbee.com; 198-11 Gwanhun-dong; d/tw/ondol ₩100,000/120,000/140,000; Ⓜ Line 3 to Anguk, Exit 6; ❋@✆) This hotel has a great location close to Insa-dong-gil. Its double beds are huge and the rooms are decorated tastefully. Many rooms come with a wide-screen TV and computer. Breakfast is coffee, toast and orange juice in your room.

Seoul Guesthouse
HANOK GUESTHOUSE $$

(서울게스트하우스; Map p42; ☑745 0057; www.seoul110.com; 135-1 Gye-dong; s/d/f ₩50,000/70,000/120,000; Ⓜ Line 3 to Anguk, Exit 3; ✆) This wooden *hanok* has a charming courtyard garden, and the English-speaking owners (who have an adorable shaggy dog Ssari) are helpful hosts. It's a delightful place to stay, but as with other *hanok,* rooms are small, bathrooms are cramped (but modern) and you sleep on a *yo* (padded quilt) mattress on an *ondol*-heated floor. It also rents out a separate *hanok* sleeping six for ₩230,000.

Moon Guest House
HANOK GUESTHOUSE $$

(Map p60; ☑745 8008; www.moonguesthouse. com; 87-1 Unni-dong; s/d from ₩60,000/80,000; Ⓜ Line 3 to Anguk, Exit 4; ❋✆) There are seven rooms at this 50-year-old *hanok,* which has been newly renovated to a high standard. Rooms are tiny and the cheapest share bathrooms, but breakfast is included in the rates and various traditional cultural experiences are offered to guests.

Sophia Guest House
HANOK GUESTHOUSE $$

(Map p42; ☑720 5467; www.sophiagh.com; 157-1 Sogyeok-dong; s/d from ₩50,000/70,000; Ⓜ Line 3 to Anguk, Exit 1; ❋✆) Rooms surround a pretty courtyard at this place run by hospitable Sophia. The main *hanok* has nine rooms (all of which share bathrooms) and there's five more rooms in an annexe building around the corner. It has an antique feel but there are TVs in the rooms and rates include breakfast.

Anguk Guesthouse
HANOK GUESTHOUSE $$

(안국게스트하우스; Map p42; ☑736 8304; www.anguk-house.com; 72-3 Anguk-dong; s/d & tw ₩50,000/70,000; Ⓜ Line 3 to Anguk, Exit 1; ❋@) Down a quiet alley, the four varnished wood rooms at this *hanok* are spread around a courtyard. All have a bathroom as well as a computer, and beds rather than *yo* mattresses. The kitchen can be used to make a DIY breakfast. Owner Mr Kim speaks English.

Doo Guesthouse
HANOK GUESTHOUSE $$

(Map p42; ☑3672 1977; www.dooguesthouse .com; 15-6 Gye-dong; s/d/tr/f ₩50,000/60,000/ 80,000/120,000; Ⓜ Line 3 to Anguk, Exit 3; ❋@✆) Mixing old and new is this enchanting *hanok* in a garden setting that has a very traditional-style room where breakfast is served. The shared bathrooms are high quality, with bidets and walk-in showers. The rooms have TVs and DVD players.

Noble Hotel
HOTEL $$

(Map p42; ☑742 4025; www.noblehotel.co.kr; 19 Unni-dong; d/tw ₩70,000/80,000; Ⓜ Line 3 to Anguk, Exit 4; ❋@) Looking for just a nice room? In a good location? Want a computer in it? And a giant LCD TV? And a whirlpool bath? And free drinks? Free body lotions? All at a cheap price? Look no further than this midrange hotel that is a cut above the average.

YMCA Tourist Hotel
HOTEL $$

(Map p42; ☑734 6884; www.ymca.or.kr/hotel; s/d/ tw/tr ₩71,500/88,000/99,000/143,000; ❋✆) We can't guarantee whether its fun to stay at the YMCA, but this 8th-floor hotel in a very central location offers a decent range of clean, simply furnished rooms, with friendly service. Breakfast is included and it's served in the popular coffee shop on the ground floor.

Inn Daewon
GUESTHOUSE $

(대원여관; Map p42; ☑787 4308; dm/d & tw ₩19,000/35,000, s ₩27,000; Ⓜ Line 3 to Gyeong-bokgung, Exit 4) As lovable as a scruffy dog, this long-running inn has the cheapest *hanok*-style accommodation, built around a covered courtyard. Everything is cramped, and guests sleep on floor mattresses, except in the dorm reached up a steep flight of stairs. Toilets and showers are shared. Daewon's greatest asset is the owner, Mr Kim, and his wife (they live next door), who are brimfull of kindness.

Beewon Guesthouse
GUESTHOUSE $

(비원장; Map p42; ☑765 0677; www.beewon guesthouse.com; 28-2 Unni-dong; dm ₩19,000, d & ondol/tr ₩50,000/60,000; Ⓜ Line 3 to An-guk, Exit 4; ❋@✆) Combining facility-filled motel-style rooms with free, guesthouse-style communal facilities, the clean and tidy Beewon is generally quiet and friendly, plastered with photos of happy past guests. Look for an orange-tiled building. Add ₩5000 to rates for stays on Friday and Saturday.

SEOUL FOR CHILDREN

Seoul is a safe and family-friendly city with plenty of interesting museums (including several devoted to kids themselves) as well as parks, amusement parks and fun events that will appeal to all age groups.

The best way to cut down on child grumbles is to mix your sampling of traditional Korean culture with things that the kids are more likely to enjoy. Fortunately, thanks to the global appeal of local pop culture, the young ones are likely to be more au fait with contemporary Korean pop culture than you! Be prepared to search out shops stocking Girls Generation posters, DVDs of the latest Korean TV soap opera, or *manhwa* (Korean print comics and graphic novels): Kyobo Bookstore is a good place to start.

Not that museums and other traditional culture centres need be boring. The National Museum of Korea and the National Folk Museum of Korea have fun, hands-on childrens sections, and the War Memorial of Korea has outdoor warplanes and tanks that make for a popular playground. Various events, some involving dressing up in traditional costumes or having a go at taekwondo, happen at Namsangol Hanok Village.

Amusements parks include the theme-park extravaganzas of Lotte World and Everland Resort (see the boxed text, p102), an easy day trip from the city. There are also scores of free city-managed parks – places such as Seoul Forest, Olympic Park and the string of bicycle-lane-connected parks that hug the banks of the Han River; each summer six big outdoor pool complexes open in the Han River Parks, too.

Korea 4 Expats.com (www.korea4expats.com) has more child-related information on Seoul.

Guesthouse Korea   BACKPACKERS **$**
(게스트하우스 코리아; Map p42; ☑3675 2205; www.guesthouseinkorea.com; 155-1 Gwongnong-dong; dm/s/d & tw from ₩19,000/33,000/44,000; Ⓜ Line 3 to Anguk, Exit 4; ✻@☎) The large, messy communal living room is furnished with comfy armchairs, free computers, a breakfast area and even a bar. Newcomers to Seoul and solo travellers can mix in and mingle easily even when there's no party raging. The rooms and dorms have air-con and modern bathrooms; private rooms also have a TV and fridge.

MYEONG-DONG & JUNG-GU

Banyan Tree Club & Spa   HOTEL **$$$**
(Map p48; ☑2256 6677; www.banyantreeclub.net; 60 Jang Chang Dan-ro; r from ₩550,000; Ⓜ Line 3 to Beotigogae, Exit 1; ✻@☎≋) Billing itself a 'sanctuary for the senses', the Banyan Tree, occupying a hilltop tower designed by feted local architect Kim Swoon Guen, offers just four rooms per floor. Calmly decorated and coolly sophisticated, each room has a giant relaxation pool and amazing views.

The Plaza   HOTEL **$$$**
(Map p48; ☑771 2200; www.hoteltheplaza.com; 23 Taepyeong-ro 2-ga; r from ₩387,200; Ⓜ Line 1 or 2 to City Hall, Exit 6; ✻@☎≋) Opposite the new City Hall, you couldn't get more central than the Plaza, which was given a striking makeover inside and out in 2010. Rooms sport a trendy design with giant anglepoise lamps, circular mirrors and crisp white linens contrasting against dark carpets. It also has some chic restaurants and a good fitness club with a 20m pool.

Westin Chosun   HOTEL **$$$**
(Map p48; ☑771 0500; www.westin.com/seoul; 87 Sogong-dong; r from ₩410,000; Ⓜ Line 2 to Euljiro 1-ga, Exit 4; ✻@☎≋) Not Seoul's most spectacular hotel, but the relaxing atmosphere and the conscientious staff keep it a cut above many. Each stylish room, decorated in soft caramel tones, comes with a rent-free mobile phone and choice of 10 types of pillows. Note that free entrance to the sports club and pool is only for executive-floor guests and those staying in suites.

Lotte Hotel   HOTEL **$$$**
(Map p48; ☑771 1000; www.lottehotelseoul.com; 30 Euljiro; r old/new wing from ₩423,500/542,800; Ⓜ Line 2 to Euljiro 1-ga, Exit 8; ✻@☎≋) The natural extension to its Myeong-dong shopping empire, this twin-towered hotel with over 1000 rooms has a marble-lined lobby long enough for Usain Bolt training runs. The new wing's standard rooms are bigger than those in the old but don't have such a modern design. There's also a ladies-only floor with a book-lined lounge. Renowned French chef Pierre Gagnaire's new restaurant is on the 35th floor.

1. Gyeongbokgung (p39)
The beautiful grounds of the 'palace of shining happiness' contain islands on an artifical lake

2. Cheong-gye-cheon (p46)
This revitalised stream runs through the centre of the capital

3. Dongdaemun Design Plaza & Park (p53)
Sculptures on display at Seoul's stylish new plaza including the haechi, symbol of the city

Metro Hotel HOTEL $$

(메트로호텔; Map p48; ☑752 1112; www
.metrohotel.co.kr; 199-33 Euljiro 2-ga; s/d from
₩115,500/126,500; ⓜLine 2 to Euljiro 1-ga, Exit
6; ❄@✉) This small, professionally run
hotel has boutique aspirations. Splashes
of style abound, beginning with the flashy,
metallic-style lobby and its laptops. Room
size and design vary – ask for one of the
larger ones with big windows (room num-
bers ending in '07'). Prices cover a Western
breakfast.

Hotel Prince HOTEL $$

(프린스호텔; Map p48; ☑752 7111; www.prince
seoul.com; Toegye-ro, Myeong-dong; d/tw/ondol
₩143,000/170,500/220,000; ⓜLine 4 to Myeong-
dong, Exit 2; ❄@✉) Rooms at this well-located
business hotel are smallish but sparkling,
with some bright primary colours to allevi-
ate an otherwise all-white regime. Online
booking discounts can make it an excellent
deal and rates include a buffet breakfast and
free wi-fi.

Pacific Hotel HOTEL $$

(퍼시픽호텔; Map p48; ☑777 7811; www.thepa
cifichotel.co.kr; 31-1 Namsan-dong 2-ga; d/tw
₩150,400/178,200; ⓜLine 4 to Myeong-dong, Exit
3; ❄@✉) Bell boys in caps greet you at this
hotel, which exudes old-fashioned elegance.
Light neutral colours, greenery and natural-
wood effects are the design style. Bathrooms
are a tad cramped, but there's a big sauna
and spa bath in the building as well as a
small rooftop garden.

Han Suites SERVICED APARTMENT $$

(Map p48; ☑2280 8000; www.hansuites.com;
2-19 Yejang-dong; studio/1-bedroom apt from
₩88,000/231,000; ⓜLine 3 or 4 to Chungmuro, Exit
4; ❄@✉) A great location, friendly and professional service and reasonable rates make
this one of the best serviced-apartment options for short or long stays. Rooms are
plainly furnished but have everything you
need. Note that many of the cheaper studios
have windows onto an internal light well so
can be rather gloomy.

Namsan Guesthouse BACKPACKERS $

(남산게스트하우스; Map p48; ☑752 6363;
www.namsanguesthouse.com; 33-3 Namsan-dong
2-ga; d & tw from ₩45,000; ⓜLine 4 to Myeong-
dong, Exit 2; ❄@✉) Now in two locations on
the slopes of Namsan, this long-running
backpacker guesthouse is a good choice.
The newer location, lower down the mountain opposite a wedding hall, offers the better rooms and some breezy terraces that allow you to mingle with fellow guests. Basic
breakfast included in the rates.

Alps Seoul GUESTHOUSE $$

(Map p48; ☑754 5111; www.alpsseoul.com; 37-1
Namsan-dong 2-ga; r from ₩70,000; ⓜLine 4 to
Myeong-dong, Exit 2; ❄@✉) If you're looking
for somewhere central and with a bit more
space to spread out than at the backpack-
er lodges, this place in a large house may
be your answer. There's a kitchen and big
bathrooms, and some antique style to the
rooms. The company also has several other
short-stay apartments around the city for
rent.

Seoul Backpackers BACKPACKERS $

(서울백팩커스; Map p48; ☑3672 1972; www
.seoulbackpackers.com; 205-125 Namchang-dong;
s/d/f ₩50,000/60,000/75,000; ⓜLine 4 to Hoe-
hyeon, Exit 4) There are no dorms, but the
cramped motel-style rooms are brightly dec-
orated and have bathroom and TV. There's
scant communal areas beyond the lobby and
tiny kitchen. From the subway exit take the
first alley on the left and then walk down the
second alley.

International Seoul Youth Hostel HOSTEL $

(Map p48; ☑319 1318; www.seoulyh.go.kr; 100-
250 San 4-5 Yejang-dong; tw/ondol/q ₩60,000/
100,000/120,000; ⓜLine 4 to Chungmuro, Exit
4; ❄@✉) The slightly isolated position, 10
minutes' walk up Namsan from the subway
exit, is compensated for at this modern hos-
tel by huge rooms, a large kitchen for self-
catering and a delightful rooftop garden.
There's also a restaurant.

WESTERN & NORTHERN SEOUL

TOP CHOICE **V Mansion** BACKPACKERS $

(Map p50; ☑010-9627 6898; http://bvseoul.
com; 262-2 Sansu-dong, Mapo-gu; s/d ₩70,000/
100,000, dm/s/d without bathroom ₩27,000/
50,000/80,000; ⓜLine 6 to Sangsu, Exit 3; ❄@✉)
Converted from a 1960s restaurant, within
a minute's walk of the Han River park in
trendy Sangsu, this is a blissful place to chill.
It offers something quite unexpected from a
Seoul backpackers – space and a big garden!
There are plans to host exhibitions of local
artists and various arty events here to help
visitors connect with Seoul's more creative
spirits. Rates include breakfast.

Jaan Guesthouse GUESTHOUSE, APARTMENT $$

(Map p50; ☑010-9627 6898; www.jaamguest
house.net; 601 MJ Bldg, 400-10 Seokyo-dong,

Mapo-gu; d/apt from ₩70,000/150,000; MLine 2 or 6 to Hapjeong, Exit 1; ❋@🛏🛜) Exactly the colourful, groovy kind of pad you'd want to stay in Hongdae. This place sleeps up to six in three rooms and can be rented out as one apartment.

Bebop House
BACKPACKERS $

(Map p50; ☑8261 4835; http://bebop-guesthouse.com; 464-50 Seogyo-dong, Mapo-gu; dm/d/tw/tr from ₩20,000/60,000/75,000/75,000; MLine 2 to Hongik University, Exit 1; ❋@🛜) A little tricky to find (check its website for directions) but a real gem that captures the youthful, arty buzz of Hongik. The whitewashed house used to be an architect's office and is decorated with very funky wallpapered walls and tons of posters. Food is provided in the kitchen for you to make breakfast.

Lee & No Guesthouse
GUESTHOUSE $$

(리앤노게스트하우스; Map p50; ☑336 4878; www.lnguesthouse.com; Hongdae; dm/s/d & tw from ₩22,000/55,000/60,000; MLine 2 to Hongik University, Exit 2; ❋@🛜) Down a quiet cul-de-sac is this four-room guesthouse run by laid-back ex-backpacker Mr Lee and his wife. Bathrooms are shared but there's a patio and breakfast included. They also have two more appealing guesthouses in the area, **Namu** and **Studio 41st**. From Exit 2, take the second left, then cross over the road to Hana Bank and walk straight for five minutes. Turn right at Grazie Espresso, and it's on your left.

Eugene's House
HANOK GUESTHOUSE $$

(off Map p42; ☑741 3338; eugenehouse.co.kr; 5-43 Hyehwa-dong; s/d from ₩90,000/110,000, s/tw without bathroom ₩60,000/110,000; MLine 4 to Hyehwa, Exit 1; ❋🛜) The friendly family who run this *hanok* homestay speak English and have another *hanok* around the corner where they also conduct various cultural experiences. These homes have larger courtyards than similar places in Bukchon, and a pleasing, lived-in quality. Rates include breakfast.

Inside Backpackers
BACKPACKERS $

(Map p42; ☑3672 1120; www.backpackersinside.com; 2nd fl, 112 Myeongryun 2-ga; s/d ₩42,000/60,000, dm/s/d without bathroom ₩16,000/27,000/44,000; MLine 4 to Hyehwa, Exit 4; @🛜) The best of several backpacker hostels in the Daehangno area, this is a friendly, clean place with plenty of character and room options. It also has rooms in a characterful *hanok* closer to the subway exit.

ITAEWON & YONGSAN-GU

Grand Hyatt Seoul
HOTEL $$$

(Map p52; ☑797 1234; www.seoul.grand.hyatt.com; Hamman-dong; r/ste from ₩363,000/550,550; MLine 6 to Hangangjin, Exit 1; ❋@🛏🛜) Making the most of its hilltop views, the Grand Hyatt oozes class. Rooms are a bit smaller than at rivals but all have been freshly renovated and sport a contemporary look. Pamper yourself in the spa or swim in the excellent outdoor pool which, come winter, is turned into an ice rink.

IP Boutique Hotel
HOTEL $$$

(Map p52; ☑3702 8000; www.ipboutiquehotel.com; 731-32 Hamman-dong; s or d from ₩262,200; MLine 6 to Itaewon, Exit 2; ❋@🛏🛜) Trying a bit too hard to be hip with its bold contemporary artworks and quirky interior design choices, this boutique wannabe slightly misses the mark. Still, it has a great location and in a city with a dearth of these kinds of places it certainly stands out.

Hotel D'Oro
LOVE HOTEL $$

(디오로호텔; Map p52; ☑749 6525; 124-3 Itaewon, Yongsan-gu; d from ₩88,000; MLine 6 to Itaewon, Exit 2; ❋@🛜) This above-average love motel has some style and attitude, verging on the hip. It offers modern equipment and furnishings, and free soft drinks rather than an expensive minibar. The entrance is up the hill off the main road.

Hamilton Hotel
HOTEL $$

(해밀톤호텔; Map p52; ☑3786 6000; www.hamilton.co.kr; 179 Itaewon-ro; s/d & tw ₩106,900/132,000; MLine 6 to Itaewon, Exit 1; @🛏🛜) This workhorse of the Itaewon strip has zero style with mainly old-fashioned, although pretty spacious, rooms. In its favour is its location, and facilities such as a sauna, gym and outdoor pool (all available to in-house guests for 50% off the regular rates).

DONGDAEMUN & EASTERN SEOUL

W Seoul Walkerhill
HOTEL $$$

(☑465 2222; www.whotels.com/seoul; Walkerhill-ro, Gwangjin-gu; r from ₩363,000; MLine 5 to Gwangnaru, Exit 2; ❋@🛏🛜) One of the city's best-designed hotels with spectacular public areas and generally fab-licious rooms with striking colour schemes and splendid river or mountain views. The spa, pool, gym, trendy restaurants and happening Woobar are so nice you probably won't want to stray far, which is just as well as it's distant from most sights.

Euijiro CO-OP
Residence
SERVICED APARTMENT $$

(Map p54; ☎2269 4600; http://rent.co-op.co.kr; 32 Euijiro 6-ga, Jung-gu; studios from ₩90,000; Ⓜ Line 2, 4 or 5 to Dongdaemun History & Culture Park, Exit 12; ✻@⊛) These smart white studio apartments provide a chic little nest high above the 24-hour hurly-burly of Dongdaemun Market. Everything is bright, modern, stylish and mini-sized – not much elbow room. Slightly more space and better facilities, including a gym, are provided at the same company's nearby **Western CO-OP Residence**, where rates start at ₩120,000.

Tokoyo Inn Seoul Dongdaemun
HOTEL $$

(Map p54; ☎2267 1045; www.toyoko-inn.com; 73 Gwanghui-dong 2-ga, Jung-gu; s/d/tw from ₩60,500/77,000/88,000; Ⓜ Line 2, 4 & 5 to Dongdaemun History & Culture Park, Exit 4; ✻@) You've got to hand it to this Japanese business hotel group for bagging a prime spot close to the future Dongdaemun Design Plaza & Park. Small, clean and well-equipped rooms (with plenty of single ones) are great value with rates including a simple breakfast.

Dongdaemun Hostel
BACKPACKERS $

(Map p54; ☎070-7785 8055; www.dongdaemun hostel.com; 43-1 Gwanghui-dong 2-ga, Jung-gu; r ₩42,000; Ⓜ Lines 2, 4 & 5 to Dongdaemun History & Culture Park, Exit 4; ⊛) A lot is crammed into the nicely decorated tiny single rooms at this backpackers guesthouse, including computers, desk and a shower-toilet cubicle. Staff are helpful and there's also a tiny shared kitchen. A basic breakfast is included in the rates.

SOUTH OF THE HAN RIVER

TOP CHOICE La Casa
HOTEL $$

(Map p58; ☎546 0088; www.hotellacasa.kr; Sinsa-dong, Gangnam-gu; r/ste from ₩193,600/471,900; Ⓜ Line 3 to Sinsa, Exit 6; ✻@⊛) The first venture into the hospitality business by classy Korean furniture and interior-design store Casamia packs plenty of chic style. The rooms are attractive and spacious with quirky details such as the travel-themed pillow cases. Rates include a buffet breakfast in its restaurant. It's also very handy for Garosu-gil.

TOP CHOICE Park Hyatt Seoul
HOTEL $$$

(Map p56; ☎2016 1234; www.seoul.park.hyatt. com; Daechi 3-dong, Gangnam-gu; r/ste from ₩407,000/572,000; Ⓜ Line 2 to Samseong, Exit 1; ✻@⊛≋) A discreet entrance – look for the rock sticking out of the wall – sets the Zen minimalist tone for this gorgeous property. Each floor only has 10 rooms with spotlit antiquities lining the hallways. Spacious rooms ingeniously combine high tech with traditional, and come with luxurious bathrooms that have quite rightly been classed among the best in Asia.

Hotel Tria
HOTEL $$

(Map p58; ☎553 2471; www.hoteltria.co.kr; Yeoksam-dong, Gangnam-gu; r/ste from ₩95,000/150,000; Ⓜ Line 2 to Yeoksam, Exit 8; ✻@⊛) Very affordable for this end of town, the 50-room boutiquey Hotel Tria has lots going for it. Opt for any room above standard and you'll get a whirlpool bath. The hotel is tucked away in the streets behind the Renaissance Hotel, a five-minute walk from the subway exit.

Jelly Hotel
LOVE MOTEL $$

(Map p58; ☎553 4737; www.jellyhotel.com; Yuksam-dong, Gangnam-gu; r ₩70,000-280,000; Ⓜ Line 2 to Gangnam, Exit 12; @⊛) The corridors are as dark as a coalmine (safeguarding guests' anonymity), but the more expensive rooms of this hip love motel are spacious, exotic and classy. Every room is different and you can check them out on the lobby screen. The most spectacular and expensive room has a full-sized pool table, a heart-shaped spa, two huge TV screens, his and hers computers, a gilt mirror and black armchairs.

Ritz Carlton
HOTEL $$$

(Map p58; ☎3451 8000; www.ritzcarltonseoul. com; Yeoksam-dong, Gangnam-gu; r from ₩423,500/496,100; Ⓜ Line 9 to Shinnonhyeon, Exit 4; ✻@⊛≋) Traditional but not old-fashioned, the Ritz Carlton wraps guests in soothing luxury with high levels of service, plenty of facilities and a European atmosphere stretching from the furniture to the food. Rooms have warm colours to contrast with the pervasive white.

Hotel Blue Pearl
HOTEL $$

(블루펄호텔; Map p56; ☎3015 7777; www .hotelbluepearl.com; 129-3 Cheongdam-dong, Gangnam-gu; d/tw ₩143,000/159,000; Ⓜ Line 7 to Cheongdam, Exit 13; ✻@⊛) Although it could do with some touching up here and there, the Blue Pearl remains a stylish mid-range hotel that is easy on the wallet for this pricey end of town. Ask for a room on the side away from the main road as they're quieter. Rooms have blinds and computers, and breakfast is included.

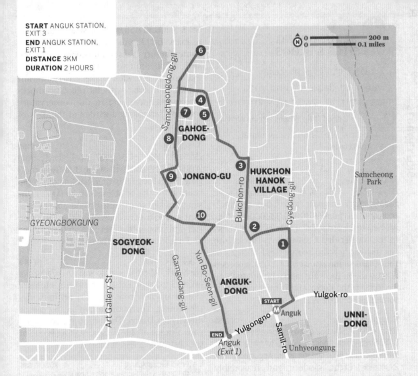

Walking Tour
Bukchon Views Walk

❯ Take in views across Bukchon's tiled *hanok* roofs on this walk around the area between Gyeongbokgung and Changdeokgung. Don't worry if you get a little lost in the maze of streets – that's part of the pleasure. Also note this description uses the new street names for the area; some maps and business addresses will have the old address system.

From the subway exit turn left at the first junction and walk 200m to ❶ **Bukchon Traditional Culture Centre**, where you can learn about the area's architecture. Turn left at the junction and then right at Bukchon-ro. On the corner is the ❷ **Bukchon Tourist Information Centre**. Walk up this major road lined with shops; 25 years ago it was a much narrower residential street leading into the hills.

Around 250m up the on the left-hand side is ❸ **11-gil, Bukchon-ro**; follow this narrow street uphill towards the parallel set of picturesque streets lined with *hanok* in ❹ **31 Gahoe-dong**. To see inside one of the *hanok* pause at ❺ **Simsimheon**.

Turn left and go a few blocks west to 5na-gil, Bukchon-ro; just to the right is a ❻ **viewing spot** across Samcheong-dong. Head south down the hill, perhaps pausing for tea at ❼ **Cha Masineun Tteul**. Further downhill is ❽ **Another Way of Seeing**, an art gallery exhibiting work by the blind.

Turn left after the ❾ **World Jewellery Museum** and then right at the junction; on the corner by another tourist information booth, walk up to ❿ **Jeongdok Public Library**, where you'll find a museum devoted to education and a small quiet park; the cherry blossoms are lovely here in spring as are the ginkgo trees turning yellow in autumn.

Return to the subway station via Yun Bo-seon-gil, which runs behind the Constitutional Court.

M Chereville
SERVICED APARTMENT $$

(Map p58; ☏532 9774; www.mchereville.net; Seomyeong-gil, Gangnam; studio/1-bedroom apt/2-bedroom apt from ₩110,000/132,000/165,000; ⓜLine 2 to Gangnam, Exit 9) Chuck dirty socks in the washer/dryer, shove dirty crocks into the dishwasher and soothe tired muscles in the steam sauna showers. All that's needed is artwork on the walls, and a bit of touching up to keep the decor and furnishings up to scratch. Reception is in Room 607.

Popgreen Hotel
HOTEL $$

(Map p58; ☏544 6623; www.popgreenhotel.com; 614-1 Sinsa-dong, Gangnam-gu; d/tw incl breakfast ₩128,840/138,820; ⓜLine 3 to Apgujeong, Exit 2; ✳@☎) Light, modern and reasonably sized rooms and bathrooms are on offer at Popgreen, with touches of style here and there from the colourful prints in the lobby and the desk staff in red and gold uniform. Rooms vary, so check out more than one.

Princess Hotel
LOVE MOTEL $$

(프린세스호텔; Map p58; ☏544 0366; Apgujeong; r from ₩80,000; ⓜLine 3 to Apgujeong, Exit 2; ✳@) If you need to be close to Apgujeong's shopping action, this easy-to-locate love motel with English-speaking reception staff is just the ticket.

✗ Eating

Dining out is one of the great pleasures of Seoul, with literally tens of thousands of options, from cheap street stalls proffering deep fried snacks and *tteokbokki* (rice cakes in a sweet sauce) to fancy restaurants serving royal Korean cuisine and seafood so fresh it's still wriggling on the plate.

GWANGHWAMUN & JONGNO-GU

TOP CHOICE Congdu
NEO-KOREAN $$$

(Map p42; www.congdu.com; Seoul Museum of History, Seamunan-ro; lunch/dinner from ₩27,000/ 45,000; ⓒ11.30am-2pm Mon-Fri, 11.30am-3.30pm Sat & Sun, 5.30-8.50pm daily; ⓜLine 5 to Gwanghwamun, Exit 7; ☎⑩) Elegantly presented, contemporary twists on Korean classics, such as pine-nut soup with soy-milk espuma (foam), are what make this restaurant a pleasure along with its relaxing atmosphere: ask for a seat in the conservatory section overlooking a garden at the back of the museum.

Tosokchon
KOREAN $$

(토속촌; Map p42; ☏737 7446; meals from ₩15,000; ⓒ10am-10pm; ⓜLine 3 to Gyeongbokgung, Exit 2) Invariably there's a line of people waiting for the bubbling *samgyetang* (ginseng chicken soup) at this venerable restaurant spread over a series of *hanok*. Tip some salt and pepper together into a small saucer and use it as a dip for the chicken.

Joseon Gimbap
KOREAN $

(조선김밥; Map p42; gimbap ₩3500; ⓒ7am-8pm; ⓜLine 3 to Anguk, Exit 1) Behind the building site for the new contemporary art museum, this quirky, tiny place is marked by a sign drawn on a T-shirt. The jumbo *gimbap* come with a range of side dishes, making it one of the best-value feeds in the city.

Balwoo Gongyang
KOREAN $$$

(발우공양; Map p60; ☏2031 2081; www.baru.or. kr; 5th fl, Templestay Information Centre, Ujeongguk-ro, Insa-dong; lunch/dinner from ₩25,000/36,000; ⓒ11.40am-3pm & 6-9pm; ⓜLine 3 to Anguk, Exit 6; ☎⑩) Make reservations three days in advance for the delicate temple-style vegetarian cuisine served here. It's all beautifully presented. For less fancy meals go down to the 2nd floor to another kitchen (open 11.30am to 8pm) where there's a buffet (₩7000) or noodle and rice dishes for around ₩4000.

Min's Club
WESTERN FUSION $$$

(민가다헌; Map p60; ☏733 2966; www.mins club.co.kr; off Insa-dong 10-gil, Insa-dong; lunch/ dinner from ₩25,000/60,000; ⓒnoon-2.30pm & 6-11.30pm; ⓜLine 3 to Anguk, Exit 6) Old-world architecture meets new-world cuisine in this classy restaurant housed in a beautifully restored 1930s *hanok* that offers European-Korean meals (more European than Korean). There's an extensive wine selection.

Tobang
KOREAN $

(토방; Map p60; Insa-dong-gil, Insa-dong; meals ₩5500; ⓒ10am-7pm; ⓜLine 3 to Anguk, Exit 6) A white sign with two Chinese characters above a doorway leads the way to this excellent-value eatery, where you sit on floor cushions under paper lanterns. Order the *sundubu jjigae* or *doenjang jjigae* for some Korean home-cooking flavour and excellent side dishes that include bean sprouts, fish, cuttlefish and raw crab in red-pepper sauce, plus a soup and rice.

Hanmiri
NEO-KOREAN $$$

(한미리; www.hanmiri.co.kr) Gwanghwamun (Map p42; 757 5707; lunch/dinner from ₩30,000/ 50,000; 11.30am-3pm & 6-10pm; Line 5 to Gwanghwamun, Exit 5;); Gangnam (Map p58; 569 7165; 2nd fl, Human Starville, Non-hyeon-dong, Gangnam-gu; lunch/dinner from ₩30,000/50,000; noon-3pm & 6-10pm; Line 2 to Yeoksam, Exit 6) Sit on chairs at tables for this modern take on royal cuisine; book one of the rooms with windows overlooking the Cheong-gye-cheon. It's gourmet and foreigner friendly. There's another branch in Gangnam.

Bibigo
KOREAN $$

(Map p42; www.bibgo.com; Saemunan-ro; meals ₩10,000-12,000; 11am-10pm; Line 5 to Gwanghwamun, Exit 6;) Traditional Korean dishes such as *bibimbap* are done fast-food style at this quite stylish operation where you can also choose the different elements of the dish, ie type of rice, topping and sauce.

Nwijo
KOREAN $$

(뉘조; Map p60; 730 9310; off Insa-dong 14-gil, Insa-dong; meals from ₩18,000; Line 3 to Anguk, Exit 6) Traditional *jeonsik* meals that tend towards vegetarian Buddhist-style cuisine are served on rustic pottery in this *hanok*. The food is fresh and has a pleasing mixture of textures.

Dhal
INDIAN $$

(Map p42; 736 4627; www.dalindia.com; Art Sonje Center, 5-gil Bukchon-ro; mains ₩15,000-25,000, lunch/dinner set menu ₩25,000/35,000; noon-3pm & 6-10pm; Line 3 to Anguk, Exit 1;) Some of Seoul's most authentic and delicious Indian food is served here in elegant surroundings – it's well worth splashing out on.

Harvest
KOREAN $$

(Map p42; 747 5056; Gye-dong-gil; meals ₩13,000-35,000; noon-3pm & 6-10pm Mon-Sat; Line 3 to Anguk, Exit 3) Four friendly brothers run this super-stylish, light-filled restaurant specialising in North Korean dishes from the province of Hwanghae. Try the chicken dish where you mix the rice with a thin consommé soup or *onjin bulgagi*. It sometimes holds Sunday flea markets on the courtyard in front of the restaurant.

Koong
DUMPLINGS $

(궁; Map p60; 733 9240; www.koong.co.kr; Insa-dong 10-gil, Insa-dong; dumplings ₩7000; 11.30am-9.30pm; Line 3 to Anguk, Exit 6) Koong's traditional Kaeseong dumplings are legendary. Enjoy them in a flavourful soup along with chewy balls of rice cake.

Gogung
KOREAN $$

(고궁; Map p60; 736 3211; www.gogung.co.kr; Ssamzigil, Insa-dong-gil, Insa-dong; meals from ₩8000-12,000; 11am-10pm; Line 3 to Anguk, Exit 6) In the basement of Ssamzigil is this smart and stylish restaurant, specialising in Jeonju (capital of Jeollabuk province) *bibimbap*, which is fresh and garnished with nuts but contains raw minced beef. The *dolsot bibimbap* is served in a stone hotpot. Both come with side dishes. Also try the *moju*, a sweet, cinnamon homebrew drink.

Osegyehyang
KOREAN $

(오세계향; Map p60; www.go5.co.kr; Insa-dong 12-gil, Insa-dong; meals from ₩7000; noon-3pm & 4-9pm; Line 3 to Anguk, Exit 6;) Run by members of a Taiwanese religious sect; the vegetarian food combines all sorts of mixtures and flavours. The barbecue-meat-substitute dish is flavoursome. Nonalcoholic beer and wine are served.

Chilgapsan
KOREAN $$

(칠갑산; Map p42; 730 7754; Sambong-gil; meals ₩6000-13,000; 11.30am-10pm; Line 1 to Jonggak, Exit 2) This convivial, sit-on-floor-cushions restaurant's speciality is excellent *neobiani*, a beef patty the size of a small pizza. Meant for sharing, it comes with a dressed green salad. The barley and rice *bibimbap* is original – you mix in *doenjang jjigae* rather than *gochujang*. Look for a building with a white frontage covered with ivy.

Sadongmyeonok
DUMPLINGS $

(사동면옥; Map p60; 735 7393; Insa-dong 8-gil, Insa-dong; dumplings ₩6000; Line 3 to Anguk, Exit 6) This bright and breezy eatery is hidden away, but is usually busy and has a long menu. It's famous for *manduguk* – because the dumplings are the largest you'll see (three make a meal). Also famous is the platter of *haemul pajeon* (seafood pancake; ₩10,000), known for its size, crispiness and the big chunks of octopus.

MYEONG-DONG & JUNG-GU

Myeong-dong Gyoja
NOODLES $

(명동교자; Map p48; www.mdkj.co.kr; Myeong-dong; noodles ₩8000; Ⓜ Line 4 to Myeong-dong, Exit 8; 🍴) The special *kalguksu* (noodles in a meat, dumpling and vegetable broth) served here is famous, so it's busy busy busy. If the place is full, there's a second branch further down the street opposite Andong Jjimdak.

Mokmyeoksanbang
KOREAN $$

(목멱산방; Map p48; Namsan Northern Circuit; mains ₩8000-10,000; ⏱ 11.30am-8pm; 🍴) Order and pay at the till, then pick up delicious and beautifully presented *bibimbap* from the kitchen when your electronic buzzer rings to pick up. The traditional-style wooden house in which the restaurant is based is named after the ancient name for Namsan (Mokmyeok); it also serves Korean teas and *makgeolli* in brass kettles.

Baekje Samgyetang
KOREAN $$

(백제삼계탕; Map p48; Myeong-dong 2-gil, Myeong-dong; mains ₩14,000-25,000; Ⓜ Line 4 to Myeong-dong, Exit 6; 🍴) This 2nd-floor restaurant, marked by a sign with red Chinese characters, offers reliable *samgyetang*, served with a thimbleful of *insamju* (ginseng wine). Put salt and pepper into the saucer and dip the pieces of chicken into it. Drink the herbal soup at the end.

Andong Jjimdak
KOREAN $$

(안동찜닭; Map p48; off Myeong-dong-gil; mains ₩17,000-27,000; Ⓜ Line 4 to Myeong-dong, Exit 7; 🛜🍴) A convivial young crowd comes here for the *jjimdak* experience, a very spicy concoction of chicken, noodles, potatoes and vegetables that comes on a platter meant for sharing.

Sinsun Seolnongtang
KOREAN $

(신선설농탕; Map p48; www.kood.co.kr; Myeong-dong-gil; meals ₩7000-8000; ⏱ 24hr; Ⓜ Line 4 to Myeong-dong, Exit 7; 🍴) *Mandu* (dumplings), tofu or ginseng can be added to the beef broth dishes served at this inexpensive chain, but purists will want to stick to the traditional version.

WESTERN & NORTHERN SEOUL

🌿 Slobbie
KOREAN $

(Map p50; ☎ 2679 9300; blog.naver.com/slobbie8; Hongdae; meals ₩8000; ⏱ 11.30am-11.30pm Mon-Sat; Ⓜ Line 2 to Hongik University, Exit 9; 🛜🍴) One of two restaurants in the Hongdae area run by social enterprise Organisa-

tion Yori, promoting a slower, healthier and more organic lifestyle; the other is **O-Yori** (Map p50; www.orgyori.com; ⏱ 11.30am-9pm Tue-Sun; Ⓜ Line 6 to Sangsu, Exit 1). Both help train young chefs from challenged backgrounds and provide jobs for single mothers. The food at Slobbie (pronounced Slow-bee) is simple, tasty Korean dishes such as *bibimbap,* while O-Yori offers a tasty pan-Asian menu.

Shim's Tapas
SPANISH $$

(Map p50; ☎ 3141 2386; Hongdae; tapas ₩5000-15,000; Ⓜ Line 2 to Hongik University, Exit 8; 🍴🛜) Three sisters are the driving force behind this adorable tapas bar. They whip up authentic and creative Spanish-style nibbles, including light-as-a-feather tortilla and homemade anchovies. Wash them down with a sangria, glass of cava or one of their fine dry martinis.

Bap
KOREAN $

(밥; Map p50; off Wausan-gil, Hongdae; meals ₩8000-20,000; ⏱ 11am-9pm Mon-Sat; Ⓜ Line 2 to Hongik University, Exit 9) Kindly ladies run this cosy place decorated in wood and brick with abundant plants. The *jeongsik* meals come with plenty of side dishes, rice and soup, so are great value and beloved by the local student population. The *bulgogi* (W20,000) serves two people.

Loving Hut
KOREAN $

(Map p50; www.lovinghut.com; mains ₩5000-6000; Ⓜ Line 2 to Sinchon, Exit 2; 🛜🍴🍴) A variety of slogans in English urge diners on to a more compassionate, meat-free life at this pastel-shaded, pleasantly modern cafe serving very tasty and good-value vegan Korean meals with rice, noodles and veggies.

TOP CHOICE Jaha Sonmandoo
KOREAN $

(자하손만두; www.sonmandoo.com; Buam-dong; mains ₩7000-10,000 ⏱ 11am-9.30pm; 🚌 1020, 7022, 7212; 🍴) Seoulites flock to this mountainside dumpling house for the steamed and boiled vegetable and beef and pork parcels. One plate is enough of these whoppers; the sweet cinnamon tea to finish is free. It's two minutes walk uphill from the bus stop on the northwest side of the fortress wall.

Deon-Jang-Yesool
KOREAN $

(된장예술; Map p42; ☎ 745 4516; meals ₩8500; ⏱ 9am-11pm; Ⓜ Line 4 to Hyehwa, Exit 3; 🍴) Serves a tasty fermented-beanpaste and tofu stew with a variety of nearly all vegetarian side dishes at bargain prices – no wonder it's well patronised by the area's student population. Look for the stone carved lions flanking the door.

ITAEWON & YONGSAN-GU

TOP CHOICE ▶ OKitchen   FRENCH, ITALIAN $$$
(Map p52; ☑797 6420; www.okitchen.pe.kr; off Itaewon-ro; mains ₩19,000-36,000; ⊙noon-2.30pm, 6-9.30pm daily; ⓜLine 6 to Itaewon, Exit 1; 🛜💷) Friendly service and set menus (starting at ₩21,000/52,000 for lunch/dinner) that balance price with quality make this one of Itaewon's surest bets for a quality meal. The chef hails from Okinawa and used to live in New York with his Korean food-stylist wife – the international sophistication shines through.

Vatos   MEXICAN $$
(Map p52; ☑797 8226; www.vatoskorea.com; off Itaewon-ro; mains ₩9000; ⊙11.30am-2pm, 5-10pm Tue-Fri, 11.30am-11pm Sat, 11.30am-10pm Sun; ⓜLine 6 to Itaewon, Exit 4; 🛜💷) These guys take their 'urban tacos' and Mexican eats to a gourmet level with delicious riffs such as tacos filled with *galbi* (beef ribs) and Korean-style pork belly. Their *kimchi carnitas* fries are good to try with their cocktails, which include a 'makgeolita', or selection of bottled US craft beers.

Le Saint-Ex   FRENCH $$$
(Map p52; ☑795 2465; www.facebook.com/lesaintex; Itaewon 2-gil; mains ₩27,000-43,000; ⊙6pm-midnight; ⓜLine 6 to Itaewon, Exit 1; 🛜💷) The blackboard menu at this very French bistro with consistently good food and service is always tempting. A heater and even blankets are available for the outside patio. The lunch sets are excellent.

Parlour   DESSERTS, BAKERY $$
(Map p52; ☑9560 9561; Hannam-dong; afternoon tea without/with champagne ₩25,000/38,000; ⊙10am-10pm; ⓜLine 6 to Hangangjin, Exit 2; 🛜💷) In the HQ of the company behind the ubiquitous Paris Croissant chain of bakery-cafes are several upscale operations of which this is the newest and most stylish. Offering an experience like Fortnum & Mason's, this is tea the English way (albeit with Kusmi-brand teas from France). Upstairs is the swank bakery cafe-confectioners Passion 5.

Buddha's Belly   THAI $$
(Map p52; ☑796 9330; off Itaewon-ro; mains ₩5000-12,000; ⊙11.30am-2am; ⓜLine 6 to Itaewon, Exit 1; 🛜💷) It's not difficult to under-

KOREA HOUSE

Scoring a hat trick for high-quality food, entertainment and shopping is **Korea House** (Map p48; ☑2266 9101; www.koreahouse.or.kr; Chungmuro; set course lunch/dinner ₩57,200/68,200; ⊙noon-2pm, dinner 5-6.30pm & 7-8.30pm Sun; ⓜLine 3 or 4 to Chungmuro, Exit 3). A dozen dainty, artistic courses make up the royal banquet. The *hanok*, the *hanbok*-clad waitresses, the *gayageum* (zither) music and the platters and boxes the food is served in are all part of the experience.

The intimate theatre stages two, hour-long traditional **dance and music performances** (shows ₩50,000; ⊙6.30 & 8.30pm), which you can see independently of eating here. Put on by a troupe of top musicians and dancers, the shows have some English commentary on a screen.

Rounding out the experience is Korea House's **shop** (⊙10am-8pm), which stocks an expertly edited selection of quality design goods, traditional crafts, books and cards.

stand why this restaurant and lounge bar is a much-recommended locals favourite. The cooking is authentic and the ambience relaxed. Its original tiny takeaway outlet is down the hill in Gyeongridan, with a few seats for dine-in customers.

Salam   TURKISH $$
(Map p52; ☑793 4323; www.turkeysalam.com; mains ₩8000-13,000; ⊙noon-10pm, closed 1st & 3rd Mon of month; ⓜLine 6 to Itaewon, Exit 3; 💷) Next to the mosque, this classy Turkish restaurant and bakery is great for a meal of hummus, kebabs and pide (Turkish pizza). If you're hungry, there's a big set menu for ₩24,000.

Tartine   BRUNCH, DESSERTS $$
(Map p52; ☑3785 3400; www.tartine.co.kr; mains ₩9000-38,500; ⊙10am-10.30pm; ⓜLine 6 to Itaewon, Exit 1; 💷) Looking for dessert? You won't go wrong with the scrumptious fruit pies and other confections at this charming bakery-cafe run by an American baker. So successful has this place been, it's expanded its operation across the alley to a bustling brunch cafe with plenty of menu options.

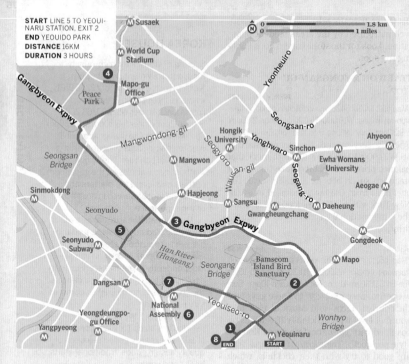

Cycling Tour
Han River Cycle Ride

❯ Dedicated cycle paths run along much
of both sides of the Han River. This 16km
route loops from Yeouido across the river to
the World Cup Stadium and back, providing
great views along the way. Walk west a block
from the subway exit to **Yeouido Park**, where
you'll find a **1 bicycle-rental stall** (first
hour ₩3000, every extra 15 minutes ₩500;
open 9am to 5pm); bring some form of photo
ID for staff to keep as a deposit.

Cycle out of the park and across the
2 Mapo Bridge, taking the blue ramp down
to the north bank of the river. Head west for
about 4km until you reach a steep cliff at
the top of which is **3 Jeoldusan Martyrs
Shrine**. Continue west under the Yanghwa
and Seongsan bridges until you reach a
small bridge across a stream. Turn right after
crossing this bridge and then left (at the sign)
to pedal uphill to reach the **4 World Cup
Stadium**.

Retrace your route back to the Yanghwa
bridge and carry your bike up the stairs to
the pathway on the west side. On an island
about halfway along the bridge is the beautifully landscaped **5 Seonyudo Park**. You'll
have to leave your bike outside if you wish to
explore the park, which has wonderful river
views.

Continue from the park back to the south
bank of the Han River and pedal back towards Yeouido. At the western tip of the island you can pause to view the **6 National
Assembly** and the ritzy **7 Seoul Marina**.
Before or after dropping off your bike have a
look at Yeouido Park, which includes a
8 traditional Korean garden.

DONGDAEMUN & EASTERN SEOUL

TOP CHOICE Gwangjang Market
KOREAN $

(광장시장; Map p54; Jongno-5ga; dishes ₩4000-10,000; ⏱5am-10pm Mon-Sat; Ⓜ Line 1 to Jongno-5ga, Exit 5) Also spelled 'Kwangjang'; during the day you'll find food and fabrics sold here as well as a great section specialising in secondhand clothes (accessed by the stairs to the upper floor outside Exit 5, open until 7pm). The best time to visit, though, is the evening, when the end towards Dongdaemun morphs into Seoul's largest food alley, with some 200 stalls specialising in dishes such as crispy, thick *nokdu bindaetteok* (mung-bean pancake; ₩5000) that are big enough to be shared by two. Pair them up with healthy bowls of *bibimbap* or *boribap* (mixed rice and barley topped with a selection of vegies).

TOP CHOICE Woo Rae Oak
NOODLES, BARBECUE $$

(Map p54; ☑2265 0151; Jugyo-dong; mains ₩11,000-43,000; ⏱11.30am-9.30pm Tue-Sun; Ⓜ Line 2 or 4 to Euljiro 4-ga, Exit 4; 🅿) Tucked away in the sewing-machine-parts section of Dongdaemun's sprawling market is this elegant old-timer specialising in *bulgogi* and *galbi* (from ₩29,000). But it's the delicious *naengmyeon* cold noodles that are the best and a great lunch with the delicious *kimchi*.

My Friend & Ala-Too
CENTRAL ASIAN $$

(Map p54; ⏱9am-10pm Mon-Sat; Ⓜ Line 1 or 4 to Dongdaemun History & Culture Park, Exit 5; 🅿) Cyrillic script on the buildings signals the location of Dongdaemun's 'Central Asian' village where you'll find Russian-speaking traders from the 'Stans, Mongolia and Russia hanging out, enjoying *shashlyk* (barbecued meat), *plov* (a meaty pilaf dish) and *lagman* (soup noodles). A good place to join in the party is this spacious, friendly joint.

APGUJEONG, GANGNAM & AROUND

TOP CHOICE Jung Sikdang
NEO-KOREAN $$$

(중식당; Map p58; ☑517 4654; http://jungsik.kr; Sinsa-dong, Gangnam-gu; lunch/dinner menu from ₩40,000/70,000; Ⓜ Line 3 to Apgujeong, Exit 3) Neo-Korean cuisine hardly gets better than this Apgujeong outpost of the New York restaurant Jungsik named after creative chef Yim Jungsik. Expect inspired contemporary mixes of traditional ingredients and an amazing chocolate dessert on a bed of sugar straw. Book ahead and ask for a table with a view across Dosan Park.

Busan Ilbeonji
SEAFOOD $$$

(부산일번지; 2nd fl, Noryangjin Market; mains ₩15,000-30,000; ⏱10.30am-10.30pm; Ⓜ Line 1 to Noryangjin, Exit 1) Generous super-fresh fish and crab meals are a bargain here. If you're not up for the full raw-fish platter, try *kkotge* (a spicy blue-crab soup), which includes great side dishes such as garnished tofu, sweet red beans, green salad and grilled fish.

Gorilla in the Kitchen
FUSION $$$

(Map p58; ☑3442 1688; www.gorillakitchen.co.kr; Sinsa-dong Gangnam-gu; mains ₩27,000-45,000; Ⓜ Line 3 to Apgujeong, Exit 2) This smart restaurant, facing the entrance to Dosan Park, focuses on health food. Unlike other places, it has a firm handle on casual Euro dining, and most meals come up trumps. It's the perfect spot to chill over a lazy brunch on the weekend.

TOP CHOICE Samwon Garden
KOREAN $$$

(삼원가든; Map p58; ☑548 3030; www.samwongarden.com; Sinsa-dong, Gangnam-gu; mains from ₩28,000; Ⓜ Line 3 to Apgujeong, Exit 2) Serving top-class *galbi* for more than 30 years, Samwon is an Korean idyll, surrounded by beautiful traditional gardens including several waterfalls. It's one of the best places in the city for this kind of barbecued-beef meal.

Grill5Taco
MEXICAN $

(Map p58; www.grill5taco.com; Sinsa-dong, Gangnam-gu; tacos from ₩7000; Ⓜ Line 3 to Sinsa, Exit 8) A business that started as a food truck has been so successful that it now has this permanent base that caters perfectly to the on-the-go shoppers and hipsters mooching Serosu-gil. The tacos filled with a choice of spare rib, spicy pork or spicy chicken hit the spot, and if you're really hungry, open your mouth very wide for its Monster Burrito.

🍷 Drinking

From rustic teahouses and own-roaster coffee houses to craft beer pubs and cocktail bars, Seoul offers an unbelievable number of places to relax over a drink. No-frills *hof* (pubs) are common and don't miss that quintessential Seoul nightlife experience: *soju* shots and snacks at a *pojenmacha* (street tent bar).

Hongdae is home to Seoul's main clubbing scene, but Itaewon and Gangnam have a few decent choices, too. Most clubs don't start becoming busy until 10pm and only start buzzing after midnight. Friday and Saturday nights have a real party atmosphere. Except in the classiest of Gangnam clubs, dress codes are generally not too strict.

GWANGHWAMUN & JONGNO-GU

TOP CHOICE **Dawon** TEAHOUSE

(다원; Map p60;Insa-dong-8gil, Insa-dong; teas ₩7000; ⊙11am-11pm; MLine 3 to Anguk, Exit 6) The perfect place to unwind on a warm summer evening is under the shady fruit trees in this courtyard with flickering candles. In winter sit indoors in *hanok* rooms decorated with scribbles or in the garden pavilion. Small exhibition spaces surround the courtyard. The teas are superb, especially *omijacha hwachae* (fruit and five-flavour berry punch), a summer drink.

TOP CHOICE **Baekseju-maeul** BAR

(백세주마을; Map p42; ☑720 0055; www.ksdb .co.kr; MLine 2 to Jonggak, Exit 4) See the website's English pages to learn more about the excellent range of traditional rice wines available at this drinking and dining outlet for brewer Kooksoondang. There are several other branches dotted around Seoul, including in Daehangno, Sinchon and Gangnam.

Kopi Bangasgan CAFE

(커피 방앗간; Map p42; ⊙8am-11pm) Based in a *hanok*, 'Coffee Mill' is a charming spot decorated with retro pieces and the quirky, colourful artworks of owner Lee Gyeong-hwan, whom you're likely to spot painting at the counter. The bags of fair-trade roasted coffee beans have his cute drawings on, too. Apart from various coffees it also serves waffles.

Pub of the Blue Star PUB

(Map p60; off Insa-dong 16-gil, Insa-dong; ⊙3pm-midnight; MLine 3 to Anguk, Exit 6) Owned by a stage actor, this rustic hang-out, plastered with posters, is a good place to sample traditional *makgeolli* rice wine served out of brass kettles into brass bowls. Order slices of its homemade tofu and *kimchi* to eat as you drink.

Cha Masineun Tteul TEAHOUSE

(차마시는뜰; Map p42; ⊙8am-11pm) Overlooking Samcheong-dong from Bukchon is this lovely *hanok* with low tables arranged around a courtyard. It offers traditional teas and a delicious bright yellow pumpkin rice cake that is served fresh from the steamer.

Dalsaeneun Dalman Saenggak Handa TEAHOUSE

(달새는 달만 생각한다; Map p60; Insa-dong 12-gil, Insa-dong; teas ₩6500-9000; ⊙10am-11pm; MLine 3 to Anguk, Exit 6) 'Moon Bird Thinks Only of the Moon' is packed with plants and rustic artefacts. Birdsong, soothing music and trickling water add to the atmosphere. Huddle in a cubicle and savour one of its teas, which include *gamnipcha* (persimmon-leaf tea). *Saenggangcha* (ginger tea) is peppery but sweet.

Yetchatjip TEAHOUSE

(옛찻집; Map p60; Insa-dong 6-gil, Insa-dong; ⊙10am-11pm; MLine 3 to Anguk, Exit 6) Half a dozen little songbirds fly around inside the 'Old Teashop'. Ethereal music, water features and candles add to the atmosphere – even the unique toilets do their bit. Antique bric-a-brac so clutters this hobbit-sized teashop that it's hard to squeeze past and find somewhere to sit.

Dabang CAFE

(다방; Map p42; www.mulnamoo.com; Gye-dong-gil; ⊙10am-midnight; MLine 3 to Anguk, Exit 2) Sip tea or hand-dripped coffee in this minimalist, retro-styled cafe that's part of a 1930s building that includes a gallery and analogue photo studio.

MYEONG-DONG & JUNG-GU

Naos Nova WINE BAR

(Map p48; ☑754 2202; www.naosnova.net; Sowol-ro; ⊙noon-1pm; MLine 1 or 4 to Seoul Station, Exit 10; 🗐) Facing the lower slopes of Namsan, this elegant bar and restaurant occupies an angular, light-filled contemporary building. There's a fine wine and liquor list and some very tempting food to go with it, but bring your credit card as it's not cheap.

Grove Lounge CAFE, BAR

(Map p48; 1F State Tower, Namsan, Toegye-ro; ⊙11am-midnight Mon-Fri, to 10pm Sat; MLine 4 to Myeong-dong, Exit 4; 🗐) This attractive cafe-bar is a stylish and spacious spot for a reviving coffee or draft beer while lounging in comfy designer chairs. The international-style food is good, too, and includes tasty toasted sandwiches with fries.

WESTERN & NORTHERN SEOUL

TOP CHOICE **Anthracite** CAFE

(Map p50; www.anthracitecoffee.com; off Tojung-gil; ⊙11am-midnight; MLine 6 to Sangsu, Exit 4; 🗐) Based in an old shoe factory a short walk towards the river from the heart of Hongdae, this is one of Seoul's top independent coffee roaster and cafe operations. Drinks are made using the hand-drip method at a counter made from an old conveyor belt; upstairs the industrial space has been converted to an ubercool lounge.

GAY & LESBIAN SEOUL

Squished between 'Hooker Hill' and the Little Arabia strip by the Seoul Mosque, 'Homo Hill' is a 50m alley so called because of its cluster of gay-friendly bars and clubs. Most hardly have room to swing a handbag, so on warm weekends the crowds often spill onto the street. All genders and sexual persuasions will feel welcome here.

At the bottom of the hill on the left is **Trance** (Map p52; http://cafe.daum.net/trance; admission ₩10,000; ⊘11pm-5am), a basement club with pouting drag queens and late-night shows. Next door is the eternally popular **Queen** (Map p52; www.facebook.com/queenbar; ⊘8pm-5am Tue-Sun), which offers sit-and-chat zones, though it usually gets very crowded with almost everyone dancing.

Flirty friendly staff and a cosy style mark out **Always Homme** (Map p52; ⊘8pm-4am Sun-Thu, to 6am Fri & Sat); the same management runs **Why Not** (Map p52; admission ₩10,000; ⊘8pm-6am), a dance club across the alley with lights and lasers; expect plenty of K-Pop. On the same side of the street, higher up the hill is **Soho** (Map p52; ⊘7pm-5am), one of the roomier places on the strip and the main competition to Queen; most customers spend the night shuttling between the two.

Between Tapgol Park and Jongno 3-ga subway station is an area that supports around 100 gay bars and small clubs. Not all are welcoming of foreigners, or will expect patrons to pay a hefty admission for *anju* (snacks). 'One-shot bars' where you can drink without an admission fee include **Barcode** (Map p42; ⊘7pm-4am; ⒨Lines 1, 3 & 5 to Jongno 3-ga, Exit 3), run by friendly English-speaking Kim Hyoung-Jin; and **Shortbus** (Map p42; ⊘7pm-4am; ⒨Lines 1, 3 & 5 to Jongno 3-ga, Exit 3), an appealing wine and cocktail bar; both have English signs. Alternatively drop by the outdoor *pojangmacha* food stalls around Jongno 3-ga to sink cheap beer, *soju* (local vodka) and snacks with the gay community.

Lesbians tend to congregate in Sinchon and Hongdae, where you'll find **Labris** (라브리스; Map p50; Wausan-gil, Hongdae; ⊘7pm-2am Mon-Thu, to 5am Fri-Sun; ⒨Line 6 to Sangsu), an 8th-floor women-only social/dance club that attracts locals and foreigners. DJ nights are Friday to Sunday when the minimum charge for a drink and compulsory *anju* is ₩15,000. The **Rainbow Meet Market** (www.facebook.com/meetmarketseoul) organised by the Butch-Hers is a semi-regular gay-lesbian party held at **Club Myoung Wol Gwan** (Map p50) in Hongdae.

At the end of May, Seoul pins up its rainbow colours for the **Korean Queer Cultural Festival** (www.kqcf.org), culminating in a parade through central Seoul.

TOP CHOICE **Suyeon Sanbang** TEAHOUSE
(수연 산방; off Map p42; Seongbuk-dong; ⊘11.30am-10pm; ⒨Line 4 to Hangsung University, Exit 6, then bus 1111 or 2112) Seoul's most charming teahouse is based in a 1930s *hanok* that was once the home of novelist Lee Tae-jun; you'll find his portrait and books in one section of the house that flanks a peaceful garden. Apart from a range of medicinal teas and premium-quality wild green tea, it also serves traditional sweets.

Café Sukkara CAFE, BAR
(Map p50; www.sukkara.co.kr; Sanullim Bldg, Seogyo-dong; ⊘11am-midnight; ⒨Line 2 to Hongik University, Exit 9; 🖥📶) There's a brilliant range of drinks and some very tasty things to eat (try the butter chicken curry) at this shabby chic farmhouse-style cafe. It also makes its own juices and liquors – try the black shandy gaff, a mix of homemade ginger ale and Magpie Brewery dark beer.

aA Café CAFE, BAR
(Map p50; www.aadesignmuseum.com; Hongdae; ⊘cafe noon-midnight, shop noon-8pm; ⒨Line 6 to Sangsu, Exit 1; 🖥📶) The antithesis of Seoul's usual cramped cosy cafes, aA offers soaring ceilings and space, filled with designer and retro furniture. It's a pleasure to hang out here, do some web surfing and have a light bite – the food is very tasty (try the chicken salad). Browse more classic furniture pieces in the basement shop-museum. There's also a branch in Samcheong-dong.

The Cure BAR
(Map p50; blog.naver.com/thecure_bmp; Hongdae; ⊘6pm-2am Sun-Thu, 5pm-5am Fri & Sat; ⒨Line 6 to Sangsu, Exit 1) Chris, a former professional Korean table-tennis player in France (!), has an amazing collection of 1980s British music. His spacious basement bar lined with sofas and video screens is a comfy place to indulge in pop nostalgia.

Castle Praha BREWERY

(Map p50; www.castlepraha.com; Solnae 6-gil, Hongdae; noon-3pm & 5pm-2am; Line 6 to Sangsu, Exit 1) Offering one of the most extraordinary facades in Seoul, this medieval fantasy 'Bohemian bistro' has an equally bizarre dungeon-cum-cellar interior. It serves several Czech-style pilsner and dunkel brews and the Praha brand has branched out to outlets in Gangnam, Garosu-gil and Itaewon, too.

Hakrim CAFE

(Map p42; www.hakrim.pe.kr; Daehangno; 10am-midnight; Line 4 to Hyehwa, Exit 3;) Little has changed in this retro Seoul classic since the place opened in 1956, save for the price of drinks. Apart from coffee it also serves tea and alcohol. The cosy wooden booths and dark corners make it popular with couples.

Minto CAFE

(Map p42; www.minto.co.kr; Maronie 2-gil, Daehangno; 10am-midnight; Line 4 to Hyehwa, Exit 2;) This cute, youth-orientated cafe chain has two pleasant locations in Daehangno. This one, spread over five floors, offers masses of different zones and hideaway spots, each with its own decor and furniture.

Comfort Zone BAR

(Map p42; Daehangno; Line 4 to Hyehwa, Exit 4) Spacious cafe-bar that lives up to its title with comfy sofas on two colourfully decorated levels and a spacious outdoor area. Happy hour with half-price draught beers runs from 5pm to 8pm.

ITAEWON & YONGSAN-GU

TOP CHOICE **Craftworks** BREWERY

(Map p52; http://craftworkstaphouse.com; Gyeongridan; Line 6 to Noksapyeong, Exit 2) Craftworks has secured a treasured place in the heart of Seoul's real-ale lovers. You can sample seven types from its range for ₩9500 and then decide which one to savour in a pint. What with a full week of special dining nights – plus the super-popular pub quiz on Wednesday – is it any wonder that many locals have made this their local?

Takeout Drawing CAFE

(Map p52; www.takeoutdrawing.com; 11am-midnight) Gyeongridan (Line 6 to Noksapyeong, Exit 2) Hamman-dong (Line 6 to Hangangjin, Exit 3;) These guys want to use drawing 'to change the world' and we're not about to argue with that. Either of the two branches of this arty cafe are cool place to hang out

and enjoy graphic art, books, magazines and coffee with a twist (try the espresso with a spiky meringue topping), organic teas and other beverages.

District BAR, CLUB

(Map p52; www.mykinc.com; Line 6 to Itaewon, Exit 1) A department store of pleasurable intoxication, this new drinking, dining and dancing complex, behind the Hamilton Hotel, has a trio of appealing, fashion-conscious options. On the ground floor is the handsome gastro-pub **Prost** serving hearty pub-style meals and beers; up a floor is the dark and stylish cocktail and wine bar **Glam**; and up one more floor is the dance club **Mute**.

Union DJ BAR

(Map p52; off Itaewon-ro; Line 6 to Itaewon, Exit 4) Run by DJ Conan, this three-storey *soju* and beer bar, also serving dishes such as *samgyeopsal* (barbecue streaky belly pork), is a prime spot to take Seoul's musical pulse. A changing roster of local DJs keeps the vibe cool and laid-back, plus there's a breezy rooftop deck that's great when the weather's steaming.

The Brew Shop BREWERY

(Map p52; http://magpiebrewing.com; Gyeongridan; 2-10pm; Line 6 to Noksapyeong, Exit 2) A stripped-down outlet behind Baker's Table is where you can come to sample the real ales of Magpie Brewing, a fledgling microbrewery establishing a name for itself around town. Occasional beer-making classes (₩50,000 including lunch, beer tasting and take-home booklet) are held here as well as food pairings and tastings.

Berlin COCKTAILS

(Map p52; 749 0903; 11.30am-2am; Line 6 to Itaewon, Exit 1) This sophisticated gay-friendly cafe, lounge and restaurant, set away from the main Itaewon drag, has an airy terrace with a view across to the Yongsan US military base; later in the evening a DJ plays. Upstairs is the restaurant Buddha's Belly, owned by the same people.

SOUTH OF THE HAN RIVER

TOP CHOICE **Platoon Kunsthalle** BAR, CLUB

(Map p58; 3447 1191; www.kunsthalle.com; Non-hyeon-dong, Gangnam-gu; 11am-1am Mon-Sat; Line 3 to Apgujeong, Exit 3;) What's not to love about this bar-gallery-events space created like a giant's Lego set from old shipping containers. Drinks and eats are affordable. Thursday night is open stage for live-music performances and there's a wide variety of other events hosted here, from the four-times-a-year Future Shorts (http://future shorts.com) short-film events to its annual Ink Bomb tattoo and body-art convention.

Moon Jar
BAR

(Map p58; ☑541 6118; Ⓜ Line 3 to Apgujeong, Exit 3; 🛜📵) Rustic charm meets Apgujeong chic at this convivial *magkeolli* bar and cafe spread over two floors. The menu has several different types of rice wine, and there's some neat twists on the usual food accompaniments such as a five-coloured *ttekboki* rice-cake dish.

Take Urban
CAFE

(Map p58; ☑519 0001; Bongeunsa-ro, Gangnam-gu; ⊙8am-midnight; Ⓜ Line 9 to Sinnonhyeon, Exit 3) On the ground floor of a building that looks like a giant concrete beehive is this sophisticated and spacious cafe, with indoor and outdoor options, heaps of designer-style fresh bakery items and organic coffee.

Oktoberfest
BEER HALL

(Map p58; ☑3481 8881; off Seomyeong-gil, Gangnam; beers ₩4000; Ⓜ Line 2 to Gangnam, Exit 9; 📵) It's much quieter than Oktoberfest at this long-running microbrewery serving up four freshly produced brews in a large bare-brick and natural-wood cellar bar. German-style meats are served by frock-clad lasses. There are other branches around the city, including one in Hongdae.

☆ Entertainment

Seoul's many performing-arts centres and theatres offer an intriguing and surprisingly accessible menu of traditional music, dance, drama and comedy. It's also very simple to make your own entertainment in private rooms *(bang)* devoted to karaoke, playing computer games or watching DVDs.

Nightclubs

M2
CLUB

(Map p50; http://ohoo.net/m2; Hongdae; admission Sun-Thu ₩10,000, Fri & Sat ₩20,000; ⊙9.30pm-4.30am Sun-Thu, 8.30pm-6.30am Fri & Sat; Ⓜ Line 6 to Sangsu, Exit 1) Deep underground is M2, one of the largest and best Hongdae clubs. It has a high ceiling and plenty of lights and visuals. Top local and international DJs spin mainly progressive house music.

Ellui
CLUB

(Map p56; www.ellui.com; Cheongdam-dong, Gangnam-gu; admission Fri & Sat ₩30,000; Ⓜ Line 7 to Cheongdam, Exit 13) Gangnam specialises in

mega dance clubs and this industrial chic place is one of the biggest with a dazzling light-and-sound system, several dance spaces and plenty of room to move. Usually open only Friday and Saturday but keep an eye out for one-off midweek events too.

Eden
CLUB

(Map p58; www.eden-club.co.kr; Yeoksam-dong, Gangnam-gu; admission Sun, Tue-Thu ₩20,000, Fri & Sat ₩30,000; ⊙8.30pm-4am Sun, Tue-Thu, to 6am Fri & Sat; Ⓜ Line 9 to Sinnonhyeon, Exit 3) Lavish laser shows, leggy models, stratospheric drink prices and tons of security mark out Eden as the late-night haunt of Seoul's smart set.

Cinemas

FREE Cinemateque KOFA
CINEMA

(한국 영상 자료원; ☑3153 2001; www.korea-film.org; Ⓜ Line 6 to Susaek, Exit 2) Classic and contemporary Korean films are on the bill at one of the three cinemas in this home of the Korean Film Archive. See the website for directions from the subway exit.

Theatres

Sejong Centre for the Performing Arts
THEATRE

(세종문화회관; Map p42; ☑399 1111; www.sejongpac.or.kr; Sejong-daero, Gwanghwamun; Ⓜ Line 5 to Gwanghwamun, Exit 1) This leading arts complex puts on major drama, music and art shows – everything from large-scale musicals to fusion *gugak* (traditional Korean music) and gypsy violinists

Chongdong Theatre
THEATRE

(Map p48; ☑751 1500; www.chongdong.com; Jeongdong; tickets ₩30,000-40,000; ⊙4 & 8pm Tue-Sun; Ⓜ Line 1 or 2 to City Hall, Exit 2) The venue for the

GANGNAM ARCHI-TOUR

Given the generally blank historical canvas and wide-open spaces of Gangnam, architects have been able to push the envelope a bit more with their designs south of the river. Start this archi-tour opposite COEX. Hyundai Development Company commissioned Daniel Libeskind to work with Seoul-based firm Himma on its headquarters. The result, **Tangent** (Map p56; **M**Line 2 to Samseong, Exit 6), is one of Seoul's boldest architectural statements, an enormous sculpture in glass, concrete and steel, reminiscent of a painting by Kandinsky.

A short walk south of COEX along Yeongdong-daero is **Kring** (Map p56; **M**Line 2 to Samseong, Exit 1). Looking like a giant music speaker crossed with a slab of Swiss cheese, this incredible steel-clad building was designed by Unsangdong Architects; at the time of research the building was closed.

Take the subway to Gangnam where you won't miss the curvaceous stylings of the slinky **GT Tower** (Map p58; **M**Line 2 to Samseong, Exit 9) beside the major crossing of Teheran-no and Gangnam-daero. Redubbed **U-Street**, Gangnam-daero is lined with 12m-high, 1.4m-wide media poles displaying video art. Above Shinonyheon station is **Urban Hive**, which looks like an enormous concrete beehive and has the cafe Take Urban on the ground floor.

Take a taxi to Apgujeong and view the **Horim Art Center** (Map p58; www.horimartcenter.org; Dosan-daero, Apgujeong; adult/child ₩8000/5000; ⊙10.30-6pm Tue, Thu-Sun, to 8pm on Wed; **M**Line 3 to Apgujeong, Exit 3), its exterior design inspired by pottery; inside the lustrous walls is a museum devoted to this Korean art form. Finish up in front of **The Galleria (West)**, its exterior covered with 4330 mother-of-pearl-like glass discs that shimmer in daylight and are a captivating canvas for dramatic LED lighting at night.

popular nonverbal musical show *Miso*, a traditional tale about star-crossed lovers. You can also dress up in traditional costumes here an hour before the show (₩5000) or join a *janggu* drumming class (₩15,000).

National Theatre of Korea
THEATRE
(Map p48; ☎2274 3507; www.ntok.go.kr; Heungin-mun-ro, Namsan; **M**Line 3 Dongguk University, Exit 6) The several venues here are home to the national drama, *changgeuk* (Korean opera), orchestra and dance companies. Free concerts and movies are put on in summer at the outdoor stage. From September to October the complex is the location of a major theatre festival. It's a 10-minute walk from the subway station or hop on bus 2 at the stop behind Exit 6.

Hanguk Performing Arts Centre
THEATRE
(Map p42; ☎3668 0007; www.hanpac.or.kr; Marronnier Park, Daehangno; **M**Line 4 to Hyehwa, Exit 2) In this large red-brick complex, designed by Kim Swoo-geun, are the main and small halls of both the Arko Art Theatre and Daehangno Arts Theatre. Come here for a varied dance-oriented program of events and shows.

Dongsoong Arts Centre
THEATRE
(Map p42; ☎766 3390; www.dsartcenter.co.kr; Dongsung-gil, Daehangno; **M**Line 4 to Hyehwa, Exit 1)

Major theatre complex, where you can see Korean and international performance arts in a variety of genres. The complex includes a puppet theatre, smaller performance spaces and a museum devoted to *kokdu* (wooden dolls and effigies with spiritual properties).

White Box Theatre
THEATRE
(www.probationarytheatre.com; tickets ₩15,000; **M**Line 6 to Hyochang Park, Exit 2) This basement studio space is the home of the Probationary Theatre Company, dream project of Australian expat Desiree Munro. A different production plays each month. It's a two-minute walk from the subway station; take the first right heading towards Hyochang Park.

Seoul Arts Centre
PERFORMING ARTS
(서울예술의전당; SAC; ☎580 1300; www.sac .or.kr; Nambusunhwan-ro, Seochu-gu; tickets from ₩10,000; **M**Line 3 to Nambu Bus Terminal, Exit 5, then bus 12) The national ballet and opera companies are based at this sprawling arts complex housing a large concert hall and a smaller recital hall in which the national choir, the Korea and Seoul symphony orchestras and various drama companies stage shows. A couple more theatres and three art galleries complete the package. To reach the SAC, walk straight on from the subway exit and turn left at the end of the bus terminal.

National Gugak Center CLASSICAL MUSIC
(☑580 3333; www.gugak.go.kr; Nambusunhwan-ro, Seochu-gu; tickets from ₩10,000; ⓜLine 3 to Nambu Bus Terminal, Exit 5) Traditional Korean classical and folk music and dance are performed, preserved and taught at this centre, which is home of the Court Music Orchestra, the Folk Music Group, Dance Theatre and Contemporary Gugak Orchestra.

The main theatre is Yeak-dang, which puts on an ever-changing program by leading performers every Saturday usually at 4pm and 5.30pm from early January to mid-December. The 1½-hour show is a bargain and usually contains seven items including court dances, folk songs, *pansori, gayageum,* flute music and drumming. The centre is down the road from the Seoul Arts Centre.

LG Arts Centre PERFORMING ARTS
(Map p58; ☑205 0114; www.lgart.com; Yeoksam-dong, Gangnam-gu; ⓜLine 2 to Yeoksam, Exit 7) Major local and international artists and companies perform at this multi-hall state-of-the-art venue. Its seasonal CoMPAS program delivers the cream of contemporary performing arts from the around the world.

Live Music

Feel LIVE MUSIC
(Map p48; Samil-daero, Myeong-dong; ⊘8pm-3am; ⓜLine 4 to Myeong-dong, Exit 10) In an incredibly decorated cavelike space, eccentric owner Mr Shin, who's been running the place since 1990, and his friends cover anything

and everything from Elvis to Korean rock. Drinks are beer or whisky. You'll find it up on the raised pathway running beneath the cathedral.

Club Evans JAZZ
(Map p50; ☑337 8361; www.clubevans.com; Wausan-gil, Hongdae; admission ₩1000; ⊘7.30-midnight Sun-Thu, to 2am Fri & Sat; ⓜLine 6 to Sangsu, Exit 1) Appealing across the generations, Evans offers top-grade jazz and a great atmosphere. Get here early if you want a seat or book ahead. They release their own label CDs, too.

Café BBang INDIE ROCK
(카페 빵; Map p50; http://cafe.daum.net/cafeb bang; Hongdae; ⊘7pm-6am; ⓜLine 2 to Hongik University, Exit 8) Basement venue where you're sure of catching something interesting – apart from music it also hosts film screenings, art exhibitions and parties.

FF INDIE ROCK
(Map p50; ☑011-9025 3407; Hongdae; admission ₩10,000; ⊘7pm-6am; ⓜLine 6 to Sangsu, Exit 1) A top live venue with up to eight local bands playing on the weekend until midnight. Afterwards it becomes a dance club with DJs.

DGBD INDIE ROCK
(Map p50; http://cafe.daum.net/dgbd; Hongdae; admission ₩5000 or ₩10,000; ⊘8-11pm; ⓜLine 2 to Hongik University, Exit 9) Legendary live-music venue where all the top Hongdae bands have played over the years. It's standing-room only and there's a balcony.

SEOUL SHOWTIME

Running for over 15 years, with no end in sight, is Korea's most successful nonverbal performance **Nanta** (http://nanta.i-pmc.co.kr; tickets ₩40,000-60,000) Ganbuk Jeong-dong (Map p48; Jeong-dong; ⊘5 & 8pm; ⓜLine 1 or 2 to City Hall, Exit 2); Hongdae (Map p50; Yellow Stone Bldg, Seokyo-dong; ⊘5 & 8pm; ⓜLine 2 to Hongdae, Exit 9); Myeong-dong (Map p48; 3rd fl, Unesco Bldg, Myeong-dong 2-ga; ⊘2, 5 & 8pm; ⓜLine 4 to Myeong-dong, Exit 6). Set in a kitchen, this high-octane 1½-hour show mixes up magic tricks, *samulnori* folk music, drumming with kitchen utensils, comedy, dance, martial arts and audience participation. It's top-class entertainment that has been a hit wherever it plays, and is staged at three venues in Seoul.

Nanta has inspired a booming industry of equally fun productions that have tweaked the blueprint, replacing cooking with drumming, quick-draw painting, martial arts and breakdancing (called b-boying in Korea) as the main themes. Other recommended shows include **Jump** (Map p42; www.yegam.com/jump/eng; Seoul Cinema; tickets from ₩40,000; ⊘8pm Mon, 4 & 8pm Tue-Sat, 3 & 6pm Sun; ⓜLine 1, 3 or 5 to Jongno 3-ga, Exit 14), featuring a wacky Korean family all crazy about martial arts; and **Bibap** (Map p42; www.bibap.co.kr; Cinecore Bldg, B2 Gwancheol-dong; tickets from ₩40,000; ⊘8pm Tue-Sat, 5pm & 8pm Sat, 3pm & 6pm Sun; ⓜLine 1 to Jonggak, Exit 4), a comedic Iron Chef–style contest that adds beatbox and a capella into the mix.

Freebird
INDIE ROCK

(Map p50; www.clubfreebird.com; 2nd fl, Eoulmadang 2-gil, Hongdae; admission free Mon-Thu, ₩20,000 Fri-Sun; ⊘6pm-midnight; MLine 2 to Hongik University, Exit 9) One of Hongdae's longest-running live-music venues, offering a range of genres from death rock to *Sound of Music* outtakes. Usually a handful of acts play every evening. Wednesday is audition night.

Luxury Noraebang
KARAOKE

(Map p50; ☑322 3111; Eoulmadang-gil, Hongdae; room per hr ₩10,000-38,000; ⊘9am-7am; MLine 6 to Sangsu, Exit 1) Karaoke your heart out and be noticed: some rooms have floor-to-ceiling windows facing the street so you can show off your K-Pop moves. Rates rise between 6pm and 7am and everyone gets a free ice cream.

Chunnyun
JAZZ

(천년동안도; Map p42; ☑743 5555; www.chunnyun.com; Maronie 2-gil, Daehangno; admission ₩7000; ⊘5pm-3am; MLine 4 to Hyehwa, Exit 2) Enjoy two or three sessions every evening in this spacious jazz haven with black decor subtly blended with blue neon. Look for the English sign 'Live Jazz Club'.

All That Jazz
JAZZ

(p52; ☑795 5701; www.allthatjazz.kr; Itaewon; admission ₩5000; ⊘8pm-midnight Sun-Thu, to 2am Fri & Sat; MLine 6 to Itaewon, Exit 2) A fixture on the Seoul jazz scene since 1976, All That Jazz has a new more spacious location closer to the subway. Top local musicians regularly perform here and table reservations are recommended for the weekend. The live music starts at 9pm, except on Friday (8.30pm) and Saturday and Sunday (both 7pm).

Once in a Blue Moon
JAZZ

(원스인어블루문; Map p58; ☑549 5490; www.onceinabluemoon.co.kr; 85-1 Cheongdam-dong, Gangnam-gu; admission free; ⊘5pm-2am; MLine 3 to Apgujeong, Exit 3) An intimate and classy club live jazz from two groups of performers nightly, each performing two sets between 7.30pm and 12.40am.

Sport

World Cup Stadium
STADIUM

(월드컵경기장; www.seoulworldcupst.or.kr; MLine 6 to World Cup Stadium, Exit 1) Built to stage the opening ceremony and matches during the 2002 World Cup, this 66,000-seat venue is still used as a sports and events stadium. Also in the building is a **museum** (adult/child ₩1000/500; ⊘9am-6pm) about the

World Cup event; a cinema multiplex; the shopping store Homeplus; and Spoland, a sports centre with swimming pools and 24-hour sauna. Around the stadium are large parks created from landfill sites returned to a natural state and cycling tracks.

Jamsil Sports Complex
BASEBALL, STADIUM

(Map p56; ☑2240 8864; Jamsil-dong, Songpa-gu; MLine 2 & 8 to Sports Complex, Exit 6) The professional baseball matches held at the stadium here are great entertainment; games kick off around 6.30pm. Also the location of the giant Olympic Stadium built for the 1988 Games and still used for major events and pop concerts.

🔒 Shopping

Whether it's traditional items like *hanbok* (clothing) or *hanji* (handmade paper), or digital gizmos and K-Pop CDs, chances are slim that you'll leave Seoul empty-handed. Seoul's teeming markets, electronics emporiums, underground arcades, upmarket department stores and glitzy malls are all bursting at the seams with more goodies than Santa's sack.

GWANGHWAMUN & JONGNO-GU

TOP CHOICE Kyobo Bookshop
BOOKS, MUSIC

(Map p42; B1, Kyobo Bldg, Jongno; MLine 5 to Gwanghwamun, Exit 4) The flagship branch, this famous bookshop sells a wide range of English-language books and magazines, as well as stationery, gifts, electronics and CDs and DVDs in its excellent Hottracks (www.hottracks.co.kr) section.

Seoul Selection
BOOKS

(Map p42; ☑734 9565; www.seoulselection.co.kr; ⊘9.30am-6.30pm Mon-Sat; MLine 3 to Anguk, Exit 1; @) Sells new and secondhand books on Korean culture in English, along with Korean CDs and Korean movies and drama series on DVD (with English subtitles). Also serves drinks, has free internet surfing and offers English-language walking tours of Bukchon every Saturday (₩30,000).

TOP CHOICE KCDF Gallery
DESIGN, CRAFT

(Map p60; www.kcdf.kr; Insa-dong 11-gil; MLine 3 to Anguk, Exit 6) The Korean Craft and Design Federation's gallery has a shop on the ground floor showcasing some of the finest locally made products, including woodwork, pottery and jewellery. It's a great place to find a unique, sophisticated gift or souvenir.

Ssamziegil HANDICRAFTS

(Map p60; www.ssamzigil.com; Insa-dong-gil, Insa-dong; [M]Line 3 to Anguk, Exit 6) This attractive, arty four-storey complex built around a courtyard is a popular stop for one-off clothing, accessories or household goods. In the basement look for **Cerawork** (www.cerawork .co.kr), where you can paint your own design onto pottery for a unique souvenir.

Jonginamoo HOMEWARES

(종이나무; Map p42; http://jonginamoo.com; Jae-dong; ⊘10am-10pm Mon-Sat, noon-10pm Sun; [M]Line 3 to Anguk, Exit 2) Selling beautiful traditional styled furniture and decorative pieces for your home, including a variety of lamps with shades made of *hanji*.

MYEONG-DONG & JUNG-GU

Myeong-dong is home to all the major global fast-fashion labels, including Asian faves Uniqlo, Basic House and Bean Pole. The streets fill up every evening with shoppers, hawkers and people shouting out the latest sale into a megaphone. It can be an overwhelming experience that borders on sensory overload, but shouldn't be missed.

TOP **CHOICE** **Namdaemun Market** MARKET

(Map p48; www.namdaemunmarket.co.kr; ⊘24hr; [M]Line 4 to Hoehyun, Exit 5) Day and night, more than 10,000 stores deal in everything from seaweed to spectacles. Pick up an English map outlining the market's different areas from one of two **tourist information booths** (⊘8.30am-6pm). If you're hungry, there are plenty of places to eat, including noodle alley near gate 6.

Shinsegae DEPARTMENT STORE

(Map p48; www.shinsegae.com; Sogong-ro; [M]Line 4 to Hoehyeon, Exit 7) Wrap yourself in luxury inside the Seoul equivalent of Harrods. It's split over two buildings, the older part based in a gorgeous 1930 colonial building that was Seoul's first department store, Mitsukoshi. Check out local designer fashion labels and the opulent supermarket in the basement with a food court; another food court is up on the 11th floor of the new building with an attached roof garden where you can relax.

Level 5 FASHION

(Map p48; http://level5ive.cafe24.com; Level 5, Noon Sq; [M]Line 2 to Euljiro 1-ga, Exit 6) No need to root around Dongdaemun's markets for the latest hot designers; visit this floor of the Noon Sq mall, which is devoted to sponsoring up-and-coming fashion talent.

TEMPLE PROGRAMS

Visit Bongeun-sa on Thursday if you want to take part in its **Templelife program** (₩20,000; ⊘2-4pm Thu), which includes lotus-lantern making, *dado* (tea ceremony), a temple tour and Seon (Zen) meditation. Book three weeks in advance to take part in its overnight Templestay programs (₩70,000).

A similar Temple Life program is offered at **Jogye-sa** (₩20,000; ⊘10am-2.30pm) every Saturday, while shorter programs (for a donation) are available daily. Gilsang-sa in Seongbuk-dong also runs an overnight Templestay program on the fourth Saturday and Sunday of the month (₩50,000).

Åland FASHION, HOMEWARES

(www.a-land.co.kr) Myeong-dong (Map p48; Myeong-dong; [M]Line 4 to Myeong-dong, Exit 6); Hongdae (Map p50; Yellow Stone Bldg, Seokyo-dong; [M]Line 2 to Hongdae, Exit 9) This multilabel boutique mixes up vintage and garage-sale items with new designer items to wear and decorate your home. You'll find cool indie CDs and magazines, too. It also has a slick store in Hongdae (in the same building as the Nanta theatre) and an outlet shop there, too.

Lotte Department Store DEPARTMENT STORE

(Map p48; Namdaemun-ro; [M]Line 2 to Euljiro 1-ga, Exit 8) Retail behemoth Lotte spreads its tentacles across four buildings: the main department store, Lotte Young Plaza, Lotte Avenuel and a duty-free shop. Also here is a multiplex cinema, restaurants and an attached hotel.

Migliore Mall FASHION

(Map p48; Toegye-ro; ⊘11am-11.30pm Tue-Sun; [M]Line 4 to Myeong-dong, Exit 6) Always teeming with young trendsetters, this high-rise mall is packed with small fashion shops. There's an outdoor performance stage by the entrance where you watch groups and brush up on your K-Pop dance moves.

WESTERN & NORTHERN SEOUL

TOP **CHOICE** **Key** ARTS & CRAFTS

(Map p50; www.welcomekey.net; off Dabog-gil, Hongdae; ⊘noon-10pm; [M]Line 2 to Hongik University, Exit 8) Representing 48 different artists and craftspeople, several of whom also sell their goods at the Freemarket on Saturday,

LOCAL KNOWLEDGE

GALLERIES GALORE

'Visitors to Seoul are often quite surprised by the diversity of art and number of galleries here,' says Monica Cha, owner of Gallery Cha in Tongui-dong, west of Gyeongbokgung. Although some commercial galleries are south of the Han River, Seoul's eclectic contemporary art scene is concentrated around Insa-dong, Bukchon and Tongui-dong. Most galleries are free to browse, and most are closed Monday. Useful resources include the free monthly art magazine **ArtnMap** (www.artnmap.com) and *Seoul Art Guide* (in Korean).

Insa-dong

The closest subway station for the following galleries is Anguk, Exit 6.

Insa Gallery (Map p60; ☑735 2655; www.insagallery.net; Insa-dong 10-gil; ☉10am-6pm) Exhibitions change twice a month. It also has a branch in Cheongdam.

Sun Art Center (Map p60; ☑734 0458; www.sungallery.co.kr; Insa-dong 5-gil ☉10am-6pm) Specialises in early-20th-century Korean art.

Tongui-dong

The closest subway station for the following galleries is Gyeonbokgung, Exit 5.

Gallery Cha (☑730 1700; www.gallerycha.com; ☉11am-6.30pm Mon-Fri, noon-6pm Sat) Specialising in emerging Korean artists.

Jean Art Gallery (Map p42; ☑738 7570; www.jeanart.net; ☉10am-6pm Tue-Fri, to 5pm Sat & Sun) Pioneer of the Tongui-dong gallery scene. Look for the metallic butterfly sculpture between the gallery's two red-brick buildings; art inside includes a 2m-tall dotted pumpkin sculpture by Japanese artist Yayoi Kusama.

Artside (Map p42; ☑725 1020; www.artside.org; ☉10am-6.30pm Tue-Sun) Regularly exhibits contemporary art by Chinese artists.

East of Gyeongbokgung

The closest subway station for the following galleries is Anguk, Exit 1.

Artsonje Center (Map p42; ☑733 8945; www.artsonje.org/asc; adult/student/child ₩3000/1500/1000; ☉11am-7pm Tue-Sun) Supports experimental art and has an annual open call for new works. Also has a bookshop and cafe and art-house cinema.

Gallery Hyundai (Map p42 ☑287 3500; www.galleryhyundai.com; ☉10am-6pm) Two outlets close by each other here; their main gallery is in Gangnam.

Hakgojae (Map p42; ☑720 1524; www.hakgojae.com; ☉10am-7pm Tue-Sat, to 6pm Sun) Contemporary works in a converted *hanok;* look for robot sculpture on roof.

Kukje (Map p42; ☑735 8449; www.kukjegallery.com; ☉10am-6pm) There's a second gallery space off the main road. Look up to the roof to see the running woman sculpture by Jonathan Borofsky.

this small gallery and showroom offers affordable, exclusive items, from jewellery to pottery to fabric art and paintings.

🍃**Little Farmers**　　　　ACCESSORIES
(Map p50; www.littlefarmers.co.kr; Wausan-gil, Hongdae; ☉noon-9pm; Ⓜ Line 2 to Hongik University, Exit 8) Ecofriendly shoes, bags and other goods, some made from recycled products, are sold at this attractive basement store. You'll also find K-Indie CDs here and other colourful accessories.

Free & Hope Markets　　　CRAFT, MARKET
(Map p50; www.freemarket.or.kr/v3; Hongdae Playground, opposite entrance Hongik University; ☉1-6pm Sat Mar-Nov; Ⓜ Line 2 to Hongik University, Exit 9) A girl in ripped jeans selling her own hand-painted cigarette lighters; Korean garage bands and singers busking in front of adoring fans; hand-painted bottle tops, hand-painted suitcases, hand-painted everything – all these can be found in this crafters market. The Hope Market that runs here on Sunday afternoons is a traditional flea market.

Dolsilnai
FASHION

(돌실나이; Map p42; www.dolsilnai.co.kr; Myeon-gryun-dong; ☺10.30am-8pm; Ⓜ Line 4 to Hyehwa, Exit 1) Producing beautifully designed, casual *hanbok* made from natural fabrics in a variety of soft natural and pastel colours. Many of the garments for both men and women are discounted and are of a far superior quality than what you'll find in the tourist shops of Insa-dong. There's also a branch in Sinchon.

Purple Record
MUSIC

(Map p50; Wausan-gil, Hongdae; ☺10.30am-11pm; Ⓜ Line 2 to Hongik University, Exit 9) An interesting selection of music genres, including titles by K-Indie singers and bands, are stocked at this independent CD store.

ITAEWON & YONGSAN-GU

Millimetre Milligram
STATIONERY, BAGS

(Map p52; MMG; www.mmmg.net; Hannam-dong; Ⓜ Line 6 to Itaewon, Exit 3) This is the spot to pick up quirky stationery and bags, including the Austrian brand Freitag. There's a cafe as well as a basement gallery/furniture store and, on the 3rd floor, the boutique art-book and magazine shop **Post Poetics** (www.postpoetics.org; ☺1-8pm Tue-Fri, to 6pm Sat & Sun). There are MMG shops also near Anguk station in Insa-dong and on Garosu-gil.

Yongsan Electronics Market
ELECTRONICS

(Yongsan; ☺9.30am-7.30pm, partly closed 1st & 3rd Sun; Ⓜ Line 1 to Yongsan, Exit 3) If it plugs in, you can find it at this geeky universe of high-tech marvels. Computer prices are usually marked but prices on other goods are lacking, so do what the locals do – check out the prices on the web before arriving. Leave the train-station plaza via Exit 3, turn right, then right again and walk through the pedestrian overpass to enter the first building of Yongsan Electronics Town on the 3rd floor. If all this is too much, try discount electronics chain E-Mart in the nearby I'Park Mall.

What the Book
BOOKS

(Map p52; www.whatthebook.com; Itaewon-ro; ☺10am-8pm Mon-Sat, from noon Sun; Ⓜ Line 6 to Itaewon, Exit 3) Itaewon's best bookshop sells new and secondhand English-language books and a wide range of American mags.

Two Heads Are Better Than One
FASHION

(Map p52; www.steveandyonip.com; Hannam-dong; ☺11.30am-7.30pm; Ⓜ Line 6 to Hanganjin, Exit 3) The two heads collaborating on the superfashionable streetware in this boutique are local designers Steve J and Yoni P. Their T-shirts, sweatshirts and colourful printed clobber are stocked by boutiques around the world, but their flagship store is down this happening little street in Hannam-dong.

I'Park Mall
MALL

(www.iparkmall.co.kr; Yongsan; Ⓜ Line 1 to Yongsan, Line 4 to Sinyongsan, Exit 3 or 4) There's pretty much everything you need from brand-name fashion to digital goods at this mall that sprawls around Yongsan station. Up on the 9th floor is the e-Sports Stadium where e-game tournaments are staged.

DONGDAEMUN & EASTERN SEOUL

TOP CHOICE Dongdaemun Market
MARKET

(Map p54; Dongdaemun; ☺24hr; Ⓜ Line 1 or 4 to Dongdaemun, Exit 5 or 7) Take Seoul's commercial pulse at this colossal retail and wholesale market where the bargaining never stops. It's a buzz to wander the network of buildings and streets where you can buy practically anything, although it's mainly fashion that drags in customers.

TOP CHOICE Doota
DEPARTMENT STORE

(Map p54; www.doota.com; Dongdaemun; ☺10.30am-5am Tue-Sat, to 11pm Sun, 7pm-5am Mon) Cut through Dongdaemun's commercial frenzy by heading to its leading fashion mall full to the brim with domestic brands. Ten floors above and below ground are dedicated to clothing, accessories, beauty items and souvenirs. When you start flagging there's plenty of cafes and a good food court on the 7th floor.

Seoul Yangyeongsi Herb Medicine Market
TRADITIONAL MEDICINE

(Gyeongdong Market; www.seoulya.com; Jegi-dong; ☺8am-6.30pm; Ⓜ Line 1 to Jegi-dong, Exit 2) Korea's biggest Asian medicine market runs back for several blocks from the traditional gate on the main road and includes thousands of clinics, retailers, wholesalers and medicine makers. If you're looking for a leaf, herbs, bark, roots, flower or mushroom to ease your ailment, it's bound to be here.

Seoul Folk Flea Market
MARKET

(Sinseol-dong; ☺10am-6pm, closed 2nd & 4th Tue of month; Ⓜ Line 1 or 2 to Sinseol-dong, Exit 6 or 10) Spilling out of a two-storey building into the surrounding area, here you'll find a fascinating collection of artworks, collectables and general bric-a-brac from wooden masks and ink drawings to Beatles LPs and valve radios. English signs point here from the subway.

Dapsimni Antiques Market ANTIQUES
($\odot$10am-4.30pm Mon-Sat; MLine 5 to Dapsimni, Exit 2) Browse through old treasures – from *yangban* (aristocrat) pipes and horsehair hats to wooden shoes, fish-shaped locks and embroidered status insignia – stuffed inside scores of small antique shops in three separate arcades.

At the subway exit walk over to the orange-tiled Samhee 6 building behind the car park. A similar arcade on the left is Samhee 5. After visiting them, go back to Exit 2 and left along the main road for 10 minutes to reach a brown-tiled arcade, Janganpyeong, with another section behind it. You can't miss them, with stonework stored permanently outside.

SOUTH OF THE HAN RIVER

10 Corso Como Seoul FASHION
(Map p58; www.10corsocomo.co.kr; Cheongdam-dong, Gangnam-gu; MLine 3 to Apgujeong, Exit 3) This outpost of the Milan fashion/lifestyle boutique is about as delicious as Seoul retail can get. Its expert blend of fashion, art and design is seductive; if you can't afford the clothes, which include several local designers, there's a brilliant selection of international books and CDs to browse and a chic cafe.

[TOP CHOICE] D Cube City MALL
(www.dcubecity.com; Kyungin-ro, Guro-gu; MLines 1 & 2 to Sindorim, Exit 1) Seoul's malls hardly come more stylish than this new one in the previously industrial hub of Guro. The interior spaces surround a waterfall and there's plenty of multilevel outdoor terraces on which to relax in fine weather. Also here is the D-Cube Arts Centre with a concert hall and larger theatre for musicals, a very spiffy Sheraton Hotel (with fabulous views from all rooms), good restaurants and a superbly designed food Korean food court in the basement.

COEX Mall MALL
(Map p56; www.coexmall.com; Samseoung-dong, Gangnam-gu; MLine 2 to Samseong, COEX Exit) This vast mall is attached to a branch of Hyundai department store, with three hotels, a multiplex cinema, the COEX Convention Centre and World Trade Centre. Among the shopping possibilities there is a branch of the bookshop Bandi & Luni's. Next door, Evan Records is a good place to pick up K-Pop and K-Indie CDs as well as local movies and TV series on DVDs.

Galleria DEPARTMENT STORE
(Map p58; http://dept.galleria.co.kr; Apgujeongno, Gangnam; MLine 3 to Apgujeong, Exit 1) Department stores in Seoul don't get more luxurious than this. If you want to play Audrey Hepburn staring into Tiffany's, don a Helen Kaminski hat, try on a Stella McCartney dress or slip into a pair of Jimmy Choos, the east wing of fashion icon Galleria is the place to be. Dozens of top designer stores are packed into the two Galleria buildings; the west wing is covered in glass discs that turn psychedelic at night.

Central City Mall MALL
(Map p58; www.centralcityseoul.co.kr; Gangnam; MLine 3 or 7 to Express Bus Terminal, Exit 7) A branch of the department store Shinsegae anchors this popular mall next to the Seoul Express Bus Terminal. You'll also find here a food court and a six-cinema multiplex.

ℹ Information

Dangers & Annoyances

A common sight on central Seoul's streets – particularly around Gwanghwamun and Seoul Plaza – are squadrons of fully armed riot police. Student, trade-union and other protests occasionally turn violent. Keep well out of the way of any confrontations that may occur.

Drivers tend to be impatient, with *kimchi*-hot tempers, and most of them, including bus drivers, routinely go through red lights. Don't be the first or last person to cross over any pedestrian crossing. Keep two eyes out for cars parking on pavements and motorcyclists who speed along pavements and across pedestrian crossings.

Emergency

If there are no English-speaking staff available, ring the 24-hour tourist information and help line ☏1330.

Ambulance (☏119)
Fire Brigade (☏119)
Police (☏112)

Internet Access

Wi-fi is universal and often free. Most hotels offer it; if they don't, the'll have LAN cables for wired access in rooms. Charges vary from free to around ₩30,000 per day at top-end hotels. If you need a computer, look for the 'PC 방' signs, which charge around ₩2000 per hour and are invariably packed with teenage online gamers. The KTO Tourist Information Centre offers free internet access.

WANT MORE?

For in-depth information, reviews and recommendations at your fingertips, head to the Apple App Store to purchase Lonely Planet's *Seoul Travel Guide* iPhone app.

Laundry

Backpacker guesthouses and motels usually provide free use of a washing machine, although you'll usually have to pay for drying. Dry-cleaning shops are fairly common.

Left Luggage

Most subway stations and bus terminals have lockers. Small lockers cost ₩1000 a day and the ones large enough to fit a backpack are ₩2000.

Media

10 Magazine (10mag.com) Monthly magazine.
Bridge (www.bridgezine.com) Monthly paperzine.
Groove Korea (groovekorea.com) Monthly magazine.
Seoul (www.seoulselection.com) Monthly magazine.
TBS (http://tbsefm.seoul.kr) Local radio station with programs in English.

Medical Services

Most facilities don't accept international insurance so bring cash or credit cards.
Asan Medical Centre (Map p56; ☏3010 5100; http://eng.amc.seoul.kr; Songpa-gu; ☺international clinic 9am-5pm Mon-Fri; Ⓜ Line 2 to Seongnae, Exit 1) A 10-minute walk from subway exit.
International Clinic (Map p52; ☏790 0857; www.internationalclinic.co.kr; Hannam Bldg, Itaewon-ro, Itaewon; ☺9am-6.30pm Mon-Wed & Fri, to 4pm Sat; Ⓜ Line 6 to Itaewon, Exit 2) Appointments are a must.
Severance Hospital (off Map p50; ☏2228 5800; www.yuhs.or.kr; Sinchon. Seodaemun-gu; ☺international clinic 9.30-11.30am & 2-4.30pm Mon-Fri, 9.30am-noon Sat; Ⓜ Line 2 to Sinchon, Exit 3) A 15-minute walk from subway exit.

Money

Credit cards are readily accepted and many ATMs accept foreign credit cards – look for one that has a 'Global' sign or the logo of your credit-card company. Many banks offer a foreign-exchange service. There are also licensed moneychangers, particularly in Itaewon, that keep longer hours than the banks and provide a faster service, but may only exchange US dollars cash.

Post

Post offices are common and offer free internet access.
Central Post Office (Map p48; Sogong-ro, Myeong-dong; ☺9am-8pm Mon-Fri, to 1pm Sat & Sun; Ⓜ Line 4 to Myeong-dong, Exit 6).

Toilets

There are plenty of clean, modern and well-signed public toilets, virtually all free of charge. It's wise to carry a stash of toilet tissue around with you just in case there's none available.

ℹ TRANSLATION & COUNSELLING SERVICES

If you need interpretation help or information on practically any topic, any time of the day or night you call either of the following:

Tourist Phone Number (☏1330 or ☏02-1330 from a mobile phone)

BBB (☏1588 5644; bbbkorea.org)

Also very useful is the **Seoul Global Center** (Map p48; ☏2075-4180; http://global.seoul.go.kr; 3rd fl, Korea Press Centre, 124 Sejong-daero, Jung-gu; ☺9am-6pm Mon-Fri; Ⓜ Line 1 or 2 to City Hall, Exit 4), a comprehensive support centre for foreign residents in Seoul; it has volunteers who speak a range of languages, as well as full-time staff who can assist on a range of issues.

Tourist Information

There are scores of tourist information booths around the city. In major tourist areas such as Insa-dong and Namdaemun look for red-jacketed city tourist guides who can also help with information in various languages. Handy TICs include the following:

Cheong-gye-cheon Tourist Information Centre (Map p42; Sejong-daero, Gwanghwamun; ☺9am-10pm; Ⓜ Line 5 to Gwanhwamun, Exit 6)

Gyeongbokgung Tourist Information Centre (Map p42; Gwanghwamun; ☺9am-6pm; Ⓜ Line 3 to Gyeongbokgung, Exit 5)

Insa-dong Tourist Information Centre (Map p60; ☏734 0222; Insa-dong; ☺10am-10pm; Ⓜ Line 3 to Anguk, Exit 6) Two more centres are at the south and north entrances to Insa-dong-gil.

Itaewon Subway Tourist Information Centre (Map p52; ☏3785 2514; Itaewon; ☺9am-9pm; Ⓜ Line 6 to Itaewon)

KTO Tourist Information Centre (Map p42; ☏1330; www.visitkorea.or.kr; Cheong-gye-cheon-ro, Jung-gu; ☺9am-8pm; Ⓜ Line 1 to Jonggak, Exit 5) The best information centre; knowledgeable staff, free internet, and many brochures and maps.

Namdaemun Market Tourist Information Centre (Map p48; ☏752 1913; Namdaemun Market; ☺9am-6pm; Ⓜ Line 4 to Hoehyeon, Exit 5) You'll find two info kiosks within the market.

Seoul Center for Culture & Tourism (Map p48; ☏3789 7961; 5th fl, M Plaza Bldg, Myeong-dong; Ⓜ Line 4 to Myeong-dong, Exit 6) Offers guide services, free internet, culture and language programs.

Websites

Lonely Planet (www.lonelyplanet.com/south
-korea/seoul) For planning advice, author recommendations, traveller reviews and insider tips.

Seoul Metropolitan Government (http://
english.seoul.go.kr) City's official site.

Seoul Sub-urban (www.seoulsurban.com)
Explore the city by subway.

Visit Seoul (www.visitseoul.net) Official city
tourism-devoted site.

ⓘ Getting There & Away

Air

Seoul has two airports. The main international
gateway, **Incheon International Airport** (☑032-
1577 2600; www.airport.kr), is 52km west of central Seoul on Yeongjongdo island. This top-class
operation also has a few domestic connections.

The bulk of domestic flights (and a handful of
international ones) arrive at **Gimpo International Airport** (☑660 2114; http://gimpo.airport
.co.kr; West Seoul), 18km west of the city centre.

Bus

Seoul is well served by very frequent intercity
buses – outside of busy holidays you can turn
up, get your ticket and go. The prices quoted
here are for regular services – you'll pay more
for deluxe and night buses.

Seoul Express Bus Terminal (Map p58; ☑536
6460; www.kobus.co.kr, www.hticket.co.kr;
Ⓜ Line 3, 7 & 9 to Express Bus Terminal, Exit 1
for Gyeongbu-Gumi-Yeongdong Terminal, Exit 7
for Honam Terminal) Split across two separate
buildings; **Gyeongbu-Gumi-Yeongdong Terminal** serves mainly the eastern region; and **Honam
Terminal** serves the southwestern region.

Dong-Seoul Bus Terminal (Map p56; ☑455
3161; www.ti21.co.kr; Line 2 to Gangbyeon, Exit
4) Serves the eastern part of Korea (1st floor) and
major cities (2nd floor).

ⓘ CITY AIR TERMINALS

If you're flying Korean Air, Asiana or Jeju
Air, you can check in your luggage and
go through immigration at **KARST** (Map
p48; http://english.arex.or.kr/jsp/eng/index
.jsp) at Seoul station, then hop on the
A'REX train to Gimpo or Incheon. South
of the river, a similar service operates
from **CALT** (Map p56; www.calt.co.kr;
⊙5.30am-6.30pm; Ⓜ Line 2 to Samseong,
Exit 5) at the COEX Mall and includes Qa-
tar Airways, Singapore Airlines Qantas,
Air Canada and Philippine Airlines. From
here limo buses run to either airport.

Nambu Bus Terminal (off Map p58; ☑521 8550;
www.nambuterminal.co.kr; Line 3 to Nambu Bus
Terminal, Exit 5) For destinations south of Seoul.

Train

Most trains leave **Seoul Station** (Map p48;
Ⓜ Line 1 & 4 to Seoul Station), which has high-
speed Korea Train Express (KTX), *Saemaul*
(express) and *Mugunghwa* (semi-express)
services to many parts of the country. **Yongsan
Station** (Map p40; Ⓜ Line 1 & Jungang Line)
handles KTX and train connections with South
Chungcheong and the Jeolla provinces. For
current fares and detailed schedules visit the
website of the **Korea National Railroad** (www
.korail.go.kr).

East of central Seoul, long-distance services
to destinations in eastern Gyeonggi-do and
Gangwon-do leave from **Cheongnyangni Station** (청량리역; Map p40; Ⓜ Line 1 to Cheongnyangni); south of the Han River, **Yeongdeungpo
Station** (영등포역; Map p40; Ⓜ Line 1 to
Yeongdeungpo) is a major *Saemaul/Mugunghwa*
station for services heading south.

ⓘ Getting Around

To/From Incheon International Airport

BUS

City limousine buses take around an hour
to reach central Seoul depending on traffic
(₩10,000, every 10 to 30 minutes; ⊙5.30am-
10pm). There are also **KAL deluxe limousine
buses** (www.kallimousine.com), which drop passengers off at hotels around Seoul (₩15,000).

TAXI

Expect to pay around ₩65,000 for the
70-minute journey to central Seoul, but the price
can rise if traffic is jammed – meters run on a
time basis when the taxis are not moving. From
midnight to 4am regular taxis charge 20% extra.

TRAIN

A'rex express trains (www.arex.or.kr) to Seoul
Station are ₩13,800 (43 minutes), the commuter trains ₩3850 (53 minutes).

To/From Gimpo International Airport

BUS

Limousine buses (₩6500) run between Gimpo
and Incheon airports. Both City/KAL deluxe
limousine buses also run every 10 minutes to
central Seoul (₩5000/7000).

SUBWAY

Subway lines 5 and 9 connect the airport with
the city (₩1250, 35 minutes).

TRAIN

A'rex trains run to Seoul Station (₩1300, 15
minutes)

BUS SERVICES FROM SEOUL

DESTINATION	PRICE EXPRESS/DELUXE (₩)	DURATION
Busan	22,000/32,800	4hr 20min
Buyeo	14,400	2hr 40min
Chuncheon	6300	1hr 10min
Gongju	7700/8600	1hr 50min
Gwangju	16,900/29,200	3hr 30min
Gyeongju	19,500/29,000	4hr 30min
Jeonju	12,200/17,900	2hr 45min
Mokpo	19,600/29,000	4hr
Sokcho	17,000	2hr 40min

TAXI

A taxi costs around ₩35,000 to the city centre.

Public Transport

All fares can be paid using the rechargeable, touch-and-go **T-Money card** (http://eng.t-money.co.kr), which provides a ₩100 discount per trip. The basic card can be bought for a nonrefundable ₩3000 at any subway station booth, bus kiosk and convenience store displaying the T-Money logo; reload it with credit at any of the aforementioned places and get money refunded that hasn't been used (up to ₩20,000 minus a processing fee of ₩500) at subway machines and participating convenience stores before you leave Seoul.

BUS

Seoul has a comprehensive and reasonably priced **bus system** (☑414 5005; www.bus.go.kr; ⊙5.30am–midnight). Some bus stops have some route maps in English, and most buses have major destinations written in English on the outside and a taped announcement of the names of each stop in English, but few bus drivers understand English.

Long-distance-express red buses run to the outer suburbs, green buses link subways within a district, blue buses run to outer suburbs and yellow short-haul buses circle small districts. Using a T-money card saves ₩100 on each bus fare, and transfers between bus and subway are either free or discounted. Place your T-money card on the screen as you exit as well as when you get on a bus, just as you do on the subway.

SUBWAY

Seoul has an excellent, user-friendly **subway system** (www.smrt.co.kr; ⊙5.30am–midnight), which connects with destinations well beyond the city borders, including Suwon and Incheon. The minimum fare of ₩1150 (₩1050 with a T-money card) takes you up to 12km. In central Seoul the average time between stations is just over two minutes, so it takes you around 25 minutes to go 10 stops.

Most subway stations have lifts or stair lifts for wheelchairs. Escalators are common, but you'll do a fair amount of walking up and down stairs and along corridors. Neighbourhood maps, including ones with digital touch screens, inside the stations help you figure out which of the subway exits to take. The closet station and exit number is provided for all listings in this chapter.

TAXI

Ideal for short trips, regular taxis have a basic charge of ₩2400 for 2km, rising ₩100 for every 144m or 35 seconds after that if the taxi is travelling below 15km/h. A 20% surcharge is levied between midnight and 4am. Deluxe taxis are black with a yellow stripe and cost ₩4500 for the first 3km and ₩200 for every 164m or 39 seconds, but they don't have a late-night surcharge. Few taxi drivers speak English, but most taxis have a free interpretation service whereby an interpreter talks to the taxi driver and to you by phone. Orange **International Taxi** (☑1644 2255; www.internationaltaxi.co.kr) have English-speaking drivers; these can be reserved in advance for 20% extra on the regular fare and can be chartered on an hourly or daily basis for longer journeys. All taxis are metered; tipping is not required.

WATER TAXI

Reservations need to be made for **water taxis** (☑1588 3960; www.pleasantseoul.com), which can be boarded at 12 stations along the Han River: Jamsil Ferry, Ttukseom Resort, Seoul Forest, Jamweon Pier, Ichon Geobukseon Naruteo, Yeoui 119, Yeouinaru Station, Yanghwa Dangsan Station, Yanghwa Ferry, Seonyu-do, Mangwon and Nanji. Commuter services run between Yeouido and Ttsukseom and Yeouido and Jamsil (₩5000, 7am to 8.30am and 6.30pm to 7.30pm Monday to Friday). The taxis can also be hired for private tours (for up to seven passengers) from ₩50,000 to ₩130,000 for trips of 20 minutes to one hour.

Gyeonggi-do & Incheon

Includes »

Best Places to Stay

» Yonaluky (p97)
» Namchidang (p116)
» Hwaseong Guest House (p100)
» Lifou (p114)
» Harbor Park Hotel (p109)

Best Places to Eat

» Yeonpo Galbi (p100)
» Mandabok (p109)
» Deokjegung (p104)
» Palpal Yeonjangeo (p117)
» Caffe Ora (p113)

Why Go?

Within easy day-trip range of Seoul are the province of Gyeonggi-do and the metropolitan area of Incheon-gwangyeok-si, which includes Incheon and the many islands flaking into the muddy West Sea like crumbs from a doughnut. Here lie illustrious historical sites, several of them World Heritage listed: timeless temples, cultural villages, sandy beaches and tree-covered mountains that are crying out to be climbed in summer and skied in winter. The range of experiences on offer – from making pottery in Incheon to straddling the North–South border in the Joint Security Area of the DMZ – is hard to beat.

To get the most from some places, such as the island of Ganghwado, it's best to stay overnight or longer. Incheon International Airport's transport connections and location on the island of Yeongjongdo mean that you needn't even go into Seoul first to visit many places.

When to Go

Incheon

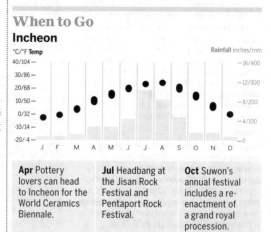

Apr Pottery lovers can head to Incheon for the World Ceramics Biennale.

Jul Headbang at the Jisan Rock Festival and Pentaport Rock Festival.

Oct Suwon's annual festival includes a re-enactment of a grand royal procession.

GYEONGGI-DO 경기도

Gyeonggi-do was designated as a province after the Korean War. The seat of regional government has been Suwon since 1967. Apart from the key places and sights listed here you can find out more about what this province offers the visitor at http://english.gg.go.kr.

The Demilitarized Zone (DMZ) & Joint Security Area (JSA)

The 4km-wide, 240km-long buffer known as the Demilitarized Zone (DMZ) slashes across the peninsula, separating North and South Korea. Lined on both sides by tank traps, electrical fences, landmines and armies in full battle readiness, it is one of the scariest places on earth. It is also one of the most surreal, since it has become a major tourist attraction with several observatories allowing you to peek into North Korea. For history buffs and collectors of weird and unsettling experiences, a visit here is not to be missed.

The place most people want to go is the Joint Security Area (JSA), 55km north of Seoul, inside of which is the truce village of Panmunjeom – there's nowhere else in South Korea where you can get so close to North Korea and North Korean soldiers without being arrested or shot, and the tension is palpable. The only way into this heavily restricted area is on an organised tour – note citizens of certain countries are not allowed on these tours. There are also strict dress and behavioural codes.

Though your tour will likely be a quiet one, the soldier 'tour guides' will remind you that this frontier is no stranger to violent incidents. One of the most notorious, in 1976, was when two US soldiers were hacked to death with axes by North Korean soldiers after the former had tried to chop down a tree obstructing the view from a watch tower. Camp Bonifas, the joint US–ROK army camp just outside the DMZ, is named after one of the slain soldiers.

Sights

The following describes the major stops on the most popular tour, offered by the USO, the US army's social and entertainment organisation, which you'll need to book at least two weeks in advance. If booking other tours, check that they include the JSA. Also ask whether time will be filled out with shopping stops, and refund/rescheduling options if a tour is cancelled – this can occasionally happen.

JSA (Panmunjeom)   MILITARY BASE

Tours kick off with a rapid-fire briefing by the soldier guides at Camp Bonifas. Next you will board specially designated buses to travel into the JSA towards the collection of blue-painted UN buildings that constitute Panmunjeom, an abandoned village where the truce between North and South Korea was signed. Official meetings between the North and South are still sometimes held here and in the main conference room; microphones on the tables constantly record everything said. Straddling the ceasefire line, this is the only place where you can safely walk into North Korea. South Korean soldiers stand guard inside and out in a

LIVING INSIDE THE DMZ

The 1953 *Korean Armistice Agreement* created two villages in the DMZ. On the south side is **Daeseong-dong** (대성동; Freedom Village), less than 1km from Panmunjeom, where around 200 people live in modern houses with high-speed internet connection and earn a tax-free annual income of over US$80,000 from their 7-hectare farms. There's an 11pm curfew, and soldiers stand guard while the villagers work in the rice fields or tend their ginseng plants.

On the North Korean side of the line is **Gijeong-dong** (기정동). The North translates this as 'Peace Village' but the South calls it Propaganda Village because virtually all the buildings are believed to be empty or just facades – the lights all come on and go off here at the same time at night. The village's primary feature is a 160m-high tower flying a flag that weighs nearly 300kg, markedly larger than the one on the South Korean side. It's believed that some workers from the nearby Kaesong Industrial Complex may now be living in Gijeong-dong.

Gyeonggi-do & Incheon Highlights

1 Fathom the bizarre terror-meets-tourism experience of a trip to the **DMZ** (p93)

2 Discover a colonial past, Chinatown and contemporary art on a walk through **Incheon** (p105)

3 Stride along the World Heritage–listed fortress wall before enjoying beef-bone soup in **Suwon** (p98)

4 Meander around **Heyri** (p96), a quirky contemporary village devoted to art and low-key architecture

5 Escape to the lovely West Sea island of **Muuido** (p113), from where you can walk to So-Muuido

6 Hike to the granite peaks and mountainside temples in **Bukhansan National Park** (p97)

7 Climb the steps to view the grotto and 10m-tall Buddha rock carving at **Bomun-sa** (p115) on the island of Seongmodo

8 Cool down in the waterpark at **Everland Resort** (p102) and be wowed by the artistic treasures of its Hoam Art Museum

NORTH KOREA

Kaesong
Gijeong-dong
DMZ **1**
Panmunjeom
Daeseong-dong
Third Infiltration Tunnel
Dorasan
Dora Observatory

Heyri
Bugeun-ri Dolmen
Gyodongdo
Odusan
Unification Observatory
Ganghwa-eup
Ganghwado
Seongmodo Oepo-ri
Bomun-sa **7**
Manisan *Gwangseongbo*
(469m)
Gim
▲ ⛩ *Jeondeung-sa*

INCHEON-
GWANGYEOK-SI

Incheon International Airport
Cheongna Free Economic Zone
Yeongjongdo
Incheon **2**
Eulwangni Beach
Jamjindo Pier
Songdo International City
Muuido **5**

To Baengnyeongdo

Simnipo Beach

Yeongheungdo
Deokjeokdo
Daebudo
Seopori Beach
Seosin-myeon
Jebudo

WEST SEA
(Yellow Sea)

CHUNGCHEONGNAM-DO

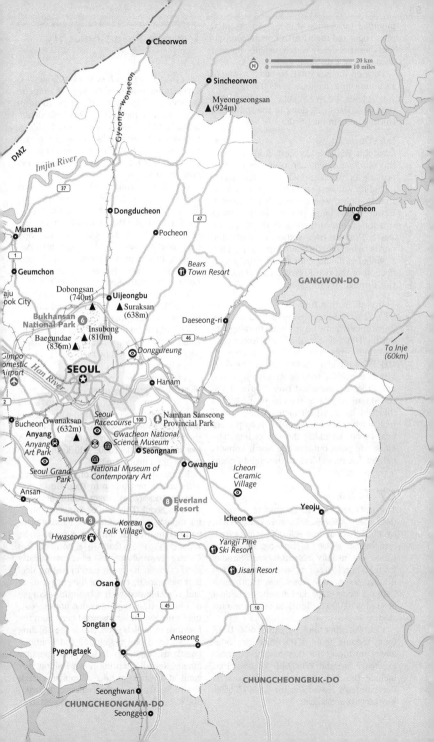

modified taekwondo stance – an essential photo op – and their North Korean counterparts keep a steady watch, usually, but not always, from a distance.

Back on the bus you'll be taken to one of Panmunjeom's lookout posts from where you can see the two villages that lie within the DMZ: Daeseong-dong to the south and Gijeong-dong in the north.

Dora Observatory OBSERVATORY

(binoculars ₩500; ⊙10am-5pm Tue-Sun) From this observatory you can peer through binoculars for a closer look at North Korea, including Kaesong city and Kaesong Industrial Complex, where cheap North Korean labourers are employed by South Korean conglomerates. At the foot of the mountain stands Dorasan train station, currently the northern terminus of South Korea's rail line – a symbol of the hope for the eventual reunification of the two Koreas and a chance to ride through to Pyongyang.

Third Infiltration Tunnel TUNNEL

(제3땅굴; ⊙9am-5pm Tue-Sun) Since 1974 four tunnels have been found running under the DMZ, dug by the North Koreans so that their army could launch a surprise attack. Walking along 265m of this 73m-deep tunnel is not for the claustrophobic or the tall; creeping, hunched over, to reach the coiled barbed wire at the end of the tunnel (blocked by a triple-concrete wall), you'll realise why they issue hard hats to protect heads from knocking the low ceiling. The guide will point out how the North Koreans painted the rocks black so they might claim it was a coal mine.

☞ Tours

The USO tour is run by Koridoor Tours (Map p58; ☎02-795 3028; www.koridoor.co.kr; cash US$80, credit card ₩96,000; ⊙office 8am-5pm Mon-Sat; Ⓜ Line 1 to Namyeong, Exit 2) The times are usually Saturday and Sunday from 7.30am to 3.30pm, with occasional additional tours on Wednesdays, 12.30pm to 7.40pm. Bring a packed lunch, or budget around ₩10,000 for lunch at the restaurant stop.

Plenty of other tour companies offer DMZ tours (Seoul's main KTO office can offer advice on these) but they tend to be more expensive; around ₩135,000 for ones that include the JSA. A recommended one is Panmunjeon Travel Center (☎02-771 5593; www.panmunjomtour.com).

Heyri & Paju Book City
헤이리 & 파주출판도시

♪ 031

Less than 10km south of the DMZ, Heyri is a charming village of small-scale contemporary buildings that couldn't be more of a contrast to the heavily fortified, doomladen border. Conceived as a 'book village' connected to the nearby publishing centre of Paju Book City, it has blossomed into a community of artists, writers, architects and other creative souls.

Get your bearings at the Tourist Information Office (☎946 8551; www.heyri.net; Gate 1; ⊙10am-6pm) where you can pick up a good guidebook (₩2000) with English descriptions of the scores of small art galleries, cafes, boutique shops and quirky private collections turned into minimuseums. Among them is the Han Hyang Lim Onggi Museum (www.heyrimuseum.com; Gate 7; ₩3000; ⊙10am-7pm Tue-Fri, 10am-8pm Sat & Sun; ☎) with a fine collection of traditional Korean pottery including many giant kimchi pots. There's also a colourful playground area devoted to the cartoon character Dalki (Gate 5; www.dalki.com) created by the Ssamzie accessories brand.

Just wandering around the village is a pleasure. Interesting pieces of architecture and sculpture abound, most created with materials that reflect and fit in with the natural environment. Roads twist naturally and the village is beautifully landscaped. Bikes (per hr/day ₩5000/13,000; ⊙10.30am-6.30pm) can be hired near Gate 3.

If you enjoy this kind of contemporary architecture, pause also in Paju Book City (www.pajubookcity.org), 10km south of Heyri towards Seoul. This hub of Korea's publishing industry is a very futuristic-looking place with more original building concepts. The Asia Publication Culture & Information Centre (www.jijihyang.org) is a particularly good example: it's partly clad in rusting steel that picks up the colours of the environment and is juxtaposed with a beautiful example of a hanok (traditional wooden homes), dating from 1834 and transposed here from the province of Jeollabuk-do. Inside the building is also an Italian restaurant and boutique guesthouse Jijihang. Paju is also popular among Koreans hunting down fashion bargains at a couple of huge shopping outlets: Premium Outlets (www.premiumoutlets.co.kr) and Lotte Outlets (http://paju.lotteoutlets.com).

WORTH A TRIP

BUKHANSAN NATIONAL PARK

Granite peak-studded **Bukhansan National Park** (북한산 국립공원; ☎031-873 2791; http://bukhan.knps.or.kr) is so close to Seoul that it's possible to visit by subway – which partly accounts for why it sees over 10 million visitors a year. It offers sweeping mountaintop vistas, maple leaves, rushing streams and remote temples. Even though it covers nearly 80 sq km, the park's proximity to the city means it gets crowded, especially on weekends.

Popular for **hiking** and **rock climbing**, the park's highest peak is Baegundae (836m), while rock climbers particularly enjoy Insubong (810m), a free-climber's dream with some of the best multipitch climbing in Asia and routes of all grades. A popular hike is to the peak of Dobongsan (740m); along the way you can visit two temples, **Gwangnyun-sa** (광륜사) and **Mangwol-sa** (망월사). Tree-shaded valleys with cooling streams also provide a chance to wallow in nature for those who'd rather not hike so far or so high. **Camping** (per 2-person tent from ₩3000; bookings via the national park website) is possible in summer or you can stay in basic **mountain shelters** (per person ₩5000).

To reach the park take subway Line 1 north from Seoul to Dobongsan station, a 45-minute journey from City Hall if your train goes all the way (not all do). Exit the station and follow the other hikers across the road, past food stalls and hiking-gear shops to reach the **Dobong Park Information Center** (☎031-909 0497; ⌚7.30am-6pm), which has a basic hiking map in English.

In between Heyri and Paju, the **Odusan Unification Observatory** (오두산 통일 공원; www.jmd.co.kr; adult/teenager/child ₩3000/1600/1000; ⌚9am-5.30pm Apr-Sep, to 5pm Oct, Mar, to 4.30pm Nov-Feb) provides another chance to gaze across the DMZ into North Korea.

Sleeping

Rates for accommodation usually rise for Friday and Saturday nights when many people visit from Seoul.

TOP CHOICE **Yonaluky** BOUTIQUE HOTEL $$$
(☎959 1122; www.yonaluky.com; Gate 8; d ₩350,000; ❄📶) Each of the seven massive, elegantly contemporary rooms at this gallery-cum-hotel have a broad outdoor private courtyard with sunken granite bath. They have kitchens, too, but rates do include breakfast served in the hotel's restaurant.

Motif #1 GUESTHOUSE $$$
(☎949 0901; www.motif1.co.kr; Gate 1; d from ₩150,000; ❄📶) The bohemian-chic home of traveller and writer Lee An-soo is typical of Heyri – packed with art, and with beautifully designed rooms that are worthy of a boutique hotel, plus a library of 10,000 books to browse. All four doubles and one family room have bathrooms, and guests can use the kitchen.

Forest Garden GUESTHOUSE $$$
(☎8071 0127, 010-4363 2660; www.forestgarden.kr; Gate 1; d from ₩200,000; ❄📶) English-speaking Mr Kim retired from the Korea Tourism Organisation and had this award-winning home that climbs up the hillside built. He and his wife allow guests to share part of it, with rooms that are very comfortable and come with TV, DVD, fridge and (for some) a balcony.

Eating & Drinking

In Heyri practically every gallery (and there are a lot of them) has an attached cafe or restaurant.

Café Between CAFE, PIZZA $$
(Gate 3; pizza ₩15,000-22,000; ⌚10am-11pm; 📶📋) On the second floor is a brick oven producing crispy pizzas while on the ground is a pleasant cafe – both have outdoor terrace seating with a view of the heart of the village.

Lachem NEO-KOREAN $$
(Gate 1; meals ₩10,000-26,000; ⌚11am-9.30pm; 📶🥕📋) Beside the gallery Jin Art is this stylish restaurant serving tasty and nicely presented modern takes on Korean dishes. The ₩10,000 set meal is vegetarian.

Foresta CAFE
(www.heyribookhouse.co.kr; Gate 3; drinks from
₩5000; ⊙noon-9pm; 🛜🖭) Inside the Hangil
Book House and overlooking a leafy glade
in the midst of Heyri is this appealing cafe,
serving gourmet coffee, smoothies, sandwiches and cakes.

ℹ Getting There & Away

Express Bus 2200 (₩2000; 45 minutes) and local
bus 200 (₩1800, 1 hour 20 minutes) both leave
from stop 16 near Hapjeong station on subway
Lines 2 and 6 in Seoul. Both pass through Paju
on the way to Heyri; the local bus also stops near
Odusan and the Premium Outlet Mall in Paju.

Suwon 수원

🎵031 / POP 1.07 MILLION
King Jeongjo, the 22nd Joseon dynasty ruler,
had the idea of moving the capital from Seoul
to Suwon, 48km south, in 1794. The fortress
wall that surrounded the original city was
constructed but the king died and power
stayed in Seoul. Named Hwaseong, Suwon's
impressive World Heritage–listed fortifications are the best reason for visiting the city,
where you'll also find the faithfully restored
palace Hwaseong Haenggung. Suwon is close
to the Korean Folk Village and Everland Resort and can be used as a base to visit both.

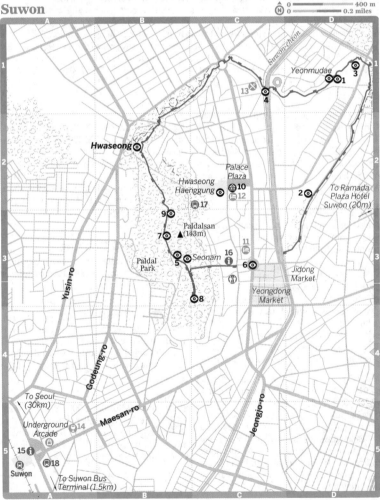

Suwon

⊙ Sights & Activities

Hwaseong
FORTRESS WALL

(화성; http://ehs.suwon.ne.kr; admission ₩1000; ⊘24hr) Suwon's fortress wall, with its command posts, observation towers, entrance gates and fire-beacon platform, was innovative for its time and makes for a fascinating two-hour historical walk. Constructed of earth and faced with large stone blocks and grey bricks, the wall stretches for 5.7km, nearly all of which has been restored. Walk outside the wall for at least part of the way, as the fortress looks much more impressive the way an enemy would see it.

Start at **Paldalmun**, also known as Nammun (South Gate), and follow the steep steps off to the left up to the **Seonam Gangu**, an observation point near the peak of Paldalsan (143m). Near the command post **Seojangdae** is the large **Hyowon Bell** you can toll (₩1000) and **Seonodae**, a tower that was used by crossbow archers.

On the wall's north side is **Hwahongmun**, a watergate over a stream. Nearby **Dongbukgongsimdon**, another watchtower, has a unique design – a high, tapering structure with rounded corners, stone base and brick tower. Further on, the **Bongdon beacon towers** were used to send messages around the country. From here the wall dips down to cross the Suwon-cheon where it breaks for the Jidong market, coming back to Paldalmun.

If you don't fancy the walk, head through the car park and up the hill at the rear of the palace to the find the 54-seat **Hwaseong Trolley** (adult/teenager/child ₩1500/1100/700; ⊘10am-5.10pm). This trolley bus, pulled by an engine-car fashioned as a Chinese dragon, winds around in and out of the fortress wall to the archery field at Yeonmudae.

Hwaseong Haenggung
PALACE

(화성행궁; admission ₩1500; ⊘9am-5pm) King Jeongjo's palace, destroyed during the Japanese occupation, has been meticulously reconstructed. Courtyard follows courtyard as you wander around the large walled complex where the king's mother held her grand 61st birthday party (61 is considered particularly auspicious and is a major date in an ancient Korean's life). Find out how detailed court records aided the reconstruction process and see how the area used to look at the **Suwon Cultural Foundation** (admission free; ⊘9.30am-6pm Mar-Oct, 9.30am-5pm Nov-Feb) on the south side of the plaza in front of the palace.

From March to November, traditional performances are held here, including a changing of the guard ceremony (2pm Sunday) and a martial arts display (11am Tuesday to Sunday). Every October a grand royal procession is reenacted during Suwon's annual **festival**.

Korean Folk Village
ARCHITECTURAL PARK

(한국 민속촌; www.koreanfolk.co.kr; adult/teenager/child ₩15,000/12,000/10,000; ⊘9am-6.30pm Mar-Oct, to 5pm Nov-Feb) About 260 thatched and tiled traditional houses and buildings from around the country make up this attractive folk village that takes at least half a day to explore. Artisans wearing *hanbok* (traditional Korean clothing) create pots, make paper and weave bamboo, while other workers tend to vegetable plots, and livestock.

Through the day traditional musicians, dancers, acrobats and tightrope walkers perform, and you can watch a wedding ceremony. Other attractions, including an **amusement park** and **horse riding**, cost extra. The village also has several restaurants and a food court.

A free shuttle bus leaves Suwon's main Tourist Information Centre (30 minutes, every hour from 11am to 3pm). The last shuttle bus leaves the folk village at 4.30pm (5pm on weekends). After that time, walk to the far end of the car park and catch city bus 37 (₩1300, one hour, every 20 minutes) back to Suwon station.

Archery Centre
ARCHERY
(10 arrows ₩2000; ◷9.30am-5.30pm, every 30min) At Yeonmudae, in the northeast corner of the fortress, is the archery centre where you can practise firing arrows. This traditional sport is one in which Koreans often win Olympic medals.

🛏 Sleeping

Although Suwon is an easy day trip from Seoul, there are several good places to stay should you choose to make it a base for seeing other sights in the region.

Hwaseong Guest House
BACKPACKERS $
(☑245 6226; www.hsguesthouse.com; dm/r ₩15,000/25,000; ✳@🛜) Run by friendly English-speaking folk, this backpackers has rooms decorated with a variety of flowery wallpaper, all of which share communal bathrooms. There's a kitchen for self-catering and several good restaurants nearby including a Japanese place downstairs. To find it turn left at Compador Bakery on Jeongjo-ro north of Paldalmun.

Suwon Hwaesong Sarangchae
GUESTHOUSE $
(수원화성 사랑채; ☑245 5555; www.sarangchae .org; d/tw/ondol from ₩30,000; ✳🛜) Tucked behind the Suwon Cultural Foundation is this professionally run place, more of a guesthouse than a hostel (you need be a party of four to take advantage of its four-bed dorm rooms). Their spacious *ondol* rooms, with repro antique furnishings and private bathrooms, are particularly nice and good value.

Ramada Plaza Hotel Suwon
HOTEL $$$
(☑230 0031; www.ramadaplazasuwon.com; d/tw from ₩200,000; ✳@🛜) About five minutes by taxi east of the fortress, the Ramada is a stylish affair with contemporary, spacious rooms and top-grade facilities, including a gym, deli and a couple of restaurants.

🍴 Eating & Drinking

Suwon is renowned for its *galbi* (beef) dishes, including *galbitang* (meaty bones in a broth). There are plenty of restaurants near the fortress walls, but the main place to meet carousing locals is close by Suwon station; lively bars cluster along and around the pedestrian street that starts between Face Shop and Paris Baguette.

Yeonpo Galbi
KOREAN $
(연포갈비; meals ₩8000-35,000; ◷11.30am-10pm) Down the steps from Hwahongmun, this famous restaurant serves up its special Suwon version of *galbitang* – chunks of meat and a big rib in a seasoned broth with noodles and leeks. Look for the building with a facade of logs.

Jondongchajip
TEASHOP $
(전동찻짚; teas from ₩6000; ◷10am-10pm) Rest your feet, sip local teas and nibble sweet rice cakes in this antique-style teashop above the archery centre. You can also order spicy snail noodles and Korean style savoury pancakes (₩1300).

Buleun Sutalk
BAR
(붉은수닭; ◷5pm-3am) Look for the iron rooster marking the entrance to this bohemian fantasy bar, with rose petals scattered on the stairs, mammoth melted candles, crystal chandeliers and plenty of scatter cushions, where you can enjoy a chilled evening with Suwon's hipsters. It's five minutes' walk northeast of the station along Maesanno on the corner where you'll find SK Telecom.

BUS DEPARTURES FROM SUWON

DESTINATION	PRICE (₩)	DURATION (HR)	FREQUENCY
Busan	21,600	5	10 daily
Daegu	18,900	3½	6 daily
Gwangju	15,300	3	every 30min
Gyeongju	20,200	4½	12 daily
Incheon	4500	1½	every 15min

TRAIN DEPARTURES FROM SUWON

DESTINATION	PRICE S/M CLASS (₩)	DURATION	FREQUENCY (DAILY)
Busan	38,600/25,900	5hr 20min	20
Daegu	27,100/18,200	3hr 10min	35
Daejeon	12,000/8100	1hr 10min	42
Jeonju	22,500/15,100	3hr	12
Mokpo	35,900/24,100	5hr	8

❶ Information

Suwon's **main tourist information centre** (☎228 4673; www.suwon.ne.kr; ☺9am-6pm Mar-Oct, to 5pm Nov-Feb) is on the left outside the railway station. **Tourist information booths** (☺9am-6pm) are located near Paldalmun at the start of the fortress walk, as well at several other points around the walls.

❶ Getting There & Away

Bus

Catch bus 5, 5-1 or 7-1 (₩1100, 15 minutes) outside Suwon train station to go to the city's **bus terminal**. For bus departures from this bus terminal, see the boxed text, p100.

Train

Subway Line 1 runs from Seoul to Suwon (₩1850, one hour) but make sure you're on a train that heads to the city after the line splits at Guro. KTO trains from Seoul are speedier (from ₩4600, 30 minutes) but not as frequent.

From **Suwon train station**, trains depart frequently to cities all over Korea; for departures, see the boxed text above.

❶ Getting Around

Outside the train station on the left, buses 11, 13, 36 and 39 go to Paldalmun (₩1100, 10 minutes). A taxi is ₩3000.

Seoul Grand Park
서울대공원

Indeed grand in scale, this park includes an excellent contemporary art museum, Korea's top zoo and the interactive Gwacheon National Science Museum. There are also hiking trails and a river that's a pleasant location for a picnic.

FREE National Museum
of Contemporary Art   MUSEUM
(www.moca.go.kr; Seoul Grand Park, Gwacheon; admission fee for special exhibitions; ☺10am-6pm Tue-Fri, to 9pm Sat & Sun Mar-Oct, 10am-5pm Tue-Fri, to 8pm Sat & Sun Nov-Feb; Ⓜ Line 4 to Seoul Grand Park, Exit 4, then shuttle bus) There's much of interest to see in this massive gallery spread over three floors and surrounded by a sculpture garden. The dazzling highlight is Nam June Paik's *The More the Better*, an 18m-tall pagoda-shaped video installation that uses 1000 flickering screens to make a comment on our increasingly electronic universe. An annexe of the museum, **UUL National Art Museum of Seoul** (www.uul.go.kr), is in the works.

Zoo   ZOO
(http://grandpark.seoul.go.kr; Seoul Grand Park, Gwacheon; adult/youth/child ₩3000/2000/1000; ☺9am-7pm Mar-Oct, to 6pm Nov-Feb; Ⓜ Line 4 to Seoul Grand Park, Exit 2) One of the largest in the world, this zoo is home to a long list of exotic creatures, including the popular African ones, and has a successful history of breeding tigers and pandas. It includes an indoor botanic garden housing a forest of cacti, numerous orchids and carnivorous pitcher plants.

**Gwacheon National
Science Museum**   MUSEUM
(www.sciencecenter.go.kr; Seoul Grand Park, Gwacheon; adult/child ₩4000/2000, planetarium adult/child ₩2000/1000; ☺9.30am-5.30pm Tue-Sun; Ⓜ Line 4 to Seoul Grand Park, Exit 5) There are over 20 different hands-on programs here – from painting with sound waves to a full-body skeleton that shows you how your bones move as you cycle – to help you discover various aspects of science. There's an extra charge for the planetarium shows (in English at 11.30am). Outdoor exhibits include a dinosaur park.

❶ Getting There & Away

Take subway Line 4 to Seoul Grand Park station (₩1000), which is 45 minutes from City Hall. Leave by Exit 2 and then either walk (10 minutes) or take an elephant-inspired **tram** (adult/youth/child ₩800/600/500) to the park entrance. Another option is to take the **cable car** (adult/youth/child ₩5000/3500/3000). A free shuttle bus runs every 20 minutes from the subway station (outside Exit 4) to the National Museum of Contemporary Art.

Anyang Art Park
안양예술공원

A short bus ride north of Anyang, 20km south of Seoul, is the **Anyang Art Park** (admission free) – 52 quirky pieces of sculpture by both Korean and international artists dotted along the rocky river bank and set among the trees of a wooded valley. Pieces include the spinning *Dancing Buddha,* the *3-D Mirror Labyrinth,* the *Anyang Crate House Dedicated to the Lost (Pagoda),* made of mulitcoloured plastic German beer crates, and the freaky *Boy + Girl* that messes with perspective. Climb up to the spiral observatory for a fantastic view across the valley, or go outside the park to explore several of the Buddhist temples that cling to the hillsides.

Back by the river is all the commercial activity typically associated with a resort area. It can get very busy here with family outings and picnics on the weekend. You could check out what's showing in the **Anyang Art Center** (☉noon-7pm) in a sleek minimalist building designed by Portuguese architect Álvaro Siza (admission varies) or go splash around in **Anyang Waterland** (안양워터랜드; www.anyangwaterland.com; adult/child ₩40,000/30,000; ☉9am-9pm). Alternatively, enjoy *mechuri* (메추리; quail roasted over charcoal), available at several stalls such as **Sunolaepang** (수노래방) with the blue awning next to the art centre.

❶ Getting There & Away

Anyang station is on Line 1 of the subway. Take Exit 1 and find the stop for bus 2, which runs a regular loop route to the park (₩800, 10 minutes), on the left outside Lotte Department Store.

WORTH A TRIP

EVERLAND RESORT

Set in lush hillsides 40km south of Seoul, this mammoth amusement park offers more than just thrill rides and fairy floss.

The main theme park, **Everland** (www.everland.com; day pass adult/teenager/child ₩40,000/34,000/31,000; ☉9.30am-10pm Sep-Jun, to 11pm Jul & Aug), is filled with fantasy buildings, fairground attractions, impressive seasonal gardens, live music and parades. Lit up at night, the park takes on a magical atmosphere and there are always fireworks. Next door is **Caribbean Bay** (adult/child from ₩35,000/27,000; ☉10am-5pm Sep-Jun, 9.30am-11pm Jul & Aug), a superb indoor and outdoor waterpark. The outdoor section is usually open from June to September (there's a higher entrance charge to the park in July and August) and features a huge wave pool that produces a mini tsunami every few minutes, and water-based thrill rides.

A free shuttle bus runs from Everland's main entrance to the **Hoam Art Museum** (http://hoam.samsungfoundation.org; adult/child ₩4000/3000, free with Everland ticket; ☉10am-6pm Tue-Sun) and you are well advised to take it. The serenely beautiful Hee Won traditional Korean gardens induce a calm frame of mind so that visitors can fully appreciate the gorgeous art treasures inside the museum, including paintings, screens and celadon.

There's so much to see here that staying over is worth considering. There are two accommodation options: **Home Bridge Hillside Hostel** (☏031-320 8849; r/ondol from ₩50,000; ❀@) is the older but quite acceptable property, while **Home Bridge Cabin Hostel** (☏031-320 9740; r from ₩130,000; ❀@) offers Heidi-esque log cabins and hotel rooms, the most expensive with balconies overlooking the park. Rates at both places are higher on Saturday nights and during July and August. However, on Sunday rates are slashed in half. Bookings can be made via the Everland website and guests can use their one-day park passes over two days.

To get here from Seoul take bus 5002 (₩2000, 50 minutes, every 15 minutes) from Gangnam. From outside Suwon's train station, hop on bus 66 or 66-4 (₩1700, one hour, every 30 minutes).

SKIING IN GYEONGGI-DO

Come the snow season (December to February) there is a handful of ski resorts an hour or less drive from Seoul. Usually there are free shuttle buses from the city – see the websites for details – but you might also want to look into travel-agency package deals that include transport, accommodation, ski-equipment hire and lift passes. For more on skiing and snowboarding in Korea, see p28. The main resorts in Gyeonggi-do:

Bears Town Resort (☎031-540 5136; www.bearstown.com) Located 50 minutes north-east of Seoul, this resort has 11 slopes, two sledding hills and nine lifts all named after bears. Accommodation includes a youth hostel and condominium; facilities include a supermarket, heated pool, sauna, bowling alley and tennis courts. English-speaking instructors, snowboarding and night skiing are all available.

Jisan Resort (☎02-3442 0322, 031-638 8460; www.jisanresort.co.kr) This popular resort, 56km south of Seoul, offers five lifts, a variety of slopes (including some for snowboarding), English-speaking instructors, night skiing and condo accommodation. The **Jisan Rock Festival** (http://global.mnet.com/valleyrockfestival/index.m) is held here each July.

Yangji Pine Resort (☎02-744 2001, 031-338 2001; www.pineresort.com) Around 40 min-utes' drive southeast of Seoul, this resort has six slopes, one sledding hill, six lifts and great views from the top. Accommodation is in a youth hostel or condo-style hotel, the latter having a heated pool and bowling alley.

Donggureung 동구릉

The 40-odd royal tombs of the Joseon dynasty (http://whc.Unesco.org/en/list/1319) are World Heritage listed and scattered across Seoul and Gyeonggi-do, with a couple also in the North Korean city of Kaesong. In these tombs, each similarly arranged on hillsides according to the rules of Confucianism and feng shui, are buried every Joseon ruler right up to the last, Emperor Sunjong (r 1907–10). Tomb entrances are marked by a simple red-painted wooden gate, stone pathway and hall for conducting rites in front of the humped burial mounds decorated with stone statuary – typically a pair of civil officers and generals, plus horses and protecting animals such as tigers and rams.

The most central tomb in Seoul is Seonjeongneung (p55). However, the largest and most attractive complex is Donggureung (http://donggu.cha.go.kr; adult/child W1000/500; ◷6am-6.30pm Mar-Oct, to 5.30pm Nov-Feb) in Guri, around 20km northeast of central Seoul. Here lie seven kings and 10 queens, including the dynasty's founder King Taejo: in contrast to the other neatly clipped plots in this leafy park, his mound sprouts rushes from his hometown of Hamhung (now in North Korea) that – in accordance with the king's

predeath instructions – have never been cut. To reach the complex take subway Line 2 to Gangbyeon to connect with bus 1, 1-1 or 1115-6, around a two-hour trip from central Seoul.

Namhan Sanseong Provincial Park 남한 산성 도립공원

The park surrounding the 17th-century temple fortress complex of Namhan Sanseong, 20km southeast of central Seoul, is famous for its beautiful pine and oak forests and wild flowers. The fortress once guarded the city's southern entrance. Numerous hiking trails wind through the trees, some of them paralleling the old fortress walls of which around 12km still remain and providing sweeping views of southern Seoul.

Take subway Line 8 to Sanseong, then taxi or take bus 9 from Exit 2 of the station to the park's South Gate, a journey of around 20 minutes.

Icheon 이천

☑ 031 / POP 195,175

The famed pottery centre of Icheon, 60km southeast of Seoul, is surrounded by mountains. Shoppers and ceramics lovers may want to stay here overnight to have time to look around or dabble in making something at a hands-on workshop, but otherwise the place can easily be visited in a day from Seoul.

◉ Sights & Activities

Seolbong Park SCULPTURE PARK
(설봉공원; ☑644 2020; http://tour.icheon.go.kr; ⏱9am-5pm) Head here first to pick up a good local area map and other tourist information at the visitors centre, and also to enjoy the parklands, variety of ceramic sculptures that surround the small lake Seolbongho, and the pottery centre **Cerapia** (www.kocef.org; admission free; ⏱9am-6pm Tue-Sun), where the **World Ceramic Biennale** is held in odd-numbered years. The park is also the venue for the annual **Icheon Ceramic Festival** (www.ceramic.or.kr; ⏱late Apr–mid-May).

Yeongworam TEMPLE
(영월암) If you have the energy, it's a steep 30-minute walk uphill from the visitors centre to this Buddhist retreat, founded back in 774 when it was known as Bugak-sa. Ancient ginkgo trees shade the brightly painted buildings, reconstructions of the originals. Moss, a giant bell and a carved cliff-face Buddha overlooking the city all make this a picturesque place to visit.

Icheon Ceramic Village NEIGHBOURHOOD
(이천 도예촌) Don't come here expecting picturesque riverside huts or wispy-bearded characters labouring over kick wheels; the Icheon Ceramic Village is a busy town with a main street full of traffic, and the many potteries are spread out over a wide urban area. The lack of rural aesthetics is compensated for by the huge selection of wares, making it a fascinating destination for ceramics lovers.

Catch a taxi (₩5000) or local bus 24-4, 24-5, 24-11 or 114-1 (₩1500, 15 minutes) from outside of the bus terminal and get off near **Songpa Pottery** (송파 도예; ☑633 6587; ⏱9.30am-7.30pm), the traditional building with blue-green roof tiles. Around here are several pottery shops. Across the road and set back from the main strip in a lovely wooden building is **Hanguk Pottery** (한국 도예; ☑638 7037; ⏱9.30am-5.30pm), where you can find the classy celadon-glazed wares of a master potter and view a traditional-style kiln.

To make your own cup or bowl visit **Namyang** (남양; ☑632 7142; per class ₩15,000; ⏱10am-5pm), where you can don a smock and sit down at a slippery mass of spinning clay, or hand-build something under the tutorage of the kindly Mr Lee and his English-speaking son. To have your efforts fired and posted home will cost approximately an additional ₩30,000 per kilogram.

Haegang Ceramics Museum MUSEUM
(해강 도자 미술관; www.haegang.org; adult/youth/child ₩2000/1000/500; ⏱9.30am-5.30pm Tue-Sun) A beautiful collection of celadon pottery is on display at this museum located back towards downtown Incheon.

Miranda Spa Plus SPA
(미란다 온천; http://mirandahotel.com/new/SPA/eng/index.asp; adult/child spa only ₩10,000/7000, all facilities ₩20,000/13,000; ⏱6am-10pm) Attached to the Miranda Hotel Icheon and just a five-minute walk from Icheon bus terminal, this large complex has ultramodern facilities with indoor and outdoor baths, including a wave pool and tube ride. Spa baths include ones where the water is infused with rice-wine, herbs, pinewood and fruit extracts. Admission is slightly higher at weekends.

Incheon Termeden SPA
(www.termeden.com; adult/child ₩32,000/22,000 Mon-Fri, ₩36,000/26,000 Sat & Sun; ⏱8am-8pm) At this German-style spa resort, around 10km south of the town centre and surrounded by a forest, the focus is on shallow Jacuzzi style pools with massage jets. There's lots of indoor and outdoor pools to choose from as well as various massages and spa therapies. A free shuttle bus runs here from SC Bank across from Icheon bus terminal.

🛏 Sleeping & Eating

Icheon's accommodation options include plenty of inexpensive motels. The town is also famous for its rice, which some claim is so good that 'it needs no side dishes'. The good news is that it is indeed pretty tasty and it's always served up with plenty of side dishes.

Miranda Hotel HOTEL $$$
(미란다호텔; ☑633 2001; www.mirandahotel.com; r ₩195,000; ✳@⏰) Incheon's snazziest hotel is located next to Spa Plus (where guests receive a 30% discount), and overlooks a small lake with a pavilion on an island. There's also a **bowling alley** (per game ₩3000, shoe hire ₩1000; ⏱10am-2am). The lobby has fine examples of locally made ceramics.

TOP CHOICE **Deokjegung** KOREAN $$
(덕제궁; ☑634 4811; meals ₩10,000-20,000; ⏱10.30am-9.30pm) On a hillside outside town, this traditional place serves a wonderful assortment of preset courses that vary by

SONGDO INTERNATIONAL CITY

One of a trio of vast free economic zones that Incheon has created out of landfill in the bay, Songdo International City (www.songdo.com) is connected to Yeongjeongdo by the 21.38km Incheon Bridge. In the works since 1994, Songdo is billed as a model urban development designed around high-tech buildings and networks, using best-practice eco-friendly principles, with a business district, convention centre and several parks. However, the economic turndowns of recent years have dented the most ambitious plans, leaving Songdo a work in progress.

The Central Park is complete but many buildings surrounding it are empty or still in the planning stages. To get an idea of the masterplan for Songdo drop by Compact Smart City (admission free; ⊙10am-8pm; MIncheon Line 1 to Central Park) where you can watch a kitschy 5D film show and see scale models of the development areas around Incheon. Outside is the photogenic Tri-bowl, Songdo's most futuristic piece of architecture that's part giant sculpture, part exhibition hall. Golfers may also want to enquire about playing a round at the waterside Jack Nicklaus Golf Club (☑850 5036; MIncheon Line 1 to Central Park) a championship 18-hole course and driving range.

The fanciest of Songdo's trio of hotels is Sheraton Incheon Hotel (☑032-835 1000; www.sheraton.com/incheon; r from ₩399,000; MIncheon Line 1 to University of Incheon; ✳@✆☀). LEED-certified and fully nonsmoking, it is next to the convention centre. A good place to eat is the foreigner-friendly What's David's? (☑833 1225; mains ₩10,000-15,000; ⊙11.30am-3pm, 5pm-midnight Mon-Fri, 11.30am-midnight Sat & Sun; MIncheon Line 1 to University of Incheon), a short walk north of the Sheraton. Across the road in the Hillstate building is the chic cafe-bar Treefish (⊙7pm-2am Tue-Sat, 3-11pm Sun).

price. The paper screens, floor seating and floral-wallpapered walls all make this a treat worth taking a taxi for.

Donggang KOREAN $$
(동강; ☑631 8833; meals from ₩10,000; ⊙9.30am-10pm) On the main road near the entrance to Seolbong Park, this restaurant looks modern from the outside but inside is decorated with traditional *giwa* (tiled) roof details, and paper and wood screens. The set menus are reasonably priced.

❶ Getting There & Away

Buses run from Dong-Seoul Bus Terminal to Icheon (₩5000, one hour, every 15 to 40 minutes). Once in Icheon most places are no more than a ₩5000 taxi ride away.

INCHEON-GWANGYEOK-SI

Incheon-gwangyeok-si (인천광역시) was hived off from Gyeonggi-do in 1981. It continues to grow with giant areas of landfill in the West Sea having been converted recently into the new urban centres of Songdo International City and Cheongna. Dozens of islands are also part of the municipality – find out more about them and other areas of Incheon at http://english.incheon.go.kr.

Incheon 인천

☑032 / POP 2.85 MILLION

This expanding metropolis and industrial port 36km west of Seoul is the place where Korea opened up to the world in 1883, ending centuries of self-imposed isolation. In 1950, during the Korean War, the American General Douglas MacArthur led UN forces in a daring landing behind enemy lines here.

Fragments of this history can be seen in Incheon today, particularly in the colourful Chinatown and Open Port areas, the most interesting areas to explore and easily accessible via subway. Come here to eat Chinese food, stroll along the Wolmido waterfront and visit the fish market at Yeonan, where you can catch ferries to China or the West Sea islands.

◉ Sights

FREE **Incheon Art Platform** ART COMPLEX
(www.inartplatform.kr; Open Port; ⊙10am-6pm Sun-Thu, to 8pm Fri & Sat) The Incheon Foundation for Arts and Culture has created gallery spaces and art residency studios in an attractive complex of early-20th-century brick warehouses, once used as part of the port. Check out the interesting exhibitions held here as well as cultural performances and events.

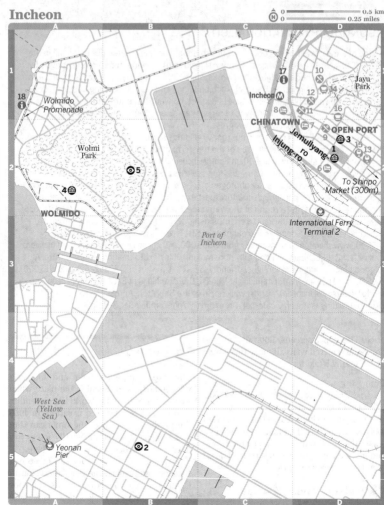

Incheon

GYEONGGI-DO & INCHEON INCHEON

Jayu Park PARK

(Open Port; M Line 1 to Incheon) Jayu means freedom and this hillside park, designed by a Russian civil engineer in 1888, is a good spot to catch the breeze. It contains a monument for the centenary of Korea–USA relations and a statue of General MacArthur.

Incheon Grand Fishery Market MARKET

(www.asijang.co.kr; Yeonan; ⊗4.30am-9pm) Even if you've already visited Noryangjin in Seoul, this fish and seafood market is still worth seeing. It's a more intimate, brightly lit place displaying hundreds of types of marine delectables, all of which you can eat on the spot at several small restaurants and cafes.

Incheon Open Port Museum MUSEUM

(인천개항장근대건축전; www.icjgss.or.kr/open _port; Open Port; adult/teenager/child ₩500/ 300/200; ⊗9am-6pm Tue-Sun) One of three former Japanese bank buildings along the same street, this has been turned into an interesting museum about the area's distinctive architecture, which dates back to the 1890s when Korea was opened up to foreign companies.

Incheon

Wolmido
NEIGHBOURHOOD

(월미도; http://wolmi.incheon.go.kr) Once an island, Wolmido was later a military base and site of the Incheon Landing Operation during the Korean war, before being transformed into a leisure area with a waterfront promenade, amusement park and plenty of love hotels. Apart from hopping on the ferry to Yeongjongdo, the best reason for coming here is to stroll around the attractive **Wolmi Park** (admission free; ⊙5am-10pm) where you'll find a replica of a traditional palace garden, walking trails shaded by leafy trees, the **Korean Emigration History Museum** (http:// mkeh.incheon.go.kr; admission free; ⊙9am-6pm Tue-Sun) and the hilltop **Wolmi Observatory** (admission free; ⊙9am-6pm Tue-Sun) offering good views.

FREE Incheon Landing Operation Memorial Hall
MUSEUM

(인천 상륙 작전 기념관; www.landing915. com; Songdo; ⊙9am-6pm Tue-Sun) Some 70,000 UN and South Korean troops took part in the surprise landing in Incheon in 1950,

supported by 260 warships. Find out about the daring attack at this sombre, strikingly designed museum around 7km south of Incheon station. The displays include newsreel films of the Korean War.

Incheon Metropolitan City Museum
MUSEUM

(인천광역시립박물관; Songdo; adult/child ₩400/free; ⊙9am-6pm Tue-Sun) Next to the Incheon Landing Operation Memorial Hall is the city's main museum offering an excellent collection of celadon pottery and some interesting historical displays.

☞ Tours

You can pick up two city-run **tours** (⌖772 4000; http://english.visitincheon.org) outside Incheon station. Contact the tourist information centre for tour departure times from the airport, which vary depending on the season.

City Tour
CITY TOUR

(3hr tours adult/child ₩7000/3500) Departs every hour between 10am and 4pm.

Ganghwa Tour
ISLAND TOUR

(8hr tours adult/child ₩10,000/5000) Two different tours offered on Saturday and Sunday from April to October.

✦ Festivals & Events

Chinese Day Cultural Festival
CULTURAL

(www.inchinaday.com) This event is held in Jayu Park and around Chinatown in April and September.

Pentaport Rock Festival
MUSIC

(www.pentaportrock.com) This three-day music fest at the end of July, featuring a mix of top international and Korean acts, is Korea's equivalent of Glastonbury.

Incheon Bupyeong Pungmul Festival
CULTURAL

(www.bpf.or.kr) Dance along to traditional folk music performances (*pungmul*) and experience other aspects of Korean culture. Held in October.

⊨ Sleeping

The following are located within walking distance of Incheon station. There are plenty more hotels and motels scattered around Incheon, including some rundown motels out at Wolmido and midrange to luxury hotels in Songdo International City.

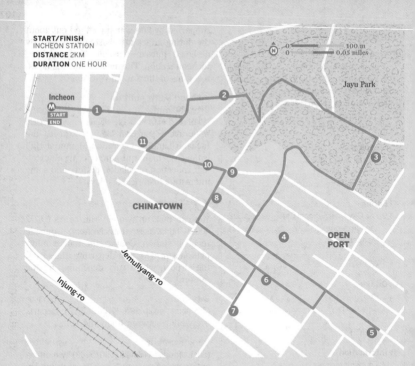

START/FINISH
INCHEON STATION
DISTANCE 2KM
DURATION ONE HOUR

Incheon

Jayu Park

CHINATOWN

OPEN
PORT

Jemullyang-ro

Injung-ro

Walking Tour
Open Port & Chinatown

> Incheon's modern history can be traced in this stroll around the areas where foreign cultures first touched the hermit kingdom of Korea in the late 19th century. Various examples of colonial architecture have been preserved here.

From Incheon station, pass through the **1 First Paeru**, an ornate gate that marks one of the entrances to Chinatown, a dazzle of red, gold and green shopfronts. Head uphill, then veer left at the junction to find the steps leading up to the **2 Third Paeru** and through Jayu Park with its statue of **3 General MacArthur**.

From the statue follow the steps downhill and the road that leads you to **4 Jung-gu District Hall**, a building that has been renovated and expanded since it was first built in 1883. Turn left and walk two blocks to admire the bottle-cap mosaic facade of the cafe-bar **5 Bboya**, then retrace your steps a block, taking a left then right turn. Along this street you'll pass three buildings from the late 19th century, one of which is the

6 Incheon Open Port Museum. Just below here are renovated brick warehouses that now house the studios and exhibition spaces of **7 Incheon Art Platform**.

Climb back up the hill to the **8 Qing & Japan Concession Area Boundary Stairs** lined with stone lanterns – at the top is a statue of **9 Confucius**. To the left a **10 mural** decorates both sides of the street illustrating historical scenes from the classic Chinese novel *The Three Kingdoms*. Turn right when you reach the main Chinatown 1st street – the profusion of red paper lanterns will clue you into whether you're in the right place.

To find out about the how the most famous Chinese dish of *jjajangmyeon* was invented in Chinatown, drop by the **11 Jjajangmyeon Museum** (www.icjg.go.kr; admission free; ⊗9am-6pm Tue-Sun). If this whets your appetite, here are plenty of places to eat around here, before returning to Incheon station.

TOP CHOICE Harbor Park Hotel
HOTEL $$$

(✆770 9500; www.harborparkhotel.com; r from ₩242,000; ❋@☎) Sporting a sleek contemporary design inside and out, the rooms at the Harbor Park provide great views of the harbour and hillsides. There's a good gym (free for guests) and tempting top-floor buffet restaurant (adult/child ₩35,000/23,000). Wi-fi is only available in the lobby.

Paradise Hotel
HOTEL $$$

(✆762 5181; www.paradisehotel.co.kr; d from ₩253,000; ❋@☎) On a hill overlooking the port, this long-established upmarket hotel has a few hip and boutique-style renovated rooms (although they have no windows). Use of the sauna (₩10,000) is 50% cheaper for in-house guests.

Hong Kong Motel
MOTEL $

(✆777 9001; r ₩30,000;❋@) Steps from the station, this love hotel is clean, well maintained and has friendly staff.

✖ Eating

In Chinatown you can sample local variations on Chinese cuisine including *jjajangmyeon* (noodles in a savoury-sweet black bean sauce), *jjampong* (noodles in a spicy seafood soup), and *onggibyeong* (crispy meat- or veg-filled dumplings baked inside large clay jars). Wolmido's promenade also offers plenty of touristy seafood restaurants; better value feasts are available at Incheon Grand Fishery Market where a raw fish platter big enough to feed four is around ₩40,000.

Mandabok
CHINESE $$$

(만다복; ✆773 3838; Chinatown; meals ₩7000-30,000; ❷11am-10pm; ▣) Guarded by a pair of terracotta warriors, this is one of Chinatown's fanciest restaurants with a refined interior and top-notch cuisine. Try the sweet-and-sour pork (₩20,000).

Pungmi
CHINESE $

(풍미; ✆772 2680; Chinatown; meals ₩5000-10,000; ❷10am-10.30pm; ▣) In business for over half a century, this is a good place to sample *jjajangmyeon* or other tasty, inexpensive dishes such as seafood fried rice.

Fog City International Café
INTERNATIONAL $$

(✆766 9024; www.fogcitycafe.com; Open Port; meals ₩15,000-30,000; ❷8.30am-midnight; ▣) If you're tired of Korean or Chinese food, drop by this appealing modern all-day cafe serving a mix of sandwiches, salads, pizza and pasta. Get here early if you want to try their *makgeolli* bread as it usually sells out.

Wonbo
CHINESE $

(원보; Chinatown; meals ₩4000; ❷11am-9pm) Big pork-filled dumplings steamed or fried are the speciality of this no-frills place.

Jageumseong
CHINESE $$

(자금성; ✆761 1688; Chinatown; meals ₩6000-15,000; ❷11am-9.30pm; ▣) Lots of red-and-gold lanterns and dragon decorations mark out this Beijing-style Chinese restaurant, which also serves spicier Szechuan dishes.

Shinpo Market
KOREAN $

(신포시장; Shinpo-dong; street eats ₩1000-10,000; ❷10am-8pm; ▣Line 1 to Dong-Incheon) Locals line up at stalls here for take-away boxes of *dakgangjeong* (spicy sweet and sour deep fried chicken). It's well worth sampling, as are other street eats available along the twin covered arcades, including giant candy-coloured *madu* (dumplings).

☕ Drinking

Café Castle
CAFE

(Chinatown; ❷11.30am-midnight) Enjoy coffee, tea and snacks at this intimate, homely cafe festooned with greenery. There's a fantastic view from its rooftop garden.

Min
BAR

(민; Open Port; ❷7pm-1am) With a painting of smiling Chinese on its outside wall this cosy bar, part of a row of colonial-era shophouses, is a hangout for students from the local art college, who sip beers and *soju* and tuck into cheap savoury pancakes.

Tochon
CAFE

(토촌; Open Port; ❷10am-10pm) Birds fly around this quirky cafe and restaurant near Jayu Park; the decor includes mock lush greenery, a water wheel, pond and fish tanks.

Bboya
BAR

(뽀야; Open Port; ❷4pm-1am) This unique cafe-bar is entirely covered both inside and out by colourful mosaics created from plastic and metal caps from beer bottles, health drinks and fruit juices.

ℹ Information

Tourist information centre (http://english. incheon.go.kr) Incheon station (✆777 1330; ❷9am-6pm); Wolmido Promenade (✆765 4169; ❷6am-9pm); bus terminal (✆430 7257;

⊙10am-6pm) The staff are very helpful at the principal office outside the subway station, with lots of excellent maps, tourist info and suggestions not only for the city, but for the surrounding islands as well. Smaller information centres are at Wolmido, in the bus terminal and at the ferry terminals.

❶ Getting There & Away

For details about Incheon International Airport see p90.

Boat

Yeonan Pier (Map p112; ☑880 3150; www. icferry.or.kr) and **International Ferry Terminal 2** (☑032-764 1820; www.icferry.or.kr) are the departure points for regular international ferries to a number of Chinese cities as well as the islands of the West Sea.

TO/FROM CHINA

Ferries link 10 Chinese ports with Incheon. They can get crowded but are a cheaper option than flying. The cheapest fares offer a thin mattress on a dormitory floor, while the more expensive fares give you a small cabin with a bunk bed and TV. Child fares are usually half the adult fare, and some companies offer students a 20% discount. Most ferries leave from Yeonan Pier, but the larger boats depart from International Ferry Terminal 2.

TO/FROM WEST SEA ISLANDS

Yeonan Pier also has a domestic ferry terminal where boats leave for Jeju-do (from ₩71,000, 13 hours) and 14 of the larger inhabited islands in the West Sea. More frequent services are provided in summer, when many holidaymakers head out to the beaches and seafood restaurants on these attractive and relaxing islands.

KOREA–CHINA FERRIES FROM INCHEON

Prices are for one-way tickets and sailing times are subject to variation.

From Yeonan Pier

DESTINATION	PHONE	WEBSITE	PRICE(₩)	DURATION (HR)	DEPARTURES
Dalian	☑891 7100	www.dainferry.co.kr	115,000-165,000	16	5pm Tue, Thu & Sat
Dandong	☑891 3322	www.dandongferry.co.kr	115,000-145,000	16	5pm Mon, Wed & Fri
Qinyindao	☑891 9600	www.qininferry.com	115,000-260,000	23	7pm Mon, 1pm Fri
Shidao	☑891 8877	www.huadong.co.kr	110,000-170,000	15	6pm Mon, Wed & Fri
Yanyai	☑891 8880	www.hanjoongferry.co.kr	120,000-140,000	15	8pm Tue, Thu & Sat
Yingkou	☑891 5858	www.yingkouferry.com	115,000-160,000	24	9pm Tue, 1pm Sat

From International Ferry Terminal 2

DESTINATION	PHONE	WEBSITE	PRICE (₩)	DURATION (HR)	DEPARTURES
Lianyungang	☑770 3700	www.lygferry.com	115,000-140,000	24	7pm Tue, 3pm Sat
Qingdao	☑777 8000	www.weidong.com	100,000-140,000	16	5pm Tue, Thu & Sat
Tianjin	☑777 8260	www.jinchon.co.kr	115,000-160,000	24	1pm Tue, 7pm Fri
Weihai	☑777 8000	www.weidong.com	100,000-140,000	13	7pm Mon, Wed & Sat

BUS DEPARTURES FROM INCHEON

DESTINATION	PRICE (₩)	DURATION (HR)	FREQUENCY
Busan	34,400	4½	hourly
Cheonan	7400	1½	every 30 min
Cheongju	9000	2	every 40 min
Chuncheon	13,000	3	every 40 min
Gongju	11,000	2½	every 80 min
Jeonju	13,400	3	hourly
Suwon	4600	1	hourly

Ferries (adult/child ₩3000/1000, 15 minutes, every 30 minutes from 7am to 9pm) shuttle between Wolmido promenade and Yeongjongdo.

Bus

Incheon's **bus terminal** (☑430 7114; www.ictr. or.kr; MIncheon Line 1 to Incheon Bus Terminal) is attached to a branch of Shinsegae department store, and has a pharmacy, post office, cinema and tourist info centre. From here you can take direct long-distance buses all over South Korea. For Seoul it's faster, cheaper and easier to connect via subway.

Subway

Subway Line 1 from Seoul (₩1600) takes around 70 minutes; the line branches at Guro so make sure you're on an Incheon-bound train.

ⓘ Getting Around

Bus & Taxi

Buses (₩1150) and taxis leave from outside Dong-Incheon and Incheon stations. For International Ferry Terminal 2, take bus 23 from Incheon station or a taxi (₩2500). To get to Songdo, hop on bus 6, 6-1 or 16 from Dong-Incheon or take a taxi (₩7000). It's a 20-minute walk from Incheon station to Wolmido, or hop on Bus 2, 23 or 45. A taxi costs ₩3000. To get to Yeonan Pier take bus 12 or 24 from Dong-Incheon, or hail a taxi (₩8000). To Yeongjongdo: Bus 306 from Incheon station goes to the airport island (₩2800, every 10 minutes).

Subway

Incheon's Line 1 runs in a north–south direction and intersects with Seoul's Line 1 subway at Bupyeong (부평). At its northern terminus the line connects with the A'rex express to Incheon International Airport at Gyeyang (계양) while in the south it terminates at the International Business District of Songdo International City. The basic fare is ₩1150 and T Money cards can be used (see p91).

Yeongjongdo 영종도

♩032

Home to Korea's busiest international airport, Yeongjongdo's best western beaches aren't disturbed by air traffic. **Eulwangni Beach** (을왕리 해수욕장) is the most popular and many motels and a resort have been built here, as well as restaurants and stores. It's an attractive place framed by hillside pine forests and strange rock formations which can get very busy on summer weekends.

Next to Eulwangni's Golden Sky International Resort is an upmarket **spa and jjimjil-bang** (spa adult/child ₩8000/5000 Mon-Fri, ₩10,000/7000 Sat & Sun; ⊙6am-8pm) and **waterpark** (adult/child ₩24,000/18,000; ⊙9am-7pm).

From Eulwangni, it's a 20-minute walk north along the road to **Wangsan Beach** (왕산 해수욕장), which has a less developed beachfront – just some fishing boats, a few restaurant shacks and watersports equipment for hire during the summer season.

At the time of research the popular seafood market at Yeongjongdo Wharf (where you'll alight if you take the ferry from Wolmido) was closed for reconstruction. From behind the market, bus 202 (₩1000, 20 minutes, hourly) will drop you near the islet of **Jamjindo** (잠진도), connected by causeway to Yeongjongdo, from where you can catch the ferry to Muuido.

🛏 Sleeping

A wide range of accommodation is available at Eulwangni Beach, including beachside camping near the pine groves. Just outside Incheon International Airport is the Airport Business District, not to be confused with Airport Town Square, two stops away on the

Yeongjongdo & Muuido

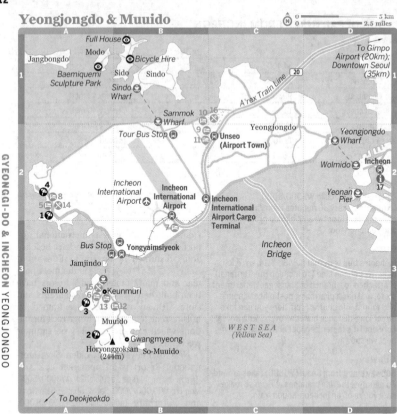

A'rex train at Unseo – the latter area has lots of small hotels if ones at the former are full. Although neither area is ideal for the beach, they are good places to crash if you have an early departure or late arrival from Incheon Airport. Rates are typically higher on the weekend. Some hotels provide a free pick-up or drop-off service, otherwise there are buses and the train.

TOP CHOICE Golden Sky
International Resort   RESORT $$$
(☑745 5000; www.goldensky.co.kr; Eulwangni Beach; apt from ₩200,000; ☎☲) The rooms at Eulwangni's fanciest resort are apartments with self-catering facilities. There's sufficient space in the studios to cram in four people (two in the bed and two on mattresses on the *ondol* floor). Sweeping views across the beach and an attached spa and waterpark are among the pluses, as well as a free shuttle bus to the airport.

Global Guesthouse   APARTMENT $$
(☑743 0253; www.globalgh.com; Airport Business District; apt ₩50,000; ☀☎) These spacious studio apartments all come with kitchenette, washing machine, cable TV and (in some rooms) wi-fi. Free pick-up from the airport is included.

Incheon Airport Hotel   HOTEL $$
(인천에어포트호텔; ☑752 2066; www.incheon airporthotel.co.kr; Airport Town Square; r from ₩89,000; ☀@) All rooms have TVs, DVD players and (ugly) fridge-sized vending machines, while deluxe ones have snazzy triangular whirlpool baths, desktop PCs and fax machines. A golf driving range is on the roof.

Carib Beach Motel   LOVE MOTEL $$
(카리브 모텔; ☑751 5455; Eulwangni Beach; s/d ₩40,000/80,000;☀) Shaped like a ship and just steps away from the beach, this love motel offers appealing views from the 'porthole' windows.

Yeongjongdo & Muuido

◉ Sights

⌂ Sleeping

⊗ Eating

ⓘ Information

✕ Eating

When the Yeongjongdo Wharf Market re-opens you'll be able to buy fish, prawns, blue crabs and other shellfish and take them to the neighbouring restaurants to have them cooked and served.

TOP CHOICE Caffe Ora INTERNATIONAL $$
(Eulwangni Beach; meals ₩15,000-20,000; ⊙10am-11pm) Overlooking the Eulwangni and Wangsan beaches, this modernist piece of architecture could be mistaken for the villain's headquarters in a James Bond movie. It's actually nothing more sinister than a high-class coffee shop, bakery and restaurant with an eye to snagging the smart Seoul set. The views, the supercool ambience and the polished service make it well worthwhile. Meals include pasta and salads.

Hoebaragi SEAFOOD $$$
(회바라기; Eulwangni Beach; meals ₩40,000-60,000; ⊙10am-10pm) The largest restaurant at Eulwangni has a large red sign. Apart from expensive assorted *hoe* (raw fish), you can try barbecue prawns, crab or shell-fish, as well as the cheaper noodle and shell-fish soups.

ⓘ Getting There & Away

Car ferries (adult/child ₩3000/1000; ⊙7am-6pm) to Yeongjongdo run every hour from Wol-mido Promenade.

A'rex trains run to Incheon International Air-port, from where you can connect to bus 301 or 316 to reach Eulwangni Beach. There's a ₩5500 toll to drive to the island via the 12.4km-long Incheon Bridge.

Muuido 무의도

☑032
If you're looking for a beachside escape within easy reach of Seoul, Muuido fits the bill perfectly. Much less developed than Yeong-jongdo, the island has several lovely beaches of which **Hanagae Beach** (하나개 해수욕장; ☑751 8833; www.hanagae.co.kr; adult/child ₩2000/1000) is the best, with plenty of golden sand, a handful of seafood restaurants and basic beach huts under the pine trees or on the beach. The chalet-style house on the beach was used in the Korean TV drama *Stairway to Heaven*. Just beyond it is the start of a 2.5km hike through dense woods to the top of **Horyonggoksan** (호룡곡산; 244m).

From Keunmuri wharf, walk for a few minutes to **Keunmuri**, a delightfully tradi-tional fishing village. Crab pots and fishing nets lie around while red peppers dry in the sun. From here it's a 1km walk over the hill to **Silmi Beach** (실미 해수욕장; ☑032-752 4466; www.silmi.net; adult/child ₩2000/1000), which has a freshwater swimming pool, campsites and huts under the pine trees. At low tide you can walk to **Silmido** (실미도), an uninhabited island where the Korean movie of that name was filmed.

Don't miss the tiny car-free island of **So-Muuido** (admission ₩1000) connected by foot bridge to Muuido's southeastern tip; the is-land's charming fishing village couldn't be more of a contrast to 21st-century Seoul.

⛵ Sleeping & Eating

Both Hanagae and Silmi beaches offer camp-ing (₩5000 per night) and basic accommo-dation in **beach huts** (from ₩30,000). Rates

DEOKJEOKDO & BAENGNYEONGDO

Deokjeokdo (덕적도), 70km southwest of Incheon, is one of the most scenic of the West Sea islands. Along its southern shore is the spectacular 2km-long **Seopori Beach** backed by a thick grove of 200-year-old pine trees, through which runs a hiking trail. The island also has many unusual rock formations; climb the highest peak, Bijobong (292m), for the grand view. There are plenty of *yeogwan* and *minbak* as well as a camping ground at Seopori Beach if you decide you'd like to stay over. Get here on the high-speed ferry (₩23,750, one hour, twice daily) from Incheon's Yeonan Pier.

If you really want to get off the beaten track, **Baengnyeongdo** (백령도) is South Korea's westernmost point, around 222km northwest of Incheon and only 12km from North Korea. Take a tour around this scenic yet heavily militarised island by boat to view the dramatic coastal rock formations for which it's best known. **Sagot Beach** is 3km long and consists of sand packed so hard that people can (and do) drive cars on it. The island is served by a high-speed ferry (₩62,500, four hours, three daily) from Incheon's Yeonan Pier.

To find out more about these and other West Sea islands see www.ongjin.go.kr.

at hotels and pensions rise on weekends and during July and August. At Keunmuri wharf there's a row of seafood restaurants.

Lifou   PENSION **$$**
(☎747 0053, 011-269 4224; www.lifou.kr; r from ₩70,000; ✳️🛜) Offering wonderful sea views, this small self-catering complex has both *ondol* and Western-style rooms that are sparkling clean and well equipped. White wicker furniture gives it a casual feel. It's run by a British-Korean couple who are a lot of fun and who open an attached bar in the summer.

Family Resort Hotel Muui Island   PENSION **$$**
(☎752 5114; www.muuiland.co.kr; 4-person unit ₩60,000-150,000; ✳️🛜) This attractive complex of self-catering units is set amid landscaped gardens with a lovely view across Keunmuri to the ocean. All rooms have double beds with more people able to sleep on the *ondol* floors.

Seaside Hotel   HOTEL **$$**
(☎752 7737; www.hotelseaside.co.kr; d ₩60,000-70,000; ✳️@) All the pleasantly decorated rooms at this hotel (both Western-style and *ondol*) have sea views – it's a little lacking in atmosphere but the price is right.

Junganghoe-sikdang   SEAFOOD **$$**
(중앙회식당; Keunmuri; meals to share ₩40,000; ⏱10am-10pm) Buy shellfish by the heap; it's enough for three or four people and includes scallops, mussels and trumpet shells. Cook it up at a barbecue set in your table, but watch out for popping shells! This simple restaurant is just before the right turn to Silmi Beach.

ℹ️ Getting There & Away

Muuido is reached via a five-minute ferry trip (₩3000 return, half-hourly until 7pm, 6pm in winter) from Jamjindo. For details of how to get to Jamjindo from Yeongjongdo see p111.

Ganghwado 강화도

☎032 / POP 57,700

For a brief period in the mid-13th century, when the Mongols were rampaging through the mainland, the island of Ganghwado became the location of Korea's capital. Situated at the mouth of the Han River, South Korea's fifth-largest island continued to have strategic importance and was the scene of bloody skirmishes with French and US forces in the 19th century as colonial powers tried to muscle in on the 'hermit kingdom'. Going even further back, Bronze Age people built many dolmen here, 70 of which have been inscribed on Unesco's World Heritage list.

It's not just Ganghwado's fascinating history that makes it worth visiting. Given over to small-scale agriculture (it's famous for its 'stamina-producing' ginseng), the island provides a welcome rural respite from the sometimes craziness of Seoul. Here egrets stalk through verdant rice fields and gulls swarm around the ferries that connect to the neighbouring island of Seongmodo, home to one of the country's most important temples, Bomun-sa, with a cliff-carved Buddha and beautiful old pines. Numerous seafood restaurants also make dining on Ganghwado a pleasure.

Ganghwado's main town, **Ganghwa-eup** (강화읍), is not particularly scenic, but is just 2km beyond the northern bridge and acts as a base for visiting all attractions on the surprisingly large island by bus. The **tourist information centre** (☎930 3515; www.ganghwa.incheon.kr; ☺9am-6pm) in the bus terminal can provide you with English maps and leaflets.

The island is big, so if time is tight, consider taking a tour: several leave from Seoul (check with the KTO Tourist Information Centre, p89) and there's also one from Incheon (p107). Also consider hiring a car or bicycle or chartering a taxi to get around.

Sights & Activities

Bomun-sa   TEMPLE

(보문사; Seongmodo; adult/youth/child ₩2500 /1700/1000; ☺9am-6pm) Situated high in the pine-forested hills of Seongmodo (steep walk, many stairs, catch your breath at the top), this temple has some superbly ornate painting on the eaves of its buildings. The grotto and 10m-tall Buddha rock carving are standouts. Korean women come here in hope of conceiving sons, and the Korean grandmothers you see aren't praying for sons for themselves but for their daughters.

Ferries (adult/child ₩2000/1000, cars ₩16,000; ☺7am-9pm Mar-Nov, 7am-5.30pm Dec-Feb) depart Oepo-ri for Seongmodo (10 minutes, every 30 minutes). On Seongmodo a bus (₩1100; hourly on weekdays, every 30 minutes on weekends) takes you near the temple.

Jeondeung-sa   TEMPLE

(전등사; ☎032-937 0125; www.jeondeungsa.org; adult/youth/child ₩1800/1300/1000; ☺6am-sunset) The Tripitaka Koreana (p152), 80,000 wooden blocks of Buddhist scriptures, was carved between 1235 and 1251 at this attractive temple surrounded by forest in the island's southeast. You can do a Templestay here and sip traditional teas at the charming teahouse **Juklim Dawan** (죽림다원; tea ₩5000; ☺8.30am-7.30pm May-Oct, 9.30am-4.30pm Nov-Apr).

Manisan   HIKING

(마니산; adult/youth/child ₩1500/800/500; ☺9am-6pm) This 469m mountain is protected within a park in the island's southwest, 14km from Ganghwa-eup. On the summit is **Chamseongdan** (참성단), a large stone altar said to have been originally built and used by Dangun, the mythical first Korean. Every 3 October on National Foundation Day (a public holiday), a colourful shamanist ceremony is held here. The 3km walk to the top from the bus stop includes over 900 steps, takes an hour, and on a fine day the views are splendid.

Hourly buses from Ganghwa-eup run to Manisan (₩1000, 30 minutes).

Ganghwa History Museum   MUSEUM

(adult/child ₩1500/1000; ☺9am-6pm Tue-Sun) Covering 5000 years of the island's history, this new museum's range of exhibits is engaging and modern. The replica of the US Navy attack on Ganghwado in 1871 takes you into the thick of the battle. Take bus 30 (₩1000, 30 minutes) or a taxi (₩6500, 15 minutes) here from Ganghwa-eup.

FREE **Ganghwa Dolmen Park**   PARK

(☺24hr) Across from the museum is Ganghwa Dolmen Park, the centrepiece of which is **Bugeun-ni Dolmen** (부근리 고 인돌), the biggest such Bronze Age stone relic, with a top stone weighing more than 50 tonnes. Cheesy small-scale replicas of other ancient relics such as Stonehenge and the Easter Island statues are also dotted around the park.

ⓘ CYCLING ON GANGHWADO

Cycling is a great way of exploring Ganghwado. Bikes can be rented from the **souvenir stall** (☎933 3692; www. kangwhahiking.com; mountain bike/ tandem per hr W5000/7000, per day W9000/15,000; ☺9am-5pm) beside the fortification Gapgot Dondae (갑곶돈대) close to the northern bridge. From here, a 15km cycle path runs alongside the seaside highway towards the southern Gangwha Choji Bridge. It's a scenic, mainly flat jaunt, though the summer sun can be scorching. Eel restaurants, rice fields, flowers and seagulls will greet you along the way. You'll also have a chance to explore several of the stone fortifications that line the coast including those at Gwangseongbo (광성보) and Chojijin (초지진).

For more on cycling and mountain biking in Korea, see p28.

Goryeogungji Palace   PALACE
(고려궁지; Ganghwa-eup; adult/child ₩900/600; ☻8.30am-6pm) In Ganghwa-eup explore the serenely quiet remains of the small palace built in 1231, once surrounded by an 18km fortress wall. The fortress was destroyed in 1866 by French troops, who invaded Korea in response to the execution of nine French Catholic missionaries. Some 2km of walls and three major gates have since been renovated. The French army burnt many priceless books and took 300 back to France; they were only returned to Korea in 2010 on a five-year renewable loan basis.

Oepo-ri   VILLAGE
(외포리) If you have been yearning for a close look at seagulls, come to this picturesque fishing village located on the west coast, about 13km from Ganghwa-eup. Flocks of the birds swoop around the ferries between Oepo-ri and Seongmodo, happily snatching snacks proffered by the delighted passengers.

Even if you stay on land, there's a quiet beauty here. The views of the harbour and mud flats seem to be cut from a Korean painting. Fishing trawlers, either sun dappled or mist cloaked, chug in and out of the port, through a backdrop of lavender-coloured islands; it's not hard to imagine that life here has been little changed for decades.

The seafood market (turn right after you get to the water) has good prices and there are decent restaurants and *yeogwan* (motels with small en suites).

Buses from Ganghwa-eup (₩1000, 30 minutes) take a scenic cross-island route to reach Oepo-ri. Ferries depart for Seongmodo, as well as other islands.

Ganghwa Imsam Spaland   SPA
(가화인삼스파랜드; ☎933 9412; Ganghwa-eup; adult/child ₩9000/7000; ☻24hr) On the southwest outskirts of Ganghwa-eup is this traditional sauna complex. The charcoal-fired saunas outside are authentic and inside there are baths and resting areas (₩10,000 per room) which can double as a great-value place to crash for the night. Catch bus 700 or 90 (₩1000) here from the terminal or hop in a taxi (₩3000).

✨ Festivals
Both the **Dolmen Cultural Festival** – celebrating this unique ancient burial ground

with festivities that include a dolmen construction re-enactment – and the **Ganghwado Azalea Festival** are held in April and May.

🛏 Sleeping
Apart from the options here, consider bedding down at one of the several *minbak* on Seongmodo, doing a Templestay at Jeondeung-sa, or renting on of the resting rooms at Ganghwa Imsam Spaland.

TOP CHOICE Namchidang   HANOK GUESTHOUSE $$$
(남취당; ☎010-9591 0226; http://kyl3850.com/pension/index.php?uid=3; Tosuk Tofu Maeul; r ₩100,000-450,000; ❄️🛜) In the south of the island, a couple of kilometres from Jeondeung-sa, this is easily one of the nicest places to stay. The purpose built *hanok* with traditional wood-fired *ondol* rooms is beautifully decorated by a couple who have had several books published about their rural life on Ganghwado. You can arrange to take a lesson in traditional painting on cotton, or sit and enjoy herbal teas. There are also free bikes to get around. Buses 2, 3 and 41 run here from Ganghwa-eup.

Ivy Tourist Hotel   LOVE HOTEL $$
(아이비호텔; ☎932 9811; Ganghwa-eup; r from ₩40,000; ❄️@) Look for this upmarket love hotel on the left not long after crossing onto the island over the northern bridge. Clean rooms have nice touches such as Jacuzzi-style jet showers.

Penthouse Motel   LOVE HOTEL $
(펜트하우스모텔; ☎934 0113; Oepo-ri; r ₩40,000; ❄️@) This love hotel in Oepo-ri will do the trick if you're looking for clean and reasonably comfortable accommodation. Rooms sport big Jacuzzi baths.

🍴 Eating
Gourmands flock to Ganghwado to sample seafood, with different fishing villages on the island renowned for certain foods. In Deurih-mi (더리미), on the east coast between the Ganghwa and Choji bridges, a dozen restaurants specialise in eel (장어), which can be served raw, salted, marinated in a special sauce and – tastiest of all – grilled over charcoal. Seonsu (선수) on the southeast coast is the place to head for herring, served raw sashimi style.

On the 2nd floor of Ganghwa-eup's bus terminal several places offer inexpensive Korean meals from 10am to 9pm.

Palpal Yeonjangeo KOREAN $$$

(팔팔연장어; ☏932 8881; Deurih-mi; meals from ₩50,000; ☺10am-9.30pm) Banquets built around grilled eel can be enjoyed at this pleasant restaurant, one of a cluster specialising in the dish along Ganghwado's east coast.

Wang Jajeong KOREAN $$

(왕자정; Ganghwa-eup; meals ₩7000-25,000; ☺10am-9.30pm) If the weather's nice you can dine on the terrace here, overlooking the walls of Goryeongungji Palace. Simple, hearty dishes such as *mukbap* (acorn jelly rice) and *kongpiji* (bean soup) are served as well as grilled beef and pork belly (from ₩23,000 per person).

Oepo Hweojjib SEAFOOD $$$

(외포횟집; ☏032-932 6662; meals ₩30,000-40,000; ☺9am-9pm; 🅿) Next to where the ferry docks from Seongmodo is this seafood restaurant where you can sit and gaze at the ocean. The set-course menus (from ₩65,000) come with a feast of side dishes.

🛍 Shopping

Ganghwa-eup Market MARKET

(강화시장; ☺8am-7pm) Near the island's main bus terminal you'll find vendors selling locally grown ginseng, mugwort products and *hwamunseok* (화문석) – reed mats with floral designs that are beautiful but expensive. Woven baskets are cheaper, easier to transport and have similar designs.

ℹ Getting There & Away

There are frequent buses from near Seoul's Sinchon station (Map p50) to Ganghwa-eup (₩2100, 1½ hours, every 10 minutes from 4am to 10pm).

Gangwon-do

Includes »

Best Places to Eat

» Daepohang (p125)

» Byoldang Makguksu (p123)

» Todam Sundubu (p135)

Best Places to Stay

» House Hostel (p125)

» Kensington Stars Hotel (p131)

» Seoraksan Tourist Hotel (p131)

» Chuncheon Tourist Hotel (p122)

» Haslla Museum Hotel (p137)

Why Go?

Mountainous Gangwon-do (강원도) gives you some of South Korea's most spectacular landscapes, up-close Demilitarized Zone (DMZ) experiences, and laid-back coastal towns and beaches on the East Sea. This is where many Seoulites escape – to get lost in the mountains, chow down on Chuncheon's fiery chicken dish *dakgalbi* or the coastal towns' raw fish, or leap into a frenzy of sports like skiing in Pyeongchang county, host of the 2018 Winter Olympics.

While the province may not have that much by way of cultural antiquities, what it does have – Gangneung's 400-year-old Dano Festival, for instance – it celebrates with zest. And Gangwon-do can be quirky too. Near Samcheok you'll find a park full of unabashed phallic sculptures standing cheek by jowl with a humble fishing village, while Gangneung has a museum dedicated to its founder's lifelong obsession with all things Edison.

When to Go
Chuncheon

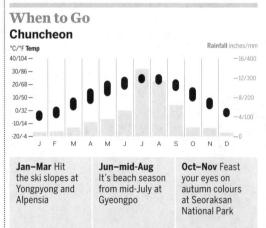

Jan–Mar Hit the ski slopes at Yongpyong and Alpensia

Jun–mid-Aug It's beach season from mid-July at Gyeongpo

Oct–Nov Feast your eyes on autumn colours at Seoraksan National Park

History

Gangwon-do is the southern half of a province that once straddled the border (the North Korean half is romanised as Kangwon-do). Some areas north of the 38th parallel belonged to North Korea from 1945 till the end of the Korean War, and it's not uncommon to come across families with relatives in North Korea.

During the war this province saw many fierce battles for strategic mountaintops. Subsequently its rich natural resources,

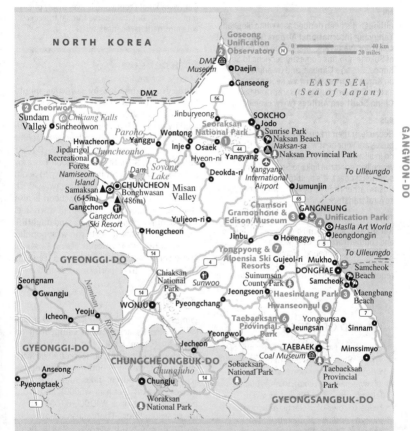

Gangwon-do Highlights

❶ Climb through the stunning, misty mountains of **Seoraksan National Park** (p127)

❷ Peer into North Korea at **Goseong Unification Observatory**, the northernmost point on the DMZ (p126), and tunnel deep into the zone at **Cheorwon** (p122), home to haunting ruins from the Korean War

❸ Get your fill of quirky Korea – gramophones galore at the **Chamsori Gramophone & Edison Museum** (p132) in Gangneung, and phallic sculptures at **Haesindang Park** (p141) in Sinnam

❹ Crawl around in a real North Korean submarine at the **Unification Park** (p136)

❺ Marvel at the limestone wonders of cathedral-like cave **Hwanseongul** (p140)

❻ Make a pilgrimage to the mountaintop altar to Dangun in **Taebaeksan Provincial Park** (p141)

❼ Take the kids skiing at the 2018 Winter Olympic venues in Pyeongchang's **Yongpyong & Alpensia Ski Resorts** (p137)

such as coal and timber, were industrialised, spurring the development of road and rail links. When many coal mines closed in the 1990s, the province had to create alternative employment opportunities, such as tourism.

ℹ Getting There & Away

AIR

Although it's been derided as a white elephant, **Yangyang International Airport** (www.airport.co.kr/doc/yangyang_eng) along the coast south of Sokcho now has domestic services to Seoul's Kimpo, Busan's Gimhae, and Gwangju airport on **Korea Express Air** (www.keair.co.kr), as well as less frequent flights to Harbin and Dalian on **China Southern Airlines** (www.csair.com).

BUS

Because of their frequency and wide coverage, buses are your best way in and out of Gangwon-do in all areas except the Chuncheon region, which has good rail links to Seoul. From the southeast coast, it's best to bus to cities like Busan rather than go by train, which may require several transfers.

TRAIN

Korail (www.korail.com) only covers the western and southern areas of Gangwon-do, with links to Chuncheon, Gangneung, Wonju, Taebaek and several other towns. Services may be infrequent and require transfers depending on your destination.

WORTH A TRIP

ISLAND OF TREES

Chuncheon is known for the filming of *Winter Sonata*, and part of the series was set on **Namiseom island** (남이섬; www.namisum.com), in an artificial lake southwest of Chuncheon. It's home to rows of majestic redwoods, ginkgos and pines, making it ideal for strolling. The island is also home to roaming deer, ostriches and various waterfowl, and hosts rotating art and photography exhibits. It's a touristy park with plenty of *Sonata* kitsch – it calls itself the Naminara Republic and visitors need 'passport' tickets (adults/kids ₩8000/3000), which include a return ferry trip (⊙7.30am-9.30pm) – but it's a fine spot for a breath of fresh air. To get there, hop on a train from Chuncheon to Gapyeong (₩3000, 17 min) and then walk 1.6km (25 min) or bus it (₩1200, 3 min) to Gapyeong Wharf.

ℹ Getting Around

Bus routes are excellent, while train lines cover only the southeast of the province and, in the west, Chuncheon and Gangchon. You can rent a car in cities like Chuncheon, Sokcho, and Gangneung; highways are excellent, though tolls and speed cameras are frequent. **Kumho Rent A Car** (www.kumhorent.com) is a relatively pricey rental agency but it will serve foreign travellers with international licenses.

Chuncheon 춘천

✍033 / POP 275,000

While it's surrounded by gorgeous mountains, the charms of Gangwon-do's capital are mostly artificial: shimmering lakes created by dams, the fiery chicken dish *dakgalbi,* and well-loved (if schmaltzy) settings for the enormously popular TV drama *Winter Sonata* (see p377). Still, it's a good base for outdoor activities and its proximity to Seoul makes it a popular weekend getaway. With several universities here, Chuncheon is also shaking off some of that small-town feel with a burgeoning shopping and nightlife scene. In late May it hosts the very popular **Chuncheon International Mime Festival** (www.mimefestival.com), which is a raucous collection of street performances and even water fights.

◉ Sights

Jungdo ISLAND

(중도) Directly across from Chuncheon on Uiam-ho (Uiam Lake), the little island of Jungdo is packed in true Korean style with enough recreational options to occupy a schoolful of children. Take your pick from bicycle rental (per hour ₩5000) and boat hire (motorboat rides ₩40,000-80,000), rowing or waterskiing. There's also an outdoor swimming pool (⊙Jul-Aug), sports fields and picnic areas.

There are a couple of restaurants and a general store on the island, but most visitors bring their own picnic. Camping (per tent ₩3000) and simple self-catering pension accommodation (✍242 4881; www.gangwon dotour.com; r ₩22,000-55,000;❄) are available; rates rise by ₩11,000 on weekends.

Note that Jungdo will be closed during the construction of a Lego Land theme park on the island.

To get to Jungdo, take bus 74 or 75 heading south from downtown Chuncheon (₩1200, 10 minutes). The ferry pier is off the main road. Ferries (adult/child return

Chuncheon

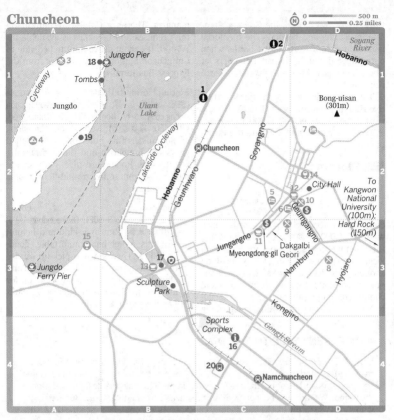

Chuncheon

₩6100/3900, bicycles ₩1000 extra; ☻every 30 min, 9am-6pm Mon-Fri, 9am-6.30pm Sat & Sun) take five minutes.

Uiam Lake   LAKE
(의암호) A bicycle path skirts the lake from Ethiopia Café (p123) round to the

Korean War Memorial, the **Soyang River Maiden** statue and beyond. The memorial is dedicated to a Korean War battle, when outnumbered South Korean defenders at Chuncheon held back the invading North Koreans.

The route makes a particularly attractive ride just before sunset. There's **bicycle rental** (per hr/day ₩3000/15,000, ID required; ⊙9am-7pm) from a stall opposite the Ethiopia Café.

🛏 Sleeping

TOP CHOICE Chuncheon Tourist Hotel
BUSINESS HOTEL $$

(춘천관광호텔; ☎257 1900; 30-1 Nagwon-dong, www.hotelchuncheon.com; d/ste from ₩77,000/110,000; 🌢@🛜) Opened in 2012, this friendly hotel stands out for its central location steps away from the Myeongdong shopping district (yes, the same name as the one in Seoul), its 43-inch flatscreen TVs and comfy beds, large spiffy rooms, and especially Mr Tony, its gregarious English-speaking

manager. There's a Chinese restaurant on the premises and breakfast is available for ₩7000. It's about a two-minute taxi ride to Chuncheon Station or 10 minutes from the Express Bus Terminal.

Sejong Hotel Chuncheon
HOTEL $$

(춘천 세종 호텔; ☎252 1191; www.chunchon sejong.co.kr; d/tw from ₩133,100, deluxe from ₩175,450; 🌢🌢@🛜) Nestled on the slope of Bonguisan, this hotel offers unrivalled views of Chuncheon and the surrounding countryside. Rooms are nice, with all the mod cons, and some ground-floor rooms have a patio.

Grand Motel
MOTEL $

(그랜드모텔; ☎243 5021; Okcheondong 39-6; r ₩35,000; 🌢@) Run by a kind and helpful family, this motel has comfortable, good-sized rooms. There's a free pick-up service from the bus terminal and train station, and the family can also provide information for sightseeing in Chuncheon and nearby. Rates rise by ₩5000 on Saturday.

A DIFFERENT SIDE TO THE DMZ

Say 'DMZ' (Demilitarized Zone) and most people think of Panmunjeom (see p93). But the little-touristed town of **Cheorwon** (철원; www.cwg.go.kr/english) presents a more haunting version. Under North Korea's control from 1945, it saw fierce fighting during the Korean War and was built anew after the war, as part of South Korea. But even today it abounds with army trucks and military checkpoints. It's one way to see the DMZ without paying an exorbitant fee and being hustled onto coaches.

Most of the war sites lie within the Civilian Control Zone that spans 20km from the border, so visitors must present identification and register with the **Hantangang Tourism Office** (한탄강 관광지 관리사무소; ☎450 5558) at the Iron Triangle Memorial Hall (철의 삼각 전적관) for an official 2½-hour **tour** (adult/youth/child ₩4000/3000/1000; ⊙9.30am, 10.30am, 1pm & 2.30pm or 2pm in winter, closed Tue). You must have your own vehicle or hitch a ride. There's usually a tour shuttle bus (₩8000) available on weekends. If not, a three-hour taxi ride to cover the sights would be about ₩100,000. Bring your passport.

The first stop is the **Second Tunnel**, dug by North Korea in 1975. About 1km of it lies in South Korea and it's large enough for purportedly 16,000 soldiers to stream through per hour. A 150m staircase leads down to the tunnel, then it's a well-lit, albeit damp, 500m stretch to where the tunnel was discovered, just 300m from the border.

The next stop is the **Cheorwon Peace Observatory**, 1km from the DMZ. There are coin-operated binoculars for gazing at North Korea and its 'propaganda village' Seonjeon. A short drive down the road is the petite **Woljeong-ri Station**, left as a memorial to the railway line between Seoul and Wonsan, and housing the battered, twisted remains of a bombed train.

After passing a few battle-scarred buildings, the tour ends at the former Labor Party (that is, Communist Party) **HQ**. The surviving facade is evocative, but its associations are less than pleasant: when Cheorwon was part of North Korea, many civilians were imprisoned and tortured here.

Buses from Dong-Seoul run to Sincheorwon (₩8700, 2 hours, every 10 to 15 minutes), where a taxi will get you to the Iron Triangle Memorial Hall in about 15 minutes.

GET YOUR ADRENALIN ON

With rushing rivers, rugged mountains and fairly unspoiled scenery, Gangwon-do's northwest has become a hotbed for kayaking, canoeing and rafting trips from mid-April to October. Trips from **Cheorwon** (철원; www.cwg.go.kr/english) make forays onto the Hantangang (*gang* means river) in the Sundam Valley, while those from **Inje** (인제; www.inje.go.kr) head to the Naerincheon river. Neither course is extremely difficult unless monsoon rains whip them up; at the time of research, Cheorwon was beset by a prolonged drought and water levels were very low.

Kayaking and rafting trips cost ₩30,000 (three hours) to ₩55,000 (seven hours) – add ₩5000 in the peak season – including instruction, and most companies offer pick-up from Seoul. Companies based in Cheorwon include **Hanleisure** (☑455 0557; www.hanleisure.com) and **Sundam Leisure** (☑452 3034; www.leports114.com). In Inje, try **X-Game** (☑462 5217; www.injejump.co.kr), which also offers bungee jumping (₩40,000 to 45,000).

Intercity buses serve Cheorwon from Seoul's Express Bus Terminal (₩12,000, two hours, hourly). Inje can be reached from Dong-Seoul (₩12,200, two hours, every 30 minutes).

GANGWON-DO CHUNCHEON

🍴 Eating

Chuncheon's gastronomical pride and joy is *dakgalbi* (닭갈비; chicken pieces), *tteok* (rice cakes) and vegetables cooked with spicy chilli paste on a sizzling hot iron plate in the middle of the table. Off the downtown Myeongdong shopping area, Dakgalbi Geori (닭갈비 거리; Dakgalbi St) is a lively street with more than 20 restaurants (meals around ₩10,000) offering such fare. Most places will only serve *dakgalbi* to at least two diners, and a serving for two is often enough to feed three. If you can't decide which spot to try, go with **Jangwon Myeongga** (장원명가; ☑254 6388; ⊘10am-midnight) on the east side of the street around the middle of the block.

Byoldang Makguksu   NOODLES $$
(별당막국수; ☑254 9603; meals ₩5000-35,000) Housed in a 40-year-old building, this atmospheric restaurant serves up delicious *makguksu*, a Gangwon-do speciality. The buckwheat noodles are served cold, garnished with vegies, pork slices and half a hard-boiled egg. You can have it dry or add broth from a kettle, as well as mustard, sugar and vinegar to taste; go easy on the *gochujang* (red pepper paste) if you don't want it too spicy. Set back from the main road on a side street, the restaurant has a vertical red sign with white lettering and a parking lot out front.

Wangmandu   DUMPLINGS $
(왕만두; ☑241 5480; meals ₩3000-5000) This hole-in-the-wall eatery is a good place to fill up on its namesake dish (large steamed dumplings), as well as *mandu* (dumplings) served fried (군만두), in soup (만두국) or in soup with rice cakes (떡만두국). There's also *naengmyeon* (buckwheat noodles in cold broth) and *bibimbap* (rice topped with egg, meat, vegetables and sauce). Go up the lane beside Dunkin' Donuts and it's on the right at the first intersection – look for the red sign with white lettering outside.

🍺 Drinking

Party-goers can head to the back gate of **Kangwon National University** (Gangwon-dae humun; 강원대 후문). There are plenty of bars and cafes, or try **Hard Rock** (☑243 0516; 628-12 Hyoja-Samdong), which has an impressive beer menu. It's on the main strip running parallel to the main road near the back gate.

Ethiopia Café (이디오피아; ⊘10am-9pm) is the main establishment at the lakefront, near the Memorial Hall for Ethiopian Veterans of the Korean War with its triple-pointed roof. Myeongdong shopping street has plenty of cafes that fill up with young people; **Creme Cake Café** (크림 케익 카페; ☑244 8795) above KFC has better cakes than most. Facing the city hall, **Dill** (☑254 9978; ⊘10.30am-10.30pm; 🖥) serves pasta, pork cutlet, seafood rice, and dainty tea sets.

TOP CHOICE **Jackson Bill**   BAR
(☑010-2540 7754; 50-6 Joyang-dong) This loveable watering hole between Myeongdong and Dakgalbi Geori feels like the sort of place where everyone knows your name. Drawing

a mix of expat teachers and Koreans, veteran bartender and owner Mr Oh has 8000 vinyl records and takes requests; he'll dig out oldies from the '70s and '80s if you like. Look for photos of the records on the sign at street level and head up to the bar on the 2nd floor.

R. Mutt 1917   CAFE
(🏠254 1917; www.artncompany.kr; ⊙10am-11pm) Part of the Art n Company gallery, this stylish hillside cafe dedicated to Marcel Duchamp commands lovely views of Uiham Lake from its patio. Rotating painting and sculpture exhibitions are held here. It's in the MBC broadcasting building; from downtown, take a taxi (₩3000 to ₩4000) since the closest bus stop is down the hill.

🛍 Shopping
Chuncheon's main shopping area is the Myeongdong-gil pedestrian lane. There's an extensive underground arcade with all manner of shops running parallel to it under Jungangno street.

ℹ Information
Not far from downtown, a large **tourist information centre** (🏠244 0088; www.chuncheon.go.kr, http://en.gangwon.to; @) inside a blockish brown brick building, is well stocked with information for the whole province. There is also a smaller **tourist information office** (🏠250 3896) at the bus terminal.

ℹ Getting There & Away
Bus
The **express and intercity bus terminals** are beside each other. Departures from the former include Daegu (₩17,500, four hours, 11 daily) and Gwangju (₩22,800, 4½ hours, four daily). For bus departures from the intercity bus terminal, see the boxed text below.

Train
ITX trains run on the Gyeongchun Line from Seoul's Cheongnyangni train station (₩6000,

one hour, hourly) and Yongsan Station (₩9800, 75 min, hourly) to Chuncheon Station, also stopping at Namchuncheon in Chuncheon, which is a little closer to downtown. From either station it's a quick taxi ride to downtown Chuncheon.

Seoul's Gyeongchun metro line also runs trains from Sangbong to Namchuncheon and Chuncheon stations (₩2600, 1 hour, 15 min).

ℹ Getting Around
Inexpensive taxis are handy for shuttling around Chuncheon.

Samaksan 삼악산
The highest mountain near Chuncheon, **Samaksan** (ticket office 🏠262 2215; adult/youth/child ₩1600/1000/600; ⊙sunrise-sunset) offers incredible views of the town and surrounding lakes. The hike up to the peak (645m) can be strenuous and takes at least two hours, passing pretty waterfalls near the base and several temples.

To get to the ticket office, take bus 3, 5, 50 or 50-1 (₩1200, 15 minutes) heading south along Jungangno in Chuncheon. Get off after about 10km, when you see the green road sign saying 'Seoul 79km'.

Sokcho 속초
🏠033 / POP 100,000
Despite its proximity to Seoraksan National Park, **Sokcho** (http://sokcho.gangwon.kr) is more of a fishing town than a tourist town. The main commercial activity – and its attendant aromas – are clustered along the waterfront. For most domestic tourists the main draw is the chance to sup on fresh raw fish with the tang of salt in the air. The beaches also get crowded on New Year's Eve when people gather to watch the first sunrise of the year.

Sokcho is only about 60km from the border and was part of North Korea from 1945 to the end of the Korean War. Most of the

BUS DEPARTURES FROM CHUNCHEON

DESTINATION	PRICE (₩)	DURATION	FREQUENCY
Cheongju	14,900	3½hr	1 daily
Cheorwon	13,200	2½hr	7 daily
Dong-Seoul	6400	70min	every 20min
Gangneung	11,100	3½hr	every 30min
Sokcho	12,500	2hr	every 1–1.5hr

coastline is lined with barbed wire. At night, remember that lights in the water are to attract squid; lights on the beaches are to detect infiltrators.

There are small **tourist information booths** (☑639 2689; ☺9am-6pm, closed Jan) outside the express and intercity bus terminals.

🛏 Sleeping

In July and August room rates can double or triple. You can also camp on the beach then (₩4000 to ₩8000 per night, shower ₩1300).

TOP CHOICE House Hostel HOSTEL $$

(더하우스 호스텔; ☑633 3477; www.thehouse -hostel.com; s/d ₩20,000/35,000, Jul & Aug s/d ₩40,000/55,000; 🅰@🛜) Within five minutes' walk of the intercity bus terminal, this is everything good budget accommodation should be. It combines the niceties of Korean motel rooms – water dispenser, minifridge and basic toiletries – with amenities such as bike rentals, free laundry and free breakfast (cereal, bread, coffee and tea). The quirky common lounge and charming, light-filled breakfast room are great for meeting travellers, and the English-speaking young owner is helpful with travel advice.

The Class 300 BUSINESS HOTEL $$

(더클래스300; ☑630 9000; www.theclass300. com; 1288-22 Joyang-dong; d from ₩70,000; 🅰@🛜) Although it's relatively far from central Sokcho, the Class 300 is one of the classier joints in town, with stylish decor (though a tad worn), relatively soft beds, and English-speaking staff. There's a breakfast buffet on the 15th floor with good views of the city and beach.

Good Morning Family Hotel HOTEL $$

(굿모닝가족호텔; ☑637 9900; www.hotelgood morning.net; Sokcho Rd; r ₩60,000; 🅰@) This spiffy nine-storey hotel is one of the nicest near the beach. Rooms have contemporary dark-wood floors, tasteful decor and floor-to-ceiling windows to take advantage of the view. Rates rise by ₩20,000 on Saturday.

Big Star Motel MOTEL $

(큰별 모텔; ☑637 4477; www.bigstarmotel.com; Yeongnanghaean-gil; r ₩30,000; 🅰@) Sitting snugly beside the Sokcho Lighthouse, this motel has very nice rooms with a brand-new feeling. Expect to pay about ₩10,000 more for a sea view. Rates rise by ₩20,000 Saturday.

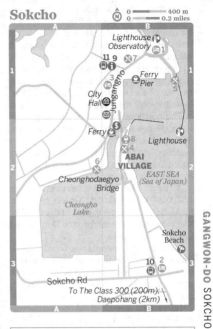

Sokcho

Sokcho

🛏 Sleeping

✕ Eating

🍷 Drinking

ℹ Information

ℹ Transport

✕ Eating

The mainstay of the local cuisine is *modeumhoe* (모듬회; assorted raw fish), served with *banchan* (side dishes), *ssam* (vegetable leaves) *ganjang* (soy sauce) with wasabi, and spicy soup. The best place to soak up the atmosphere and flavours is on the water-front. At the southern harbour of **Daepo-hang**, you can poke around the market stalls or bump elbows with the locals at casual eateries where the proprietor will kill, slice and serve your meal within minutes of scooping it live out of the tank. Alternatively partake of a more civilised (though not necessarily quiet) meal at a seafood restaurant.

The northern harbour of **Dongmyeong-hang** offers a similar but tamer experience, as the stalls have been moved into a proper building, with a communal eating hall upstairs. You can also take away your meal to eat on the breakwater.

A large platter of *modeumhoe* costs ₩30,000 to ₩100,000. Order from the tanks, or tell your hosts your budget and let them assemble a meal for you. Don't forget the *soju* (local vodka).

Another local speciality is squid *sundae* (sausage). *Sundae* is usually made with a pork casing, but here squid is stuffed with minced noodles, tofu, onion, carrot, seaweed and seasoning, then sliced and fried in egg.

Daepohang is south of Sokcho, on the way to Naksan (p127). Take bus 1, 1-1, 7, 7-1, 9 or 9-1 (₩1300, 10 minutes) heading south and get off at the giant parking lot for the harbour. Dongmyeonghang is near the intercity bus terminal.

Wangsibri   BBQ **$$**
(왕십리; ☏636 7849; meals ₩10,000; ⊙3pm-midnight) If seafood isn't your thing, fill up at this no-frills all-you-can-eat barbecue joint, where locals perch on stools and feast till closing time.

Jinyang Hoetjip   SEAFOOD **$$**
(진양횟집; ☏635 9999; meals ₩10,000-20,000) A modest establishment celebrated for its squid *sundae*. It also serves raw fish platters, including *mulhoe* (seasoned raw fish in water). The restaurant has fish tanks interspersed with greenery out front.

Abai Shikdang   SEAFOOD **$$**
(아바이식당; ☏635 5310; meals ₩10,000-30,000) A fine place to try squid *sundae* in Abai, a collection of vintage seafood restaurants between the canal and the sea. To get there, take the old-fashioned ferry (a floating platform attached to a cable) across the harbour and walk under the elevated bridge road on the other side.

Cafe Nadoo   CAFE
(☏635 9773; drinks ₩4000; ⊙10am-9pm; ☎) Also in the old-timey Abai district, this chic spot hewn from raw concrete serves coffee, tea and lemonade.

🛈 Getting There & Away
Air
Yangyang International Airport (see p126) has connections to Seoul, Busan, and other cities in Korea as well as Harbin and Dalian in China.

Bus
Buses leave Sokcho **express bus terminal** for Seoul Gangnam (₩17,000, 2½ hours, every 30 minutes). For bus departures from Sokcho **intercity bus terminal**, see the boxed text below.

🛈 Getting Around
Many buses (1, 1-1, 7, 7-1, 9 and 9-1) connect the intercity bus terminal, via the town's main street Jungangno, to the express bus terminal and Daepohang. Buses 7 and 7-1 go to the Seoraksan area, while buses 9 and 9-1 link Sokcho with Naksan and Yangyang.

Around Sokcho
GOSEONG UNIFICATION OBSERVATORY 고성 통일 전망대
While this area was part of North Korea from 1945 to 1953, today this **building** (☏682 0088; www.tongiltour.co.kr; adult/child ₩3000/1500, parking ₩3000; ⊙9am-4pm, to 5.30pm Jul 15-Aug 20) is the closest most South Koreans can get to glimpsing that world. There are binocu-

---

BUS DEPARTURES FROM SOKCHO

DESTINATION	PRICE (₩)	DURATION (HR)	FREQUENCY
Busan	39,100	7½	11 daily
Chuncheon	12,500	2	hourly
Daegu	24,100	3½	5 daily
Dong-Seoul	16,100	4	hourly
Gangneung	6000	1	every 20min

lars (₩500 for two minutes) installed on the viewing deck, and inside the observatory is a large map labelled (in Korean only) with mountain names and the locations of military installations (red text for North Korea, white text for South Korea). Kiosks here sell liquor, cash, postage stamps and other souvenirs from North Korea.

On a clear day, you can get a good view of Kumgangsan (p318), about 20km to the west. The North-bound highway and railroad fell quiet after South Korea suspended Kumgangsan tours in July 2008, when a South Korean tourist was shot by North Korea.

Despite the solemnity of the place, the parking lot is cluttered with souvenir shops and restaurants. On the other side of the lot is the Korean War Exhibition Hall, which provides something of a primer on the war.

DMZ MUSEUM 박물관

This large **museum** (☎680 8463; www.dmz museum.com; adult/child ₩2000/1000; ☺9am-5.30pm Mar-Oct, 9am-5pm Nov-Feb) is also inside the Tongil Security Park, on the left side of the road as you approach the Goseong Unification Observatory. It has a surprising amount of English in its narration of the history of the DMZ, as well as exhibits like US POW letters and extensive photos.

❶ Getting There & Away

From downtown Sokcho or the bus stop right outside the intercity bus terminal, catch bus 1 or 1-1 (₩5020, 1½ hours, 44km, every 15 minutes) headed north. Get off at Machajin (마차진; a round-trip taxi from Sokcho might cost ₩35,000) and walk about 10 minutes up to the Tongil Security Park (통일안보공원). Here you present identification and purchase your admission ticket. If you don't have your own vehicle, the staff might be able to help you hitch a ride, but don't count on it. It's 10km to the observatory; pedestrians, bicycles and motorbikes are not allowed.

NAKSAN PROVINCIAL PARK
낙산 도립공원

This small coastal **park** (☎670 2518; http://eng.yangyang.go.kr; admission free) south of Sokcho is home to the temple **Naksan-sa** (낙산사; ☎672 2448; adults/youth/kids ₩3000/1500/1000; ☺5am-7pm), established in AD 671 and enjoying glorious sea views all around. A majestic 15m-tall statue of the Goddess of Mercy, Gwaneum, presides over the East Sea from a promontory. Notably it has never fallen victim to the forest fires that have periodically razed the temple buildings (most recently in 2005).

Most of the temple complex has been stoutly rebuilt since the last fire and the surrounding pine forest is recovering as well. Immediately below the statue is a small shrine, with a window strategically constructed so that a kneeling devotee can look up and gaze upon the statue's face. Further down a side path is a pavilion with a glass-covered hole through which you can see the sea cave below.

Below the temple is **Naksan Beach** (낙산해수욕장), considered one of the best on the east coast and phenomenally busy in the summer, when accommodation prices can triple. At other times it's a pleasant place to stay if you want to avoid Sokcho's fishing-town feel.

🛏 Sleeping

Euisangdae Condotel   MOTEL **$**
(의상대콘도텔; ☎672 3201; www.euisangdae .com; r ₩40,000-70,000; ❉@✿) It doesn't look like much from the outside, but rooms are clean and sharp and enjoy great views right on the beachfront. They also come with kitchenettes and desktop computers.

Naksan Beach Hotel   HOTEL **$$**
(낙산비치호텔; ☎672 4000; www.naksanbeach .co.kr; r ₩90,000; ❉@✿) The most upmarket option, with comfortable rooms and decent restaurants. A seawater sauna is sometimes available. Ask for a room at the front to get a great view of the sunrise. Rates rise by ₩60,000 on Saturday.

❶ Getting There & Away

Bus 9 and 9-1 (₩1500, 15 minutes, every 15 minutes) can be picked up outside either of Sokcho's bus terminals, heading in the direction of Yangyang. Get off at Naksan Beach. You can approach Naksan-sa via the beach, or walk backwards along the highway and follow the signs to approach it from the landward side.

Seoraksan National Park
설악산 국립공원

☎033

This **park** (☎636 7700; http://seorak.knps.or.kr; adult/youth/child ₩2500/1000/600; ☺sunrise-sunset) is one of the most beautiful and iconic on the entire Korean Peninsula. Designated by Unesco as a Biosphere Protection site, it boasts oddly shaped rock formations, dense forests, abundant wildlife, hot springs and ancient Shilla-era temples. Seoraksan (Snowy Crags Mountain) is the third-highest mountain in South Korea, with its highest

Seoraksan National Park

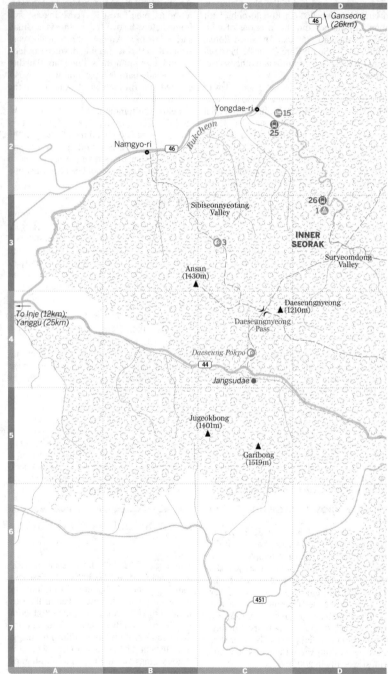

Ganseong
(26km)

Yongdae-ri

15
25

Namgyo-ri

Bukcheon

Sibiseonnyeotang
Valley

26
1

INNER
SEORAK

Suryeomdong
Valley

3

Ansan
(1430m)

To Inje (12km);
Yanggu (25km)

Daesenngnyeong
(1210m)

Daeseungnyeong
Pass

Daeseung Pokpo

Jangsudae

Jugeokbong
(1401m)

Garibong
(1519m)

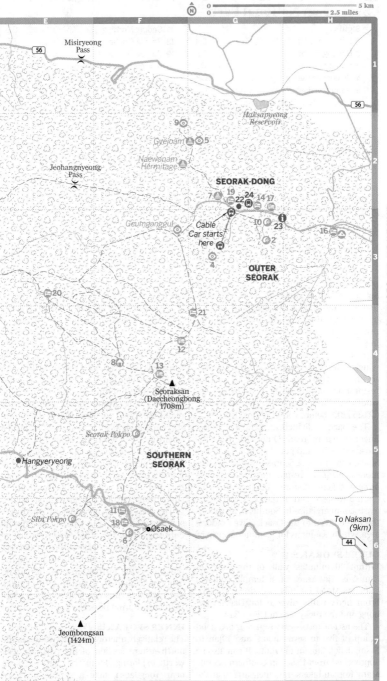

N

0 — 5 km
0 — 2.5 miles

56 Misiryeong Pass

Haksapyeong Reservoir

56

9

Gyejoam 5

Naewonam Hermitage

Jeohangnyeong Pass

SEORAK-DONG

7 19 22 24 14 17
10 23
16
Geumganggul Cable Car starts here
2
4

OUTER SEORAK

20

21

12

8 13

Seoraksan (Daecheongbong 1708m)

SOUTHERN SEORAK

Seorak-Pokpo 1

Hangyeryeong

Sibi Pokpo

11
18
6 Osaek

To Naksan (9km)

44

Jeombongsan (1424m)

Seoraksan National Park

peak, Daecheongbong, standing at 1708m. Set against this landscape are two stately temples, Sinheung-sa and Baekdam-sa.

Peak season is July and August, while in mid-October visitors flock to see the changing colours of the autumn leaves – best appreciated over a bottle of *meoruju* (wild fruit wine). Given the park's size (nearly 400,000 sq km), sections are sometimes closed for restoration or preservation, or to prevent wildfires. Check with the **Visitor Centre** (☑636 7700) before you head out.

The park is divided into three sections, unconnected by road: Outer Seorak is the most accessible and popular area, nearest to Sokcho and the sea. Seorak-dong has hotels, motels, *minbak,* restaurants, bars, *noraebang* and general stores; Inner Seorak covers the western end of the park and is the least commercialised; Southern Seorak is the name given to the Osaek (Five Colours) area, which is famous for its mineral springs.

OUTER SEORAK 외설악

Within 20 minutes' walk of the park entrance is **Sinheung-sa**, a temple complex that has stood on this site since AD 652. From here, paths diverge for Daecheongbong and the rocky face of Ulsan Bawi.

The ascent to **Daecheongbong** is a solid tramp of five to seven hours and 10km to 14km, depending on the route. It can also be approached from Osaek in Southern Seorak. Many Korean hikers time their arrival at the

peak to catch the sunrise. There are mountain shelters of varying quality en route (see p131).

A shorter but still strenuous hike is the two-hour, 4.3km route to **Ulsan Bawi**, a spectacular granite cliff that stands at 873m. The trail passes **Heundeul Bawi**, a massive 16-tonne boulder balanced on the edge of a rocky ledge, which can be rocked to and fro by a small group of people. It's a popular spot for photos. From here, it's a hard-going but rewarding climb (including an 808-step metal staircase) to Ulsan Bawi. There are stupendous views all the way to Sokcho on a clear day – well worth the effort.

An easier option is the hour-long hike to a couple of waterfalls: **Yukdam Pokpo**, a series of six small falls, and the 40m-high **Biryong Pokpo**. The 2km hike starts at the stone bridge beyond the cable-car station.

The least taxing and quickest way to get some good views is to ride the 30-minute **cable car** (☑636 7362; adult/child return ₩8500/5500; ☺8.30am-5pm, to 6pm in summer), which drops you a 20-minute walk from the remains of the fortress **Gwongeumseong**, believed to date back to the 13th century. The cable car runs every 20 minutes, more frequently during peak season.

INNER SEORAK 내설악

The relatively uncrowded river valleys in the northwestern section of the park are well worth exploring. From the park entrance near Yongdae-ri, take a shuttle bus (see p132) or hike 6.5km to the serene temple of **Baekdam-sa** (☏462 2554; ☉sunrise-sunset), which faces east and is best appreciated in the morning. From there, you can ramble along the Suryeomdong Valley for an hour or two, or even connect to Outer Seorak (seven hours, 14km).

Alternatively, from Namgyo-ri there's a splendid 2½-hour hike in the Sibiseonnyeotang Valley to **Dumun Pokpo**. After another two hours uphill you can turn right for a 30-minute hike up **Ansan** (1430m) or turn left for **Daeseungnyeong** (1210m), which takes the same amount of time. You can also approach Ansan from the south, via a hiking trail from Jangsudae.

SOUTHERN SEORAK 남설악

It's easier to hike up Daecheongbong from **Osaek Mineral Water Spring** in the south, though the climb is still steep and difficult. Budget four hours up and three hours down, then soak away the strain in the hot-spring pools. You can also descend on the other side to Seorak-dong (six hours).

🛏 Sleeping

The widest range of accommodation is at Seorak-dong. Accommodation rates can double in July and August, and also tend to inflate in October. At other times, the upmarket hotels offer significant discounts. Basic camping (₩3500 to ₩7000) facilities are available in Seorak-dong, Jangsudae and Osaek. There are four mountain **shelters** (₩5000-8000) along the Outer Seorak routes to Daecheongbong – at Jungcheong, Yangpok, Huiungak and Socheong. Reservations are accepted only for **Jungcheong** and **Huiungak** (☏672 1708; http://english.knps.or.kr/), which is just 100m below the peak. **Suryeom-dong shelter** (☏462 2576) is located on the trail from Baekdam-sa. Check for shelter closures at http://english.knps.or.kr/Experience/Shelters/Default.aspx.

SEORAK-DONG 설악동

TOP CHOICE **Seoraksan Tourist Hotel** HOTEL **$$**
(설악산관광호텔; ☏636 7101; www.seorakhotel.com; r ₩121,000, ste ₩165,000; ❈@✿) Steps away from the outbuildings of Sinheung-sa temple, the only hotel inside the park has its own private access road and restaurant. Rooms are clean and pleasant, and some have fantastic views of the mountains. This property also stands out for its English-speaking manager, who is very hospitable and informative.

TOP CHOICE **Kensington Stars Hotel** LUXURY HOTEL **$$$**
(켄싱턴호텔; ☏635 4001; www.kensington.co.kr; d & ondol ₩209,000, tw ₩330,000; ❈@✿) Just 300m from the park entrance, tucked into the crook of a majestic Korean mountain, is this unexpected English oasis – with Edwardian armchairs in the lobby, and red double-decker buses parked outside. The floors have different themes such as movies and sports, and autographed memorabilia abound; check out the Beatles records in the Abbey Road lounge. Rooms are suitably plush and those at the front have great views.

Seorak Morning MOTEL **$$**
(설악의 아침; ☏632 6677; www.seorakmorning.com; r ₩40,000; ❈P) The former Meorujang has been transformed into a sharp-looking *pension*, with bright and cosy rooms. The owners speak a little English.

Mount Sorak Youth Hostel HOSTEL **$**
(설악산 유스호스텔; ☏636 7116; www.sorakyhostel.com; dm/f ₩25,000/50,000, Fri & Sat ₩30,000/75,000; ❈@) The cheapest option for solo travellers, but you'll have to bus it to the park entrance (₩1200, five minutes, every 10 minutes).

INNER SEORAK

The road from Yongdae-ri to the park entrance (1km) is flanked by farmhouses, **minbak** (per room ₩20,000) and restaurants. It's a good place to spend the night if you'd like to wake up to your own slice of rural Korean idyll.

SOUTHERN SEORAK

Seorak Oncheonjang HOTEL **$$**
(설악온천장; ☏672 2645; www.sorakjang.com; r ₩30,000; ❈@✿) This motel has pleasant rooms spread over two neat white buildings, with the lobby in the rear one. The *oncheon* (summer & fall only) is free for guests, as is internet use. Owner Mr Lim can speak some English. Rates rise to ₩40,000 on Friday and Saturday, and go up to ₩70,000 during peak periods.

Green Yard Hotel HOTEL **$$**
(그린야드호텔; ☏672 8500; r & ondol from ₩90,000; ❈@) The only high-end hotel, this mountain chalet–inspired complex has smart rooms with all the creature comforts. The *oncheon* (guests/nonguests ₩5000/9000) looks a little industrial from the entrance, but has lovely outdoor bath areas.

GANGWON-DO SEORAKSAN NATIONAL PARK

✕ Eating & Drinking

As in many national parks, the restaurants around Seoraksan serve popular fare such as *sanchae bibimbap* (₩5000) and *sanchae jeongsik* (banquet dishes; ₩8000), both of which feature local vegetables.

Seolhyang
CAFE

(drinks ₩7000; ⊙8am-6.30pm) Inside the park and on the outskirts of Seorak-dong, this charming traditional Korean cafe built with thick logs sits by a bridge leading to the main pavilion of Sinheung-sa temple. It's the perfect spot to refuel with a coffee and a cookie or two.

ⓘ Information

The **Visitor Centre** (☑636 7700; ⊙10am-5pm) at the entrance to Outer Seorak has some information in English as well as maps.

ⓘ Getting There & Away

The access road to Outer Seorak branches off the main coast road at Sunrise Park, halfway between Sokcho and Naksan. From outside Sokcho's intercity bus terminal or opposite its express bus terminal, catch bus 7 or 7-1 (₩1100, 20 minutes, every 10 minutes), which terminates at Seorak-dong.

Buses from Sokcho's intercity bus terminal run every hour to Osaek (₩4000) and Jangsudae (₩5400). From Dong-Seoul, there are also eight buses daily to Osaek (₩18,800). At Osaek, buy your bus ticket at the general store about 10m from the bus stop.

Also from Sokcho's intercity bus terminal, buses bound for Jinburyeong (six daily from 6.30am to 5.50pm) make stops at Yondae-ri (₩6600) and Namgyo-ri (₩7000). From Yongdae-ri, it's a 1km walk to the park entrance. There, you can hike or take a shuttle bus (adult/child one way ₩1800/1000, 15 minutes, every 20 minutes) to Baekdam-sa; it runs from 7am to 5.30pm.

Gangneung 강릉

☑033 / POP 200,000

Gangneung (www.gangneung.go.kr) is the largest city on the Gangwon-do coast. Its pockets of attractiveness lie towards the sea, particularly near Gyeongpo, while its cultural hotspots – well-preserved Joseon-era buildings and the 400-year-old shamanist Dano Festival (see boxed text, p132) – are matched by quirky modern attractions, such as a museum lovingly dedicated to Thomas Edison and a North Korean submarine on display in nearby Jeongdongjin (see p136). With natty motels and a decent bar scene as well, the town is a good place to linger for a few days if you're looking for an experience that's off the beaten track without being too small-town.

The **tourist information centre** (☑640 4537; www.gntour.go.kr) is beside the bus terminal, with English-, Mandarin- and Japanese-speaking staff. There is also a small booth in front of the train station, and another at Gyeongpo Beach. The main shopping area is downtown, in the warren of lanes near Jungang Market.

◉ Sights

Chamsori Gramophone & Edison Museum
MUSEUM

(참소리 축음기 에디슨 과학 박물관; ☑655 1130; www.edison.kr; adult/youth/child ₩7000/6000/5000; ⊙9am-5pm; ⊕) This whimsical museum is a sheer delight. It combines the two loves of private collector Son Sung-Mok: gramophones and Thomas Edison. There are hundreds of antique gramophones (or phonographs, as Edison termed them) and music boxes, as well as a colourful collection of Edison's other inventions and related devices, from cameras and kinetoscopes to toys, TVs and typewriters. Some of these items are

---

GETTING INTO THE SPIRIT

The highlight of Gangneung's calendar is the shamanist **Dano Festival** (Danoje; 단오제), celebrated for one week on the fifth day of the fifth lunar month (usually in June). It's one of the biggest holidays in Korea and has been recognised by Unesco as a 'Masterpiece of the Oral and Intangible Heritage of Humanity'. For foreigners, it's a great opportunity to revel it up Korean-style, while learning about some of the country's oldest spiritual beliefs.

Danoje is the climax of a month-long series of shamanist and Confucian ceremonies for peace, prosperity and bountiful harvests. On the first day there's a lantern parade to welcome a mountain spirit, who unites with his 'wife', another spirit dwelling in Gangneung. During the festival people present their wishes to both, while female shamans perform the *dano gut* ritual. On the final day the people send off the male spirit back to the mountain.

GRAMOPHONES & GIZMOS GALORE

Ask Mr Son Sung-Mok about any item in his Chamsori Gramophone & Edison Museum, and he'll tell you a story about it. He has amassed over 10,000 gramophones, Edison inventions and their technological descendants from around the world, only a fraction of which are on public display.

Mr Son's best story just might be the one about his very first gramophone, a Columbia G241 made in the 1920s and given to him by his parents when he was a boy in Wonsan (in what is today North Korea). When the family fled south during the Korean War, the 12kg phonograph was the only possession he lugged along. It now takes pride of place beside the entrance to the museum shop.

As for Mr Son's favourite story, he'll point at the American coin-slot phonograph on the museum's second floor in the middle of the main gallery; it's tall like a grandfather clock. Dating from the 1900s, it's the only one of its kind left, so when it came up for auction in Argentina, Mr Son was determined to get it. Even falling victim to an armed robbery en route didn't stop him from making it to the auction and putting in a successful bid.

Mr Son's fascination with gramophones extends to the man who invented and patented the phonograph, Thomas Edison. Mr Son notes that Edison didn't do well in school yet was curious enough to learn on his own. Through this museum, Mr Son hopes to inspire Korean children to be likewise curious and interested in many things. He also has plans for a children's museum, a movie museum and perhaps a school to train curators.

Gramophones are still his first love, though, whether he's tinkering with one, savouring its music or looking for new acquisitions. A consummate collector for over 40 years, he avers, 'I will keep collecting till I die'.

the only one of their kind. Though the tour is in Korean only, the guide demonstrates the use of some antique music boxes and other contraptions – good fun for children and anyone interested in 'retro' technology.

Take bus 202 for Gyeongpo and get off at the Gyeongpo Beach stop (five minutes after Seongyojang).

Ojukheon
HISTORIC BUILDING

(오죽헌; ☎648 4271; adult/youth/child ₩3000/ 2000/1000; ◷8am-6pm) Revered as the birthplace of the paragon of Korean womanhood, Sin Saimdang (1504–51), and her son, the philosopher and government official Yi Yulgok (1536–84), this complex contains one of the oldest surviving Joseon-dynasty homes. The sprawling space has the feel of an elegant park, with buildings nestled amid punctiliously maintained gardens, lotus pools and the black-stemmed bamboo groves for which the property is named.

Sin Saimdang was an accomplished poet and artist, and is traditionally regarded in Korea as a model daughter, wife and mother. Her visage graces the ₩50,000 note – a move that irked some women's groups, who say it reinforces the idea that women should devote themselves to their children at home as Sin did, teaching her son the Confucian classics.

Yi Yulgok, also known by his pen name Yiyi, appears on the ₩5000 note, with Ojukheon on its front and back. Yi won first prize in the state examination for prospective government officials and went on to serve the king. Unfortunately his advice to prepare against a possible invasion by Japan was ignored – to the kingdom's peril after Yi's death, when the Japanese invaded in 1592.

Many of Sim's paintings are on display at Ojukheon, including a delicate folding screen with eight studies of flowers and insects. The building Eojegak preserves a children's textbook which Yi authored and hand-wrote, *Gyeokmongyogyeol*.

Ojukheon is 4km from downtown Gangneung. From right outside the bus terminal, take bus 202 (₩1200, 10 minutes, every 30 minutes) and make sure it's the one heading to Gyeongpo (경포). The bus stop outside Ojukheon is well signposted.

Gangneung Seongyojang
HISTORIC BUILDING

(강릉선교장; ☎640 4799; adult/youth/child ₩3000/2000/1000; ◷9am-6.30pm) Dating back to the late Joseon dynasty, this national cultural property was for 300 years the home of a *yangban* (aristocratic) family. It was built for a descendant of the brother

Gangneung

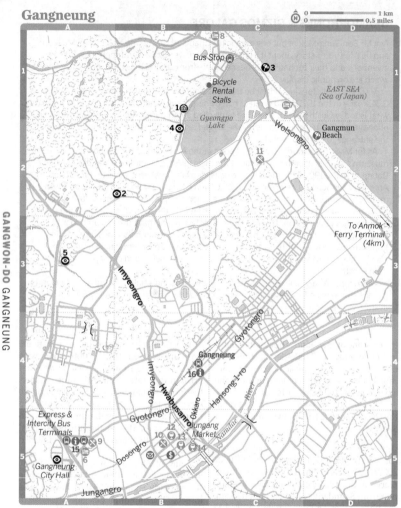

GANGWON-DO GANGNEUNG

of King Sejong (the monarch who invented *hangeul*, the Korean phonetic alphabet), and has been restored in keeping with the original floor plan and architectural style.

The complex includes residential quarters, a library and a pavilion overlooking a lotus pond. It's very pretty but somewhat lifeless, like a movie set; in fact, a number of Korean films and TV shows have been shot here. The servants quarters has unfortunately been turned into a gift shop, but you can try your hand at some traditional games outside.

To get here, take bus 202 and get off about five minutes after Ojukheon.

Gyeongpo Beach   BEACH
(경포해수욕장) The largest beach on the east coast, and the third-busiest in South Korea, has 1.8km of flat, white sand running down to moody, steel-grey waters. It's besieged by visitors during the official season (13 July to 20 August). At other times, the noisy strip of beachside restaurants and motels doesn't detract too much from the charm of the wind-twisted pine trees. There is a small **tourist information booth** (☑640 4537; ⊙9am-5pm).

Gangneung

⊙ Sights

**Gyeongpo Lake &
Gyeongpodae Pavilion**   HISTORIC BUILDING
(경포호, 경포대) Immediately behind Gyeongpo Beach is Gyeongpoho (Gyeongpo Lake), which attracts local residents looking for a little peace and quiet. It hosts a Cherry Blossom Festival in early April.

There's a 4km bicycle path along the lakeshore, passing some traditional pavilions. The most prominent of these is Gyeongpodae, from which it is poetically said that you can see five moons: the moon itself and its four reflections – in the sea (now obscured by pine trees), in the lake, in your obligatory glass of alcohol, and in your own mind.

There are **bicycle rental stalls** (per hour ₩3000) at the northern end of the lake. Gyeongpodae is a short walk from the Chamsori Gramophone & Edison Museum.

🛏 Sleeping

MGM Hotel   HOTEL $$
(MGM호텔; ☎644 2559; www.mgmhotel.co.kr; d from ₩66,000, deluxue tw from ₩77,000; ❄@) North of Gyeongpo Lake but close to the shore, the MGM sure ain't Vegas but it's comfortable enough, with relatively soft beds and all the mod cons (go for the deluxe

rooms). There's an on-site spa with large baths, too. Staff can speak a little English. Prices can double in summer. Rates rise by ₩11,000 on weekends.

Equus Motel   MOTEL $$
(에쿠스모텔; ☎643 0114; r without/with computer ₩30,000/40,000; ❄@) This love motel has sleek rooms that are the best value for money around the bus terminal. Rooms have neat black decor and enormous TVs, and better rooms come with treadmills and whirlpool baths. No English is spoken here. Rates rise by ₩10,000 on Saturday.

Hotel Hyundai Gyeongpodae   HOTEL $$$
(호텔현대 경포대; ☎651 2233; www.hyundaihotel.com/gyeongpodae/index.jsp; r ₩140,000, ste ₩300,000; ❄) Perched on a hill overlooking Gyeongpo Beach, this hotel was undergoing a major renovation at the time of research but was scheduled to reopen in 2014.

✕ Eating & Drinking

There are heaps of raw-fish and seafood restaurants along the beach, but Gangneung's prized speciality is *sundubu* (순두부), soft or uncurdled tofu made with sea water in **Chodang**, the 'tofu village'. At its plainest, *sundubu* is served warm in a bowl, with *ganjang* (soy sauce) on the side. It can also be prepared in *jjigae* (순두부찌개; stew) or *jeongol* (순두부전골; casserole).

TOP CHOICE **Todam Sundubu**   KOREAN $
(토담 순두부; ☎652 0336; www.todamsoondubu.com; meals ₩6000-10,000) In Chodang, this rustic eatery serves up simmering *sundubu* inside a quaint wooden house with floor seating. Look for the white vertical sign with red lettering beside Heogyun-Heonanseolheon Park (허균 허난설헌 유적공원). To get to Chodang, take bus 206, 207 or 230 (₩1200, 30 minutes) from outside the bus terminal.

Terarosa   ITALIAN $
(테라로사; ☎648 2760; www.terarosa.com; meals ₩6000-10,000) If it's good coffee or bread-packed breakfasts you're craving, check out this cosy cafe that roasts and brews about 20 varieties of coffee, bakes its own bread and serves sandwiches, pasta, and wraps with chilli con carne.

Haengun Sikdang   KOREAN $
(행운 식당; ☎643 3334; meals ₩6000-8000) Offers good, simple fare like *kimchi jjigae* (*kimchi* stew) or *doenjang jjigae* (soybean

paste stew); if you like squid or octopus, try the stir-fried *ojing-eo bokkeum* (오징어볶음) or *nakji bokkeum* (낙지볶음). Look for the light-brown sign and blue umbrella outside.

Bumpin' Bar
BAR

(☎644 3574; ⏰7pm-1am; @) This gem, down an alley opposite Terarosa, lives in a ramshackle wooden house with a low ceiling. Park yourself at the beautiful bar, constructed of old pine planks from a Buddhist temple, and make a request from the owner's vinyl collection of classic rock.

Rush
BAR

(☎070-8202 3233; 31-2 Gunghak-dong) This laid-back basement club has a stage with live music every weekend. Its burgers (₩7000) are worth a try if you're craving a break from Korean food.

Warehouse
BAR

(☎017-230 6389; 9-1 Seongnae-dong; ⏰8pm-3am Mon-Sat) This relocated 2nd-floor nightspot has a large bar, a pool table and, on weekends, a busy dance floor. Look for the sign above SK Telecom's corner shop.

❶ Getting There & Away

Boat

Gangneung now has a ferry to the island of Ulleungdo (p168). Services depart from the **Anmok Ferry Terminal** (☎653-8670; one-way/return ₩49,000/98,000) at 8.40am or 9am daily (2½ hours). To get to the terminal, take buses 202 or 303 (₩1200) from the bus terminal or a taxi (₩6000, 15 minutes).

Bus

Gangneung's **express** and **intercity bus terminals** share the same building, near the entrance to Hwy 7. Express buses to Seoul (₩14,000, 2½ hours) from Gangneung head to Dong-Seoul (every 40 minutes) and Gangnam (every 20 minutes). For intercity departures, see the boxed text below.

Train

Seven *Mugunghwa* (semi-express) trains connect Gangneung (₩21,300, 6 hours) daily with Seoul's Cheongnyangni station via Wonju. There's also a special 'seaside train' to Samcheok (p140).

❶ Getting Around

Buses 202 and 303 (every 25 minutes) connect the bus terminal with the train station. For bus 202, check that it's heading downtown (시내); otherwise it goes to Gyeongpo (경포). A reference sheet in English is available at tourist information centres.

Around Gangneung

The coast south of Gangneung has a couple of unique sights that merit a day trip if you have the time. Where else can you get inside a North Korean submarine?

◉ Sights

Unification Park
HISTORIC SITE

(통일 공원; ☎640 4469; adult/youth/child ₩3000/2000/1500; ⏰9am-5.30pm Mar-Oct, 9am-4.30pm Nov-Feb) The park consists of two areas: a seafront display of a warship and a North Korean submarine, and an underwhelming 'security exhibition hall' on a distant hillside with military planes parked outside it. You won't miss much if you skip the hall and head to the seafront area.

The 35m-long submarine was spying on military facilities near Gangneung in 1996 when it ran aground off Jeongdongjin. The commander burnt important documents (the fire-blackened compartment is still visible) and the 26 soldiers made a break for shore, hoping to return to North Korea. It took South Korea 49 days to capture or kill them (except one, who went missing); during the manhunt 17 South Korean civilians and soldiers were killed and 22 injured.

BUS DEPARTURES FROM GANGNEUNG

DESTINATION	PRICE (₩)	DURATION (HR)	FREQUENCY
Chuncheon	16,600	2½	every 40min
Daejeon	15,800	3½	10 daily
Samcheok	5000	1	every 10min
Sokcho	7600	1½	every 20-30min
Wonju	7600	1½	hourly

The **warship**, while considerably larger than the submarine, has a less dramatic story: built in America in 1945, it saw action in WWII and the Vietnam War, and was donated to South Korea in 1972. Its interior has been refurbished for an exhibition on Korean naval history.

Unification Park is 4km north of the Jeongdongjin train station along the coastal road. As you exit the train station, turn left and look for the bus stop along the row of restaurants. Take bus 111, 112 or 113 (₩1200, 10 minutes, hourly).

Haslla Art World   ARTS CENTRE
(하슬라아트월드; ☏644 9419; www.haslla.kr; 33-1 Gangdong-myeon, Jeongdongjin-ri San; adult/child ₩10,000/9000; ☺8.30am-6pm; 🅟) Sitting atop a hill, this park has contemporary Korean sculptures set amid a pleasant 11-hectare garden with winding paths and boardwalks. On a clear day, there are incredible sea views. It's a nice ramble for an hour or so, but the artworks are generally underwhelming, albeit quirky. They include enormous mid-air stones suspended by cables, as well as cow dung art by Choi Ok-yeong. Round up your visit with some traditional Korean tea at the Sea Café (a drink is included in the admission price).

The adjacent Haslla Museum Hotel has five art galleries, with exhibitions on subjects such as Pinocchio; they're also open to ticket holders.

The park is 1.5km north of the Jeongdongjin train station. Take bus 11, 112, 113, or 114 (₩1200, five minutes, hourly), and walk up a steep slope to the park entrance.

🛏 Sleeping

TOP CHOICE **Haslla Museum Hotel**   HOTEL **$$$**
(하슬라호텔; ☏644-9411; www.haslla.kr; d from ₩184,000; 🅧🅰🅦) This architectural oddity by the Haslla Art World is an oasis of design: beds are shaped like large wooden bowls, rooms are furnished with quirky pieces of art, and all have great ocean views. Rates rise to ₩246,000 on weekends and prices can nearly double during peak times in summer.

❶ Getting There & Away

BUS
Bus 109 (₩1600, 45 minutes, every one to two hours) leaves from the bus stop outside Gangneung's bus terminal for Jeongdongjin, which

is 20km south. Buses 111, 112 and 113 (₩1200, 35 minutes, hourly) leave from downtown Gangneung.

TRAIN
Eleven trains daily connect Jeongdongjin to Gangneung (₩2500, 15 minutes). Jeongdongjin is also a stop on the 'seaside train' that runs between Gangneung and Samcheok (see p140).

❶ Getting Around

Local buses are infrequent; taxis are a better option. A trip between any of the sights costs ₩5000 to ₩8000.

Yongpyong & Alpensia Ski Resorts
용평 알펜시아 스키 리조트
☏033
The alpine venue for the 2018 Winter Olympics to be held in Pyeongchang county, **Yongpyong** (☏335 5757; www.yongpyong.co.kr; 🅟) is one of Northeast Asia's better ski resorts, though to many foreign travellers it will seem the size of a molehill. The surrounding buildings manage to be charming without being kitschy, and on a clear day it's possible to glimpse the East Sea from the slopes.

With an average of 250cm of snow, the season runs from November to March and there are 31 slopes for skiers and snowboarders, plus mogul bumps, cross-country trails and two half-pipes. It also hosts an **International Ski Festival** in February. A lifts-and-gondola day pass costs ₩72,000/55,000 (adult/child), while a day's ski equipment rental is ₩26,000/20,000 (adult/child). Snowboards cost ₩34,000 for daytime hire. Four-hour ski classes (in English) for a group of 10 are ₩55,000/44,000 (per adult/child).

The main venue for the Winter Games will be **Alpensia** (☏339 0000; www.alpensia.com; 🅟), hosting the ceremonies, as well as ski jumping, luge and other sports. It's a good place for family skiing and kids who are learning to ski, and there's an area reserved for snowboarders. Alpensia is about a 10-minute drive from Yongpyong, and is very small, with only six runs and no expert trails. Prices (adult/child) for lift tickets are ₩65,000/48,000, ski rental ₩26,000/20,000 and board rental ₩30,000/23,000.

Sleeping

Dragon Valley Hotel
LUXURY HOTEL $$$

(드래곤밸리호텔; ☑335 5757; www.yongpyong. co.kr; r ₩250,000, ste ₩530,000; ✳☀☎) The nicest hotel in Yongpyong, this is close to the slopes and has attentive staff and good rooms.

Holiday Inn Alpensia
Pyeongchang Suites
LUXURY HOTEL $$$

(☑339 0000; www.holidayinn.com; d from ₩154,600, ste from ₩181,000; ✳☎) Right at the foot of Alpensia's slopes, this large new Holiday Inn complex has Western, Korean-style and wheelchair-accessible rooms. Room design is utilitarian but modern. There are cafes, restaurants and shops in the complex.

Yongpyong Hostel
HOSTEL $

(용평호스텔; ☑335 5757; www.yongpyong.co.kr; dm ₩11,000, r up to 14 people ₩70,000; ✳) Hidden among the pines like a Swiss chalet, this is a good budget option that's only three minutes from the slopes. It doesn't have any lounges to socialise in, but it's a good place to crash. It's open November to March and 14 July to 19 August.

Getting There & Away

From Gangneung's intercity bus terminal, take a bus to Hoenggye (₩2300, 30 minutes, every 10 to 15 minutes), from where you can catch a free **shuttle bus** (10 minutes, 15 daily, operates 5.30am to 11.30pm) for Yongpyong. The latter are violet and marked with the resort name. They wait across the street, to the left as you exit from the bus terminal at Hoenggye. A taxi from Hoenggye to Yongpyong costs ₩7000.

Buses run to Hoenggye from Dong-Seoul (₩13,800, hourly). The resort also has a **private shuttle bus** (☑02-2201 7710, round-trip adult/ child ₩28,000/22,000) operating twice daily from Seoul's Jamsil Station (2½ hours).

Odaesan National Park
오대산 국립공원

This **park** (☑332 6417; http://english.knps.or.kr; admission free; ☺9am-7pm) has great hiking, superb views and two prominent Buddhist temples, Woljeong-sa and Sangwon-sa. Like Seoraksan, Odaesan (Five Peaks Mountain) is a high-altitude massif; the best times to visit are late spring and early to mid-autumn, when the foliage colours are richest.

There are two main entrances to the park: from the south at Dongsan-ri and from the northwest at Sogeumgang. The former leads to the temples and the main hiking trail.

Sights & Activities

Woljeong-sa
TEMPLE

(월정사; ☑339 6800; www.woljeongsa.org; admission incl Sangwon-sa adult/youth/child ₩2500/ 1000/400; ☺5am-9pm) The Shilla-era temple was founded in AD 645 by the Zen Master Jajang to enshrine relics of the historical Buddha. Although it fell victim to fires and was even flattened during the Korean War, one treasured structure that has survived from the Goryeo dynasty is the octagonal nine-storey pagoda in the main courtyard, with the figure of a kneeling bodhisattva before it. The younger buildings around it are decorated with intricate religious art. There is a **museum** (☺9.30am-5.30pm Apr-Oct, 9.30am-4.30pm Nov-Mar, closed Tue) of Joseon-era Buddhist art and you can arrange a temple stay (p386) here.

Sangwon-sa
TEMPLE

(상원사; ☑332 6666; www.woljeongsa.org; admission incl Woljeong-sa adult/youth/child ₩2500/ 1000/400) Ten kilometres beyond Woljeongsa is Sangwon-sa, where the hiking trail begins. The temple's intricately decorated bronze bell was cast in AD 725 and is the oldest bell in Korea (and one of the largest as well). Another prized object is the wooden statue of the bodhisattva of wisdom Munsu (in Sanskrit, Manjusri) – made in the 15th century, it is said, on the order of King Sejo after the bodhisattva cured his skin disease.

Hiking Trails
HIKING

The main hiking trail begins at Sangwon-sa and is a fairly steep 6.5km climb to the highest peak **Birobong** (1563m), about three hours round-trip. Gung-ho hikers can continue from Birobong along a ridge to **Sangwangbong** (1493m), then back down to the road and to the temple (12.5km, five hours).

A separate trail runs 13.3km from Sogeumgang to **Jingogae**, passing several waterfalls, including **Guryong Pokpo** and **Nagyeong Pokpo**, and **Noinbong** (1338m). The route takes about seven hours one way. The trail linking Jingogae to the western half of Odaesan is currently closed for restoration.

Sleeping & Eating

A small **minbak village** with restaurants is on the left side of the access road, about 1km from the turnoff from Hwy 6. It's a 40-minute walk south of Woljeong-sa, or you can take the bus. Halfway between the

Odaesan National Park

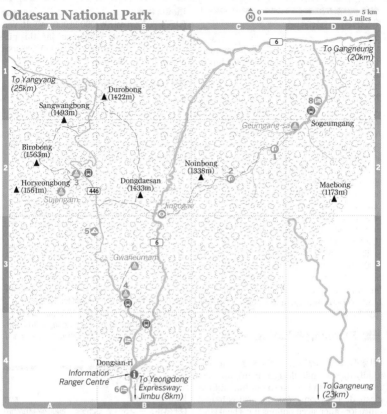

temples is **Dongpigol Camping Ground** (per tent ₩3000-6000). Sogeumgang also has a **minbak village** and **camping ground**.

Kensington Flora Hotel   LUXURY HOTEL **$$$**
(켄싱턴 플로라호텔; ☎330 5000; www.kensingtonflorahotel.co.kr; r ₩180,000, ste ₩280,000; ✳✳✳) Formerly known as the Odaesan Hotel, this tall deluxe hotel is about 2.5km from the southern park entrance, with sweeping views all around. Rooms are suitably plush and during low season discounts of up to 50% are possible.

ⓘ Getting There & Away

To get to the southern park entrance near Dongsan-ri, take an intercity bus from Gangneung (₩4000, 50 minutes, every 10 minutes) to Jinbu. At Jinbu, local buses (₩1200, 12 per day) run from the bus terminal to Woljeong-sa (20 minutes) and Sangwon-sa (another 20 minutes). Look out for the white buses towards the rear of the terminal lot. Bus schedules are

Odaesan National Park

◉ Sights

ⓛ Sleeping

helpfully posted at all these stops, or you can get them from Gangneung's tourist information centres.

To get to Sogeumgang, take local bus 303 (₩1200, 50 minutes, hourly) from right outside the Gangneung bus terminal. It drops you at the *minbak* village; it's 500m to the park ranger station and the hiking trail begins another 500m beyond.

Samcheok 삼척

☎033 / POP 80,000

Sedate little Samcheok is the gateway to an unusual mix of sightseeing spots. Within an hour's bus ride are spectacular limestone caves, an inimitable 'penis park' (phallic sculptures, not body parts) and pretty beaches tucked away in quiet coves. The town has a rousing Full Moon Festival in February, with tug-of-war competitions.

The only sightseeing spot in town is the **Mystery of Caves Exhibition** (동굴 신비관; ☎574 6828; adult/youth/child ₩3000/2000/1500; ⊙9am-6pm Mar-Oct, 9am-5pm Nov-Feb; 🖭), in a building that resembles a wedding cake dripping with brown icing. The exhibits (some in English) contain elaborate detail on cave formation and there's a 20-minute IMAX film at 10.30am, 2pm and 3pm.

The **tourist information centre** (☎575 1330; http://eng.samcheok.go.kr; ⊙9am-6pm) is beside the express bus terminal. Detailed bus schedules are available in English for buses to Hwanseongul and Haesindang Park (p140).

🛏 Sleeping & Eating

Star Motel　　　　　　　　　　MOTEL $
(한일장; ☎574 8277; r ₩30,000; ❄@) Run by a kindly *ajeossi* (middle-aged man), this motel is starting to look worn out but still has clean, decent rooms. Ask the nearby tourist office for other sleep options if it's booked.

Eunmi Gamjatang　　　　　　KOREAN $
(은미 감자탕; ☎574 5333; meals ₩5000-8000) This friendly eatery specialises in hearty *gamjatang* (meaty bones and potato soup) served in a *jeongol* (hotpot) or *ttukbaegi* (뚝배기; earthenware dish); you'll need at least two people to order it. Solo diners can try the *galbitang* or *yukgaejang* (spicy beef soup with vegetables).

Buona Pizza　　　　　　ITALIAN $$
(☎574 8030; meals ₩7000-18,000; 🖭) If you need a break from Korean cuisine, this pizzeria across from Samcheok Post Office does a decent enough job.

❶ Getting There & Away

Bus

The express and intercity bus terminals sit beside each other. Express buses to Seoul (₩15,900, 3½ hours) run to Gangnam (every 35 minutes) and Dong-Seoul (hourly). For intercity bus departures, see the boxed text below.

Train

A special 'seaside train' runs between Samcheok and Gangneung. Train carriages have been remodelled so that passengers face the extra-large windows looking out to sea (instead of the conventional front-back arrangement). From Samcheok, the train makes stops at Donghae, Jeongdongjin and several beach stations before terminating at Gangneung (₩12,000 or ₩15,000, one hour 20 minutes). The sea views are lovely, but the route also passes some unattractive stretches of industrial landscape.

Trains depart Samcheok at 12.10pm and 3.42pm, and return from Gangneung at 10.24am and 2.10pm. There are extra services in May and August.

Around Samcheok

Hwanseongul　　　　　　　　CAVE
(환선굴; ☎570 3255; adult/youth/child ₩4000/2800/2000; ⊙8.30am-6.30pm Mar-Oct, 9.30am-5.30pm Nov-Feb) One of the largest caves in Asia, with almost 2km of steel stairways that take visitors through cathedral-sized caverns – up, down and around its varied formations. As with many caves in Korea, while Hwanseongul's natural beauty is breathtaking, garish lighting and kitschy names have been added to 'enhance' the experience. Some nifty formations to look

BUS DEPARTURES FROM SAMCHEOK

DESTINATION	PRICE (₩)	DURATION (HR)	FREQUENCY
Busan	28,200	4½r	3 daily
Daegu	28,300	5	6 daily
Gangneung	5000	1	every 15min
Sokcho	11,000	3½	3 daily
Taebaek	6000	1	hourly
Wonju	12,600	3½	1 daily

out for are the heart-shaped hole over the correspondingly named Bridge of Love, the rimstone that resembles a fried egg, and a difficult-to-spot calcite growth that resembles a tiny statue of the Virgin Mary.

Bus 60 (₩2900, 45 minutes, departures 8.20am, 10.20am, 2.20pm) heads from Samcheok's intercity bus terminal for the cave. The last bus leaves the cave at 7.30pm.

Haesindang Park
PARK

(해신당 공원; ☏570 3568; adult/youth/child ₩3000/2000/1500; ☉9am-6pm Mar-Oct, 9am-5pm Nov-Feb, closed Mon) Of all the things you'd expect to find in a fishing village like Sinnam (신남), odds are a 'penis park' is not one of them. There are over 50 phallic sculptures, some taking the form of park benches or drums. These carvings were entered for a contest in Samcheok's now-defunct Penis Sculpture Festival; today they attract joshing *ajumma* and *ajeossi* (married or older women and men). There's an elaborate series representing the 12 animals of the Chinese zodiac and outside the park stands a red lighthouse with the same, uh, peculiarities.

The phallic obsession originates with a local legend about a drowned virgin whose restless spirit was affecting the village's catch. A fisherman discovered that she could be appeased if he answered the call of nature while facing the ocean, so the village put up phalluses to placate her. A small shrine to this spirit stands at the seaward end of the park.

The park also contains the Fishing Village Folk Museum (어촌 민속 전시관), focusing on the history of fishing and shamanist rituals in the region, and sexual iconography in other cultures.

From Samcheok's intercity bus terminal, take bus 24 (₩1700, 40 minutes, 20km, hourly) from the platform on the right. You can enter Haesindang Park from the top of the headland (where there's a huge parking lot) or from the entrance in Sinnam. The easier walk is to start at the top, work your way down and exit at the village.

Beaches

The closest beaches are Samcheok Beach (삼척 해수욕장), found immediately to the north of town, and Maengbang Beach (맹방 해수욕장), about 12km south. The former has shallow waters, making it popular with families, and the usual assortment of motels and restaurants. Maengbang Beach has no

buildings, although tented stalls spring up during beach season (10 July to 20 August). It's less frantic than Samcheok Beach, but the downside is that it's about a 2km walk (20 minute) from the bus stop.

Bus 11 (₩1200, 20 minutes, five daily) runs from Samcheok's intercity bus terminal to Samcheok Beach. Maengbang Beach is on the route for bus 21, 23, and 24 (₩1200, 25 minutes).

Taebaek 태백

☏033 / POP 51,000

This dinky mountain town is the main jumping-off point for visitors to Taebaeksan Provincial Park. The train station, bus terminal, tourist information centre (☏550 2828; http://tour.taebaek.go.kr; ☉9am-5pm), accommodation and motels are bunched up around a small roundabout just off the town's main street. Taebaek has longer winters and cooler summers than the rest of the country. It hosts the lively Taebaeksan Snow Festival at the end of January, with giant ice sculptures, sledding and igloo restaurants.

ⓘ Getting There & Away

Buses connect Taebaek to various destinations such as Dong-Seoul (₩23,800, 3 hours, hourly), Samcheok (₩6000, 1¼ hours, hourly), and Busan (₩30,700, 4 hours, six daily). Six trains run to Gangneung (₩6800, two hours) and five to Seoul's Cheongnyangni station (₩15,500, 4 hours) daily.

Taebaeksan Provincial Park 태백산 도립공원

The centrepiece of this park (☏550 2740; adult/youth/child ₩2000/1500/700; ☉sunrise-sunset) is Taebaeksan (Big White Mountain) – for shamanists, one of the most sacred mountains in Korea. The summit is Janggunbong (1568m), and nearby is Cheonjedan (천제단), an altar connected with Korea's mythical founder Dangun. The stark stone structure stands 3m high and is believed to have been used since the Shilla dynasty. Ceremonies are performed here on New Year's Day and during the Taebaek folk festival (Taebaekje; 태백제) from 3 to 5 October. There is a shrine to Dangun (단군성전), with a rare outdoor statue of its namesake, about 800m from the park entrance.

Cheonjedan is a 4.5km hike northwest from the park entrance; allow 2½ hours to get there. The other peak, Munsubong (1546m), is 4km from the park entrance and 3km from Cheonjedan. The park is especially crowded during Taebaekje and when the royal azaleas bloom in June. Most of the hiking signs are in Korean only.

Near the park entrance is a shrine of a different sort: **Taebaek Coal Museum** (태백 석탄 박물관; www.coalmuseum.or.kr; ☏552 7720; admission included with park entrance fee; ☺9am-5pm; 🐾), with a mine-head contraption at one end. The extensive exhibits document the history of coal mining in Korea and this region, which used to be the country's main coal-mining area.

If you're spending the night, the prefab-looking tourist village beside the park entrance is a nicer option than the town.

❶ Getting There & Away

Bus 33 leaves from Taebaek's bus terminal (₩1200, 25 minutes, every 30 minutes).

Wonju 원주

♫033 / POP 306,000

The closest major town to Chiaksan National Park, **Wonju** (http://english.wonju.go.kr/) is home to several universities and military bases. If you must spend the night, there are decent restaurants and love motels around the express bus terminal. There is no tourist information centre here.

❶ Getting There & Away

From the express bus terminal buses run to Seoul Gangnam (₩10,000, 1½ hours, every 10-15 minutes), Gangneung (₩7600, 1½ hours, hourly) and Gwangju (₩28,000, 4 hours, every 2 hours). Buses from the intercity bus terminal head to Cheongju (₩8400, 1½ hours, hourly).

Trains (₩7900, 2½ hours, hourly) run between Wonju and Seoul's Cheongnyangni station.

Chiaksan National Park
치악산 국립공원

This **park** (☏732 5231; http://english.knps.or.kr; free admission, parking ₩2000; ☺sunrise-sunset) may be the smallest of the national parks in Gangwon-do, but it offers challenging **hikes**

Chiaksan National Park

and is a very doable weekend trip from Seoul. A popular but strenuous route starts from **Guryong-sa** (구룡사; Nine Dragon Temple) up to 1288m-high Birobong (three hours, 5.6km); it's possible to continue another 5.4km (two hours) down to **Hwanggol** (황골). There are also hiking trails from **Geumdae-ri** and **Seongnam-ri**, running about 6km to the peak Namdaebong (1181m).

The main *minbak* and restaurant village is outside the Guryong-sa entrance. There are **camping grounds** (Geumdae-ri ☏731-1289; ₩9000) in summer available at **Daegok** near Guryong-sa and Geumdae-ri. There are no mountain shelters.

❶ Getting There & Away

To get to Guryong-sa, exit Wonju's intercity bus terminal and take a taxi (₩2200) to Wonju train station. Take bus 41 (₩1200, 40 minutes, every 25 minutes), which drop you at the car park near the park entrance. Guryong-sa is 800m in.

Bus 82 runs a loop service to Hwanggol (₩1200, 30 minutes, hourly), while bus 21 runs to Geumdae-ri and Seongnam-ri (₩1200). At Hwanggol, the bus can be picked up at the stop opposite the Italian restaurant Pino.

Gyeongsangbuk-do

Best Places to Stay

» Taegu Grand Hotel (p146)
» Sarangchae (p160)
» Nahbi Guest House (p160)
» Rak Ko Jae Hahoe (p175)
» Design Motel A2 (p166)

Best Places to Eat

» Bulgogi Myeongya (p162)
» Gaejeung (p148)
» Kisoya (p162)
» Dijon (p148)
» 99 Sikdang (p171)

Why Go?

Korea's cultural warehouse, Gyeongsangbuk-do (경상북도) is a region resplendent both in natural beauty and heritage sites, including many fascinating temples, ancient pagodas, rock-carved Buddhas and tombs. Gyeongju is often called 'the museum without walls' for its historical treasures, many of which are outdoors. The oddly symmetrical *tumuli* (burial mounds) in the centre of town are serene pyramids – stately reminders of the dead they still honour.

The region's major city, Daegu, is a sprawling place with an excellent medicinal herb market, a downtown drenched in neon and superb restaurants. Elsewhere, don't miss Haein-sa, a must-see temple-library amid gorgeous mountain scenery that contains the Tripitaka Koreana, 1000-year-old wooden tablets inscribed with sacred Buddhist texts and ingeniously preserved in a building so ahead of its time that modern science hasn't improved it. Off the coast is the rugged island of Ulleungdo, with seemingly endless opportunities to enjoy spectacular coastal landscapes.

When to Go

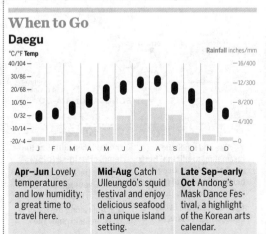

Daegu

Apr–Jun Lovely temperatures and low humidity; a great time to travel here.

Mid-Aug Catch Ulleungdo's squid festival and enjoy delicious seafood in a unique island setting.

Late Sep–early Oct Andong's Mask Dance Festival, a highlight of the Korean arts calendar.

History

At the centre of South Korea, this area was once the capital of the Shilla empire (57 BC–AD 935), and as such was a central part of Korean government and trade. During this almost 1000-year-long empire, the Shilla rulers created alliances with China to defeat Japanese threats, as well as to repel other Korean invaders. During this time Confucian laws were widely adopted and informed all aspects of Korean life, including who, where and when a person could marry.

Daegu 대구

♩053 / POP 2.45 MILLION

South Korea's fourth largest city is a pleasant and progressive place with a fascinating traditional-medicine market, some excellent eating options and a humming downtown that's good fun to explore. The city is a popular place for exchange students and English teachers, and the large student population gives Daegu a young and carefree feel.

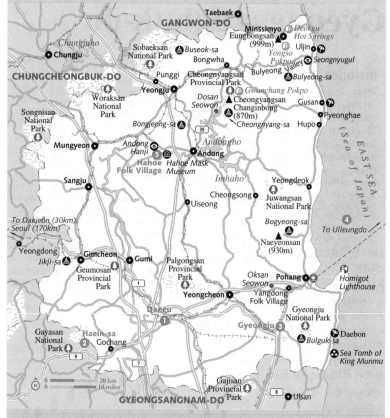

Gyeongsangbuk-do Highlights

① See and smell the fascinating **medicinal herb market** (p145) in Daegu before partaking of great eating in the city's downtown

② Marvel at the 80,000-plus wooden tablets of

the Buddhist sutras at the temple **Haein-sa** (p152)

③ Slip back into the Shilla era in **Gyeongju** (p154), the 'museum without walls'

④ Walk along the rocky coastline and enjoy the

stunning scenery and great seafood of **Ulleungdo** (p168)

⑤ Admire centuries-old architecture and an unchanged way of life in **Hahoe Folk Village** (p175)

A simple, two-line subway system makes getting around easy, and Daegu is also a great hub for day trips; be sure to check out Haein-sa (p152) and Jikji-sa (p153), both of which offer temple stays for those wishing to immerse themselves in traditional local culture.

◉ Sights

FREE **Daegu National Museum**   MUSEUM
(국립 대구 박물관; Map p146; ☎768 6051; http://daegu.museum.go.kr; ☺9am-6pm Tue-Fri, to 7pm Sat, Sun & holidays, closed Mon) Following a total refit in 2010, this excellent museum now enjoys English labelling throughout most of its collection – and what a collection. Armour, jewellery, Buddhist relics from various different eras, Confucian manuscripts, clothing and textiles are all beautifully displayed in well-lit glass cases and there's normally at least one or two temporary exhibits here as well. From Banwoldang subway, take bus 414 or 349 to Daegu National Museum, or from Dongdaegu station take bus 414 from the bus stop across the road on the bridge. The electric boards inside the bus will announce 'Nat'l Museum' when you're there.

FREE **Bullo-dong Tumuli Park**   PARK
(불로동 고분 공원; off Map p146; ☎940 1224; ☺9am-6pm) If you're already in the north end of the city, stop by Bullo-dong Tumuli Park, an enormous open space covering some 330,000 sq metres. The grassy hillocks that rise like bumps across the valley are *tumuli* (burial mounds, similar to those in Gyeongju). Dating from the 2nd to the 6th century AD, the *tumuli* are for both nobles and commoners – the higher the location on the hill, the higher the status of the person.

Greenvill   BATHHOUSE
(그린빌 찜질방 사우나; Map p148; admission sauna ₩5000, sauna & bed ₩7000; ☺24hr; Ⓜ Line 1 or 2 to Banwoldang, Exit 1) This centrally located bathhouse and *jjimjil-bang* is not large, but has a soothing mixture of hot, warm and cold tubs. The spacious *jjimjil-bang* has a scorching-hot room (81°C) and an ice-cold room. It's a 24-hour facility, so guests can sleep overnight, making it a great budget sleeping option if you're just spending one night in town. Take the lift to the basement.

DAEGU'S HERBAL MEDICINE MARKET

This **market** (한약 시장; Map p148; Ⓜ Line 1 or 2, Banwoldang, Exit 4), west of the central shopping district, has a history as vast as its scope. It dates from 1658, making it Korea's oldest and still one of its largest. Begin at the **Yangnyeong Exhibition Hall** (☎257 4729; admission free; ☺9am-5pm, closed Sun) for an introduction to *insam* (ginseng), reindeer horns and the people who popularised them – there's usually someone who speaks English at the tourist booth outside who'll show you around. Then head out to the street to stock up on everything from lizards' tails to magic mushrooms (the latter only with a prescription); you might also catch a glimpse of someone receiving acupuncture. On the days ending with 1 or 6 (except the 31st), *yangnyeong sijang* (a wholesale market) takes place downstairs in the exhibition hall.

Life Spa   BATHHOUSE
(수목원 생활 온천; off Map p146; www.lifespa.kr; admission ₩10,000; ☺24hr; Ⓜ Line 1 to Jincheon) Located in western Daegu, this spa is a beautiful facility with 1100 sq metres of tubs and sweat rooms, a fitness centre and rooftop pools. Take the subway to Jincheon station, Exit 3. Walk to the intersection and turn right. From here, it's a quick taxi ride; ask for *'sumokwon saengwol oncheon'* (수목원 생활 온천).

☞ Tours

Palgongsan tours   BUS TOUR
(Map p146; adult/youth ₩6000/4000) Travellers with limited time might consider this tour, with six daily departures starting at 10am. Jump on and off the bus at some of the area's best sites. Buy a ticket and get on the bus at the Dongdaegu station tourist information booth.

🛏 Sleeping

Novotel Daegu City Center   LUXURY HOTEL $$$
(대구 노보텔; Map p148; ☎664 1101; www.novotel.com/7038; r from ₩142,000; Ⓜ Line 1, Jungangno, Exit 3; 🕸@🛜) There's a real lack of sleeping options in Daegu's busy downtown and, if you want to sleep in comfort, this

Daegu

sleek and modern high-rise Novotel is your best bet. Reception is on the 8th floor and so all the rooms have great views, even if they can be a little on the small side. Other attractions include a sauna, a superb breakfast buffet (₩22,000) and a smart terrace bar for evening drinks.

Taegu Grand Hotel
LUXURY HOTEL $$$
(대구 그랜드 호텔; Map p146; ☑742 0001; www.taegugrand.co.kr; r from ₩274,000; MLine 2, Beomeo, Exit 3; ※@🖥) This immaculate property blends minimalism with style and touches like king-sized beds and widescreen TVs. The location is great and the rooms are extremely comfortable, and there are more liveried bellboys and pruned bonsai trees than you'll know what to do with.

Danim Backpackers
HOSTEL $
(다님; off Map p148; ☑8270 7532 9119; www.danim backpackers.com; dm incl breakfast ₩20,000; MLine 1 or 2 to Banwoldang, Exit 9; ※@🖥) This

brand new youth hostel is just what Daegu has been crying out for. With just 12 beds in two dorms (one of which is female only), it's a tiny place with the feel of an apartment, but it's got all the necessary facilities, including a great location a short stroll away from the neon-drenched streets of downtown, a communal kitchen, free use of laundry facilities, a rooftop, free PC use and a decent breakfast. Staff are English speaking and very keen to help, and there's even a small bar down the road for guests to hang out in.

Jingolmok Guesthouse
HOSTEL $
(진골목; Map p148; ☑8270 7504 4115; www. danimbackpackers.com; Jingolmok dm/tw incl breakfast ₩20,000/50,000; MLine 1 or 2 to Banwoldang, Exit 15; ※@🖥) The second property in Daegu from the team behind Danim Backpackers, Jingolmok is located in the heart of the herbal medicine market amid traditional courtyard houses and boasts

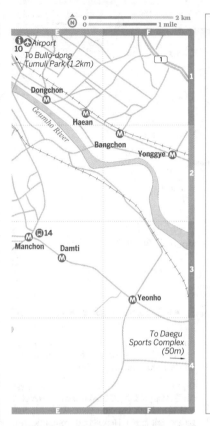

three dorms and a twin bedroom. The price includes the use of a communal kitchen, PC use and access to a great roof terrace.

Rojan Motel　　　　　　　　　MOTEL **$**
(로잔 모텔; Map p146; ☎766 0336; r ₩25,000; 🚇Line 2 to Beomeo, Exit 4; ❄) One of the best deals in Daegu – if not the whole region – is this spotless, no-frills motel, which offers clean, crisp sheets and a private bathroom. Credit cards accepted, but there's no internet. The location is good, with easy access to downtown and plenty of nearby restaurants.

Hera Motel　　　　　　　　LOVE HOTEL **$$**
(헤라모텔; Map p146; ☎958 2200; d/tw from ₩50,000/70,000; 🚇Line 1 to Dongdaegu, Exit 1; ❄@) Very conveniently located next to Dongdaegu station, this fabulously kooky love hotel is a reliable choice in an area dominated by downtrodden inns with ₩30,000 rooms. Enormous rooms with queen-sized beds, widescreen TVs and modern bathrooms (including cushions in the bath tubs and rain showers) make a stay here comfortable, even if the decor can be garish. Turn right out of Dongdaegu station, walk down to the pedestrian bridge, but do not cross. Walk right down the steps to the street. It's straight ahead on the right.

Hotel Ariana　　　　　　　　　HOTEL **$$**
(호텔 아리아나; Map p146; ☎765 7776; www.ariana.co.kr; r from ₩120,000; 🚇Line 2 to Beomeo, Exit 4; ❄🛜) This smart and well-run property has fairly anodyne rooms, but they're comfortable and spacious and the location is good, near the Deurangil restaurant district and an easy bus ride to downtown. Each room has a double and single bed and the staff is friendly, even though their English is limited. There's no breakfast served here, but there's the good Caffe Boccaccio on the ground floor, which does coffee, pastries and even pizzas.

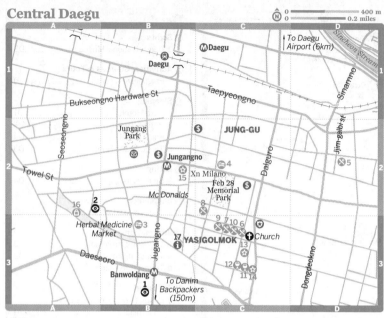

Central Daegu

✗ Eating

Around the Yasigolmok downtown district
(Map p148) you'll find literally hundreds of
cafes, bars and nightclubs – endless choice
for all forms of entertainment. A couple of
other areas worth checking out for good
restaurant selection include Deurangil (Map
p146), which specialises in Korean *hanu*
beef as well as a variety of other Asian cuisines, and the busy area around Gyeongbuk
University, which is full of student bars and
restaurants serving cheap and delicious
chicken dishes.

TOP CHOICE Gaejeong KOREAN $
(개정; Map p148; dishes ₩5000-10,000; ⊙11am-
10pm; MLine 1 to Jungangno, Exit 2; 🖥) This
excellent-value place serves up divine but
healthy traditional Korean food over three
floors, so even if it's packed they'll usually
be able to find you a seat. If you come here,
don't hesitate to order the special rice with
vegetables in a stone pot – surely one of the
best dishes in Daegu!

Geumgok Samgyetang KOREAN $$
(금곡 삼계탕; Map p148; mains ₩12,000;
⊙11am-10pm; MLine 1 to Jungangno, Exit 2; 🖥)
A local favourite in easy walking distance
of the downtown markets. Order one of the

three menu items: ginseng-infused chicken,
barbecue chicken, or a half-order of the lat-
ter (₩6000) – all are sublime.

Dijon FRENCH $$$
(디존; Map p148; ☎422 2426; mains from ₩27,000;
⊙11.30am-10pm, last order 9pm; MLine 1 to Jungangno, Exit 2; 🖥) Here's that romantic restaurant you were looking for. Come here for
French and Mediterranean dishes like grilled
snapper with mussels in lemon butter sauce,
or roast pork with apple-cider sauce. First im-
pressions inside the door are tasteful: a dimly
lit ambiance, a hint of garlic in the air, a rose
on every table and professional service.

Into EUROPEAN $$
(인투; Map p148; dishes ₩9000-14,000; ⊙noon-
11pm; MLine 1 to Jungangno, Exit 2; 🖥) A tiny
European-style cafe that serves fine pastas
and tasty salads. With just four dining ta-
bles, it looks and smells like someone's
home kitchen. French and Italian dishes are
the specialities with a menu that changes
regularly and a full set meal available daily
for ₩22,000.

Bongsan Jjim-galbi KOREAN $$
(봉산 찜갈비; Map p148; dishes from ₩7000;
⊙10am-10pm; MLine 1 to Jungangno, Exit 2;
🖥) Located on Daegu's famous *jjim-galbi*

Central Daegu

🍷 Drinking

The central shopping district is teeming with *hof* (local pubs), singing rooms, bars and cafes. There's a small gay district with a few bars near the Express bus terminal.

Buddha　　　　　　　　　　　　　BAR

(부다; Map p148; ⊙5pm-5am; Ⓜ Line 1 or 2 to Banwoldang, Exit 3) One of the city's funkiest bar-restaurants. Wine bottles and candles line the entrance, there's a hint of incense in the air and private rooms are created by sheer drapes. Remove your shoes at the entrance. It's between the Bus pub and G2 club.

Bus　　　　　　　　　　　　　　BAR

(버스; Map p148; ⊙5pm-10am; Ⓜ Line 1 or 2 to Banwoldang, Exit 3) This unmistakable bus-turned-pub is on a side street right near G2 club. It's a popular hangout with students and serves food and drink all night.

☆ Entertainment

There is a huge Xn Milano complex that houses the **Hanil Gukjang cinema** (Map p148; Ⓜ Line 1 to Jungangno, Exit 2), where there are often English-language movies.

G2　　　　　　　　　　　　　　CLUB

(Map p148; admission before/after 10pm ₩15,000/ 20,000; ⊙8pm-9am; Ⓜ Line 1 or 2 to Banwoldang, Exit 3) Bump around in trance-inducing, blacklit darkness. The funk, hip-hop and reggae are ear-splitting – just the way most of the crowd wants it.

Frog　　　　　　　　　　　　　CLUB

(Map p148; admission ₩15,000, US soldiers ₩8000; ⊙9pm-6am; Ⓜ Line 1 or 2 to Banwoldang, Exit 3) Five floors of hip-hop and electronic music for you and a few thousand of your closest friends.

🛍 Shopping

Daegu is a shopper's dream. In addition to good prices on brand-name goods (clothes, shoes, bags etc) at the various department stores and amid the neon of downtown, Daegu has numerous speciality markets that make for a fascinating stroll even if you're not going to part with any won.

Seomun Market　　　　　　　　MARKET

(서문시장; Map p146; ⊙9am-6pm Mar-Oct, to 5pm Nov-Feb, closed 2nd & 4th Sun; Ⓜ Line 2 to Seomun Market, Exit 1) Start at this hulking, multistorey complex with over 4000 stalls in six sections. Bustling but orderly, it's been one of Korea's big-three markets since 1669,

(slow-cooked beef ribs) street, this quaint restaurant has been serving spicy steamed beef for 40 years. The friendly owner, Mr Choi, speaks English and is happy to accommodate customers who prefer less spice in their food.

Seokryujip　　　　　　　　KOREAN $$

(석류집; Map p146; ☑ meals from ₩10,000; ⊙10am-10pm; Ⓜ Line 2 to Beomeo, Exit 3) Dog or goat, which do you prefer? Try both at this delightful traditional dining room and see for yourself if Korea's fabled stamina-producing food really works. From the main street, it's just next to the SK petrol station – look for the traditional tiled roof.

Gimbapjjang　　　　　　　NOODLES $

(김밥짱; Map p148; dishes ₩2000-5000; ⊙10am-2am; Ⓜ Line 1 to Jungangno, Exit 2) Nearly across the street from Gaejeong, *naengmyeon* (냉면; buckwheat noodles in an icy broth) and *mandu* (만두; dumplings) are on the menu at rock-bottom prices. There's no English menu, but there is a pictorial one.

DAEGU BUS DEPARTURES

Departures from the express bus terminal

DESTINATION	PRICE (₩)	DURATION	FREQUENCY
Andong	9000	1½hr	every 20min
Busan	9300	1¾hr	hourly
Daejeon	13,000	2hr	hourly
Dongseoul	24,400	4hr	hourly
Gyeongju	4600	50min	every 40min
Jinju	12,500	2¼hr	hourly
Seoul	24,100	4hr	every 10min

Departures from the intercity bus terminals

DESTINATION	TERMINAL	PRICE (₩)	DURATION (HR)	FREQUENCY
Andong	Bukbu	9300	1½	every 30min
Busan	Seobu	9200	2	every 1½ hr
Chuncheon	Bukbu	19,500	5½	5 daily
Gyeongju	Dongbu	4600	1	every 15min
Haein-sa	Seobu	6600	1½	every 40min
Jinju	Seobu	8600	2	hourly
Pohang	Dongbu	8900	1½	every 10min
Tongyeong	Seobu	12,800	2½	every 50min

even if the current buildings have little of that historic character. Outside the subway exit, turn 180 degrees and walk around the corner.

Yasigolmok   MARKET
(야시골목; Map p148; MLine 1 to Jungangno, Exit 2) This is the heart of Daegu's shopping district, with clothing and fashion outlets, bustling day and night.

ⓘ Information

Daegu has a **tourist information centre** (☑053 1330, 627 8900; ◷9am-6pm) at all major transit points and destinations including the airport, outside Dongdaegu station, at Duryu Park (all Map p146), in the central shopping district and by the herbal medicine market (both Map p148). All have helpful English-speaking staff, comprehensive local maps in English and reams of pamphlets.

ⓘ Getting There & Away

Air

Asiana and Korean Air connect Daegu with Seoul and Jeju. International destinations include Shanghai, Bangkok and Beijing.

Bus

There are five bus terminals in Daegu (all Map p146): an **express (Gosok) bus terminal** (☑743 3701; MLine 1 to Dongdaegu, Exit 4) by Dongdaegu train station, plus **Dongbu (East)** (☑756 0017; MLine 1 to Dongdaegu, Exit 4), **Seobu (West)** (☑656 1583; MLine 1, Seongdangmot, Exit 3), **Nambu (South)** and **Bukbu (North)** (☑357 1851; MLine 2, Duryu, Exit 1) intercity terminals. Note that buses to some destinations leave from multiple terminals, so it may be worth checking departure times of several terminals if you're looking for a bus at a specific time.

The express bus terminal is four separate buildings, each housing different companies. For departures from the express bus terminal and the intercity bus terminals, see the boxed text above.

Train

Dongdaegu station on the east side of the city is the main station for long-distance trains. It's near the express bus terminal. Daegu station, closer to downtown, is mostly for *Tonggeun* (commuter-class) and *Mugunghwa* (semi-express) trains.

You'll find good connections to Seoul and Busan. KTX (high-speed) trains run every 10 to 30 minutes to Seoul (₩37,500, two hours). A frequent KTX service to Busan is available (₩14,400, one hour), though consider *Saemaul* (express; ₩10,600, 1¼ hours) or *Mugunghwa* (₩7200, 1½ hours) services to increase your departure options without adding a significant amount of travel time. Check www.korail.go.kr for schedules and fares.

❶ Getting Around

To/From the Airport

Daegu's airport is northeast of the city, about 2km from the express bus terminal. From downtown, take Line 1 to Ayanggyo station, Exit 3, and catch bus 401, 101 or Express 1. A taxi from the airport to the centre will cost around ₩10,000 and take about 20 minutes.

Bus & Subway

Local bus fares are ₩1200, but can vary with longer routes. To get to Deurangil from central Daegu or Dongdaegu station, take bus 401. From Dongdaegu train station, exit the building and walk right to the pedestrian bridge. Do not cross the bridge, instead walk right down the stairs. The bus stop is down the road. Two subway lines crisscross the city centre; tokens also cost ₩1200.

Around Daegu

PALGONGSAN PROVINCIAL PARK
팔공산 도립공원

Just 20km north of Daegu, this park is sprawling, mountainous and well visited. Its highest peak, Palgongsan ('Mountain of the Eight Meritorious Officers'; 1192m) received its name at around the end of the Shilla period after eight generals saved Wang-Geon, the founding king of the Goryeo kingdom.

Donghwa-sa　　　　　　　　TEMPLE
(동화사; admission ₩3000; ⊙9am-6pm) The park's most popular destination is the province's leading temple, with a history stretching back to AD 493.

FREE Gatbawi　　　　　　　SHRINE
(갓바위; www.seonbonsa.org) Gatbawi is a medicinal Buddha shrine and national treasure, some 850m above sea level and said to date back to AD 638. This Buddha is famed for the flat stone 'hat' hovering over its head, 15cm thick. Incense wafts and mountain mist make it quite a spiritual experience. Plan on a challenging, though enjoyable, two-hour (return) hike from the Gatbawi bus stop; bus 401 (₩1200) runs here from outside Dongdaegu station. About 20 minutes into the hike, the trail leads to a small temple. For a longer though less-steep hike, pick up the dirt trail behind the temple. For a shorter but steeper walk up stone steps, turn left at the small pagoda in the temple compound. Note: the trails are often packed on weekends.

GYEONGSANGBUK-DO AROUND DAEGU

Palgongsan Provincial Park

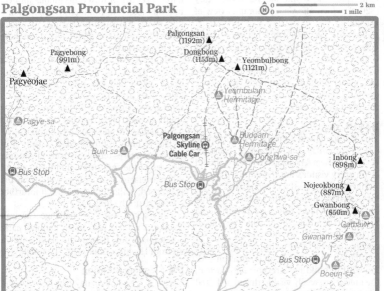

TRIPITAKA KOREANA

The Tripitaka Koreana, also known as the Goryeo Buddhist canon, is one of the world's most significant Buddhist sacred texts. Tripitaka literally means 'three baskets', representing the three divisions of Buddhism: the Sutra (scriptures), Vinaya (laws) and the Abhidharma (treatises).

The Tripitaka Koreana has been preserved on more than 80,000 beautifully carved woodblocks, which took 16 years to complete. The first set of blocks, completed in 1087, was destroyed by Mongolian invaders in 1232. A reconstructed set, the one on display today, was completed in 1251. From carefully selecting appropriate birch wood, then soaking it in brine and boiling it in salt before drying it, to locating and constructing a sophisticated repository, the techniques involved were so complex and the artwork so intricate that they remain an inspiration today. The woodblocks are housed and preserved in the 15th-century hall, **Janggyong Pango**, a masterpiece of ingenuity in its own right; its techniques include charcoal beneath the clay floor and different-sized windows to minimise variations in humidity. Despite the ravages of Japanese invasion and fires that destroyed the rest of the temple complex, the repository remained standing with the woodblocks preserved intact.

During the 1970s, President Park Chung-hee ordered the construction of a modern storage facility for the woodblocks. The facility was equipped with advanced ventilation, temperature and humidity control. However, after some test woodblocks began to grow mildew the whole scheme was scrapped. Today the four storage halls and woodblocks are inscribed on the Unesco World Heritage list to ensure their continued preservation. In a bold attempt to ensure accessibility to more people, Haein-sa's monks have completely transcribed the works onto digital formats and translated the classical Chinese text into modern-day Korean.

Palgongsan Skyline Cable Car CABLE CAR
(return ₩6500; ☺9.45am-sunset) The quickest way to ascend Palgongsan. The 1.2km-long ride drops you at the observatory (820m), which affords a panoramic view of Daegu.

Bus 401 (₩1200) runs between Dongdaegu station and the tourist village below Gatbawi. Bus 급행 (Geuphaeng; ₩1300) connects Donghwa-sa and the bus stop near Dongdaegu station, running at least once every 12 minutes and taking 50 minutes to complete the journey.

HAEIN-SA 해인사

This Unesco World Heritage–listed **temple** (☑055-934 3105; www.haeinsa.or.kr; admission ₩3000; ☺8-11am & noon-5pm Wed-Mon) should be on every visitor's not-to-be-missed list.

Haein-sa holds 81,258 woodblock scriptures, making it one of the largest Buddhist libraries of its kind. Known as the Tripitaka Koreana (see p152), the blocks are housed in four buildings at the temple's upper reaches, complete with simple but effective ventilation to prevent deterioration. Although the buildings are normally locked, the blocks are easily visible through slatted windows.

As well as being one of Korea's most significant temples, Haein-sa is also one of the most beautiful. Part of its beauty lies in the natural setting of mixed deciduous and coniferous forest surrounded by high mountain peaks and rushing streams. At prayer times (3.30am, 10am and 6.30pm) the place can feel otherworldly.

The main hall, Daegwangjeon, was burnt down in the Japanese invasion of 1592 and again (accidentally) in 1817, though miraculously the Tripitaka survived. It escaped a third time, during the Korean War, when a South Korean pilot working for the Allied forces refused to allow them to bomb it.

The recently refurbished **Haein-sa Museum** showcases temple treasures including replicas of the scriptures, Buddhist art and other artefacts. It is a short walk from the main road, while the temple itself a further kilometre up the hillside.

Hikers will want to challenge Gayasan (1430m), the main peak in the national park, and a pretty one, though the 1100m stretch up from Haein-sa is known to be tough.

🛏 Sleeping & Eating

Haein-sa is a popular day trip from Daegu, but there are options to spend the night.

Haein-sa
TEMPLESTAY $

(http://80000.or.kr; weekdays/weekends ₩30,000/50,000) Probably the most interesting sleeping option is to stay at the temple itself. Don't expect luxury – men and women sleep in separate *ondol* (underfloor-heated) dorms, but it's a worthwhile option to experience the otherworldly 3.30am prayer service.

Gobau
GUESTHOUSE $

(고바우; ☎932 5599; r ₩30,000; meals ₩10,000) A beautiful place to stay with kind owners. Rooms are simple, comfy, clean and floor-heated, with yellow linoleum. Try the **restaurant** (◯7am to midnight) where *sanchae jongsik* (산채 정식; rice with vegetables) is the main dish. It's in the centre of Haein-sa, up the hill beyond the bus terminal.

Haeinsa Tourist Hotel
HOTEL $$

(해인사 관광 호텔; ☎933 2000; d/tw/ste ₩95,000/110,000/230,000; ✼) The most comfortable option in Haein-sa is at top of the hill opposite the bus terminal, with fountains, a polished lobby, coffee shop, restaurant and sauna – even if it is often eerily deserted. The hotel offers a weekday discount.

Jeonju
KOREAN $$

(전주; www.jjbab.com; dishes ₩8000-15,000; ◯7am-9pm; ☺) Who would have imagined bus-terminal food could be this good? On the 2nd floor above the tiny terminal, this place serves tasty *bibimbap* (비빔밥; vegetables, meat and rice), a good-value set menu with Bulgogi and stir-fried shitake mushrooms.

❶ Getting There & Away

Although it's in Gyeongsangnam-do, Haein-sa is most easily accessed by bus (₩6600, 1½ hours, every 40 minutes) from Daegu's Seobu (South) intercity bus terminal. While the bus terminates at Haein-sa's small bus terminal at the top of the hill, tell the driver you're going to Haein-sa temple and they will drop you one stop earlier – look out for the traditional-style building on your right with 'shopping centre' written on it in English and follow the crowds 1.2km up the hillside to the temple complex. All the hotels and the restaurants are around the bus terminal, a further 500m uphill along the main road.

JIKJI-SA 직지사
♩054

Jikji-sa (☎436 6174; www.jikjisa.or.kr; adult/youth/child ₩3000/2000/1500; ◯7am-6.30pm Mar-Oct, 7am-5.30pm Nov-Feb) is a postcard-pretty temple in a quiet forest. The delicate paintings on the temple buildings have a refinement and grace that is very appealing, as are the giant timbers that support the structures, and the faded, cracked wood.

Of the 40 original buildings, about 20 still exist, the oldest dating from the 1602 reconstruction. Highlights include the **Daeungjong**, with stunning Buddhist triad paintings on silk (1774) that are national treasures, and the rotating collection in the temple's **Buddhist art museum** (☎436 6009; admission ₩2000; ◯9am-5.30pm Mar-Oct, to 4.30pm Nov-Feb, closed Mon).

⬛ Sleeping & Eating

Many visitors day trip to Jikji-sa, while some join the **Templestay program** (☎429 1716; http://eng.templestay.com; per night ₩50,000). There's a well-established tourist village by the bus stop with *minbak* (private homes with rooms for rent), *yeogwan* (budget motels) and restaurants.

❶ Getting There & Away

Jikji-sa is reached via Gimcheon (population 152,000), about 20 minutes by bus. Local buses 11, 111, and 112 (₩1400) depart every 10 minutes from Gimcheon's **intercity bus terminal** (☎432 7600). The temple complex is a pleasant 15-minute walk from the bus stop.

Gimcheon can be reached by train on the line connecting Daegu (50 minutes) and Seoul. If you're using KTX from Seoul, transfer at Daejeon and take a local line to Gimcheon. For bus departures from Gimcheon, see the boxed text below.

GYEONGSANGBUK-DO GYEONGJU

BUS DEPARTURES FROM GIMCHEON

DESTINATION	PRICE (₩)	DURATION (HR)	FREQUENCY
Andong	11,000	2	every 1-2hr
Daegu	4900	1¼	every 30min
Daejeon	6000	1¼	hourly
Gochang*	6300	1¼	hourly

*for Haein-sa & Gayasan National Park

Gyeongju 경주

054 / POP 280,000

Known as 'the museum without walls', Gyeongju holds more tombs, temples, rock carvings, pagodas, Buddhist statuary and palace ruins than any other place in South Korea.

Most visitors touring the city centre are taken aback by the distinctive urban landscape created by round grassy tombs – called *tumuli* – and traditional architecture with colourful hip roofs set against a canvas of green rolling mountains.

Two of Gyeongju's most not-to-be-missed sites – Bulguk-sa and Seokguram – are in the outlying districts and are within reach via public transport. Gyeongju covers a vast area – some 1323 sq km – so you should plan on several days of travel if you want to visit some of the lesser-known

places. Bus transport out to these areas is satisfactory, though personal transport is a better option if you value speed and some flexibility.

In 57 BC, around the same time that Julius Caesar was subduing Gaul, Gyeongju became the capital of the Shilla dynasty, and it remained so for nearly a thousand years. In the 7th century AD, under King Munmu, Shilla conquered the neighbouring kingdoms of Goguryeo and Baekje, and Gyeongju became the capital of the whole peninsula. The population of the city eventually peaked at around one million people, but the Shilla eventually fell victim to division from within and invasion from without.

The city began a cultural revival in the late 20th century – with much preservation and restoration work thanks to President Park Chung-hee in the 1970s.

Gyeongju

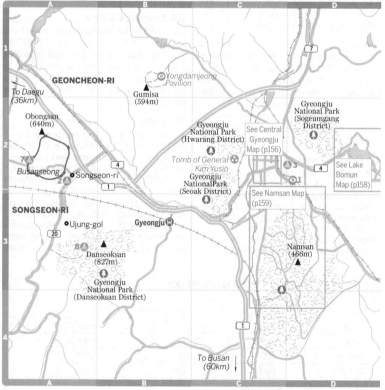

◉ Sights

Central Gyeongju is compact, encompassing the bus and train terminals (20 minutes' walk apart) and, between them, sights, lodgings and dining.

About 5km east of the centre is Bomunho, a lakeside resort with a golf course, luxury hotels and posh restaurants. A 16km drive southeast brings you to Bulguk-sa, one of Korea's most famous temples. From here it's a quick ride to Seokguram, a mountain grotto with a historic Buddha.

CENTRAL GYEONGJU

FREE **Gyeongju National Museum** MUSEUM (국립경주박물관; Map p159; ☑740 7500; http://gyeongju.museum.go.kr; ☉9am-6pm, to 9pm Sat & holidays Mar-Dec) Arguably the best history museum in Korea, the Gyeongju National Museum is where you can appreciate

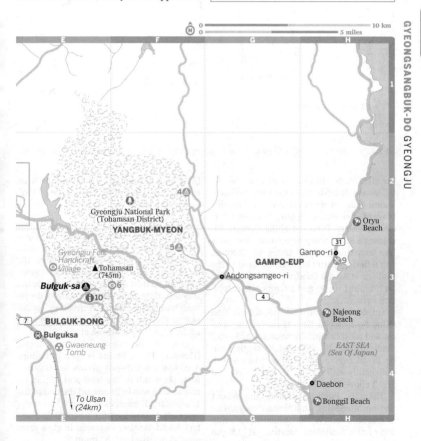

Central Gyeongju

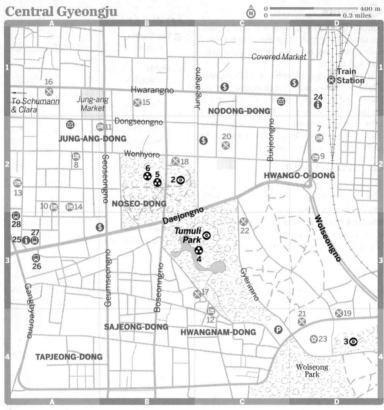

the significance of this ancient city in one fell swoop. In addition to the main archaeological hall, where there are dazzling displays of jewellery, weaponry and other ceremonial items from the Shilla dynasty, including a 5th-century gold crown that looks like something out of Game of Thrones, you'll find an entire building devoted to the findings at Anapji Pond, an art hall focusing on Buddhist works and a temporary exhibition hall.

Outside the main hall, the Emille Bell (King Seongdeok's Bell) is one of the largest and most beautifully resonant bells ever made in Asia. It's said that its ringing can be heard over a 3km radius when struck only lightly with the fist. Unfortunately, you aren't allowed to test this claim.

There is English labelling throughout and an interesting multilingual audioguide is available too (₩3000). English-speaking tours run Saturdays starting at 1.30pm

(March to November). The museum is an easy 150m walk from the east side of Wolseong Park and is well signed.

Tumuli Park
PARK

(대릉원 Map p156; admission ₩1500; ◷9am-10pm) The huge, walled park has 23 tombs of Shilla monarchs and family members. From the outside, they look like grassy hillocks – much more subtle than the Egyptian pyramids, but they served the same purpose; many of the *tumuli* have yielded fabulous treasures, on display at the Gyeongju National Museum. On colder days, the park closes at sunset.

One of the tombs, Cheonmachong (Heavenly Horse Tomb), is open to visitors. A cross-section display shows its construction. The tomb is 13m high and 47m in diameter and was built around the end of the 5th century. Facsimiles of the golden crown, bracelets, jade ornaments, weapons and pottery found here are displayed in glass cases around the inside of the tomb.

Central Gyeongju

Noseo-dong Tombs TOMBS
(노서동 고분; Map p156) Across the street and closer to the main shopping area is the Noseo-dong district, where there are other Shilla tombs for which there is no entry fee. **Seobongchong** and **Geumgwanchong** are adjacent tombs built between the 4th and 5th centuries. They were excavated between 1921 and 1946, the finds including two gold crowns. Across the road is **Bonghwadae**, the largest extant Shilla tomb at 22m high and with a circumference of 250m; adjoining it is **Geumnyeongchong**. Houses covered much of this area until 1984, when they were removed.

Bunhwang-sa PAGODA
(분황사; Map p154; admission ₩1500; ⊙sunrise–sunset) This large pagoda was built in the mid-7th century during Queen Seondeok's reign, making it the oldest datable pagoda in Korea. It's a rare example of one made from brick.

The magnificently carved Buddhist guardians and stone lions are a main feature; it is unique in that each entrance is protected by two guardians.

To get here, follow the willow-lined road across from the Gyeongju National Museum until you reach the first intersection. Turn right at the intersection and then take the first lane on the right. The walk will take about 20 to 25 minutes and is well sign-posted.

Cheomseongdae OBSERVATORY
(첨성대; Map p156; ☑772 5134; admission adult/teen/child ₩500/300/200; ⊙8am-6pm Apr-Oct, 9am-6pm Nov-Mar) Southeast of Tumuli Park in the attractive sprawl of Wolseong Park is the Far East's oldest astrological observatory, which was constructed between AD 632 and 646. Its apparently simple design conceals amazing sophistication: the 12 stones of its base symbolise the months of the year. From top to bottom there are 30 layers – one for each day of the month – and a total of 366 stones were used in its construction, corresponding (approximately) to the days of the year. Numerous other technical details relate, for example, to the tower's position in relation to certain stars.

There's a free visitor centre, with a digital display about the building's construction in English, just outside the entrance.

FREE **Banwolseong** RUINS
(반월성; Castle of the Crescent Moon; Map p154) A few minutes' walk south from Cheomseongdae, Banwolseong is the site of a once-fabled fortress. Now it's attractive parkland, where you can see some walls and ruins. The only intact building is **Seokbinggo** (Stone Ice House; early 18th century, restored 1973), which was once used as a food store.

Anapji Pond POND

(안압지 연못 Map p154; admission ₩1500; ☺8am-sunset Sep-May, 7.30am-7pm Jun-Aug) Today, this is a popular spot for couples to take prewedding photos. From June to early August, magnificent lotus blossoms seem to fill the horizon.

In the past, it was a pleasure garden to commemorate the unification of the Korean Peninsula under Shilla. The buildings here burned in 935 and many relics ended up in the pond itself, to be rediscovered only when it was drained for repair in 1975. Thousands of well-preserved relics were found including wooden objects, a die used in drinking games, scissors and a royal barge – you can see them in the Gyeongju National Museum.

EASTERN GYEONGJU

TOP CHOICE **Bulguk-sa** TEMPLE

(불국사; Map p154; www.bulguksa.or.kr; adult/youth/child ₩5000/4000/3000; ☺6.30am-6pm Apr-Oct, 7am-5pm Nov-Mar) On a series of stone terraces about 16km southeast of Gyeongju, set among gnarled pines and iris gardens that would make Van Gogh swoon, this temple is the crowning glory of Shilla architecture and is on the Unesco World Cultural Heritage list. The excellence of its carpentry, the skill of its painters (particularly the interior woodwork and the eaves of the roofs) and the subtlety of its landscapes all contribute to its magnificence.

The approach to the temple leads you to two national-treasure **bridges**. One of these bridges has 33 steps, representing the 33 stages to enlightenment. Two more national treasures are the pagodas standing in the courtyard of the first set of buildings that

somehow survived Japanese vandalism. The first, **Dabotap**, is of plain design and typical of Shilla artistry, while the other, **Seokga-tap**, is much more ornate and typical of the neighbouring Baekje kingdom. The pagodas are so revered that replicas appear in the grounds of the Gyeongju National Museum.

You can reach Bulguk-sa from central Gyeongju via buses 10 or 11 (₩1800). There's a **tourist information booth** (☎746 4747) in the car park, near the bus stop.

FREE **Golgul-sa** TEMPLE

(골굴사; Map p154; ☎744 1689; www.sunmudo.com; ☺8am-6pm) Finally, a temple where you can do more than just look around. The Buddha carved out of solid rock by Indian monks in the 6th century is kind of interesting but the real draw here is *sunmudo,* a Korean martial art that blends fighting skills with meditation. Short 20-minute demonstrations take place at 3pm Sundays at Sunmudo University on the temple grounds and *sunmudo* training is available through the **Templestay program** (per night incl meals ₩50,000). Reservations are recommended though not always necessary. Most of the program is taught in English.

From Gyeongju intercity bus terminal, take a bus towards Gampo-ri or Yangbuk-myeon (bus 100 or 150) and ask the driver to drop you off at Andongsamgeo-ri, where the turn-off to the temple goes off to the left. Golgul-sa is a 20-minute walk down the road.

Bomunho Resort RESORT

(보문 단지; Map p158) Bomun is a tourist district around an artificial lake some 5km east of central Gyeongju. Tradition-seekers will find the tandem bikes, paddle boats, conference centres and such less appealing, but it is home to Gyeongju's top-end lodgings. The lake and extensive parklands are great for strolling or bike riding, though the area doesn't have the character of the town centre.

Traditional dancing and musical performances are held on a regular basis from April to October at **Bomun Outdoor Performance Theatre**, located below the information centre by the lake.

Sonje Museum of Contemporary Art MUSEUM

(선재 아트 센터; Map p158; ☎745 7075; www.artsonje.org; admission ₩3500; ☺10am-6pm, closed Mon) This modern art museum behind the Hilton Hotel is the sister to Artsonje Center Seoul and holds three exhibition spaces with

Lake Bomun N 0 — 1 km / 0 — 0.5 miles

BOMUNHO RESORT
To Gyeongju (4km)
Commodore Hotel
Gyeongju Chosun
Lake Bomun
Information Centre
Bumun Outdoor Performance Theatre
Myeonghwal Fortress Site
Sonje Museum of Contemporary Art
Gyeongju Hilton
Hansol-jang
To Gyeongju National Park (2km)

seasonal exhibitions plus a permanent collection containing paintings, sculpture and mixed media. It's a worthwhile stop if you're already in the area.

Seokguram   GROTTO
(석굴암; Map p154; adult/child/youth ₩3500/2500/2000; ⊙6.30am-6pm Apr-Oct, 7am-5.30pm Nov-Mar) In the mountains above Bulguk-sa is the famous grotto of Seokguram, also on the Unesco World Cultural Heritage list. Chipmunks dance in the thick woods leading up to the rotunda, where sits an image of the Sakyamuni Buddha surrounded by over three dozen guardians and lesser deities. This Buddha's position looking out over the East Sea (visible in clear weather) has long made him regarded as a protector of his country.

Seokguram was quite a feat of engineering when it was constructed in the mid-8th century. Huge blocks of granite were quarried far to the north at a time when the only access to the Seokguram site (740m above sea level) was a narrow mountain path. Seokguram can be a magical place, especially when it is raining and the mists cloak the mountaintops.

Buses run hourly between the car parks for Bulguk-sa and Seokguram (₩1600, 15 minutes). From the Seokguram car park, it is a 400m walk along a shaded gravel track and up the stairs to the grotto. Alternatively, there is a hiking trail between the Seokguram ticket office and Bulguk-sa (about 3.2km).

Girim-sa   TEMPLE
(기림사; Map p154; admission ₩4000; ⊙8am-8pm) About 3.5km down the road from Golgul-sa, Girim-sa is one of the largest complexes in the vicinity of the Shilla capital. Its size (14 buildings and growing) compares with that of Bulguk-sa, but the compound lacks a 'wow' factor, which might explain why it receives comparably fewer visitors.

From Golgul-sa, there is no public transport to Girim-sa. If you're without personal transport, the choices are walking 3.5km down the road alongside rice paddies, or asking for a lift.

SOUTHERN GYEONGJU (NAMSAN) 남산
This mountain, south of the city centre, is one of the region's most rewarding areas to explore, a place where you can easily combine the athletic with the spiritual. It's beautiful, and strewn with relics, active

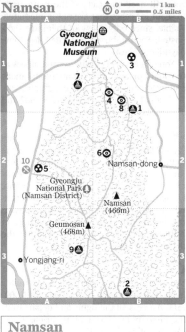

Namsan

◎ Top Sights
Gyeongju National Museum.............. B1

◎ Sights
1 Bori-sa.. B1
2 Chilbulam..B3
3 Mangdeok-sa.....................................B1
4 Ongnyong-am B1
5 Samneung...A2
6 Sangsabawi..B2
7 Sangseonam Hermitage....................A1
8 Tapgol..B1
9 Yongjangsaji A3

⊗ Eating
10 Sigol Yeohaeng A2

temples, monasteries and sites for impromptu religious observance. Among the relics that have been found here are 122 temple sites, 64 stone pagodas, 57 stone Buddhas, and many royal tombs, rock-cut figures, pavilions and the remains of fortresses, temples and palaces.

You can choose from hundreds of paths, many of which run alongside streams that tumble down the mountain. The paths and tracks are well trodden, though at times you will need to head off the main trails to scout for relics that are not immediately visible, since only a few of them are signposted. See the boxed text, p161, for some day-hike suggestions.

You can also check with tourist offices at Gyeongju or Bomunho for additional maps and information about trail conditions.

Buses 11, 500, 501, 503, 505, 506, 507 and 591 all pass by Namsan.

FREE **Samneung** ROYAL TOMBS
(삼릉; Map p159; ⊙24hr) The reason to come to this pine grove is to start a hike up Namsan. On your way up, you may pass the *tumuli* of three Shilla kings. Another tomb, located away from the others, is said to contain King Gyeongae, who was killed when robbers raided Poseokjeongji during an elaborate banquet, setting the stage for the dynasty's collapse.

☞ Tours

Numerous Korean-language **tour buses** (6-9hr tours excl lunch & admissions; ₩10,000-16,000) access all the sights and depart from the intercity bus terminal at various times each morning. Ask at the nearby tourist information kiosk for exact timings and costs.

🛏 Sleeping

Lodgings are everywhere, so finding a room in and around the bus and train stations to match your budget won't be a problem. Higher-end lodgings and restaurants are at Bomunho, with some less expensive options just east from the lake.

TOP CHOICE **Sarangchae** HANOK GUESTHOUSE $
(사랑채; Map p156; ☎773 4868; www.kjstay.com; s/d incl breakfast ₩30,000/35,000, s/d without private bathroom ₩25,000/30,000;@🅟🛜) This charmingly traditional yet simple guesthouse to one side of Tumuli Park has existed for 120 years and offers cosy rooms with *ondol* or beds scattered around a courtyard. The friendly owner speaks English and offers plenty of advice for visitors, including free maps. There's free laundry, a left-luggage room and even log fires in the courtyard on some nights. It's by far the best place for a taste of local colour in Gyeongju and reservations are normally essential.

Nahbi Guest House HOSTEL $
(나비 게스트 하우스; Map p156; ☎010-9700-3047, 070-8719-9500; www.nahbiguesthouse.com; dm/s/d ₩16,000/25,000/39,000; 🅧@🛜) This brand new youth hostel is located right in the centre of town, clearly signposted on the fourth floor of a building on the main drag (look for the wine bottles that greet you on the staircase and listen out for the enthusiastic sound of ping pong being played). With seven rooms that run from doubles and twins to a family room and three dorms (two of which are female-only), there's plenty of choice, not to mention a spacious social area with table football, a good kitchen, free PC use and laundry facilities for a mere ₩3000. Staff speak English and are extremely helpful. Overall this is Gyeongju's best hostel and a very welcome addition to the sleeping options.

Gyeongju Guest House HOSTEL $
(경주 게스트 하우스; Mapp156; ☎745-7101; www.gjguesthouse.com; dm/tw/tr ₩16,000/45,000/60,000; 🅧@🛜) Another new hostel just a short distance from the train station is gleamingly presented, with a spacious and modern communal area, a sparkling kitchen and very clean dorm and room accommodation. Staffs' English appeared to be lacking, but otherwise this is another solid budget option.

Gyeongju Hilton LUXURY HOTEL $$
(힐튼 호텔; Map p158; ☎745 7788; www.hilton.com; r from ₩121,500; 🅧🛜🅧) A real Miró hangs in the lobby of this art deco Hilton by the lake. It has a sauna, squash courts, pool and gym, not to mention spacious rooms with marble bathrooms. Definitely a good choice if you're looking for smart comfort.

Commodore Hotel Gyeongju Chosun HOTEL $$$
(조선호텔; Map p158; ☎745 7701; www.chosunhotel.net; r from ₩144,000; 🅧@) Perhaps the best located of the lakeside hotels, with some of the most attractive grounds, the Commodore is nevertheless rather less than impressive on the inside, where rooms need a bit of updating. That said there is nice woodwork in the rooms, Gyeongju green and terracotta-coloured motifs downstairs, and one of the city's favourite spas.

Bellus Tourist Hotel HOTEL $$
(벨루스 호텔; Map p156; ☎741-3335; r from ₩50,000; 🅧@🛜) Right in the centre of town, wedged between the love hotels around the bus stations and the bustle of downtown is this solid option, which will suit those who want to avoid love hotels and seek in-

NAMSAN DAY HIKES

Central Namsan

There are numerous trails through Namsan (Map p159), the most convenient starting at Samneung. Whichever route you take, be sure to include detours – necessary to hunt for relics off-track. There's virtually no English signage, but with some *hangeul* skill you should do fine.

Three-hour course Head up from Samneung, breaking to take in several relief carvings and statues along the way, to the hermitage **Sangseonam** (상선암), where you'll find lovely views across the valley and maybe a monk chanting. Continue up past the rock formation **Badukbawi** (바둑바위) and along the ridge to **Sangsabawi** (상사바위), then walk back the way you came.

Five-hour course Instead of doubling back from Sangsabawi, continue on to the summit of **Geumosan** (금오산, 468m) to **Yongjangsaji** (용장사지, Yongjang temple site), where you can view the seated Buddha image carved in stone and the three-storey stone pagoda. Descend to **Yongjang-ri** (용장리, Yongjang village), from where you can catch a bus back to central Gyeongju.

Eight-hour course Follow the route as far as Yongjangsaji, but instead of heading down towards Yongjang-ri, head across the ridge to **Chilbulam** (칠불암, hermitage of seven Buddhas), Namsan's largest relic with images carved in natural rocks and stone pillars. From here it's mostly downhill towards the road and about another kilometre to **Namsan-ni** (남산리, Namsan village) on the eastern side of the park, from where it's an easy bus ride back to town.

Northeastern Namsan

Take local bus 11 from Gyeongju and get off as soon as the bus crosses the river, about 2.5km past the Gyeongju National Museum. Off the main road is a fork – take the left branch and you can wind your way to **Bori-sa** (보리사), a beautifully reconstructed nunnery set amid old-growth trees and ancient images. It is possible to head over the hill behind Bori-sa to **Tapgol** (탑골, Pagoda Valley), but it's a rough climb. It's easier to backtrack down to the fork and take the other branch. Follow the river for several hundred metres until you come to a small village. Turn left here and head up the road through Tapgol and you'll reach the secluded hermitage **Ongnyong-am** (옥룡암). In the upper corner are ponderous boulders covered with Korea's greatest collection of relief carvings.

Returning to the bridge and looking towards the main road, you will see two stone pillars standing in a thicket of trees amid rice paddies. These pillars are all that remain standing of **Mangdeok-sa**, a huge Shilla-era temple complex. From there it's an easy trip back towards the National Museum, about 20 minutes. Depending on your route, this itinerary might take you a half-day.

For more on hiking in Korea, see p27.

room wi-fi. Otherwise the rooms are rather cell-like, with little or no charm and old bathrooms, but English is spoken and the accommodation is at least clean.

Hanjin Hostel HOSTEL **$**
(한진 여관; Map p156; ☑ 771 4097; http://hanjinko rea.wo.to; dm/s/tw ₩15,000/25,000/40,000; ☎) Open since 1977 (and rather showing its age), this centrally located hostel is run by the friendly English-speaking Clint Kwon, who can give excellent local advice and even works part time as a guide. The rooms are

dingy, but the walls are covered with paintings and the bathrooms were about to be renovated when we last visited. The dorms have brand new beds in them, making them a good deal. The kitchen, courtyard and roof deck are great places to chat with other travellers and laundry is available for ₩6000 per load.

Taeyang-jang Motel LOVE HOTEL **$**
(태양장 여관; Map p156; ☑ 773 6889; r/ste ₩30,000/40,000; ❉ @) Right near the Hanjin Hostel, this spotless motel has a rock garden

in the lobby and a friendly owner. Rooms are spacious, with good bathrooms and all modern conveniences including huge widescreen TVs and in-room PCs.

Show Motel LOVE HOTEL $$
(쇼모텔; Map p156; ☑771 7878; r from ₩60,000; ✳@) One of the snazziest of the multiple flashing love hotels behind the bus terminal. There's lots of attention to detail in the rooms from desktop computers and spacious interiors to saunas in the bathroom and complimentary drinks. Large bathrooms and general cleanliness make up for the incredibly gaudiness of the decor.

Arirang-jang Yeoinsuk GUESTHOUSE $
(아리랑장 여인숙; Map p156; ☑772 2460; r ₩20,000) Shabby but inexpensive, this place has tiny, odd-shaped *ondol* rooms. It's located close to the train station, right behind the bakery.

✖ Eating

Gyeongju provides plenty of good eating opportunities with the greatest concentration of choice in the city centre. Southeast of Tumuli Park is a street full of **ssambap restaurants** (쌈밥), where you order lots of side dishes which you wrap up in lettuce and other leaves.

TOP CHOICE Dosolmaeul KOREAN $$
(도솔마을; Map p156; mains ₩15,000; ⊙11.30am-9pm Tue-Sun; 🖹) Definitely the most atmospheric place to eat in Gyeongju, this traditional family-run courtyard restaurant by the side of Tumuli Park has a delicious and wide-ranging menu featuring lip-smacking dishes such as steamed octopus with hot sauce or sea food, meat ball and vegetable stew. The best deal however is the ₩18,000 traditional Korean set dinner for two, a delicious feast of around 20 small dishes.

Bulgogi Myeongga KOREAN $$
(불고기 명가; Map p156; mains ₩6000-25,000; ⊙10am-10pm; 🖹) Right in the heart of town is this excellent place, where the main attraction is the delicious all-you-can-eat *bulgogi* (marinated barbecued meat) for ₩10,000 per person. In actual fact, unless you're starving, the ₩7,000 *bulgogi* will be more than enough. In addition there's a great raw beef *bibimbap* and a vegetarian *bibimbap* too, not to mention very jolly and attentive staff.

Kisoya JAPANESE $$
(기소야; Map p156; meals ₩8000-30,000; ⊙10am-3pm & 5-10pm; 🖹) Spotless and friendly Kisoya serves up a mouth-watering array of Japanese dishes with a Korean slant. Mains run from bento boxes to sashimi and noodle soups. Don't miss the superb chicken filet bento box.

Daebak Jip KOREAN $
(대박집 Map p156; mains ₩2000-10,000; ⊙11am-2pm) A good place to eat late, this delicious local hangout does excellent barbecue pork and beef dishes at low prices. The service is very friendly, even if there's no English menu or English spoken – the pictorial menu saves the day on that front.

Sigol Yeohaeng KOREAN $
(시골 여행; Map p154; meals ₩5000-12,000; ⊙9am-9pm) Opposite the entrance to Samneung, this 20-year-old restaurant specialises in *mukun kimchi* (묵은 김치), a spicy noodle-and-broth dish made with *kimchi* aged at least three years.

Pyeongyang NOODLES $$
(평양; Map p156; meals ₩7000-20,000; ⊙11am-9pm; 🖹) This bustling place always attracts crowds of locals who come here for the excellent Pyongyang Cold Noodles as well as the spicy *bulgogi*. It's got a pleasant outdoor seating area complete with a garden and a little fountain. Ask for the English menu.

Kuro Ssambap KOREAN $$
(구로쌈밥; Map p156; per person ₩10,000; ⊙11am-9pm) Eclectic collection of birds, rocks, figurines, pottery and other folk arts make this a unique place to dine on this strip of otherwise rather similar *ssambap* restaurants just to the north of Wolseong Park. Orders include 28 refillable side dishes.

Sukyeong Sikdang KOREAN $$
(숙영 식당; Map p156; mains from ₩9,000; ⊙11am-8.30pm; 🖹) Since 1979, this cosy restaurant with a delightfully cluttered and rustic interior has been serving tasty *pajeon* (파전; green onion pancake) made from organic ingredients and homemade *dongdongju* (동동주; rice wine). It's near the east wall of Tumuli Park.

Gampo Hogung Raw Fish Center SEAFOOD $$$
(감포 호궁 회센타; Map p154; crab meals from ₩30,000 person; ⊙7am-midnight) King crab and raw fish are the specialities of this bustling restaurant near the Gampo harbour.

Crab dinners start with a small selection of side dishes and finish with a pot of spicy fish soup that tastes better after adding a splash of soy sauce. It's customary to negotiate the price of a crab meal before going inside, although English isn't spoken, so come with a Korean friend or prepare for some interesting bargaining.

☆ Entertainment

There are outdoor traditional dance and music performances every Saturday during April, May, September and October (3pm to 5pm) on the performance stage in Wolseong Park. More regular traditional performances are held at Bomunho between April and October. Weekend performances of Korean dance and music at Bomunho start at 7.30pm or 8.30pm with additional Thursday and Friday shows in May, July and August. Check with the tourist office for information about what's going on while you're in town.

ℹ Information

There are central **tourist information kiosks** (Map p156; express bus terminal ☎772 9289; train station ☎772 3843) as well as in the car park near Bulguk-sa (Map p154), all with English-speaking staff and comprehensive English-language maps.

For planning advice, author recommendations, traveller reviews and insider tips, see **Lonely Planet** (http://www.lonelyplanet.com/south-korea/gyeongsangbuk-do/gyeongju).

ℹ Getting There & Away

Air

There is no airport at Gyeongju itself, but the airports at Busan (Gimhae) and Ulsan are readily accessible. Ulsan's airport is closer, but Gimhae has more flights.

Bus

Gyeongju's **express bus terminal** (Map p156; ☎741 4000) and **intercity bus terminal** (p156; ☎743 5599) are adjacent to one other. For departures from the express and intercity bus terminals, see the boxed text below.

Train

Gyeongju has a new KTX service with regular services from here to Seoul (₩41,000, two hours) and Busan (₩12,000, 30 minutes), but it serves the out-of-town Singyeongju station, rather than the conveniently central Gyongju Train Station. Arriving at Singyeongju station, takes buses 50, 60, 61, 70, 201 or 700 to the city centre.

From Gyeongju **Train Station** (Map p156; ☎743 4114) there are services to Pohang (₩2600, 30 minutes, every one to two hours) and Daegu (₩5000, 1 hour 20 minutes, hourly), but you need to go to Daegu and change trains to reach Seoul or Busan from here.

ℹ Getting Around

To/From the Airport

Several direct buses link Gyeongju with both the Ulsan airport (₩4900, four daily) and Busan's Gimhae airport (₩9800, 10 daily). Buses leave from Gyeongju's main intercity bus terminal.

GYEONGSANGBUK-DO GYEONGJU

GYEONJU BUS DEPARTURES

Departures from the express bus terminal

DESTINATION	PRICE (₩)	DURATION (HR)	FREQUENCY
Busan	4900	1	hourly
Daegu	4600	1	every 40min
Daejeon	18,600	3	2 daily
Seoul	29,000	4½	hourly

Departures from the intercity bus terminal

DESTINATION	PRICE (₩)	DURATION (HR)	FREQUENCY
Busan	4500	1	every 15min
Daegu	420	1	every 40min
Ulsan	3100	1	4 daily
Pohang	4900	1	every 40min

Bicycle

Hiring a bicycle for a day is a great way of reaching the sites in Gyeongju. There are some bike trails around Namsan (but it's rather hilly) and Bomunho. There are bicycle rental shops everywhere, including several scattered around the centre of town and one opposite the Gyeongju National Museum. The rates are approximately ₩3000 to ₩4000 hourly or ₩12,000 to ₩15,000 daily.

Bus

Many local buses (₩1500) terminate just outside the intercity bus terminal, alongside the river. For shorter routes (eg to Bulguk-sa), buses can be picked up along Sosongno and Daejeongno.

Buses 10 (which runs clockwise) and 11 (counterclockwise) run a circuit of most of the major sights including Bulguk-sa, Namsan and Bomunho, as well as the bus terminals and Gyeongju train station (every 15 minutes). Bus 150 departs from the train station to the eastern sights, via the Bomunho Expo arena (every 30 minutes). Bus 100 makes a similar initial route.

Taxi

If your time is limited and you want to cover a lot of ground in a short time, taxis are often available for day hire outside the train and bus stations. Rates are negotiable but hover around ₩150,000/200,000 for five/seven hours.

Around Gyeongju

YANGDONG FOLK VILLAGE
양동 민속 마을

Getting here is not easy, but your journey to this Joseon-dynasty village will be rewarded with an up-close, intimate look at superb traditional architecture in a decidedly uncommercial setting. Designated as a cultural preservation area, the entire village (replete with stone walls, straw-thatched roofs and green gardens) is a photographer's dream.

Set aside a half-day to admire the 180 or so houses typical of the *yangban* class – a largely hereditary class based on scholarship and official position. Most of the homes here are still lived in, so you need to observe the usual courtesies when looking around; some of the larger mansions stand empty and are open to the public. There are descriptive plaques with English explanations outside some of the more important structures. If buildings are locked, you may be able to ask for a key nearby. There are no entry fees to any of the buildings.

When it's time for a break, try one of the area teashops, like **Uhyangdaok** (우향다옥; dishes ₩5000-15,000; ☺noon-10pm), which is in a rustic building with simple treats like green tea, wine and light meals. No English is spoken here but the owner goes to much effort to ease communication. If you want to stay the night, there are two small *ondol* rooms (₩30,000) for rent. Early breakfast is possible but you need to ask ahead of time.

From Gyeongju, buses 200, 201, 202, 203 and 206 will get you to within 1.5km of Yangdong. From the bus stop, follow the train line and then go under it. There's only one road into the village, about a 30-minute walk.

OKSAN SEOWON & AROUND 옥산 서원
☑054

Established in 1572 in honour of Yi Eonjeok (1491–1553), Oksan Seowon was one of the most important seowon, or Confucian academies. It was enlarged in 1772 and was one of the few to escape destruction in the 1860s. However, an early-20th-century fire destroyed some of the buildings here; today only 14 structures remain.

◉ Sights

FREE **Dongnakdang**   HISTORIC SITE
(독락당; ☺by appointment) A 10-minute walk beyond Oksan Seowon up the valley road will bring you to Dongnakdang, a beautiful collection of well-preserved buildings, constructed in 1515 and expanded in 1532 as the residence of Yi Eon-jeok after he left government service. The walled compound is partly occupied by descendants of Master Yi himself.

Due to past vandalism, the family requests visitors to book appointments in advance (ask at tourist offices). They will open up the inner rooms and answer any questions (in Korean).

🛏 Sleeping & Eating

Oksan Motel   MOTEL $
(옥산 모텔; Map p154; ☑762 9500; www.oksan motel.com; r from ₩30,000; ❋) About 500m from Dongnakdang, the Oksan has modern *ondol* or bedrooms with a shower, and a patio in front of the property.

Sanjang Sikdang   KOREAN $$
(산장식당; Map p154; ☑762 3716; chicken/duck stew for 2-4 people ₩30,000/35,000) This place specialises in free-range duck and chicken. *Tojongdak baeksuk* (토종닭 백숙) and *orihanbang baeksuk* (오리한방 백숙) are

chicken and duck stews served with rice porridge. Note: stews take up to 50 minutes to prepare, so you can relax in the outdoor seating area or have a Korean speaker call before you arrive. It's between Dongnak-dang and the Oksan Motel.

❶ Getting There & Away

Bus 203 (₩1800, six daily departures) to Angang-ri connects Gyeongju train station and Oksan Seowon.

SONGSEON-RI 송선리

Close to the summit of the thickly forested Obongsan (640m), **Bokduam hermitage** (Map p154) features a huge rock face out of which 19 niches have been carved. The three central niches hold a figure of the historical Buddha flanked by two bodhisattva (Munsu and Bohyeon); the remainder house the 16 arhat monks who have attained Nirvana. The carving is recent and although there's an unoccupied house up here, the actual hermitage was burned down in 1988 after an electrical fault started a blaze. There is also a statue of Gwanseeum, the Goddess of Mercy, just beyond the rock face. Just below the hermitage is a stunning viewpoint from the top of a couple of massive boulders. It's a great place for a picnic lunch.

The trail is easy to follow, but bring water as there are no springs along the way. The walk up will take around an hour. From the bus stop in Songseon-ri, follow the creek up along the narrow road about 500m to a small temple, **Seongam-sa**. The trail starts just to the left of this temple and is well marked in Korean.

A further 3.8km up the road from the bus stop for Bokduam and Jusaam, remote **Sinseon-sa** near the top of Danseoksan (827m) was used as a base by General Kim Yu-shin in the 7th century. It has seen some renovation work since then. About 50m to the right as you face the temple are some ancient rock carvings in a small grotto; it's believed to be one of the oldest cave temples in Korea. It's about a two-hour circuit walk from the bus stop. There's a little village along the way, about 2.5km from the bus stop.

Bus 300 (₩1800, every 25 minutes) travels to Obongsan and stops near Jusaam. If you're looking for a more direct route to Sinseon-sa, take bus 350 (₩1800, every one to two hours) and get off at Ujung-gol (우중골). From the intercity bus terminal tourist information booth, catch either bus at the stop near Paris Baguette.

Pohang 포항

♪054 / POP 508,000

If you've ever wanted to swim on a beach in full view of the world's second-largest steel plant, Pohang is the place for you. A large and rather bland city best known as home to Posco (Pohang Iron & Steel Company), Pohang does actually boast a pretty decent beach, though a fairly unpleasant smell pervades much of the place. Most people pass through here on the way to the island of Ulleungdo, but it's a convenient place to spend the night, with plenty of accommodation choice and beachside restaurants open until sunrise.

◉ Sights

Bogyeong-sa   TEMPLE
(보경사; admission ₩2500; ◷7am-7pm) You'll need a full day to explore the offerings in and around this temple. About 30km north of Pohang, Bogyeong-sa is a gateway to a beautiful valley boasting 12 waterfalls, gorges spanned by bridges, hermitages, stupas and the temple itself. There are good **hikes** including Naeyeonsan (930m). The 20km return trip to the summit – Hyangnobong – from Bogyeong-sa takes about six hours.

The well-maintained trail to the gorge and waterfalls branches off from the tourist village. It's about 1.5km to the first waterfall, 5m-high **Ssangsaeng Pokpo**. The sixth waterfall, **Gwaneum Pokpo**, is an impressive 72m and has two columns of water with a cave behind it. The seventh waterfall, about 30m high, is called **Yeonsan Pokpo**.

Further up the trail, the going gets difficult; the ascent of Hyangnobong should only be attempted if the day is young.

The temple is 15 minutes' walk from where the buses from Pohang terminate, and there's a tourist village with souvenir shops, restaurants, *minbak* and *yeogwan*.

Bus 500 (₩1600, 45 minutes, every 30 to 90 minutes) runs between Pohang's intercity bus terminal and the temple, though some require a transfer at Cheongha. The easiest route is to catch one of three or four buses that travel directly to the temple; check with the tourist office to find out the latest timings. Otherwise, take bus 500 to Cheongha, get off at the tiny terminal and wait for a connecting bus (₩1200, 15 minutes, every 10 to 90 minutes). A taxi from Cheongha to the temple costs ₩15,000.

Pohang

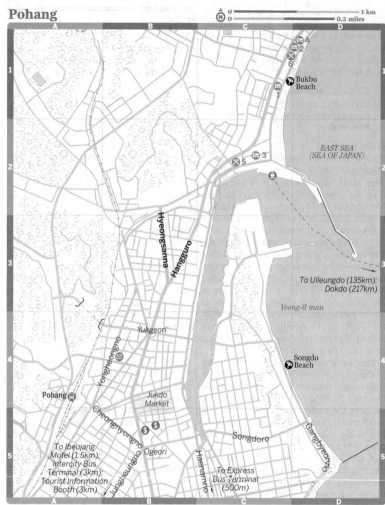

EAST SEA (SEA OF JAPAN)

Bukbu Beach

To Ulleungdo (135km); Dokdo (217km)

Yeong-il man

Songdo Beach

Yukgeori

Jukdo Market

Pohang

Songdoro

Ogeori

To Ibeujang Motel (1.5km); Intercity Bus Terminal (3km); Tourist Information Booth (3km)

To Express Bus Terminal (500m)

Hyeongsanno

Hangguro

Yongheongno

Cheongnyongno

Jungheungno

Haenanno

Gangbyeonno

GYEONGSANGBUK-DO POHANG

🛏 Sleeping

Design Motel A2
BOUTIQUE HOTEL $$

(디자인 모텔 A2; ☎249 5533; r/ste from ₩50,000/60,000; ❄🤶) Right on the beachfront, this hotel with a design sensibility and boutique pretensions offers slightly more imaginative accommodation than its neighbours, with free coffee and popcorn, bathtubs in the middle of the rooms and 3D TVs. Each room is decorated differently (choose carefully from the room menu) and those with sea frontage really make the most of their views.

Blue Ocean Motel
HOTEL $$

(블루오션 모텔; ☎232 2100; s/d/ste ₩50,000/60,000/80,000, add ₩20,000 weekends & summer season; ❄@) Another place with a prime location right on the beachfront, the Blue Ocean has comfortable and tasteful – if rather forgettable – rooms with PCs and all creature comforts, many with great views of the sea.

Motel Pacific
HOTEL $$

(모텔 퍼시픽; ☎252 8855; r from ₩40,000; ❄@) Also on the beachfront strip, this clean and efficiently run place has well-equipped

Pohang

🛏 Sleeping

⊗ Eating

rooms with fridge, TV and ocean views from many. There are in-room PCs in the pricier rooms but, alas, no wireless.

Manstar Motel   HOTEL $$
(맨스타 모텔; ☎244 0225; r ₩40,000-45,000; ❄@) Down a street off the main drag, the Manstar has decent rooms for budget travellers, seashell-design baths and the kind owner speaks English. Some rooms have a computer.

Ibeujang Motel   LOVE HOTEL $
(이브장 모텔; ☎283 2253; d from ₩35,000; ❄) Small but clean rooms with bright furnishings and huge old-school TVs are what you get here, the red lamps being the only hint that this is a love hotel. It's very conveniently located for the Intercity Bus Terminal.

🍴 Eating

For fresh seafood head to Bukbu Beach, where there's a string of restaurants with your meal waiting in tanks along with some good barbecue options. Pohang's unique dish is *mulhoe* (물회), a spicy soup with raw fish.

Yuk Hae Gong   SEAFOOD $$$
(육해공; dishes from ₩25,000; ⊙noon-5am) Take a seat in the outdoor patio overlooking the beach and enjoy barbecued shellfish, called *jogae gu-e* (조개 구이). Shells filled with seafood, cheese and onion look, smell and taste wonderful. It's often brimming with a boisterous late-night crowd – look for the restaurant with a gravel patio floor. If full, many nearby shops have a similar menu.

Jju Jju Mi   KOREAN $$
(쭈쭈미; servings from ₩7000; ⊙5-10pm) Come here for unique *samgyupsal* (삼겹살): tangy pork on a skewer, cooked up at your table on a rotisserie. It's behind the Manstar Motel.

ℹ Information

Bukbu Beach, adjacent to the ferry terminal, is 1.7km long, making it one of the longest sandy beaches on Korea's east coast. There's no English spoken at the **tourist information booth** (☎245 6761; ⊙9am-6pm Mon-Sat Jul & Aug, until 5pm Sep-Jun) outside the **intercity bus terminal**, but there are plenty of English-language brochures and maps. A booth outside the **ferry terminal** is not regularly staffed. Buses 105 and 200 go to Bukbu Beach and the ferry terminal from the intercity bus terminal.

POHANG BUS DEPARTURES

Departures from the intercity bus terminal:

DESTINATION	PRICE (₩)	DURATION (HR)	FREQUENCY
Andong	12,700	2	every 1-2hr
Busan	7700	1½	every 10min
Daegu	6700	2	every 10min
Seoul	23,300	4½	every 30min

Departures from the express bus terminal:

DESTINATION	PRICE (₩)	DURATION (HR)	FREQUENCY
Daejeon	19,800	3¼	hourly
Gwangju	25,800	4	5 daily
Masan	11,400	2¼	5 daily
Seoul	27,000	4½	every 40min

❶ Getting There & Away

Air

Asiana and Korean Air both have daily Seoul-Pohang services.

Boat

See p172 for details of ferries travelling to Ulleungdo.

Bus

For buses departing from Pohang's **intercity bus terminal** (☑272 3194) and the express bus terminal (a five-minute taxi ride from the intercity bus terminal), see the boxed text, p167.

Train

There are a few trains per day from **Pohang station** (☑275 2394) to Seoul (*Saemaul*; ₩39,900, five hours).

❶ Getting Around

Local buses cost ₩1000/1500 (regular/deluxe). Bus 200 runs between the airport and the intercity bus terminal.

Ulleungdo 울릉도

☑054 / POP 10,235

This island, the top of an extinct volcano that rises majestically from the sea floor and has incredibly steep cliffs as a result, offers some of the most spectacular scenery in Korea; think mist-shrouded volcanic cliffs, traditional harbour towns and a breathtaking jagged coastline.

In the rainy season the green hues are even more vivid, saturating the hills like an overtoned colour photograph. In autumn, the hills are a patchwork of reds, greens and yellows from the turning leaves.

Located 135km east of the Korean Peninsula, Ulleungdo today is mainly a fishing community that sees enough tourism to warrant a sprinkle of (sadly) fairly mediocre hotels and far better restaurants.

⊙ Sights & Activities

Dodong-ri   PORT

(도동리) Dodong-ri is the island's administrative centre and largest town. Like a pirate outpost, its harbour is almost hidden away in a narrow valley between two forested mountains, making it visible only when approached directly. It's also the island's main tourist hub, meaning the greatest selection of lodging and dining options.

Behind the ferry terminal, a spiral staircase leads to a seaside **walking trail** (Map p170) offering spectacular views of the sea crashing into jagged rocks. About 1.5km down the path, you'll find a **lighthouse** and, if you choose, a trail leading to Jeodong-ri (it's a two-hour return trip). The one-hour return walk to the lighthouse should be on every traveller's must-do list, but you'll need a flexible schedule as the path is closed when ocean tides are too strong.

Mineral Spring Park   PARK

(약수 공원) The highlight of this park, a 350m climb above Dodong-ri, is the **cable car** (Map p170; return ₩8000; ⊙6am-8pm) across a steep valley to Manghyangbong (316m). The ride up affords stunning views of the sea and a bird's-eye view of Dodong-ri. Visit either early or late in the day to avoid crowds, and try to avoid the weekends entirely, if possible.

The park's namesake *yaksu gwangjang* (mineral-water spring) is near the top. The water has a distinctive flavour (think diet citrus soda-meets-quartz) and some claim drinking it has all sorts of medicinal benefits.

Taeha-ri   MONORAIL

(태하리; Map p169) In the northwest corner of the island about 20km from Dodong-ri, Ulleungdo's most recent tourist investment is a **monorail** (admission ₩5000; ⊙8am-5pm). The six-minute, 304m ride up a sharp cliff (39-degree angle) drops you off at the base of a 500m trail leading up to **Hyangmok Lighthouse** (향목 등대) and a terrific view of the northern coastline.

Buses to Taeha-ri leave the Dodong-ri terminal (₩1600, 40 minutes, every 40 minutes).

Namyang-dong   VIEWPOINT

(남양동; Map p169) The coastal road from Dodong-ri to Taeha-ri leads through Namyang, a tiny seaside community with spectacular cliffs covered with Chinese juniper and odd rock formations.

Sunset Point Pavilion (Ilmoljeon Mangdae) is a steep 15-minute walk above the town, commanding great views of the ocean and the sunset. To get there, follow the western creek out of town and cross the bridge after the school. A small trail continues up to the pavilion.

Jeodong-ri   PORT

(저동리; Map p169) Jeodong-ri is a fishing village with picturesque sea walls, fishing nets, and seagulls. The boats with the lamps strung around like oversize holiday lights are for catching squid.

Ulleungdo

Bongnae Pokpo WATERFALL
(봉래폭포 Map p169; admission ₩1400; ⊙6am-
7pm Apr-Oct, 8am-5pm Nov-Mar) A steep 1.5km
walk from Jeodong-ri is Bongnae Pokpo.
Source of the island's drinking water, the
waterfall is quite spectacular during the
summer.

On the return trip, cool down in **Cheo-
nyeon Natural Air Conditioner** (천연 에어
컨), a cave that maintains a year-round temperature of 4°C.

Buses serve the car park from Dodong-ri
via Jeodong-ri (₩1700, 15 minutes, every 40
minutes).

Boat Trips

A **round-island tour** (₩25,000; ⊙departs 9am
& 3pm) is a great way to admire Ulleungdo's
dramatic landscape. Tours depart from Dodong-ri ferry terminal (Map p170) and last
around two hours.

Other sightseeing boats run to **Jukdo**
(Map p169; ₩16,000; ⊙10am & 3pm), a nature

preserve 4km from Ulleungdo. Visitors are
welcome to take a picnic to eat on the island.
It takes about 1½ hours including walk or
picnic time.

With a reservation and sufficient demand, speedy boats (₩50,000, 3¼ hours) run
out to **Dokdo**, but you can't go onto the
island (see the boxed text, p171).

During the annual **squid festival** (three
days in mid-August), you may be able to
board boats and even ride a vessel out to sea.
The rest of the year it's interesting to watch
the boats in the evening when they head out
to sea with their lanterns glaring.

Hiking

Various pathways lead to the summit of
Seong-inbong (984m; Map p169), but the
two main routes run from Dodong-ri (about
five hours return) or Nari-bunji (four to five
hours return).

From Dodong-ri, take the main road towards **Daewon-sa** (Map p170). Just before

Dodong-ri

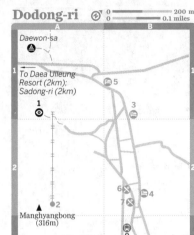

```
0          200 m
0         0.1 miles
```

Daewon-sa

To Daea Ulleung
Resort (2km);
Sadong-ri (2km)

Manghyangbong
(316m)

Harbour

you reach the temple, there is a fork in the trail and a sign (in Korean) pointing the way to Seong-inbong (a steep 4.1km).

From **Nari-bunji** (Map p169), enter the thick forest, adhering to the right-hand path, and you'll arrive at fields of chrysanthemum. Further on you'll pass a traditional home. Finally, at the entrance to the virgin forest area and picnic ground, the steep ascent of Seong-inbong takes you (one hour) through a forest of Korean beech, hemlock and lime.

Just below the peak, as you descend to Dodong-ri, is a trail off to the right, down to Namyang-dong (1½ hours).

If you're not up for a major hike, try the 5km return trip from the Nari basin bus stop to **Sillyeong Su** (신령수; Map p169), a mountain spring. The walk cuts through a thick forest and is an easy one-hour stroll while waiting for the van to take you back to Cheonbu for a connection back to Dodong-ri.

🛏 Sleeping

Ulleungdo has lots of choices for those on a budget, but is still very poorly set up for those wanting more comfort or luxury. Room rates rise steeply in peak season (from ₩50,000 to ₩100,000 in July, August and holidays) – coinciding with a flood of boisterous Korean travellers on package tours – so book-ahead. The hotels listed are all in or around Dodong-ri.

Khan Motel   HOTEL **$$**
(칸 모텔; Map p170; ☎791 8500; www.motelkhan. com; d from ₩75,000; ✳@) One of the best options on the island is this classy if rather minimalist place with both *ondol* and Western-style rooms. The rooms are on the small side, though the large TVs and computers are pluses. The owner is a great resource for guests looking for hard-to-find ferry tickets during the busy travel season.

Daea Ulleung Resort   HOTEL **$$$**
(대아 리조트; off Map p170; ☎791 8800; www. daearesort.com; r/ste from ₩160,000/230,000; ✳@⊠) Definitely the island's most expensive property, this impressive resort has amazing mountaintop views of the sea, but the rooms here are rather overpriced for what they are: rather unexciting and on the small side, albeit perfectly comfortable and clean. From mid-July to August there's an outdoor swimming pool, which is when room rates shoot up in price. The hotel is in Sadong-ri, a ₩4000 taxi ride from Dodong-ri.

Hotel Ulleungdo   HOTEL **$$**
(울릉도 호텔; Map p170; ☎791 6611; ondol/r ₩50,000/80,000; ✳) While it's the only hotel

in Dodong-ri officially accredited for tourism, the Ulleungdo remains a large *yeogwan* with lots of simple but clean *ondol* rooms. It's a popular choice for groups who want to economise by sharing a room and don't mind the minimal furnishings.

Pension Skyhill   PENSION **$$**
(스카이힐 펜션; Map p170; ☎791 1040; d/ondol from ₩65,000/55,000; ❊) Near the top of town, it's a popular destination for groups of university students, so the rooms and communal areas – such as a shared kitchen and rooftop barbecue facilities – look a little worn out. However, it's a convenient stroll from several restaurants and one of the cheapest deals in town.

🍴 Eating & Drinking

Outdoor seafood stalls are ubiquitous in Ulleungdo. There are a few scattered *mandu/naengmyeon/gimbap* shops, where you can eat for as little as ₩3000, and some casual restaurants by the harbour with outdoor seating. Unless otherwise indicated, all the restaurants listed are in Dodong-ri.

Nokdu Bindaeddeok   KOREAN **$$**
(녹두 빈대떡; Jeodong-ri; dishes from ₩10,000; ❧9am-8pm) Definitely the coolest and most unique of the island's eating options is this friendly place with outdoor floor seating under trees, overlooking a landscaped garden filled with statues, pagodas and a crane. The food is delicious; try the crispy *bindaetteok* (빈대떡; mungbean pancake) and a platter of homemade *muk* (묵; acorn jelly) mixed with spicy onions and carrots. Nokdu Bindaeddeok is on the path leading to Bongnae Pokpo just outside Jeodong-ri. Look for two Korean totems in front of a black gate.

99 Sikdang   SEAFOOD **$$**
(99 식당; Map p170; dishes ₩6000-23,000; ❧6.30am-10pm; 🅰) One of the island's most famous restaurants – its owner will tell you proudly about its many appearances on Korea's famously food-obsessed TV channels – this is a place to delight in seafood barbecue and dishes such as *ojing-eo bulgogi* (오징어 불고기; squid grilled at the table with vegetables and hot pepper sauce) and *ttaggaebibap* (딱개비밥; shellfish with rice).

Yong Gung   SEAFOOD **$$**
(용궁; Map p170; dishes from ₩16,000; ❧8am-10pm; 🅰) Sit near the seafront with a bottle of *soju*, a platter of raw fish and watch the ocean crash onto the rocky shoreline at this ramshackle but quietly charming place. Mr Jeong (who speaks passable English) and his brother run the place and personally catch the seafood on offer by diving for sea creatures each morning. It's about 500m from the ferry terminal on the seaside walking trail.

Sanchang-hoe Sikdang   SEAFOOD **$$**
(산창회식당; Map p170; mains ₩7000-18,000; ❧6pm-midnight) Downstairs from Sanchangjang Yeogwan, it specialises in *honghapbap* (mussel rice) served with a locally-cultivated mountain plant called *myeong-e* (명이) and a generous bowl of *miyeokguk* (미역국; seaweed soup).

ℹ Information

The helpful **information booth** (Map p170; ☎790 6454; ❧9am-6pm) by the Dodong-ri ferry terminal occasionally has English speakers on duty, but this can't be relied upon. You can change money or withdraw cash from the 24-hour bank machine at Nonghyup Bank in Dodong-ri.

WAITING FOR DOKDO

In 1905, during the Japanese occupation, Japan annexed Dokdo – fishing grounds marked by two small, rocky islands – and renamed it Takeshima. Korea protested, but as a colony did not have much say. Following WWII, US general Douglas MacArthur designated the island part of Korea, and US forces erected a monument there to Korean fishermen accidentally killed nearby by American ordnance. However, Japan destroyed the monument in 1952, prompting Korea to send a defence unit and Japan to put the island under surveillance.

In August 2012 Lee Myung Bak became the first sitting South Korean President to visit Dokdo, causing tension between South Korea and Japan and bringing the disputed claims back to international prominence. While the two countries remain economically close and otherwise enjoy good relations, the disputed issue of Dokdo's ownership doesn't seem to be going anywhere quickly.

ℹ️ Getting There & Away

Ferry

You can get to Ulleungdo by **ferry** (☎242 5111; www.daea.com) from Pohang (standard/1st class ₩58,800/64,400, three hours). There is one departure daily year-round (weather permitting), and there are two daily departures during the summer months. If assigned seats are unavailable you have the option of buying a floor-seating ticket in a common room for a slight discount. It's possible to take vehicles on the standard daily ferry, the *Sunflower* (₩5000 per vehicle), but not on the supplementary summer ferry, the *Ocean Flower*.

It is best to reserve your tickets to and from the island, especially during summer – ask at a tourist office someone to do this for you. Otherwise you can buy your ticket at the terminal first thing in the morning, but go early and expect to wait.

ℹ️ Getting Around

Bus

Buses run between Dodong-ri and Jeodong-ri every 30 minutes (₩1100, 10 minutes). Eighteen daily buses go from Dodong-ri via Namyang-dong (₩1700, 25 minutes) to Cheonbu-ri (₩1700, 65 minutes), where you can transfer to Nari-bunji via a van (₩1100, 10 minutes, eight daily). Timetables are posted at the Dodong-ri bus terminal.

Taxi

Taxis, usually 4WD, regularly ply between Dodong-ri and Jeodong-ri (₩5000). All day trips can be arranged for about ₩150,000.

Andong 안동

☎54 / POP 184,000

Famous for its mackerel, its strong *soju* and its wooden masks, Andong makes a good base for exploring the numerous historical and cultural sights outside the city. The city itself has a very laid-back vibe and is strikingly friendly, with a good selection of places to eat and stay.

⊙ Sights & Activities

Andong Folk Village   VILLAGE
(안동 민속 마을) On a hillside above the town, Andong Folk Village is a repository for homes moved to prevent them from being submerged by the construction of Andong Dam in 1976. Relocated and partially reconstructed traditional-style buildings range from peasant farmhouses to elaborate mansions of government officials with multiple courtyards. The village looks so authentic that the TV network KBS has used it as a set for historical dramas on multiple occasions. The village is about 4km east of Andong, close to the dam wall on the opposite side of the river from the main road. Take buses 3, 3-1 or 3-2 (₩1200) from next to the tourist office and hop off at *minsokchon* (folk village). A taxi costs about ₩6000.

Andong Folklore Museum   MUSEUM
(안동 민속 박물관; ☎821 0649; admission ₩1000; ☉9am-6pm Mar-Oct, until 5pm Nov-Feb)

ANDONG'S MASKED BALL

In late September/early October, masks and their admirers come from all over the world to join in a host of mask-related festivities. In Hahoe Folk Village (24km from Andong), masked dancers perform traditional dances in the pine forests to the delight of crowds. Andong City has numerous mask-related shows, and a mask-making contest pits artisan against artisan in a delightful 'mask off'. Firework displays are another popular attraction.

Every weekend at 3pm from May to October (as well as Sunday at 3pm in March, April and November), **Byeolsingut Talnori** performances take place in a small stadium near Hahoe's car park. These shows are a must-see; plus, they're free, although donations are demanded by hard-working *halmeoni* (grandmas). If you can't make it to a performance, you can view many masks at the Hahoe Mask Museum.

According to legend, the Hahoe mask tradition came about when the residents of Hahoe got frustrated with their hoity-toity noble clan. One clever craftsman carved a likeness of one of the most obsequious, much to the delight of his peers. Byeolsingut Talnori is a traditional dance style created by the common folk for the common folk to satirise the establishment. Characters wear masks representing social classes including corrupt monks and the rich, some with bulging eyes and crooked mouths. The conflicts among them are portrayed in amusing combinations of popular entertainment and shamanism. Accompanying the dance are the sounds of *nong-ak*, a traditional farmers musical percussion quartet. For more information, visit www.maskdance.com or Andong's tourist office (p175).

Andong

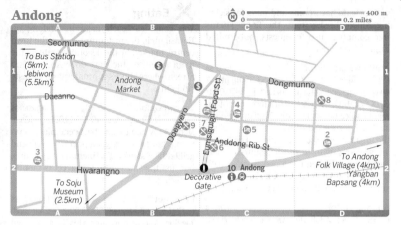

Just next door to the folk village, it offers clear displays of Korea's folk traditions from birth through to death.

FREE **Soju Museum** MUSEUM
(소주 박물관; www.andongsoju.net; ⊙9am-5pm Mon-Sat) The heady 45% *soju* of Andong may or may not be to your taste, but its significance has been preserved with its designation as an intangible cultural property. On the grounds of the Andong Soju Brewery, the museum houses a couple of displays that detail the distilling process, the drinking ceremony and a history of *soju* labels. A (thimble-sized) taste of the liquor is given at the end of your visit.

The museum is in the south of Andong, across the Nakdong River, and is best reached by taxi (₩5000). Catch bus 34 or 36 (₩1200, 10 minutes) from the stop opposite and down the road from the train station, near an elementary school.

FREE **Jebiwon** SHRINE
(제비원; ⊙24hr) The body and robes of this Buddha are carved on a boulder over 12m high, on top of which are the head and hair – carved out of two separate pieces of rock.

Catch bus 54 (₩1200, every 30 minutes) from opposite and down the road from the railway station and ask the driver to drop you off at Jebiwon. Moving on to the next destination requires some imaginative travel techniques because there are no obvious bus stops on the street. You can stand on the street and wait for a bus or taxi, or ask anyone nearby for directions to Andong or Yeongju, which is 45km north. Don't be surprised if someone offers you a lift.

Andong

🛏 **Sleeping**
  1 Andong Hotel.............................C1
  2 Andong Park Hotel D2
  3 Happy Guesthouse A2
  4 Munhwa Motel...........................C1
  5 Sharp Motel................................C2

🍴 **Eating**
  6 Jaerim Galbi...............................C2
  7 Lavender C2
  8 Loving Hut..................................D1
  9 Mammoth Bakery B2

ℹ **Information**
  10 Tourist Office............................C2

🎭 Festivals & Events

Andong Mask Dance Festival (held at the end of September to early October) is a great time to visit Andong. It brings together a colourful array of national and international mask dance troupes. It is usually held in tandem with **Andong's folk festival**, showcasing performances of traditional music and dance. Check with the tourist office for details.

🛏 Sleeping

TOP CHOICE **Happy Guesthouse** HOSTEL **$**
(해피 게스트하우스; ☏010 8903 1638; s/d incl breakfast ₩25,000/40,000; ✳@) This brand new hostel is the first of its kind in Andong and a welcome change to the pricier motels that crowd the town's centre. Incense infuses the traditional downstairs dining room, while upstairs there are spotless new rooms

with private bathrooms and mats for sleeping rolled directly onto the floor. There's free computer use for guests, but limited English is spoken.

Andong Park Hotel
HOTEL $$

(안동 파크관광 호텔; ☎853 1501; http://www.andongparkhotel.com; d/tw/VIP ₩50,000/60,000/70,000; ❄@🕾) Andong's establishment choice boasts friendly English-speaking staff and surprisingly reasonable prices given the quality of accommodation. The suites are spacious, with their own lounges, smart bathrooms with old-fashioned wooden bath tubs, and flatscreen TVs. Standard rooms are smaller, but well maintained and clean.

Andong Hotel
HOTEL $

(안동 호텔; ☎858 1166; www.andonghotel.net; s/d/ste from ₩40,000/50,000/70,000; ❄@🕾) Perhaps the best choice in town, the Andong Hotel is set right in the centre of Andong and despite an incredibly kitschy decor capable of making any African dictator feel right at home, it has spacious rooms (the suite are huge!), good bathrooms, desktop PCs in each room and helpful staff.

Munhwa Motel
MOTEL $$

(문화 모텔; ☎857 7001; s/d ₩35,000/45,000; ❄@) With its smart and surprisingly unhideous room decor, this unfussy motel in the centre of town is good value. The owners are very friendly, though they speak no English and some rooms have internet access via PCs.

Sharp Motel
LOVE HOTEL $$

(샾 모텔; ☎854 0081; s/d ₩40,000/50,000; ❄@) Centrally located and offering good standard, relatively tasteful rooms, all with huge flatscreen TV, in-room PCs and fridges, the Sharp is a love hotel, but not obviously so.

✗ Eating

You could eat each meal in Andong on Eumsiguigil, the restaurant row in the town centre, marked by the decorative gate off the main street, or the next door Andong Rib Street, where there's a proliferation of tasty rib joints.

Jaerim Galbi
KOREAN $$

(재림 갈비; servings ₩9000-19,000; ⊙10am-11pm; 🎟) A good value barbecue place serving up pork ribs, *bulgogi*, prime beef rib and grilled beef steaks. The menu is very simple but just the smell from the street is mouthwatering.

Lavender
INTERNATIONAL $$

(라벤더; set meals ₩8000-20,000; ⊙11am-10pm Tue-Sun) White and airy, this is a civilised pasta and salad place – pastas come with garlic bread, salad and coffee.

Yangban Bapsang
KOREAN $$

(양반 밥상; meals ₩8000-18,000; ⊙10am-9pm) Mackerel served golden, skin crispy, flesh tender – melts on the tongue the way mackerel was meant to. Not far from the Andong Folk Village, it's across the street from the entrance to the wooden bridge.

Loving Hut
VEGAN $

(러빙 헛; ₩5000-8,000; ⊙noon-10pm) This simple place may look like nothing special but will thrill vegans and vegetarians with its *bibimbap*, *kimchi* stew, cold noodles and even a vegan burger.

Mammoth Bakery
BAKERY $

(맘모스 베이커리; coffee ₩3000, breads ₩1000-4000; ⊙8am-11pm) Friendly owner with good espresso and fresh tasty treats. If the weather is nice, enjoy your drink on the outdoor patio.

BUS DEPARTURES FROM ANDONG

DESTINATION	PRICE (₩)	DURATION	FREQUENCY
Busan	15,300	2½hr	every 30-60min
Daegu	9300	1½hr	every 30min
Daejeon	14,100	3hr	every 30min
Dongseoul	15,700	3hr	every 30min
Gyeongju	12,000	1¾hr	7 daily
Juwangsan	7400	35min	6 daily
Pohang	12,700	2hr	every 2hr
Ulsan	14,700	2¾hr	8 daily

TRAIN DEPARTURES FROM ANDONG

DESTINATION	PRICE (₩)	DURATION (HR)	FREQUENCY
Daegu	7400	2	1 daily
Dongdaegu*	7800	2	3 daily
Gyeongju	7900	2	3 daily
Seoul	22,500	4	8 daily
Seoul	15,200	5½	2 daily

* transfer to Busan

ⓘ Information

The **tourist office** (☏852 6800; www.andong. go.kr; ☺9am-6pm) is outside the train station. The staff are very helpful and English is spoken.

ⓘ Getting There & Away

Bus

Andong has a brand new **bus terminal** (☏857 8296; www.andongterminal.co.kr) around 5km from the town centre. To get into town take bus 0, 1, 2,11, 46, 51 or 76 (₩1200) and get out at Andong station, or it's a quick ₩5000 cab ride.

Train

For departures from Andong train station, see the boxed text above.

ⓘ Getting Around

The tourist office hands out a helpful local bus timetable with English explanations. The town is small enough to get around on foot, and local buses serve all the sights.

Hahoe Folk Village
하회 민속 마을

Now a Unesco World Heritage site, **Hahoe Folk Village** (Hahoe Minsok Maeul; admission ₩2000; ☺9am-6pm Mar-Oct, 9am-sunset Nov-Feb) is the outstanding attraction of the region around Andong. Arrive early in the morning and the mystical beauty of this creates the illusion that you are in another time.

Walk down the dirt road and you'll pass small garden plots of squash vines, corn and green chilli peppers, all overshadowed by riverbank escarpments. Down the road, farm fields stretch out to the horizon. On your left is a magnificent village of centuries-old homes, so impeccable in design you'd swear you were living in the Joseon dynasty.

While other Korean folk villages can be tourist productions, this one has 230 residents maintaining old ways, and the government helps with preservation and restoration. There is a tourist information booth at the entrance to the village, and a lotus pond that (in season) is filled with beautiful blooms. Remember to respect people's privacy if you step beyond the entrance gates.

Two kilometres back in the direction of Andong, **Hahoe Mask Museum** (admission ₩2000; ☺9.30am-6pm) houses a remarkable collection of traditional Korean masks, as well as masks from across Asia and countries as diverse as Nigeria, Italy and Mexico. Two daily buses to and from Hahoe follow a bumpy dirt road and make a 10-minute stop at **Byeongsan Seowon** (admission free; ☺9am-6pm Apr-Oct, 9am-5pm Nov-Mar), a former Confucian academy dating from 1572.

Many homes in Hahoe have *minbak* rooms for rent from around ₩50,000. But for more luxury and privacy, try **Rak Ko Jae Hahoe** (☏054-857 3410, 010-8555 1407; www.rkj.co.kr; s/d incl breakfast ₩120,000/180,000; ❇☏), a four-room, upmarket guesthouse facing the river and blending seamlessly with the surrounding thatched-roof *hanok* (traditional wooden homes). Each traditional room comes with modern comforts like cable TV and a fridge plus an odd *hinoki* (pine) bathtub. There's a mud-walled *jjimjil-bang* as well, for that true traditional bathing experience.

Bus 46 (₩1800, 50 minutes, eight daily) runs out to Hahoe from Andong.

Cheongnyangsan Provincial Park
청량산 도립공원

Beyond Dosan Seowon, this **park** (admission free; ☺8.30am-6pm) boasts spectacular views and tracks wandering along cliff precipices. In addition to the mountain Cheongnyangsan, the summit of which is Changinbong

(870m), there are 11 scenic peaks, eight caves and a waterfall, **Gwanchang Pokpo**. A spiderweb of tracks radiates out from Cheongnyang-sa and most are well marked. The largest temple in the park is **Cheongnyang-sa** and there are a number of small hermitages. Built in AD 663, the temple is quite scenic, sitting in a steep valley below the cliffs. **Ansimdang**, at the base of the temple, is a pleasant teahouse.

It takes about five hours to complete a round trip of the peaks, returning to the bus stops, or about 90 minutes to the temple and back again.

Across the street from the park entrance, there are a dozen *minbak,* shops, restaurants and the **Cheongnyangsan Museum** (admission free; ⊙9am-6pm), a modest effort with artefacts related to the area's agricultural history and clean public toilets.

From Andong, bus 67 (₩2200, one hour, six daily) continues past Dosan Seowon to the park.

Juwangsan National Park
주왕산 국립공원

Far to the east of Andong and reaching almost to the coast, the 106-sq-km **Juwangsan National Park** (admission ₩2000; ⊙sunrise-1hr before sunset) is dominated by impressive limestone pinnacles that seem to appear from nowhere. Beautiful gorges, waterfalls and cliff walks also feature, and with any luck you'll see an otter or protected Eurasian flying squirrel, among the 900-plus wildlife species here.

◉ Sights & Activities

Most of the visitors to the park are content to see the **waterfalls** and **caves**, but for a more rigorous experience you can try hiking up from **Daejeon-sa** to **Juwang-san** (720m; 1¼ hours), once known as Seokbyeongsan or 'Stone Screen Mountain', along the ridge to **Kaldeunggogae** (732m, 15 minutes) and then down to **Hurimaegi** (50 minutes), a beauty spot, before following the valley back to Daejeon-sa (1¾ hours).

On the way back down take the side trip to **Juwanggul Cave**; the track first passes **Juwang-am Hermitage**, from where a steel walkway takes you through a narrow gorge to the modest cave.

Also within the park is **Naewonmaeul**, a tiny village where craftspeople do woodworking.

🛏 Sleeping & Eating

The *minbak* village *(minbakchon)* opposite the Juwangsan bus terminal has 50-plus properties of varying quality, so shop around before paying. The room rates can double on weekends and in July, August and October.

Hyangchon Sikdang-Minbak   B&B **$**
(향촌 식당 민박; ☑873 0202; r from ₩35,000) With the largest sign near the park entrance, this *minbak* and restaurant is hard to miss. It also has some of the area's nicest rooms. Downstairs in the **restaurant**, the *jeongsik* meal (₩10,000) comes with soup and a colourful array of leafy side dishes from the local mountains, some of which are picked by the owner.

Bangalo Minbak   CHALET **$$**
(방갈로 민박; ☑874 5200; r weekdays/weekends ₩30,000/60,000) About 500m from the park entrance, this place has a log-cabin exterior with central courtyard. Rooms have *ondol* or beds and there's also a simple onsite **restaurant**.

BUS DEPARTURES FROM JUWANGSAN

DESTINATION	PRICE (₩)	DURATION
Andong	7300	1½hr
Busan	18,900	3¾hr
Cheongsong	1600	20min
Dongdaegu	15,500	3hr
Dongseoul	23,200	5hr
Yeongcheon*	12,400	2hr

* transfer to Gyeongju

Juwangsan National Park

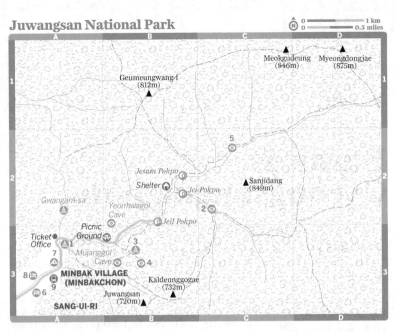

Juwangsan National Park

Campground　　　　　CAMPGROUND $
(☏873 0014; sites adult/youth/child ₩2000/
1500/1000) The campground, on the other
side of the stream, has basic facilities and
rents tents (₩5000 to ₩10,000).

❶ Information

The main gateway to the park is the town of
Cheongsong, about 15km away. At the park
entrance, the **information centre** (☏873 0014;
2nd fl, bus terminal; ◔9am-5.30pm) has English
and Korean maps detailing hiking routes, distances and estimated calories burned. Be sure
to check here for local trail conditions.

❶ Getting There & Away

Virtually all buses to Juwangsan stop in Cheongsong (₩1500, 20 minutes, every 30 minutes).
Check the timetable inside the Juwangsan **bus
terminal** for detailed schedules.

Busan & Gyeongsangnam-do

Best Places to Stay

» Ibis Ambassador Hotel (p185)

» Paradise Hotel (p185)

» Westin Chosun Beach Hotel (p185)

» Dong Bang Hotel (p197)

Best Places to Eat

» Dongnae Halmae Pajeon (p186)

» Jagalchi Fish Market (p187)

» Busan's tent bars (p191)

» Zio Ricco (p198)

Why Go?

The best sites in Korea either awe with beauty or deepen our understanding of the culture. Busan and Gyeongsangnam-do (부산과경상남도) do both.

Underrated Busan's easily accessible mountains and beaches, as well as its colourful seafood and drinking scene make it very easy to love. It's home to the world's largest shopping and entertainment complex, and a world-class cinema centre that's dazzling to behold.

Gyeongsangnam-do's natural beauty, inspired by verdant mountains and coastal towns untouched by tourist development, is closer than you think, thanks to an efficient transport system. Hop on a bus and you'll be rewarded with outstanding hiking trails on Jirisan, glorious temples in hideaway locations and lush rice paddies in just about every rural community. For marine treasures, board a ferry and go island-hopping around Tongyeong. On land or by sea, Gyeongsangnam-do is accessible, affordable and waiting to be explored.

When to Go

Busan

Apr–May Cherry blossoms make spring a great time for hiking.

Jul–Aug Haeundae and Gwangan beaches in full swing.

Oct Busan International Film Festival runs through mid-October.

History

Gyeongsangnam-do has a long history of warfare, though it's difficult to beat the Imjin War for destruction, treachery and the birth of an icon. In 1592 the Japanese were eager to secure a land route to China. The Joseon government refused assistance, so the Japanese attacked. Led by Toyotomi Hideyoshi, the Japanese landed 160,000 troops at several places including Busan, Sangju Beach and Jinju, where the Koreans made a valiant yet unsuccessful stand against a superior enemy.

The war's star was Admiral Yi Sun-sin, a brilliant tactician credited with the development of the turtle ship, an ironclad vessel instrumental in harassing Japanese supply lines. Despite his significant wartime contributions, Yi was arrested in 1597 for disobeying orders thanks to a clever ruse

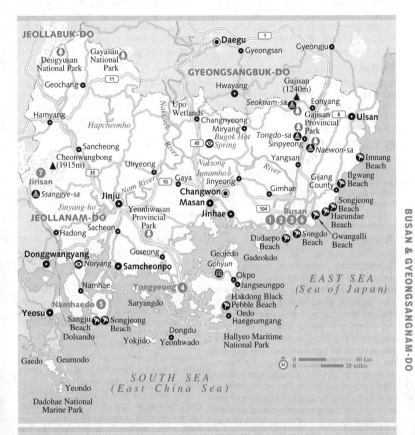

Busan & Gyeongsangnam-do Highlights

1 Shock your taste buds with Busan seafood specialities like raw fish at **Jagalchi Fish Market** (p187)

2 Clink glasses of gut-warming soju in Busan's colourful **tent bars** (p191)

3 Get architecturally and cinematically inspired at the **Busan Cinema Centre** (p191)

4 Go island-hopping off the coast of **Tongyeong** (p195)

5 Take in terraced rice paddies and misty temples on the picturesque island of **Namhaedo** (p199)

6 Rejuvenate your body at **Spa Land** (p183), one of the world's largest hot spas

7 Explore **Jirisan** (p200), one of the best places to hike in Korea

concocted by the Japanese, who were eager to see the good admiral removed from the war. With Yi behind bars, the Japanese launched a massive assault that destroyed all but 13 of Korea's 133 vessels. Shaken by the loss, the king released Yi and put him in charge of the tattered navy. In a classic case of size doesn't matter, the admiral destroyed or damaged 133 Japanese vessels. One year later, Yi defeated a Japanese armada near Namhaedo that cost the invaders 450 ships. It also cost Admiral Yi his life. In September of 1598, Hideyoshi died and the Japanese leadership lost its appetite for the war.

ℹ Getting There & Away

International travellers with direct routes to Busan typically come through Japan by air (see p192) or by sea (see p193). Most train travellers stop at Busan station, a glassy facility close to the city centre.

ℹ Getting Around

For regional trips, the bus is a superior option with departures from Seobu and Dongbu bus terminals, both close to subway stations. By air, most travellers land at Gimhae International Airport, about 30 minutes west of central Busan.

Busan 부산

🎵051 / POP 3.6 MILLION

Bursting with mountains, beaches, hot springs and seafood, South Korea's second-largest city is a rollicking port town with tons to offer. From casual tent bars and chic designer cafes to fish markets teeming with every species imaginable, Busan has something for all tastes on land or sea. The mountains criss-crossing the city and the coastline define the urban landscape, while events like the Busan International Film Festival underline the city's desire to be a global meeting place. The people can be brash but down-to-earth, caring little for the airs of Seoul, which seems like a distant cousin that's just way too big and complex. Note that Busan is within the boundaries of Gyeongsangnam-do province but is a separate administrative unit with its own telephone area code.

◎ Sights & Activities

Beomeo-sa   TEMPLE

(범어사; Map p184; www.beomeosa.co.kr; ⊙8.30am-5.30pm; Ⓜ Line 1 to Beomeosa, Exit 5) This magnificent temple is perhaps Busan's best sight. Despite its city location, Beomeo-sa is a world away from the urban jungle, with beautiful architecture neatly set against an extraordinary mountain backdrop. It's a busy place, as the path leading to the temple is the northern starting point for trails across Geumjeongsan. Before heading back to the city, visit the restaurants near the bus stop to enjoy *pajeon* (파전; green onion pancake) for ₩7000.

At street level from the station spin 180 degrees, turn left at the corner and walk 200m to the terminus. Catch bus 90 (₩1200, 20 minutes, every 15 minutes from 8am to 8pm) or take a ₩3000 taxi to the temple entrance.

Geumjeong Fortress   HISTORIC SITE

(금정산성; Map p184) Travellers climbing **Geumjeongsan** (Geumjeong Mountain) expecting to see a fort will be disappointed because there isn't one. Geumjeong fortress is a stone wall with four gates. Not all is lost because this is where you'll find some of the city's best hiking. Outdoor enthusiasts seeking an intimate experience with nature should avoid the mountain on holidays and weekend mornings – peak times for maddening crowds of fashionable hikers.

Most hikers start at the north end of the trail that begins with a steep climb along the left side of Beomeo-sa. This trail leads to **Bukmun** (북문; North Gate). The 8.8km hike from Beomeo-sa to **Nammun** (남문; South Gate) is a comfortable walk with a couple of steep stretches.

The least arduous route is by **cable car** (Map p184; one way/return adult ₩4000/7000, child ₩4000/2500; ⊙9am-6.30pm) inside **Geumgang Park** (Map p184; admission free; ⊙9am-6pm Mar-Oct, 9am-5pm Nov-Feb) at the southern base of the mountain. From the cable car, it's a 10-minute walk to the South Gate.

The cable car is a 15-minute walk from Oncheonjang station on Line 1, Exit 1. Walk left towards the overhead pedestrian crosswalk. Cross the street, walk down the left staircase and turn right at the first corner. Down the street, there's a sign pointing to Geumgang Park.

FREE Seokbul-sa   TEMPLE

(석불사; Map p184; ⊙7am-7pm) Hard to find, difficult to reach and a wonder to behold, this temple is a hermitage carved into rock. Two massive boulders stretching 20m in height jut out from the mountainside to form a U-shaped enclave with three rock facings, which is now a place of worship. Inside the enclave, Buddhist images have been meticulously etched into stone. Visually powerful in scale and impact, it's the kind of work that moves first-time visitors to exclaim 'wow' as they step back and arch their necks to get the full picture.

The most interesting – and strenuous – route to Seokbul-sa is to add it to your Geumjeongsan hike (be sure to carry plenty of water). From **Nammum** (남문; South Gate), the path indicated by the **Mandeokchon** (만덕촌) sign leads to a collection of restaurants and a foot volleyball court in **Nammun Village** (남문마을). Keep going straight until you can't go any further, then turn right onto a narrow path. Eventually this leads to a larger path heading down the mountainside. Look for a sign that reads 석불사 입구 (Seokbul-sa entrance) which points you down a steep, rocky trail. Way down at the bottom, turn right at the cement road and walk uphill to the temple.

On the way back, you can either return to Nammun gate, and then follow the signs to the cable car, or keep walking down the cement road from the temple and you'll end up near Mandeok subway station on Line 3. Bottom line: add 4km and two to three hours to the Geumjeongsan hike to experience one of the most unique temples in Busan.

Haeundae   BEACH
(해운대해수욕장; Map p186) Beautiful Haeundae is the country's most famous beach. During the peak travel season in August, umbrellas mushroom across the 2km beach while frolickers fill the water with inner tubes rented from booths behind the beach. It's a fun family outing with 500,000 friends, though the marketing bumph portraying Haeundae as a world-class resort is bunk. Take Line 2 to Haeundae station, Exit 3 or 5, and walk to the beach.

Gwangalli   BEACH
(Map p182; 광안리해수욕장) Gwangalli is the best option for access and quality among Busan's seven other beaches, namely Dadaepo, Songdo, Songjeong, Ilgwang, Imnang and Pebble Beach. Although the wall of commercial development behind the beach diminishes the daytime experience, Gwangalli really shines at night. The multicoloured light show illuminating the Gwangan Bridge is grand. The shortest route to Gwangalli is Line 2 to Geumnyeonsan station, Exit 3.

Rotate 180 degrees at street level and turn right at the corner; the beach is five minutes down the road. Or take Line 2 to Gwangan station, Exit 5.

Igidae   PARK
(이기대; Map p182; Ⓜ Line 2 to Namcheon, Exit 3) If the trails of Geumjeongsan seem more like work than pleasure, there are opportunities to explore Busan's natural beauty at a more leisurely pace. Igidae is a nature park that's ideal for a two-hour stroll. On the way up **Mt Jangsan** (225m), you'll come to the first of three plateaus that provide panoramic views of the city. There are a myriad of trails to choose from, just be sure you eventually get over to the sea and follow the boardwalk that zigzags along the coastline. The park is a 20-minute walk down the road from the subway station. Pick up the trail behind the pier and outdoor driving range.

Taejongdae Park   PARK
(태종대유원지; Map p182) On the southern tip of **Yeongdo** (영도; Yeong Island) is another chance to experience the city's rugged coastline. Walk down the stone steps and you'll come to a tiny beach, featuring jagged cliffs, thick pine forests, odd rock formations and a lighthouse. The slow but convenient Danubi tram (adult/child ₩1500/600) can save your feet but you'll have to line up; otherwise count on a two-hour walk. From Exit 6 at Nampo station, catch bus 38 (₩1200) on the Jagalchi side of the street or take a taxi (₩18,000).

BUSAN IN FILM

Haeundae (2009) is about a tsunami that crashes onto Busan's most famous beach. The story follows a standard disaster movie plot line: a geologist predicts a calamity by tracking seismic activity in the East Sea but nobody listens. When the inevitable tide is set to destroy Haeundae, the geologist goes to the beach to see his ex-wife.

Gritty and disturbing, *Chingu* (2001) is the story of four school friends, boys whose lives move in radically different directions as men. Two friends end up in rival gangs, leading to a compelling courtroom scene.

Busan

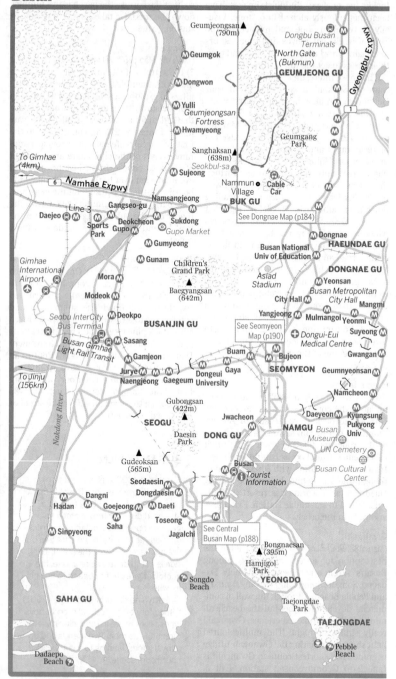

Geumjeongsan▲
(790m)

Dongbu Busan
Terminals

Geumgok

North Gate
(Bukmun)

GEUMJEONG GU

Gyeongbu Expwy

Dongwon

Yulli
Geumjeongsan
Fortress

Hwamyeong

Geumgang
Park

Sanghaksan
(638m)
Seokbul-sa

To Gimhae
(4km)

Sujeong

Nammun
Village

Cable
Car

BUK GU

Namhae Expwy

See Dongnae Map (p184)

Namsangjeong

Gangseo-gu

Daejeo

Line 3

Deokcheon

Sports
Park

Gupo

Gupo Market

Sukdong

Dongnae

HAEUNDAE GU

Busan National
Univ of Education

Gumyeong

Gunam

Children's
Grand Park

Asiad
Stadium

DONGNAE GU

Yeonsan

Busan Metropolitan
City Hall

Mangmi

Gimhae
International
Airport

Mora

Modeok

Baegyangsan
(642m)

City Hall

Yangjeong

Yeonmi

Mulmangol

Suyeong

Seobu InterCity
Bus Terminal

Deokpo

BUSANJIN GU

See Seomyeon
Map (p190)

Dongui-Eui
Medical Centre

Gwangan

Busan Gimhae
Light Rail Transit

Sasang

Buam

Bujeon

To Jinju
(156km)

Gamjeon

Jurye

Naengjeong

Dongeui
University

Gaegeum

Gaya

SEOMYEON

Geumnyeonsan

Namcheon

Nakdong River

Gubongsan
(422m)

Jwacheon

Daeyeon

NAMGU

Kyungsung
Pukyong
Univ

SEOGU

Daesin
Park

DONG GU

Busan
Museum

UN Cemetery

Gudeoksan
(565m)

Busan
Tourist
Information

Busan Cultural
Center

Seodaesin

Dongdaesin

Dangni

Goejeong

Daeti

Hadan

Saha

Toseong

Sinpyeong

Jagalchi

See Central
Busan Map (p188)

Bongnaesan
(395m)

Hamjigol
Park

YEONGDO

Songdo
Beach

Taejongdae
Park

SAHA GU

TAEJONGDAE

Dadaepo
Beach

Pebble
Beach

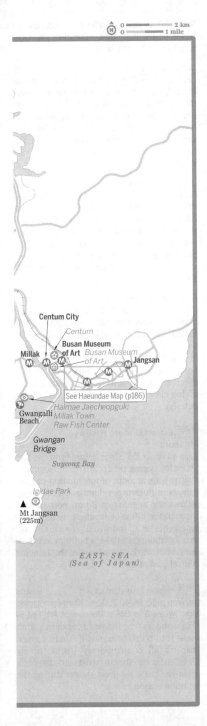

See Haeundae Map (p186)

Centum City

Centum

Busan Museum
of Art · Busan Museum
of Art

Millak · Millak Town · Jangsan

Halmae Jaecheopguk;
Gwangalli · Millak
Beach · Raw Fish Center

Gwangan
Bridge

Suyeong Bay

Igidae Park

▲ Mt Jangsan
(225m)

EAST SEA
(Sea of Japan)

Busan Cinema Center CINEMA

(☏780 6000; www.dureraum.org; ⏱9am-9pm; Ⓜ Line 2 to Centum City, Exit 12) This $150 million new showpiece venue for the Busan International Film Festival (p185) is an architectural delight, with the longest free cantilever roof in the world. It especially dazzles in the evening, with 127,000 LED lights streaming across its concave surfaces. The complex has a 4000-seat outdoor cinema with the country's largest screen, a 1000-seat indoor theatre, as well as three smaller film venues. It regularly screens a mix of Korean and foreign films.

Spa Land SPA

(www.shinsegae.com; Shinsegae department store; adult/youth weekdays ₩12,000/9000, weekends ₩14,000/11,000; ⏱6am-midnight; Ⓜ Line 2 to Centum City, Exit 3) You can't really experience Busan unless you've been to a public bath. Spa Land is one of the largest spas in Asia. The bathing area itself isn't particularly impressive or large, but has hot and cold *jjimjil-bang* (sauna) rooms. Beyond it, however, is a mall-like assortment of relaxation rooms of various temperatures and scents, as well as an outdoor foot bath. Drinks and light snacks are available with costs charged to your locker key. Before leaving, go to the checkout desk; a scanner reads your key to determine the bill. Kids under 13 are not permitted; last entry is 10.30pm.

Hurshimchung SPA

(허심청; Map p184; www.hotelnongshim.com; adult/youth/child ₩8000/6000/4000; ⏱5.30am-10pm; Ⓜ Line 1 to Oncheonjang, Exit 1) With 4300 sq metres of floor space, Hurshimchung is the second-largest place to take the plunge. The domed roof and ornate features make this a great place to relax, wash and exfoliate. Part of the Nongshim Hotel, it's a 10-minute walk from the station.

FREE **UN Cemetery** CEMETERY

(Map p182; ☏625 1608; www.unmck.or.kr; ⏱9am-6pm Jun to Sep, to 5pm Oct-May; Ⓜ Busan Station) This is the only United Nations cemetery in the world and is the final resting place of 2300 men from 11 nations including the UK, Turkey, Canada and Australia that supported the South in the 1950–53 Korean War. The US has a large wall of remembrance here; there's also a moving photo exhibit and flag ceremonies (10am and 5pm May to September, 10am and 4pm October to April) carried out by UN guards. From Busan station take bus 134 and get off at the UNMCK stop.

Dongnae

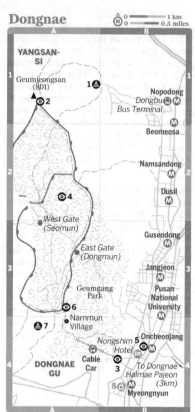

N 0 ——— 1 km
0 ——— 0.5 miles

YANGSAN-SI

Geumjeongsan (801)

1

Nopodong

Dongbu
Bus Terminal

2

Beomeosa

Namsandong

4

Dusil

West Gate
(Seomun)

Guseodong

East Gate
(Dongmun)

Jangjeon

Geumgang
Park

Pusan
National
University

6

Nammun
Village

7

Oncheonjang

Nongshim **5**
Hotel

Cable
Car

3

To Dongnae
Halmae Pajeon
(3km)

8

Myeongnyun

**DONGNAE
GU**

Dongnae

Children's Grand Park
PARK

(Map p182; 어린이대공원) The path in cuts through a forest and circles around a small lake, eventually leading to a kids' amusement park. For a more strenuous four-hour outing, pick up a trail leading to the 642m peak of **Baegyangsan** (백양산; Baegyang

Mountain). A taxi (₩5000 from Seomyeon) to the park's main gate is the most practical way to start your journey.

Yongdusan Park
PARK

(용두산 공원; Map p188) In the centre of this humble park stands the 118m **Busan Tower** (Map p188; adult/child ₩4000/3500; ⊙8.30am-10pm Apr-Sep, 9am-10pm Oct-Mar; MLine 1 to Nampo, Exit 1). If the haze is not too thick, daytime views of container-ship traffic in the harbour provide a sense of the port's vast scale of operations.

Jagalchi Fish Market
MARKET

(자갈치 시장; Map p188) Anyone with a love of seafood and a tolerance for powerful odours could easily spend an hour exploring the country's largest fish market. Waterfront warehouses, tiny shops and elderly women perched on street corners sell an incredible variety of seafood. Take Line 1 to Jagalchi, Exit 10.

Busan Aquarium
AQUARIUM

(Map p186; ☏740 1700; www.busanaquarium .com; adult/youth/child ₩19,000/17,000/15,000; ⊙10am-8pm Mon-Thu, 9am-10pm Fri, 9am to 10pm Fri-Sun, Jul 21-Aug 28; MLine 2 to Haeundae, Exit 3 or 5) In Haeundae, the aquarium is a large fish tank with 40,000 creatures. The aquarium also hosts a shark diving class open to nondivers (see p30 for details).

FREE Busan Modern History Museum
MUSEUM

(Map p188; ☏253 3845; ⊙9am-6pm; Tue-Sun; MLine 1 to Jungang, Exit 3 or 5) This museum has a surprising amount of information in English about Busan's development. The exhibit follows the opening of Busan port in 1876 through the influx of Japanese, and its later emergence as an industrial powerhouse. It's in a Japanese colonial-era building north of Yongdusan Park, 300m west of the Jungang central post office.

FREE Busan Museum of Art
MUSEUM

(off Map p182; ☏740 2602; ⊙10am-8pm, closed Mon; MLine 2 to Busan Museum of Art, Exit 5) One wonders why the word 'modern' didn't make it into this huge facility's name given that it's all contemporary works, nearly all of them by Korean artists. It's hardly a must-see but it's a good shelter during the typhoon season.

☞ Tours

Mipo Wharf (Map p186), the small pier at the eastern end of Haeundae beach, is home for ocean tours.

Return trips run to nearby islands like Oryukdo (round trip adult/child ₩18,000/9000, start at 9am, schedule varies) and one-way trips to the coastal ferry terminal in Jungang-dong (adult/child ₩17,000/9000, start at 9am, schedule varies).

From Taejeongdae, a noisy two-hour cruise runs along the coast with views of Igidae (round trip adult/child ₩10,000/7000, 9am to 5pm).

City Tour Busan   BUS TOUR

(www.citytourbusan.com; 1hr 40min tours adult/ child ₩10,000/5000; ⊘every 40min) This operator runs two daytime bus tours that whisk you to the sights. The Haeundae route includes two beaches and the UN Cemetery. The Taejeongdae bus heads south with stops at Yongdusan Park and Gukje market. One evening bus tour (7pm departure) drives towards Haeundae for a night view of Gwangan bridge. All buses start at Busan station. Ticket purchases are on the bus.

★☆ Festivals & Events

In August special events are held on the city's beaches as part of the **Busan Sea Festival**, including the **Busan International Rock Festival** (www.rockfestival.co.kr; Dadaepo beach).

The **Busan International Film Festival** (www.bif&f.kr) is the city's most significant festival and the largest of its kind in Asia. Launched in 1996, some 196,000 people attended the 16th edition in 2011, which screened 307 films, including 86 world premieres, from 70 countries. The festival is held in early to mid-October and screenings are held at five theatres, focusing on the massive Busan Cinema Centre (p191) in the Centum City district.

Also in October, the **Busan International Fireworks Festival** (www.bff.or.kr) lights up the skies over Gwangalli Beach and the already dazzling Gwangan Bridge on two Saturday nights.

🛏 Sleeping

Seomyeon is the most convenient place to stay to see most of Busan's sights. If you want to splash out at the beach, try Haeundae. Rates jump up in price in July and August.

TOP CHOICE **Ibis Ambassador**
Busan City Centre Hotel   BUSINESS HOTEL **$$**

(파라다이스 호텔; off Map p190; ☑930 1110; www.ibishotel.com; d from ₩99,000; ⑤Line 1 to Bujeon, Exit 1; ✳@☎) Towering over Bujeon market, the Ambassador wins for its location (a five-minute walk from Seomyeon), cheery staff, and understated, chic rooms, which have LCD TVs and views of downtown. There's a decent breakfast buffet, as well as a Starbucks and convenience store on street level.

TOP CHOICE **Paradise Hotel**   LUXURY HOTEL **$$$**

(파라다이스 호텔; Map p186; ☑749 2111; http:// paradisehotel.co.kr; tw from ₩199,000; ⑤Line 2 to Haeundae, Exit 3 or 5; ✳@☎≋) Fantastic views of Haeundae Beach, grovelling service and decent on-site dining make the Paradise stand out. The rooms are somewhat worn, and the casino (Busan's first) seems ridiculously small if you've been to Las Vegas, but amenities like the outdoor rooftop hot spring make up for that.

Westin Chosun
Beach Hotel   LUXURY HOTEL **$$$**

(웨스틴 조선 비치 호텔; Map p186; ☑749 7000; www.starwoodhotels.com; d from ₩230,000; Ⓜ Line 2 to Haeundae, Exit 3 or 5; ✳@☎≋) Busan's oldest international hotel gets better with age. A hint of retro shaken, not stirred, with modern touches, creates a James Bond – a la Sean Connery – dashing cool. It's a little removed from the main action on Haeundae Beach.

Pobi Guesthouse   HOSTEL **$**

(포비 게스트 하우스; ☑746 7990; www.pobi house.com; dm from ₩22,000; Line 2 to Haeundae, Exit 3; ✳@☎) A few minutes' from Haeundae Beach, Pobi is a large, recently renovated hostel with dorms of four to 12 beds as well as private rooms. From the exit, take a right at the first corner and walk down past the Haeundae Market entrance; it's on the left.

Indy House   HOSTEL **$$**

(Map p186; ☑070 8615 6442; www.indyhouse.net; dm ₩22,000, tw ₩60,000; ✳@☎; Ⓜ Line 2 to Haeundae, Exit 1) Now in a beautifully redesigned space in Haeundae, Indy gets positive reviews for cleanliness and friendliness, two features not always available in Busan's budget accommodation market. There's a modest free breakfast, too.

Haeundae

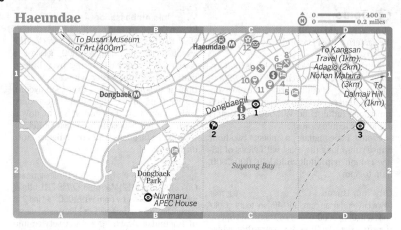

Haeundae

◎ Sights

🛏 Sleeping

✕ Eating

🍸 Drinking

🎭 Entertainment

ℹ Information

**Toyoko Inn Busan
Seomyeon**   BUSINESS HOTEL **$$**
(토요코인 부산서면; off Map p190; ☎638 1045; www.toyoko-inn.com; d/tw ₩58,300/80,300; Ⓜ Line 1 or 2 to Seomyeon, Exit 8; ✳@🛜❄) One of several branches of the Tokyo Inn in Busan, this property caters to Japanese businessmen and offers rather cramped, no-frills rooms and a modest but free breakfast. It's a few minutes' walk from central Seomyeon.

Blue Backpackers   HOSTEL **$**
(Map p190; ☎010 5019 3962; www.blueback packers.com; dm ₩20,000; r ₩35,000; Ⓜ Line 1 or 2 to Seomyeon, Exit 7; ✳@🛜) The owners have moved uptown with a bigger hostel in a central location. Budget rooms are a 10-minute walk behind the Lotte Hotel in Seomyeon. Check the web for details.

Lotte Hotel   LUXURY HOTEL **$$$**
(롯데 호텔; Map p190; ☎810 1000; www.lot tehotelbusan.com; d/tw from ₩340,000; Ⓜ Line 1 or 2 to Seomyeon, Exit 5 or 7; ✳@🛜❄) The top business-class hotel in Seomyeon has beautifully redesigned contemporary rooms but the older ones are uninspiring. There's also a casino here but like the one at the Paradise Hotel it's small and less than thrilling.

Angel Hotel   HOTEL **$$**
(엔젤 호텔; Map p190; ☎802 8223; www.angel hotel.co.kr; d/tw ₩50,000/65,000; Ⓜ Line 1 or 2 to Seomyeon, follow underground signs to Judies Taewha Exit; ✳@🛜) Location is the best feature of this unpretentious property with few amenities and rooms bordering on small. Stay here for the price and central Seomyeon location.

✕ Eating

TOP CHOICE **Dongnae Halmae Pajeon**   KOREAN **$$$**
(동래 할매 파전; ☎552 0791; http://english. dongraepajun.co.kr; meals ₩18,000-35,000; ⏰noon-10pm; Ⓜ Line 1 to Dongnae, Exit 2) Dongnae is famous for *pajeon* (파전; green onion pancake) and this is one of the most attractive places to experience a classic Busan dish. Large wooden tables and rich earthy

colours blend traditional design with modern touches. From the station, walk to the first light. Cross the street, walk right and turn left at the first road beside KT Plaza. Turn right past the motels. The restaurant is on the left. Or it's a short taxi ride from the subway.

Yetnal Jjajang
KOREAN $

(옛날짜장; Map p190; ☎809 8823; meals from ₩4000; ⊙9.30am-10.30pm; Ⓜ Line 1 or 2 to Seomyeon, Exit 7) A sterling example of a successful restaurant owner who won't update the interior. According to superstition, the good fortune a successful shop enjoys could be lost if the interior were changed. Consequently, some shoddy-looking restaurants, like this one, serve great food. The famous *jjajangmyeon* (black bean-paste noodles) and *jjambbong* (spicy seafood soup) are excellent.

Podo Cheong
BARBECUE $

(포도청; Map p190; ☎806 9797; per serving ₩6500-7000; ⊙noon-midnight; Ⓜ Line 1 or 2 to Seomyeon, follow underground signs to Judies Taewha Exit) It's not the best *sutbul galbi*

(숯불갈비; charcoal-fired barbecue) restaurant but it is good. The main draw at this busy place is the backyard barbecue feel in the outdoor patio. Lean *moksal* (목살; pork chop) tastes great, though most Koreans will choose *samgyeopsal* (삼겹살; fatty pork).

Loving Hut
VEGETARIAN $

(Map p190; ☎808-7718; www.lovinghut.co.kr; meals ₩4500-6000; ⊙11am-9pm; Ⓜ Line 1 or 2 to Seomyeon, Exit 3 from the underground mall; ☎✐💻) This cosy spot in Seomyeon serves up yummy vegetarian treats like *bibimbap*, soft tofu pot stew, fried noodle, and homemade vegan ice cream.

Haeundae Bapjip
KOREAN $

(해운대밥집; Map p186; ☎746 6654; meals ₩5000-7000; ⊙11am-9pm; Ⓜ Line 2 to Haeundae, Exit 3 or 5) This humble, friendly eatery tucked away in an alley behind the Haeundae Market serves up delicious *soksoegui* grilled pork (석쇠구이) that you wrap in lettuce. From the market, go south at the mobile phone shop across from Save Zone and then bear left.

BUSAN'S SPECIALITY FOOD

Busan is a coastal city, so it's not surprising that seafood flavours much of the local cuisine. Raw fish, called *hoe* (회; sounds like 'when' without the 'n'), a popular dish enjoyed with a group of friends, is widely available and affordably priced (compared to most cities). Busan is one of the country's favourite raw-fish destinations.

A typical *hoe* dinner starts with appetisers like raw baby octopus still wiggling on the plate. A platter of sliced raw fish is the main course. Fish is dipped into a saucer of *chogochujang* (초고추장), a watery red-pepper sauce, or soy sauce (간장) mixed with wasabi (와사비). The meal is customarily finished with rice and a boiling pot of *maeuntang* (매운탕; spicy fish soup).

Most Koreans say *hoe* has delicate taste and smooth texture. Western travellers may find the taste bland with a slightly tough texture. A small platter starting at ₩40,000 is rarely sufficient for a pair of raw-fish aficionados. Japanese sushi is popular, called *chobap* (초밥). Raw fish is best accompanied with *soju* (local vodka).

The **Jagalchi Fish Market** (자갈치 시장; Map p188; Ⓜ Line 1, Jagalchi, Exit 10) opposite Nampo-dong is the city's sprawling wholesale and retail centre for all things fishy. Head to the newly constructed market and pick your favourite live sea creature from any of the 1st-floor vendors. Expect to pay a minimum of ₩15,000 and for a modest fee (₩3000 per person) they'll prepare your dinner and serve it upstairs in the restaurant.

Millak Town Raw Fish Centre (민락타운 회 센터; Ⓜ Line 2, Gwangan, Exit 5) is at the northeast end of Gwangalli beach. Purchase a fish for ₩10,000 to ₩30,000 and walk upstairs to eat; the woman selling you the fish will indicate which floor. Inside the seating area, your fish will be prepared and served for ₩10,000 per person.

Myeongseong Chobap (명성 초밥; Map p188; sushi sets from ₩12,000; raw fish ₩30,000-60,000; Ⓜ Line 1, Jungang, Exit 3 or 5) is a popular Japanese-style restaurant serving *chobap* and *sushi* courses (생선회 코스; raw fish set menu). Located in Jungang-dong, it's 100m north of the Tower Hotel with 'sushi' written on the signboard.

Central Busan

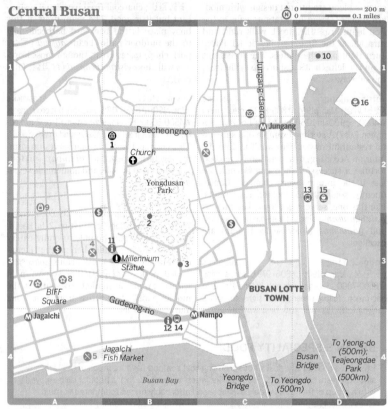

Geumsu Bokguk SEAFOOD $$$

(금수 복국; Map p186; meals ₩10,000-40,000; ⊘24hr; ⓂLine 2 to Haeundae, Exit 3 or 5) This celebrated blowfish eatery is a good spot for anyone who wants to experience a seafood delicacy and earn themselves some bragging rights: 'I ate poisonous fish and survived'. It's on a lane opposite the Paradise Hotel, surrounded by a car park and a few pine trees. Look for the red metal beams on the roof.

Halmae Jaecheopguk SEAFOOD $$

(할매 재첩국; Map p182; ☑751 7658; per serving ₩7000; ⊘24hr; ⓂLine 2 to Gwangan, Exit 5) Hungover in Gwangan beach? Do what many Koreans do and stumble over to this restaurant respected for hangover remedies disguised as food. *Jaecheopguk* (재첩국; marsh clam soup) is a clear shellfish broth. Located on Gwangan's one-way street, behind Beach Bikini on the beach road.

O'Taco MEXICAN $$

(오타코; ☑627 8358; www.otaco.co.kr; meals ₩5000-15,000; ⊘9am-10pm; ⓂLine 2 to Kyungsung-Pukyong, Exit 3; 🖥) A branch of this chain near the bars in Kyungsung-Pukyong makes decent tacos, enchiladas, quesadillas and other Mexican standards.

B&C Bakery BAKERY $

(Map p188; meals from ₩3000; ⊘9am-10pm; ⓂLine 1, Nampo, Exit 1) Stock up on tasty carbohydrates before exploring Nampo-dong's back alleys.

🍷 Drinking

GWANGALLI BEACH

Thursday Party BAR

(drinks from ₩3000; ⊘5pm-5am) This Western-style bar on the beach road is a regular meeting place for expats and locals. Cheap draught beer, curry-flavoured popcorn and bartenders who take musical requests make this a fun place.

Central Busan

◎ Sights
1 Busan Modern History Museum.........B2
2 Busan Tower B3
3 Escalator to Tower B3
    Jagalchi Fish Market....................(see 5)

⊗ Eating
4 B&C Bakery A3
5 Jagalchi Fish Market............................A4
6 Myeongseong Chobap C2

⊗ Entertainment
7 CINUS Busan Theatre...........................A3
8 Daeyeong Cinema Theatre..................A3

⊕ Shopping
9 Gukje Market A2

⊕ Information
10 Immigration Office...............................D1
    Tourist Information ....(see 16)
11 Tourist Information Centre B3
12 Tourist Information Centre B4

⊕ Transport
13 City Tour Busan D2
14 City Tour Busan B4
15 Coastal Ferry Terminal D2
16 International Ferry Terminal..............D1

Fuzzy Navel   BAR

(Map p186; drinks from ₩4000; ☺7pm-6am; 🎤) The recipe is simple: take one shack and decorate liberally with beach-bum graffiti. Add Plexiglas windows and presto, one of the city's most interesting concoctions.

HAEUNDAE BEACH
Noran Mahura   BAR

(노란 마후라; drinks ₩4000; ☺2pm-sunrise) It's a tent restaurant on Cheongsapo (청 사포), an out-of-the-way harbour where people come for a drink to watch the sunset and unexpectedly stay for the sunrise. Snacks include *garibi* (가리비), barbecued shellfish with a salsa-like sauce that tastes great. It tastes even better with *soju* at sunrise. Catch a ₩4000 taxi from Haeundae beach.

U2   CLUB

(Map p186; drinks ₩4000; ☺7pm-3am, to 5am Fri & Sat) Finding a bar that plays George Thorogood isn't easy. Luckily, Busan has one and this is it: a rock-and-roll bar with bourbon, scotch and beer. It's opposite the Novotel Hotel.

KYUNGSUNG-PUKYONG UNIVERSITIES

The commercial district in front of Kyungsung and Pukyong universities (Map p182) is an electric party district with eating and drinking options catering to 40,000 hungry, thirsty and frugal students.

TOP CHOICE Nogada/Radio Bar   BAR

(노가다; ☏625 0735; drinks ₩8000; ☺5pm-1am; Ⓜ️Line 2 to Kyungsung-Pukyong, Exit 1) Architectural flair in Busan? Nogada, aka Radio Bar, is like a design oasis in an urban desert. With hundreds of vinyl records behind the bar and a large barn-like space for drinking and live shows, this rough-hewn watering hole is easy to fall in love with. It's in the Gol Mok (골목) complex of restaurants and galleries above a wine bar. From the station exit, turn right at the first street then right again at the second street. When you see a camping-themed bar on your right with a kayak on the wall, look for a tall, slender tower on your left. The little lane leads to Gol Mok.

Fully Booked   CAFE

(☏010-4469 9658; drinks ₩2500-9000; ☺7pm-midnight Tue-Thu, 7pm-1am Fri, Sat 2pm-2am, 2pm-midnight Sun; Ⓜ️Line 2 to Kyungsung-Pukyong, Exit 1) Expats gather at this friendly cafe (which also serves up used paperbacks, beer, wine, and panini sandwiches) to play cribbage and Scrabble. From the subway exit, take the first right then first left and walk three blocks. It's on the second floor above the real-estate agency with bright yellow signage.

Ol' 55   BAR

(drinks ₩4000; ☺7pm-2am Tue-Thu, to 5am Fri & Sat, closed Sun; Ⓜ️Line 2 to Kyungsung-Pukyong, Exit 3; turn right at the first street) A testosterone-charged tavern, ale to match budget and taste, a prohibition on hip-hop music, and women who play billiards in high-heel shoes and cut-offs. It's under the Family Mart.

Vinyl Underground   BAR

(drinks ₩4000; ☺7pm-5am; Ⓜ️Line 2 to Kyungsung-Pukyong, Exit 3; turn right at the first street) Bring your A-game to this hip-hopping dance club that's wall-to-wall flesh late Fridays and Saturdays. Mingle with locals sporting the latest music video-inspired club wear and the baddest home boyz to come out of Saskatchewan. It's near Ol' 55.

BUSAN & GYEONGSANGNAM-DO BUSAN

Seomyeon

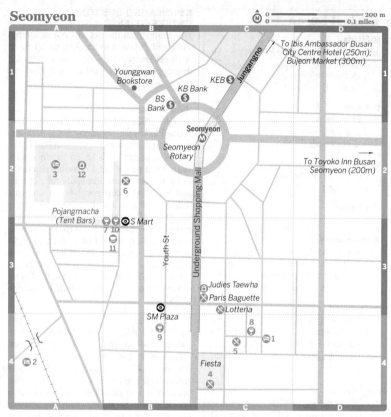

0 — 200 m
0 — 0.1 miles

To Ibis Ambassador Busan
City Centre Hotel (250m);
Bujeon Market (300m)

Younggwan
Bookstore

KEB

KB Bank

BS
Bank

Seomyeon

Seomyeon
Rotary

To Toyoko Inn Busan
Seomyeon (200m)

6

Pojangmacha
(Tent Bars)

S Mart

7 10

11

Youth St

Underground Shopping Mall

Judies Taewha
Paris Baguette
Lotteria

8

1

SM Plaza

9

5

Fiesta
4

2

Seomyeon

SEOMYEON

Guribar
BAR

(Map p190; drinks ₩5000; ⊘8pm-5am) On the corner behind Lotte department store, this hip young *pojangmacha* tent bar plays dance music and has beer, cocktails and snacks.

First House
BAR

(첫집; Map p190; drinks ₩3000; ⊘6pm-5am, closed 2nd & 4th Mon) Next to Guribar, First House is a tent bar run by the friendly Mrs Ahn, and dishes out *soju*, beer and seafood.

Lotte Hotel Lobby Lounge
LOUNGE

(Map p190; drinks ₩15,000) Here's the upscale lizard lounge you've been looking for. Palm trees, comfy chairs and live muzak created by a pianist. Throw in a decent Irish coffee and you've got the perfect place to impress a date.

Fuzzy Navel
BAR

(퍼지네불; Map p190; drinks ₩5000; ⊘4.30pm-6am) A party for the 20-something crowd on Seomyeon's Youth St. It's on the 4th floor. Another Fuzzy Navel is near the Podo Cheong meat restaurant and Angel Hotel.

Hana Bang Teahouse
TEAHOUSE
(하나방; Map p190; drinks ₩5000; ☺10am-11pm) This shop has a good selection of teas, though the interior is modern, spacious and, for people who don't like floor seating, more relaxing. This 2nd-floor shop is hard to see from street level. On the road running behind Lotte department store; look for a sign with the phone number 806 0011.

☆ Entertainment

Cinemas

There's no shortage of theatres showing first-run English-language movies (with Korean subtitles) including multiscreen cinemas in Nampo-dong next to BIFF Sq (Map p188).

Busan Cinema Centre
THEATRE
(☎780 6000; www.dureraum.org; ☺9am-9pm; Ⓜ Line 2 to Centum City, Exit 12) Outside the Busan International Film Festival, this new complex (see p191) plays a mix of Korean and foreign films in its smaller venues. The website listings are in Korean only, so get a Korean speaker to call for info.

Megabox
THEATRE
(Map p186; Sfunz Bldg, Haeundae; Ⓜ Line 2 to Haeundae, Exit 1) This 10-screen facility, 100m from the station, is a venue for the Busan International Film Festival.

Live Music

Monk
JAZZ
(drinks ₩4000; ☺6pm-2am; Ⓜ Line 2 to Kyung-sung-Pukyong station, Exit 3) Before and after jazz sets (often starting at 7.30pm, Wednesday to Saturday), Monk can be an empty sound stage with a few offbeat characters. When the live music hits the stage, the place is full of offbeat characters. From the subway station, turn right at the first street. It's down the road and around the corner from Ol'55 in the Kyungsung-Pukyong area.

Busan Cultural Centre
CLASSICAL MUSIC
(Map p182; http://culture.busan.go.kr; Ⓜ Line 2 to Daeyeon, Exit 3 or 5) With three halls and a fairly active schedule, it's possible to attend a Busan Philharmonic Orchestra concert, or a show by any of the other musical and dance companies that perform here. The English website provides little useful information. Check the Busan City website calendar page (http://english.busan.go.kr/) for a listing of current events at the centre and across the city.

🛍 Shopping

Shinsegae Centum City
DEPARTMENT STORE
(http://english.shinsegae.com; Ⓜ Line 2 to Centum City, Shinsegae Exit) With 5.5 million sq feet of space, it's the world's largest shopping and entertainment behemoth, out-muscling Macy's in New York for the Guinness World Record. After shopping, pick your favourite

---

INSIDE THE COVERED WAGON

Spend time walking at night on a busy Busan street and you're likely to come across a *pojangmacha*, an orange piece of Korean street culture. Literally meaning 'covered wagon', these food-and-drink carts draped in a tarpaulin are more than a convenient late-night street pub. They're an institution that delivers a unique social and sensory experience.

According to Mrs Ahn, the woman who runs First House (p190), a *pojangmacha* in Seomyeon, 'people who love drinking come to the covered wagon because they feel comfortable'. Comfort, in this case, does not mean physical amenities, as most *pojangmacha* are equipped with bench seating, dim lighting and off-site washrooms that require a short stumble to a nearby car park. Comfort instead means a respite from the outside world.

Inside the *pojangmacha*, traditional barriers that prevent Koreans from socialising easily give way to conviviality. As customer talk rambles on between shots of *soju* and whiffs of cigarette smoke, Mrs Ahn sits behind the counter watching over a charcoal grill. Plumes of smoke rise to the top of the tent. The aroma of grilled chicken anus (닭똥집), sea eel (곰장어구이) and mackerel (고등어) commingled with the plasticky smell of a decades-old tarpaulin induce childhood memories of an overnight camping trip. It all seems like another world.

method of relaxation: see a movie, go ice skating, clean up in the spa (see p183), eat sushi in the food park or work on your golf swing at the driving range.

Bujeon Market
MARKET

(off Map p190; M Line 1 to Bujeon, Exit 5) The city's largest downtown market and best place to buy in-season fruit and vegetables.

Gukje Market
MARKET

(Map p188; M Line 1, Nampo, Exit 1) West of Nampo-dong; has hundreds of small booths with a staggering selection of items, from leather goods to Korean drums.

Lotte Department Store
DEPARTMENT STORE

Seomyeon (Map p190; M Line 2 to Seomyeon, Exit 5 or 7); Dongnae (Map p184; outside Myeongnyun station; M Line 1 to Myeongnyun, Exit 1) Upmarket retailer with the newest store in Haeundae, beside Shinsegae (Map p182).

ⓘ Information

Emergency

Fire & rescue ☑119
Police ☑112

Internet Access

Busan is one of the most wired cities on the planet. The post office has free internet access and there's free wi-fi on local buses, at bus stops and on subways.

In addition, the city has provided free Dynamic Busan hotspots at 25 tourist locations such as Jagalchi Market and Haeundae Beach. Getting online, however, can sometimes be tricky with a foreign computer or mobile device.

Medical Services

Dong-Eui Medical Centre (☑867 5101; www .demc.kr/eng; ⊙8.30am-4.30pm Mon-Fri, 8.30am-noon Sat; M Line 1 to Yangjeong, Exit 4) English-speaking staff at this large medical complex can help travellers. Outside the exit, take local bus 8.

Money

Most banks exchange currency, though the level of service varies; your chances of finding reasonably efficient service are greatest at the Korea Exchange Bank (KEB). For international withdrawals, your best bet is a KB Kookmin Bank ATM. Look for the yellow asterisk and 'b' logo, and the 'global' ATM inside.

Gimhae International Airport currency exchange domestic terminal (⊙9.30am-4.30pm); international terminal (⊙8.30am-9pm).

Post

Central post office (Map p188; ⊙9am-8pm Mon-Fri, to 1pm Sat & Sun; M Line 1 to Jungang, Exit 9)

Tourist Information

Busan station office (☑441 6565; ⊙9am-8pm) There's knowledgeable staff and a modest selection of maps.

Gimhae International Airport desk domestic terminal (☑973 4607; ⊙6.30am-last flight); international terminal (☑973 2800; ⊙7am-9pm) Try these when you need help finding a bus into the city.

Haeundae office (Map p186; ☑749 4335; ⊙9am-6pm) A great selection of material; beside the Busan Aquarium on Haeundae beach.

International ferry terminal (Map p188; ☑465 3471; ⊙9am-6pm) Useful information when you're coming from Japan.

Kangsan Travel (off Map p186; ☑747 0031; www.kangsantravel.com; ⊙9am-noon, 1-6pm Mon-Fri, 10am-3pm Sat; M Line 2 to Jangsan, Exit 9) Provides English-language services geared towards expats. The agency is on the 4th floor, above Starbucks.

Websites

Busan Haps (http://busanhaps.com) Free magazine covering entertainment, nightlife and other attractions in Busan.

Busan Life (http://bfia.or.kr/webzine/) Local news and event information.

City government (http://english.busan.go.kr) For basic socio-economic and travel data.

Gyeongsangnam-do (http://english.gsnd.net) Learn about Gyeongsangnam-do's sites and geography.

Lonely Planet (www.lonelyplanet.com/south-korea/gyeongsangnam-do/busan) For planning advice, author recommendations, traveller reviews and insider tips.

ⓘ Getting There & Away

Domestic travellers often come to Busan via a KTX train service (see p193) though there are good bus connections (see p193) from most major destinations.

International travellers, especially those arriving from Japan, can fly directly to **Gimhae International Airport** (☑974 3114; www .gimhaeairport.co.kr), 27km west of Seomyeon, Busan's city centre. There are also frequent ferry connections with Japan (see p193).

Air

International flights are mostly to Japan (Tokyo, Osaka, Nagoya and Fukuoka), with departures to Beijing, Hong Kong, Bangkok, Manila and Vladivostok.

On domestic routes, the Busan-to-Seoul run on Korean Air, Asiana or AirBusan (one hour, every 30 minutes from 7am to 9pm) usually requires reservations for weekend and holiday travel. Most of the flights from Busan to Seoul land at Gimpo airport, which has few international connections. If you're flying out of the country, you'll need to catch the train link from Gimpo to Incheon International (see p90) or book early for a seat on one of the four to six daily flights to Incheon via Korean Air or Asiana. Flights also connect Busan and Jeju-do (one hour, every 30 to 90 minutes from 7am to 8pm).

Bus

There are hourly buses from the airport's domestic terminal to regional cities including Gyeongju (₩9000), Masan (₩6800) and Ulsan (₩7900).

DEPARTURES FROM DONGBU Intercity (☑508 9966) and **express** (☑508 9955) buses depart from the Dongbu terminal (Map p184) at Nopo-dong station on Line 1.
WESTBOUND DEPARTURES FROM SEOBU Seobu intercity bus terminal (☑322 8301) is outside Sasang station on Line 2 with street-level access through a no-name department store.

Boat

To find the **International Ferry Terminal** (Map p188; ☑63 3068; www.busanpa.com) from Jungang station, take Exit 12 and walk towards the containers visible down the road and cross the major street. Continue straight and turn right past the immigration office; the terminal is about 150m down the path.

First-floor booths in the International Ferry Terminal sell tickets to four distant Japanese cities (one-way fares): Fukuoka (☑466 7799, ₩90,000, departs 10.30pm, six hours, check in by 7pm); Shimonoseki (☑462 3161, ₩95,000, departs 7pm, 13 hours); Osaka (☑462 5482, ₩129,350, departs 3pm Sunday, Tuesday, Thursday, 18 hours) and Tsushima (☑465 1114, ₩75,000, schedules vary, 1¾ to 2¾ hours, departures every day except Tuesday). Discounted tickets are available at travel agencies.

For a quick trip to Fukuoka on the Kobee and Beetle hydrofoils (☑441 8200), go to the 2nd floor. There are 10 to 13 daily departures (one way/return ₩115,000/230,000, three hours) depending on the season.

Train

Most trains depart from and arrive at Busan's downtown station. There are departures from Gupo, a western station with easy subway access to Line 3 that saves the hassle of going downtown. Between Busan and Seoul, KTX is the quickest service with most trips taking three hours or less (adult/child ₩53,300/26,600, every 30 to 60 minutes).

Saemaul services take five hours to reach Seoul (adult/child ₩40,700/20,300, six daily departures). The *Mugunghwa* service is only about 30 minutes slower and quite a bit cheaper (adult/child ₩27,300/13,600, eight daily departures).

BUSAN BUS DEPARTURES

Departures from Dongbu terminal

DESTINATION	PRICE (₩)	DURATION	FREQUENCY
Gyeongju	4500	50min	every 10min
Pohang	7700	80min	every 10min
Samcheok	28,200	4hr	4 daily
Seoul	32,800	4½hr	every 30min
Tongdosa	2000	25min	every 20min

Westbound departures from Seobu intercity bus terminal

DESTINATION	PRICE (₩)	DURATION (HR)	FREQUENCY
Gohyeon	13,400	2¾	every 30-40min
Hadong	10,800	2½	every 2hr
Jinju	7300	1½	every 10-20min
Namhae	11,300	2½	hourly
Ssanggyae-sa	14,000	3½	twice daily
Tongyeong	10,800	1¾	every 20-30min

If you're heading to Japan, a **Korea-Japan Co-Ticket** (aka Korea-Japan Joint Ticket) provides discounted travel between the two countries. It covers Korea Rail services, the ferry crossing between Busan and Fukuoka or Shimonoseki and Japan Rail services. The application procedure is slightly complicated and tickets must be reserved seven days in advance; see www.korailtours.com for details.

❶ Getting Around

To/From the Airport

An airport limousine from Gimhae International Airport (www.airport.co.kr) runs to the major hotels in Haeundae (adult/child ₩6000/3500, one hour, every 20 minutes).

A taxi from the airport to Seomyeon takes 30 minutes and costs ₩20,000, depending on traffic. A 10-minute taxi from Deokcheon station costs ₩7000.

The most economical link between the airport and city is a ₩1400 bus: the 307 from Deokcheon or Gupo stations or 201 from Seomyeon station (opposite Lotte department store).

The Busan-Gimhae Light Rail line connects Sasang station and the airport (₩1500, 15 minutes).

Bus

Adult cash fares are ₩1200/1600 for regular/express buses. Slight discounts are available when paying with a Hanaro card.

Subway

Busan's four-line subway uses a two-zone fare system: ₩1200 for one zone and ₩1400 for longer trips. Purchasing a Hanaro (₩6000 plus travel credits, available at ticket booths) is handy for long stays: you get a small discount on fares and avoid the hassle of buying a ticket for each trip. A one-day subway pass costs ₩4000. Subway trains generally run between 5.10am and 12.30am.

Taxi

Basic taxi fares start at ₩2200 (with a 20% premium at night). Avoid black and red deluxe taxis if possible, because the fares can run high.

Gajisan Provincial Park
가지산 도립공원

This park has three sections. The northernmost section, not far from Gyeongju, is known for rocky terrain. This is where you'll find **Gajisan** (Mt Gaji; 1240m), the park's highest peak. **Tongdo-sa**, one of the country's most commercialised Buddhist temples, is in the smallest of the three sections.

◉ Sights

Seoknam-sa
TEMPLE

(석남사; Map p179; adult/youth ₩1700/1000; ◔3am-8pm) An easy day trip from Busan, the temple of Seoknam-sa, home to female monks training in Zen meditation, is a visual masterpiece. The 800m walk from the park entrance cuts through a heavily wooded forest where patches of sunlight struggle to break through the thick canopy of foliage. Just before the temple, the path forks right over a bridge to a Korean-only map and starting point for a 6.4km hike to Gajisan.

Buses depart Busan's Dongbu intercity terminal for the temple (₩3200, 50 minutes, every 20 minutes).

Tongdo-sa
TEMPLE

(통도사; Map p179; adult/youth/child ₩3000/1500/1000; ◔8.30am-5.30pm) One of the country's most important Buddhist temples, Tongdo-sa is noted for a *sari,* a crystalline substance thought to develop inside the body of a monk who leads a pure life. The *sari* is enshrined in a fenced area outside the main hall and cannot be seen. It is a focal point of devotion, which is why Tongdo-sa does not have a Buddha statue in the main hall, a rarity in Korea.

Tongdo-sa Museum
MUSEUM

(www.tongdomuseum.or.kr; adult/youth ₩2000/1000; ◔9am-5pm Nov-Feb, to 6pm Mar-Oct, closed Tue) This museum houses a collection of Buddhist paintings with limited viewing hours (9am to 11.30am and 1pm to 5pm) to minimise light exposure. There are 30,000 artefacts with full-day access including gongs, roof tiles and wooden printing blocks. Before entering, place your shoes in a bag at the front door.

Buses depart Busan's Dongbu intercity terminal for the temple (₩2100, 30 minutes, every 20 minutes). From the terminal near Tongdo-sa, walk left and turn right at the first corner; the temple is past the parade of shops, restaurants and motels.

Geojedo 거제도

☏055 / POP 230,000

Now connected to the mainland by the 8km Busan-Geoje Fixed Link bridge, Korea's second-largest island is famous for its massive shipbuilding industry and its natural beauty. The coastal scenery varies between pastoral and industrial, with the best views in and around **Haegeumgang** (해금강). Getting around the island can be tricky but a local bus tour (see p195) can help.

◉ Sights & Activities

Oedo Botania   ISLAND
(외도; ☑070 7715 3330; www.oedobotania.com; adult/youth/child ₩8000/6000/4000; ⊙8.50am-7pm, arrive by 5.30pm) The island's busiest tourist attraction is a tiny island-cum-botanical garden 4km off the coast. It's popular with Korean travellers, but unless you absolutely adore manicured gardens, long waits (if ferries are cancelled or delayed) and pushy lines, consider avoiding this place.

Historic Park of Geoje POW Camp   MUSEUM
(거제도 포로수용소유적공원; ☑639 8125; adult/youth/child ₩4500/3000/1500; ⊙9am-6pm Apr-Oct, to 5pm Nov-Mar, 8.30am-6.30pm 20 Jul-15 Aug) In Gohyun, this is a modest but worthwhile museum because it provides hard-to-find information about this unique aspect of the Korean War. Just by the gate is a **tourist info centre** (⊙9am-6pm; @) that has maps but no English-speaking staff.

About halfway between Jangseungpo and Haegeumgang, the **black-pebble beach** in Hakdong (학동) is a cosy destination for family outings and romantic getaways. Summer crowds flock to the 1.2km beach to laze and fish off the pier. During the rest of the year, you'll have the place to yourself.

About 30 minutes by car from Hakdong, **Haegeumgang** is a collection of breathtaking rocky islets and a jagged coastline, part of the **Hallyeo Maritime National Park**, which is famous for stirring sunrises and sunsets.

🛏 Sleeping & Eating

There's a collection of motels a few blocks from the Gohyun intercity bus terminal. You'll have no problem finding a place to eat in Hakdong, if you like raw fish.

Venus Motel   MOTEL $
(비너스 모텔; ⊙637 9586; r from ₩40,000; ❋🛜) The Venus has small rooms with private bathrooms. If full, there are other motels nearby.

Geoje Tiffany Pension   PENSION $$
(거제 티파니 리조텔; ☑636 8866; http://geojetiffany.co.kr; r from ₩50,000; ❋) Hakdong has an impressive selection of motels of varying quality, some closer to the beach than

others. Geoje Tiffany Pension is beside the beach. Nothing fancy, just nice, clean rooms with bathroom and a short walk to nearby restaurants.

Palm Tree Pension   PENSION $$$
(☑6362241; www.palm-tree.co.kr; standard/deluxe ₩80,000/150,000, weekend ₩120,000/170,000; ❋🛜🛜) Beautiful and private, the Palm Tree is a gorgeous three-storey building with balconies overlooking the sea. The snazzy boutique rooms (from ₩290,000 with breakfast) have kitchenettes and Jacuzzis. It's in a secluded area and a couple of kilometres from the pebble beach and restaurants.

Daega Supbul   BARBECUE $$
(대가숯불갈비; ☑636 6612; servings from ₩9000; ⊙8am-9.30pm) For barbecued meat try Daega Supbul, a floor-seating restaurant with tender *samgyeopsal* (삼겹살; fatty pork). It's about 200m to the right as you exit from the Tiffany motel.

❶ Getting There & Around

From the Gohyun intercity bus terminal there are frequent connections to Busan's Seobu terminal (₩13,400, 2¾ hours, every 30 to 40 minutes) and Tongyeong (₩3100, 25 minutes, every 15 minutes).

Outside Gohyun, the island's biggest city, public transport is not well developed. Although there are local buses, connections are inconvenient so personal transport on the island is recommended. It's now relatively easy to drive to and from Busan thanks to the Busan-Geoje Fixed Link bridge but you'll have to pay the ₩10,000 toll for cars.

An alternative is the **Geoje Blue City bus tour** (☑681 6188; www.geojebluecitytour.com; ₩15,000, attraction admissions not incl; Tue-Sun), which takes in the main sights as well as industrial plants such as the Daewoo Shipbuilding and Marine Engineering, depending on the day. Tours with English commentary leave at 9am from the Gohyun bus terminal and return around 5.30pm. Reservations are required.

Tongyeong 통영

☑055 / POP 134,000

On the southern tip of Goseong Peninsula, Tongyeong is a coastal city wedged between Namhaedo and Geojedo. Most of the picturesque sights are in and around **Gangguan** (강구안), a pretty harbour just made for sunset strolls. Visiting Tongyeong's truly spectacular sights – any one of the 190 or so islands dotting the coastline – usually requires an overnight stay and early-morning ferry departure to some of the most pristine territory in the province.

There are three tourist information booths (open 9am to 6pm). Outside the express bus terminal and on Gangguan harbour, there's a decent selection of material though you'll need to rely on body language because no one speaks English. You'll usually find English-speaking staff in the booth outside the Excursion Terminal.

◉ Sights & Activities

Gangguan   HARBOUR

(강구안) It's not the only harbour in the city but Gangguan is the prettiest. It's also a busy pier anchored by a promenade that serves multiple civic functions including dock, basketball court and picnic ground for package-tour travellers who aren't squeamish about a midmorning *soju* pick-me-up. Towards the north end of the promenade, there are four turtle ship replicas (admission free; ⊙10am-5pm) and the Jungang Live Fish Market (중앙활어시장), an open-air building with grannies selling produce and seafood out of plastic tubs.

The harbour is a good starting point for two strolls. Set aside at least one hour to walk along Seoho Bay (서호만) in the early evening to get a brilliant neon show. Walking past the passenger ferry terminal (여객선 터미널) towards the Chungmu and Tongyeong Grand bridges, you could pass through the Undersea Tunnel (해저 터널). It's a dull site but a worthwhile stop to take in the panoramic view from the other side of the bay. The second walk takes you up Namsan, the small mountain opposite the Gangguan pier. Up top, a pavilion provides a panoramic view of the harbour.

Ferry Excursions   ISLANDS

On the south side of the bay, the Excursion Terminal (유람선 터미널) runs ferry trips to nearby islands including Maemuldo (매물도; ₩13,200, ⊙hourly departures 11am-2pm) and Jeseungdang (제승당; ₩4,100; ⊙hourly departures 7am-6pm), as well as the best of the lot, Yeonhwado (연환도; return ₩16,600; ⊙five departures daily), which is ideal for seaside hikes of about three hours. Often boisterous, guided tours provide an up-close look at stunning rock formations, historical insights (all in Korean) and a chance for adults to cut loose.

Hallyeosudo Cable Car   OUTDOORS

(한려 수도 조망 케이블카; www.ttdc.co.kr; one way/return adult ₩9000/5000, child ₩5500/3000; ⊙9.30am-5pm, to 6pm Jul & Aug, closed 2nd & 4th Mon) Stretching out 1975m, it's Korea's longest cable-car ride. Near the top of Mireuksan (461m) the view of Hallyeo Maritime National Park is dramatic. If you're up for a hike, buy a one-way ticket, walk down the back end of the mountain and head towards the Undersea Tunnel. Allow one to two hours from the mountaintop to Gangguan. Pick up a map and travel tips from the info booth near the ticket window. Note: if you're coming here on the weekend, arrive early because wait times can be long. It's about a ₩5000 taxi ride from the coastal ferry terminal.

🛌 Sleeping

Near Gangguan, there is a handful of motels on or near the lane next to the KB bank, which is where Tongyeong's seedy side comes to life at night.

Napoli Motel   MOTEL $$

(나폴리모텔; ☎646 0202; http://tynapoli.co.kr; d from ₩40,000; ❄@) This serviceable motel by the northern end of the Gangguan promenade has fairly modern rooms with harbour views and some bathrooms with bathtubs. Expect to pay ₩70,000 and up in July and August. The signs say 'Napole Motel'.

Nexun   MOTEL $$

(넥슨모텔; ☎643 6568; d ₩50,000; ❄@) Though it's just a motel, a modern design makes it one of the nicer properties near the Passenger Ferry Terminal. From terminal's north driveway, cross the street and go straight ahead into the lane.

✕ Eating & Drinking

Ddungbo Halmae Gimbap   KOREAN $

(뚱보 할매 김밥; per serving ₩4500; ⊙7am-2am) Hungry travellers with limited Korean skills come here because there's no need to speak or read: this place only serves *chungmu gimbap* (충무 김밥), a spicy squid-and-radish dish. The waitress will ask how many servings you want and if necessary she'll use her fingers to count. One serving of this spicy dish, which will test the red-pepper tolerance of the hardiest Korean food lover, should be enough for a single person. It's in front of the turtle ships and has a white sign with the founder's photo.

Prowstar Espresso Coffee CAFE
(drinks ₩3500; ☺10.30am-10.30pm) This cosy cafe is on a corner of the Gangguan harbour beside an entrance to the Jungang Live Fish Market. It serves up espressos, smoothies, cocoa and cookies – just in case you're in need of some foreign comfort food.

ⓘ Getting There & Around

The express bus terminal is on the city's northern fringe. Local buses 10, 20, 30 and 40 (₩1100) run to Gangguan. Buses 60 to 66 go to the cable car. A taxi from the bus terminal to Gangguan costs ₩6000. From Gangguan, buses 10 to 15 drive by the Excursion Terminal. Ask the driver for the cable-car stop. From there, it's a 15-minute uphill walk. A taxi to either location from Gangguan costs about ₩6000.

Express buses connect Tongyeong with Jinju (₩7100, 1½ hours, every 10 to 20 minutes), Busan (₩10,800, 2½ hours, every 30 minutes) and Gohyeon on Geojedo (₩3100, 25 minutes, every 15 minutes).

Jinju 진주

☏055 / POP 341,000

Famous for *bibimbap*, bullfighting and its role in the Japanese invasions of the 16th century, Jinju is a breezy, laid-back metropolis with a park-like fortress by the Namgang River. Thanks to excellent bus connections, it's a refreshing day trip from Busan.

◉ Sights & Activities

Jinju's interesting sights are north of the Namgang River. East of the Jinju Fortress, Jungangno separates two worlds: a traditional market to the east and modern trappings like coffee shops, bars and cinemas to the west. Jinju is the largest city in the area and a convenient transport hub from which to explore the province's western region.

Jinju Fortress HISTORIC SITE
(Jinjuseong; adult/youth/child ₩2000/1000/600; ☺ticket office 9am-6pm Sun-Fri, to 7pm Sat, gates 5am-10pm) This fortress is the city's most interesting and historically important site. Local street signs call it a castle but it's actually a well-preserved fortress that was partially destroyed during the Japanese invasion of 1592. It was here that one of the major battles of the campaign was fought, in which 70,000 Koreans lost their lives. Inside the fortress walls, traditional gates and shrines dot the grassy knolls of this heavily wooded park. Enter the fortress from the North Gate, not far from a large E-Mart department store, or the East Gate. The information booths (open 9am to 6pm) have a decent selection of material, though the staff can't speak English.

Inside the fortress, the **Jinju National Museum** (☏742 5951; http://jinju.museum.go.kr; admission free; ☺9am-6pm Tue-Fri, to 7pm Sat, Sun & holidays, closed Mon) specialises in artefacts from the Imjin War (임진왜란), a seven-year bloody tussle between Joseon and Japan's Toyotomi Hideyoshi shogun that began with the latter invading the former in 1592. There's a nifty 3D animated video portraying the invasions; ask for the English-language earphone narration.

✲ Festivals & Events

In October several important festivals take place, including the **Nam River Lantern Festival**. Weekly **bullfights** are held every Saturday at **Jinyangho Lake Park** (진양호 공원; admission free; ☺fights 1.30-6pm Mar-Nov). Catch bus 16, 26, or 116 (₩1200) opposite the express bus terminal.

⌚ Sleeping

TOP CHOICE **Dong Bang Tourist Hotel** BUSINESS HOTEL $$$
(동방호텔; ☏743 0131; www.hoteldongbang.com; d from ₩145,200, ste from ₩296,450; ❀❀⊛) Jinju's only business-class hotel has perfectly cosy rooms with superb views of the Namgang River, although the decor feels somewhat 1980s. The cordial, English-speaking staff here make this a very handy property to use as a base for touring the region. Prices jump in July and August. It's a 15-minute walk from Jinju Fortress and downtown.

Asia Lakeside Hotel BUSINESS HOTEL $$$
(아시아레이크사이드호텔; ☏746 3734; www.asiahotel.co.kr; d/tw from ₩145,000, ste from ₩385,000; ❀@⊛) On the outskirts of the city, the Lakeside overlooks Jinyang Lake, an artificial reservoir, in a bucolic setting. Rooms are spacious though worn, and there's an alfresco buffet surf and turf dinner. It's a nice escape from the city but it isn't convenient to downtown (count on paying ₩7000 for a taxi).

Jinju

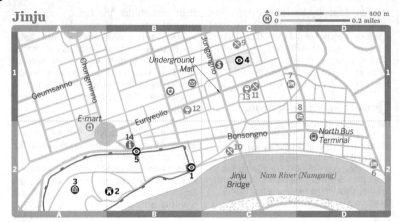

Jinju

⊙ Sights
1 East Gate............................B2
2 Jinju Fortress.....................B2
3 Jinju National Museum A2
4 Jungang Market..................C1
5 North Gate.........................B2

🛏 Sleeping
6 Dong Bang Tourist Hotel D2
7 Jageum Seong C1
8 Movie Motel.......................D1

✗ Eating
9 Cheonwhang Sikdang C1
10 Eel Restaurants..................C2
Jeil Sikdang....................(see 4)
11 Zio Ricco C1

🍷 Drinking
12 Beast Bar B1
13 La Vigne............................C1

ⓘ Information
14 Tourist Office.....................B2

Movie Motel   MOTEL $$
(무비 모텔; ☎743 4114; d ₩50,000; ❄@)
It doesn't look like much on the outside,
but this property has many of the in-room
amenities that you'd expect in a top-end
motel, like wide-screen TVs, whirlpool tubs
and free internet. When you exit the bus
terminal, cross the street and walk right
on the first road that runs perpendicular
to the main street. Look out for the neon
outside.

Jageum Seong   SPA $
(자금성; ☎743 8841; jjimjil-bang ₩8000; ⏱24hr;
❄) In Jinju's red-light district, this *jjimjil-
bang* is probably the city's cheapest sleep
option. Take a long bath, splash in the tubs,
relax in the *jjimjil-bang* and sleep on the
floor. Next morning, take another bath. Exit
the bus terminal, cross the street and walk
up the first road that runs perpendicular to
the main street. Turn left at the small chil-
dren's playground. It's in the tall building
down the road.

✗ Eating & Drinking

For something different, try one of the eel
restaurants along the waterfront near the
fortress. The quality and price (₩15,000
to ₩20,000 per person) is similar at all of
them.

TOP CHOICE Zio Ricco   ITALIAN $$$
(meals ₩10,000-20,000; ⏱10am-11pm) With low
chairs and cool music, Zio Ricco is a popular eatery with the locals and expats. Pasta
and pizza are the specialities; they're decent
enough, and make for a nice break from Korean food if you need one. Up on the second
floor, the restaurant owner sometimes plays
sax with a surprisingly good rock band on
Saturday nights from 6pm.

Cheonwhang Sikdang   KOREAN $$$
(천황식당; ☎741 2646; meals ₩7000-20,000;
⏱9.30am-9pm, closed 1st & 3rd Mon) Housed in
a vintage wooden building from the postwar
era with a white-tile interior, Cheonwhang
is the place for Jinju *bibimbap*, a bowl of
vegies, rice and raw beef served with

seongjiguk (beef-blood soup). Look for the tile roof, wooden doors, and grey-white exterior. It's on a corner.

Jaeil Sikdang   KOREAN $

(제일식당; meals from ₩6000; ⊙8am-9pm) This famous eatery inside the traditional market serves only two dishes. Until 9.30am, it's *haejangguk* (해장국), a vegetable soup thought to cure hangovers. Thereafter, it's *bibimbap* (비빔밥), a scrumptious rice and vegetable dish that's served with a rich, flavourful broth and, if you so desire, a helping of raw beef as well. Jaeil Sikdang is buried inside the market but the locals know where it is.

La Vigne   WINE BAR

(bottles from ₩28,000; ⊙10am-2am, closed Sun) With over 400 bottles, you're likely to find a vintage to match your budget and taste in this delightful wine bar. Some half-bottle options are available, though the choices aren't always so palatable. Find a seat facing the window to enjoy a quaint street view.

Beast Bar   BAR

(drinks ₩4000-7000; ⊙6pm-6am) This small but convivial watering hole serves up domestic and foreign beer, attracting a blend of expat teachers and Korean salarymen. Two dart machines are by the bar, and K-Pop is on the stereo.

ⓘ Getting There & Around

Air

The closest airport is in Sacheon, 20km from Jinju. Two daily flights connect with Gimpo airport in Seoul via Korean Air, which also runs one daily flight to Jeju Island (as does Asiana). Local buses connect Jinju's north-end bus terminal to Sacheon airport (₩1700, 30 minutes).

Bus

There's an express bus terminal south of the river with services running to Seoul (₩22,000, every 20 minutes), Deagu (₩12,500, hourly) and Gwangju (₩14,300, hourly). Most travellers use the terminal north of the river. For departures from the north terminal, see the boxed text below.

Train

The train station is south of the Namgang River. *Mugunghwa* connections include Dongdaegu (adult/child ₩10,300/5100, three hours, one daily), Daejeon (adult/child ₩20,200/10,100, five hours, one daily) and Seoul (adult/child ₩30,500/15,200, seven hours, one daily).

Namhaedo 남해도

🎵 055 / POP 67,000

Namhaedo is the country's third-largest island, famous for garlic and a slower pace of life, so clearly evident in the countryside where some farmers continue to use oxen to plough fields. Driving in from the mainland through the picturesque valleys, you might think you're in southern France. Rugged ocean views, tiny fishing ports untouched by tourist development and charming roadside diversions are best appreciated by travellers with their own transport and an unhurried sense of exploration.

◉ Sights & Activities

Some decent **beaches** are on the southern coast, including **Sangju** (상주 해수욕장) and **Songjeong** (송정 해수욕장). While highly ranked on Korean search engines, Sangju is underwhelming but good for families since offshore rocks ensure most waves are small. The stand of trees here creates an illusion of isolation.

BUS DEPARTURES FROM JINJU (NORTH TERMINAL)

DESTINATION	PRICE (₩)	DURATION (HR)	FREQUENCY
Busan	8500	1½	every 10-20min
Hadong	4700	1	every 2-3hr
Namhae	5400	1½	every 15-30min
Ssanggyae-sa	7300	2	3 daily
Tongyeong	7100	1½	every 20min

Between Namhae City and Sangju beach, **Boriam** (보리암) is a Buddhist hermitage on Geumsan famous for spectacular sunrises. About 16km from Sangju, there's an architectural oddity: the **German Village** (독일마을) is a hillside hamlet of homes designed with a German motif. Behind the village, spend 30 minutes walking through the **Horticultural Art Village** (원예 예술촌), a public garden with outdoor art. On the way to the German Village from Sangju, **Mijo** (미조) is a rustic fishing port with superb countryside food. **Daraengi Village** (다랭이 마을) is famed for its over 100 terraced rice paddies descending precipitously toward the ocean. It's a picturesque, otherworldly spot if you have the time to explore the remote southwest part of the island.

While it's easiest to get around Namhae with your own wheels, a **bus tour** (see p200) can take you to some of the main sights.

There's a part-time **tourist information centre** in the Namhae bus terminal, but little English is spoken there.

Sleeping & Eating

Byzantine Motel   LOVE HOTEL **$$**
(비잔틴 모텔; ☑864 5120; standard/special ₩40,000/50,000; ❄@) If you need to sleep in Namhae City, the Byzantine Motel is down a side road outside the bus terminal. It's a standard love hotel, but rooms are slightly above average. From here, the city centre is a 10-minute walk. If lost, ask anyone to point the way to the Baskin Robbins icecream shop.

Oasis Pension   PENSION **$$**
(오아시스펜션; ☑862 8107; standard/ocean view ₩50,000/70,000; ❄🛜) If you're spending the night, try this pension where most rooms come with a double bed and a basic kitchen. Prices jump to ₩200,000 during the first week of August when the beach is packed. It's along the road running parallel to the beach.

Dajeong Sikdang   KOREAN **$**
(다정식당; meals from ₩7000; ⊙6am-8pm) In Mijo, Dajeong Sikdang is a simple restaurant with outstanding *twenjang jjigae* (된 장찌개; soybean stew). The soft tofu, superb balance of vegetables and seafood is a welcome treat for travellers who need a break from spicy food. Facing the police station, walk left, turn left at the lane opposite the post office and then right at the first lane.

ℹ Getting There & Around

There are frequent bus connections to Namhae from Seobu terminal in Busan and Jinju. Leaving the island, four daily buses run to Hadong (₩4800, one hour, four daily), Jinju (₩5400, 1½ hours, every 15 to 60 minutes) and Busan (₩12,500, 2¼ hours, every 30 to 60 minutes).

Local buses to Sangju (₩2400, 40 minutes, every 30 to 50 minutes), Mijo (₩3200, 60 minutes, every 30 to 50 minutes), and Daraengi (₩2200, 30 minutes, hourly) from Namhae are available but the return trip can involve long roadside waits. Private transport is the only practical way to Boriam. Follow the road signs up to the car park (₩4000). Driving close to the hermitage is possible though traffic is restricted, so expect delays during summer and on weekends. Alternatively, park the car and enjoy a two-hour hike or catch a shuttle bus (adult/child ₩1000/free, 30 minutes, every 30 minutes).

To see the island by bus, the **Namhae Sarang Tour** (☑864 0052; ₩20,000) departs from Namhae bus terminal at 9am, hitting German Village, Boriam temple and Daraengi Village, returning at 5.30pm. Get a Korean speaker to call and reserve.

Jirisan National Park – East 지리산 국립공원

☑055

This **park** (Map p201; admission free; ⊙2hr before sunrise-2hr after sunset) offers some of Korea's best hiking opportunities, with 12 peaks over 1000m forming a 40km ridge. Many peaks are over 1500m high, including **Cheonwangbong** (1915m), the country's second-highest mountain. There are three principal park entrances, each with a temple. Two of the three temples, Ssanggye-sa and Daewon-sa, are in Gyeongsangnam-do. From the west, Hwaeom-sa is accessible via Gurye in Jeollanam province (see p212).

The **Jirisan Bear Project** (see the boxed text, p379) was established with the aim to build up a self-sustaining group of 50 wild bears in Jirisan.

◉ Sights & Activities

Ssanggye-sa   TEMPLE
(쌍계사; Map p179; ☑883-1901; www.ssang gyesa.net; adult/youth/child ₩2500/1000/500; ⊙8am-6pm) The visual imagery of this temple is a feast for the eyes, and like any exquisite dinner should be consumed with deliberation in order to enjoy each and every morsel. Stone walls supporting

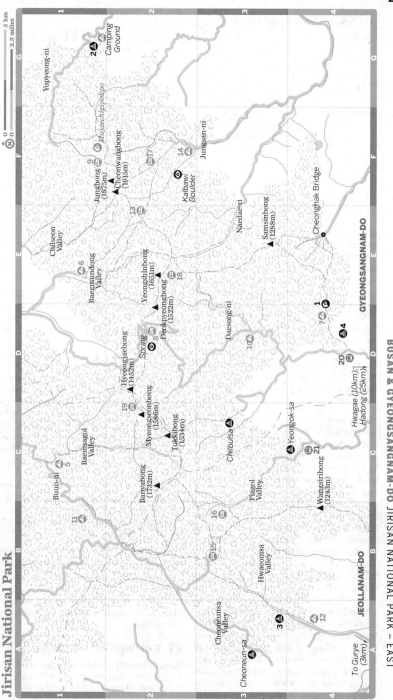

Jirisan National Park

Jirisan National Park

BUSAN & GYEONGSANGNAM-DO JIRISAN NATIONAL PARK – EAST

GYEONGSANGNAM-DO

JEOLLANAM-DO

Yupyeong-ni

Camping Ground

2

Mujaechigipokpo

Jungbong (1875m)

Cheomwangbong (1915m)

Kalbawi Boulder

Jungsan-ni

17

14

13

9

Chilseon Valley

Baegmundong Valley

Yeongshinbong (1651m)

Naedae'ri

Samsimbong (1288m)

Cheonghak Bridge

6

Deokpyeongbong (1522m)

18

Spring

8

Hyeongjaebong (1452m)

Daesong-ni

1

10

7

4

20

19

Myeongseonbong (1586m)

Tokkibong (1534m)

Chilbul-sa

Yeongok-sa

21

5

Buun-ni

Baemsagol Valley

Banyabong (1732m)

Piagol Valley

Wangsiribong (1243m)

Hwagae (10km); Hadong (25km)

11

16

15

Hwaeomsa Valley

Cheoneunsa Valley

Cheoneun-sa

3

12

To Gurye (3km)

5 km
2.5 miles

Jirisan National Park

multiple levels of buildings notched into the mountainside, combined with mature trees and a trickling creek, create a pleasant sensory experience. Three gates mark the path to the main hall; take the time to read the signs to appreciate the symbolism of your visit. To the left of the main hall is a smaller pavilion dedicated to the Chinese Zen master Haeneng; it's the original temple. One of the most attractive sanctuaries in the province, it's a long day trip from Busan. For a more relaxing pace, consider an overnight stopover in Jinju, Namhae or Hadong and an early-morning departure to the temple.

Hiking Trails
HIKING

It's impossible to describe the myriad of trails within this great park. The traditional course runs east to west (Daewon-sa to Hwaeom-sa), which experienced Korean hikers say requires three days. Some Lonely Planet readers have suggested an alternate three-night route that puts hikers in position for a sunrise view on top of Cheonwangbong. The route starts with a night at the Nogodan shelter. The next two nights are spent at the Baemsagol camping ground and Jangteomok shelter. On the final day, follow the trail to Jungsan-ni and then catch a bus to Jinju or Busan.

Travellers with less ambitious plans, but who want to experience Jirisan's beauty, hike the popular trail to **Buril Pokpo** (불일폭포; Buril Falls). Starting from Ssanggye-sa, the mildly challenging trail (2.4km each way, three hours return) winds through a forest along a rippling creek. About two-thirds along the way, just when you've noticed the sound of the creek has disappeared, the trail bursts onto an open field. At the foot of the falls, there's a rocky pool where hikers meditate to regain their chi.

🛏 Sleeping

There are nine **camping sites** (from ₩3000): Hwangjeon, Daewon-sa, Jungsan-ri, Baemsagol 1 and 2, Dalgung, Daeseonggyo, Buril Pokpo and Baengmu-dong. Facilities are basic.

There are also nine **shelters** (₩5000-8000). From west to east, they are: Nogodan 1 and 2, Piagol, Yeonhacheon, Byeoksoryeong, Seseok, Jangteomok, Chibanmok and the Rotari shelter. Jangteomok has enough space for 135 bodies, and sells torches, noodles and drinks. Seseok is the largest shelter, with space for 190 people. For overnight hikes bring bedding, food, tea and coffee, as most shelters have limited supplies.

Multiday treks require a hiking plan and bookings if you plan on staying at any of the shelters. Online reservations can be made at the website of **Korea National Park Service** (http://english.knps.or.kr).

Gilson Minbak
INN **$$**

(길손민박; ☎884 1336; ondol ₩40,000-70,000) This place has clean rooms with private bathrooms. It's a brown-beige building on a small road off to the right as you walk up to the temple admission gate. No English is spoken here.

❶ Getting There & Away

Buses to Ssanggye-sa often pass through Hadong, a small village and useful transfer point in the region. If you can't get a direct bus to

Ssanggye-sa, travel to Hadong and catch one of the frequent buses to the temple (₩2500, 30 to 60 minutes, every 45 to 90 minutes). En route to Ssanggye-sa from Hadong, buses pass a large bridge and shortly thereafter make a quick stop in Hwagae; don't get off there. Further down the road (usually the next stop), the bus stops beside a concrete bridge. Do get out here, cross the bridge and follow the winding road to the park entrance. Return tickets are purchased inside the seafood restaurant beside the bridge. The signboard lists times for several destinations, though most travellers are best served by heading to Hadong, where frequent buses connect with Busan (₩13,300, 2½ hours, every 30 to 60 minutes) and Jinju (₩7300, 1½ hours, every 30 minutes).

Jeollanam-do

Best Places to Eat

» Minsokchon (p208)

» House Filled with Happiness (p223)

» Jeonsama (p219)

Best Places to Stay

» Yuseongwan (p217)

» Hotel 1004 (p225)

» The Ocean Resort (p214)

Why Go?

This beautiful southwest province is one of Korea's least developed and greenest. The heartland of Jeollanam-do (전라남도) has rolling hills, the towering Sobaek Mountains to the east and 6100km of coastline to the south and west, with over 2000 islands offshore – less than 300 of which are inhabited.

With a warmer and rainier climate than its provincial mainland neighbours, bountiful Jeollanam-do is all about agriculture – the province is famous for its food and green tea, celebrated in several festivals. For all of its rural atmosphere, Jeollanam-do has urban elements that are common to the rest of Korea; think high-speed train lines and expanding cities, chief of which is Gwangju, Korea's sixth-largest metropolis with its own separate government and telephone code. Despite all this, the province retains a rebel edge, and is proud of its ceramic and artistic traditions, its exiled poets and prodemocracy martyrs. Jeollanam-do rewards the intrepid and really does have something for everyone.

When to Go
Gwangju

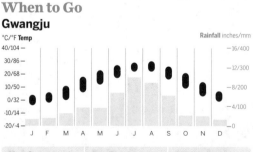

May Summer offers a chance for visitors to cool off at the beaches.

Sep The Gwangju Biennale brings the glamour of the art world to town.

Oct It's *kimchi* EVERYTHING during the eponymous festival in Gwangju.

History

Far from Seoul during the Joseon era, Jeollanam-do was a place of exile, often used as a dumping ground for political and religious dissidents. The tradition of political dissent has continued; the province was a hotbed of opposition to the military governments that ruled South Korea in the 1960s and '70s. Students and trade unionists led countless prodemocracy protests and demonstrations, until army tanks crushed an uprising in Gwangju city in May 1980 (see p355). Today about 25% of households in the province are farms, versus a national average of 7%.

Gwangju 광주

♪ 062 / POP 1.46 MILLION

Gwangju (http://english.gjcity.go.kr) may look like any other city with its shop-filled central area, an attractive riverside, busy restaurants, pubs and bars – all encircled by apartment blocks – but within this everyday exterior resides the heart of an artist and the soul of a revolutionary. Civic Gwangju emphasises the arts and the city has an important place in the history of Korea's democracy and human-rights movement.

◉ Sights & Activities

FREE **Gwangju National Museum** MUSEUM
(국립광주박물관; ☎ 570 7014; ⊙ 9am-6pm Tue-Sun) The Gwangju National Museum's collection traces the region's prehistoric beginnings to the modern day, via artifacts, paintings and calligraphy. When there aren't any visiting exhibitions, look out for the Chinese ceramics salvaged from a 14th-century shipwreck. Bus 55 (₩1200, 20 minutes, every 30 minutes) runs from Geumnamno to the National Museum.

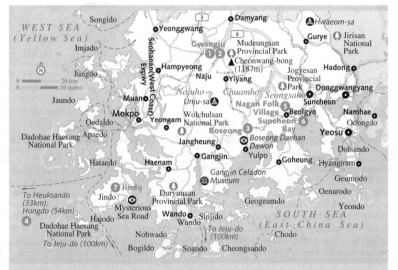

Jeollanam-do Highlights

① Visit **Gwangju** (p205) for its vibrant arts and nightlife scene, urban hiking opportunities, and solemn memorials

② Learn everything there is to know about bamboo at the **Damyang Bamboo Crafts Museum** (p211)

③ Savour the scenic location and flavours of the photogenic **Daehan Dawon Tea Plantation** (p216) in Boseong

④ Voyage to the scattered, unspoilt islands of **Heuksando** (p225) and fabled **Hongdo** (p225)

⑤ Marvel at the thatched-roofed houses of the immaculately preserved fortress town of **Nagan Folk Village** (p213)

⑥ Spot migratory birds feasting in the rich wetlands at **Suncheon Bay** (p212)

⑦ Partake in the mysterious 'parting of the sea' phenomenon known as the Ganjuyuk Gyedo in **Jindo** (p219)

JEOLLANAM-DO GWANGJU

Gwangju

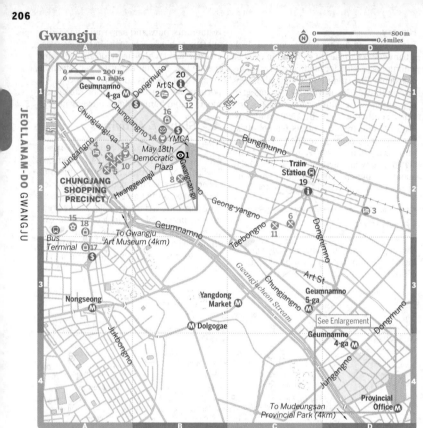

Gwangju Art Museum
MUSEUM

(광주시립미술관; ☎529 7126; adult/youth/child ₩500/300/200; ◷9am-6pm Tue-Sun) Part of an art plaza with concert and performance halls, this three-storey museum displays highlights from the avant-garde Gwangju Biennale (p208) as well as quality paintings and installations from the likes of Nam Jun Paik.

Gwangju Folk Museum
MUSEUM

(광주민속박물관; ☎525 8633; adult/youth/child ₩500/300/200; ◷9.30am-6pm, Tue-Sun) This retro-looking museums uses dioramas, models, sound effects, videos and more to show off Jeollanam-do's traditional culture and practices. Topics cover the vast ground between *kimchi*, weddings and shamanism. Historical photographs at the end reveal how quickly Koreans have morphed from feudal farmers to 21st-century city dwellers.

The museum district is northwest of downtown. Take bus 48 (₩1200, 10 minutes, every 15 minutes) from outside the bus ter-

minal and get off at the Gwangju Art Museum stop (Munhwa Yesul Hoegwan). Bus 95 (₩1200, 20 minutes, every 15 minutes) from the YMCA also runs here. It's a 15-minute walk through a tunnel under the expressway to Gwangju National Museum. Bus 50 (₩1200, 20 minutes, every 30 minutes) runs from the train station to the Folk Museum.

FREE Mudeungsan Provincial Park
PARK

(무등산도립공원; ☎265 0761) Overlooking Gwangju, Mudeungsan Provincial Park is a gorgeous green mountain range with a spider's web of well-signed trails leading to the peak, Cheonwang-bong (1187m), and up to the towering rocky outcrops called Ipseok-dae and Seoseokdae that are visible from miles away.

There are three major Buddhist temples in the park, most of which were rebuilt after being destroyed in the Korean War. The easiest to reach is Wonhyo-sa, a short walk

Gwangju

from the bus stop. The small but ornate temple has a sculpture garden with several bronze figures standing sentry and a fabulous bronze bell dating to 1710. Further south is **Jeungsim-sa**, the park's largest temple with a Shilla-era iron Buddha backed by red-and-gold artwork, housed in an insignificant-looking shrine behind the main hall. The tiny shrine perched on a rock next to it is dedicated to the Shamanist Mountain God. Further up is the smaller temple of **Yaksaam**.

Around 250m before Jeungsim-sa, **Uijae Misulgwan** (☑222 3040; admission ₩1000; ⊙9.30am-5.30pm Tue-Sun) is an art gallery that displays landscape, flower and bird paintings by the famed Heo Baek-ryeon (1891–1977), whose pen name was Uijae. His rebuilt house is a short walk away. About halfway between Uijae and Jeungsim-sa is the **Chunseolheon tea plantation** that Uijae established, now cultivated by Jeungsim-sa monks.

A popular route is to begin at Wonhyosa, climb up to Seoseokdae and Ipseokdae, down past Jeungsim-sa and Uijae, and then down to the bus stop; the hike takes about five hours. If you're pressed for time, just visit Jeungsim-sa and Uijae. The road leading from the bus stop to Uijae has been newly developed, with modern restaurants, cafes and way too many outdoor-clothing stores.

Take the cleverly named bus 1187 (the height in metres of Cheonwang-bong) which terminates near Wonhyo-sa; you can catch the bus (₩1200, every 20 minutes) from the bus terminal or outside the YMCA. Bus 51 (₩1200, every 20 minutes) from the YMCA runs to the Jeungsim-sa area.

FREE **May 18th National Cemetery** MEMORIAL
(국립 5.18 민주묘지; ☑266 5187; www.518. org; ⊙8am-6pm Mar-Oct, to 5pm Nov-Feb) This sombre memorial park, opened in 1997, is the final burial place for victims of the May 18 Democratic Uprising of 1980 (p355), one of the most tragic incidents in modern Korean history. Officially, the casualties include 228 dead or missing and 4141 wounded, but the real numbers are believed to be much higher. A small but emotionally charged museum shows photographs, blood-stained flags, and a hard-hitting film that gives a dramatic account of the traumatic events that still scar the country's political landscape.

On the right, a memorial hall displays photographs of the ordinary folk – from students to grandmothers – who paid the ultimate price during the military government's crackdown. A five-minute walk through the memorial garden leads to the reinstated original cemetery, where the victims were first hurriedly buried without proper ceremony. The bodies were later reinterred in the new cemetery.

Take bus 518 (₩1200, one hour, every 30 minutes), which can be picked up at the bus terminal, train station, Gwangju Hospital or along Geumnamno.

Mudeung Stadium STADIUM
(www.tigers.co.kr, in Korean; Mudeung; tickets from ₩7000) Catch the Kia Tigers professional baseball team in action and check out the differences between the Korean

and American games. You won't find pea-nuts or Cracker Jack but vendors do sell dried squid, sushi, fried chicken and Kore-an beer. Stock up on snacks from the street vendors outside the stadium, where prices are cheaper. You're permitted to bring in food, beer, coolers and cameras. Take buses 51 and 95 from the YMCA or bus 38 from the terminal. You can also take the subway to Nongseong station and walk 30 minutes north to the stadium. Games usually start at 5pm or 6.30pm.

Asian Culture Complex CULTURAL BUILDING
(아시아문화중심도시홍보관; http://.cct.go.kr) This massive US$680 million arts com-plex in the old Provincial Hall and May 18th Democratic Plaza is currently under construction. Set to open in 2013, it will house galleries, performance spaces, a library and plazas. The Kunsthalle Gwang-ju, a temporary gallery with details of the project and a performance art space is next door.

⭐🎪 Festivals & Events

The **Gwangju Biennale** (www.gb.or.kr) is a three-month contemporary art festival that takes place every two years (due to be held in autumn 2014). Based at the Biennale Ex-hibition Hall, near the Gwangju Folk Mu-seum, it features more than 500 artists and foreign curators from 60 countries.

🛏 Sleeping

The usual mixture of cheap *yeogwan* and love motels can be found around the train station; smart new motels surround the bus terminal and the downtown Chungjang nightlife district. New luxury hotels such as the Holiday Inn and Ramada are in the Sangmu district near City Hall.

KIMCHI FESTIVAL

Every October, Gwangju hosts a five-day *kimchi* (pickled vegetables) extravaganza with a fairground, market stalls, pottery making, folk music and a *hanbok* (traditional clothing) fashion show. The festival is the best oppor-tunity to make, taste, purchase or just enjoy the visual sensation of Korea's most famous dish in all its hundreds of varieties. Shuttle buses run to the often-changing venue.

Geumsoojang Tourist Hotel HOTEL $$$
(금수장 관광 호텔; ☎525 2111; www.geumsoojang.co.kr; r 110,000-240,000; ※) This warm and inviting hotel with English-speaking staff is close to the train station and offers hefty 50% discounts if you book through its website. The in-house restaurant serves up a delicious rendition of the Korean *hanjeon-sik* (banquet; ₩50,000). Go with an empty stomach and a huge appetite.

Windmill Motel MOTEL $
(윈드밀 모텔; ☎223 5333; Chungjang district; r ₩30,000-40,000; ※@) Perfectly situated on the west end of the Chungjang nightlife district, Windmill has a slight love motel feel with dark corridors, but the rooms are clean, tidy and spacious with flat-screen TVs, fridges and water coolers.

Bando Motel MOTEL $$
(반도 모텔; ☎227 0238; r ₩35,000-45,000; ※) This basic but clean motel is hidden in an al-ley between Art St and Geumnamno, behind the NH Bank building and just steps from the action of Chungjang (minus all the noise).

Ballade Motel MOTEL $$
(발라드 모텔; ☎363 1751; Chungjang district; r ₩35,000-45,000; ※@) The pick of the bunch near the bus terminal, Ballade impresses with its ode to spotless rooms kitted out with a sofa, large TV and PCs. Prices jump by ₩10,000 on the weekend. It's 500m east of the Shinsegae Department Store.

🍴 Eating

TOP CHOICE Minsokchon KOREAN $$
(민속촌; ☎224 4577; meals ₩7000-17,000; ⏱11.30am-midnight) A popular, attractive and cheery restaurant with *so galbi* (소갈비; beef) and *dwaeji galbi* (돼지갈비; pork) sizzling on table barbecues. The *galbitang* (갈비탕) is ex-cellent with chunky, lean meat, and there are also the usual suspects such as *bibimbap*. If this Chungjang restaurant has a long queue outside, try the branch in Gwangsan-gil.

Moojin Joo KOREAN $$$
(무진주; ☎224 8074; meals ₩8000-50,000; ⏱11.30am-midnight) Located opposite Minsok-chon, this classy restaurant has wooden inte-riors and calligraphy on the walls. But all that matters little when you start digging into their pork-focused dishes. Try the *mudan bossam* (모둔보쌈), you wrap soft slices of pork with *kimchi* and assorted vegetable leaves. Lunch deals (₩10,0000) offer great value.

Cafe Bari E
ITALIAN $$

(dishes from ₩12,000; ☻10am-10pm; @☎) Local fashionistas flock to this sleek corner cafe/restaurant to dig into thin-crust pizzas, pastas and healthy salads whilst flicking through fashion magazines. There's a wide range of drinks including coffee, juice and German draft beer. Those not hip enough to have their own iPads can surf the net on the in-house Macbooks.

Mick Jones's Pizza
PIZZA $

(pizza slice ₩3200-4700; ☻11am-10pm) For a cheap and tasty meal, grab a piece of pie and beer at this brightly coloured, NYC-inspired joint.

Yeongmi
KOREAN $$$

(영미; meals ₩20,000-32,000) The most popular of the many duck restaurants in Duck St alongside Hyundai department store. The speciality is *oritang* (오리탕), which is meant for sharing, and bubbles and thickens away at your table together with a pile of vegetables.

Hyundai Department Store
FOOD COURT $

(현대백화점; ☻10am-8pm) Near Gwangju train station, it has a bright and clean food court (meals ₩4000 to ₩7000) in the basement.

🍷 Drinking

Chungjang, the city's buzzing, semipedestrian shopping district, is also Gwangju's prime nightlife spot with hundreds of bars, nightclubs, restaurants and cafes, particularly in the narrow alleys south of Hwanggeumgil St.

TOP CHOICE Ethnic Café
THEME BAR

(☏234 0901; drinks ₩5000-9000; Chungjang district; ☻2pm-2am) This unique, Middle Eastern–themed pub is set in a cave-like, candle-lit basement with a reflecting pool in the centre of the room. Remove your shoes and sit on pillows on the floor and enjoy a conversation while the chill-out music plays quietly in the background. There's also sheesha on offer.

Speakeasy
BAR

(drinks ₩4000-8000; ☻7pm-3am Thu-Sun) This second-floor bar hidden down an alley is a favourite with foreigners and has a good selection of imported beer. A live band rocks the house Fridays and Saturdays though the mood can be muted on other days. From the front of Burger King go left for 40m and down the alleyway.

GREEN TEA

The 'well-being wave', the name given to the trend towards healthy food and drinks, has boosted sales of *nokcha*, green tea, which was introduced in the 7th century. Like ginseng it is used as a flavouring for a wide variety of products from ice cream, chocolates, cakes and milk shakes to noodles, pasta and *hotteok* (sweet pita bread). Some spas even offer green-tea baths.

Korean Buddhist monks have always regarded green tea as an ideal relaxant and an aid to meditation, especially when prepared, served and drunk in the correct ceremonial way known as *dado*. They usually settle any disputes over a cup of green tea.

Korean green tea is only grown in the southern provinces and has a subtle flavour but experts can tell when and where the tea was picked. Green tea, like wine, is a blend of flavours, a mix of aroma and taste, with its own special vocabulary and rituals.

Chasaengwon
TEAHOUSE

(차생원; Art St; ☻9am-5pm) A traditional Korean teahouse offering a variety of teas, cakes and a large selection of tea sets and other supplies.

☆ Entertainment

The bus terminal **U-Square** and the adjoining **U-Square Cultural Centre** houses an IMAX theatre and multiscreen cinema, performance halls, stores, video arcade, pool hall, art gallery, cafes, restaurants and a massive floor with Korean and Western food options. U-Square is a 1km walk north of Nongseong subway station.

🔒 Shopping

Chungjang is bursting with youth-oriented clothing, shoes and accessory stores along the street and below ground in the Chunggeum underground shopping arcade. Larger department stores are downtown near the train station.

Shinsegae Department Store
MALL

(☻10am-8pm) Brand names such as Vuitton and Dior rub shoulders with an art gallery and basement food court/supermarket at this large but somewhat sterile mall. There's also a Starbucks, the favourite haunt of local *doenjangnyeo,* as some Koreans might say (*doenjangnyeo* is a derogatory term for young women who only care about style and fashion). It's 200m east of the bus terminal.

E-Mart HYPERMART
(◔10am-10pm, to midnight Fri & Sat) Stock up on cheap food, drinks and supplies at this hypermarket, next door to Shinsegae.

Art Street STREET
(Yesurui Geori) This cobblestoned road is famous for its art galleries, studios, workshops, teashops and stores selling *hanbok* (traditional Korean clothing), *hanji* (handmade paper), art books, ethnic jewellery, calligraphy brushes, tea sets and dolls.

ⓘ Information

Central post office (Chungjangno) Free internet.

Citibank (Jukbongno; ◔9am-4pm Mon-Fri) Global ATM with high daily withdrawal limit.

Global ATM (Bus Terminal) Near the ticket booths.

Gwangju Bank (Shinsegae Department Store) Foreign exchange.

Gwangju International Centre (☏226 2733; www.eng.gic.or.kr; KEB Bldg; ◔10am-1pm & 2-6pm Mon-Sat) This expat organisation offers guidebooks, tourist information, Korean-language classes, tours and social events.

KEB (Geumnamno) Global ATM.

Standard Chartered Bank (Geumnamno) Global ATM and foreign exchange.

Tourist information centres Bus terminal (☏360 8733); Geumnamno (☏062 1330; ◔9am-9pm); Gwangju airport (☏942 6160); train station (☏522 5147)

ⓘ Getting There & Away
Air
Seven Gwangju–Seoul and nine Gwangju–Jeju flights run daily.

Bus
Express and intercity buses to more than 100 destinations depart from the U-Square complex, 1km north of the Nongseong subway station.

Train
KTX trains (₩38,900, three hours, five daily) run between Gwangju and Yongsan station with a transfer required. Trains also run to Mokpo and Yeosu from Gwangju as well as the Gwangju-Songjeong train station, west of Gwangju past the airport. Take a subway to Songjeon-ni station (₩1200).

ⓘ Getting Around
To/From the Airport
Bus 1000 (₩1200, 30 minutes, every 15 minutes) runs from the airport to the bus terminals and Geumnamno. You can also take the subway (₩1200). A taxi costs around ₩9000.

Bus
Gwangju has over 80 city bus routes, and most run past the bus terminal that has bus stops on all sides. Bus 17 (₩1200, 20 minutes, every 15 minutes) runs between the bus terminal and Gwangju train station.

Subway
Currently there is one line that stretches west to the airport and beyond with plans for a second line in the works. A single ride is ₩1200; trains run from 5.30am until midnight.

Around Gwangju

The intriguing **Unju-sa** (운주사; ☏061-374 0660; www.unjusa.org; adult/youth/child ₩3000/2000/1000; ◔7am-7pm Mar-Oct, 7am-6pm Nov-Feb) occupies a river valley and its hillsides in Hwasun-gun, 40km south of Gwangju. The compound has an almost primeval feel, with the temple set against a backdrop of forests and hills. Clamber up hillsides to discover various statues and carvings. Legend has it that the site originally housed 1000 Buddhas and 1000 pagodas, built because, according to traditional geomancy, the southwest of the country lacked hills and needed the pagodas to 'balance' the peninsula. The remaining 23 pagodas and some 100 Buddhas still make up the greatest numbers of any Korean temple. According to another legend they were all built in one night by stonemasons sent down from heaven, but another theory is that Unju-sa was the site of a school for stonemasons.

Whatever their origins, many works are unique and some are national treasures. Back-to-back twin Buddhas face their own pagodas, while another pair of Buddhas lying on their backs are said to have been the last works sculpted one evening; the masons returned back to heaven before the Buddhas could be stood upright.

To reach Unju-sa, catch bus 218 or 318-1 from Gwangju bus terminal (₩3000, 1½ hours, every 30 minutes). Check with the driver as only some of the buses go all the way to Unju-sa. The last bus back to Gwangju leaves around 8.10pm.

BUS DEPARTURES FROM GWANGJU

Express bus destinations

DESTINATION	PRICE (₩)	DURATION (HR)	FREQUENCY
Busan	16,100	4	every 40min
Daegu	13,000	3	every 40min
Daejeon	10,700	2½	every 30min
Incheon Airport	30,900	4½	every 30min
Jeonju	6300	1¼	every 30min
Seoul	16,900	4	every 10min

Intercity bus destinations

DESTINATION	PRICE (₩)	DURATION	FREQUENCY
Beolgyo	8300	1½hr	every 30min
Boseong	7800	1½hr	every 30min
Gangjin	9300	1½hr	every 30min
Haenam	10,500	2hr	every 30min
Jindo	11,400	3hr	hourly
Mokpo	5400	50min	every 20min
Songgwang-sa	7000	1½hr	8 daily
Suncheon	6400	2hr	every 30min
Wando	15,400	2½hr	hourly
Yeongam	6400	1½hr	every 20min
Yeosu	9700	2hr	every 20min

The **Damyang Bamboo Crafts Museum** (담양대나무박물관; ☏061-381 4111; adult/youth/child ₩1000/700/500; ⊙9am-6pm) in Damyang, north of Gwangju, has an amazing range of bamboo products, both ancient and modern. Furniture, exquisitely woven baskets – even a bamboo teapot and bamboo jewellery – are more interesting than you'd expect. Bamboo has 101 uses and the displays and shops here prove it. A few of the 46 kinds of bamboo grow behind the museum.

A two-minute walk down the road is the busy but superb **Bakmulgwan Apjip** (박물관앞집; meals ₩12,000-32,000; ⊙10am-9.30pm) The *daetongbap* (대통밥) is excellent – rice and nuts cooked inside a bamboo stem, bamboo-shoot *doenjang,* and a dozen side dishes are served up with free bamboo-leaf tea. The side rooms have glorious views over the rice fields.

If you haven't had enough of a bamboo fix, head to the **Bamboo Culture Experience** (Juknokwon; 죽녹원; adult/youth/child ₩2000/1500/1000; ⊙9am-7pm), a lush bamboo forest set on a hill.

Try to visit Damyang on the 2nd, 7th, 12th, 17th, 22nd or 27th of each month, as the bamboo market is held on these days. A **bamboo crafts festival** is held in early May.

Bus 311 (₩2100, 40 minutes, every 15 minutes) runs between Gwangju bus terminal and Damyang, dropping off at the museum and the Bamboo Culture Experience. Bus 303 runs from Gwangju train station to Damyang. If you end up in the Damyang bus terminal it's a 15-minute walk to the museum.

Jogyesan Provincial Park
조계산도립공원

This **park** (☏061-755 0107; adult/youth/child ₩3000/2000/free; ⊙8am-7pm Mar-Oct, 8am-5pm Nov-Feb) revolves around two noteworthy temples, their beauty complemented by the attractive surrounding forest.

To the west, 70km from Gwangju, **Songgwang-sa** (www.songgwangsa.org) is considered one of the three jewels of Korean Buddhism (along with Tongdo-sa and

Haein-sa, in Gyeongsangnam-do). Featured in the *Little Monk* movie, it is a regional head temple of the Jogye sect, by far the largest in Korean Buddhism. It is also one of the oldest Zen temples in Korea, founded in AD 867, although most of the buildings date from the 17th century. Songgwang-sa is known for having produced many prominent Zen masters over the years, and today the temple is home to a community of monks.

On the eastern side of the mountain is Seonam-sa, a quieter hermitage dating back to AD 529, where the monks study and try to preserve the old ways. Below Seonam-sa is Seungseongyo, one of Korea's most exquisite ancient granite bridges, with a dragon's head hanging from the top of the arch.

A spectacular 16km hike over the peak of Janggunbong (884m) connects the two temples. The walk takes six hours if you go over the peak, or four hours if you go around it. Either route is fantastic.

A weekend Templestay (see p386) is available at Songgwang-sa. Accommodation and restaurants are also available by the car park

---

WORTH A TRIP

SUNCHEON-MAN: ONE FOR THE BIRDS

If you're staying at or near Songgwang-sa, one place you might want to consider making time to see is Suncheon-man (순천만; ☎061-749 3006; www.suncheonbay.go.kr; adult/youth/child ₩2500/1500/100). In 2006 this bay became the first coastal estuary in Korea to be inscribed on the Ramsar list of protected wetlands. Apart from admiring the view of the beautiful reed-studded river estuary and surrounding beaches, birdwatchers can spot the hooded crane, black-faced spoonbills and swans, all of which stop by during their migrations.

There's an eco museum and walkways through the rustling reeds that lead up to an observation hut on a neighbouring hill. If you'd like to get closer to the wildlife, take a birdwatching boat (₩4000, 35 minutes, six daily). To get here, take bus 67 (₩1500, 30 minutes, every 20 minutes) from Suncheon bus terminal. Buses run from Gwangju to Suncheon.

---

at Songgwang-sa. Lodgings here range from ₩30,000. There's also a tourist village near Seonam-sa.

From Gwangju buses (₩5600, 1½ hours, every 1½ hours) run to Songgwang-sa. Bus 1 to Seonam-sa (₩1100, 1½ hours, every 50 minutes) and bus 111 to Songgwang-sa (₩1100, 1½ hours, hourly) runs from Suncheon.

Jirisan National Park – West 지리산국립공원

While the bulk of this national park lies in the neighbouring province of Gyeongsangnam-do (p200) it is best approached from this direction if you plan to visit Hwaeom-sa (☎061-783 9105; www.hwaeomsa.org; adult/youth/child ₩3800/1800/1300; ☻6am-7pm). Founded by priest Yeongi in AD 544 after his return from India, this ancient temple dedicated to the Birojana Buddha is enveloped by the beautiful natural surroundings of the park. Last rebuilt in 1636, it has endured five major devastations in its history, including the Japanese invasion of 1592.

On the main plaza is Gakgwang-jeon, a huge two-storey hall. Inside are paintings that are national treasures, nearly 12m long and 7.75m wide, featuring Buddhas, disciples and assorted holies. These are displayed outdoors only on special occasions. Korea's oldest and largest stone lantern fronts Gakgwang-jeon, which was once surrounded by stone tablets of the Tripitaka Sutra (made during the Shilla era). These were ruined during the Japanese invasion. Many pieces are now preserved in the temple's museum.

Up many further flights of stairs is Hwaeom-sa's most famous structure, a unique three-storey pagoda supported by four stone lions. The female figure beneath the pagoda is said to be Yongi's mother; her dutiful son offers her tea from another lantern facing her.

The temple is about 25 minutes' walk from the bus stop. It is possible to continue from the temple and along Hwaeom-sa Valley. After about 2½ to three hours the trail begins to ascend to a shelter, Nogodan Sanjang (a strenuous four-hour hike). From the shelter the trail continues to rise until you are finally on the long spine of the Jirisan ridge. For hiking details and a map see the section starting on p200.

Templestays (see p386) are possible at Hwaeom-sa. A large tourist village is at the

Jogyesan Provincial Park

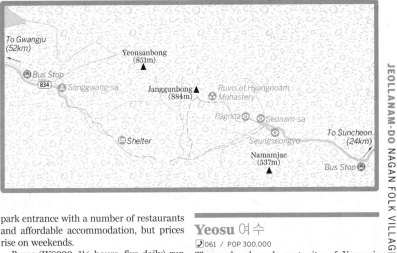

park entrance with a number of restaurants and affordable accommodation, but prices rise on weekends.

Buses (₩8000, 1½ hours, five daily) run from Gwangju bus terminal to Jirisan National Park and Hwaeom-sa.

Nagan Folk Village
낙안읍성민속마을

Among Korea's many folk villages, **Nagan** (061-749 3893; adult/youth/child ₩2000/1500/1000; 9am-6pm) is unique for its setting, surrounded by 1410m of Joseon-period fortress walls, built to protect the inhabitants from marauding Japanese pirates. It's Korea's best-preserved fortress town, crammed with narrow, dry-stone alleyways leading to vegetable allotments, and adobe and stone homes thatched with reeds. Some of these are private homes while others house working artisans (with wares for sale) or are *minbak* (private homes with rooms for rent, from ₩40,000), restaurants or souvenir shops. Some points of interest are labelled in English and there's the inevitable folk museum.

The **Namdo Food Festival** (www.namdofood.or.kr/www/page/), which receives 200,000-plus attendees, is usually held here early in October – it features 300 Korean dishes, eating contests and traditional cultural events.

Catch a bus (₩1500, 15 minutes, every 30 minutes) from Beolgyo. Buses also run from Suncheon (₩1500, 40 minutes, every 30 minutes).

Yeosu 여수
061 / POP 300,000

The molar-shaped, port city of Yeosu is halfway along Korea's steep, island-pocked and deeply indented southern coast. Its bustling city centre is nothing special, but its shoreline, peppered with cliffs, islands and peninsulas, is spectacular. Yeosu hosted the **2012 World's Fair International Exposition** (www.expo2012.or.kr) and some of the purpose-built sights and facilities remain post-expo.

◎ Sights

FREE **Odongdo**　　　　　　　　　　ISLAND
(오동도; 690 7301; 9am-5.30pm) This small, craggy island, a favourite destination for locals, is joined to the mainland by a 750m causeway that can be traversed by a **road train** (adult/youth/child ₩500/400/300). The island is one large botanical garden with bamboo groves and camellia trees, which are full of birdsong and can be walked round in 20 minutes. Take the lift up to the **lighthouse observatory** (admission free; 9.30am-5.30pm) for the best harbour views.

Shops, restaurants, a dancing musical water fountain, a turtle-ship replica and boat trips around the harbour or around Dolsando are also available.

City buses 2, 8, 9, 10, 13, 15, 17 and 107 all stop at the causeway entrance. Otherwise it's a 30-minute walk from Jangang-dong Rotary.

Yeosu

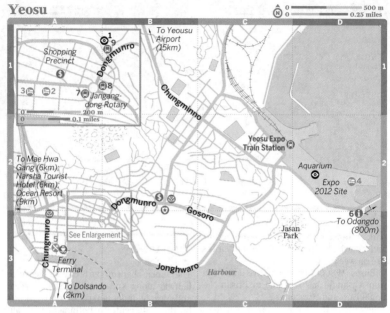

Yeosu

FREE **Jinnamgwan**　　　　　　　HISTORIC BUILDING
(진남관; ⊙9am-5pm) In the centre of town
stands this national treasure, Korea's largest single-storey wooden structure (75m
long and 14m high). The beautiful pavilion,
first constructed in 1599 with 68 pillars
supporting its massive roof, was originally
used for receiving officials and for holding ceremonies. Later it became a military
headquarters.

On the right, a small but modern **museum** (admission free) focuses on Admiral Yi
Sun-sin (1545–98) and has maps explaining
his naval tactics and victories over Japan in
the 1590s.

Expo 2012 Site　　　　　　　　HISTORIC SITE
(Chungminno; http://eng.expo2012.kr; ⊙9am-
6pm) The Expo 2012 (aka World's Fair) site
wasn't all dismantled after the festivities
ended. At the time of research, the tourism board had plans to keep the **Korean
Pavilion** and the hugely popular **aquarium**
running. Admission prices were yet to be
confirmed.

🛏 Sleeping

There's no shortage of budget and midrange
motels, most clustered around the harbour.
Newer, midrange hotels can be found in
Hak-dong.

The Ocean Resort　　　　　　　RESORT **$$$**
(☑689 0000; theoceanresort.co.kr; Yeocheon; r
from₩312,000; ❄@🅿♨) The Ocean Resort is
a five-star luxury hotel complex with sleek,
minimalist decor and top-notch amenities

and facilities. Located 9km west of downtown, the resort also contains **ParaOcean Water Park** (adult/child ₩50,000/40,000, sauna ₩12,000 extra; ⏰9am-8pm). Open year-round, this indoor-and-outdoor park has several pools, water slides, a lazy river and a hot-spring sauna. The resort also has a new hotel-style tower across the road, with rooms from ₩150,000.

Narsha Tourist Hotel   HOTEL $$
(나르샤 관광호텔; ☎686 2000; Hak-dong; www.narshahotel.com; r ₩80,000-120,000; ❄@) This is probably the best of the waterfront hotels in Hak-dong, with polished staff accompanying the carpeted modern rooms. If the rooms here are too pricey, stroll along the street and look out for places such as the Bellagio and the Sun House (rooms from ₩50,000).

MVL Hotel   HOTEL $$$
(☎660 5800; www.mvlhotel.com; r from ₩225,000; ❄@) The glossy 'Most Valuable Life' hotel (really!) was set up onsite for VIPs at Expo 2012. The pricey rooms are ultramodern with sleek fittings, plush beds and views of the bay.

Motel Sky   MOTEL $$
(모텔스카이; ☎662 7780; Sikdang 1-golmuk; r ₩40,000-50,000; ❄@) A friendly welcome awaits you at this dated but well-maintained motel. The 6th floor has the best views and more expensive rooms have computers.

Motel T   MOTEL $$
(☎665 5757; Sikdang 1-golmuk; r ₩50,000-60,000; ❄@) The owner claims to have the cleanest rooms in the strip and he's probably right. Plus features include big TVs and large rooms, some with sea views.

✗ Eating

The harbour front is loaded with restaurants serving fresh fish and seafood, although none of them are cheap. A row of new restaurants and bars surround Soho Yacht Marina in Hak-dong.

TOP CHOICE Mae Hwa Gang San   KOREAN $$$
(매화강산; ☎692 1616; meals ₩20,000-25,000; ⏰10am-10pm) Lovers of red meat will have reason to rejoice at this friendly, family-run, Korean barbecue restaurant serving such favourites as *bulgogi* and *galbi*. This popular place is housed in a modern structure overlooking the waterfront in Hak-dong.

Gubaek Sikdang   KOREAN $$$
(구백식당; ☎662 0900; meals ₩10,000-23,000; ⏰7am-8pm) The *ajumma* (married or older women) staff are friendly and used to dealing with foreigners. *Saengseongui* (생선구이; grilled fish) with rice and refillable side dishes is the best deal.

ℹ Information

Gyodong post office (Chungmuro) Free internet access.

Korea Exchange Bank (near Jangang-dong Rotary) Exchanges foreign currency.

Nice Bank Global ATM inside the train station.

Tourist information centre (☎664 8978; www.yeosu.go.kr) At the entrance to Odong-do pedestrian causeway.

Wooribank (⏰8am-5.30pm Mon-Fri) Exchanges foreign currency, has an ATM.

Yeosu post office (Gosoro)

ℹ Getting There & Away
Air
Yeosu airport, 17km north of the city, has flights to Seoul and Jeju-do.

Boat
The ferry pier for island ferries is at the western end of the harbour. Ferries leave for Geomundo (₩36,600, two hours) at 7.40am and 1.40pm, and for Sado (₩11,500, one hour) at 6am and 2.20pm.

Bus
The express bus terminal and intercity bus terminal are together, 4km north of the port area. For bus departure details, see the boxed text, p216.

Train
KTX trains from Yongsan in Seoul run to Yeosu Expo Station (₩43,100, three hours, eight daily). There are also *Saemaul* (₩39,300, five hours, one daily) and *Mugunghwa* (₩26,400, six hours, six daily) services.

ℹ Getting Around
Bus
The express and intercity bus terminals are 4km north of the port. Cross the pedestrian overpass to Pizza Hut and from the bus stop, almost any bus (₩1100, 15 minutes) goes to Jangang-dong Rotary. From the train station the same situation applies. Bus 35 (₩3000, 40 minutes, every 30 minutes) runs to and from Jangang-dong Rotary and the airport.

BUS DEPARTURES FROM YEOSU

DESTINATION	PRICE (₩)	DURATION (HR)	FREQUENCY
Busan	13,500	4	hourly
Gangjin	14,200	3	every 30min
Gwangju	9800	2¼	every 30min
Mokpo	19,000	3½	hourly
Seoul	20,500	5	hourly

Taxi

Taxis are cheap and plentiful with fares starting at ₩2300.

Dolsando 돌산도

This large scenic island is connected to Yeosu by a beautiful bridge that is dramatically lit at night. Perched halfway up on a cliff on its southern tip is a popular temple and small monastery called **Hyangiram** (향일암; ☎061-644 3650; adult/youth/child ₩2000/1500/1000; ◷8am-6pm), which has superb coastal views over clear blue seas when the mist disperses.

It's a steep 10-minute walk from the bus stop through the tourist village up to the temple, passing through narrow clefts in the rock. Outside some shrines are stone turtles facing out to sea.

Walk to the right and down the access road for about 50m for the signposted walk up **Geumosan** (323m). Climbing up the 350 steps takes about 20 minutes, and your reward is a fantastic vista of distant islands and a 360-degree view from the rocky summit. Carry on and the loop track will bring you back down to Hyangiram (about 25 minutes).

Every restaurant in the tourist village sells locally made *gatkimchi* (갓김치; pickled mustard leaves), which has a mustard taste; even if you don't usually like *kimchi* you might find you like the mildish ones here. If the weather's fine, find a restaurant where you can sit outside under covered shelters for sea views. There are also some pensions and *minbak* if you're inclined to stay.

Buses 111, 113 and 116 (₩1100, one hour) run from outside Jinnamgwan to Hyangiram. Check the times as the timetable has gaps.

Boseong 보성

☑061

This town is the gateway to the famous **Boseong Daehan Dawon Tea Plantation** (대한다원; ☎853 2595; adult/child ₩3000/2000; ◷9am-6pm), spectacularly set on a hillside covered with curvy row after row of manicured green tea bushes.

If you dine in the plantation's **restaurant** (meals ₩4000-6000), overlooking the tea bushes, you can choose from *jajangmyeon* made with green-tea noodles, *bibimbap* with green tea-rice or other green-tea themed favourites. Downstairs you can sip on a cup of green tea, slurp green-tea shakes or guzzle green-tea ice cream. A shop sells green tea in leaf, teabag or powder form plus green-tea biscuits, soap...you get 'tea' picture?

Get on the road past the plantation and walk 1km up the hill to the **Korea Tea Museum** (한국차 박물관; ☎852 0918; www.koreateamuseum.kr; adult/child ₩1000/500; ◷10am-5pm) where you can learn everything there is to know about tea and even partake in a traditional tea ceremony (₩2000, 30 minutes).

Local buses to the tea plantation continue to Yulpo Beach, where **Yulpo Haesu Nokchatang** (율포 해수 녹차탕; ☎853 4566; adult/child ₩5000/3000; ◷6am-8pm, last entry 7pm) offers you the chance to bathe in green-tea water or seawater.

ⓘ Getting There & Around

From Boseong bus terminal take any bus bound for Yulpo Beach (₩1100, 10 minutes, every 30 minutes) to reach the Boseong Daehan Daewon Tea Plantation. Buses pass through Boseong every 30 minutes along the Mokpo-to-Suncheon route.

Gangjin 강진

♪061

One of the most important ceramic centres in Korea, Gangjin has been associated with celadon (glazed green ceramic) for over 1000 years. Gangjin is specifically known for etched celadon, in which shallow patterns are cut out of the piece while it's still wet and filled in with special glazes through an inlay process.

Gangjin Celadon Museum (강진청자박물관; ☑430 3718; adult/youth/child ₩2000/1500/1000; ☉9am-6pm) is 18km south of Gangjin and 300m from the road. There is little English explanation but the exquisite examples of Goryeo-dynasty celadon speak for themselves. Even 800-year-old pieces look startlingly contemporary. At the back are **pottery workshops**, where visitors can watch artisans at work on various processes. On the right is an excavated kiln site, discovered in 1968, that dates back to the 12th century. The museum and shops outside sell modern-made Goryeo celadon (the Seoul airport sells similar pieces for 10 times the price). The **Gangjin Ceramic Festival** is held here during midsummer.

To get here, take a local bus from Gangjin bus terminal for Maryang and get off at the museum (₩1950, 25 minutes, every 40 minutes). Gangjin is a major transport hub for southern Jeollanam-do; for bus departure details, see the boxed text below.

Duryunsan Provincial Park 두륜산도립공원

♪061

◉ Sights & Activities

Daedun-sa TEMPLE
(대흥사; ☑535 5775; adult/youth/child ₩3000/1500/1000; ☉sunrise-sunset) One highlight of this park, southeast of Haenam, is a major

Zen temple complex. The temple is thought to date back to the mid-10th century, but it remained relatively unknown until it became associated with Seosan, a warrior monk who led a group against Japanese invaders between 1592 and 1598. The backdrop of mountains against the temple is said to be a silhouette of Buddha lying down on his back. A museum houses a Goryeo-dynasty bell, other Buddhist treasures and a tea-ceremony display (Seosan was also a tea master). The temple is a 30-minute walk from the bus stop. Weekend Templestays are available.

The peak, **Duryunbong** (630m), provides a dramatic backdrop. To climb it, turn left after the temple museum. It takes 1½ hours to reach the top, and you are rewarded with a very picturesque view of Korea's southern coastline. Head back via the other trail and turn right at the first junction (20 minutes); it's another hour back down to Daedun-sa, via Jinburam.

For an easier ascent, walk back down the access road from the bus stop and turn right up the road for 800m to the **cable car** (☑534 8992; return ₩8000; ☉7am-7pm). It takes you 1.6km up **Gogye-bong** (638m) but does not operate on windy days.

🍴 Sleeping & Eating

Haenam Youth Hostel HOSTEL $$
(☑533 0170; dm/r ₩10,000/50,000; ✻@) A three-minute walk beyond the cable car is the best budget option, with clean modern rooms. Dorms have bunk beds while private rooms have *yo* (padded quilt mattresses on the floor); all rooms have bathrooms. Staff speak English.

TOP CHOICE **Yuseongwan** HANOK GUESTHOUSE $
(유산관; ☑534 2959; d ₩40,000) This idyllic traditional inn, built around a courtyard and filled with art, is inside the park

BUS DEPARTURES FROM GANJIN

DESTINATION	PRICE (₩)	DURATION	FREQUENCY
Boseong	4200	45min	every 30min
Gwangju	9300	1½hr	every 40min
Mokpo	5100	1hr	every 30min
Seoul	30,700	4½hr	6 daily
Wando	6100	1hr	every 30min
Yeosu	14,100	2hr	every 30min

BUS DEPARTURES FROM HAENAM

DESTINATION	PRICE (₩)	DURATION (HR)	FREQUENCY
Busan	24,100	6	hourly
Gwangju	10,500	1¾	every 30min
Jindo	5400	1	every 40min
Mokpo	5800	1	hourly
Seoul	32,800	5	hourly
Wando	5800	1	hourly

about two-thirds of the way between the car park and Daedun-sa. It offers breakfast (₩8000) and dinner (₩10,000). Just ahead of Yuseongwan is a rest stop with floor seating above the gurgling stream – it's a perfect place to stop for an ice cream or *maekgolli*.

Jeonju Restaurant KOREAN $$
(meals from ₩8000; ⊙9am-10pm) This place is famous for mushrooms – choose *pyogojeongol* (mushroom casserole) or *sanchaehan jeongsik* (minced beef, seafood, mushrooms and vegetables). Look for the English sign halfway along the line of restaurants leading to the ticket office.

🛈 Getting There & Around

Access to the park is by bus (₩1100, 15 minutes, every 40 minutes) from Haenam bus terminal; for bus connections, see the boxed text above.

Wando 완도

📱061 / POP 55,000

Another island now connected by a bridge to the mainland, Wando is scenic with ever-changing views of scattered offshore islands. This quiet fishing village is not the most ex-citing city on the south coast, the main reason to visit is to catch a ferry to Jeju-do or the nearby picturesque islands.

◉ Sights

Myeongsasim-ni BEACH
The best and most convenient swimming beach is on neighbouring Sinjido, an island now joined to Wando by an impressive bridge that is lit up at night. Take a bus (₩1700, 15 minutes, hourly) from the bus terminal to this sandy beach lined with pine trees.

Gugyedeung Park PARK
(📞554 1769; adult/youth/child ₩1600/600/300; ⊙9am-5pm) On Wando's south coast is a tiny park that offers views of distant cliffs and offshore islands, a pebbly beach and a 1km nature trail that runs through a thin slither of coastal woodland. Swimming is dangerous. The Seobu (western side) bus (₩1100, 10 minutes, hourly) runs from Wando bus terminal. Get off at Sajeong and walk 600m down to the park entrance.

🛏 Sleeping

Motels topped by neon signs run all the way along the western side of Wando-eup harbour. Listed rates often drop during slow periods.

BUS DEPARTURES FROM WANDO

DESTINATION	PRICE (₩)	DURATION (HR)	FREQUENCY
Busan	30,000	6	5 daily
Gwangju	15,400	2¾	every 40min
Haenam	5800	1	every 1½hr
Mokpo	11,200	2	3 daily
Seoul	35,100	6	4 daily
Yeongam	9000	1½	hourly

Grand Motel
MOTEL **$$**

(그랜드 모텔; ☑535 0100; r ₩40,000-60,000; ❈) Wando's latest motel addition is a spiffy one with large rooms, sea views on one side and free use of the in-house sauna.

Dubai Motel
MOTEL **$$**

(두바이 모텔; ☑553 0688; r ₩35,000-50,000; ❈@) There's no desert in sight but this green waterfront hotel has smart rooms, most with offensive floral wallpaper and harbour views. Pricier rooms have PCs.

Naju Yeoinsuk
GUESTHOUSE **$**

(나주여인숙; ☑554 3884; r ₩17,000) Rock-bottom prices are charged at this green, basic pad that couldn't be closer to the ferry terminal. All *ondol* rooms have bathrooms, although with plastic tubs rather than sinks.

✗ Eating & Drinking

Wando's speciality is raw seafood but *saeng-seongui* (생선구이; grilled fish) and *jang-eogui* (장어구이; grilled eel) are cooked-food options. There are plenty of lookalike restaurants on the seafront boulevard heading west from Dubai Motel. Take a stroll through the busy **fish market** and stock up on dried fish and squid.

Jeonsama
KOREAN **$$$**

(전사마; meals ₩9000-50,000; ⏰11am-10pm) Korean restaurants that have been featured on TV are sometimes as underwhelming as their advertising overwhelms...not this joint. The seafood-heavy menu is all good but try what we dub as a Korean version of the surf-and-turf: *bulgogi* cooked with abalone (전복불고기; ₩13,000). Wrap it up in a piece of kelp with *kimchi*. Yum.

Kim's Cafe
CAFE **$**

(coffee ₩3000-4000) This cute-as-pie white cottage looks totally out of place on a street filled with grey, weathered shops. But that shouldn't stop you from having a latte on outdoor deck or in the side garden. A small selection of cakes is available.

❶ Getting There & Away

Boat

From **Wando Ferry Terminal** (☑554 8000), **Hanil Car Ferries** (☑554 8000; ₩30,000-53,000) depart for Jeju-do daily at 8am, 9am, 3pm, 4pm or 5pm. The earliest, less-direct ship takes five hours; travel time on the other ships is three to 3½ hours. Other ferries run to a dozen nearby islands including Cheongsando.

Wando

Bus

For bus departures from Wando, see the boxed text, p218.

❶ Getting Around

From Wando bus terminal, one local bus heads west (Seobu bus) while another heads east (Dongbu bus). Both go to the bridge to the mainland before heading back to Wando. The ferry terminal is a 25-minute walk from the bus terminal or a short taxi ride.

Jindo 진도

☑061 / POP 43,000

Korea's third-largest island (http://jindo.go.kr), south of Mokpo and connected to the mainland by a bridge, boasts some of the world's largest tides. The island is famous for an unusual natural phenomenon: for a few days each year (usually in spring), the tide drops extremely low, exposing a 2.8km-long, 40m-wide causeway that connects Jindo to the tiny island of Modo-ri.

BUS DEPARTURES FROM JINDO

DESTINATION	PRICE (₩)	DURATION HR)	FREQUENCY
Busan	29,600	6	8.15am & 12.50pm
Gwangju	11,000	2¾	every 30min
Mokpo	6000	1¼	every 30min
Seoul	29,000/33,600	6	6 daily

Some 300,000 people make the crossing each year – in long rubber boots (available for rent, naturally).

The experience is known as the Ganjuyuk Gyedo (Mysterious Sea Road) and has long been celebrated among Koreans in legend. With the spread of Christianity in Korea, the similarity to the Israelites' crossing of the Red Sea has only brought more enthusiasts. The **Jindo Sea Parting Festival** (Jindo Yeongdeung) is held every spring to coincide with the crossing and includes folk music and dances, a Jindo dog show and fireworks. To get to the site, take a bus to Haedong (₩2600, 30 minutes, six daily).

The **Jin-do Dog Research Centre** (진 도개시험연구소; ☎540 6312; admission free; ☉9am-6pm) is dedicated to the study and training of this unique breed of Korean canine (see p378). Training sessions are held at 10am, 11am, 3.30pm and 4.30pm from Monday to Saturday and at 3.30pm and 4.30pm on Sunday. Otherwise, the dogs can be viewed in their pens. The centre is

a 20-minute walk from the bus terminal – walk back along the main road from the terminal into Jin-do-eup for 1km and at the blue sign (in English) turn right. A taxi there costs ₩4000.

ℹ Getting There & Around

Buses connect Jindo-eup (Jindo's main town) with many places; for details, see the boxed text above.

Wolchulsan National Park
월출산국립공원

East of Yeongam, 42-sq-km **Wolchulsan** (☑061-473 5210; adult/youth/child ₩2000/1000/500; ☉5am-7pm Mar-Oct, 8am-6pm Nov-Feb), Korea's smallest national park, invites a day of hiking. There are crags, spires and unusual shaped rocks around every corner as well as an 8m Buddha rock carving, steel stairways and a 52m steel bridge spanning two ridges. Beautiful and rugged rock formations include **Cheonwangbong** (809m), the park's highest peak.

The popular route is the 8km, six-hour hike from Dogap-sa in the west to Cheonhwang-sa in the east or vice versa. Tracks are well signposted, but steep and strenuous in places due to the rocky terrain. Bring lots of water. **Dogap-sa** is a gorgeous temple complex where you'll find a painting, amusingly, detailing a scene from the 2002 World Cup. It's at the back of the main hall. If you're not up for a huge hike, head to the more popular Cheonhwang-sa end and hike an hour up a rocky path to the suspension bridge from where sprawling views of the surrounding country unfold.

The gateway to the park is Yeongam, from where buses run the 11km to Dogapsa (₩1250, 20 minutes, 9.30am and 2.10pm) in the west and the 4km to Cheonhwang-sa (₩1100, 10 minutes, five daily). Consider taking a taxi from Yeongam.

GRANDMA BBONG & THE PARTING OF THE SEA

Grandma Bbong is a folk hero on Jindo, a sort of Korean version of Moses. According to legend, a family of tigers was causing so many problems on Jindo that all the islanders moved to nearby Modo, but somehow Grandma Bbong was left behind. She was broken-hearted and prayed to the Sea God to be reunited with her family. In answer to her fervent prayers, the Sea God parted the sea, enabling her to cross over to Modo and meet her family again. Sadly, she died of exhaustion shortly afterward. Statues, shrines and paintings of her can be seen throughout Jindo.

Mokpo 목포

📞061 / POP 250,000

The sprawling port city of Mokpo, set on a small peninsula jutting out into the West Sea, is the end of the line for trains and expressway traffic, and a starting point for sea voyages to Jeju-do and the western islands of Dadohae Haesang National Park. Korea's National Maritime Museum is appropriately located here, and the craggy peaks of Yudalsan Park rear up in the city centre and offer splendid sea, city and sunset views.

Mokpo is the hometown of late South Korean president and Nobel Peace Prize recipient Kim Dae-jung. Come October, it's also the base of the Formula 1 race, held at a racetrack 15km south of town. It's a surprisingly vibrant, hip, youthful city with a large population of expats working as English teachers or in the shipping industry.

◉ Sights

Most of the city is on the south side of the peninsula at the mouth of the Yeongsan River. The old city centre is on the southwest side of the peninsula, between the train station and ferry terminal. Moving east, museums and other tourist attractions are clustered in the Gatbawi Culture District. On the eastern edge of town before the bridge to the mainland is Hadang, a newer neighbourhood of smart hotels, restaurants, bars, shops and the waterfront Peace Park.

Gatbawi Culture District　　NEIGHBOURHOOD
(갓바위공원) This area, 4km northeast of downtown, has a swathe of museums and art galleries, situated between rocky hillsides and a wide river. We list some of the best ones to visit.

National Maritime Museum
(국립해양유물전시관; 📞270 2000; admission free; ◷9am-6pm Tue-Sun) This is the only museum in Korea dedicated to the country's maritime history. The highlights are two shipwrecks, one dating from the 11th century and the other from the early 14th century. Thousands of priceless items of Korean and Chinese celadon, coins and other trade items were salvaged from them. Fascinating film footage shows the treasures being salvaged, and part of the actual boats has been preserved. It has excellent English signage.

Culture & Arts Center
(📞274 3655; admission free; ◷9am-6pm) A grand four-floor atrium building that displays the work of local artists who work in all genres – from traditional ink to colourful modern splodges, from photographs to the Asian art of growing bonsai trees. The centre also houses a 700-seat performance hall.

Namnong Memorial Hall
(남농기념관; adult/child ₩1000/500; ◷9am-6pm Tue-Sun) This hall contains a collection of paintings by five generations of the Huh family, including work by Huh Gun, a master of Namjonghwa, a Korean art style associated with the Southern School of China.

Mokpo Natural History Museum
(목포자연사박물관; 📞276 6331; adult/youth/child ₩3000/2000/1000; ◷9am-6pm Tue-Sun; ♿) This fabulous museums is aimed at children, with large dinosaur skeletons, live lizards and fish, and thousands of colourful but dead butterflies.

Mokpo Ceramic Livingware Museum
(목포생활도저박물관; 📞276 8480; adult/youth ₩3000/2000; ◷9am-6pm Tue-Fri, to 7pm Sat & Sun) Traces the history and uses of Korean ceramics, from ancient pottery to biotechnology.

Further past the maritime museum is the riverside **Gatbawi Rocks** which have been heavily eroded into shapes that are supposed to look like two monks wearing reed hats. A pier extends into the river so you can get a good look at this city icon.

Carry on from Gatbawi Rocks to hike up the rock-strewn hills behind the museums. East of Gatbawi Rocks is **Peace Park**, a lovely waterfront promenade that's popular with walkers and young couples. On weekends it's packed with street vendors and bike rental stands.

Catch bus 15 (₩1100, 15 minutes, every 30 minutes) from outside the train station (across the overbridge). A taxi costs ₩5000 from the train station.

FREE **Mokpo Modern History Museum**　　MUSEUM
(목포근대역사관; 📞279 8728; ◷9am-6pm; Tue-Sun) This museum, set in a beautiful colonial building, showcases Mokpo's growth through the years via a large collection of historical photos. Unearth other colonial-era buildings in the area around the

Mokpo

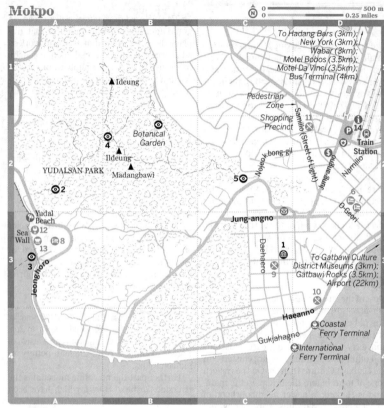

JEOLLANAM-DO MOKPO

museum and cross the street to the fabulous House Filled with Happiness (p223) for coffee or lunch.

FREE Yudaisan Park   PARK
(유달산; ☎242 2344; ☉8am-6pm) This attractive park filled with rocky cliffs and pavilions offers splendid views across the island-scattered sea. The park entrance, guarded by a statue of Admiral Yi, is just 20 minutes' walk from the train station or ferry terminal.

Follow the main path for 45 minutes to reach **Madangbawi** (great views and two rock carvings), followed by **Ildeung** (228m). Turn left just before the white **Soyojeong** (소요정) pavilion to head down to **Yudal Beach**. Turn left at the sign to Arirang Gogae (아리랑고개) and then follow the sign to **Nakjodae** (낙조대) pavilion. From there it's a 10-minute walk down the steps to the beach.

The beach is just a tiny patch of sand, rocks and seaweed, so the main attractions are the island views (partially spoiled by a bridge) and the few bars and restaurants. Sightseeing trips (adult/child ₩11,300/10,300) depart from the ferry terminal and cruise around the nearby islands.

Bus 1 and most of the other buses that pass by can take you back to downtown.

🛏 Sleeping

There are countless love motels and *yeogwan* around the bus terminal and between the train station and ferry terminal. More modern hotels are in Hadang.

FREE 1 Motel   MOTEL $$
(에프원호텔; ☎242 5700; r ₩50,000-60,000; ❄@) The best accommodation between the train station and the ferry terminal is this dark high-rise. Modern, clean rooms have sofas, heated toilet seats and ultrafast PCs.

Mokpo

Motel Da Vinci   MOTEL **$$**
(287 0456; r ₩40,000-60,000; ❄@) A flashing bank of LED lights along the side of the building dazzles passersby come night time. Thankfully, the interiors are less bling and are head and shoulders above the competition in the area. Twin rooms, for example, come with two PCs and spa tubs. Opposite Motel Bobos.

Baek Je Hotel   HOTEL **$$**
(백제관광호텔; Namillo; 245 0080; r ₩40,000-60,000;❄@) Location, location, location. The Baek Je is a 10-minute walk from the train station and the ferries and has compact rooms with dark-wood decor.

Motel Bobos   MOTEL **$$**
(283 2210; r ₩40,000; ❄@) This sleek black and silver tower is clean, sharp and stumbling distance from the Hadang nightlife area. Look for the rooftop yellow English sign. Opposite the Motel Da Vinci.

Shinan Beach Hotel   HOTEL **$$**
(신안비치호텔; 243 3399; www.shinanbeachhotel.com; r from ₩99,500; ❄) Traditionally seen as Mokpo's top hotel, it towers over Yudal Beach and is old-fashioned classy. Rooms (mainly *ondol* or twin) have large windows; but the sky lounge is disappointing. Discounts during low season though prices double during peak.

✕ Eating

You'll find many seafood restaurants in front of the ferry terminal along Haeanno. Smart new restaurants and chains are in Hadang. For some great street food, head towards Yudal Beach, where every evening around dusk vendors set little seaside stalls along Jeonghoro. The shopping precinct opposite the train station has bakeries, cafes and pizza joints rubbing shoulders with Korean restaurants.

TOP CHOICE **House Filled with Happiness**   CAFE **$$$**
(dishes ₩14,000-20,000; 9am-9pm) Housed in a colonial Japanese home, the irony of the cafe's name will soon be forgotten when you take delight in the eclectic decor: a mix of country, modern and antique styles. It all meshes together in a cozy haze once you start tucking into burgers, pizzas, pastas, beers and coffee. If the weather is fine, grab an outdoor seat facing the compact but verdant garden.

Miyashi   JAPANESE **$$$**
(미야시; meals ₩10,000-20,000; 11.30am-9am) Located in Hadang opposite the Motel Da Vinci, this popular Japanese restaurant has great-value lunch deals. Sets such as sushi, tempura and sashimi come with a large selection of Japanese-style *banchan* (side dishes). English menu. Prices double at dinner.

Namupo   KOREAN **$$**
(나무포; meals ₩7000-30,000; 10am-midnight) Not in a seafood mood? Try the *galbi* (갈비) grills at this clean local favourite located in the city centre. There's also a range of fan faves such as *bibimbap* and *naengmyeon*.

Namhae   KOREAN **$$$**
(남해; 242 9998; Haeanno; meals ₩10,000-60,000; 10am-10pm) Of the many seafood restaurants near the ferry port, this popular place stands out. Specialties include octopus, spicy noodle soup, crabs and sashimi. Dishes are for sharing. Look for the black and gold building.

🍷 Drinking

Mokpo's entertainment and nightlife district is the pedestrian zone along Rose St in Hadang, crammed wall-to-wall with bars, restaurants, cafes, discos and karaoke clubs. Nearby are several cinemas.

Beach Gallery BAR

(까페비치갤러리; Yudal Beach; ⊙noon-4am) This bar with nightly outdoor live music in summer draws an older crowd. Up the way is **Old Man & the Sea** (drinks ₩4000-9000; ⊙11.30am-late), a cafe/restaurant where you can watch the sun set from the top deck. If you're expecting rum there though, you'll be as sorely disappointed as Hemingway was when *Death in the Afternoon* was panned by critics. The 7-Eleven below has outdoor plastic tables and chairs and is hugely popular with students looking for a quick, cheap *soju* hit.

New York BAR

(☑733 8658; Rose St; drinks from ₩7000-10,000; ⊙6pm-5am) New York is a favourite expat haunt with a wide selection of pricey imported beer and whisky in dark-wood environs. Attentive staff are quick to top up your beer snacks while you gorge on pub grub.

Wabar BAR

(Hadang; drinks from ₩5000; ⊙6pm-4am) OK, so it's a chain. But this one stands out for its large size and buzzy crowd. The concept is the same as the rest: bottles of frosty imported beer are nestled on tables in beds of ice. The house light and dark beers are actually really good. On Rose St, 200m before New York.

❶ Information

Global ATM At the train station.

KB Bank (Jung-angno) Foreign exchange and global ATM.

Post office (Jung-angno) Free internet access; behind it is an historic Japanese colonial building.

Tourist information centre (☑270 8599) At the train station.

❶ Getting There & Away

Air

Flights to and from Seoul Gimpo operate once daily from the **Muan International Airport** (☑455 2114; muan.airport.co.kr), 25km north of the city. International flights operate to Shanghai and Macau.

Boat

Mokpo's **Coastal Ferry Terminal** (연안여객선 터미널) handles boats to smaller islands west and southwest of Mokpo.

The **International Ferry Terminal** (국제 여객선 터미널) has two sailings a day to Jeju-do. Slower car ferries leave at 9am and take 4½ hours. The faster, pricier *Pink Dolphin* leaves at 2pm, taking three hours. Fares start at ₩30,000 and vary based on class; under 12s' fares are half-price. Contrary to its name, there are no international routes from this terminal.

Bus

Mokpo's bus terminal is some distance from the centre of town. Turn left outside the bus terminal, then left at the end of the road and walk down to the main road where bus 1 (₩1100, 10 minutes, every 20 minutes) stops on the left. It runs to the train station, the ferry terminals and then on to Yudal Beach.

Train

KTX provides a fast service to Seoul's Yongsan station (₩42,100, 3¼ hours, 14 daily), as well as *Saemaul* (₩39,200, 4½ hours, two daily) and *Mugunghwa* (₩26,300, 5½ hours, five daily) services. Less frequent trains also serve Gwangju, Boseong and Yeosu.

BUS DEPARTURES FROM MOKPO

DESTINATION	PRICE (₩)	DURATION	FREQUENCY
Busan	21,300	5hr	7 daily
Gwangju	5400	1¼hr	every 20min
Haenam	5800	1hr	hourly
Incheon Airport	37,400	4½hr	3 daily
Jindo	6000	2hr	every 45min
Seoul	29,200	4½hr	every 40min
Wando	11,200	2hr	3 daily
Yeongam	3800	30min	every 20min
Yeosu	12,300	3½hr	hourly

ℹ Getting Around

It's a 15-minute walk from the train station to the ferry terminals or to the entrance to Yudalsan Park.

Airport buses (₩3000, 30 minutes) depart from near the train station and are timed to meet flights. They also stop by the bus terminal.

Local bus 1 (₩1100, 10 minutes, every 20 minutes) serves the bus terminal, ferry terminals, train station and Yudal Beach. Bus 15 (₩1100, 15 minutes, every 30 minutes) runs to the Gatbawi Park museums from the bus and train stations. Taxis are cheap and plentiful.

Dadohae Haesang National Park
다도해해상국립공원

Consisting of over 1700 islands and islets and divided into eight sections, Dadohae Haesang (Marine Archipelago) National Park occupies much of the coast and coastal waters of Jeollanam-do. Some of the isles support small communities with fishing and tourism income; others are little more than tree-covered rocks.

Mokpo is the gateway to the western sector, including Hongdo and Heuksando, the most visited and scenic of the islands. In July and August the boats there get full so book ahead.

Hongdo   ISLAND

(홍도; Red Island; visitor fee ₩1000) The most popular and beautiful of the islands west of Mokpo is Hongdo. Some 6km long and 2.5km wide, it rises precipitously from the sea and is bounded by sheer cliffs, bizarre rock formations and wooded hillsides cut by ravines. The island is ringed by islets and sunsets can be spectacular, but the only way you can see most of it is by boat, because with the exception of the villages, Hongdo is a protected nature reserve; entry is prohibited. You can however, climb a surrounding hill for views. There's a small pebbled beach on the south of the island.

Ferries to Hongdo arrive at a spanking new ferry-terminal building in Ilgu village, which is protected by a tiny cove. Boat tours

(₩22,000, two hours, 7.30am and 2.30pm) around the island are the way to appreciate the island and its rocky islets and arches though the Korean commentary gets a little grating. Towards the end of the tour, a small boat pulls up and fishermen slice up live fish into plates of sashimi (₩35,000).

Ilgu has several *minbak* and new motels, all charging about ₩35,000 to ₩50,000 per night. Try **Hotel 1004** (☏061-246-3758; r ₩40,000; ✱), with its sea-facing rooms with balconies. Restaurants serve up seafood from ₩15,000 and a small supermarket beside Hotel 1004 serves the town.

Heuksando   ISLAND

(흑산도) Heuksando, on the way to Hongdo, is the larger, more populated and more accessible of the two islands. Views from its peaks show why Dadohae Haesang means 'marine archipelago'. Fishing villages are linked by trails, but walking around the island would take around nine hours. Fortunately, local buses (₩1100, hourly) circle most of the island – a recommended trip is up the **Bonghwadae** peak, on the north coast hill, Sangnasan. You can also jump on tour buses (₩15,000) for 1½ hour circuit around the island. If you're in a group, you can do a taxi tour (₩60,000).

The largest village, **Yeri**, formerly a whaling centre, is where ferries dock and is home to several basic accommodation options of *minbak* and *yeogwan*. Seafood restaurants are plentiful but prices, ranging from ₩10,000 to ₩60,000, are higher than the mainland.

ℹ Getting There & Away

The same ferries serve Heuksando, 90km west of Mokpo, and Hongdo, another 20km further away. Leaving from Mokpo's Coastal Ferry Terminal, ferries run to Heuksando (adult/child one way ₩34,300/17,150, two hours) and continue on to Hongdo (adult/child one way ₩42,000/21,000, 2½ hours). Ferries depart Mokpo at 7.50am, 8.10am, 1pm and 4pm.

There are two ferries per day between Hongdo and Heuksando (₩10,300, 9.50am and 2.50pm), with additional boats during summer months.

Jeju-do

Best Places to Stay

» Hotel Little France (p247)

» The Seaes Hotel & Resort (p253)

» Ssari's Flower Hill (p240)

» Seongeup Folk Village Traditional Houses (p245)

» Baume Couture Boutique Hotel (p232)

Best Places to Eat

» Dasi Boesi (p240)

» Saesom Galbi (p248)

» Yetnalpatjuk (p245)

» Harubang Pizza (p257)

» Haejin Seafood Restaurant (p233)

Why Go?

The tropical charms of Jeju-do (제주도), Korea's largest island, have long made it the country's favourite holiday destination. Since Jeju-do was inscribed as one of the new seven wonders of nature in 2011, the world is also discovering more about its beautiful beaches, volcanic geography, lush countryside, and ancient culture that includes traditions, dress, architecture, a dialect separate from the mainland and 18,000 gods.

The islanders' warm hospitality will instantly put you in a relaxed mood, but there's plenty on Jeju to appeal to those who prefer to be active. Hike up South Korea's highest mountain, Hallasan, or the incredible tuff cone Seongsan Ilchulbong rising straight from the sea. Meander along one of the Jeju Olle Trails. Plunge into blue oceans to view coral as colourful as the sunsets, and dig into Jeju's unique cuisine, including seafood caught by Jeju's famous *haeneyo* (female free divers).

When to Go

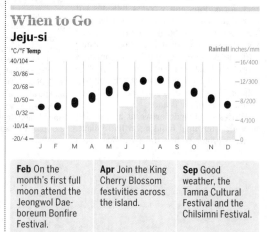

Jeju-si

Feb On the month's first full moon attend the Jeongwol Daeboreum Bonfire Festival.

Apr Join the King Cherry Blossom festivities across the island.

Sep Good weather, the Tamna Cultural Festival and the Chilsimni Festival.

Travel Itinerary

If time is short, make Seogwipo, the island's second-largest city on the south coast, your base. From here you can visit Hallasan National Park as well as Seongsan Ilchulbong. Jeju-si, the island's capital, is closer to the airport but is not as scenic a city.

With a week or more it's possible to take in all of Jeju's top sights, as well as visit one of the smaller islands such as Udo, or lounge on a lovely deserted beach. Get off the beaten track by staying at a small village pension or guesthouse.

JEJU-DO FOOD & DRINK

Jeju speciality meats include *heukdwaeji*, pork from the local black-skinned pig; *kkwong* (pheasant); and *basme* (horse) served in a variety of ways including raw.

All kinds of fish and seafood are available from restaurants and direct from *haenyeo*, the island's famous female divers; try *galchi* (hairtail), *godeungeo* (mackerel) or *jeon-bok* (abalone), often served in a rice porridge (*jeon-bok-juk*). *Okdomgui* is a tasty local fish that is semidried before being grilled.

Hallabong tangerines are common; also look out for prickly-pear jam, black *omija* tea and honey. Hallasan *soju* (local vodka) is smoother than some.

Getting Around

» **Car** Road signs are in English and the hire cost is reasonable (around ₩60,000 a day). You must be 21 years old and have a current International Driving Permit.

» **Bicycle/Scooter** It's possible to pedal or scooter your way around the island (250km) in three to five days. The designated cycleway is relatively flat, much of it parallel to the beautiful coast. Pack rain gear. Bicycles (₩10,000 per day) and scooters (₩15,000 to ₩25,000 per day) can be hired in Jeju-si, Seogwipo and a few other places.

» **Bus** Services radiate from Jeju-si and Seogwipo and cover most of the island, running round the coast and across the centre roughly every 20 minutes. Pick up an English bus timetable from the airport tourist office.

» **Taxi** Charge is ₩2200 for the first 2km; a 15km journey costs about ₩10,000. You can hire a taxi driver for around ₩100,000 a day.

DON'T MISS

Colourful and lively **five-day markets**, which occur every five days, are scattered around the island and well worth attending to buy local agricultural produce.

Fast Facts

» **Population** 568,000

» **Telephone area code** 064

» **Area** 1848 sq km

» **Number of oreum (parasitic volcanic cones)** 368

Planning Your Trip

July and August are peak season; hotels and car hire get booked up and rates are higher. Visit after 1 September and you'll avoid the crowds and pay less; the weather is still good and you'll have the beaches mostly to yourself.

Resources

» Jeju Special Self-Governing Province: http://english .jeju.go.kr

» Jeju Weekly: www.jeju weekly.com

» Jeju World Natural Heritage: http://jejuwnh .jeju.go.kr

» Jeju Provincial Tourism Association: www.hijeju .or.kr

JEJU-DO

History

According to legend, Jeju-do was founded by three brothers who came out of holes in the ground and established the independent Tamna kingdom. Early in the 12th century the Goryeo dynasty took over, but in 1273 Mongol invaders conquered the island, contributing a tradition of horsemanship, a special horse (*jorangmal*) and quirks in the local dialect. During the Joseon period, Jeju was used as a place of political and religious exile.

The Japanese colonisation period of the early 20th century can be traced through abandoned military bases and fortifications on the island. From 1947 to 1954, as many as 30,000 locals were massacred here by right-wing government forces in events collectively labelled the 'April 3 Incident' (see p231).

Recent decades have seen Jeju's economy shift from mainly agriculture to tourism. In 2006 the island was made into a special autonomous province, giving it a level of self-government that is encouraging further economic development. The World Conservation Congress was held here in September 2012 and ambitious carbon-free electricity generation ventures are being tested. Jeju has come under fire from conservationists and other protesters for the planned Korean Naval base at Gangjeong on the island's southern coast.

JEJU-SI

POP 414,000

Chances are that you'll end up spending a day or two in the island's capital, Jeju-si (제주시), as this is the main entry to point to Jeju,

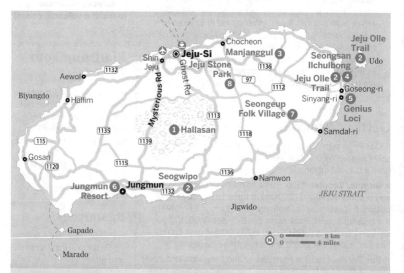

Jeju-do Highlights

① Hike to the summit of **Hallasan** (p254), South Korea's highest mountain.

② Walk the island bit by bit along the **Jeju Olle Trail** (p244); several good ones are accessible from **Seogwipo** (p245), a beautifully situated town with two amazing waterfalls.

③ Go underground at **Manjanggul** (p239), part of the world's largest lava-tube cave system.

④ Watch the sunrise from atop the volcanic tuff cone **Seongsan Ilchulbong** (p240).

⑤ View Seongsan Ilchulbong from Ando Tadao's serene meditation hall **Genius Loci** (p241).

⑥ Visit the beaches, waterfalls, museums and luxury resorts of **Jungmun Resort** (p252).

⑦ Step back in time at **Seongeup Folk Village** (p244), a community of traditional volcanic rock and thatched houses.

⑧ Learn about the volcanic forces that created the island at **Jeju Stone Park** (p230), an amazing showpiece of natural and man-made stone art.

LOCAL KNOWLEDGE

JEJU'S OFFBEAT GEMS

Darryl Coote, assistant editor of *The Jeju Weekly,* has lived on the island since 2009. His job regularly takes him off the tourist trail to some of the island's quirkier and more intriguing sights. Following are his top recommendations:

Kim Young Gap Gallery Dumoak (p243) This talented photographer died from Lou Gehrig's disease in 2005 but his former home is one of the island's best art galleries.

Jeju April 3 Peace Park (p231) Part of Jeju's 'dark tourism' trail, highlighting a tragic chapter in the island's recent history.

Jeju Peace Museum (www.peacemuseum.co.kr; adult/youth & child ₩6000/4000; ☉8.30am-6pm) Gama Oreum is a parasitic volcano that hides an underground fortress created by the Japanese Army in the final stages of WWII. Explore some of the 2km of tunnels at this museum on Jeju's west side.

Ahop-gut Maeul Experience Yard (http://ninegood.go2vil.org) In the west Jeju village of Nakcheon-ri, on Route 13 of the Olle Trail, is perhaps the island's quirkiest sight; an outdoor art installation scattered with 1000 wooden chairs and sculptures.

either by air or sea. The city centre, 4km east of Jeju International Airport, has a few historic structures, plenty of shopping, and lively bars and restaurants opposite the old City Hall – all fine, but nothing extraordinary.

Closer to the airport is the suburb of Shin-Jeju, where you'll find more accommodation, restaurants and bars. The most interesting sights, such as Jeju Stone Park and Jeju Loveland, are out of town, but easily accessed either by bus or taxi.

◉ Sights & Activities

CITY CENTRE

Tapdong Promenade & Waterbreak PROMENADE

(제주시해안; Map p234; Tapdong haean-ro) Jeju-si itself doesn't have a beach but along the Tapdong seafront runs this pleasant promenade; at the eastern end walk along the mosaic-decorated sea wall or shoot some hoops on the outdoor basketball courts. There's also a small **amusement park** and an outdoor **band shell** that hosts summer music and dance performances.

Yongduam Rock VIEWPOINT

(용두암; Map p234; Coastal Rd) 'Dragon Head Rock' (so-called because the volcanic lava rocks are supposed to resemble a dragon), attracts coachloads of tourists. It's a nice walk along the coast here from town, which includes crossing a small suspension bridge over a scenic ravine. Besides rock watching, plane spotting is another popular activity; aeroplanes fly just a few hundred metres overhead on their final approach to the island.

Jeju Mokgwana ARCHITECTURE

(제주 목관아; Map p234; http://mokkwana.jejusi.go.kr; Gwandeok-ro; adult/youth/child ₩1500/800/400; ☉9am-6pm) The island's administrative centre under the Joseon dynasty, destroyed during Japanese rule, has been reconstructed. The cluster of historical buildings have an austere style that is designed to promote virtue. You can have a go at **traditional archery** (☉10am-noon Sat Apr-Jun & Sep-Oct), as well as watch displays of centuries-old **martial arts** (☉2-4pm Sun Apr-Jun & Sep-Oct).

Outside the main gate is the 15th-century pavilion **Gwandeok-jeong** (관덕정; Map p234), Jeju's oldest building, once used as a training place for soldiers.

Samseonghyeol Shrine SHRINE

(삼성혈; Map p234; www.samsunghyeol.or.kr; Namseong-ro; adult/youth/child ₩2500/1700/1000; ☉8am-6pm Mar-Oct, to 5.30pm Nov-Feb) The main feature of this unusual shrine, originally built in 1526, is three holes in the ground. Legends say that three brothers, Go, Bu and Yang, came out of the holes and founded the Tamna kingdom with help from three princesses who arrived by boat together with cattle and horses. An English version of a 15-minute film about the legend is shown in the exhibition hall.

The shrine also houses the spirit tablets of the island's first ancestors who are honoured with food and music in a ceremony held in April, October and December. At the entrance are two of the 45 remaining original *dolharubang* (grandfather rock; see the boxed text, p233), which are over 250 years old.

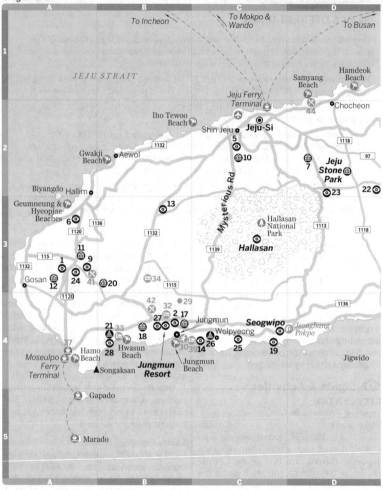

JEJU STRAIT

To Incheon

To Mokpo &
Wando

To Busan

Jeju Ferry
Terminal

Iho Tewoo
Beach

Samyang
Beach

Hamdeok
Beach

Chocheon

Shin Jeju

Jeju-Si

Gwakji
Beach

Aewol

Jeju
Stone
Park

Biyangdo

Hallim

Mysterious Rd

Hallasan
National
Park

Hallasan

Geumneung &
Hyeopjae
Beaches

Gosan

Jungmun

Seogwipo

Jeongbang
Pokpo

Wolpyeong

Jigwido

Moseulpo
Ferry
Terminal

Hamo
Beach

Hwasun
Beach

Jungmun
Beach

**Jungmun
Resort**

Songaksan

Gapado

Marado

Folklore & Natural History Museum
MUSEUM

(민속자연사박물관; Map p234; Sinsan Park, Namseong-ro; adult/youth/child ₩1100/500/free; ⊙8.30am-6pm) Wide-ranging eco-museum with well-labelled exhibits on Jeju-do's varied volcanic features, including volcanic bombs, lava tubes and trace fossils. Fortunately the volcanoes have all been dormant thousands of years, although earthquakes were felt in the 16th century. Other highlights to look out for are excellent wildlife films, the bizarre oar fish and panoramas of the island's six ecological zones.

OUTSIDE JEJU-SI

Jeju Stone Park
MUSEUM, PARK

(Map p230; www.jejustonepark.com; adult/youth/child ₩5000/3000/free; ⊙9am-6pm, closed 1st Mon of month) Creating a park dedicated to rocks on rock-littered Jeju might sound a snooze, but you'll quickly reassess that opinion after viewing this beguiling sculpture park. Covering nearly 327 hectares, the park is still being developed, but there's already plenty to see including the **Jeju Stone Museum** (in which you can learn all about the volcanic forces that created Jeju) and the **Obaek Jang-goon Gallery** displaying artworks inspired by Jeju's

sacres on the island between 1947 and 1954 that resulted in up to 30,000 deaths and the destruction of many villages. The reasons behind the massacres are complex and the museum takes both a factual and artistic approach that heightens the emotional impact. The park is on the Jeju City Tour Bus route.

Halla Arboretum
GARDENS

(한라 수목원; Map p230; http://sumokwon.jeju. go.kr; Hwy 1100; admission free; ☺9am-6pm) Also known as Halla Botanical Garden, this tranquil oasis includes 100,000 individual plants, trees and shrubs comprising 1100 species. The 15-hectare arboretum is divided into 11 separate gardens, including evergreens, tropicals, herbs, a bamboo forest and a four-season flowering garden. Meandering footpaths wind through the beautifully landscaped gardens, ponds and greenhouses. Bus 70 (₩1000) will drop you off here.

Jeju Museum of Art
MUSEUM

(제주도립미술관; Map p230; http://jmoa.jeju. go.kr; Hwy 1100; adult/youth/child ₩1000/500/300; ☺9am-6pm Tue-Sun, to 8pm Jul-Sep) View interesting permanent and temporary exhibits of contemporary visual art at this excellent gallery next to Jeju Loveland. The beautifully designed building appears to float on a pool of water.

Saryeoni Forest
FOREST

(사려니; Map p230; Jejuforest.kfri.go.kr; admission free) On the eastern border of Hallasan National Park, this 15km forest path, on the Jeju City Tour Bus route, is shaded by temperate broad-leaf evergreen trees such as maple, hornbeam and konara oak.

Iho Tewoo Beach
BEACH

(이호테우해변; Map p230) The nearest beach to Jeju-si along the west coast is blessed with an unusual mixture of yellow and grey sand, which means that you can build two-tone sandcastles. There's shallow water that makes for safe swimming. A pair of red and white horse-shaped lighthouses is also a feature.

Buses (₩1000, 20 minutes, every 20 minutes) run from Jeju-si's intercity bus terminal to Heon-sa Village, from where the beach is a 150m walk.

🛏 Sleeping

There are dozens of hotels and motels along or near the seafront in Tapdong. Plenty more can be found in Shin-Jeju, which is closer to the airport. Unless mentioned, breakfast is included in the rates.

environment. Three walking courses snake past the outdoor exhibits, ranging from replicas of the original 48 *dolharubang* to an enchanting forest scattered with hundreds of *dongjasok* (pairs of stone tomb guardians). It's a stop on the Jeju City Tour Bus route.

Jeju April 3 Peace Park
MUSEUM, PARK

(Map p230; http://jeju43.jeju.go.kr; admission free; ☺9am-6pm Tue-Sun) Labelled a 'sanctuary for reconciliation, prosperity, peace and civil rights', the museum here chronicles the events that led up to and followed what is called the 'April 3 Incident' – a series of mas-

Jeju-do

TOP CHOICE Baume Couture Boutique Hotel

HOTEL $$$

(off Map p234; ☑798 8000; www.baume .co.kr; Singwang-ro, Shin-Jeju; r from ₩210,000; ❋@🛜⛱) This boutique hotel is Jeju-si's most stylish place, decorated in neutral tones, with Philippe Starck lamps in the lobby, a comfy lounge and a view of Hallasan, weather permitting, from its rooftop pool (open July and August).

Ocean Suites Jeju Hotel

HOTEL $$$

(Map p234; ☑720 6000; www.oceansuites.kr; Tapdong; r from ₩181,500; ❋@🛜) Large, well-equipped, modern rooms, with wooden floors, most of them sea-facing, make this hotel appealing. The bar and restaurant also have good views. Breakfast is extra.

Ramada Plaza Jeju

HOTEL $$$

(Map p234; ☑729 8100; www.ramadajeju.co.kr; Tapdong; r ₩407,000; ❋@🛜⛱) A pricey but classy option, the Ramada makes the most of its seafront location and nautical design that gives guests the illusion they're at sea on a luxury liner. Prices rise on weekends and rooms with sea views cost more.

Backpackers in Jeju
BACKPACKERS $

(Map p234; ☑773 2077; City Hall; r ₩56,000, dm/s without bathroom ₩25,000/40,000; ❄@☎) Handy if you want to be in the heart of the Shi-Cheong party district. It's a foreigner-friendly place with a bit more quirky style than your average Korean backpackers, such as mosquito-net tents over the beds and a cafe-bar in the basement.

HK Jeju
BACKPACKERS $

(Map p234; ☑727 0027; www.hkjeju.com; Tapdong; dm/s/tw ₩15,000/39,000/55,000; ❄@☎) The young, clued-up staff speak English and are friendly at this appealing backpackers joint that occupies an old-fashioned hotel. A bit of colourful paint brightens things up, and there's a big kitchen and free laundry.

Tapdong Hotel
MOTEL $

(탑동호텔; Map p234; ☑723 3600; Haejing-ro; r ₩40,000; ❄@) One of the better-value motels near the seafront, with spacious rooms and bathrooms with claw-footed tubs. Rooms with computer are ₩10,000 extra. Staff are friendly and speak basic English. Breakfast isn't included.

December Hotel
MOTEL $$

(off Map p234; ☑753 8400; www.jejudecember. co.kr; Samnu-ro, Shin-Jeju; r ₩55,000; ❄@) Useful inexpensive option close to the restaurants and bars of Shin-Jeju, as well as a short taxi ride to the airport.

✖ Eating

Apart from the following, **Seomun Market** (Seomun-ro) is good for beef barbecues, while **Dongmun Market** (Dongmun-ro) is best for fresh seafood: reckon on around ₩30,000 per meal at the small restaurants at either.

TOP CHOICE Haejin Seafood Restaurant
SEAFOOD $$

(해진횟집; Map p234; ☑757 4584; Sashimi St; meals ₩10,000-60,000; ⊙noon-10pm; 🅿) Of the many restaurants overlooking the harbour, Haejin is the largest and one of the most popular places to try Jeju-do's raw seafood specialities like cuttlefish, eel, squid, octopus, sea cucumber and abalone. The set meal (₩30,000) feeds two people.

Bagdad Café
INDIAN $$

(off Map p234; ☑757 8182; Shi-Cheong; meals ₩9000-15,000; ⊙noon-11pm; ☎🅿) Named after the movie, this top date spot has good music, English-speaking staff and a pleasant outside terrace making it a great place to relax and enjoy a meal. The Indian food is tasty but not Jeju-si's best. Look for the pink building two blocks west of Jungang-ro.

Winnie's Brunch/Pub
BRUNCH $

(Map p234; Jungang-ro; meals ₩6000-12,000; ⊙10.30am-12.30pm Thu-Tue; ☎🅿) Vegemite and toast and 'chip butties' (a sandwich of chips) are just some of the things that homesick travellers may appreciate about Winnie Park's relaxed cafe-bar, apart from the affable Winnie herself. It's also an all-vegetarian menu.

Rajmahal
INDIAN $$

(off Map p234; ☑749 4924; Sungwang-ro, Shin-Jeju; meals ₩30,000-40,000; ⊙11.30am-11pm; 🅿) The city's best Indian restaurant does authentic tandoori, curries, biriyani and naan, as well as a decent selection of vegetable dishes; lunch thali meals are a great deal at ₩15,000 or ₩13,000 for a vegetarian version.

Dombegogi
BARBECUE $$

(돔베고기; Map p234; ☑753 0008; meals ₩9000-30,000; ⊙noon-2am) One of the better options on a street dedicated to Korean barbecue restaurants serves up the island's tastiest speciality, black-pig pork. Dishes are huge and meant for sharing.

DOLHARUBANG

An ever-present symbol of Jeju-do are volcanic stone statues known as *dolharubang* (grandfather rock). The original *dolharubang* were carved around 1750 and placed outside the island's fortresses; 47 of these still exist – two can be seen outside Samseonghyeol Shrine in Jeju-si.

It's generally believed the statues were set to ward off evil, but they may have also been fertility symbols – they certainly look phallic! They are nearly life-sized with a helmet-style hat, bulging eyes, a squashed nose and hands on their stomach, one slightly higher than the other. Taking home your own *dolharubang* is easy as they are sold in all shapes and sizes as souvenirs.

Jeju-si

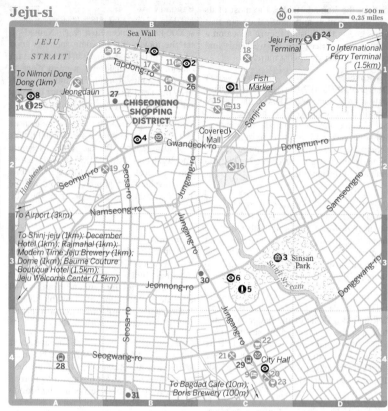

Cooking Story Bob
ITALIAN $$

(쿠킹스토리밥; Map p234; ☑726 4004; Yongduam; meals ₩20,000-40,000; ⊘10am-3pm & 5-10pm; ☎⑩) There are great coastal views from this stylish pizzeria and steakhouse overlooking Yongduam Rock. Outdoor tables make it also a pleasant spot for a glass of wine or coffee and cake.

Zapata's
MEXICAN $

(Map p234; Shi-Cheong; meals ₩3000-9000; ⊘noon-11pm; @⑩) Serves nearly authentic tacos, burritos, fajitas and quesadillas, plus it has excellent lemon margaritas and a large selection of tequilas and Mexican beer.

E-Mart Food Court
KOREAN $

(Map p234; Tapdong; meals ₩5000-10,000; ⊘10am-11pm) This workaday food court on the 5th floor has sea views and plenty of cheap eats. The basement supermarket is ideal for self-catering.

🍷 Drinking

The prime nightlife spots are Shi-Cheong, the semi-pedestrian area west of City Hall and Shin-Jeju around Singwan-ro.

Jeju Chocoart
CAFE

(Map p234; www.jejuchocoart.com; cnr Jungang-ro & Seogwang-ro; ⊘11am-11pm) Equal parts cafe, confectionery and patisserie, this is a magnet for coffee lovers and chocoholics. The milkshakes are especially tasty.

The Factory
BAR

(Map p234; off Jungang-ro; ⊘7pm-4am Tue-Sun) Named after Andy Warhol's studio, the Factory is a dark and moody bar that attracts artists, musicians and other hipsters. It's a favourite haunt for Jeju's expat community. There's occasional live music.

Nilmori Dong Dong
CAFE, BAR

(off Map p234; www.nilmori.com; Coastal Rd; ⊘11am-11pm; ☎⑩) On the coastal road

Jeju-si

JEJU-DO JEJU-SI

behind the airport is this sophisticated cafe-bar that often stages art and craft exhibitions and other events. The Western-style food is also pretty good. There's also pleasant self-catering accommodation at **Jeju Pension Oda** (☑712 2005; www.jejuoda.com) in the same building. A taxi here from Shin-Jeju is around ₩5000.

Boris Brewery BREWERY
(off Map p234; ☑726 4141; off Jungang-ro; ⊙noon-2am) Award-winning Spanish brewer Boris de Mesones has moved on from Modern Time Jeju Brewery to set up this operation closer to the City Hall nightlife nexus.

Modern Time Jeju Brewery BREWERY
(off Map p234; ☑748 4180; Singwang-ro, Shin-Jeju; ⊙noon-2am Mon-Sat, 4pm-2am Sun) Several types of locally brewed beer are offered here; our favourite is the crisp, copper, slightly floral pale ale. An extensive menu features tasty Western pub grub (from ₩12,000).

☆ Entertainment

Dome NIGHTCLUB
(off Map p234; ☑749 8990; Singwang-ro, Shin-Jeju; admission ₩20,000; ⊙7pm-late) This flashy club offers shows featuring exotic dancers before midnight, then a DJ and spectacular laser light shows into the early hours.

Jeju Race Park HORSE RACING
(제주경마장; ☑741 9114; www.kra.co.kr; admission ₩800; ⊙12.30-5pm Sat & Sun, to 9pm Sat & Sun Jul & Aug) Watch *jorangmal*, Jeju descendants of horses brought to the island by invading Mongols centuries ago, race around this track, 15km southwest from Jeju-si along Hwy 1135. The facilities are first class with foreigners even getting their own lounge.

Cross-island buses (₩1500, 30 minutes, every 20 minutes) between Seogwipo and Jeju-si stop outside the racetrack. A taxi from Jeju-si costs ₩10,000.

ⓘ Information
Jeju post office (Map p234; Gwandeok-ro; ⊙9am-6pm Mon-Fri, 1-6pm Sat)

Jeju Welcome Center (off Map p234; www.ijto.or.kr; 23 Seondeok-ro, Shin-Jeju; ⊙9am-6pm) Tourist information; internet access.

KTO tourist information office (☑742 0032; 1st fl, Jeju International Airport terminal) Free internet.

Tourist information centres Jeju-si ferry terminal (Map p234; ☑758 7181; ⊙6.30am-8pm); Jeju International Airport (☑742 8866; ⊙6.30am-8pm); Yongduam Rock (Map p234; ☑750 7768; ⊙9am-8pm) Free internet access at the airport and Yongduam Rock centres. There is a seasonal tourist kiosk in Jeju-si by the band shell at Tapdong.

TOPIC PHOTO AGENCY / CORBIS ©

1. Ulleungdo (p168)
All the remains of an extinct volcano, this island has some of the best scenery in Korea

2. Heyri (p96)
This charming village near the publishing centre of Paju Book City is devoted to books

3. Seoraksan National Park (p127)
Designed as a Biosphere Protection site, this stunning park has forests, temples and wildlife

4. Hahoe Folk Village (p175)
Centuries-old Joseon-era homes have been preserved in this beautiful region

❶ Getting There & Away

Air

Flights connect Jeju-si with several mainland cities, plus a handful of international destinations in China, Japan and Taiwan. From Gimpo in Seoul there are flights every 10 to 15 minutes from dawn to dusk; except during the busy summer season, it's rarely necessary to prebook. Advance one-way fares can start as low as ₩18,900 from Seoul, Busan (₩15,200) and Cheongju (₩16,600); you may be able to get discounts simply by asking, or by bartering between airlines.

Airlines serving Jeju-do include the following:

Air Busan (☏1588 8009; www.flyairbusan.com)

Asiana (☏1588 8000; www.flyasiana.com)

Eastar Jet (☏1544 0080; www.eastarjet.com)

Jeju Air (☏1599 1500; www.jejuair.net)

JinAir (☏1600 6200; www.jinair.com)

Korean Air (Map p234; ☏1558 2001; www.korean air.co.kr)

T'way Air (☏1688 8686; www.twayair.com)

Boat

Comfortable ferries sail between Jeju-si and four ports on the peninsula. Most ships have three classes: 3rd-class passengers sit on the floor in big *ondol*-style rooms; 2nd class gets you an airline-style seat; and 1st class gets you a private cabin with bed and private bathroom.

Ferries berth at either Jeju Ferry Terminal (Map p234) or the International Ferry Terminal (off Map p234), 2km further east. City bus 92 (₩1000, every 20 minutes) runs to and from both ferry terminals, but a taxi is more convenient. Contrary to the latter terminal's name, there are currently no international routes.

❶ Getting Around

To/From the Airport

Jeju International Airport (Map p230; ☏742 3011; www.airport.co.kr/doc/jeju_eng/) is 1km from Shin-Jeju and 4km from central Jeju-si. The limousine airport bus 600 (every 20 minutes) drops off and picks up passengers at major hotels and resorts all round the island. Buses 100, 300 and 500 (₩1000, 15 minutes, every 20 minutes) shuttle between the airport, Jeju-si and Shin-Jeju.

Bicycle & Scooter

I Love Bike (Map p234; ☏723 7775; bicycle per day ₩7000-30,000; ☽7am-8pm) English speaking; large choice of bikes.

Mr Lee (Map p234; ☏758 6640, 010-699 8562; Seosa-ro; scooter per day ₩20,000; ☽8am-7pm) Recommend for scooter and bike rental.

Bus

Streams of city and round-island buses originate from the intercity bus terminal (Map p234) on Seogwang-ro; tourist information offices can provide a timetable. Fares start at ₩1000.

Car

Car-rental agencies include the following:

Avis (☏726 3322; www.avis.co.kr)

Jeju Rent-a-Car (☏747 3301; www.jejurentcar.co.kr)

FERRIES FROM JEJU-SI

DESTINATION	SHIP'S NAME	TELEPHONE; WEBSITE	PRICE FROM (₩)	DURATION	FREQUENCY
Incheon	Ohamana	☏725 2500; www.cmcline.co.kr	65,000	13hr	Tue, Thu, Sat
Mokpo	Namhae	☏723 9700; http://seaferry.co.kr	26,500	4hr 20min	Tue-Sun
Mokpo	Pink Dolphin	☏758 4234; http://seaferry.co.kr	49,650	3hr 10min	daily
Mokpo	Rainbow	☏758 4234; http://seaferry.co.kr	26,500	4hr 40min	Mon-Sat
Samchunpo	Jeju World	☏753 9333; http://seaferry.co.kr	30,000	10hr	Tue, Thu & Sat
Wando	Blue Narae	☏751 5050; www.hanilexpress.co.kr	24,000	1hr 40min	Sun-Fri
Wando	Hanil Car Ferry I	☏751 5050; www.hanilexpress.co.kr	24,000	2hr 50min	Mon-Sat
Wando	Hanil Car Ferry II	☏751 5050; www.hanilexpress.co.kr	24,000	5hr	daily

JEJU-DO JEJU-SI

ℹ **JEJU CITY TOUR BUS**

An easy and economical way to see some of Jeju-si's sights in a day is to hop on and off the Jeju City Tour Bus (adult/child ₩5000/3000; ⊙every hr 8am-5pm), which runs a circuit around 19 stops starting and finishing at Jeju City Hall. Key stops include Jeju City Hall, Saryeoni Forest, Jeju Stone Park, Jeju April 3 Peace Park, Dongmun Market, Gwandeok-jeong, Yongduam Rock and Jeju International Airport.

EASTERN JEJU-DO

The following destinations can all be accessed off Hwy 1132 as it heads east from Jeju-si around the coast to Seogwipo. Buses (₩1000 to ₩3000, every 15 to 25 minutes from 5.40am to 9pm) shuttle between Jeju-si and Seogwipo stopping at or near all of these destinations.

Samyang Beach
삼양해수욕장

The first beach east along Hwy 1132 from Jeju-si is Samyang, which is jet black when wet. In summer join the locals and bury yourself in the iron-rich sand for a therapeutic sand bath, said to relieve dermatitis, arthritis and athlete's foot.

Serving good Western food (in particular brunch) is The Lighthouse (☑758-3500; BeachJoa Pension; mains ₩10,000-20,000; ⊙11am-10pm Mon-Sat, 12.30-10pm Sun), which also offers floor-to-ceiling views of the beach.

Gimnyeong Beach
김녕해수욕장

The white sand of small Gimnyeong Beach contrasts with the black-lava rocks and wind turbines spinning round nearby. West of the beach is a small harbour and the Gimnyeong Sailing Club (김녕세이 링클럽; ☑011-639 5379), where you can sail in a dinghy or a cruiser. Just take the boat out, or lessons can be arranged. The harbour is a perfect spot for novices to learn to sail.

Run by a friendly old lady, Emerald Pension Castle (에메랄드펜션개슬; ☑782 1110; r ₩50,000-80,000) has super sea views.

Manjanggul 만장굴

About 2.5km off Hwy 1132 is Manjanggul (jejuwnh.jeju.go.kr; adult/24yr & under ₩2000/1000; ⊙9am-6pm), the main access point to the world's longest system of lava-tube caves. In total the caves are 13.4km long, with a height varying from 2m to 30m and a width of 2m to 23m; in this section you can walk around 1km underground to a 7m lava pillar, the cave's outstanding feature. The walk takes 40 minutes as the floor is pitted and full of puddles.

As you venture inside the immense black tunnel with its swirling walls and pitted floor, it looks like the lair of a giant serpent and it's hard to imagine the titanic geological forces that created it aeons ago, moulding rock as if it was Play-Doh. Take a jacket, as the cave ceiling drips and the temperature inside is a chilly 10°C. The lighting is dim so a torch (flashlight) is a good idea.

On the way to Manjanggul you'll pass the popular Gimnyeong Maze Park (김녕 미로공원; www.jejumaze.com; adult/youth/child ₩3300/2200/1100; ⊙8.30am-7pm Mar-Oct, to 6pm Nov-Feb), which is as much fun for adults as for children. Created by American expat Fred Dunstin from 2232 Leyland cypress trees, it's fiendishly clever and a real challenge.

It's quicker to walk to the cave from the bus stop on Hwy 1132 (around 30 minutes) than wait for the irregular connecting bus (₩1000, five minutes).

Woljeong Beach
월정해수욕장

This small white sandy beach is so little known that it's not on most maps. Sea World Pension (시월드펜션; ☑784 7447; www.seaworldpension.com; r from ₩60,000; ❄⊙) has smart rooms with kitchens and balconies steps from the sand. There are several taverna-style cafes fringing the beach, too.

To reach here, get off the bus at the Manjanggul stop, continue walking east along Hwy 1132 for 500m, then turn left down the access road to the beach.

Sehwa-ri & Hado-ri
세화리, 하도리

The highlight of the small fishing town of Sehwa-ri is the Haenyeo Museum (해녀박물관; www.haenyeo.go.kr; adult/youth ₩1100/500; ⊙9am-6pm), which does an

HAENYEO: JEJU'S FREE DIVERS

Jeju is famous in Korea for its women, in particular the hardy *haenyeo*. Statues celebrate these women free divers all along the coast and it's not uncommon to spot the real deal preparing to dive on the seashore or bobbing in the ocean.

For centuries, Jeju women have been engaged in this form of fishing to gather seaweed, shellfish, sea cucumbers, spiky black sea urchins, octopus and anything else edible. Working as cooperatives and sharing their catch, they use low-tech gear – polystyrene floats, flippers, nets, knives and spears – and no oxygen tanks. Until recently they didn't wear wetsuits, either, despite diving for long hours in all weather. They are able to hold their breath underwater for up to two minutes and reach a depth of 20m. Great physical stamina is a prerequisite and yet many of the *haenyeo* are in their 60s if not older.

With around 5000 *haenyeo* on Jeju (down from a peak of 30,000 in the 1950s), it's a dying profession; daughters these days are not keen to follow in their mothers' flippers. However, since 2008, at Hallim (p257), a school has been helping to preserve the legacy by teaching anyone who wants to learn the *haenyeo*'s free-diving skills. Call ☎011-691 6675 to find out how to take part in a one-day experience.

Brenda Paik-Sunoo's book *Moon Tides: Jeju Island Grannies of the Sea* and the 2004 movie *My Mother the Mermaid* both provide more insights into the lives of *haenyeo*.

---

excellent job explaining the history and culture of these amazing *haenyeo* women (see the boxed text above); buses plying the Jeju-si to Seongsan route stop near the museum entrance.

TOP CHOICE **Dasi Boesi** (다시버시; ☎783 5575; meal for 2 people ₩12,000-20,000; ☺10am-9pm) serves delicious feasts of grilled mackerel and tofu stew as well as black-pork *bulgogi*. It's a 10-minute walk from the museum, next to the five-day market on the waterfront.

About 10km south around the coast from Sehwa-ri, you're likely to have the beautiful beach at Hado-ri to yourself. The aptly named **Ssari's Flower Hill** (☎782-5933; www .seoul110.com/jeju/jeju_en.html; s/tw incl breakfast ₩40,000/50,000; ✻@⌨) is a great base for touring the area. It's managed by a friendly Japanese woman and bike rental is available (₩5000 per day).

Seongsan-ri & Sinyang-ri
성산리, 시냥리

A must-see destination, Seongsan-ri (Fortress Mountain Village) and the neighbouring village of Sinyang-ri are at the extreme eastern tip of the island at the foot of a spectacular extinct volcano that rises straight out of the ocean. Black-sand beaches are nearby, as is the lovely island of Udo and the peninsula Seopji-koji, with its new giant aquarium and the breathtaking architecture of Japanese master Ando Tadao.

◉ Sights & Activities

Seongsan Ilchulbong VOLCANO
(성산일출봉; jejuwnh.jeju.go.kr; adult/youth & child ₩2000/1000; ☺4am-7pm) One of Jeju-do's most impressive sights is this 182m tuff volcano, shaped like a giant punchbowl. The crater is a forested Lost World ringed by jagged rocks, though there's no lake because the rock is porous.

From the entrance, climbing the steep stairs to the crater rim only takes 20 minutes. Doing it in time to catch the sunrise is a life-affirming journey for many Koreans – expect plenty of company. To do the sunrise expedition, you'll have to spend the night in Seongsan-ri. The path is clear, but if you're concerned bring a torch. Not an early riser? It's also a popular daytime hike. The **Seongsan Sunrise Festival**, an all-night New Year's Eve party, is held here every 31 December.

At the eastern base of the volcano, a staircase leads down to the lovely little black-sand **Ilchulbong Beach**, tucked into a crescent-shaped cove backed by weather-beaten lava cliff walls and boulders. On the left side of the cove you'll find a small restaurant run by Jeju-do's famous *haenyeo* female divers; for details, see p243. The *haenyeo* put on a free performance of their skills every day at 1.30pm and 3pm. Next to the restaurant, small **speedboats** (선착장; per trip ₩10,000) can whisk you out to sea for another perspective on Ilchulbong.

To the right of the Ilchulbong ticket office is the small temple of **Dongam-sa**.

Phoenix Island   RESORT, ARCHITECTURE
(www.phoenixisland.co.kr; Seopji-koji; adult/youth/
child ₩2000/1500/1000; ☺9am-6pm) Coachloads of tourists disgorge here daily to view
the scenic location that has been used in several Korean TV dramas and movies. While
the ambling cliff-edge pathways past the fake
church and whitewashed lighthouse are attractive, the real stars of the peninsula are a
couple of pieces of contemporary architecture
by Ando Tadao. The award-winning Japanese
architect designed the **Glass House** (housing
the restaurant Mint as well as a gallery and
coffee shop) and the amazing **Genius Loci**
(adult/child ₩2000/1000; ☑9am-6pm), a gallery
with site-specific works that aid meditation.
Both buildings are angled to frame Seongsan
Ilchulbong, providing yet more perspectives
on the supermodel volcano. A taxi here from
Seongsan-ri is around ₩5000.

Aqua Planet Jeju   AQUARIUM, MUSEUM
(www.aquaplanet.co.kr; adult/youth/child general
admission ₩37,600/35,100/32,600, Marine Science Museum only ₩1600/1500/1400; ☺10am-
7pm) Just outside Phoenix Island is this
brand-new aquarium, an impressive facility with a 10,800-tonne tank, the largest in
East Asia. You can see here some 500 different species, including manta rays, sea lions,
30 African penguins and two white sharks;
in July and August five times daily local
haenyeo put on diving shows in the tank.
Russian synchronised swimmers and six
dolphins are part of a show in the attached

Ocean Arena, covered in the general admission ticket, as well as a **Marine Science Museum**, a restaurant and food court.

Sea Life Scuba   DIVING
(제주성산포해양스쿠버리조트; ☑782 1150;
Seongsanpo; ☺7am-6pm) Mr Park speaks some
English and can take you diving inside underwater caves and around coral reefs. A day
trip with two dives costs ₩150,000, including guide and all equipment.

Sinyang Beach   BEACH
(신양해수욕장) This crescent-shaped 1.5km
beach is sheltered and is great for windsurfing; in summer you can rent sailboats and
windsurfers and take lessons in both.

🛏 Sleeping

There's plenty of accommodation in Seonsan-
ri; you'll also find grannies on the main road
to the Ilchulbong offering *minbak* rooms. If
your budget doesn't run to the Phoenix Island resort, then the adjacent small town has
minbak and restaurants, too.

Phoenix Island   SELF-CATERING $$$
(☑731 7000; www.phoenixisland.co.kr; r from
₩300,000; Seopji-koji; ❄@☺☎) The enormous
and comfortable self-catering apartments
at this resort complex are great for families
or groups of friends to share. You have ac-
cess to plenty of facilities on-site, plus the
park, nearby beaches and beautiful views of
Seongsan Ilchulbong.

WORTH A TRIP

UDO 우도

The largest of 62 islets surrounding Jeju-do, and supposedly shaped like a sprawled-out
cow, **Udo** (Cow Island), 3.5km off the coast from Seongsan-ri, is a beautiful, relaxing
place despite throngs of tourists and tour buses, particularly on weekends. The high-
lights are the black-lava cliffs at Tolkani and the lighthouse that you can walk up to (15
minutes) for panoramic views of patchwork fields and brightly painted roofs, and gor-
geous Hongjodangoe Haebin Beach, a brilliant white coral-sand beach.

A great way to see the island's sights is following the 15.9km Route 1-1 of Jeju Olle
Trail. Should you wish to stay over, there are plenty of *minbak* and guesthouses here as
well as places to eat.

Entry to the island, which is a provincial maritime park, is included when you buy your
ferry ticket. **Car ferries** (☑782 5671) cross to either **Cheonjin** or **Haumokdong** ports
on Udo from Seongsan port (return ₩5500, 10 minutes, at least hourly from 7.30am to
6pm). The ticket office is at the far end of Seongsan port, a 15-minute walk or a short
taxi ride from Seongsan-ri.

Once on Udo plenty of operations close to either port will rent you a bicycle (two
hours ₩5000), a scooter (per hour ₩15,000) a quad bike (per hour ₩30,000) or golf
cart (per hour ₩30,000) to get around. Alternatively there's a hop-on, hop-off tourist
bus (₩5000, every 30 minutes).

Seongsan Ilchulbong

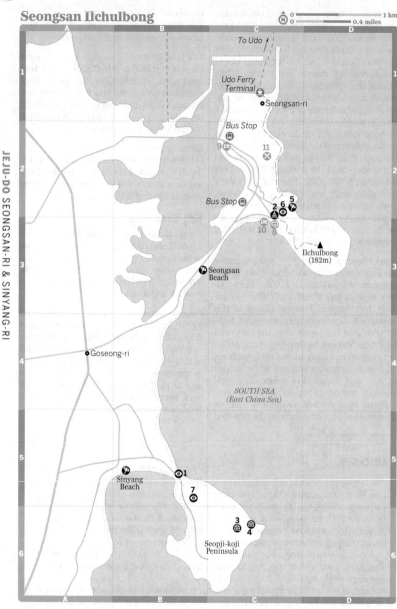

To Udo

Udo Ferry Terminal

Seongsan-ri

Bus Stop

9

11

Bus Stop

2 6 5

10

Seongsan Beach

Ilchulbong (182m)

Goseong-ri

SOUTH SEA (East China Sea)

Sinyang Beach

1

7

3 4

Seopji-koji Peninsula

Bomulseom   PENSION $$
(보물섬; ☏784 0039; www.jejubms.com; r from ₩50,000; ❄@☎) This hilltop pension has well-kept and -equipped self-catering rooms with enclosed balconies and good views. In July and August its outdoor pool is available.

Seongsanpo Village   HOTEL $$
(성산포빌리지; ☏782 2373; r ₩40,000; ❄@) Sit out on a balcony with a wonderful view of the sea and anything going on along the harbour. It also has a good restaurant on the ground floor.

Seongsan Ilchulbong

◉ Sights
1	Aqua Planet Jeju	B5
2	Dongam-sa	C2
3	Genius Loci	C6
4	Glass House	C6
5	Ilchulbong Beach	C2
6	Ilchulbong Ticket Office	C2
7	Phoenix Island	B5

◎ Activities, Courses & Tours
8	Sea Life Scuba	C3
	Speedboat Dock	(see 5)

◎ Sleeping
9	Bomulseom	C2
	Phoenix Island	(see 7)
10	Seongsanpo Village	C3

◎ Eating
11	Haeddeuneun	C2
	House of Women Divers	(see 5)
	Mint	(see 4)

◎ Drinking
	Café It Suda	(see 6)

✗ Eating & Drinking

There's a cluster of restaurants and fast-food places at the entrance of Seongsan Ilchulbong if the following don't appeal.

Haeddeuneun SEAFOOD $$
(해뜨는; ☑782 3380; Hando-ro, Seongsan-ri; mains from ₩10,000; ☺8am-9pm; 🅿) Set a little way apart from the cluster of touristy restaurants at the foot of Seongsan Ilchulbong, this one provides good views of the Sunrise Peak and a menu covering all common local options, including abalone rice porridge, sea-urchin soup and seafood hotpot.

Mint INTERNATIONAL $$$
(☑731 7000; www.phoenixisland.co.kr; Seopji-koji; set lunch/dinner from ₩36,000/56,000; 🛜🅿) Dining inside Ando Tadao's Glass House is a delightful experience and best enjoyed during the day when you can take full advantage of floor-to-ceiling views of the coast through the windows. The menu offers high-grade local produce such as black-pork neck and steak.

House of Women Divers SEAFOOD $$
(Ilchulbong Beach; mains ₩10,000-20,000; ☺9am-6pm) Left of Ilchulbong Beach is this small restaurant run by Jeju-do's famous *haenyeo* female divers, who serve fresh raw octopus, conch, abalone and other delicacies.

Café It Suda CAFE $
(Seongsan-ri; coffee & snacks from ₩3000; ☺9am-7pm; 🛜🅿) There are plenty of chain cafes near the volcano but this independent, artsy cafe has bags more charm. Plus it sells Jeju Olle Trail souvenirs and other attractive local items.

❶ Getting There & Away

Buses (₩3000, 1½ hours, every 20 minutes) run to Seongsan-ri from Jeju-si and Seogwipo bus terminals. Make sure that the bus goes right into Seongsan-ri as a few stick to the main road and drop you 2.5km from town.

From the **Udo ferry terminal** (우도여객선 터미널) boats sail to Udo and Jangheung (one way adult/child ₩36,000/18,000, two hours 20 minutes, one to two daily) in Jeolla-do; see www.jhferry.com for details.

Samdal-ri 삼달리

The reason for pausing at this coastal village between Sinyang-ri and Pyoseon Beach is to view the stunning images at the **Kim Young Gap Gallery Dumoak** (김영갑갤러리두모악; www.dumoak.com; adult/teenager/child ₩3000/2000/1000; ☺9.30am-6pm Thu-Tue, daily Jul & Aug). Kim (1957–2005) was a talented, self-taught photographer who lived on the island for 20 years and documented its landscape. In the last years of his life he moved into an abandoned school, which he transformed into his studio (now the museum) and created a lovely sculpture-filled garden outside.

Across the road from the gallery, have a drink or a bite to eat at the pleasant **Orum Café** (blog.naver.com/orumcafe; mains ₩7000-10,000; ☺9.30am-9pm Thu-Tue; 🛜), which has an English-speaking chef.

From Samdal-ri bus stop on Hwy 1132 the gallery is a 1.4km walk; it's also on Jeju Olle Trail Route 3.

Pyoseon 표선

This small, quiet town has a huge expanse of white sandy **beach** that, at low tide, stretches as far as the eye can see; in the middle a lagoon forms. If you like plenty of space, this is the beach to visit.

Near the beach, the educational **Jeju Folk Village** (제주민속촌; www.jejufolk.com; adult/youth/child ₩8000/5500/4000; ☺8.30am-6pm) gathers together traditional buildings from across the island (some reconstructions, others hundreds of years old) in an attractively designed park. Various sections cover Jeju's culture from shamans to *yangban* (aristocrats), and the differences between mountain, hill-country and fishing villages. The modern construction has been done in authentic style, and at various places you can watch craftsmen at work and buy their products. Also here are country-style restaurants serving inexpensive noodle and rice dishes, traditional song and dance performances and, oddly, an ostrich farm.

Next to the folk village is the luxury **Haevichi Hotel & Resort Jeju** (☑780 8000; www .haevichi.com; r/unit from ₩401,000/300,000; ❄@🛜🏊), owned by Hyundai Motors, which accounts for the display cars in the lobby. The rooms, all of which have balconies and many with sea views, are very chic and spacious; the self-catering units in the 'resort' side of the complex sleep up to four. Facilities include several restaurants, outdoor swimming pools and a *jjimjilbang* (luxury sauna; guests/nonguests ₩10,000/20,000).

Seongeup Folk Village
성읍민속마을

A 10-minute bus ride north of Pyoseon lies this former provincial capital, where government assistance has encouraged the preservation and renovation of the traditional rock-walled, thatched-roofed houses. Modern intrusions include souvenir shops, restaurants and car parks, but most of it still looks fantastically feudal. Unlike Jeju Folk Village, Seongeup is the real deal with people living and working here still.

The core of the village is surrounded by a fortress wall punctuated by ornate entrance gates; **Namoon** (the south gate) is the main gate. Some inhabitants offer free guided tours of their compound, but afterwards they want you to buy local products such as black *omija* tea or paper-thin dried fish called *myeongtae*. Just ramble down the narrow lanes and discover the place for yourself; if the gate poles are down, you are welcome to enter. Look out for the Confucian school and the 1000-year-old zelkova tree.

JEJU OLLE TRAIL

Launched by former Korean journalist and Jeju native Suh Myeong-sook in 2007, the **Jeju Olle Trail** (☑762 2170; www.jejuolle.org) is one of the great success stories of local tourism. The first route starts in Siheung near Seongsan-ri, and a further 25 routes of between 5km and 22.9km meander mainly along Jeju's coast (but also with some inland diversions) and three outer islands (Udo, Gapado and Chujado). Around one million people hiked an Olle route in 2011, creating jobs and providing an income for many local businesses.

Olle is the local word for a pathway that connects a house to the main street, signifying one of the project's aims to open up Jeju's unique culture and scenery to visitors. Although you could hike all the 430km of trails in around a month, the Olle's philosophy is one of slow, meandering travel. 'We recommend you don't rush,' says the Jeju Olle Foundation's Soojin Ivy Lee, 'its not a race...we like people to feel spiritual healing and tranquility.'

If you hike any of the trails, it's worth investing in a passport (₩12,000) that comes with an excellent English-language guidebook providing detailed information on many sights and places to stay and eat along the routes. The passport also gets you discounts at many places. Along with unique locally made souvenirs, such as the *ganse* horse dolls and keychains (made from recycled fabrics), the passports are available at seven Jeju Olle Information Centres dotted around the island, including the foundation's head office in Seogwipo on Trail 6, as well as 30 local Family Marts, another 30 guesthouses and cafes. Buy the passport online and you can pick it up from the Olle information desk at the airport.

The four-day **Jeju Olle Walking Festival** (www.ollewalking.co.kr) generally occurs each October or November and includes many special events. The foundation is always looking for volunteers for this and other ongoing projects. The *Jeju Weekly* also has full reports of all the Olle Trails; see www.jejuweekly.com/news/articleList.html?sc_sub_section_code=S2N63.

Seongeup is also a good place to buy *galot* (traditional Jeju workclothes) and naturally dyed fabrics. Shops include Garotmandenjip on the village central road, and Sokgungyehtusanpum (속궁예토 산품) next to Namoon car park.

Sleeping & Eating

TOP CHOICE Seongeup Folk Village Traditional Houses
SELF-CATERING **$$**

(☎760 3578; cottage from ₩60,000; ❋) The village offers comfortable accommodation in six volcanic-stone and thatched-roof cottages. Inside they have two bedrooms with *ondol* (heated) floors and *yo* (padded quilt) on raised platforms; the bathrooms and kitchens are modern and tastefully decorated.

TOP CHOICE Yetnalpatjuk
KOREAN **$$**

(옛날팥죽; mains ₩5500-8500; ☉10am-7.30pm; ☎) Just outside the village walls to the northwest, next to the bus stop from Pyoseon, this convivial place serves several delicious soups including some made from lotus flowers, pumpkin and seaweed, along with tasty side dishes, all on rustic pottery.

Gwandangnae Sikdang
KOREAN **$$**

(관당네식당; mains from ₩12,000; ☉8am-9pm) The ebullient owner of this restaurant, next to Namoon car park, is a national celebrity for his succulent black-pig pork dishes; a massive banquet for two is ₩35,000.

❶ Getting There & Away

Regular buses shuttle between Pyoseon and Seongeup (₩1000, 10 minutes, every 20 minutes). A taxi is ₩7000.

SOUTHERN JEJU-DO

If you only have a short time in Jeju, make this area your base; it has the best climate and coastal scenery plus easy access to central Jeju-do for Hallasan National Park.

Seogwipo 서귀포

POP 154,000

Jeju-do's second-largest city is beautifully situated on a rocky volcanic coastline, dotted with lush parks, a deep gorge and two of the country's most famous waterfalls. The clear blue waters and mild water temperatures make Seogwipo Korea's best scuba-diving destination and it's also an ideal base for hiking.

GATE POLE MESSAGES

Jeju-do has traditionally described itself as having lots of rocks, wind and women, but no beggars, thieves or locked gates. In the island's villages, instead of locked fences in front of homes you'll often see a *jeongnang* gate, two stone pillars that support three wooden poles between them. Three poles straight across means 'We're not home, please keep out'. Two down and one across means 'We're not home, but we are within shouting distance'. If all the poles are on the ground, it means 'We're home, please come in'.

The town centre (up a steep slope from the harbour) is full of motels and hotels. The main bus terminal and other attractions are clustered around the World Cup Stadium, 6km west of town in Shin Seogwipo. Jungmun Resort is also within easy day-trip distance.

◉ Sights

Cheonjiyeon Pokpo
WATERFALL

(천지연폭포; adult/youth & child ₩2000/1000; ☉7am-10pm) This lovely 22m-high waterfall is reached after a 10-minute walk through a beautifully forested, steep gorge. After heavy rain the waterfall can be impressive, but at other times it's more noisy than wide. Well worth visiting in the evening, too, when the illuminated gorge takes on a romantic atmosphere.

Jeongbang Pokpo
WATERFALL

(정방폭포; adult/youth/child ₩2000/1000/600; ☉7.30am-6.30pm Mar-Oct, to 5.30pm Nov-Feb) Said to be the only waterfall in Asia that falls directly into the sea, Jeongbang Pokpo is a 15-minute walk east of the town centre. Legend has it that around 219 BC, the falls were visited by sorcerer Xu Fu (Seo Bok in Korean); he had been sent on a mission by the Chinese emperor to find the elixir of life, believed to exist on Hallasan. An inscription on the rock near the falls (saying 'Xu Fu passed here') may have been carved by the man himself. You can learn more at the **Seobok Exhibition Hall** (admission free; ☉9am-6pm) next to the falls, then stroll around the pretty Chinese garden.

Seogwipo

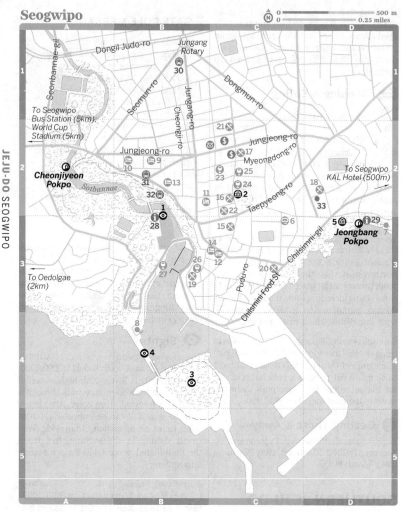

JEJU-DO SEOGWIPO

Saeyeon-gyo & Saeseom BRIDGE, ISLAND
(새연교, 새섬; admission free; ⊙dawn-11pm)
This attractive cable-stayed **bridge** at the
mouth of Seogwipo Harbour provides access to densely wooded **Saeseom** (Sod
Island), around which runs a shady 1.1km
trail. It's a favourite spot to stroll at sunset
and the bridge is also nicely illuminated at
night.

Lee Jung-Seop Art Gallery & Park MUSEUM
(www.seogwipo.go.kr/JSLee; Lee Jung-Seob St;
adult/youth/child ₩1000/500/300; ⊙9am-6pm)
On the street that is named after him and

decorated with images from his distinctive
paintings and drawings, is this small museum devoted to Lee Jung-Seop (1916–56).
Outside, in a lovely manicured lawn with
fragrant trees, is the traditional Jeju house
in which the Pyongyang-born artist lived for
a short time in 1951. A four-day festival is
held in September and October to celebrate
Lee and every Saturday a **flea and craft
market** takes place on the street.

World Cup Stadium STADIUM
(제주 월드컵 경기장; Map p230; Shin Seogwipo) Six kilometres west of central Seog-

Seogwipo

wipo, the graceful soccer stadium built for the 2002 World Cup is the centrepiece of an entertainment complex that includes a multiplex cinema, E-Mart discount store, **Water World** (admission ₩25,000; ⊙11am-11pm) water park, **Dak Paper Doll Museum** (adult/youth ₩6000/5000; ⊙9am-7pm) and **International Eros Museum** (adults only, admission ₩7000; ⊙9am-9pm), one of Jeju's trio of museums devoted to sex (see the boxed text, p248).

🏃 Activities

For more about diving, see p30.

Oedolgae　　　　　　　　　　　　WALKING
(외돌개) At the junction of Routes 6 and 7 on the Jeju Olle Trail, about 2km west of Seogwipo, is this impressive 20m-tall volcanic basalt pillar jutting out of the ocean. Like other unusual-shaped rocks there's a legend associated with it – a Korean general is said to have scared away Mongolian invaders by dressing the rock up to look like a giant soldier. Oedolgae (meaning 'Lonely Rock') is a pleasant walk through pine forests to a beautiful cliffside lookout at Sammae-bong Park. Bus 8 (₩1000, five minutes) runs to Oedolgae.

Big Blue 33　　　　　　　　　　　DIVING
(☑733 1733; www.bigblue33.co.kr; Chilispri 4-Ro; ⊙9am-7pm) Run by German expat Ralf Deutsch, a diving enthusiast who speaks English, German and Korean (see the boxed text, p32). A two-tank dive trip costs ₩105,000 with all equipment and guide. A five-day NAUI certification course costs ₩500,000.

Seogwipo Submarine　　SUBMARINE TOUR
(www.submarine.co.kr; submarine tours adult/teenager/child ₩51,500/41,000/30,500) Don't dive? Then hop aboard one of these popular submarine tours down to a depth of 30m around Munseom island. Tours run at least every 40 minutes from 9.20am to 4pm. Ask at the tourist information centre next to Cheonjiyeon Pokpo for a discount ticket coupon. Reservations are recommended July and August.

🛏 Sleeping

TOP CHOICE Hotel Little France　　HOTEL $$
(☑7324552; www.littlefrancehotel.co.kr; r ₩60,000-90,000; ❋@☎) This modern, stylish hotel is a cut above others in its class and provides

JEJU'S SEX MUSEUMS

Although attitudes are changing, Koreans tend to be conservative about sex. Pornography, for example, is illegal. So how come Jeju-do has not one but three highly graphic museums devoted to sex? Chatting to locals, a couple of answers come up. The first is that the island gives tax breaks to anyone who runs a museum (which also accounts for why Jeju has so many so-called 'museums'). Secondly, many honeymooning and vacationing visitors are already in the mood for frisky fun – which is where these museums step in to provide inspiration and, in one case, a very healthy education.

The original sex museum **Jeju Loveland** (www.jejuloveland.com; Hwy 1100; admission ₩9000; ⊙9am-11pm), an erotic theme park created by art students and graduates of Seoul's Hongkik University, features hundreds of sexy and frequently comic sculptures, soft-core art galleries and adult-toy stores. It's located next door to the Jeju Museum of Art.

Far better is the **Museum of Sex & Health** (www.sexmuseum.or.kr; admission ₩12,000; ⊙10am-8pm) in Gamsan-ri, Southern Jeju. This huge complex has extensive sections devoted to sex education and sex culture from around the world. Laudable for its inclusivity, covering usually taboo subjects in Korea such as homosexuality, it also has some very, ahem, imaginative arty installations. Buses shuttling between Jungmun and Hwasun along Hwy 1132 stop in front of the museum.

Completists will want to visit the **International Eros Museum** (p246); its collection of mainly oriental erotic arts and crafts is impressive, too, even including some very kinky scenes involving bestiality. Definitely for adults only!

---

guests with a choice of four room styles: modern, oriental, antique and royal classic. The management is friendly and speaks English.

Backpacker's Home　　　　BACKPACKERS $
(☑763 4000; www.backpackershomejeju.com; dm ₩23,000; ✲@🛜) Seogwipo's best backpackers' hostel offers spacious dorms, each with its own bathroom, sleeping four in sturdy pine bunks. Rates include breakfast. There are also English-speaking staff, a great outdoor terrace cafe-bar and bike rental (₩10,000 a day).

Seogwipo KAL Hotel　　　　HOTEL $$$
(☑733 2001; www.kalhotel.co.kr; r from ₩200,000; ✲@🛜⛲) Set in pleasant grounds around 2km west of the town centre, this luxury option has an overall design of muted colours and pastels. Bathrooms are on the small side. Add ₩50,000 for ocean views and another 20% on weekends.

Shinsung Hotel　　　　MOTEL $$
(신성호텔; ☑732 1415; www.shinsunghotel.com; r ₩50,000; ✲@) A classy motel with a hard-to-miss metal-and-chequerboard exterior. Rooms include a computer and Jacuzzi. Some rooms have balconies and those with a sea view cost ₩10,000 extra, even if it's too misty to see the sea.

Sun Beach Hotel　　　　HOTEL $$
(☑732 5678; www.hotelsunbeach.co.kr; Taepyeong-ro; r incl breakfast ₩90,000; ✲🛜) A reasonable option if you're into retro and hanker for these midrange tourist hotels that resemble a grand dame somewhat past her prime but still retaining an air of faded gentility.

Benikea Crystal Hotel　　　　HOTEL $$
(☑732 8311; www.jejucrystal.com; 16 Joongung-ro; r ₩100,000; ✲🛜) Rates are cheaper online for this decent hotel. Don't be fooled by the grand piano in the lobby, though; the rooms, which have balconies, are old-fashioned.

Wooseong Motel　　　　HOTEL $
(우성모텔; ☑732 5700; r ₩25,000; ✲) Simple but well-kept rooms are cheerful and welcoming. Rooms on the 4th floor, such as room 405, have sea views. The owners don't speak English, but are friendly.

✗ Eating

TOP CHOICE **Saesom Galbi**　　　　BARBECUE $$
(새솜 갈비; ☑763 2552; mains ₩12,000-30,000; ⊙11am-11pm; 🛜🅿) Perched on a cliff overlooking the harbour, this is a great place to sample a blow-out beef or black-pork barbecue. The waitresses will make sure you get your meat grilled just right.

Ankori Pakori
KOREAN $

(안거리 박거리; ☏763 2552; mains ₩7000-8000; ⊙10am-9pm) This simple, family-run restaurant offers fabulously tasty, great-value meals. Single diners will get *bibimbap* (rice, egg, meat and vegies with chilli sauce) with tons of side dishes, but if there's two or more of you, the *jeonsik* (set meal) includes sliced pork and grilled fish.

Semmudukbaegi
SEAFOOD $$

(삼무뚝배기; ☏733 2360; Chilsmini Food St; mains ₩10,000-15,000; ⊙10am-9pm) Fish restaurants cluster around the harbour along 'Chilsmni Food St'; this is a good one for the usual range of seafood dishes such as abalone rice porridge and *okdomgul* (fried fish).

Namhaegulbap
KOREAN $$

(남해굴밥; Donghong-jungang-ro; mains ₩8000; ⊙11am-9pm) Meaning 'southern sea oyster and rice', this simple place, a short taxi ride or walk east from the city centre, serves plenty of bivalve dishes including a tasty oyster pancake. Its cold noodle dishes are served in bowls made of ice; try the *kongguksu*, a soy-milk and cucumber soup over noodles with half a boiled egg.

Kkomjirak
INTERNATIONAL $$

(꼼지락; Lee Jung Seob St; mains ₩7000-10,000; ⊙noon-11pm Mon-Sat; 🛜📶) Of the many convivial cafes that have popped up along this arty street, this is the best option, serving a great brunch of bagel, scrambled eggs, bacon and salad from noon to 2pm. Other dishes include vegetable curry and pork cutlet.

Meokbo Bunsik
DUMPLINGS $

(먹보분식; meals ₩2000-5000; ⊙24hr) Handy for late-night snacking is this cheap diner with homemade *mandu* (만두; dumplings) steaming in big pots outside and *gimbap* on the menu.

Tok Sung Won
CHINESE $$

(덕성원; ☏762 2402; dishes ₩5000-40,000; ⊙11am-8.30pm; 📶) At this popular restaurant you'll find all your favourite Chinese dishes plus exotic specialities like fried pheasant and sea slug. Rice and noodle dishes are great value with huge portions perfect for sharing.

Seogwipo Mae-il Olle Market
MARKET $

(서귀포매일올레시장; Jungjeong-ro; ⊙6am-6pm) Browse stalls of wonderful fruit and live seafood direct from local orchardists and fishermen. It's a good place to pick up snacks for a picnic.

🍷 Drinking

🔺TOP CHOICE Maybe
CAFE, BAR

(Lee Jung Seob St; drinks ₩2000-5000; ⊙11.30am-1am; 🛜📶) Creatively decorated inside with tables spilling onto the street, Seogwipo's most laid-back cafe is a great place to chill and make friends with locals.

Pyeonuijeom
CAFE, BAR

(편의점; drinks ₩2000-5000; ⊙10.30am-4am) Quirky and informal, 'Rose Marina' is a tumbledown waterfront shack with a deck decorated with snowboards, kayaks and giant trees growing through the floorboards. Drinks are cheap and there's a great music selection.

Hear the Wind Sing
CAFE, BAR

(http://blog.naver.com/windsing1; Lee Jung Seob St; ⊙8am-midnight; 🛜📶) A relaxed place with a travel theme and soothing music and decor serving a good selection of caffeinated drinks and alcohol. There's also a small selection of food, including tasty pasta dishes for lunch and a steak hamburger for dinner.

Milano
PUB

(밀라노; beers/cocktails ₩3000/5000; ⊙7pm-4am) Sit inside on the red seats or outside near the barbecue (meals ₩8000 to ₩25,000) under the trees with harbour views.

G Bar
BAR

(beer & cocktails ₩5000-12,000; ⊙7pm-5.30am) Super-chic, jet-black cocktail lounge that caters to young professionals.

ℹ Information

Family Mart (Myeong-dong-ro) Global ATM.

Jeju Bank (Jungjeong-ro) Global ATM with a ₩1,000,000 withdrawal limit.

Tourist information centre (관광 안내소; ☏1330; next to Cheonjiyeon Pokpo ticket office; ⊙10am-9pm) Free internet access and global ATM. A smaller tourist kiosk is located at Jeongbang Pokpo waterfall.

ℹ Getting There & Around

The fastest way here from Jeju-si is on the cross-island buses (₩3000, one hour and 20 minutes, every 20 minutes), although you can also come either way around the coast and take the more expensive Airport Limousine Bus (₩7500, one hour and 20 minutes, every 20 minutes) from the airport.

Tap-sa (p265)
pagoda temple inside Maisan
Provincial Park; its stone towers all
present religious ideas

2. Triumphal Arch (p308)
The Pyongyang landmark celebrates
Kim Il-sung's speech to Koreans at the
end of Japanese occupation in 1945

3. Jirisan National Park (p200)
The mountains of Jirisan offer some
of the best hiking in Korea

Seogwipo bus terminal is 6km west of the town centre, next to the World Cup Stadium; frequent buses (₩1000, 10 minutes) link from here to the town. Seogwipo itself is small enough to walk around, but taxis are plentiful and cheap. Local buses can be picked up at Jungang Rotary.

Scooter & Free Zone (스쿠터 앤 프리존; ☑762 5296; 50/125cc scooter per 24hr ₩20,000/25,000, bicycle/electric bicycle ₩10,000/15,000; ☉9am-7pm) rents bicycles, electric bikes and scooters.

Jungmun Resort & Vicinity
중문 휴양지

Located a 25-minute bus ride west of Seogwipo, Jungmun Resort is South Korea's primary tourist resort, with a beach backed by swaying palm trees, dramatic black volcanic cliffs, waterfalls, luxury hotels, casinos, restaurants and museums.

If you spot couples wearing matching outfits, riding tandem bicycles or stuffing food into each other's mouths here, they're likely to be honeymooners. The resort is also ideal for families, with plenty of kid-friendly activities and sights. The pleasant beach isn't the most scenic on Jeju but it's well set up for those seeking activities rather than relaxation.

Tourist information and free internet access is available from the KTO-run **Jungmun tourist information centre** (☑1739 1330; ☉9am-7pm summer, to 6pm rest of year) at the main entrance to the resort, and from the **tourist information centre** (☑738 1393; ☉9am-5pm) at the main entrance to Jusangjeollidae.

⊙ Sights

Cheonjeyeon Pokpo WATERFALL
(천제연폭포; adult/youth & child ₩2500/1370; ☉sunrise-sunset) Jungmun's top natural attraction is this legendary waterfall, a three-tier cascade tucked deep inside a forested gorge. Above soars an arched footbridge decorated with sculptures of the seven nymphs who served the Emperor of Heaven and who, it is said, used to slide down moonbeams to bathe here every night.

Jusangjeollidea GEOLOGICAL FEATURE
(주상절리대; adult/youth & child ₩2000/1000; ☉9am-5pm) Just south of the International Convention Centre is a dramatic 2km stretch of coastline, known for hexagonal and rectangular rock columns that look as if they

were stamped out with a cookie cutter. The formations are the result of the rapid cooling and contraction of lava as it poured into the sea. Either walk to the viewing platform here (on Jeju Olle Trail Route 8) or view the rocks from the sea on one of the boat tours from the resort.

Yeomiji Botanical Garden GARDENS
(여미지식물원; www.yeomiji.or.kr; adult/youth/child ₩8000/6000/4000; ☉9am-6pm) Off the Jungmun Resort access road, this impressive botanical garden has a huge indoor section with areas that mimic rainforests, deserts and other landscapes. The surrounding outdoor plantings and designs include Italian, Japanese, palm and herb gardens.

Museum of Africa MUSEUM
(www.africamuseum.or.kr; adult/youth/child ₩6000/5000/3000; ☉9am-10pm Jul & Aug, to 7pm rest of year) Housed in a building modelled after the Grand Mosque of Djenné, this surprisingly good attraction features a fine collection of African tribal art, as well as gorgeous contemporary photography of the continent's people and animals by Kim Jung-man. There are occasional live-music and dance performances by African musicians and kids will love the cute stuffed toy animal 'safari'. It's at the far eastern end of the resort, close to the entrance to Jusangjeollidea.

Yakcheon-sa TEMPLE
(약천사; ☑738 5000; admission free; ☉sunrise-sunset) Although this Buddhist temple was only constructed between 1987 and 1997, it is one of Jeju-do's most impressive buildings. The ornate hall is filled with vibrant murals of scenes from Buddha's life and illustrations of his teachings, and the main hall has galleries that overlook a 3m-tall statue of Buddha. Overnight Templestays are offered every first and third weekend of the month; there's also a daily two-hour Templelife program. The temple is near Wolpyeong, around 2km east of Jungmun and on the 600 Limousine bus route. It's also not far from the end of Jeju Olle Trail Route 7 and the start of Route 8.

Sound Island Museum MUSEUM
(adult/child ₩700/5000; ☉9am-6.30pm) Somewhat more educational and interactive than Jungmun's other so-called 'museums' is this tribute to sound and music from around the world. There's a giant piano you can play

with your feet (like Tom Hanks in *Big*) and you can marvel at the world's biggest mobile of seashells.

Teddy Bear Museum   MUSEUM
(www.teddybearmuseum.com; adult/youth/child ₩8000/7000/6000; ☺9am-8pm) A supremely kitsch, world-beating gathering of stuffed teddies in poses ranging from Mona Lisa to Elvis.

🏃 Activities

Besides the following activities, there are also casinos at the Hyatt Regency, Lotte and Shilla hotels.

Jungmun Beach   BEACH
(중문해수욕장) The resort's palm-fringed beach becomes crowded in July and August when it's patrolled by lifeguards. Walk up the steps to the Hyatt Regency Hotel, continue along the boardwalk and down the steps to reach an even more scenic and secluded beach: aquamarine water and golden sand backed by sheer black cliffs eroded into cylindrical shapes.

The waves and wind here make Jungmun one of the best beaches on Jeju for windsurfing and parasailing. Operators are based between Pacific Land and the International Convention Centre. **Kayaks** and **boogie boards** (per 2hr kayak/boogie board ₩15,000/5000) can also be hired on Jungmun Beach.

Shangri-la   CRUISE
(☏738 2888; cruise per 30min/1hr from ₩40,000/60,000) Pacific Land, which runs the ageing dolphinarium overlooking Jungmun Beach, also offers a variety of cruises that will give you a sea view of the incredible geological creations along the coast.

Jeju Jet   CRUISE
(☏739 3939; www.jejujet.co.kr; per ride ₩25,000) Get your thrills speeding up and down the coast in one of these jet boats. The same company can also arrange parasailing trips.

Daeyoo Land   HORSE RIDING
(대유랜드; ☏738 0500; www.daeyooland.net; activities ₩25,000-165,000) This private retreat several kilometres north of Jungmun offers 4WD tours and horse riding. Pheasant hunting and target shooting are also available.

Jungmun Beach Golf Club   GOLF
(☏738 4359; green fees ₩90,000-130,000) Of the many golf courses on the island, this one perched on a seaside cliff, is one of the most scenic.

🛏 Sleeping

Minbak (private homes with rooms for rent), pensions and restaurants are strung out along Hwy 12 near the access road to the resort, while luxury hotel resorts are down towards the beach.

TOP CHOICE The Seaes Hotel & Resort   HOTEL $$$
(☏735 3000; www.seaes.co.kr; r/ste from ₩300,000/410,000; ❄@🛜) Just 26 traditional stone-wall and thatched cottages (all mod cons inside) set in lovely landscaped gardens form this compact resort next to the convention centre. Rates include breakfast. Its Cheon-Jae-Yeon restaurant is very good too, while for a coffee in something more stylish than Jungmun's Starbucks you could amble over to its Olle cafe.

Hyatt Regency Jeju   HOTEL $$$
(☏733 1234; www.jeju-regency.hyatt.com; r from ₩356,950; ❄@🛜🏊) This white, beehive-shaped edifice is the closest hotel to the beach with the best sea views. The stylish rooms feature minimalist decor. The wonderful outdoor swimming pool features a swim-up bar hidden behind a waterfall, though it's only open in July and August (there's also an indoor pool).

Shilla Jeju   HOTEL $$$
(☏738 4466; www.shilla.net; r from ₩393,250; ❄@🛜🏊) The Shilla drips designer cool with muted blue, coral and beige colours, modernist artworks, and connected indoor and outdoor pools.

Lotte Hotel Jeju   HOTEL $$$
(☏731 1000; www.lottehoteljeju.com; r from ₩400,000; ❄@🛜🏊) Las Vegas comes to Jeju-do with this over-the-top resort; the gardens have windmills, a boating lake and swimming pool surrounded by fake rocks. A nightly outdoor show involves music, lights, fountains, volcanoes and dragons. There are plenty of kid-friendly activities and Hello Kitty fans will want to book one of the seven themed rooms (from ₩726,000).

Gold Beach Minbak   MINBAK $$
(골드비치민박; ☏738 7511; r ₩50,000; ❄) A 10-minute walk to the beach is this motel with smart wood-panelled rooms with balconies and kitchenettes. Room 305 is one of the best. Look for a peach-and-green building above a restaurant, 200m east of the Jungmun Beach access road.

Eating

Jeju Mawon
KOREAN $$$

(📞733 1000; www.jejumawon.com; mains ₩15,000-45,000; ⏰11am-10pm) Occupying part of the Joseon-style palace Jeju Korea House, this traditional restaurant serves, among other things, horsemeat dishes – a speciality of the island.

Island Gecko's
INTERNATIONAL $$

(📞739 0845; www.geckosterrace.com; mains ₩10,000-15,000, drinks ₩3000-8000; ⏰10am-2am) This popular expat hang-out features Western comfort foods like Philly cheese steaks, burgers and pizza. Staff speak English and there's even a bus pick-up service. It's about 2km inland from Jungmun; just ask any taxi driver.

Ha Young
BARBECUE $$

(📞738 6011; mains ₩25,000-50,000; ⏰10am-10pm) Just east of the Gold Beach Minbak is Jungmun's most popular Korean barbecue restaurant specialising in Jeju-do's famous black pig. Look for the tall grey building with a patio and blue fairy lights.

ℹ️ Getting There & Away

Frequent buses (₩1000, 20 minutes, every 20 minutes) shuttle between Seogwipo and the Jungmun Beach access road, 1km from the beach.

Sanbangsan & Yongmeori Coast 산방산, 용머리해안

A steep, 10-minute walk up the south-facing side of the dramatic, craggy **Sanbangsan** (395m) is a stone Buddha in an atmospheric cave called **Sanbang-gul-sa** (산방굴사; adult/youth & child ₩1000/500; ⏰8.30am-7pm). It's been a sacred site since Goryeo times, and the water flowing from the ceiling is said to be magically curative. Lower down, by the ticket office, are other shrines and statues of more recent origin.

Across the road, a footpath leads downhill to the spectacular **Yongmeori coast** (adult/youth & child ₩2000/1000, incl Sanbang-gul-sa ₩2500/1500), a spectacular oceanside trail of soaring cliffs, pockmarked by erosion into catacombs, narrow clefts and natural archways. *Haenyeo* sell freshly caught seafood, which you can scoff with *soju* on the rocks (₩20,000 per person). Note the walk along the cliffs closes during very high seas.

At the coastal trail exit is a replica of the **Hamel Memorial** (admission included in Yongmoeri coast ticket) housed in a replica of a Dutch merchant ship. Hendrick Hamel (1630–92), one of the survivors of a shipwreck near Jeju in 1653, was forced to stay in Korea for 13 years before managing to escape in a boat to Japan. Later he was the first Westerner to write a book on the 'hermit kingdom'.

Buses (₩2500, 45 minutes, every 40 minutes) leave from Seogwipo bus terminal for Sanbangsan. You can also walk here along Jeju Olle Trail Route 10 from **Hwasun Beach**.

🛏️ Sleeping & Eating

Joyful Guesthouse
GUESTHOUSE, CAFE $$

(📞792 5551; www.ijoyful.net; Hwasun; dm/s/d ₩18,000/25,000/40,000; ❄️@🛜) Beside the beach and the open-air swimming pool (open July and August), this pleasant guesthouse and cafe (open 8am to 10pm) has clean *ondol* rooms and bunkbed dorms.

🏆 TOP CHOICE Lazybox Café & Guesthouse
GUESTHOUSE, CAFE $$

(📞792 1254; www.lazybox.co.kr; ⏰10am-7pm; ❄️@🛜) At the foot of Sanbangsan, this stylish cafe serves fair-trade coffee, freshly squeezed juices and homemade cakes. The owners, escapees from Seoul, also run an equally charming guesthouse (dorm ₩20,000), 2km away in Sage, which also has a cafe.

CENTRAL JEJU

Hallasan National Park 한라산국립공원

Hiking up 1950m **Hallasan** (www.hallasan .go.kr; admission free), South Korea's highest peak, is well worth the effort. The densely wooded dormant volcano, the world's only habitat for Korean firs, is beautiful throughout the seasons, with hillsides of azaleas flowering in April and May being a particularly notable sight. If you're lucky, you might spot small roe deer. Be prepared for bad weather that can arrive in the blink of an eye and for snow in winter.

On Hallasan, refreshments are available at the Jindallaebat emergency shelter on the Seongpanak Trail and at the Witse-oreum

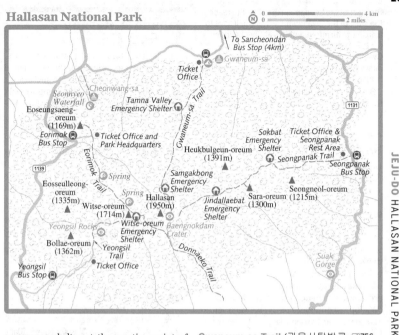

JEJU-DO HALLASAN NATIONAL PARK

emergency shelter at the meeting point of the Eorimok, Yeongsil and Donnaeko Trails; all shelters have toilets. There's a **camping ground** (per tent per night from ₩3000) at the Gwaneum-sa entrance. The shelters are for emergency use only and cannot be used for overnight stays.

🏃 Activities

There are five main trails up Hallasan but only Seongpanak and Gwaneum-sa provide access to the peak and views of the crater lake. Free maps are available from the information centres at each of the main trail entrances, but the paths are very clearly marked so it's difficult to get lost. Besides, you'll seldom be climbing alone.

The following climbing times indicated are generous. However, set out early – if you don't reach the uppermost shelters by certain times (usually around 1pm), rangers will stop you from climbing higher. There are also a couple of shorter trails lower down the mountain if you don't have time for the full climb.

Seongpanak Trail (성판악탐방로; ☎725 9950; 9.6km; 4½hr) This popular route, offering the most gradual ascent, also has a side trail to Sara-oreum Observatory.

Gwaneum-sa Trail (관음사탐방로; ☎756 9950; 8.7km; 5hr) Most scenic of the four trails, but the steepest, which can make it murder on your knees coming down.

Eorimok Trail (어리목탐방로; ☎713 9953; 4.7km; 3hr) Starts after a 15-minute walk from the Eorimok bus stop, with a steep climb up through a deciduous forest (gorgeous coloured leaves in autumn). Halfway up, the dense trees give way to an open, subalpine moorland of bamboo, grass and dwarf fir trees.

Yeongsil Trail (영실탐방로; ☎747 9950; 3.7km; 2½hr) Wetter than the Eorimok Trail but has grand scenery – panoramas of green *oreum* (craters) and pinnacle rocks atop sheer cliffs as you hike through a dwarf fir forest, before reaching the mixed deciduous and evergreen forest lower down.

Donnaeko Trail (돈내고탐방로; ☎710 6920; 7km; 3½hr) This southern course provides coastal views of Seogwipo and runs through a red pine forest.

ℹ️ Getting There & Away

Bus 5.16 between Jeju-si and Seogwipo will take you to the Seongpanak, Gwaneum-sa and Donnaeko Trails. The bus stops directly opposite the start of the Seongpanak Trail, but to reach the start of the Gwaneum-sa Trail you'll have to transfer to an infrequent bus at Sancheondan (산천단) or walk 4km to the trailhead, past Gwaneum-sa Temple. Similarly it's around a 3.5km walk to the start of the Donnaeko Trail from the main road.

Bus 1100 to the Eorimok and Yeongsil Trails runs between Jeju-si and Jungmun along the West Cross-Island Hwy (Hwy 1139).

Sangumburi 산굼부리

Halfway between Jeju-si and Seongeup Folk Village, **Sangumburi** (www.sangumburi .net; adult/youth & child ₩3000/1000; ⊙8.30am-6.30pm) is an impressive volcanic crater, the second largest on the island, 350m in diameter and 100m deep. It only takes five minutes to walk up and another five minutes to circumnavigate the crater rim. That's all that's allowed, so it's a short stop. The crater is lush and forested with over 420 varieties of plants. In the distance, across the plains, are more of Jeju-do's *oreum* (craters). Buses (₩2000, 30 minutes, hourly) between Jeju-si, Seongeup and Pyoseon stop at the entrance to the crater.

WESTERN JEJU-DO

Frequent buses connect the main towns along Hwy 1132, but if you want to see inland sights, you're better off with your own transport or taking taxis.

Moseulpo 모슬포

Near the island's southwest tip, this sizeable fishing port is a good base for the area, being at the junction of Routes 10 and 11 on the Jeju Olle Trail, as well as the jumping-off point for Gapado and Marado.

Springflower Guesthouse (☎010-6816 8879; http://gojejuguesthouse.com; dm/d & tw/f ₩18,000/40,000/70,000; ❄@🛜), run by a friendly British-Korean couple, is a convivial place to stay, with the motto 'don't worry, be happy'; it's well set up for travellers and rates include breakfast.

To eat, you really can't go wrong at the seafood restaurants, many run by the fishermen's families. At **Mulguroeg** (물꾸럭; meals ₩8000; ⊙10am-9pm), which means 'octopus' in the local dialect, order the delicious *hanchimulhe,* a gazpacho-style soup with slivers of raw squid.

Gapado & Marado 가파도, 마라도

Jeju Olle Trail Route 10-1 (5km, two hours) encircles Gapado (pop 400), the nearer and larger of the two pizza-flat volcanic islands to Moseulpo. Taking even less time to walk around is windswept Marado (pop 200), Korea's most southerly point.

From Moseulpo, **ferries** (☎794 3500) depart twice daily for both Gapado (adult/child return ₩8000/4000, 10 minutes) and Marado (adult/child return ₩15,500/10,000, 20 minutes); call to check departure times as they frequently change with the seasons and weather.

Inland Sights

As well as the following, also check out the Jeju Peace Museum and the Ahop-gut Maeul Experience Yard in Nakcheon-ri (see p229).

👁 Sights

FREE O'Sulloc Tea Museum   MUSEUM
(오설록 녹차박물관; www.osulloc.com; ⊙10am-5pm) Overlooking the verdant plantation of one of Korea's largest growers of *nokcha* (green tea), this museum displays a collection of ancient tea implements, some of which date back to the 3rd century. You can stroll the fields, shop for its products, and enjoy green tea, a slice of green-tea cake and green-tea ice cream in its stylish cafe.

Jeju Glass Castle   THEME PARK
(유리의성; www.jejuglasscastle.com; adult/youth/child ₩9000/8000/7000; ⊙9am-6pm) This fascinating theme park features more than 350 glass sculptures created by worldwide artists, including the world's largest glass ball and the world's largest glass diamond. Highlights include an all-glass labyrinth, a mirror room covered in more than 5000 mirrors, glass *dolharubang* statues and a two-storey-tall glass beanstalk. Glass-blowing and glass-making glasses are also run here.

Spirited Garden   GARDENS
(생각하는 정원; www.spiritedgarden.com; adult/youth/child ₩9000/6000/5000; ⊙8am-6.30pm, to 10pm late Jul–mid-Aug) *Bunjae* (bonsai) trees may seem esoteric, but this bonsai park has some excellent examples, some 500 years old. It's the life's work of Mr Sung Bum-young, and has hosted dignitaries from all over the world.

PODO HOTEL & PINX GOLF CLUB

Whether you come to play golf at the **Pinx Golf Club** (☏792 8000; green fees week/weekend ₩110,000/144,000), admire the award-winning architecture by Japanese-Korean architect Itami Jun, or simply relax and enjoy the gently rounded *oreum*-scattered scenery of Central Jeju-do, a stay at the **Podo Hotel** (☏793 7000; www.thepinx.co.kr/podohotel; Western/Korean r incl breakfast from ₩300,000/385,000; ✳@🛜) has much to recommend it. There are only 26 rooms at the hotel, each with luxurious features such as *hinoki* wood baths and beautiful views from private terraces. Rates are higher on weekends and holidays.

Jeju Museum of Contemporary Art   MUSEUM
(제주현대미술관; www.jejumuseum.co.kr; adult/teenager/child ₩1000/500/300; ⏱9am-6pm Thu-Tue) At the heart of the Artists Village in Jeoji is this excellent art gallery. Permanent exhibitions of works by Kim Heng-sou and Park Kwang-jin are supplemented by regularly changing shows of other artists. The village is dotted with sculptures and engaging pieces of modern and traditional architecture where various artists live and work.

✖ Eating

Harubang Pizza   ITALIAN **$$**
(피자굽는돌하르방; ☏773 7273; mains ₩13,000-39,000; ⏱11am-8pm Tue-Sun) Tasty 1m-long pizzas topped with potato, sweet potato, pork *bulgogi* and *kimchi* are served in this old farmhouse, jazzed up with colourful murals, between Jeju Glass Castle and O'Sulloc Tea Museum. Next door is **Mayflower**, a self-serve cafe in a building crafted from whitewashed driftwood.

Hallim 한림

On the northwest coast this laid-back town is close by several lovely beaches including **Geumneung** (금능해변) and **Hyeopjae** (협재해변), both with white sand and crystal-clear waters, perfect for snorkelling.

Hallim Park (한림공원; www.hallimpark.co.kr; adult/youth/child ₩9000/600/5000; ⏱8.30am-7.30pm summer, to 6pm rest of year) offers a botanical and bonsai garden, a mini folk village, and two walks through a lava-tube cave – virtually a one-stop Jeju! The caves, **Hyeopjae** and **Ssangyong**, are part of a larger, 17km-long lava-tube system and are said to be the only such caves in the world to contain both stalagmites and stalactites.

Westbound circular buses (from Jeju-si ₩3000, 50 minutes; from Seogwipo ₩4500, 80 minutes) stop directly at the park entrance.

Jeollabuk-do

Includes »

Best Places to Stay

- » Seunggwangje (p262)
- » Jeonju Traditional Life Experience Park (p262)
- » Tirol Hotel (p265)

Best Places to Eat

- » Gapgiwon (p262)
- » Traditional Culture Centre (p262)
- » Hwarim Hoegwan (p264)

Why Go?

The southwestern province of Jeollabuk-do (전라북도) is Korea's rice bowl. As Korea's agricultural heartland, this fertile, green area has influenced Korean cuisine more than any other part of the country. For foodies, no trip to Korea is complete without eating your way through Jeollabuk-do. The provincial capital city of Jeonju is a must-stop for any fan of Korean food, especially for its most well-known export, *bibimbap,* a dish of rice, meat and vegetables served up by countless restaurants nationwide and abroad. Rural Jeollabuk-do is an outdoors-lover's paradise. Much of this province is parkland. With unspoilt national and provincial parks covering its beautiful mountains, this rural province offers some of Korea's finest get-away-from-it-all hikes and scenery. To top it all off, there are sandy beaches in West Sea islands such as Seonyudo and skiing on the slopes of Muju when you get tired of the rich cultural backdrop of temples and folk villages. What's there not to like?

When to Go

Jeonju

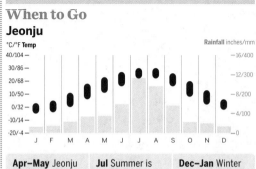

Apr–May Jeonju comes alive when the international film festival hits town.

Jul Summer is the best time to hit the beaches and islands.

Dec–Jan Winter means you'll be able to hit the slopes.

History

The Donghak rebellion, led by Chon Pong-jun, took place mainly in Jeollabuk-do in 1893 when a ragtag force of peasants and slaves seized Jeonju fortress and defeated King Gojong's army, before being destroyed by Japanese forces. Their demands included the freeing of slaves, better treatment of the *chonmin* (low-born), the redistribution of land, the abolition of taxes on fish and salt, and the punishment of corrupt government

officials. Jeollabuk-do and Jeollanam-do were one joint province until 1896; Jeonju was the capital of this combined province.

Jeonju 전주

♪063 / POP 643,000

Jeonju, the provincial capital, is famous for being the birthplace of both the Joseon dynasty and Korea's most well-known culinary delight, *bibimbap* (rice, meat, egg and

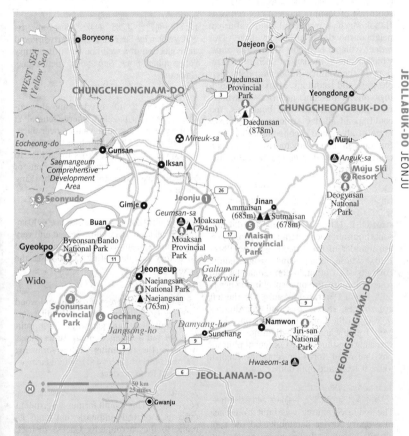

Jeollabuk-do Highlights

① Get lost exploring the back alleys of the fascinating **Jeonju Hanok Maeul** village (p260)

② Ski or snowboard the slopes at **Muju Ski Resort** (p265)

③ Zip round **Seonyudo** (p270) on a bicycle before relaxing on the beach

④ Amble through pretty **Seonunsan Provincial Park** (p268) to a giant Buddha carving on a cliff

⑤ Be amazed by the unique rock-pinnacle temple in **Maisan Provincial Park** (p264)

⑥ Visit the impressive Moyang Fortress and eerie dolmen sites in **Gochang** (p268)

vegetables with a hot sauce). Centrally located, the city is the perfect base from which to explore Jeollabuk-do as it's the regional hub for buses and trains. The central historical folk village has many outstanding *hanok* (traditional wooden homes) housing museums, cute teahouses and artisan workshops.

◉ Sights & Activities

Jeonju Hanok Maeul   NEIGHBOURHOOD
(전주한옥마을; http://hanok.jeonju.go.kr) Just southeast of Jeonju's modern city centre is Hanok Maeul, a wonderful historical urban neighbourhood untouched by time. This *maeul* (village) has more than 800 *hanok*, which is one of the largest such concentrations in the country. Residents retain their old ways and traditions. Many of the buildings contain museums, galleries, workshops, restaurants, teahouses and boutiques. You could spend all day exploring the narrow maze of alleys and architecture. Pick up a free English map at any tourist information centre. We've listed several places within the village to visit.

Gyeonggijeon
(경기전; ☑281 2790; Taejo-ro; adult/student/child ₩1000/700/500; ◷9am-6pm) Originally constructed in 1410, reconstructed in 1614 and containing a replica portrait of Yi Seong-gye, the founder of the Joseon dynasty (1392–1910), whose family came from Jeonju. Portraits of six other Joseon monarchs, and palanquins, are also on display in the newly built **Royal Portrait Museum**. On the left are shrines, storehouses and guardrooms relating to the Confucian rituals once held here. Treating ancestors with utmost respect was a cornerstone of the Confucian philosophy that ruled Korea for centuries. English tours at 10am and 3pm daily.

Jeondong Catholic Church
(전동성당; ☑284 322; Taejo-ro; admission free) The red-brick church was built by French missionary Xavier Baudounet on the spot where Korean Catholics were executed in 1781 and 1801. Built between 1908 and 1914, the architecture is a fusion of Asian, Byzantine and Romanesque styles. The stained-glass windows portray early martyrs.

Traditional Wine Museum
(전통술박물관; ☑287 6305; admission free; ◷9am-6pm Tue-Sun) Housed in a beautiful old *hanok,* the museum has a *gosori* (tradi-

tional still) and occasional classes on making *soju* (Korean vodka). You can also taste and buy traditional Korean liquors.

Jeonju Korean Paper Institute
(전주전통한지원; ☑232 6591; admission free; ◷9am-5pm) See sheets of *hanji* (handmade paper) being manufactured in the institute, housed in a gloriously atmospheric *hanok* down an alley. A slop of fibres in a big tank magically solidifies into paper. Purchase handmade paper products at the gift shop.

Gangam Calligraphy Museum
(강암서예관; ☑285 7442; admission free; ◷10am-5pm Tue-Sun) Houses the artwork and art collection of a well-known 20th-century calligrapher, Song Sung-yong (pen name, Gangam).

Omokdae
(오목대) On a hill overlooking the entire village is a pavilion where General Yi Seong-gye celebrated a victory over Japanese pirates in 1380, prior to his overthrow of the Goryeo dynasty. Cross the bridge to **Imokdae** (이목대), a monument to one of Yi Seong-gye's ancestors written by King Gojong.

Jeonju Hyanggyo
(전주향교; ☑288 4548; admission free; ◷10am-7pm) Stroll around a well-preserved and very atmospheric Confucian shrine, school and dormitory complex dating to 1603 (see the boxed text, p262).

Pungnam-mun   GATE
(풍남문) An impressive stone-and-wood gateway is all that remains of Jeonju's fortress wall and four gateways. First built in 1398 but renovated many times since, it marks the beginning of the sprawling **Nambu Market** (남부시장), where farmers' wives sell fresh produce.

Jeonju Gaeksa   HISTORIC BUILDING
(전주 객사) This rebuilt former government office is a central landmark that lends its name to the surrounding Gaeksa district, Jeonju's primary shopping and nightlife area.

Deokjin Park   PARK
(덕진공원; ☑281 2436; admission free; ◷5am-11pm) Join Korean couples who hire paddleboats in this charming park, in the north of the city, to view the lotus lilies in July. Buses 69, 70, 87 and 88 run here.

Jeonju

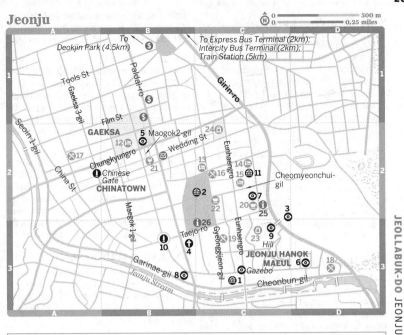

Jeonju

◎ **Sights**

◎ **Sleeping**

◎ **Eating**

◎ **Drinking**

◎ **Shopping**

◎ **Information**

🎇 Festivals & Events

Jeonju International Film Festival   FILM
(www.jiff.or.kr) Nine-day event every April/May
focusing mainly on indie, digital and experimental movies. Around 200 films from 40
countries shown in local cinema multiplexes.

Jeonju Sori Festival   MUSIC
(www.sorifestival.com) A week-long international music festival held every August in
the Hanok Maeul. The focus is on traditional
Korean music.

HYANGGYO & SEOWON

Hyanggyo were neighbourhood schools established by *yangban* (aristocrats) in the 1500s to prepare their sons for the *seowon* (Confucian academies), where the students took the all-important government service exams. The pupils studied Chinese characters and key Confucian texts. Over 600 *seowon* were spread across the country, making Korea more Confucian than China. In the 1860s Regent Heungseon Daewongun forced most of them to close as he reasserted the king's authority, but the buildings remain as symbols of Koreans' unwavering passion for education.

🛏 Sleeping

Budget and midrange hotels are located in the Gaeksa district; cheaper love motels surround the bus terminals and train station. For a truly unique experience, stay in a *hanok*: you'll find many littered around the Hanok Maeul. Look down alleys for English signs that say 'guesthouse'. Rooms start at ₩50,000.

Benikea Jeonju Hansung Tourist Motel
HOTEL **$$**

(전주한성관광호텔; ☑288 0014; www.hotel hansung.kr; Gaeksa; s/d incl breakfast ₩50,000/ 60,000; ❄@) This recently renovated hotel in the heart of the Gaeksa district offers Western and *ondol*-style rooms with TV and fridge. It's sparkling clean and modern, and staff speak English. Rooms facing the main drag can be noisy on weekends.

TOP CHOICE Seunggwangje
HANOK GUESTHOUSE **$$**

(승광제; ☑284 2323; r from ₩60,000; ❄) Live like a king at Jeonju's best *hanok*. The tiny rooms have TV, fridge, *yo* (padded quilt or mattress on the floor) and small, modern bathrooms. It's owned by English-speaking Lee Seok, a grandson of King Gojong, who lives in the adjoining *hanok*. It's a special place down an alley with royal photographs on display.

Jeonju Traditional Life Experience Park
HANOK GUESTHOUSE **$$$**

(전주한옥생활체험관; ☑287 6300; www.jj hanok.com; r ₩70,000-130,000; ❄) Stay in tiny bare rooms and sleep on a *yo* in this newly built but traditional-style *hanok*. Prices include a Korean-style breakfast and free use of a bicycle. There are also cultural activities such as kite-making and tea etiquette on offer.

Jeonju Guesthouse
HOSTEL **$**

(☑286 8886; dm ₩19,000-30,000, d ₩60,000-70,000; ❄@⏣) The town's only hostel is nothing special – pine-wood-heavy rooms look hastily put together – but it's a popular place to meet fellow travellers and the location on the edge of the Jeonju Hanok Maeul can't be beat.

Good Morning Motel
LOVE MOTEL **$**

(굿모닝모텔; ☑251 9948; r ₩30,000-35,000; ❄@) This big, blue, no-fuss motel has helpful staff and spacious rooms with modern, clean bathrooms. Rooms vary, so look at more than one – some have round, heated waterbeds. It's 50m east of the express bus terminal.

🍴 Eating & Drinking

For traditional fare, head to the restaurants and teahouses of Hanok Maeul. Modern restaurants, bars and Western fast-food chains are located in the Gaeksa district, Jeonju's prime nightlife spot.

Gapgiwon
KOREAN **$$**

(갑기원; bibimbap ₩12,000-1,3000; ⏲10am-9pm) You can put Jeonju's *bibimbap* claim-to-fame to the test in this Hanok restaurant. The version here comes served with raw or cooked beef and a dazzling array of *banchan* (side dishes). If you've got a big party and big stomachs, splash out for a *hanjeongsik* (banquet) meal (₩120,000).

Veteran
KOREAN **$**

(베테랑; dishes ₩4000-6000; ⏲10am-9pm) This 'veteran' of the Jeonju dining scene has been dishing out delicious *mandu* (만두; dumplings) and only four noodle dishes such as *kalguksu* (칼국수) since 1977. The setting is decidedly no-frills but who cares with food this cheap and good!

Sambaekjip
KOREAN **$**

(삼백집; meals ₩5000; ⏲24hr) This restaurant specialises in *kongnamul gukbap* (콩나물 국밥), a local Jeonju dish of rice, egg, bean sprouts and seasoning cooked with broth in a stone pot. It's said to be a hangover cure and comes with side dishes.

Traditional Culture Centre
KOREAN **$$$**

(전통문화센터; ☑280 7000; meals ₩10,000-200,000; ⏲11am-9pm) A stylish, upmarket restaurant popular with the older, well-heeled set offers Jeonju *bibimbap, galbi jeongsik*

(갈비정식; ribs and side dishes) or a full-on *hanjeongsik* (한정식; banquet). Next door is a teashop and a hall that hosts traditional music and dance shows.

Story
CAFE $
(83 Gyeonggijeon-gil; drinks ₩3000-4500; ⊙10am-10pm) This lovely little coffeehouse offers coffees, espresso drinks and tea against a backdrop of mismatched furniture.

Daho Teahouse
TEAHOUSE $
(다호찻집; teas from ₩4000; ⊙11am-midnight) The best of the *hanok* teahouses is down an alleyway and has rustic, goblin-sized rooms overlooking an attractive garden where birds flit around. Listen to ethereal music as you sip the excellent teas, such as *daechucha* (대추차; red date) and pink *omijacha* (오미자차; dried five-flavour berries).

Deepin
BAR $
(☑231 9695; Gaeksa; drinks from ₩3000; ⊙7pm-4am; ☎) A foreigner-friendly watering hole, this tiny, dark and smoky bar is the local expat hang-out with comfy couches, cool music and cheap beer. From the Jeonju Gaeksa, cross the main road, turn right, take the first left and go to the end of the street; Deepin is on the left, just past the bricked Wedding St.

🛍 Shopping
The bustling Dongbu and Nambu Markets sell everything under the sun. Malls and indie fashion outlets are dotted around the youthful Gaeksa district, surrounded by beauty shops and Western restaurants.

Craft Treasures Centre
CRAFT
(공예품전시관; ☑285 4403; Taejo-ro; ⊙10am-7pm) A large complex of shops that sell lanterns, boxes, ties, clothing and paper products. The courtyard is a pleasant spot for a rest.

ℹ Information
Citibank (Daedong-gil) Global ATM and foreign-currency exchange.
Jeonju website (www.jeonju.go.kr)
KB Bank (Paldal-ro) Global ATM and foreign-currency exchange.
Main post office (⊙9am-6pm Mon-Fri, to 4.30pm Sat)
Shinhan Bank (Paldal-ro) Global ATM and foreign-currency exchange.
Tourist information centre Main (☑282 1338; Taejo-ro); bus terminal (☑281 2739; outside Express bus terminal); Taejo-ro (☑232 6293; Gyeonggijeon entrance) Free internet access.

JEOLLABUK-DO JEONJU

BUS DEPARTURES FROM JEONJU

Express bus terminal destinations

DESTINATION	PRICE (₩)	DURATION (HR)	FREQUENCY
Busan	15,400	4	hourly
Daegu	17,300	3½	every 2hr
Daejeon	5400	1½	every 30min
Gwangju	6300	1¼	every 30min
Seoul	12,200	3	every 15min

Intercity bus terminal destinations

DESTINATION	PRICE (₩)	DURATION	FREQUENCY
Buan	7000	1hr	every 15min
Daedunsan	9000	1¼hr	5 daily
Gochang	6000	1½hr	hourly
Gunsan	5200	1hr	every 15min
Gurye (Jirisan)	9000	2hr	10 daily
Gyeokpo	8300	2hr	13 daily
Jeongeup	3900	1hr	every 15min
Jinan	4200	50min	every 20min
Muju	9000	1½hr	hourly

ⓘ Getting There & Away

Bus

For bus departures from the express and inter-city bus terminals, see the boxed text, p263.

Train

There is one direct KTX (Korea Train Express; ₩30,900, two hours, 6.05pm) from Seoul and three trains to/from Yongsan station (₩30,600, two hours, 5.40am, 8.05am, 10.35am) in Seoul. *Saemaul* (express; ₩25,000, three hours, 8.35am) and *Mugung-hwa* (semi-express; ₩16,800, 3½ hours, six daily) also run from Yongsan. Trains also run south to Jeollanam-do.

ⓘ Getting Around

Numerous buses (₩1100) such as 5-1, 5-2 and 79 run from near the bus terminals and along Girin-ro to the city centre, while buses 12.60, 508, 536, 552 and others run to the train station. Taxis are plentiful and cheap (fares start at ₩2200).

Geumsan-Sa & Moaksan Provincial Park 금산사, 모악산도립공원

☑063

This **park** (☎548 1734; adult/youth/child ₩3000/2000/1000; ☺8am-7pm), which contains Moaksan mountain (794m), is only 40 minutes from Jeonju and is a popular destination for hikers on weekends. The main attraction is **Geumsan-sa**, a temple that dates back to AD 599. To stay in the temple (₩80,000 including meals), contact the **tourist information office** (☎548 1330, 010-9476 0796; ☺9am-6pm, closed 2 weekdays per week). The **Maitreya Hall** is a three-storey wooden structure built in 1635 that retains an air of antiquity. Inside is an impressive Mireuk-sa Buddha, the Buddha of the Future. On the left is a museum and a hall with carvings of 500 unique Buddha helpers. Near the entrance, sip soothing tea in the serene, Zen-style atmosphere of **Sanjang Dawon** (산중다원; teas ₩5000-8000).

The usual climbing route up Moaksan goes past the temple, up Janggundae and along the ridge to the peak. The hike is relatively easy and you can be up and down in three hours.

Overlooking the car park on the left is **Hwarim Hoegwan** (화림회관; meals ₩1000-215,000), a restaurant where you can sit inside or outside under the wisteria. Choose between local black pig (흙돼지주물럭), *tokkitang* (토끼탕; spicy rabbit soup) or roast *ori* (오리; duck).

Geumsan-sa and Moaksan are easily reached by bus from Jeonju. Local bus 79 (₩1700, 45 minutes, every 40 minutes) can be picked up along Girin-ro, Jeonju's main street. Don't get on buses that go to the other end of Moaksan park; ask for Geumsan-sa, from where it's a 20-minute walk to the temple.

Daedunsan Provincial Park 대둔산도립공원

☑063

Yet another of Korea's beautiful parks, **Daedunsan** (☎263 9949; admission free; ☺8am-6pm) offers craggy peaks with spectacular views over the surrounding countryside. Although relatively small, it's one of Korea's most scenic mountain areas.

Aside from the superb views, the climb to the summit of Daedunsan (878m) along steep, stony tracks is an adventure in itself, as you cross over a 50m-long cable bridge stretched precariously between two rock pinnacles and then climb up a steep and long steel-cable stairway. Vertigo sufferers are advised to take the alternative route! Otherwise, a five-minute **cable-car ride** (one way/return ₩5000/8000) saves you an hour of uphill hiking.

Daedunsan Tourist Hotel (☎263 1260; fax 263 8069; r ₩65,000-75,000; ✳@) has an *oncheon* (hot-spring bath) and a sauna (₩5000) that is perfect for soaking your aching hiking muscles. You can relax further, playing pool or four-ball in the bar (open 1pm to midnight) or sitting in an armchair with a view.

Many restaurants serve *sanchae bibimbap* (산채비빔밥; rice, egg, meat and mountain vegies) and the usual country-style food.

Daedunsan can be reached by bus from Jeonju (₩5900, 1¼ hour, five daily) or from Seodaejeon bus terminal in Daejeon (₩3500, 40 minutes, five daily).

Maisan Provincial Park 마이산도립공원

☑063

This is a must-see **park** (☎433 3313; adult/youth/child ₩2000/1500/900; ☺sunrise-sunset). Maisan means 'Horse Ears Mountain', which refers to two extraordinary rocky peaks as they appear from the access town of Jinan. The east peak, **Sutmaisan** (Male Maisan), is 678m while the west peak, **Ammaisan** (Female Maisan), is slightly taller at 685m. Both ears are made of conglomerate rock, which is rare in Korea. Only Ammaisan can be scaled. It's a steep half-hour climb, but grinning grandmas make it to the top without any problem.

Tap-sa (탑사; Pagoda Temple), at the base of the female ear, has a unique sculptural garden of 80 stone towers or pinnacles that were piled up by a Buddhist mystic, Yi Kapmyong (1860–1957). Up to 15m in height, they represent religious ideas about the universe and miraculously they never seem to crumble, although no cement has been used. The diverse stone towers are an intriguing sight, evoking the atmosphere of a surreal world.

En route to Tap-sa is **Unsu-sa** (은수사), a temple with a Dangun shrine, a centuries-old pear tree and attractive gardens, and you can even bang the big drum.

An easy 1½-hour, 1.7km hike with a splendid view at the top starts by Tap-sa and takes you back to the car park at the entrance. In April the cherry trees around the nearby lake burst into blossom.

Frequent buses (₩4200, 50 minutes, every 20 minutes) run along the scenic route from Jeonju to the small town of Jinan (진안). From Jinan, buses (₩1200, five minutes, hourly) run to the Maisan Provincial Park entrance, from where it's a 40-minute walk to Tap-sa.

Deogyusan National Park & Muju Ski Resort
덕유산국립공원, 무주리조트

☑063

Deogyusan National Park (☑322 3174; http://deogyu.knps.or.kr/eng; adult/youth/child ₩3200/1200/600; ☺sunrise-sunset) is a year-round playground offering skiing, hiking, biking and golf.

The park is best known as the home of **Muju Ski Resort** (☑322 9000; www.mujuresort.com). Opened in 1990, Muju is the only Korean ski resort located in a national park, with 30 runs including the highest altitude and longest slope (6.1km) in the country. Snowboarding, sledding, night and mogul skiing and lessons in English are on offer. The ski season runs mid-December to April.

When the snow melts, lace up your hiking boots and explore the park on foot. The tourist village at **Gucheon-dong** is the start of the park's best hike (1¾ hours, 6km) that follows the river and valley past 20 beauty spots to a small temple, **Baengnyeon-sa** (백련사). Fairies are said to slide down rainbows to bathe in the pools. The enchanting trail continues to a strenuous, steep, 1½-hour ascent of **Hyangjeokbong** (1614m). Yew trees, azaleas and alpine flowers adorn the summit.

In the northwest of the park is **Jeoksang Sanseong**, a fortress rebuilt in the 17th century. Encircled by the 8km wall are the ruins of a Joseon-dynasty archive, a reservoir and **Anguk-sa** (안국사), a temple built in the 1860s. Buses only run along the main road to Gucheon-dong, so you must get off at the access road and walk (4km) or hitchhike.

Although winter is the high season, a few of the shops, restaurants, bars and attractions here are open year-round, including the **gondola** (adult/child return ₩12,000/9000; ☺9.30am-4.30pm) to the peak of **Seolcheonbong** (1520m). **Mountain bikes** (per hour adult/child ₩10,000/8000; ☺9am-7pm) can be hired to ride round a special track.

Muju is home to the **Muju Firefly Festival** (http://english.firefly.or.kr), an environmental awareness event that is held in mid-June. **Taekwondo Park** (www.tpf.kr), a theme park devoted to Korea's national sport, is set to open by the time this book is published.

🛏 Sleeping & Eating

The resort has top-notch dining, drinking and sleeping options in all price ranges; the best place to stay in the park is **Tirol Hotel** (티롤호텔; ☑320 7200; www.mujuresort.com; r from ₩380,000; ❄@), with its Austrian-styled chalets and condominium apartments. Cheaper *minbak* accommodation (private homes with rooms for rent) is located in the tourist village near the park entrance. For the best deals here, buy a package that includes accommodation, ski and equipment hire, transport and lift tickets.

❶ Getting There & Away

The nondescript town of Muju is the gateway to Deogyusan National Park and Muju Ski Resort. Muju is connected by bus to Daejeon (₩700,

Deogyusan National Park

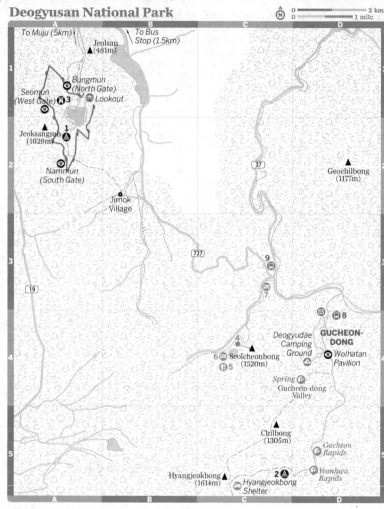

Deogyusan National Park

one hour, hourly), Geumsan (₩2800, one hour, hourly), Jeonju (₩9000, 1½ hours, hourly), Seoul (₩14,700, three hours, six daily) and other cities.

From Muju, take the Gucheon-dong bus (₩3500, 30 minutes, 10 daily), which drops you near the tourist village, or take the resort shuttle bus (free, one hour, six daily, more frequent in ski season).

Naejangsan National Park
내장산국립공원

📞063

The mountainous ridge in this **park** (📞538 7875; http://naejang.knps.or.kr/eng; adult/youth/ child ₩3000/1200/700; ☉sunrise-sunset) is shaped like an amphitheatre. A spider's web of trails leads up to the ridge, but the fastest way up is by **cable car** (adult/child one way ₩4000/3000, return ₩7000/4000; ☉9.30am-5.30pm). The hike around the rim is strenuous, but with splendid views on a fine day. The trail itself is a roller-coaster ride, going up and down six main peaks and numerous small ones before you reach Seoraebong (622m), from where you head back down to the access road.

There are metal ladders, bridges and railings to help you scramble over the rocky parts. Give yourself four hours to hike around the amphitheatre, with an hour more for breaks and a picnic. If you find the hike too difficult, turn right at any time and follow one of the many trails back down to **Naejang-sa**.

An easy and picturesque 2km walk from Naejang-sa goes through Geumsong valley, which becomes a steep ravine before leading to a cave, a natural rock arch and a waterfall.

A tourist village clusters around the **park entrance**, but it's not usually busy except in October. **Camping** (per person ₩2) is available before the tourist village. The **tourist information centre** (📞537 1330) has free internet access.

Naejangsan National Park

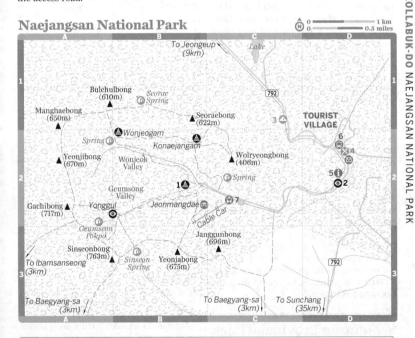

JEOLLABUK-DO NAEJANGSAN NATIONAL PARK

Naejangsan National Park

Buses (₩3000, one hour, every 15 minutes) run from Jeonju to Jeongeup. From just outside the bus terminal on the left, local bus 171 (₩1300, 30 minutes, every 20 minutes) runs to Naejangsan National Park. It's a 2km, 20-minute walk between the ticket office and the cable-car terminal.

Gochang 고창

☑063

Perched on a hill overlooking the small village of Gochang, **Moyang Fortress** (모양성; ☑560 2710; adult/youth/child ₩1000/800/600; ☺9am-7pm Mar-Oct, to 5pm Nov-Feb) is an impressive structure built in 1453 during the Joseon dynasty. The ivy-covered, 1.6km-long fortress wall with three gates surrounds a complex of reconstructed buildings including a prison and pavilion. A local legend says that if a woman walks three times around the wall with a stone on her head during a leap year, she will never become ill and will enter paradise. To the right of the fortress is the **Pansori Museum** (☑560 2761; adult/youth/child ₩800/500/free; ☺9am-6pm Tue-Sun), with memorabilia on this unique solo opera musical form.

The hills surrounding Gochang are eerily filled with thousands of dolmen, prehistoric tombs from the Bronze and Iron Ages now registered with Unesco. It's worth visiting the **Gochang Dolmen Site** (adult/youth/child ₩3000/2000/1000; ☺9am-5pm Tue-Sun), where you can wander trails leading in and around the huge boulders dotting the lush green hills.

Buses serve Gochang from Jeonju (₩6000, 1½ hours, hourly) and Gwangju (₩5000, one hour, every 30 minutes). To get to the Gochang Dolmen Site, take bus 5 (₩1150, 20 minutes, five daily) from the Gochang bus terminal.

Seonunsan Provincial Park
선운산도립공원

☑063

This pretty **park** (☑563 3450; adult/youth/child ₩3000/2000/1000; ☺sunrise-sunset) has always been popular with monks and poets alike. A 20-minute walk along a rocky, tree-lined river brings you to **Seonun-sa** (선운사). Just behind the temple is a 500-year-old **camellia forest** that flowers around the end of April, although a few blooms linger into summer.

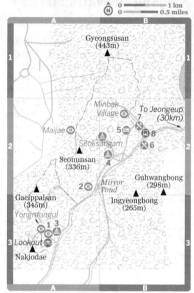

Seonunsan Provincial Park

Seonunsan Provincial Park

◉ Sights
1 Buddha Rock Carving A3
2 Camellia Forest A2
3 Dosol-am Hermitage...........................A3
4 Seonun-sa..B2

◉ Sleeping
5 Seonunsan Youth Hostel B2

◉ Eating
6 Food Stalls B2
7 Restaurants B2

◉ Transport
8 Bus Stop B2

Another 35 minutes further on is **Dosol-am hermitage** and just beyond is a giant **Buddha rock carving** dating to the Goryeo dynasty; the amazing image is carved into the cliff face and is 15m high. Despite centuries of erosion the Buddha is still an impressive sight, a testament to the faith of ancient times. On the right is a very narrow grotto, and next to it stairs lead up to a tiny shrine and a great view. From the Buddha, you can climb **Nakjodae** and carry on to **Gaeippalsan** and **Seonunsan**, with views of the West Sea, before heading back down to Seonun-sa.

The tourist village near the park entrance has a handful of lodgings, restaurants and shops. The **Seonunsan Youth Hostel** (선운산유스호스텔; ☎561 3333; r ₩50,000-60,000; ❄) has friendly English-speaking staff and clean rooms that fill up fast on weekends.

Buses (₩6000, 1½ hours, hourly) run from Jeonju to Gochang, from where buses (₩3000, 30 minutes, hourly) run to Seonunsan.

Byeonsan Bando National Park 변산반도국립공원

☎063
This coastal **park** (☎582 7808; http://byeonsan.knps.or.kr; adult/youth/child ₩2000/800/500; ☉sunrise-sunset) contains the large temple of **Naeso-sa** (내소사), originally built in 633 and last renovated in the 19th century. Take a close look at the main hall, especially the lattice doors, the painting behind the Buddha statues, and the intricately carved and painted ceiling with musical instruments, flowers and dragons among the motifs. You can do a Templestay here. Such is the popularity of this temple that the path leading to the temple has a Family Mart and a cute cafe serving espresso coffees.

Hike up the unpaved road to **Cheongnyeonam** (청련암; 20 minutes) for sea views; another 15 minutes brings you to the ridge where you turn left for Gwaneumbong. From the peak follow the path, which goes up and down and over rocks for an hour until you reach **Jikso Pokpo** (직소폭포), a 30m-high waterfall with a large pool. Another pretty spot is **Seonyeotang** (선녀탕, Angel Pool). From there walk along the unpaved access road past the ruins of **Silsang-sa** (실상사), destroyed during the Korean War. Note that return buses are infrequent. For a more challenging hike head up **Nakjodae**, which is famous for its sunset views.

Also part of the national park, beaches along the coast attract crowds in summer. **Byeonsan Beach** is a wide beach of fine sand, clear water and backed by pine trees. Further south, **Gyeokpo Beach** has dramatic stratified cliffs and caves, as well as seafood restaurants. The beach is safe for swimming but the sea disappears at low tide. Gyeokpo is also the starting point for ferries to the island of **Wido**, which has a sandy beach; every house in the little fishing village of Jinli is a *minbak*-cum-restaurant.

Take a bus from Jeonju to Buan (₩4700, one hour, every 15 minutes) and then a local bus to Naeso-sa (₩2000, one hour, every 30

JEOLLABUK-DO BYEONSAN BANDO NATIONAL PARK

Byeonsan Bando National Park

minutes). Buses (₩8300, two hours, 13 daily) also run from Jeonju to Gyeokpo Beach and the ferry terminal.

Ferries (☑581 0023) go from Gyeokpo to Wido (₩9000 one way, 40 minutes, three daily September to April, six daily May to August).

Gunsan & Seonyudo
군산, 선유도

☑063

The industrial port city of **Gunsan** was a former Japanese colonial town and now boasts Korea's largest collection of period buildings. Visit the well-curated **Gunsan Modern History Museum** (군산근대역사박물관; ☑450 4384; admission free; ☺9am-5pm Tue-Sun) to learn about the city's rich past before grabbing a tourist map to seek out remaining colonial buildings stretching out around the waterfront. A taxi from the bus terminal to the museum costs ₩5000.

A 43km ferry trip from Gunsan brings you to the relaxing tropical island of **Seonyudo**, situated amid 60 mostly uninhabited small islands. When the tide is in and the sun is out, the views from here are unbelievably beautiful. Today there are more bicycle-hire stalls than fishing boats; you can hire bicycles (₩3000 per hour) to pedal around the laid-back fishing villages on Seonyudo and the three islands that are linked to it by bridges. Six-person *bungbungka* (auto rickshaws; per hour ₩30,000) take pensioner parties on fun tours.

The main attraction is the 1.6km beach, a 10-minute walk from the ferry pier, on a spit of soft sand with great island views on both sides. All the island's peaks can be hiked for panoramic views of islands: just look out for a trail or steps leading up to the top.

You'll find plenty of inexpensive restaurants and *minbak* (rooms from ₩40,000) in the main fishing village just before the beach.

Buses (₩5200, one hour, every 15 minutes) leave from Jeonju for Gunsan. Ferries (one way adult/child ₩16,650/8500, 1½ hours, 9am, 11.30am, 1.30pm and 4.10pm) leave from the **Yeonan Yeogaek** (Gunsan Coastal Ferry Terminal; 연안여객터미널; ☑467 6000), a 15-minute, ₩9000 taxi ride from the Gunsan bus terminal.

Chungcheongnam-do

Includes »

Best Places to Eat

» Gudurae Dolssambap
(p283)

» Mushroom (p276)

» Gomanaru (p279)

Best Places to Stay

» Lotte Buyeo Resort (p283)

» Hisikdang (p285)

» Kum-Kang Tourist Hotel
(p279)

Why Go?

Much of the buzz in the region has focused on a new administrative city of Sejong, but until it gets up and running, it's Daejeon that's the capital manqué, with flashy KTX services, all the trappings of modern Korean life and all of its lack of urban charms as well. More interesting are the small towns left in its wake: little Geumsan is the hub of the ginseng industry, while Gongju and tiny Buyeo were once capitals of the ancient Baekje dynasty. The latter towns have retained a surprising number of old fortresses, tombs and relics. Daecheon Beach in the south is widely considered to be the best on the western coast, while travellers preferring some solitude can hop on a ferry to one of the nearby islands. To the north is Taean Haean Marine National Park, dotted with more islands, beaches and the promise of wind-whipped fresh air – just what most day-trippers from Seoul are looking for.

When to Go
Daejeon

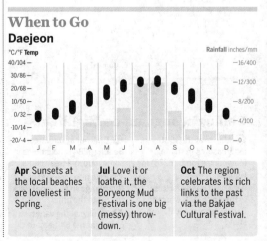

Apr Sunsets at the local beaches are loveliest in Spring.

Jul Love it or loathe it, the Boryeong Mud Festival is one big (messy) throwdown.

Oct The region celebrates its rich links to the past via the Bakjae Cultural Festival.

History

When the Baekje dynasty (57 BC–AD 668) was pushed south by an aggressive Goguryeo kingdom in AD 475, this is where the Baekje ended up, establishing their capital first in Ungjin (modern-day Gongju), then moving further south to Sabi (modern-day Buyeo). Its culture was fairly sophisticated, but after Sabi fell to the joint army of Shilla and China in AD 660, the region passed into obscurity.

Daejeon 대전

📞042 / POP 1.5 MILLION

The fifth-largest city in South Korea, Daejeon is the locus of science and technology and government administration, spread across a cookie-cutter landscape of looming apartment buildings, squat research establishments and traffic-snarled streets. It's large enough to merit its own telephone code, subway and KTX trains, but

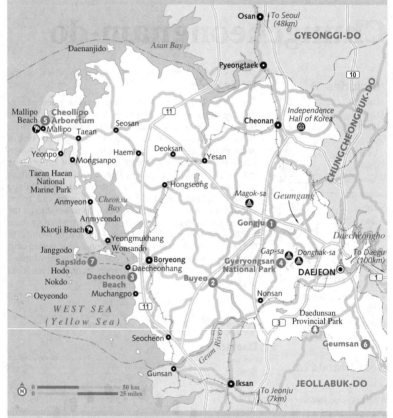

Chungcheongnam-do Highlights

❶ Marvel at the 1500-year-old treasures from King Muryeong's tomb (p278) in **Gongju**

❷ Climb up the fortress in **Buyeo** (p280) where the Baekje army made its last stand

❸ Chill out at **Daecheon Beach** (p284) and indulge in some mud spa treatments

❹ Hike from one end of **Gyeryongsan National Park** (p276) to the other

❺ Rejoice at the variety of flora at the 64-hectare

Cheollipo Arboretum (p286)

❻ Go gaga over ginseng in the trading town of **Geumsan** (p281)

❼ Unwind at a beachfront hut in tiny **Sapsido** (p285)

it possesses few attractions for travellers other than the Yuseong Hot Springs and the nearby Gyeryongsan National Park and Daedunsan Provincial Park in Jeollabuk-do (p264).

Daejeon's transformation from small town into overgrown suburb of Seoul began in the 1970s, when science institutes began to set up shop (including KAIST, aka the 'MIT of South Korea'). In the decades since, it's shown no signs of slowing down or acquiring any graces. Though it's less abrasive than Seoul can be, there's little reason to linger unless you're either teaching English here or using it as a base to explore the rest of the province.

◉ Sights & Activities

Daejeon's attractions, such as they are, belong strictly in the 'if you have time to kill or kids to amuse' category. The 'old downtown' area of Eunhaeng-dong (은행동) is near Daejeon train station and Jungang Market, while the 'new downtown' of Dunsan-dong (둔산동), 5km from Eunhaeng-dong, is home to City Hall, the unimaginatively named Government Complex, and new shopping and entertainment areas.

Yuseong Hot Springs　　　NEIGHBOURHOOD
(유성 온천) The cluttered western neighbourhood of Yuseong has many hotels and *oncheon* (hot-spring spas) that draw their water from sources 350m underground. **Yousung Spa** (☎820 0100; admission ₩5000; ⏰5am-10pm), at the eponymous hotel (유성 호텔), has indoor and outdoor pools, with small waterfalls. Across the road is the spiffier **Hotel Riviera** (호텔 리베라; ☎824 4050; admission ₩13,000; ⏰6am-10pm), with sauna and spa facilities.

Take bus 102 or 106 (₩1200, 25 minutes, every 15 minutes) from outside the express bus terminal. After the bus passes Chungnam University, look out for Hotel Hongin on the left side of the road and get off at the stop for Yuseong Spa station, Exit 6. Walk backwards to the intersection and turn left, following Oncheonmunhwa-gil to the hotels.

🛏 Sleeping

The motel clump around the Dongdaejeon intercity bus terminal has some seedy corners but new motels come up all the time.

Limousine Motel　　　LOVE MOTEL $
(리무진모텔; ☎621 1004; Youngtap 3-gil; r ₩40,000; ❋@) A love motel with all the trim-

mings: spacious rooms with huge flat-screen TV, bathtub, contemporary furnishings and windows that can be shuttered for complete privacy. Weekend rates ₩10,000 extra.

Jinju Park　　　MOTEL $
(진주파크; ☎624 4776; Yongjeon Gosok 1-gil; r ₩20,000;❋) Next to Limousine Motel, this *yeogwan* (motel with small private bathroom) in a pink three-storey building has the cheapest, tiniest rooms around. The flat-screen TVs are larger than the windows! Weekend rates ₩5000 extra.

🍴 Eating

For cheap bites, visit the food outlets in the Daejeon bus terminal complex. Dunsandong is packed with Korean faves such as barbecue and fried chicken.

Yeongsuni　　　KOREAN $
(영순이; ☎633 4520; meals ₩4000-15,000) Choose from a range of hearty set menus with *shabu kalguksu* (샤브칼국수), where you cook your own meat and noodles in a spicy mushroom and vegetable soup. More elaborate sets come with seafood (해물), *sangchussam* (상추쌈; grilled meats wrapped in vegetable leaves) or *bossam* (보쌈; steamed pork and *kimchi* eaten *ssam*-style; served with the set menu). Look for a mushroom-headed caricature giving the thumbs up.

Daejeon

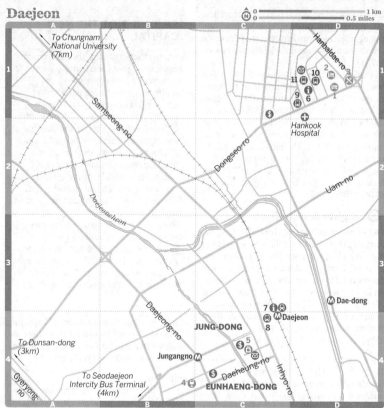

CHUNGCHEONGNAM-DO DAEJEON

Daejeon

🛏 Sleeping
1	Jinju Park	D1
2	Limousine Motel	D1

🍽 Eating
	Subuk Sikdang	(see 9)
3	Yeongsuni	D1

🍷 Drinking
4	Brickhouse	B4

🛍 Shopping
5	Jungang Market	C4

ℹ Information
6	Tourist Information Centre	D1
7	Tourist Information Centre	C3

ℹ Transport
8	Bus Stop	C4
9	Bus Stop	D1
10	Dongdaejeon Intercity Bus Terminal	D1
11	Express Bus Terminal	D1

Subuk Sikdang   KOREAN $
(수북식당; Yongjeongosok 4-gil; meals ₩5000-8000) Right next to the express bus terminal, this restaurant has plenty of Korean comfort food, such as *kimchi jjigae* (*kimchi* stew), *galbitang* (beef-rib soup) and *bibimbap* (rice with vegetables, meat and egg).

Daejeon Cantina   MEXICAN $
(www.facebook.com/daejeoncantina; meals from ₩8000; ☺6pm-late Tue-Sun) A cavernous bar-restaurant run by a chirpy Mexican. As expected, the food is authentic. Even if you don't fancy Mexican, you can expect sports on TV, live bands and a variety of other

expat-oriented events. To find it, walk backwards about 50m from the bus stop at Time-World Galleria and go up the lane across the road. Pass Lucky Strike on the corner two lanes ahead and hang a right at the next lane. Walk ahead 100m and keep an eye out for a yellow sign on the 2nd floor of a building to the left.

Drinking

There are two lively areas: in the 'old downtown' of Eunhaeng-dong, near Jungangno subway, and in the 'new downtown' of Dunsan-dong near the mall TimeWorld Galleria. The area around Chungnam National University has bars and cheap restaurants.

Brickhouse   BAR
(☑223 6515; www.facebook.com/groups/2101638 0541; drinks from ₩5000; ◎9pm till late Wed-Sun) Rollicking sports bar, big-screen TVs and all. Even when games aren't on, regulars come by for darts and pool, or just good pub grub.

Lucky Strike   BAR
(Dunsan-dong; drinks from ₩4000-12,000) The snug wooden bar plays lots of classic rock and the bartenders make some fine cocktails (try the mojitos). To find it, walk backwards about 50m from the bus stop at TimeWorld Galleria and go up the lane across the road. Lucky Strike is on the corner two lanes ahead.

Shopping

Bargain buys can be found at the sprawling Jungang Market, while young people clog the pedestrianised streets of Eunhaeng-dong. The more upscale shopping area is in Dunsan-dong around TimeWorld Galleria.

ℹ Information

Chungnam National University Hospital
(☑220 7114; www.cnuh.co.kr; Munhwaro)
Daejeon website (www.daejeon.go.kr/language/english)
KB Bank (Daejeong-no) Exchanges foreign currency and has a global ATM.
Post office There are post offices on Inhyoro and opposite Dongdaejeon intercity bus terminal.
SC (Jungangno) Exchanges foreign currency and has a global ATM.
Shinhan Bank (Dongseo-ro) Exchanges foreign currency. Another branch in the Daejeon bus terminal complex.
Tourist information centre Dongdaejeon inter-city bus terminal (☑632 1338); Daejeon train station (☑221 1905); Seodaejeon train station (☑523 1338)

ℹ Getting There & Away

Air
The nearest airport is at Cheongju (p292), 40km north. Buses run from Dongdaejeon intercity bus terminal to the airport (₩3500, 45 minutes, six daily). There are also buses to Incheon International Airport (₩24,300, three hours, every 20 minutes).

Bus
Daejeon has three bus terminals: Seodaejeon (west) intercity bus terminal, and Dongdaejeon (east) intercity bus terminal and the express bus terminal, both located in the new Daejeon bus terminal complex. See p276 for bus times.

Train
Daejeon train station serves the main line between Seoul and Busan. KTX trains run from Seoul (₩23,700, 50 minutes, every 20 minutes) in the early mornings and evenings, and from Busan (₩26,700, two hours, every 30 minutes) all day. From Seoul, there are also hourly *Saemaul* (16,000, 1¾ hours) and *Mugunghwa* (₩10,800, two hours) services to Daejeon.

Seodaejeon train station, in the west of the city, serves the lines to Mokpo and Yeosu. There are KTX (₩23,800, 45 minutes, four daily) trains from Seoul, and KTX (₩23,400, one hour, five daily) and *Mugunghwa* (₩10,600, two hours, five daily) trains from Yongsan Station (Seoul) to Seodaejeon.

ℹ Getting Around

Bus
City buses are very regular and bus stops have GPS-enabled signs with arrival information. From outside the express bus terminal, useful buses (₩1200, every 10 to 15 minutes) include the following:
Bus 2, 201, 501 or 701 (15 minutes) To Daejeon train station and Eunhaeng-dong. The bus stop for the latter is along Jungangno after Daejeon train station.
Bus 102 or 106 (25 minutes) To Yuseong.
Bus 106 (20 minutes) To City Hall and Dunsan-dong. The bus stop for the latter is just after TimeWorld Galleria.
Bus 701 (35 minutes) To Seodaejeon intercity bus terminal.

Subway
Daejeon's subway line (per trip ₩1200) has 22 stations. Useful stops for travellers are Daejeon station, Jungangno (near Eunhaeng-dong), City Hall and Yuseong Spa.

Taxi
Cheap and plentiful. Fares start at ₩2300.

CHUNGCHEONGNAM-DO DAEJEON

BUS DEPARTURES FROM DAEJEON

Express bus terminal departures

DESTINATION	PRICE (₩)	DURATION (HR)	FREQUENCY
Busan	22,300	3¼	every 2hr
Daegu	13,400	2	every 2hr
Gwangju	15,600	3	hourly
Seoul	9200	2	every 30min

Dongdaejeon intercity bus terminal departures

DESTINATION	PRICE (₩)	DURATION	FREQUENCY
Cheongju	3600	50min	every 15min
Gongju	4000	1hr	every 40min

Seodaejeon intercity bus terminal departures

DESTINATION	PRICE (₩)	DURATION	FREQUENCY
Boryeong	11,500	3hr	hourly
Buyeo	6300	1¼hr	every 30min
Daedunsan	3500	40min	3 daily
Jeonju	5700	1½hr	9 daily

Gyeryongsan National Park 계룡산국립공원

☑041

This **park** (☑825 3003; http://gyeryong.knps.or .kr/Gyeryongsan_eng/; adult/youth/child ₩2000/ 700/400; ☺6am-7pm) is one of the smallest parks in South Korea and it's possible to hike from one end to the other in less than a day. The name is just as unassuming – Gyeryongsan means 'Rooster Dragon Mountain', because locals thought the mountain resembled a dragon with a rooster's head. There are two park entrances: the eastern one closer to Daejeon, and the western one closer to Gongju.

EASTERN ENTRANCE

A gentle 15-minute climb from the entrance is the nunnery **Donghak-sa**, said to have been founded during the Shilla era, although the buildings date only from the early 19th century. From here, you can hike up to the pagodas at **Nammaetap**, then on to **Sambulbong** (775m) and the peak **Gwaneumbong** (816m), before returning to Donghak-sa via the waterfall Eunseon Pokpo. The route is about 6.5km; allow four hours in all. Alternatively, from Gwaneumbong you can push on west to **Yeoncheongbong** (738m) and descend to the western park entrance via the temple Gap-sa (3.5km, 2½ hours).

The tourist village has restaurants, accommodation and a **tourist information centre**; the latter provides handy schedules (Korean only) for buses to Daejeon, Gongju and other towns. For accommodation, head up the lane beside the park entrance to **Geurintel** (그린텔; ☑825 8210; r ₩40,000-50,000; ✴), which has better rooms than its drab exterior suggests. **Camping** (☑825 3005; per night ₩3000-6000) is also available.

The mushroom-shaped restaurant **Mushroom** (머쉬룸; meals ₩7000-24,000) looks like an escapee from a Disney film set and serves its namesake ingredient in *beoseot jeongol* (버섯전골) or with *ssambap* (머쉬 룸쌈밥; rice and lettuce wraps). Single diners can try the *beoseot deopbap* (버섯덮밥; mushrooms with sauce on rice) or *sanchae bibimbap* (*bibimbap* made with mountain vegetables). Mushroom meals may include meat.

From outside Daejeon's express bus terminal, take bus 102 or 106 and get off at the bus stop for Yuseong Spa station, Exit 6.

Walk up to the street corner and turn right, heading for the bus stop for Yuseong Spa station, Exit 5. Bus 107 (₩1200, 25 minutes, every 20 minutes) goes to the eastern end of the park.

WESTERN ENTRANCE

The temple Gap-sa is an easy 15-minute walk from the entrance. The main hall contains three gleaming Buddha statues, while a smaller shrine houses three shamanist deities – Chilseong, Sansin and Dokseong. The temple is also known for its bronze bell, crafted in 1584, with both Shilla and Joseon characteristics. From Gap-sa you can ascend Sambulbong directly; en route are the small waterfall Yongmun Pokpo and the small hermitage Sinheungam (3km, 2¾ hours).

The tourist village is very small, consisting only of a few restaurants, shops and Kyeryongsan Gapsa Youth Hostel (계룡산갑사 유스호스텔; ☏856 4666; www.kapsayouthhostel .com; dm/f ₩13,000/45,000;❄), where guests sleep on a *yo* (padded quilt). Weekend rates rise by ₩3000 (dorm) and ₩15,000 (room). Restaurants serve vegetable-laden meals, such as *sannamul jjigae baekban* (산나물 찌개백반; wild vegetable stew with rice and side dishes) and *pyogo beoseot deopbap* (표 고버섯 덮밥; shiitake mushroom with sauce on rice).

From Gongju's local bus terminal, take a bus for Gap-sa (₩1200, 30 minutes, hourly), the western park entrance, or Donghak-sa (₩1200, 30 minutes, four daily), the eastern park entrance.

Gongju 공주

041 / POP 121,600

Once the capital of Korea's oldest dynasty Baekje, dusty Gongju came to national attention in 1971 with the discovery of the Baekje king Muryeong's tomb. These days it's more often mentioned in the same breath as its native son, Major League baseball player Park Chan Ho. The town

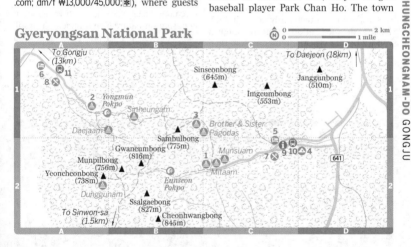

Gyeryongsan National Park

is divided by the river Geumgang: the old part in the south, where all the Baekje monuments are, seems to be drifting along at its own pace, while the new part in the north looks much like any Korean town, with modern high-rises and love motels.

◉ Sights

Tomb of King Muryeong   ARCHAEOLOGICAL SITE
(백제 무령왕릉; Muryeongwangneung; ☎856 0331; adult/youth/child ₩1500/1000/700; ◌9am-6pm) On a hillside lie seven ancient Baekje tombs, including that of King Muryeong. No grand mausoleums here – the tombs are modest and grass covered, looking like gentle hillocks. They're sealed for protection, but the aptly named **Replica Museum** contains full-size replicas of the tombs that you can enter. Look for the intricate tomb murals in Tomb No 6, the only such example known among Baekje sites.

The museum also has replicas of some artefacts from King Muryeong's tomb, which was discovered, miraculously intact, in 1971. There's detailed information in English and it's best to visit the museum first, then take a wander around the tombs. To see the actual artefacts, visit the Gongju National Museum.

Bus 125 (₩1100, 15 minutes, every 15 minutes) from the new intercity bus terminal travels here. Catch bus 1 or 25 (₩1100, five minutes, every 15 minutes) from Gongsanseong to the tombs, or walk the distance in about 20 minutes. A taxi costs ₩2500.

Gongsanseong   FORTRESS
(공산성; adult/youth/child ₩1200/800/600; ◌9am-6pm Mar-Oct, 9am-5pm Nov-Feb) This commanding hilltop fortress is a reminder of a time when Gongju (then called Ungjin) was Baekje's capital. It was during the Joseon dynasty that the original mud structure was rebuilt into today's stone fortress.

Within the walls lie numerous pavilions and building sites. The best views are in the northwest overlooking the river, from an observation platform or **Manharu Pavilion** near the temple **Yeongeun-sa**, whose warrior monks fought valiantly against the Japanese in the 1590s.

At the main entrance gate of **Geumseoru**, a 10-minute Baekje changing-of-the-guard ceremony takes place hourly between 11am and 4pm on Saturday and Sunday in April, May, June, September and October. A good time to visit is in the late afternoon, to catch the sunset glow upon Geumseoru; linger for dinner at Gomanaru (see p279) and you'll also enjoy a stunning floodlit view of the fortress.

Gongju

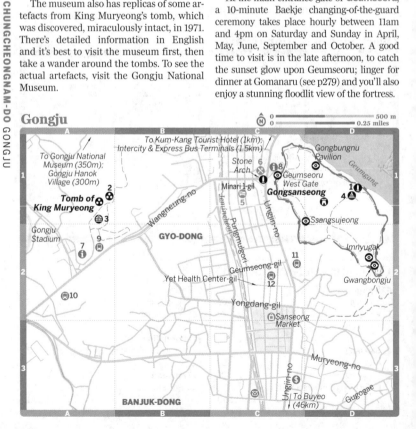

FREE **Gongju National Museum** MUSEUM
(국립공주박물관; ☑850 6300; http://gongju
.museum.go.kr; ◷9am-6pm Tue-Fri, 9am-7pm Sat
& Sun) This excellent museum exhibits the
treasures discovered in the tomb of King
Muryeong. Only a few hundred of the 2906
tomb artefacts are on display here, but together with some videos (with English subtitles) they paint a vivid picture of Baekje
culture. The museum's exhibits include the
intricate and distinctive gold diadem ornaments that you'll see images of all over
Gongju, as well as many small decorative
objects, jewellery and Chinese ceramics. A
re-created **hanok village** was under construction beside the museum. When complete, there will be restaurants, a hotel and
cultural activities on offer.

The museum is a 15-minute walk north
from the royal tombs or a ₩2500 taxi ride
from the fortress entrance.

✖ Festivals & Events

Baekje Cultural Festival CULTURAL
(www.baekje.org) Gongju hosts this extravagant festival in October each odd-numbered
year, with a huge parade, games, traditional music and dancing, and a memorial
ceremony for its erstwhile kings. The
festival is held in Buyeo in even-numbered
years.

⌷ Sleeping

Kum-Kang Tourist Hotel HOTEL **$$**
(금강관광 호텔; ☑852 1071; www.hotel-kum
kang.com; r incl breakfast ₩40,000-50,000; ✳@)
Located on the northern side of the river,
this excellent hotel has neat rooms with
large bathrooms and is a class above the
usual love motels.

I-Motel MOTEL **$**
(아이 모텔; ☑853 1130; Bldg 7, Minari 2-gil; r
₩35,000; ✳@) One of a dozen motels clus-
tered opposite the fortress, this one is run
by a friendly older couple, and has a homey
feel with clean rooms, huge TVs and com-
puters. Look for the huge 'I' sign surrounded
by swans.

✖ Eating & Drinking

There's a cluster of *naengmyeon* eateries
(serving buckwheat noodles in cold broth)
around the stone arch in front of Gong-
sanseong, offering meals from ₩4000 to
₩6000. There are also numerous eateries
around the intercity bus terminal. If you're
itching for a drink, head to the back gate
of Gongju National University (공주대 후
문; Gongjudae humun), which has scads of
bars, cheap eateries and cafes servicing the
university crowd.

Gomanaru KOREAN **$$**
(고마나루; Ungjin-no; meals ₩6000-40,000; ◱)
Get a table by the window with a fortress
view at this charming restaurant. Locals
come for the *ssambap* (assorted ingredients
with rice and lettuce wraps) and *dolsotbap*
(hotpot rice). The smoked duck specialities
are good, too.

ⓘ Information

Gongju website (www.gonju.go.kr)
Tourist information centre (☑856 7700)
Beside the car park at the Gongsanseong
entrance and a smaller booth near the path
to King Muryeong's tomb. Enquire at the
former about the bus tours in English, held
every Sunday and second and fourth Saturday
from April to November. The tour is free, but
museum and fortress admission charges
still apply.

CHUNGCHEONGNAM-DO GONGJU

BUS DEPARTURES FROM GONGJU

DESTINATION	PRICE (₩)	DURATION	FREQUENCY
Boryeong	7100	1¾hr	every 30min
Buyeo	4000	45min	every 30min
Cheonan	5000	1hr	every 30min
Daejeon	4000	1hr	every 10min
Seoul	7700	1¾hr	every 40min

❶ Getting There & Away

The old intercity bus terminal south of Gosan-seong has buses to Seoul and Daejeon. The new intercity and express bus terminals are together north of the river. For departures from the terminals, see the boxed text above.

Around Gongju

🎵 041

MAGOK-SA

A pleasant half-day trip from Gongju, this utterly serene **temple** (마곡사; 🎵841 6221; www.magoksa.or.kr; adult/youth/child ₩2000/1500/1000; ◷6am-6.30pm) enjoys a pastoral setting beside a river. It was founded near the end of the Baekje dynasty in the 7th century and, like most Korean temples, has had its buildings restored and reconstructed through the years. Unlike most temples, however, its extant buildings are being allowed to age gracefully, and there are quite a few atmospheric halls, stumpy pagodas and pavilions.

The elaborate entry gates Cheonwang-mun and Haetalmun feature colourful statues of various deities and bodhisattvas. Cross the 'mind-washing bridge' to reach the main hall, behind which stands a rare wooden two-storey prayer hall, Daeungbojeon.

From Magok-sa, three hiking trails head up the nearby hills (there's a signboard with a map, in Korean only), passing small hermitages. The longest trail (10km, 4½ hours) hits the two peaks, **Nabalbong** (나발봉; 417m) and **Hwarinbong** (활인봉; 423m).

If the idyllic, hassle-free setting is appealing, there are two sharp motels nearby. **Cello Motel** (첼로 모텔; 🎵841 7977; ❄) and **Magok Motel** (마곡모텔; 🎵841 0042; www.magokmotel.com; ❄) are along the access road to the temple, with good rooms at ₩40,000

(add ₩10,000 on weekends). It's also possible to arrange a Templestay at Magok-sa.

The tourist village is small. The restaurants serve typical country fare (₩10,000 to ₩25,000): *sanchae bibimbap, pyogo jjigae jeongsik* (표고찌개정식; shiitake mushroom stew with side dishes) and *tokkitang* (토끼탕; spicy rabbit soup). The one opposite Cello Motel is particularly good.

Magok-sa is 25km from Gongju. Buses (₩1100, 45 minutes, hourly) run from Gongju's local bus terminal and the temple is a 20-minute walk from the tourist village along a road flanked by a stream.

Buyeo 부여

🎵 041 / POP 84,000

It's smaller and more of a backwater than Gongju, yet Buyeo has just as many historical Baekje sites and relics. King Seong, a statue of whom presides over the roundabout in the town centre, moved the capital here in AD 538, when it was known as Sabi. It lasted till AD 660, when the combined Shilla-Tang army destroyed it.

Today Buyeo is a compact, walkable town, saddled with fewer Korean chain stores than most. New buildings cannot be taller than five storeys and it's the kind of place where you'll stumble across children playing in the streets after school.

◉ Sights

Busosanseong   FORTRESS
(부소산성; adult/youth/child ₩2000/1100/1000; ◷7am-7pm Mar-Oct, 8am-5pm Nov-Feb) This mountain fortress covers the forested hill of Busosan (106m) and shielded the Baekje capital of Sabi within its walls. Structures such as the **Banwollu Tower** offer lovely views of the surrounding countryside. The fortress is best approached from the southern entrance off Wangungno.

One shrine, Samchung-sa, is dedicated to three loyal Baekje court officials, including General Gyebaek. Despite being outnumbered 10 to one, he led his army of 5000 in a last stand against the final Shilla and Chinese onslaught in AD 660. The Baekje army dauntlessly repulsed four enemy attacks but were defeated in the fifth – the *coup de grâce* for the kingdom.

In response, it is said, on the northern side of the fortress 3000 court ladies threw themselves off a cliff into the river Baengmagang, rather than submit to the conquering armies. The rock where they jumped is now called Nakhwa-am, 'falling flowers rock', in their honour; it also offers the best view of the area.

From Nakhwa-am there's a rocky and somewhat steep path down to the tiny temple at the bottom of the cliff, Goran-sa. Behind it is a spring that provided the favourite drinking water of Baekje kings. Slaves collecting the water had to present it along with a leaf from a nearby plant that only grows near here, to show that the water came from this spring.

At Goran-sa, ferries (adult/child one way ₩4000/2200, return ₩6000/3000, ☺sunrise-sunset) head to Gudurae sculpture park (구두래공원). The trip takes 10 minutes. From Gudurae it's a 15-minute walk to the town centre.

FREE Buyeo National Museum MUSEUM
(국립부여박물관; ☎833 8562; http://buyeo.museum.go.kr; ☺9am-6pm Tue-Sun) This museum houses one of the best collections of Baekje artefacts. It has extensive English captions, making it a good place to get a primer on pre-Baekje and Baekje culture. The highlight of the collection is a glittering Baekje-era incense burner. Weighing 12kg, the burner and its pedestal are covered with incredibly intricate and well-preserved metalwork, crested with the legendary *bonghwang* bird.

Baekje Royal Tombs ARCHAEOLOGICAL SITE
(백제왕릉; adult/youth/child ₩1000/600/400; ☺8am-6pm Mar-Oct, 8am-5pm Nov-Feb) Dating from AD 538 to 660, these seven royal tombs are less impressive than those in Gongju (p278), but you can peer into Tomb No 1, where paintings on the walls and ceiling have

GAGA OVER GINSENG

It's stumpish and a woody colour, with wispy roots trailing from its ends. Use your imagination and you might see the shape of a body, complete with limbs, perhaps even a head-shaped tip with thinning 'hair'. No wonder the Chinese call it ginseng (literally, 'man root'). To the Koreans it's *insam* (인삼), and they have been cultivating it for over 1500 years. It's credited with myriad health benefits, from relieving pain and fatigue to curing cancer and improving sexual stamina.

Most foreigners encounter ginseng in *samgyetang* (ginseng chicken soup), but it's an ingredient in many dishes and also ingested in tea, liquor or capsules, or by the slice. The centre of the Korean ginseng business is Geumsan (금산; www.geumsan.go.kr), which despite its size (population 22,000) handles 80% of the ginseng trade. There are hundreds of stores, from mom-and-pop operations to wholesalers, and you'll find ginseng sold raw (*susam*), as an extract, in shampoo and soap, and in tea, candy, biscuits and chocolate. The street vendors make fresh *insam twigim* (인삼튀김; fried ginseng in batter; ₩1500), which you can wash down with *insam makgeolli* (인삼막걸리; rice wine made with ginseng; ₩2000).

If you're buying ginseng, the most prized variety is *hongsam* or red ginseng (홍삼), which is four to six years old and has been steamed and dried to concentrate its medicinal properties. More common is *baeksam* or white ginseng (백삼), a less processed four-year-old version. One *chae* (750g) of ginseng costs ₩10,000 to ₩75,000, depending on its quality and grade.

The best days to visit Geumsan are on market days every 2nd, 7th, 12th, 17th, 22nd and 27th days of the month. In September the town hosts a 10-day Insam Festival, with tours and activities to show how ginseng is grown, harvested, processed and served.

To get to Geumsan, take an intercity bus from Daejeon's Dongdaejeon intercity bus terminal (₩3800, one hour, every 15 minutes) or Seoul's Express Bus Terminal (₩11,700, 2¾ hours, every two hours). After you exit the Geumsan bus terminal, turn left and follow the canal for about 10 minutes. When you see SAE-Kumsan Hospital, turn right onto the road Bihoro. The market lies ahead, after you cross the wide road Insamno.

CHUNGCHEONGNAM-DO BUYEO

Buyeo

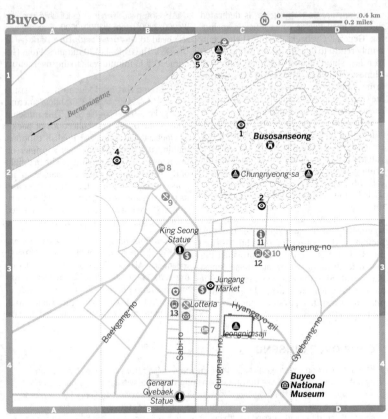

been restored. This is the only tomb here with a painted interior and it depicts the four celestial creatures that guard the compass points (dragon, tiger, tortoise and phoenix).

There's an on-site **museum** with a small-scale model of the oldest tomb, believed to be that of King Seong (who installed the Baekje capital at Buyeo). Outside is the now-empty temple site, where the famous Baekje incense burner was unearthed in 1993. The tombs are on a hillside 3km east of Buyeo. Take a bus (₩1100, five minutes, every 30 minutes) from Wangungno, opposite Busosanseong. It heads to Nonsan (논산) and has no number.

Baekje Cultural Land　　　THEME PARK
(백제역사문화관; ☏830 3400; www.bhm.or.kr; adult/youth/child ₩4000/3000/2000; ☺9am-6pm, closed Mon) This newly opened 'theme park', north across the river, is devoted to Baekje culture and has performances, re-creations of palaces, houses and other structures of the period, and a 'living' village featuring art and craft demonstrations. The open-air space is brutally hot in summer. The ticket includes entry to the informative **Baekje Historical Museum**. Buses are irregular, so grab a taxi (₩7000) from town.

🛏 Sleeping

There are plenty of motels clustered around the bus terminal in the centre of town. Many look rundown, but aren't as seedy as they appear.

Lotte Buyeo Resort　　　HOTEL $$$
(롯데부여리조트; ☏939 1000; www.lottebuyeoresort.com; r from ₩270,000; ❄@≋) Located opposite Baekje Cultural Land, this high-end condo-style hotel by conglomerate Lotte is a hunk of gleaming glass and concrete complete with ultraplush and modern rooms on par with the best in Seoul. A shopping complex was being built next door at the time of research.

Arirang Motel　　　MOTEL $$
(아리랑 모텔; ☏832 5656; r ₩50,000-80,000; ❄@) It looks as generic as its neighbours, but this motel has sleek, large rooms with modern decor. Deluxe rooms have an attached living room! It's run by a cheerful *ajumma* (middle-aged woman); staff will clean the room daily if you stay for more than one night.

Samjeong Buyeo Youth Hostel　　　HOSTEL $
(삼정부여유스호스텔; ☏835 3101; dm/f ₩16,000/44,000; ❄≋) You're as likely to stumble upon a bunch of kids on a field trip as you are a wedding party at this airy hostel. Dorm rooms have two double bunks and good bathrooms. Family rooms are of motel standard and have twin beds.

🍴 Eating & Drinking

The road between Gudurae sculpture park and the town centre is lined with restaurants and cafes.

Gudurae Dolssambap　　　KOREAN $$
(meals ₩7000-19,000) This quirky, cosy establishment is decorated with classic movie posters (in Korean) for *Ben Hur* and *Spartacus*. The menu here features delicious *dolsotbap* and *ssambap*, or get the best of both worlds with *dolssambap* (hotpot rice and lettuce wraps), served with succulent fried pork. English menus are available.

House of Baekje　　　KOREAN $$
(백제의 집; meals ₩7000-18,000) This busy restaurant serves generous banquet-style meals. The house specialities are dishes with duck, such as *ori mabap* (오리마밥; rice cooked in a stone pot with *bulgogi*). Hungry diners can order the *jeongsik* version of their dishes (ie with an abundant spread of side dishes).

ℹ Information

Buyeo website (www.buyeo.go.kr)
Tourist information centre (☏830 2523) with English-speaking staff is beside the entrance to Busosanseong and at the Buyeo National Museum.

ℹ Getting There & Away

For bus departures from Buyeo bus terminal, see the boxed text below.

BUS DEPARTURES FROM BUYEO

DESTINATION	PRICE (₩)	DURATION	FREQUENCY
Boryeong	4800	1hr	8 daily
Cheongju	8600	2½hr	every 45min
Daejeon	6600	1hr	every 20min
Gongju	4000	45min	every 30min
Seoul	14,400	2¾hr	every 30min

Boryeong 보령

📞 041 / POP 93,350

Boryeong is the gateway to Daecheon Beach (10km away) and the harbour Daecheon-hang (a further 2km), from where ferries sail to a dozen rural islands. The buses that connect Boryeong bus terminal and train station with Daecheon Beach continue to the harbour.

ℹ️ Information

The **tourist information centre** (📞 932 2023; www.boryeong.chungnam.kr) is inside Dae-cheon train station (yes, it's in Boryeong, not Daecheon Beach). Interpretation services for English (📞 010-5438 4865), Chinese (📞 010-2031 2270) and Japanese (📞 010-5098 7799) are available.

ℹ️ Getting There & Away

Bus

For bus departures from Boryeong, see the boxed text below.

Train

The train station is located across a field from the bus terminal. Regular *Saemaul* (17,400, 2¾ hours, seven daily) and *Mugunghwa* (₩11,700, 2¾ hours, nine daily) trains run between Daecheon station and Yongsan station in Seoul.

Daecheon Beach
대천해수욕장

📞 041

This popular strip of almost golden-hued sand runs 3.5km long and is about 100m wide during low tide. The main hub of activity is at its southern end, near the **Civil Tower Plaza** (시민탑 광장), but in summer the entire stretch gets overrun with beachgoers, especially during the increasingly bacchanalian Boryeong Mud Festival (see the boxed text, p285).

Though it's well-supplied with motels, restaurants, bars, cafes and *norae-bang* (karaoke rooms), Daecheon Beach is less a proper town than a resort outpost, surrounded by rice paddies and the sea. Developed only in the 1990s, it has all the aesthetic finesse of a tawdry Las Vegas – think neon nightscapes and plastic palm trees, with more hotels and amenities in the works. If it gets too touristy, head to the harbour **Daecheonhang** (대천항), which has more rustic seafood restaurants.

🏃 Activities

In summer there's lots to do at the beach: waterskiing, canoeing, windsurfing, horse-and-carriage rides, and speedboat, banana-boat and jet-ski rides.

Boryeong Mud Skincare Center   SPA
(보령 머드체험관; 📞 931 4022; adult/child ₩5000/3000; ⏰8am-6pm) A modern facility with a sauna, mud bath and aroma spa. Massages and mud packs cost up to ₩20,000 extra, and you can buy mud soaps and other cosmetics from the shop. All the products are made from local mud, said to be full of health-giving minerals. It's on the beachfront near the Civil Tower Plaza; if you're approaching from Boryeong, it's to the left of the access road.

🛏️ Sleeping

The older establishments are near Civil Tower Plaza, while Fountain Plaza (분수광장) to the north has newer outfits. Prices are an additional ₩10,000 to ₩20,000 on weekends and easily triple in summer.

Motel Coconuts   MOTEL $$
(모텔코코넛스; 📞 934 6595; r ₩50,000;❄🀄) Decorated in bright colours and with funky bed-linen prints, this motel has a contemporary zing lacking in most of its competitors. Rooms on the upper level might have a snatch of sea view. It's beside the Lotteria to the left of the access road from Boryeong.

BUS DEPARTURES FROM BORYEONG

DESTINATION	PRICE (₩)	DURATION (HR)	FREQUENCY
Buyeo	4800	1	hourly
Daejeon	11,200	2½	hourly
Jeonju	8900	2½	7 daily
Seoul	10,400	2½	hourly

MUD, GLORIOUS MUD

Every July Daecheon Beach is the principal venue for the nine-day **Boryeong Mud Festival** (www.boryeongmudfestival.com), which since its debut in 1997 has grown to attract over 1.5 million attendees. What began as a way of promoting the health benefits of the mud, which is rich in germanium and other minerals, has since developed a reputation for the unabashed, alcohol-fuelled frolics of expats, US GIs and international travellers, who make up about half the festival crowd.

After being baptised in a vat of the oozing grey stuff, participants can enter the 'mud prison' and get doused with buckets of warmed mud. There's a mud super-slide, a mud rain tunnel and a very muddy game of soccer played on the mudflats. Every evening there's a concert or rave on the beach and the festival is bookended by parades and fireworks.

Many English-speaking volunteers are on hand and there are free lockers, a campsite and basic clean-up facilities, making this one of the most foreigner-friendly events held in Korea. Accommodation gets booked up months in advance, even in Boryeong, so many come for the day or on tours run by outfits such as **Adventure Korea** (www.adventurekorea.com).

Singung Motel　　　　　　　　MOTEL **$$**
(신궁 모텔; ☏931 0900; r ₩50,000; ❄@) Only the higher floors have sea views, but this motel is quiet yet close to the main strip. Rooms are small, clean and comfortable. It's to the right of the access road, behind Opera Motel.

Legrand Fun Beach Hotel　　　　HOTEL **$$$**
(레그랜드 펀비치; ☏939 9000; www.fun-beach.com; r/ste ₩90,000/126,000; ❄@☒) The priciest option in Daecheon Beach has carpeted rooms with contemporary decor and cables for internet access. Its waterpark (admission from ₩33,000) has numerous rides and a full sauna.

✖ Eating

Restaurants lining the beachfront have aquariums of fish, eels, crabs and shellfish outside, and you can get a platter of *modeumhoe* (모듬회; assorted raw fish) or *jogae modeumgui* (조개 모듬구이; mixed shellfish), to be barbecued at your table, for ₩30,000 to ₩40,000. Try the local speciality *kkotgejjim* (꽃게찜; steamed blue crab), or round off your meal with some spicy *haemultang* (해물탕; assorted seafood soup). Grab a seat on the upper floor to enjoy the sunsets over the sea.

❶ Information

The **tourist information centre** (☏931 4022; ⊙8am-8pm) is in the Boryeong Mud Skincare Center. For interpretation services, call the numbers given for Boryeong (p284).

❶ Getting There & Away

Buses (₩1600, every 10 minutes) run from Boryeong bus terminal and Daecheon train station in Boryeong to Daecheon Beach and on to Daecheonhang (harbour). All the places mentioned here are at the Civil Tower Plaza; get off at the first stop in Daecheon Beach, opposite Legrand Fun Beach Hotel. A taxi will cost ₩20,000.

Sapsido 삽시도

☏041

If you like undeveloped beaches, farmhouse villages surrounded by rice paddies and the salty smell of fish, skip out to this small island, just 13km from Daecheon. There isn't much to do here except hit the beach or wander from the Witmaeul marina (윗마을 선착장) where the ferry stops to the main village near Sulttung marina (술뚱 선착장). You'll see locals mending fishing nets, collecting shellfish at low tide or working in the rice paddies.

The pace speeds up in summer, with three beaches and over 50 *minbak* drawing visitors from the mainland. The nearest beach to Sulttung is **Geomeolneomeo Beach** (거멀너머 해수욕장), a 15-minute walk past the primary school. Curving between two rocky headlands, this flat, wide beach is backed by sand dunes and fir trees. Except at high tide, you can clamber over the rocks on the left to the smaller **Jinneomeo Beach** (진너머 해수욕장).

Along the southern coast is the sweeping **Bamseom Beach** (밤섬 해수욕장), the largest of the three. Follow the road to the

Sapsido

CHUNGCHEONGNAM-DO TAEAN HAEAN NATIONAL MARINE PARK

left of the *minbak* village at Witmaeul marina. None of the beaches have restrooms or showers.

There are plenty of *minbak* but prices spike in summer. A fab choice is **Hisikdang** (히식당; ☑010-3920-7140; r ₩50,000; ✳), with basic *ondol* cottages right on Geomeolneomeo Beach. Another option is the centrally located **Haedotneun** (해돋는민박; ☑935 1617; r ₩50,000), a cheery red-brick *minbak* with rooms that are of motel standard, equipped with a fridge and kitchenette.

Most visitors bring a picnic or eat at their *minbak*. **Haedotneun** (meals ₩6000-25,000) has a homey dining area in the front room and the menu depends on the catch of the day.

ℹ Getting There & Around

Ferries (☑934 8896; one way adult/child ₩9900/4900) run from Daecheon Ferry Terminal to Sapsido at 7.30am, 1pm and 4pm. The trip takes 40 minutes, longer if the ferry is rerouted to other islands first. The inbound ferry goes to Witmaeul marina in the south and departs from Sulttung marina in the north. The island has no public transport (and indeed, hardly any cars). It's a 40-minute walk from one end of the island to the other.

The last ferry returns directly to Daecheon at 5.25pm. If you take an earlier one at 8.10am or 1.45pm, the return trip takes 1½ to two hours as the ferry stops at other islands – Janggodo, Godaedo and Anmyeondo – en route.

The Daecheon Ferry Terminal (대천 연안 여객선 터미널) is at the harbour Daecheonhang. Buses for Daecheon Beach all continue to the harbour. Other ferries from Daecheon (adult

₩4500 to ₩16,800, child ₩2300 to ₩8100) run to even more remote islands – Hojado, Wonsando, Hodo, Nokdo and Oeyeondo – where few foreigners have ventured. Ferries may be delayed or cancelled on misty or rainy days.

Taean Haean National Marine Park
태안해안국립공원

☑041

This beautiful **marine park** (☑672 9737; http://taean.knps.or.kr; admission free; ☉sunrise-sunset) covers 327 sq km of land and sea, with 130 islands and islets, and over 30 beaches. It was badly hit by South Korea's worst-ever oil spill in December 2007, but the coast has been cleaned up and fishing and tourism have resumed with aplomb.

The largest island is **Anmyeondo** (안면도; www.anmyondo.com, in Korean) and of its many beaches, one of the best is **Kkotji Beach** (꽃지해수욕장), a gentle 3.2km-long stretch that's a glorious 300m wide at low tide and popular with photographers at sunset. You can get there by bus (₩1100, 15 minutes, hourly) from the bus terminal at the island's main town, **Anmyeon** (안면).

You can get to Anmyeon by bus from Seoul (₩11,500, 2¾ hours, hourly), Daejeon (₩11,600, three hours, three daily) and Taean (₩2500, one hour, every 30 minutes). But the most picturesque journey is to take a ferry from Daecheon Ferry Terminal (₩8050, six daily) or Sapsido (₩7600, three daily) bound for Yeongmokhang (영목항). The journey takes 45 minutes to two hours depending on the ferry route. Once you disembark at Yeongmokhang, turn right and then fork left for the two-minute uphill walk to the bus stop. The bus for Anmyeon (₩2500, one hour, hourly) takes a rugged, circuitous route along backcountry roads between rice paddies and rustic farmhouses.

Closer to the town of **Taean** (태안; www.taean.go.kr) is **Mallipo Beach** (만리포), not quite as stunning as Kkotji but still an attractive getaway, fringed by pine trees. While development is ramping up around the beachfront it's still a peaceful option compared to Daecheon and Kkotji.

Avid gardeners or photographers may want to head another 2.5km up the road to the privately owned **Cheollipo Arbore-**

HE CAME, HE SAW, HE PLANTED

The Cheollipo Arboretum has gained international recognition as an outstanding botanical institution, yet it was founded and built by a man without formal training in that field. American Carl Ferris Miller was a banker in Seoul when he bought his first plot of farmland in Cheollipo in the 1970s, intending it as a weekend retreat. He began planting trees and studying botany on his own – then gradually acquired more land and more plant specimens. By the time he died in 2002 at the age of 81, Cheollipo Arboretum had become an exquisite showcase of over 7000 botanical species from over 60 countries, laid out with diligent care across 64 hectares of lush coastal property.

Miller had settled in South Korea after the Korean War and became a naturalised Korean citizen in 1979, renaming himself Min Byung Gal. He also relocated several Korean *hanok* (traditional wooden homes) to the arboretum in order to preserve them. After his death, he was buried, fittingly, in his beloved gardens.

tum (천리포수목원; ☏672 9982; www.chollipo .org, in Korean; Mon-Fri ₩7000, Sat & Sun ₩8000; ◷9am-4.30pm, closed Nov-Mar), an impressive garden that grew out of an American-turned-Korean-citizen's dedication to his plants (see the boxed text above).

There are motels along all these beaches, with rooms starting from ₩40,000. The Cheollipo Arboretum has *hanok* rooms starting from ₩80,000.

You can get to Mallipo Beach by local bus (₩1850, 25 minutes, hourly) from Taean's bus terminal, or directly from Seoul (₩12,000, three hours, seven daily). Taean is well served by buses from Seoul (₩10,000, 2¼ hours, every 30 minutes) and Daejeon (₩11,000, 2¾ hours, hourly).

Chungcheongbuk-do

Best Places to Eat

» Sangdangjip (p291)
» Satgatchon (p296)
» Doljip Sikdang (p299)

Best Places to Stay

» Birosanjang (p294)
» Hotel Lin (p291)
» Rivertel (p299)

Why Go?

The only landlocked province in the South, Chungbuk (충청북도) as it's known informally, is largely mountainous and agricultural. The province is a sleepy sort of place and its major cities are not particularly compelling, though bibliophiles may be inclined to make a pilgrimage to Cheongju, where in 1377 Buddhist monks printed the world's oldest extant book with moveable metal type.

The province's charms can better be appreciated in its smaller towns and three national parks, which are also home to an assortment of intriguing Buddhist sites. There's plenty to see and do here: climb the azalea-covered peaks of Sobaeksan, descend into the otherworldly caverns of Gosu Donggul, or simply savour the views along the river and at nearby Chungju Lake. Visit Guin-sa, a Buddhist temple ensconced in a tight valley, as imposing as the mountain slopes on either side of it. If you have a few days to while away, this is the place to do it.

When to Go
Cheongju

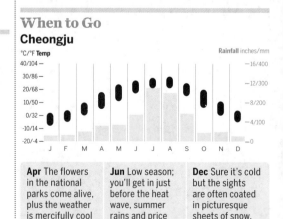

°C/°F Temp | Rainfall inches/mm

Apr The flowers in the national parks come alive, plus the weather is mercifully cool for hiking.

Jun Low season; you'll get in just before the heat wave, summer rains and price hikes.

Dec Sure it's cold but the sights are often coated in picturesque sheets of snow.

Cheongju 청주

♩043 / POP 668,000

Like most provincial capitals, Cheongju (http://english.cjcity.net) – not to be confused with nearby Chungju – is not terribly captivating. Its primary claim to fame is as the place where the world's oldest book was printed using moveable metal type.

As a modern city it's somewhat redeemed by a youthful vibe, thanks to its universities, but if not for its proximity to Songnisan National Park and presidential villa Cheongnamdae, there'd be little reason to stop here.

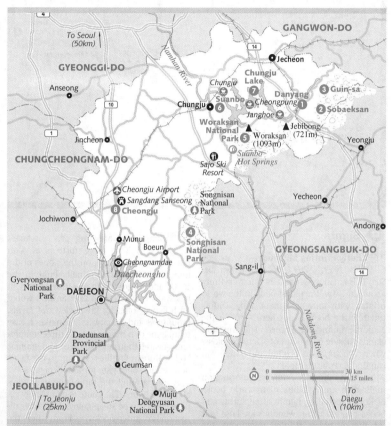

Chungcheongbuk-do Highlights

❶ Wake up to glorious mountain views in **Danyang** (p298)

❷ Hike up nearby **Sobaeksan** (p300), where azaleas bloom in May

❸ Sign up for a Templestay at bustling **Guin-sa** (p300), a modern but awe-inspiring hillside temple complex

❹ Admire the gold-plated Buddha at Beopju-sa in **Songnisan National Park** (p293), then overnight at a charming *yeogwan* (motel) beside a burbling river

❺ Meditate on ancient Buddhist carvings and the evocative ruins of Mireuksaji at **Woraksan National Park** (p297)

❻ Soothe your stresses at an *oncheon* (hot-spring spa) in **Suanbo** (p296)

❼ Admire the scenery as you cruise down **Chungju Lake** (p295)

❽ Learn all about the *Jikji*, the first book printed by movable type, in the province's capital of **Cheongju** (p293)

Cheongju

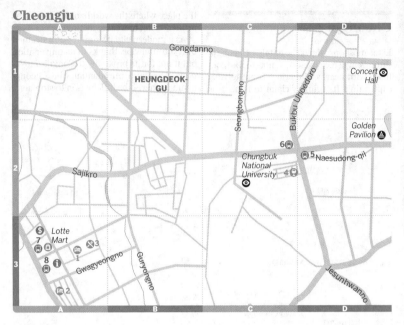

CHUNGCHEONGBUK-DO CHEONGJU

👁 Sights

FREE **Early Printing Museum** MUSEUM
(고인쇄박물관; ☎269 0556; ⊙9am-6pm Tue-Sun) This small museum tells you everything about the *Jikji*, the oldest book in the world printed with moveable metal type. Unfortunately the book is not here – it's in the National Library of France. The museum stands beside the site of Heungdeok-sa, where the *Jikji* was printed and where you can find a replica temple.

The museum has extensive information in English and exhibits many early books of Korea, including handwritten sutras and books printed using woodblocks. Look out for Korea's oldest printed document, the Dharani Sutra, dating back to at least AD 751. It's accompanied by the wood blocks used in its creation. Book nerds will be enthralled by the slightly creepy Korean-speaking wax models that replicate the various steps in the creation of the *Jikji*.

To get there, catch bus 831 or 831-1 (₩1150, 15 minutes) from the bus stop opposite the tourist information centre. Get off at the bus stop beside the pedestrian bridge with green and yellow arches. The museum is about 50m ahead on the left.

FREE **Sangdang Sanseong** FORTRESS
(상당 산성) This large fortress is 4km northeast of Cheongju, on the slopes of the mountain Uamsan. Originally built in the 1590s and renovated in the 18th century, it has walls that stretch 4.2km around wooded hillsides, offering great views of farms, mountains and the city. Its size makes it easy to imagine that it once housed three temples and several thousand soldiers and monks. Today, Korean families decamp to the fields outside the south gate for family picnics.

A hike around the top of the wall takes about 1½ hours. The route is completely exposed and can be steep-going. The easier direction is counter-clockwise. From where the bus drops you, walk back along the road and look on the left for a paved path that ascends to the top of the wall. Along the walk, there are hardly any signs or resting places, and no food stalls, vending machines or toilets – so bring your own water and a hat. If you're up for a challenge, follow the path beside the pond and up the steep hill on the right to do a clockwise circuit. There are restaurants (p291) and shops near the bus stop.

Bus 862 (₩1150, 30 minutes, hourly) goes from the Cheongju Stadium bus stop and goes up to the fortress. To get to the stadi-

um, hop on any bus heading downtown to Sajing-no (사직로) from outside the intercity bus terminal. The stadium bus stop is just after a five-storey golden pavilion. A taxi from the bus terminal should cost ₩15,000. The last bus back to town leaves at 9.50pm.

🎊 Festivals & Events

Jikji Festival   CULTURAL FESTIVAL
(www.jikjifestival.com) Cheongju hosts the Jikji Festival every September with a demonstration of ancient printing techniques, exhibitions of old printed books, and traditional music and drama performances.

🛏 Sleeping

There are *a lot* of love motels around the bus terminals if you care to shop for price and varying degrees of 'look at me!' decor.

TOP CHOICE **Hotel Lin**   MOTEL $$
(모텔린; ☎231 0207; r ₩40,000-50,000; ❋@) It may have faux castle exteriors but the interiors are Santorini-inspired and a huge class above its neighbours. White walls accompany large beds and ultramodern bathrooms complete with cute touches such as floral-patterned sinks and colourful tiling. Some rooms even have plexiglass-encased models of Santorini houses.

Plaza Motel   MOTEL $$
(프라자모텔; ☎234 1400; d/tr ₩40,000/ 50,000; tr with computer ₩60,000; ❋@) Run by a genial older couple who will offer to clean your room *(cheong so)* every day and ask to keep the room key when you go out. The rooms in this clean, no-frills hotel feature wooden laminate flooring, fleur-de-lis wallpaper and water dispensers. The triples are cavernous and can sleep five (two on floor bedding).

🍴 Eating & Drinking

You can scrounge up cheap eats (everything from fried chicken to *bulgogi*) and bars galore in the downtown shopping area around Seongan-gil or with the students near Chungbuk National University (충대 중문; Chungdae jungmun). To get to the latter, take any bus headed downtown from outside the intercity bus terminal and get off at the stop for Sachang Intersection, which is after the Cheongju High School stop.

Sangdangjip   KOREAN $$$
(상당집; meals ₩6000-25,000) Opposite the bus stop at Sangdang Sanseong, this popular restaurant makes its own tofu in a giant cauldron inside the entrance. A light starter is *dubujijim* (두부지짐; steamed tofu); for a fuller meal, try the *jeongol* (전골; hotpot)

BUS DEPARTURES FROM CHEONGJU

Express bus terminal destinations

DESTINATION	PRICE (₩)	DURATION (HR)	FREQUENCY
Busan	16,600	3½	9 daily
Daegu	8000	2½	hourly
Dong-Seoul	9000	1¾	every 30min
Seoul	9400	1¾	every 5–10min

Intercity bus terminal destinations

DESTINATION	PRICE (₩)	DURATION	FREQUENCY
Chuncheon	16,400	3¾hr	11 daily
Chungju	8200	1½hr	every 20min
Daejeon	3600	50min	every 15min
Danyang	16,800	4hr	6 daily

or *duruchigi* (두루치기; spicy stew). Although the chief ingredient is tofu, dishes may include meat. If you don't have time for a meal, sample free tofu soup near the cauldron.

Cheongju House KOREAN $$$

(청주본가; ☑231 0588; meals ₩6000-35000) Meat-lovers can check out the range of *galbi* (beef ribs) and *samgyeopsal* (streaky pork belly) here. For something easier on the arteries, there's *naengmyeon* (buckwheat noodles in cold broth), *galbitang* (beef-rib soup) and *ttukbaegi bulgogi* (뚝배기불고기; beef simmered in an earthenware dish). Look out for a red sign with an image of a house.

The Bugle PUB

(beer from ₩3000, shots from ₩4000; ⊘6pm-late) A stalwart on the local bar scene, the rock-music den known as Pearl Jam has morphed into an Irish pub though there's still occasional live music on weekends. There's Guinness on tap, lots of imported beer, and bar bites such as burgers and Tex-Mex food (₩9000 to ₩12,000) as well as brunch on weekends. The friendly owner Andy speaks excellent English.

❶ Information

The **tourist information centre** (☑233 8431; ⊘9am-6pm) is outside the intercity bus terminal in a two-storey blue-green building. There's free internet access and English-speaking staff.

❶ Getting There & Away

Air

Cheongju airport (☑210 6110) has flights to Jeju-do and China. It's 18km from the city. Take bus 747 from outside the intercity bus terminal (₩1150, one hour, hourly). A taxi costs ₩20,000.

Bus

For departures from the express and intercity bus terminals, see the boxed text above.

Train

Cheongju station (청주역; ☑232 7788) connects primarily with Daejeon (₩2900, 40 minutes, eight daily), while Jochiwon station (조치원역) connects to Seoul (₩7700, 1½ hours, every 30 minutes). From the intercity bus terminal, take bus 717 to Cheongju station, or 502 to Jochiwon. Fast KTX trains to/from Cheongju arrive at the Osong station (오송역). There are trains to Seoul (₩16,900, 55 minutes, 18 daily) and Daejeon (₩8200, 16 minutes, 25 daily). Buses 500, 511 and 519 from the intercity bus terminal get you there.

Around Cheongju

◎ Sights

Cheongnamdae HISTORIC BUILDING

(청남대; ☑043-220 5677; http://chnam.cb21.net; adult/youth/child incl return shuttle bus ₩8000/7000/7000; ⊘9am-6pm Tue-Sun) Once the holiday home of South Korean presidents, this villa is no Camp David, but it's a beautiful lakeside park, with 185 hectares of well-manicured grounds and 2.3km of paths along the lakefront and across the gently rolling hills. You can linger in the Choga-jeong Pavilion where President Kim Dae-jung liked to sit, or look over the golf course that President Roh Tae-woo favoured but President Kim Young-sam disapproved of (too many associations with corruption). Wander the trails around the compound and gawk at the musical fountain (ABBA features on the soundtrack).

Cheongnamdae was built in 1983 by President Chun Doo-hwan (he whose takeover of power sparked the Gwangju Uprising in 1980). Twenty years later, the much-loved President Roh Moo-Hyun opened it to the public. While Korean visitors are simply curious about where their presidents used to vacation, for foreign visitors it's probably the parkland that's more attractive than the surprisingly modest two-storey villa. Where the bus stops, there's a building with a hagiographic exhibition (mostly Korean) on all the presidents as well as displays of former items used by the presidents in residence (polo mallets, Colgate shaving cream, cutlery etc).

Take local bus 311 (₩1450, 50 minutes, 15km, hourly) from outside Cheongju's intercity bus terminal to the final stop at Munui. Walk out of Munui's small bus depot and turn left. In a few minutes you'll reach the car park and ticket office for the shuttle bus (15 minutes, every 30 minutes) to Cheongnamdae, which operates 9am to 4.30pm February to November, 9am to 3.30pm December and January.

Songnisan National Park
속리산국립공원
043

With forested mountains and rocky granite outcrops, this **park** (542 5267; http://songni.knps.or.kr/eng; adult/youth/child ₩4000/200/1000; 6am-7pm) covers one of central Korea's finest scenic areas. Though it often goes by the touristy catchword Chungbuk Alps, its name has a more solemn meaning – 'Remote from the Ordinary World Mountain', referring to the temple **Beopju-sa**, which dates back to AD 553. The temple lies about 1km from the park entrance and has a 33m-high gold-plated Maitreya Buddha statue, a unique five-storey wooden pagoda, a weather-worn Shilla-era bodhisattva statue and an enormous iron cauldron, once used for cooking for up to 3000 monks. Temple stays are offered.

Beyond the temple, hiking trails run up to a series of 1000m-high peaks. A popular hike is the relatively easy 6km climb up **Munjangdae** (1033m). Back in 1464 King Sejo was carried up in a palanquin; using your own feet, it's three hours up and two hours down. You can also return via Sinseondae, further south via Birobong or, for the truly gung-ho, push on to the highest peak **Cheonhwangbong** (1058m).

There is a **tourist information centre** (542 5267) diagonally across the road from the bus terminal.

THE PRINTED WORD, MADE BY MONKS

While the Gutenberg Bible needs no introduction, the *Jikji* languished for many years in obscurity, even though it is the oldest book in the world printed with moveable metal type. It was printed in 1377 (78 years before the Gutenberg) at the temple of Heungdeok-sa in modern-day Cheongju. In the mid-19th century it was acquired by a French official in Korea, who took it to France. After it was put on display at the 1900 World's Fair in Paris, it disappeared without fanfare from the public eye, and it was only in 1972 that Korean historian Park Byeng-Sen rediscovered it at the National Library of France.

The *Jikji* itself is a small book: 38 sheets of thin mulberry paper, each one measuring just 24.6cm x 17cm. Its full title is *Baegun hwasang chorok buljo jikji simche yojeol* – that is, an anthology of the monk Baegun Gyeonghan's teachings on Seon Buddhism (more commonly known in the West as Zen Buddhism). It's the second and only extant volume of a two-volume collection of these teachings, delivered at Heungdeok-sa in the 1370s. The last page of the book indicates that it was printed by two of Baegun's disciples, Seokchan and Daldam, with funding from a nun named Myodeok.

The *Jikji* has been exhibited at international book fairs since 1972 and South Korea lobbied till it was admitted to Unesco's Memory of the World Register in 2001. However, the book still resides within the National Library of France, along with other cultural relics from Korea's early dynasties. Understandably South Korea would like to see the book returned, but there's no indication that's likely to happen.

Songnisan National Park

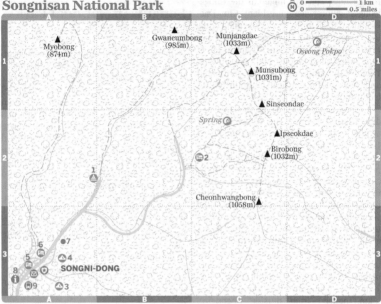

🛏 Sleeping & Eating

Two camping grounds (₩1000) are available. There are plenty of motels in the lanes to the left of the main road (looking towards the park entrance). Lining the main road to the park entrance are many restaurants, offering the usual tourist-village fare: *sanchae jeongsik* (산채 정식; banquet of mountain vegetables), *beoseot jeongsik* (버섯 정식; mushroom set menu) and *sanchae bibimbap* (*bibimbap* with mountain vegetables). Prices range from ₩6000 to ₩35,000.

TOP CHOICE **Birosanjang** GUESTHOUSE **$$**
(비로산장; ☎011-456 4782, 043-543 4782; r with shared bathroom ₩40,000, Sat & Sun ₩50,000, summer ₩60,000) If only every national park had this – a homely, delightful *yeogwan* right beside a gurgling river in the middle of the park. There's nothing fancy here, just nine *ondol* (heated-floor) rooms and meals such as *bibimbap* (rice with vegetables, meat and egg; ₩8000) and *sanchae jeongsik* (₩15,000) whipped up by the friendly owner, who speaks a little English. Ask to try their refreshing *makgeolli* (fermented rice wine). It's on the trail between Beopju-sa and Sinseondae so *don't* lug a heavy backpack in. The local police station will help keep your luggage. Reservations are recommended.

Eorae Motel MOTEL **$**
(어래모텔; ☎543 3882; r ₩35,000;❄) The closest budget option to the park entrance. Rooms are clean and adequate, with wood laminate floors and *ondol* rooms available.

Lake Hills Hotel Songnisan HOTEL **$$$**
(레이크힐스호텔속리산; ☎542 5281; www.lakehills.co.kr; ₩150,000;❄) The area's 'nicest' digs, right by the park entrance, are a little

dated, with balconies and faded carpets. The back rooms face the woods. Rates are discounted during low season.

ⓘ Getting There & Away

Buses leave Cheongju's intercity bus terminal (₩8000, 1¾ hours, every 40 minutes) for Songnisan National Park. There are also direct buses to the park from Dong-Seoul (₩15,900, 3¾ hours), Seoul Gangnam (₩15,000, 3½ hours) and Daejeon (₩7200, 1¾ hours).

Chungju 충주

📞043 / POP 202,000

Chungju (www.cj100.net/english) might be the town where UN Secretary-General Ban Ki-moon grew up, but there are really only three reasons to come to here: to get the bus to the Chungju Lake ferries or Woraksan National Park, to attend the World Martial Arts Festival or because you really, *really* like apples (there's an Apple Festival every October).

A **tourist information centre** (📞850 7329) is inside the bus terminal.

🛏 Sleeping & Eating

Unlike most towns, there are no motels around the bus terminal. There's a clump of love motels opposite the train station, in an area otherwise populated by car workshops. From the bus terminal (turn right as you exit) it's a 15-minute walk or five-minute taxi ride (₩2200) across a treeless urban landscape.

Good eats aren't easy to scare up in Chungju but there are some good options along the road to the left as you exit from the bus terminal. For self-caterers, there's a Lotte Mart beside the train station.

Titanic Motel   LOVE MOTEL $
(타이타닉모텔; 📞842 5858; r without/with computer ₩30,000/35,000; ❄@) The castle-inspired Titanic has decent rooms with all the usual love-motel trimmings.

Gamjatang   KOREAN $$$
(감자탕; meals ₩6000-35,000) Serves a very hearty version of its namesake dish (a rich, spicy peasant soup with meaty bones and potatoes).

Bohae Galbi   KOREAN $$
(보해갈비; 📞848 2595; meals ₩6000-15,000) This place specialises in barbecue and also has *bulgogi* (barbecued beef slices, served with rice) and *seolleongtang* (beef and rice soup).

ⓘ Getting There & Away

Bus

For bus departures from Chungju, see the boxed text below.

Train

Chungju receives only one direct train from Seoul (₩13,500, 2¾ hours). Alternatively, take a train from Seoul to Jochiwon station (조치원역, ₩8000, 1½ hours, every 30 minutes) and change to a train for Chungju (₩6000, 1¼ hours, eight daily).

Around Chungju

📞043

CHUNGJU LAKE 충주호
👁 Sights & Activities
**Cheongpung Cultural
Heritage Complex**   HISTORIC SITE
(📞641 4301; adult/child ₩3000/2000; ⊙9am-6pm) When the area around here was flooded to create the Chungju dam and lake, a number of villages were submerged (the residents were resettled, of course).

In order to preserve some of the rich heritage, 43 cultural properties, several private residences and over a thousand artefacts were relocated here from Cheongpung, a historic port during the Joseon dynasty. You can take the ferry to Cheongpung, get off and walk up the hill to the complex.

CHUNGCHEONGBUK-DO CHUNGJU

BUS DEPARTURES FROM CHUNGJU

DESTINATION	PRICE (₩)	DURATION (HR)	FREQUENCY
Cheongju	8000	1½	every 30min
Daejeon	9500	2¼	hourly
Danyang	7800	1½	11 daily
Seoul	7500	2	every 20min

MARTIAL ARTS FIESTA

Every September/October, Chungju hosts a week-long **World Martial Arts Festival** (☑850 6740; www.martialarts .or.kr), alongside a cultural festival with food stalls, music and dance. Over 2000 martial arts exponents from 30 countries come to demonstrate their amazing and varied skills. It's a chance to see both traditional Korean martial arts, such as *hapkido* and *takkyeon*, and a slew of snappy moves such as Chinese *wushu*, Malaysian *silat*, Brazilian *capoeira*, Indian *kalan* and Uzbekistan *kurash*.

Chungju Lake Cruise   CRUISE
(☑851 5771; www.chungjuho.com) The artificial Chungju Lake was formerly a valley that was deliberately flooded in 1985. This cruise across the lake is a scenic way to make your way towards Danyang. There are numerous routes but the most popular cruise (adult/child one way ₩17,000/8500, return ₩24,000/12,000; fast boat 1½ hours, ferry 2¼ hours) is from Chungju Dam to Janghoe via Cheongpung (and in reverse); the rocky cliffs are most dramatic between the latter stops.

The cruises get very busy on weekends and there's pre-recorded sightseeing commentary (Korean only), so it may not be the most relaxing experience – though the placid scenery is beautiful.

❶ Getting There & Away
From Janghoe you can continue to Danyang by bus (p299).

Ferries depart hourly in summer and every other hour in winter, though this is subject to weather conditions, water levels and passenger volume, so you need to enquire at the tourist information centre in **Chungju** (☑850 7329) or **Danyang** (☑422 1146) before you head to the terminal.

To get to the Chungju Dam ferry terminal (충주댐 선착장) take bus 301 (₩1150, 30 minutes, seven daily) from opposite the Chungju bus terminal. A taxi will cost ₩15,000.

SUANBO 수안보
This tiny spa resort has baths, restaurants and motels clustered snugly across several streets, and a small ski resort less than 2km away. The town looks as if it's seen better days, but it can be lively during high season. If you're headed to Woraksan National Park, this makes a better base than Chungju.

The modest **Sajo Ski Resort** (사조스키 리조트; ☑846 0750; www.sajoresort.co.kr; lift pass ₩30,000, ski rental ₩26,000) has seven slopes and three lifts, and offers night skiing. Near the slopes are the **Hanwha Resort** (www .hanhwaresort.co.kr) and a youth hostel (both closed in low season), but you can stay in Suanbo and use the free shuttle buses during ski season.

There is a **tourist information centre** (☑845 7829) at the entrance to town.

🛏 Sleeping & Eating

Suanbo Sangnok Hotel   HOTEL $$$
(수안보상록호텔; ☑845 3500; www.san gnokhotel.co.kr; r ₩120,000, ste ₩220,000; ❄@≋) To the right of the entrance to Suanbo stands this upmarket hotel, with a good onsite restaurant, a tennis court and a nightclub. The carpeted rooms are smart and modern. The main attraction here is the *oncheon* (nonguests/guests ₩7000/4000).

Suanbo Royal Hotel   HOTEL $$
(수안보로얄호텔; ☑846 0190; r ₩90,000; ❄@) This blockish concrete-and-glass hotel looks sterner but newer than the others on the main road. Rooms are cosy and warm, and there's an *oncheon* (nonguests/guests ₩6000/4000).

Restaurants specialise in rabbit (*tokki*; 토끼), duck (*ori*; 오리) and pheasant (*kkwong*; 꿩) meals, such as *tokki doritang* (토끼도 리탕; rabbit stew) and *kkwong jeongsik*, meant for at least two diners. Also popular is *sanchae deodeok jeongsik* (산채더덕정식), a set meal with mountain vegetables and a herbal root similar to ginseng. **Satgatchon** (삿갓촌식당; ☑846 2529; meals ₩6000-50,000) has *kkwong shabu shabu* (꿩샤브샤브) with pheasant served in seven different ways: kebabs, dumplings, meatballs, barbecued, *shabu shabu*-style, raw and in soup. To find it, walk down the side road by Suanbo Sangnok Hotel to the bridge and turn left. Walk ahead 50m and it's the restaurant to the right with a wooden man sculpture standing at the door.

❶ Getting There & Away
From outside Chungju's bus terminal, catch bus 240 or 246 (₩1250, 35 minutes, 21km, every 40 minutes) to Suanbo's main street. You can also return via a more comfortable intercity

bus (₩2300, 30 minutes). Tickets for this bus are sold at the grocery store beside the bus 'terminal', which consists of a yellow and blue sign planted beside some orange seats. Other intercity buses go to Daegu (₩14,700, 2½ hours, 11am and 7.20pm), Dong-Seoul (₩11,300, 2½ hours, hourly) and Woraksan National Park (₩1300, 30 minutes, every two hours).

Woraksan National Park
월악산국립공원

Spread across two serene valleys, this **park** (043-653 3250; http://worak.knps.or.kr; admission free; sunrise-sunset) offers fine hiking through picturesque forests, with pretty waterfalls, ancient Buddhist structures and, if you climb high enough, views all the way to Chungjuho. Woraksan (Moon Crags Mountain) is also home to the endangered long-tailed goral.

A road runs through the park; the bus that plies it stops at the villages of Mireuk-

ri in the south, Deokju in the middle and Songgye-ri in the north. Around 1km from Mireuk-ri lie the remains of **Mireuksaji**, a small Buddhist temple which was built in the late Shilla or early Goryeo period. Although a new temple has been constructed beside it, the stark, weather-beaten ruins – an enigmatic Buddha statue, stone lantern and five-storey pagoda – can be quite atmospheric.

The most popular of the hiking routes starts from Deokju. A gentle path leads past **Deokjusanseong**, a late Shilla-era fortress that has been partly restored, up to **Deokju-sa** temple. The trail continues for 1.5km to **Ma-aebul**, a rock face with a Buddha image, then it's pretty tough going for 3.4km more to the summit of **Yeongbong** (1097m). Allow about 3½ hours to get from Deokju-sa to Yeongbong. You can also approach Yeongbong from Songgye-ri (three hours, 4.3km).

There are shops, restaurants and pensions and *minbak* at all three of the villages, Songgye-ri being the most developed. There's camping (₩2000 per night) at Deokju and Datdonjae, but no mountain shelters.

Getting There & Away

Bus 246 (₩4600, one hour, six daily) leaves from outside Chungju's bus terminal for Mireuk-ri. It can also be picked up in Suanbo's main street (₩1300, 30 minutes). Bus 222 (₩4600, 45 minutes, six daily) from Chungju's bus terminal goes directly to Songgye-ri. Bus stops and place names in the park are not well signposted, so ask the bus driver to alert you for your stop.

Woraksan National Park (map)

Woraksan National Park

Sights
1 Deokju-sa B3
2 Deokjusanseong B3
3 Ma-aebul (Rock-cut Buddha) B2
4 Mireuksaji B4

Sleeping
5 Datdonjae Camping Ground B3
6 Deokju Camping Ground A3

Information
7 Park Office A2

Transport
8 Bus Stop B3
9 Bus Stop A4

Danyang 단양

♩043 / POP 37,000

A little gem of a resort town, Danyang (http://english.dy21.net) is cosied right up to the mountains of Sobaeksan National Park, at a bend in the river Namhangang. This is small-town Korea at its most charming: you can stay at a riverfront motel and explore limestone caves, hiking trails and a one-of-a-kind Buddhist temple, basking in mountain views wherever you go. It's a great place to dawdle for a couple of days.

Danyang

Danyang

🛏 Sleeping
Hotel Luxury	....	(see 1)
1 Rivertel	....	B1

🍽 Eating
2 Doljip Sikdang	....	A1
3 Gimbap Heaven	....	A2
4 Kujib Ssogari	....	B2

ℹ Information
5 Tourist Information Centre	....	B1

ℹ Transport
6 Danyang Bus Terminal	....	B1

The annual highlight is the 10-day **Royal Azalea Festival** in May. Hikers come to see the flowers bloom on Sobaeksan, while the riverside comes alive with concerts, fireworks, food stalls and a funfair.

Tourist information centres (♩422 1146) with English-speaking staff are across the bridge and in the Danyang Danuri building next to the bus terminal.

👁 Sights & Activities

Gosu Donggul   CAVE

(고수동굴; ♩422 3072; adult/youth/child ₩5000/3000/2000; ☉9am-5pm) This stunning limestone cave is a rabbit's warren of metal catwalks and spiral staircases running through 1.7km of dense, narrow grottoes. It's quite an intimate experience where you get up close with the rock formations. Unlike garishly lit caves, Gosu Donggul feels old and drippy – perhaps not as old as its 150,000 years, but it's certainly authentic.

There are few explanatory signs, except for a few earnest exhortations to, 'for a moment, look back please!'. Walkways are narrow – definitely not for the claustrophobic. The cave is about a 10-minute walk from Danyang. Cross the bridge to the tourist information centre and follow the road to a busy tourist village. The cave entrance is tucked away up a stone staircase behind the village. At the latter, you can refresh yourself with a cup (or jar) of local flavours like *omija* (five-flavour berry), honey (꿀; *kkul*) or yam (마; *ma*) drinks.

Dansim Mugung   PARAGLIDING

(단심무궁 패러글라이딩; ♩010-9072 4553; http://cafe.daum.net/dypara, in Korean) Offers paragliding (₩100,000) from Yangbaeksan, the peak overlooking the town that's topped by an astronomical observatory.

Aquaworld   AMUSEMENT PARK

(아쿠아월드; ♩420 8370; adult/child Mon-Fri ₩29,000/22,000, Sat & Sun ₩33,000/29,000; ☉9am-9pm) Tamer options than caving or paragliding are to go swimming at Daemyung Resort's indoor water park or drop by its **sauna** (adult/child ₩10,000/8000; ☉7am-8pm), which has mineral baths and jade, charcoal or amethyst saunas.

🛏 Sleeping

Most of the riverside motels are dated and faded but can't be beat for location.

BUS DEPARTURES FROM DANYANG

DESTINATION	PRICE (₩)	DURATION	FREQUENCY
Chungju	7900	1½hr	2 daily
Daejeon	17,400	3½hr	4 daily
Guin-sa	3300	30min	hourly
Seoul	12,700	2½hr	every 30min

Rivertel
MOTEL $$

(리버텔; ☎422 2619; www.erivertel.com; r ₩35,000-70,000; ❄@) Despite the shabby exterior and the worn red carpet, this place has the cheapest rooms-with-a-view – they're pleasant though none too large. The owner speaks some English and plenty of travel information is available at the reception desk. We were told a renovation would be impending. When completed, the property will be renamed Guesthouse Danyang with a ground-floor cafe and rooms costing ₩50,000 to ₩80,000 (including breakfast).

Hotel Luxury
MOTEL $$

(럭셔리 호텔; ☎421 9911; www.hotel-luxury .co.kr; r ₩50,000, ste ₩70,000; ❄@) This spanking new outfit brings love-motel chic to Danyang, with stylish rooms decorated in bold (read: garish!) colours. The VIP suite sleeps three (₩80,000) and comes with a whirlpool bath. Rooms cost an extra ₩20,000 on weekends.

Daemyung Resort
RESORT $$$

(대명리조트; ☎421 8321; www.daemyungresort .com; r ₩78,000-135,000, ste ₩102,000-160,000; ❄@) This condominium is equipped with full facilities such as Aquaworld, noraebang (karaoke room), billiard rooms and a restaurant. The rooms can sleep up to four persons. Enquire about the low-season packages available, which come at significant discounts.

✖ Eating

Doljip Sikdang
KOREAN $$

(돌집식당; meals ₩6000-15,000) This busy restaurant has private dining rooms and serves elaborate jeongsik, with main-course options such as suyuk (수육; boiled beef slices) and locally grown maneul (마늘쌈정식; garlic wrap) or beoseot jjigae (버섯찌개; mushroom stew). Lighter options

are doenjang sotbap (된장솥밥; claypot rice with fermented bean paste, jujube and vegetables) or dolsot bibimbap (bibimbap in a stone hotpot).

Gimbap Heaven
KOREAN $

(김밥천국; meals ₩2000-6000) Scrounge up dirt-cheap eats in this small chain restaurant. There's a range of ramyeon (instant noodles in soup) and udong (thick white noodle broth), served with kimchi. There's also pork cutlets, assorted rice dishes and of course, half-a-dozen variations of gimbap (Korean sushi).

Kujib Ssogari
KOREAN $$$

(그집쏘가리; ☎423 2111; meals ₩8000-80,000) This riverfront restaurant serves the mandarin fish ssogari raw (쏘가리회; ssogari hoe) or as a spicy soup (쏘가리매운탕; ssogari maeuntang). A milder option is the catfish bulgogi (메기불고기; megi bulgogi).

❶ Getting There & Away

Boat

The closest ferry terminal for the Chungjuho ferry (p296) is at Janghoe. After you exit the terminal, turn right at the main road and walk down for about 100m. Beside the trail entrance to Woraksan National Park is the waiting point for the bus to Danyang (₩2100, 30 minutes, 21km, every 2½ hours). It's marked with a circular red sign that reads '단양버스정류소'.

Bus

A new bus terminal (☎421 8800) complex is in front of the bridge. Local buses don't have numbers but signs (Korean only) indicating the destination at the front of the bus. For intercity bus departures, see the boxed text above.

Train

The train station is in old Danyang, about 3km from the main town. Eight trains run daily from Seoul's Cheongnyangni station (₩12,000, three hours). A taxi into town costs ₩5000, the local bus ₩1150.

Sobaeksan National Park
소백산국립공원

☑043

This **park** (☑423 0708; admission free; http://sobaek.knps.or.kr/Sobaeksan_eng; ☺2hr before sunrise-2hr after sunset) is the third largest in South Korea and the daintily named Sobaeksan (Little White Mountain) is one of the highest mountains in the country. While the climbs are not particularly steep, they can be demanding, wending through dense forests, picturesque valleys and even a waterfall.

The main trail (7km, 2½ hours) heads from the park entrance at Darian to the highest peak of **Birobong** (1439m), famous for royal azaleas which bloom in late May. Views are incredible from the grassy mountaintop. It can also be approached from the campground at Samga (5.7km, 2½ hours).

From Birobong, you can push on to the three peaks of **Yeonhwabong** (2.5km to 6.8km); the National Astronomical Observatory is here but not open to visitors.

◉ Sights

FREE **Guin-sa**   TEMPLE
(구인사; ☑420 7315; www.temple.cheontae.org) This stately complex's 30-odd buildings are wedged into a valley, with steep, forested slopes on either side. The gold-roofed buildings are as elaborate as you'd expect, very close together and connected with elevated walkways. While wandering around, you may very well stumble upon monks chanting and drumming away. The communal kitchen serves free vegetarian meals (6am to 7.30am, 11.30am to 1.30pm and 6.30pm to 9.30pm) and Templestays are held twice a month.

Sobaeksan National Park

The temple is the headquarters of the Cheontae sect of Korean Buddhism, which was re-established by Sangwol Wongak in 1945. Strangely, the most opulent structure is the three-storey hall dedicated to him (대조사전) at the rear of the complex. From there, it's a steep climb of 30 minutes to his tomb atop the hill.

🛏 Sleeping & Eating

There is a delightful *minbak* village at Darian and many also have restaurants. They are spread out so it doesn't feel too crowded or noisy. Rooms cost from ₩40,000 and you can wake up right next to the mountains.

There are campsites here (₩11,000). Camping (₩2000) is also available at Samga. Take the bus (₩1150, every 30 minutes) heading to Yeongju (영주).

ℹ Getting There & Away

Buses (₩1150, 10 minutes, hourly) leave from the stop outside Danyang's bus terminal for Darian (다리안). Direct buses (₩3300, 30 minutes, hourly) head from Danyang's bus terminal to the tourist village at the base of Guin-sa from where a free shuttle drops you near the entrance.

From Guin-sa, there are hourly buses to Seoul (₩13,000, three hours).

North Korea

Best Places to Stay

» Koryo Hotel (p311)
» Yanggakdo Hotel (p311)
» Minsok Folk Hotel (p315)
» Emperor Hotel (p321)

Best Places to Eat

» Pyongyang Number One Duck Barbecue (p312)
» Pizza Restaurant (p312)
» Lamb Barbeque Restaurant (p312)
» Chongryu Hotpot Restaurant (p312)

Why Go?

No country in the world provokes a similar reaction to North Korea. Now on its third hereditary ruler, this nominally communist state and by-product of the Cold War has defied all expectation and survived a quarter of a century since perestroika dismantled the rest of the once-vast Soviet empire.

The death of Kim Jong-il in late 2011 has seen the highly repressive police state back in the headlines as nervous governments around the world watch his son Kim Jong-un take over the reins of a nuclear-armed state with an enormous army. Most people don't even know that it's possible to travel here, and indeed the compromises required to do so are significant. You'll be accompanied by two government minders at all times and only hear a one-sided account of history. Those who can't accept this might be better off staying away – but those who can will have a fascinating trip into another, unsettling world.

When to Go

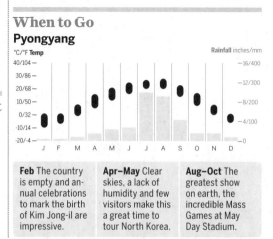

Pyongyang

Feb The country is empty and annual celebrations to mark the birth of Kim Jong-il are impressive.

Apr–May Clear skies, a lack of humidity and few visitors make this a great time to tour North Korea.

Aug–Oct The greatest show on earth, the incredible Mass Games at May Day Stadium.

Tours

All North Korean tours are ultimately arranged by Ryohaengsa, the national travel agency. However, these tours are best bought via agencies in Beijing specialising in travel to the DPRK; travel agencies offering tours to North Korea include the following:

Koryo Tours (www.koryotours.com)

Lupine Travel (www.lupinetravel.co.uk)

New Korea Tours (www.newkoreatours.com)

North Korea Travel (www.north-korea-travel.com)

Regent Holidays (www.regent-holidays.co.uk)

VNC Travel (www.vnc.nl)

Young Pioneer Tours (www.dprk.youngpioneertours.com)

SET YOUR BUDGET

The cost of a trip to North Korea is considerable. Visitors have to pay the government for their guides and buy all their food and board in advance as part of an all-inclusive tour. The only real way to cut costs is to join a group tour and share the expenses between many travellers. It's difficult to travel to North Korea for less than €1000 for five days. However, if you arrange your own group, it's possible to request the cheapest hotels in the country and save some money.

Itineraries

» **Five Days** The standard tour of North Korea gives you a couple of days visiting the extraordinary monuments of Pyongyang, a day trip to Kaesong and the DMZ, and sometimes a visit to the mountains at Myohyangsan.

» **10 Days** Trips of more than a week can be exhausting, but very rewarding. As well as doing everything in the five-day itinerary, groups will have the opportunity to visit truly remote and little-visited cities such as Nampo, Wonsan or Hamhung, a great chance to see real life in North Korea.

AT A GLANCE

» **Currency** Locals use North Korean Won but travellers must use euros, Chinese RMB or US dollars

» **Language** Korean

» **Visas** Needed by everyone and normally issued the day before you travel by the North Korean embassy in Beijing

Fast Facts

» **Area** 120,540 sq km

» **Population** 25,000,000

» **Capital** Pyongyang

» **Telephone** North Korea's country code is ☎850. It's not permitted for travellers to bring mobile phones into North Korea

» **Internet** Unavailable anywhere in the country

Exchange Rates

Australia	A$1	KPW 138
China	RMB1	KPW 21
Euro Zone	€1	KPW 173
Japan	Y100	KPW 172
UK	UK£1	KPW 215
USA	US$1	KPW 138

Resources

» Koryo Tours: www.koryogroup.com

» North Korean Economy Watch: www.nkeconwatch.com

» North Korean Refugees: www.northkoreanrefugees.com

» Lonely Planet: www.lonelyplanet.com/north-korea/pyongyang

PYONGYANG

♫02 / POP 3.25 MILLION

It's no exaggeration to say that the North Korean capital is unlike any other on earth. An ideological statement forged in concrete, bronze and marble, Pyongyang (평양; 'flat land') is the ultimate totalitarian metropolis, built almost entirely from scratch following its destruction in the Korean War.

Every visit to North Korea focuses heavily on the capital. Your guides will be falling over themselves to show you monuments, towers, statues and buildings that glorify Kim Il-sung, Kim Jong-il and the Juche idea. These include the Triumphal Arch, the Tower of the Juche Idea and the Mansudae Grand Monument, a rendering of the Great Leader and the Dear Leader in bronze to which every visitor is expected to pay floral tribute.

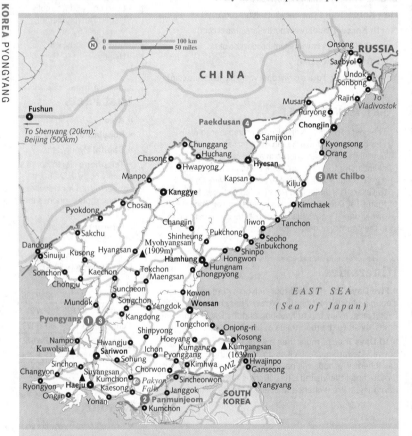

North Korea Highlights

❶ Marvel at the architecture, monuments and general totalitarian weirdness of **Pyongyang** (p305)

❷ Feel the full force of Cold War tensions during a visit to **Panmunjom** (p315) in the Demilitarized Zone (DMZ), where an uneasy armistice holds

❸ Visit Pyongyang between August and October to see the incredible **Mass Games** (p313), a gymnastic spectacle featuring thousands of athletes and dancers in perfect formation

❹ Explore the remote far north and Korea's highest peak and holy mountain **Paekdusan** (p319)

❺ Enjoy pristine mountain walks and some lovely beaches along the coast in and around **Mt Chilbo** (p320)

DON'T LEAVE HOME WITHOUT...

Anything medical or electrical that you will need during your stay; this includes simple everyday products such as painkillers, tampons, condoms, memory cards and batteries. Such basic items are sometimes available, but their price and quality can be quite different from elsewhere. Bringing a bag of fruit or energy snacks from China is a great idea for snacking between sights and sharing with other members of your tour group. Small change in euros and yuan (€1 and 1 yuan notes) are a huge help, as there's rarely hard-currency change in shops. Small token gifts for your guides will be appreciated, though they are not essential (and a cash tip will be expected whatever else you give them). Popular gifts include cigarettes (for male guides only), chocolates and quality beauty products. Most of all, bring a sense of humour and an open mind – you'll need both to make North Korea enjoyable and rewarding.

While these are all impressive, if surreal, the real delights of Pyongyang are to be had in the quieter moments when you can get glimpses of everyday life. A gentle stroll on Pyongyang's relaxed Moran Hill, for example, is a great chance to see the locals having picnics, playing music and idling away sunny afternoons. As you wander the streets between sights, you'll still be able to find a semblance of normality surviving in the capital. You just have to look hard for it.

History

It seems incredible to think it, given its stark, thoroughly 20th-century appearance, but Pyongyang is ancient, stretching back to when the Goguryeo dynasty built its capital here in AD 427. By the 7th century the kingdom of Goguryeo had started to collapse under the strain of successive, massive attacks from Sui and Tang China. Cutting a deal with the Tang Chinese, the Shilla kingdom in the South was able to conquer Goguryeo in 668, creating the first unified Korea.

The city was completely destroyed by the Japanese in 1592 and then again by the Manchus at the beginning of the 17th century. Pyongyang remained a relative backwater until the arrival of foreign missionaries in the 19th century, who constructed over 100 churches in the city. Pyongyang was once again destroyed during the Sino-Japanese War (1894–95) and remained neglected until the occupying Japanese developed industry in the region.

The US practically wiped out Pyongyang between 1950 and 1953, and it rose from the ashes in the late 1950s as the ideological theme park it is today. Few historic buildings remain, but there are some in evidence, including a couple of temples and pavilions, the Taedong Gate and a few sections of the ancient city's inner and northern walls.

◉ Sights

Pyongyang is divided into East and West Pyongyang by the Taedong River. Most sights, museums and hotels are in West Pyongyang, which is focused on Kim Il-sung Sq (which faces the Tower of the Juche Idea across the river). A large area of the city, known to foreign residents as the 'forbidden city', is back behind the Kim Il-sung Sq west of Changgwang St and is a closed-off area for senior party members and their families.

Pyongyang's sights divide neatly into two categories: the impressive yet fairly pointless proliferation of statues, monuments and museums glorifying the Kims and the far more interesting slices of daily North Korean life to be found in excursions to funfairs, cinemas, parks and on public transport. You don't have to be a genius to work out which your guides will prefer to show you, or to guess which most tour groups will enjoy the most.

Mansudae Grand Monument   MONUMENT
Every itinerary features this larger-than-life bronze statue of the Great Leader, to which a statue of Kim Jong-il was added in 2012 following the Dear Leader's death.

This is no memorial but rather was unveiled in 1972 to celebrate his 60th birthday. It was originally covered in gold leaf but apparently at the objection of the Chinese who were effectively funding the North Korean economy, this was later removed in favour of the scrubbed bronze on display today.

Pyongyang

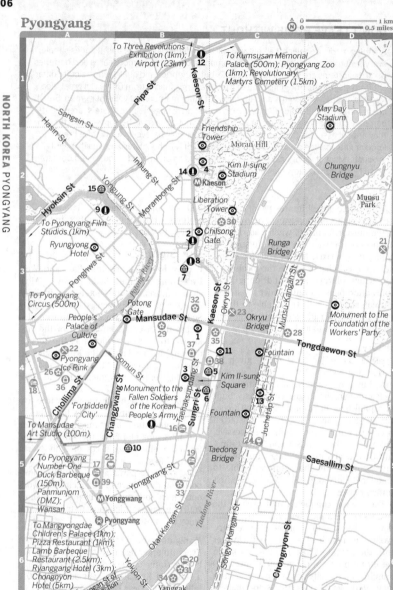

As the epicentre of the Kim cult, visitors need to be aware of the seriousness (officially at least) with which North Koreans consider this monument and the respect they believe foreigners should accord it. Your tour leader will usually buy flowers and elect one member of the group to place them at the statue's feet. As this is done, the whole group will be expected to bow. Photographers will be instructed never to photograph one part of the monument – all pictures should be of the entire statue to avoid causing offence.

Pyongyang

Chollima Statue MONUMENT

Just north of the Mansudae Grand Monument is the Chollima Statue – a bronze statue of the Korean Pegasus, the steed Chollima. It's an interesting example of how the Kim regime has sought to incorporate traditional Korean myths into its cult. According to legend, Chollima could cover hundreds of kilometres a day and was untameable. Kim Il-sung appropriated the myth in the period of reconstruction following the Korean War so that the zeal of the North Korean workers to rebuild their shattered nation and construct monuments to the leadership became known as 'Chollima Speed'. Indeed, when North Korea broke through to the quarter-finals of the World Cup in 1966, it was apparently because Kim senior had urged them to play 'Chollima football'.

Kumsusan Sun Memorial Palace MAUSOLEUM

Kim Il-sung's residence during his lifetime, the Kumsusan Palace remains so in death. At the time of writing the embalmed corpse of Kim Jong-il was believed to be being added to the top-floor viewing chamber where North Koreans come en masse to pay their respects to the Great Leader. The palace is eerie, with bricked-in windows and a vast and empty plaza before it. Just getting to the viewing chamber is adventure enough. First of all you'll need to be dressed smartly (shirts, ties and trousers for men, modest dress for women), then you'll go through airport-style security, allowed to take only your wallet and camera with you, pass along miles of slow red travelators and then be dusted off by both automatic shoe cleaners and a giant clothes-dusting machine. In the sombre Hall of Lamentations you'll hear an English-language audio guide narrating the Korean people's grief at Kim Il-sung's death. This completed, you'll finally ascend to the viewing chamber itself, where you'll proceed to the glass bier and bow three times (once on each side, but not bowing when you're standing behind the Great Leader's head). If

PYONGYANG HIGHLIGHTS

» Take the lift to the top of the **Tower of the Juche Idea** for a magnificent view of the sprawling cityscape on a clear day

» Ride the impressively deep and spectacularly adorned **Pyongyang metro** with the locals

» See where Kim Il-sung lies in state at the **Kumsusan Sun Memorial Palace** (p308), which makes Lenin's mausoleum look like a shoebox

» Escape the relentless grandeur of the city centre and have a walk on relaxed **Moran Hill**

» Enjoy an unforgettable night of bizarrely coordinated dance at the stunning **Mass Games** (p313)

you had any doubt that your trip to North Korea would keep you in dinner-party anecdotes for decades to come, the Kumsusan Memorial Palace will quash them.

Just as eerie is the **Tower of Immortality**, under which the traffic to the palace must pass from central Pyongyang. This tower, one of hundreds throughout the country, bears the legend 'The Great Leader Comrade Kim Il-sung will always be with us'. The writing on the monument was being amended at the time of writing to include mention of Kim Jong-il.

Tower of the Juche Idea   MONUMENT
On the other side of the Taedong River from Kim Il-sung Sq, this tower honours the North Korean philosophy of Juche, and was unveiled to mark the president's 70th birthday in 1982. Indeed, the tower is made up of 25,550 granite blocks – one for every day of Kim's life until his 70th birthday. The tower stands at 170m and a trip to the top by lift (€5) is well worth it, providing a great view over the capital on a clear day. For the best views go in the morning, as the sun is still in the east, lighting up the western, more interesting side of the city.

Triumphal Arch   MONUMENT
Your guides will tell you with barely concealed glee that the Triumphal Arch is 3m higher than its cousin in Paris, making it the largest of its kind in the world.

The arch marks the site where Kim Il-sung first addressed the liberated Koreans after the end of Japanese occupation in 1945.

The gloss you hear will omit the fact that the Soviets liberated Pyongyang, not Kim Il-sung's partisans, who themselves gave full credit to the Soviets at the time. An impressive **mural** a short walk away details the event according to the legend and pictures a young Kim addressing a wildly enthusiastic local population. Set back from the arch is the Kim Il-sung Stadium, where you'll often see pioneers and school children practising for the mass games and military parades.

Kim Il-sung Square   SQUARE
Pyongyang's central square is where North Korea's massive military parades normally take place. The plaza is ringed by austere-looking buildings: most impressive of these is the **Grand People's Study House**, the country's largest library and national centre of Juche studies, where any North Korean over 17 can come for free lectures.

With over 30 million books, finding what you want is inevitably quite a challenge – and you will be proudly shown the impressive system of conveyor belts that can deliver books in seconds. You'll also normally visit a reading room, a classroom, the intranet room and a room full of late-'80s cassette recorders.

Other buildings on the square include the **Korean National Art Gallery**, which is worth a visit to see the postwar North Korean socialist realist art collection. There are 14 rooms of prewar Korean art that are of very high quality too. There's also the ho-hum **Korean Central History Museum** on the opposite side of the square. There's a great view from the riverside bank across the Taedong to the Tower of the Juche Idea, where groups usually go to take photos. There's also the Austrian joint venture **Ryongwang Coffee Shop** here, where you can get a decent cappuccino.

Mangyongdae Children's Palace ARTS CENTRE
This centre for extracurricular activity – from martial arts to the playing of traditional instruments – makes for a great visit. The palace visit will include displays of incredibly talented martial artists, gymnasts and musicians, all beaming at you with permanent smiles as they perform. The tour usually culminates in the main auditorium with a stellar display by fantastically regimented youth. The grand finale is usually a loyalty song to Kim Jong-il. As well as the larger and more modern Mangyongdae Children's Palace, there's a smaller, older Children's Palace in the centre of Pyongyang near Kim Il-sung Square.

Pyongyang Metro
UNDERGROUND

Visiting the impressive Pyongyang metro is definitely a highlight of the capital. The network, which is made up of two lines, has a simultaneous function as a nuclear bunker in the event of the long-awaited American invasion. Stations are deep below ground, and you can even see blast doors that will close if Pyongyang ever comes under nuclear bombardment. Most tours include a visit to just the two most photogenic stations, but it's more and more common to do an 'extended' trip that runs all the way to Kaeson station next to the Triumphal Arch.

Moran Hill
PARK

This is Pyongyang's top recreation ground for the masses. Couples wander, families picnic and there are people playing guitars and sometimes even dancing in an incongruously relaxed area of the capital. It's particularly busy on a Sunday and a lovely place to stroll and absorb something of daily life.

Victorious Fatherland Liberation War Museum
MUSEUM

Perhaps the best museum in Pyongyang; here you'll see the key battles of the Korean War depicted vividly in dioramas, and there's some fascinating military hardware ranging from war-damaged tanks and aircraft to torpedo boats used by both sides. These huge trophies of war were all placed in the basement and the museum was then built around them. Nearby, opposite the little Potong tributary of the Taedong, there's the impressive Monument to the Victorious Fatherland Liberation War, unveiled in 1993 to mark the 40th anniversary of the war's end. The sculptures reflect the different battles of the war; the Victory Sculpture is the centrepiece.

Korean Revolution Museum
MUSEUM

A visit to the museum behind the Mansudae Grand Monument is sometimes included on itineraries. Despite the museum's rather misleading name, its main function is to document the death of Kim Il-sung (including a film of the extraordinary public reaction to it) and the succession of Kim Jong-il during the turbulent 1990s. One of the more bizarre items on display is a tin of Nivea hand cream that the Dear Leader thoughtfully gifted to factory workers with sore hands.

Party Founding Museum
MUSEUM

Located on the southern slope of Haebang Hill is this museum that originally housed the Central Committee of the Korean Workers' Party, as well as Kim Il-sung's office from where he 'led the building of a new democratic Korea'. Next door is the Great Leader's conspicuously modest residence, used after coming to power (and before he had numerous palaces built for him).

Three Revolutions Exhibition
MUSEUM

A surreal, enormous exhibition complex, this is North Korea's answer to Florida's Epcot theme park. The sprawling site details the 'three revolutions' Kim Il-sung brought about in postwar Korea: ideological, technical and cultural. The six halls detail advances

THE MYSTERY UNDERGROUND

Visiting the Pyongyang metro normally involves a one-stop trip between Puhung (Rehabilitation) and Yonggwang (Glory) stations. Nearly all visitors, from tour groups to then US Secretary of State Madeleine Albright, were given the same show trip, giving rise to a rumour that power cuts and lack of repair have meant that the rest of the system no longer functions on a day-to-day basis. In fact today the whole system (admittedly just 17 stations) is used, although it's likely that during the years of austerity in the late 1990s much of it was closed to make energy savings.

The entire system's construction was overseen by the Great Leader, who offered his 'on-the-spot guidance'. The Pyongyang Metro guide, produced for the 1973 opening of the network, describes his wise words on opening the new network in 1973:

'The Great Leader President said to officials in a thoughtful tone "I think it is difficult to build the metro, but it is not to cut the tape." Hearing his words, which considered the trouble of builders first, the participants in the opening ceremony felt a lump in their throats and gave enthusiastic cheers, waving bundles of flowers.'

One very telling museum is the Metro Museum, next to the Tower of Immortality. It details the construction of the metro system in enormous detail, but focuses throughout on the roles played by Kim Il-sung and Kim Jong-il, with almost no technical information, although there is a very cool diorama.

across the board in electronics, heavy industry, light industry, agriculture and technology (advances appear to be fairly slim, though, with all the technical exhibits looking more like a display of antiques). The world's weirdest planetarium can be found within the electronics industry hall, which looks like a silver rendering of Saturn. There's also an interesting outdoor display of vehicles produced in North Korea.

Pyongyang Film Studios   FILM STUDIOS

Several films a year are still churned out by the country's main film studios in the suburbs of Pyongyang. Kim Il-sung visited the complex around 20 times during his lifetime to provide invaluable on-the-spot guidance, while Kim Jong-il visited more than 600 times during his life, such was his passionate interest in films.

Like all things North Korean, the two main focuses are the anti-Japanese struggle and the anti-American war. The main complex is a huge, propaganda-filled suite of office buildings where apparently postproduction goes on, even though it feels eerily empty. A short uphill drive takes you to the large sets, however, which are far more fun. Here you'll find a generic ancient Korean town for historic films (you can even dress up as a king or queen and be photographed sitting on a 'throne' carpeted in leopard skin), a 1930s Chinese street, a Japanese street, a South Korean street (look for the massage signs that illustrate their compatriots' moral laxity) and a fairly bizarre range of structures from a collection of 'European' buildings. Some groups have been lucky and seen films being made during their visit, although you're more likely to find it empty.

Pyongyang Zoo   ZOO

Worth a visit for the opportunity to see locals enjoying themselves in an informal setting, Pyongyang zoo has a good aquarium and reptile house and a large array of animals, most of whom look pretty forlorn. Worst off are the big cats, nearly all gifts of long-dead communist bigwigs around the world – the wonderful lions, tigers and leopards are kept in woefully inadequate compounds and many have lost the plot as a result. The zoo's two elephants and its hippo all look exceptionally lacklustre as well.

There's more fun to be had with the baboons and a collection of lemurs, while perhaps the oddest thing is the huge cage of domestic cats. It's very relaxed here; you'll find North Korean families on outings and this is one of the few environments where you can communicate with locals in a relatively carefree way.

Mangyongdae   NEIGHBOURHOOD

Located a kilometre from the centre of Pyongyang, Mangyongdae has long been a destination for day-trippers from the capital, due to its idyllic setting amid the gentle hills

SHOULD YOU VISIT?

North Korea is a police state with a human-rights record that is the worst on earth. Concentration camps, executions, state-orchestrated terror and mass control by a vast propaganda machine are a daily reality for millions here. All the revenue from your trip will go directly to the government, and given the cost of just one traveller's tour this totals a sizeable amount. So should you visit, and is it morally acceptable to do so?

The case against visiting, as outlined above, is strong. On the other hand, those who argue that you *should* visit point out that tourism is one of the few ways of encouraging openness in the DPRK, of letting people see that the West is interested and, more importantly, friendly – not an insignificant fact for a population brought up on a relentless diet of anti-US propaganda.

Part of the fascination of travelling in North Korea is trying to divine the real from the fake and attempting to see past the ideology. While you may be horrified, amazed or awestruck by what you see in North Korea, you won't be able to help yourself seeing the world from a different perspective once you've been here.

If you do decide to come, the one thing you should never do is visit with the intent of stirring up trouble or making any kind of protest – your guides and any North Koreans having contact with your group will suffer very serious consequences and you'll achieve nothing more than a speedy deportation. If you do come, listen to the version of history given to you by the guides, accept that this is their version (however untrue) and leave serious criticism until you are back at your hotel.

THE GENERAL SHERMAN & USS PUEBLO

During the 'hermit kingdom' phase of the Joseon dynasty, one of Korea's first encounters with Westerners was the ill-fated attempt of the American ship, the *General Sherman*, to sail up the Taedong River to Pyongyang in 1866. It arrogantly ignored warnings to turn around and leave, and insisted on trade. When it ran aground on a sandbar just below Pyongyang, locals burnt it and killed all those on board including a Welsh missionary and the Chinese and Malay crew. An American military expedition later pressed the Seoul government for reparations for the loss, otherwise the incident was virtually forgotten in South Korea. However, northerners have always regarded it with great pride as being their first of many battles with, and victories over, the hated Yankee imperialist enemy.

Also of great pride to the North Koreans is the 'fact' that none other than the Great Leader's great-grandfather had participated in burning the ship. Today, all that is left of the *General Sherman* is a plaque. The site is overshadowed by the nearby ship the USS *Pueblo,* a US surveillance vessel that was seized by the North Koreans off the east coast of Korea in January 1968 during a heightening of tensions between the North and South. You can step aboard and hear another lecture on the violations of the ceasefire agreement by the US, and on the embankment look out for the recent addition of an alleged US submersible captured by the North Koreans in 2006.

where the Sunhwa River flows into the Taedong. The suburb also houses the place of Kim Il-sung's birth.

Kim Il-sung's birthplace is a collection of traditional huts: a typical Korean peasant house with a thatched roof and a block of living rooms, as well as a small barn, most of which looks as if it were built in the past few decades. The emphasis is very much on the president's humble origins, and indeed, it's an open question as to whether Kim Il-sung was really born here at all.

The **Mangyongdae Revolutionary Museum**, located nearby, continues the theme of the Great Leader's childhood and makes the point that all his family members were Korean patriot revolutionaries of the humblest possible order.

The **Mangyongdae Funfair** is a pleasant oasis built around the base of Song Hill, where you can relax with some day-trippers from the capital. You can throw a ball at American imperialists at the coconut shy, take a ride on a North Korean roller coaster and nauseate yourself on the Mad Mouse (a harmless-looking mini roller coaster that throws you about horribly).

🛏 Sleeping

Pyongyang has a range of hotels, including the newly completed ginormous pyramid of the Ryugyong Hotel, designed to be the world's largest luxury hotel in the 1980s, abandoned halfway through construction during the economic collapse in the 1990s and finally finished in 2012 (though still not open at the time of writing). Even though you can't stay there, it's visible from almost all over the city and may soon be on offer to tour groups.

Yanggakdo Hotel HOTEL $$$
(☎ 381 2134; fax 381 2930/1; Yanggakdo; ❄ ❄) This is where most tour groups stay, a massive mid-'90s tower on its own island right in the middle of Pyongyang. The rooms are already showing their age but they are spacious and comfortable, with great views over the city from most. As well as a pool and sauna, there are numerous restaurants, a microbrewery, a bowling alley, a golf course, a billiards lounge, a karaoke lounge, several shops, a casino and a (rarely open) foreigners-only disco. One advantage of the Yanggakdo is that you can wander around outside without your guides as the grounds are so large, something you aren't able to do in other hotels in Pyongyang.

Koryo Hotel HOTEL $$$
(☎ 381 4397; fax 318 4422; Changgwang St; ❄ ❄) Pyongyang's other first-class hotel, this striking 1985 orange-bronze twin-towered structure is more commonly used for business travellers, journalists and NGO staff, although some tour groups stay here too. Each of its twin towers has a revolving restaurant on top, though only one of them is open as, in a spectacular failure of forethought, the other overlooks the highly secretive 'forbidden city'. The rooms are quirky, with curious alcoves for sitting in, and small bathrooms, but it's comfortable, clean and has several bars, restaurants and shops to occupy guests, although avoid the overpriced ground-floor coffee shop!

Potonggang Hotel HOTEL $$$
(☏381 2229; fax 381 4428; Saemaul St; ❄☎) Famously the only hotel in North Korea to get CNN, the pink-painted Potonggang was owned by the late Unification Church leader Reverend Moon, and has the best rooms in the city. However, it's rare for groups to stay here as it's about 4km from the city centre. It nevertheless offers some good restaurants, a bar, pool, karaoke and indoor golf.

Haebangsan Hotel HOTEL $$
(Sungri St) Centrally located, this hotel has decent enough rooms, a good shop, pool tables and an office for booking international train tickets.

Pyongyang Hotel HOTEL $$
(Sungri St) Popular with foreign residents in the capital mainly for its excellent Arirang restaurant (supposedly one of the city's best, though tourists aren't usually taken there), the Pyongyang Hotel is basic, though some floors have been redone to a good standard.

Chongnyon Hotel HOTEL $$
(Chongchun St; ☎) The 'Youth' Hotel is in the bizarre sports district around Chongchun St, and while it boasts an outdoor pool and a lurid karaoke room, its rooms are damp and depressing.

Ryanggang Hotel HOTEL $$
(Chongchun St) Also in the sports district of Chongchun St, this place is one of the cheapest hotels in the city and it shows: there's a revolving restaurant that doesn't revolve, beds are hard and rooms are extremely dusty.

✖ Eating

Pyongyang has by far the best restaurants in North Korea, though that's not saying a huge amount. Almost all tour groups will eat out at least once a day, usually twice. Any restaurant you are taken to will be run by Korean International Travel Company (KITC) and therefore the exclusive preserve of foreigners and the local elite – there are popular local restaurants, such as those on Changgwang St, but foreign tour groups will not usually be taken there. There are some options that are not run by KITC and frequented by locals that can be visited, but tour groups will have to pay for their own meals (and for those of their guides).

On tours all eating out will be included in your price, although there are extra charges for additional beers or specialities such as the local favourite, cold noodles.

Pyongyang Number One Duck Barbeque is one of the best places in town, and will often be where groups go on their last evening. Here you'll be served up delicious strips of duck meat you cook at your table.

The **Lamb Barbecue Restaurant** has some of the friendliest and most boisterous staff in the country, and once the delicious lamb barbecue has been served at your table the waitresses will burst into song and encourage diners to dance with them.

The **Chongryu Hotpot Restaurant** opposite the Romanian Embassy is nearly always on the itinerary. It's a pleasant place where you make your own hotpot dish on little individual gas stoves. There's a second branch of this restaurant housed in a boat-shaped restaurant overlooking the Potong River by the ice rink. Tourists are charged extra if they eat at the latter, though, as it's one of Pyongyang's top restaurants.

Pyongyang's first pizza joint, imaginatively called **Pizza Restaurant** (Kwangbok St), caused a sensation when it opened in 2009 after Kim Jong-il reportedly sent a team of chefs to Italy to learn how to make the perfect pizza. The results are pretty decent, although if you don't fancy pizza, there's a full range of pasta dishes, as well as karaoke.

Okryu, one of the city's best-known restaurants, is a recently renovated faux-traditional structure on the riverside that's famed for its cold noodles and very popular with locals. For this reason it's not usually on the schedule for groups, but you may get lucky.

Pyulmori is a refreshingly well-run joint venture restaurant, coffee shop and bar near the Koryo Hotel. You can get decent food, coffee and excellent cake here, and in the evenings it's a popular bar and expat hang-out.

Right in the centre of the city, just off Kim Il-sung Sq, is the recently opened **Viennese Coffee Shop**, a joint venture between Austrian investors and North Koreans, which means you can grab a decent cappuccino and a cake between sights.

🍷 Drinking

Nightlife in Pyongyang is almost nonexistent, although hotel bars can be rowdy, especially in high season when there are plenty of tour groups in town. The large diplomatic and NGO presence in town means that there are some private clubs where foreigners can relax away from the strictures of everyday Pyongyang life, though these are usually inaccessible to foreign tourists.

The **Diplomatic Club** by the Juche Tower is a newly refurbished complex full of bars, karaoke rooms and restaurants, and it boasts an excellent pool aimed at foreign residents, although foreign visitors are regularly taken here. More often than not though, it's deserted.

☆ Entertainment

The nature of visiting North Korea is that the most mundane, everyday things become instantly fascinating. Given that contact with locals is kept to a minimum, while in Pyongyang you should take advantage of the relatively wide choice of evening entertainment to see how the capital's residents like to relax.

The ultimate Pyongyang night out is the unforgettable **Mass Games**, a unique show that takes place nightly between August and October at the **May Day Stadium** and involves more than 100,000 participants in a dazzling display of coordinated political sloganising, gymnastics, dance, music and drama. The long-running *Arirang Mass Games,* the story of Korea's history, was finally retired in 2012 and a new show is purportedly in the works, although this was not confirmed at the time of writing. Tickets are steeply priced, starting at €80 for a 'third class' ticket and rising to €300 for VIP tickets – but the experience is worth every cent.

The **Pyongyang Circus** is a popular afternoon or evening out, though it's housed in a palatial building a million miles away from your standard big top and sawdust floor. Here you'll see a stellar display of acrobatics, some very funny clowns and some deeply sad-looking bears who skip rope while dressed in outlandish costumes.

A trip to the **Pyongyang shooting range** off Chongchun St, where all Pyongyang's sporting facilities are concentrated, makes for an unusual evening. It costs €1 for three bullets using a 2.2mm rifle or pistol, and you may be shown how to shoot by former Olympic marksmen.

The huge **Golden Lane Bowling Alley** on Munsu-Kangan St is a good chance to mix with locals and watch some stellar displays of local bowling talent.

Cinema, theatre and opera trips are also possible (although rare), and while performances aren't likely to be particularly gripping, again, it's the experience that's interesting. The two cinemas on offer are the

AN INTRODUCTION TO THE BRILLIANT COMRADE...

Following a debilitating stroke in 2008, Kim Jong-il selected his youngest son, Kim Jong-un, to be his successor, passing over his two older sons, the eldest of whom now lives in Macau and the second of whom, though apparently deemed 'too effeminate' for the top job by his father, continues to live and work in Pyongyang.

The rise of Kim Jong-un was as swift as it was surprising to North Korea watchers who didn't expect the youngest son to bypass his older siblings. When Kim Jong-il died in late 2011, there appear to have been some behind-the-scenes power struggles, but ultimately the succession went according to plan, and Kim Jong-un became the Supreme Leader of North Korea. So little was known about Jong-un that the few known facts about his life quickly became repeated everywhere: he attended a private school in Switzerland incognito and loved basketball. Even Jong-un's date of birth isn't known for certain, but he's believed to have been born between 1982 and 1984, which makes him the youngest national leader in the world today.

Since his rise, Jong-un has earned his own song and his own honorific title (the 'brilliant comrade'); he's given several speeches that have transfixed the nation given that his father never once gave a long speech in public, and he has been seen attending events with his wife by his side, identified as Ri Sol-ju, a glamorous woman about whom very little is yet known. Even more significantly for the future direction of the country, Kim Jong-un unseated the staunchly conservative Ri Yong-ho, the head of the Korean People's Army, who had formerly been an ally of his and who had helped ensure the succession following his father's death. The next day Kim Jong-un himself was appointed head of the KPA, a key role in a country where the military holds so much power. The enigmatic leader has also announced plans to remove control over the economy away from the military, a move that could spell big changes for a country with effectively no private enterprise and incredibly inefficient industries.

newly refurbished **Taedongmun Cinema** on Sungri St and the **Pyongyang International Cinema**, a six-screen complex on Yanggak Island. The biennial **Pyongyang Film Festival** (www.pyongyanginternationalfilmfestival.com) is held here in September of even-numbered years.

The main theatres are the **Pyongyang Grand Theatre**, the **East Pyongyang Grand Theatre**, the **Moranbong Theatre** and the **Mansudae Art Theatre**, although spectacles vary little from one to the other. The newly completed **People's Theatre** is part of the brand-new buildings along Mansudae St, and stages some of the most prestigious spectacles in the city.

Drama is not usually shown, and instead you'll usually see orchestras performing classical and traditional Korean music, or one of the five North Korean revolutionary operas such as *The Flower Girl* and *A Daughter of the Party*. Jump at the chance to see these, as they are sumptuous productions with very high production values.

Soccer, a very popular local spectator sport, is a good way to spend an evening with ordinary Koreans. Sadly though, foreigners are normally only allowed to attend international fixtures, though exceptions have been known. Matches are played at Yanggakdo Football Stadium.

Other sports are possible by prior arrangement, especially if you're travelling with a sports group. The **Olympic pool** and the **Changgwang Health Complex** are both open to foreigners on Saturday, while a round at the nine-hole **golf course** at the Yanggakdo Hotel will make a great anecdote for years to come.

If you're stuck in your hotel for the evening then **karaoke**, **pool** and a visit to the **sauna** are the main entertainment options, though the Yanggakdo Hotel, the most common residence of tourists in Pyongyang, also boasts a **casino**, **ten-pin bowling**, **pool tables** and a **microbrewery** serving up delicious beer. Note that the Chinese sauna at the Yanggakdo is a 'special service' sauna for tired businessmen, so it's best to stick to the normal sauna.

🔒 Shopping

Every Pyongyang sight has a small stand selling books, postcards and other souvenirs. There are good bookshops at both the Yanggakdo and Koryo Hotels and the **Foreign Language Bookshop** is the best in the city.

MOVING ON?

For tips, recommendations and reviews, head to shop.lonelyplanet.com to purchase a downloadable PDF of Lonely Planet's *China* guide.

Next door to the Koryo Hotel is **Korea Stamp**, a good place to buy North Korean stamps (spectacular propaganda pieces). T-shirts and postcards are also on sale.

Department stores are often visited, and they can be a fascinating insight into what's available. The one most regularly visited is the **Ragwon (Paradise) Department Store**, which tends to have few local shoppers or products and is consequently not that interesting. Sadly, **Department Store Number One**, the city's busiest, is currently off-limits to foreigners.

Art is another popular purchase in Pyongyang. The **Mansudae Art Studio** (Saemaul St) is a centralised art studio employing thousands of painters, embroiderers and sculptors. There's a large selection of socialist-realist art available for sale, as well as more traditional landscape paintings.

ℹ Information

There is no tourist office in Pyongyang but there are numerous English-language publications designed for visitors detailing various aspects of North Korean life. The English-language *Pyongyang Times* is an amusing weekly paper full of propaganda, although a copy makes a great curio to take home.

Hotels, as the only place the authorities are happy to have visitors spend any time, are all encompassing and will provide all necessary services. Most tourists will not need to do laundry, as trips are rarely longer than a week, although the facilities exist in all Pyongyang hotels. Most hotels also have a 24-hour doctor on call.

ℹ Getting Around

All tourists will be driven around Pyongyang either by car, minibus or coach. Using public transport is not possible, save for the metro ride between the few stations foreigners are permitted to visit on a tour (see the boxed text, p309). Foreign residents in the city have more freedom to use the extensive bus, tram, trolleybus and metro network, however.

Taxis are available outside all hotels for you to travel in with your guide, should the need arise. Reception can also book taxis for you if there are none outside the hotel.

AROUND NORTH KOREA

All tours begin and end in Pyongyang but most also include a trip to other parts of the country. Nearly all travellers visit the DMZ at Panmunjom and the nearby city of Kaesong, typically overnight. Visits to mountain resorts elsewhere on the peninsula and even the far-flung mountains in the country's northeast are also sometimes included, as are a slew of industrial cities with few traditional attractions, but that hold plenty of interest to anyone interested in North Korean daily life.

Kaesong 개성

POP 330,000

Though just a few miles from the DMZ and the world's most concentrated build-up of military forces, Kaesong is a fairly relaxed place just off the Reunification Hwy from Pyongyang. The city is dominated by a massive statue of Kim Il-sung atop a large hill, while the city's main street runs from the hill to the highway.

Once the capital of the Goryeo dynasty, Kaesong has an interesting old quarter as well as the country's most atmospheric hotel, but the KITC is not inclined to spend much time here. You are usually billeted at the hotel for the night before returning to Pyongyang having seen the DMZ, although a walk to the top of the hill with your guides is usually possible.

◉ Sights

Kaesong is a modern city with wide streets and an old town consisting of traditional tile-roofed houses sandwiched between the river and the main street. Within the town are a number of lesser tourist sights: the **Sonjuk Bridge**, a tiny clapper bridge built in 1216 and opposite, the **Songin Monument**, which honours neo-Confucian hero Chong Mong-ju; the **Nammun** (South Gate), which dates from the 14th century and houses an old Buddhist bell; the **Sungyang Seowon** (Confucian academy); and **Chanamsan**, the hill from which Kim Il-sung's statue stares down at the city (and from where there are good views over the old town).

Songgyungwan

Neo-Confucian College   COLLEGE, MUSEUM

This well-preserved college, originally built in AD 992 and rebuilt after being destroyed in the 1592 Japanese invasion, today hosts the **Koryo Museum** of celadon pottery and other Buddhist relics. The buildings sur-

round a wide courtyard dotted with ancient trees, and there are also two good souvenir shops; one selling ginseng and another selling commemorative stamps and souvenirs. It's a short drive northeast of town.

Tomb of King Kongmin   TOMB

Perhaps the best-preserved and most elaborate royal tomb in the country, the Tomb of King Kongmin (the 31st Goryeo king, who reigned between 1352 and 1374) and his queen is well worth the slow drive through the hills to get here. It is richly decorated with traditional granite facing and statuary, including some curious sheep statues and vaguely Aztec-looking altars. It's a very secluded site about 13km west of the city centre; there are splendid views over the surrounding tree-covered hills from a number of vantage points.

🛏 Sleeping

Minsok Folk Hotel   HOTEL

If you stay over in Kaesong, you'll be based at this wonderful hotel consisting of 20 traditional Korean *yeogwan* (small, well-equipped en suite rooms) all off a courtyard, and featuring a charming stream running through it. There's no electricity during the day but there's usually light in the evening and hot water. It's basic (the rice husk pillows are distinctly hard!) but fascinating and far more atmospheric than anywhere else you'll stay in the country.

Panmunjeom & the DMZ
판문점&비무장지대

The sad sight of a pointlessly divided nation remains one of the most memorable parts of any trip to North Korea. While military history buffs will really be in their element, you don't have to be an expert to appreciate the weirdness of the site where the bloody Korean War ended in an unhappy truce more than half a century ago. Seeing the situation from the North, facing off against US troops to the south is a unique chance to witness things from a new perspective.

The eerily quiet drive from Pyongyang down the six-lane Reunification Hwy – the road is deserted save for military checkpoints – gives you a sense of what to expect. Just before you exit to the DMZ, the sign saying 'Seoul 70km' is a reminder of just how close and yet how far normality is.

There are several aspects to the DMZ visit. Your first stop will be at a **KPA post** just outside the DMZ. Here a soldier will show you a model of the entire site, pointing out South Korean as well as North Korean HQ and watchtowers. Then you'll be marched (single file!) through an anti-tank barrier to rejoin your bus, and you'll drive down a long concrete corridor. Look out for the tank traps either side – huge slabs of concrete ready to be dropped into the road at any minute in the event of a US land invasion.

The next stop is the **Armistice Talks Hall**, about 1km into the DMZ. Here negotiations were held between the two sides from 1951 until the final armistice, which was signed here on 27 July 1953. You'll see two copies of the agreement on display in glass cases, along with the original North Korean and UN flags. Next door there's an exhibition of photos from the war. Outside, a plaque in red script best sums up the North Korean version of the ceasefire. It reads:

It was here on July 27, 1953 that the American imperialists got down on their knees before the heroic Chosun people to sign the ceasefire for the war they had provoked June 25, 1950.

From here you'll reboard the bus and drive to the demarcation line itself, and are re-minded in more than usually severe lan-guage about sticking together 'for your own safety'. The site consists of two sinister-looking headquarters staring at each other across the line (the North Korean is built to be the bigger of the two) and several huts built over the line for meetings. Amazingly, you can cross into South Korea a few me-tres within the huts, but the doors out to the south are closed and guarded by two soldiers. For an account of the South Korean tour to the same place, see p93.

Being at the centre of the biggest military face-off on earth is rather like being in the eye of a storm – tension is in the air but it is so peaceful that it makes the very idea of imminent combat seem ridiculous. South Korean and American soldiers eyeball their northern counterparts as they have done every day since 1953. Do not be fooled by the prevailing air of calm, though; any at-tempt to even approach the border proper will result in you being shot on the spot, possibly from both sides. In the 1980s, how-ever, a Soviet tourist found a unique way to flee the communist bloc, and defected amid gunfire from both sides. Unless you are re-ally short of time, this is not an advisable way to get to Seoul.

The other interesting sight at the DMZ is the **Korean Wall**, a US-constructed anti-tank barrier that runs the length of the entire 248km border. It has been hijacked as an emotive propaganda weapon by the North, which since 1989 has been compar-ing it with the Berlin Wall. Indeed, the issue has proven an emotive one in the South as well, where students have demanded it be dismantled. You will inspect the wall with binoculars and be shown a North Korean propaganda video that we found particu-larly funny.

Myohyangsan 묘향산

A trip to this pretty resort area just 150km north of Pyongyang provides an easy chance to experience the pristine North Korean countryside, along with an inevitable slice of personality cult. Mt Myohyang and the surrounding area of hills, mountain trails and waterfalls make for a charming trip, and if you begin to miss the relentless pomp and propaganda of Pyongyang, the **Inter-national Friendship Exhibition** (IFE) will remind you that you are still very much in North Korea.

Myohyangsan means 'mountain of mys-terious fragrance' and it's certainly no misnomer. The scenery is quite wonderful, and in summer the area is awash with flow-ers. The focus of all trips are, however, the two vast shrines that make up the IFE. Before entering, you will be asked to put on shoe covers in keeping with the rev-erential attitude shown by one and all. A member of your group may be honoured with the task of opening the vast doors that lead into the exhibit – after putting on cer-emonial gloves to protect the polished door knob.

Kim Il-sung's gifts are very impressive. Particularly noteworthy is the beautiful ar-moured train carriage presented to him by Mao Zedong and a limousine sent by that great man of the people, Josef Stalin. The exhibits are arranged geographically, al-though you will thankfully only be shown the highlights of over 100,000 gifts spread over 120 rooms. Gifts from heads of state are displayed on red cloth, those from other officials on blue and gifts from individuals on brown. The undeniable highlight is a stuffed crocodile holding a tray of wooden glasses, presented to the Great Leader by the Sandinistas.

The tone of the visit is very strict and sombre, so avoid the very real temptation to ice-skate across the ridiculously over-polished floor in your foot covers. The most reverential and surreal part of the exhibit is the final room, in which there is a grinning life-sized waxwork of the Great Leader, to which you will be expected to bow your head before leaving respectfully.

Next is Kim Jong-il's similarly spectacular warehouse where gifts given to him have been housed in a vault built into the cave wall, recalling the secret lair of one of the Bond villains. Kim Jnr has gifts from Hyundai and CNN, as well as a good-luck note from Jimmy Carter and a basketball from Madeleine Albright. Indeed, some parts of the exhibit look like any upmarket electronics showroom – row after row of wide-screen televisions and stereo equipment donated by industrialists.

Having completed a tour of both exhibits, the perfect way to unwind from the seriousness is with some walking on the beautiful mountain trails. Sangwon Valley is the most common place for a hike and is directly northeast of the IFE.

Don't miss **Pyohon Temple**, the most historically important Buddhist temple in western North Korea. The temple complex dates back to 1044, with numerous renovations over the centuries. It's just a short walk from the IFE, at the entrance to Sangwon Valley. It features several small pagodas and a large hall housing images of Buddha, as well as a museum that sports a collection of wood blocks from the Buddhist scriptures the Tripitaka Koreana.

It is common for tours to visit the **Ryongmun Big Cave** either prior to or after a visit to Myohyangsan. This 6km-long limestone cave has some enormous caverns and a large number of stalactites. Enjoy sights like the Pool of Anti-Imperialist People's Struggle, the Juche Cavern and the Mountain Peak of the Great Leader.

🛏 Sleeping

Hyangsan Hotel HOTEL
Tourists are usually put up here, a 15-storey pyramidal building with a fake waterfall attended by plastic deer in the lobby. It's in a rather poor state of repair but totally fine. In keeping with North Korean hotel tradition, there is a revolving restaurant on the top floor, complete with net curtains, from which absolutely nothing is visible in the evenings due to the hotel's isolated mountain location.

Hamhung 함흥

North Korea's massively industrial second city is now open to tour groups and it's a great place to visit, boasting such North Korean delights as a fertiliser factory and a collective farm. Tours inevitably begin with a **Kim Il-sung Statue** on the central street, and include a visit to the monumental **Hamhung Grand Theatre**, the largest theatre in the country (and sadly only viewable from the outside at present) and the far more interesting **Home of Ryi Song Gye**, an impressive complex of historic buildings set in attractive gardens and to which a particularly bawdy tale is attached. The suburbs of Hamhung are made up of factory after factory, the air is horribly polluted and chimneys belch noxious yellow fumes into the air. The **Hungnam Fertiliser Factory** can sometimes be visited, where you will be shown how ammonia is made deep inside the enormous industrial complex, an experience like no other, even by North Korean standards. Some way outside the city is the **Tongbong Co-operative Farm**, which can also be visited by groups. While you're unlikely to see any actual farming (except from a distance), you will be able to visit a kindergarten, a quite beautifully presented gift shop and see the inside of a collective-farm worker's home.

Accommodation in Hamhung is in the **Sin Hung San Hotel** on the city's main drag. The rooms are basic, but there's running water and some unique interiors to enjoy. Otherwise, there's the **Majon Beach Guesthouse**, which is rather isolated some way out of town but enjoys beach access and similarly spectacular interiors in its main building.

Wonsan 원산

POP 300,000
This port city on the East Sea is not a big tourist draw but makes for an interesting stop en route to Kumgangsan from Pyongyang. As it's not usually a destination, it reflects real North Korean life to a good extent. The city is an important port, a centre of learning with 10 universities and a popular holiday resort for Koreans, with lovely sand beaches at nearby Lake Sijung and Lake Tongjong.

The city is surrounded by verdant mountains and is full of high-rise buildings in its centre. The two main tourist hotels are next door to each other on the waterfront: the **Songdowon Tourist Hotel** and the

Tongmyong Hotel are second class but boast absolutely first-class '70s socialist interiors. The restaurant at the Tongmyong Hotel is also far better than average.

The suburb of Songdowon, on the northwestern shore of the city, boasts a clean sandy beach where the Jokchon Stream runs into the East Sea and some antique metallic diving boards. Foreigners have to swim at the 'foreigners only' beach, but interaction with North Koreans is possible on the small pier. Also in Songdowon is the Songdowon Schoolchildren's Camp, where you can meet holidaying schoolkids, see a very curious collection of disintegrating taxidermy and a rather colourful waterslide. In the centre of town, visitors are shown a very dull disused train station and adjacent hotel where Kim Il-sung arrived and met with workers and students in the 1940s.

Kumgangsan 금강산

South of the port city of Wonsan on the east of the Korean peninsula, the most dramatic scenery in the entire country begins to rise. Kumgang is divided into the Inner, Outer and Sea Kumgang regions. The main tourist activities are hiking, mountaineering, boating and sightseeing. The area is peppered with former Buddhist temples and hermitages, waterfalls, mineral springs, a pretty lagoon and a small museum. Maps of the area are provided by park officials to help you decide where you want to go among the dozens of excellent sites.

If your time here is limited, the best places to visit in the Outer Kumgang Region are the Samil Lagoon (try hiring a boat, then rest at Tanpung Restaurant); the Manmuisang Area (fantastically shaped crags); and the Kuryong and Pibong Falls (a 4.5km hike from the Mongnan Restaurant).

In the Inner Kumgang Region, it's worth visiting the impressively reconstructed Pyohon Temple, founded in AD 670 and one of old Korea's most important Zen monasteries. Hiking in the valleys around Pyohon Temple or, really, anywhere in the park is rewarding and memorable. Pirobong (1639m) is the highest peak out of at least a hundred.

The usual route to Kumgangsan is by car from Pyongyang to Onjong-ri via Wonsan along the highway (around 315km, a four-hour drive). Along the way to Wonsan, your car or bus will usually stop off at a teahouse by Sinpyeong Lake. From Wonsan, the road more or less follows the coastline south, and you'll get glimpses of the double-wired electric fence that runs the entire length of the east coast. There may also be a stop for tea at Shijung Lake.

Your final destination is the village of Onjong-ri and the Kumgangsan Hotel. The hotel is quite a rambling affair consisting of a main building and several outer buildings that include chalets, a shop, a dance hall and bathhouse (fed by a hot spring).

Nampo 남포

POP 730,000

On the Taedong delta, 55km southwest of Pyongyang is Nampo, North Korea's most important port and centre of industry. Nampo has made its name for being the 'birthplace of the Chollima movement', after the workers at the local steel plant supposedly 'took the lead in bringing about an upswing in socialist construction' according to local tourist pamphlets. Sadly there's nothing much to see in the town itself.

The reason tourists come here (usually on an overnight stop en route to Kaesong) is to see the West Sea Barrage, built across an 8km estuary of the Taedong, which solved the irrigation and drinking-water problems in the area. The impressive structure, built during the early 1980s and opened in 1986, is nevertheless a rather dull visit – in every way a classic piece of socialist tourism. You'll drive across it, then up to a hill at the far end from where you'll get good views and enjoy a quick video at the visitor centre. You'll then drive down to the sluice gates and watch them open, ostensibly the highlight of the trip.

It's now common to include Nampo in an overnight trip from Pyongyang; your group will sleep some way outside the city at the Ryonggang Hot Spring House, a former government guesthouse now open to tourists. It's a unique place – some 20 well-appointed villas with several bedrooms each are spread out in the sprawling grounds, each room containing its own spa bath where you can take the waters in your room for a maximum of 15 minutes a time – it's not clear what will happen if you stay in for longer than 15 minutes but the guides make it clear it would be bad.

On the other side of the West Sea Barrage, there are nice beaches about 20km from Nampo. Here, if you are lucky enough to go, you will see the locals enjoying volleyball and swimming.

Sinchon 신천

This small, nondescript place is often visited on trips between Nampo and Kaesong. It's interesting to stop here, as this is a small North Korean town and it's easy to get a sense of daily life from passing through.

The reason you're here is to visit the **Sinchon Museum**, which details the atrocities allegedly carried out here against civilians during the Korean War. That US atrocities were committed here and in other places is not in question (both sides frequently violated the Geneva Convention), but the typically hyperbolic portrayal of these sad events does little to restore the dignity of those who suffered.

On arrival you'll be given a long lecture about how Americans 'never change' and how the bloodthirsty US soldiers enjoyed carrying out the murder of some 35,000 people here.

The museum presents 'historic' paintings of American brutality (which apparently was endlessly complex and ingeniously esoteric: people having their heads sawn open, a man being pulled in two by two cows attached to either arm, people being burned at the stake).

Following the museum, the standard tour includes laying a wreath at a memorial next door and then travelling to the site of two barns where mothers and children were allegedly burned alive by the US Army. Sinchon is sadly emblematic of North Korea's lack of will to move on from the horror of the Korean War, and its determination to memorialise its dead as a propaganda tool. There is no hotel in Sinchon, but from here it's a three-hour drive to Kaesong.

Paekdusan 백두산

One of the most stunning sights on the Korean peninsula, Paekdusan (Mt Paekdu) straddles the Chinese–Korean border in the far northeastern tip of the DPRK. Apart from it being the highest mountain in the country at 2744m, and an amazing geological phenomenon (it's an extinct volcano now containing a crater lake at its centre), it is also of huge mythical importance to the Korean people.

Paekdusan is not included on most tours, as it involves chartering an internal flight to Samjiyon and then travelling an hour and a half into the mountains from there.

However, if you have the time and money to include a visit on your trip, you will not be disappointed. It's also possible to approach Paekdusan from the Chinese side of the border on a ferry and bus tour from Sokcho in South Korea.

The natural beauty of the extinct volcano now containing one of the world's deepest lakes is made all the more magical by the mythology that surrounds the lake, both ancient and modern. The legend runs that Hwanung, the Lord of Heaven, descended onto the mountain in 2333 BC, and from here formed the nation of Choson – 'The Land of Morning Calm', or ancient Korea. It therefore only seems right and proper that four millennia later Kim Jong-il was born nearby 'and flying white horses were seen in the sky' according to official sources. In all likelihood, Kim Jong-il was born in Khabarovsk, Russia, where his father was in exile at the time, but the all-important Kim myth supersedes such niggling facts.

Trips here are strictly organised as this is a sensitive border region and a military zone. Having arrived at the military station at the bottom of the mountain, you'll be checked in and will take the funicular railway up the side of the mountain. From here it's a 10-minute hike up to the mountain's highest point, past some superb views down into the crater lake. You can either walk down to the shore of Lake Chon (an easy hike down, but somewhat tougher coming back up!) or take the cable car (€7 per person return) for the easy option. Bring warm clothing; it can be freezing at any time of year, with snow on the ground year round.

Much like Myohyangsan, an area of great natural beauty is further enhanced by revolutionary 'sights' such as **Jong-il peak** and the **Secret Camp**, the official birthplace of Kim Jong-il and from where Kim Il-sung supposedly directed some of the key battles during the anti-Japanese campaigns of WWII, despite the fact that no historians outside the DPRK have ever claimed that the area was a battle scene.

North Korea's current history books also claim that he established his guerrilla headquarters at Paekdusan in the 1920s, from where he defeated the Japanese. To prove this, you'll be shown declarations that the Great Leader and his comrades carved on the trees – some so well preserved you might think that they were carved yesterday.

The North Korean book *Kim Jong-il in His Young Days* describes the Dear Leader's difficult childhood during those days of ceaseless warfare at Paekdusan:

> His childhood was replete with ordeals. The secret camp of the Korean People's Revolutionary Army in the primeval forest was his home, and ammunition belts and magazines were his playthings. The raging blizzards and ceaseless gunshots were the first sounds to which he became accustomed. Day in and day out fierce battles went on and, during the breaks, there were military and political trainings. On the battlefield, there was no quilt to warmly wrap the newborn child. So women guerrillas gallantly tore cotton out of their own uniforms and each contributed pieces of cloth to make a patchwork quilt for the infant.

The Dear Leader's birthplace is a nondescript log cabin that you aren't allowed to enter (though you can peer in through the windows), and it's a bit of a let-down after a long drive. But with the revolutionary sites out of the way you can enjoy the real reason to come here, the glories of nature: vast tracts of virgin forest, abundant wildlife, lonely granite crags, fresh springs, gushing streams and dramatic waterfalls.

◉ Sights

Samjiyon, the slightly sinister new resort town where most travellers stay overnight on the visit to Paekdusan, also boasts a couple of attractions – most notably the **Samjiyon Grand Monument**, which must be the most impressive paean to the leadership in the country outside Pyongyang. Set in a huge clearing in the woods with views to Mt Paekdu and overlooking a large lake, the monument commemorates the battle of Pochombo, where the anti-Japanese forces first moved from guerrilla tactics to conventional warfare and took the town of the same name. The centrepiece of the monument is a 15m-high statue of a 27-year-old Kim Il-sung, as well as a smaller version of Pyongyang's Juche Tower and several large sculptures of various revolutionary scenes. Elsewhere in Samjiyon there's the **Paekdu Museum**, a very ho-hum recreation of all the sights of the region and a small **Children's Palace**, where groups will sometimes be shown a performance.

🛏 Sleeping

Hotels in this area include the **Pegaebong Hotel** just outside the resort town of Samjiyon, a decent option with modern rooms and hot running water in its newest wing. Further away, you can also stay in the town of Hyesan, at the second-class **Hyesan Hotel**.

❶ Getting There & Away

Paekdusan is only accessible from around late June to mid-September; at all other times it is forbiddingly cold and stormy. Access to the mountain is by air only, followed by car or bus. These charter flights can hold up to 40 people, for around €4600 per plane and per round-trip flight. In a decent-sized group it isn't unreasonable, but it's rather pricey for a solo trip.

Mt Chilbosan 칠보산

The area around Mt Chilbosan is one of the most beautiful places in North Korea. It's also incredibly remote – the only way to get here in reasonable time is to charter a flight from Pyongyang to Orang airport (approximately €4600 return per plane and usually combined with a trip to Paekdu), from where Mt Chilbo is a three-hour drive down a rather Mediterranean-looking coastline of high jagged cliffs, small fishing villages and sandy beaches. The World Tourism Organization has pioneered a **homestay program** here, though it's some way from what you might imagine from the term 'homestay' – a Potemkin village of large traditional-style houses (as well as some 'European' style ones) where one family lives in part of the house, and guests in the other. While it does feel rather contrived, it's still one of the best opportunities in the country to meet and talk with North Koreans, though the main problem is communicating, unless you speak some Korean or Chinese. There's a restaurant and a shop in the homestay and another restaurant on the nearby beach where squid barbecues are often laid on. Elsewhere in Chilbosan there's the **Wae-chilbo Hotel**, where Americans must stay, as they're currently not allowed to visit the homestay.

There's little to do here save enjoy the spectacular scenery, and you'll usually be driven around the attractive valleys, peaks and viewpoints of Mt Chilbosan, including a stop at various beaches and the **Kaesim Buddhist Temple**, which dates from the 9th century.

Chongjin 청진

Jump at the chance to visit Chongjin (tours rarely go there), North Korea's third-largest city and a great way to see how North Koreans really live. This huge industrial centre and port is a world away from gleaming Pyongyang, and despite a few attempts to ape the capital's socialist grandeur around the city centre, it's a poor, ugly, polluted and depressing place. Coming here is definitely fascinating though – most locals have never even seen foreigners and this is about as 'real' an experience of the country as you'll ever get. The rules about photography are very strict here, your guides will become far more stern and you'll see little of the city save what you glimpse out of the bus as it races through the city's deserted avenues at high speed.

The only two sights currently on offer are the Kim Il-sung Statue on the town's main square, where you'll be expected to bow after presenting flowers, and the adjacent Revolutionary Museum, where you'll hear the strange story of how locals were burned alive protecting trees with revolutionary slogans on them during a forest fire.

It's usually just possible to visit Chongjin on an overnight stop after visiting Mt Chilbo. Accommodation is at the imaginatively named Chongjin Hotel, which has a very friendly manager and a team of frustrated singers working in the restaurant as waitresses who love to perform songs and dance for the guests after dinner. There's usually no hot water in the rooms but there's a communal sauna for a wash. Chongjin is an hour's drive north of Orang airport, and while trains run here from Pyongyang, foreigners aren't able to travel on them.

Rajin-Sonbong 라진-선봉

This eccentric corner of North Korea, right on the border with China and Russia, has been designated a 'free trade zone' since 1991, but the name seems to be something of a joke as there's very, very little going on. The two towns of Rajin and Sonbong (sometimes referred to collectively as Rason) are both unremarkable industrial ports surrounded by attractive hills, wetlands and forest.

There's little to see or do. The Chinese-owned five-star Emperor Hotel is here (possibly the country's best, as the only five-star hotel in North Korea), although its casino (the main attraction for many Chinese) has closed so it's even quieter than usual. Rajin-Sonbong also boasts what must be the world's worst zoo: on our last visit it contained three ducks, an exceptionally large turkey, some foxes we couldn't see, a picture of a monkey, three bears – one of which was missing an arm – and a cow tied to a fence (we couldn't decide whether the cow was part of the display or just passing through).

Despite the lack of things to do, Rajin-Sonbong is uniquely beautiful, with its rocky cliffs, lakes and sandy coastline, but it feels like the end of the universe, and it's very unusual to come here these days. There are two guesthouses for tourists who don't stay at the Emperor.

UNDERSTAND NORTH KOREA

North Korea Today

When Kim Jong-il, who had led North Korea since his own father's death in 1994, died suddenly in December 2011, the world held its breath and nervously wondered how the various factions in the country's leadership would realign themselves with the Dear Leader no longer in the picture.

In the event, Kim Jong-il's rapid elevation of his third son, Kim Jong-un, following a stroke he is believed to have suffered in 2009, ended up being a very timely act. Kim Jong-un's assumption of the leadership was every bit as smooth as Kim Jong-il would have liked it to have been; he is the third member of the Kim clan to rule this secretive nation. In his late 20s, the Swiss-educated Jong-un inherited a country with an enormous number of problems in almost every field. Food shortages, low industrial production, international sanctions and diplomatic isolation are just a few of the most pressing issues, though there are many, many more. Yet Kim Jong-un's avuncular manner, smiling face and the speeches he's given have massively boosted his popularity among a people that hadn't heard their last leader's voice more than once throughout his reign. With a voice and manner reminiscent of his grandfather, Kim Jong-un has visibly earned the respect and loyalty of a nation that has grown up with enormous reverence for the late Great Leader.

On the international scene, Kim Jong-un's rule has been marked by confusing signals. While on the one hand 2012 saw North Korea apparently returning to the Six Party Talks with China, Russia, Japan, the US and South Korea following an agreement to exchange food aid for a moratorium on uranium enrichment, missile testing and the admission of IAEA inspectors, the North immediately afterwards announced the launch of a satellite to mark the 100th anniversary of Kim Il-sung's birth on 15 April 2012, drawing furious criticism from around the world on the grounds that the launch broke the terms of the moratorium agreement. The launch went ahead and failed, and the North Koreans got neither food aid nor the satellite they wanted, managing instead simply to cement their international isolation.

The centennial festivities of 15 April 2012, which celebrated 100 years since the birth of Kim Il-sung, were something of a coming-out party for Kim Jong-un, who became the Supreme Leader just months beforehand. A march of over a million people in central Pyongyang culminated in a speech by the 'brilliant comrade' to the masses. However, North Korea watchers agree that it's impossible to know how much Kim Jong-un is a figurehead or how much real power he has, the power struggles within the notoriously paranoid and secretive North Korean elite being totally beyond the understanding of the outside world.

For the vast majority of North Koreans, however, life has changed little in decades. While the terrifying famine and unspeakable sufferings of the 1990s may now be a distant memory, for most people day-to-day life remains incredibly hard: fear of arrest or denouncement is never far away, food is never plentiful, consumer goods remain unimaginable luxuries for most citizens, propaganda is ubiquitous and relentless, electricity is scant, work is demanding, and often weeks on end will be spent doing back-breaking work in the rice fields during transplantation and harvesting seasons. North Koreans have almost no control over their destinies, and about the only option most normal citizens have to change their lives is the dangerous option of escaping across the border to China, and eventually South Korea.

Against all odds though, the country has survived over two decades since the end of the Cold War, and the Kim regime still has an iron grip on the country – once more going against the predictions of many Korea-watchers. Most chillingly of all, after 60 years of total repression of all opposition, it appears there are simply no surviving networks of dissent. How long the status quo can go on remains a mystery, but the fact that North Korea is now on its third hereditary leader, has survived devastating famine, complete international isolation and recurring energy crises suggests that the quick dissolution of the 'hermit kingdom' is far from certain.

History

For an overview of Korean history before the division of the peninsula, see p339.

Division of the Peninsula

The Japanese occupation of the Korean peninsula between 1910 and 1945 was one of the darkest periods in Korean history; the occupation forces press-ganged many Korean citizens into slave-labour teams to construct factories, mines and heavy industry – particularly in the north. Moreover, the use of Korean girls as 'comfort women' for Japanese soldiers – a euphemism for enforced prostitution – remains a huge cause of resentment and controversy today in both Koreas (p354).

Most of the guerrilla warfare conducted against the Japanese police and army took place in the northern provinces of Korea and neighbouring Manchuria; northerners are still proud of having carried a disproportionate burden in the anti-Japan struggle. In fact, some modern history books would have you believe that Kim Il-sung defeated the Japanese nearly single-handedly (with a bit of help from loyal comrades and his infant son).

While his feats have certainly been exaggerated, Kim Il-sung was a strong resistance leader, although not a strong enough force to rid Korea of the Japanese. This task was left to the Red Army, who, in the closing days of WWII, entered Manchuria and Northern Korea as the Japanese forces retreated. The USA, realising that the strategic importance of the peninsula was too great for it to be left in Soviet hands, similarly began to move its troops to the country's south. Despite an agreement at Yalta to give joint custodianship of Korea to the USSR, the USA and China, no concrete plans had been made to this end, and the US State Department assigned the division of the country to two young officers, who, working from a *National Geographic* map, divided Korea across the 38th parallel.

American forces quickly took possession of the southern half of the country while the Soviets established themselves in the north, both sides stopping at the largely arbitrary dividing line. The intention to have democratic elections across the whole peninsula soon became hostage to Cold War tensions, and after the North refused to allow UN inspectors to cross the 38th parallel, the Republic of Korea was proclaimed in the South on 15 August 1948, while the North proclaimed the Democratic People's Republic just three weeks later on 9 September 1948.

The Korean War

Stalin, it is rumoured, personally chose the 33-year-old Kim Il-sung to lead the new republic. The ambitious and fiercely nationalistic Kim was an unknown quantity, although Stalin is said to have favoured him due to his youth. He would have had no idea that Kim would outlive not only him and Mao Zedong, but communism itself, to become the one of the world's longest-serving heads of state. As soon as Kim had assumed the leadership of North Korea, he applied to Stalin to sanction an invasion of the South. The 'man of steel' refused Kim twice in 1949, but perhaps bolstered by Mao's victory over the nationalists in China the same year and the USSR's own A-bomb project, he gave Kim the green light a year later.

The brutal and pointless Korean War of 1950–53 saw a powerful North Korean advance into the South, where it almost drove US forces into the sea, followed by a similarly strong counterattack by the US and the UN, which managed to occupy most of North Korea. As the situation began to look bleak for the North, Kim advocated retreating to the hills and waging guerrilla warfare against the South, unaware that China's Mao Zedong had decided to covertly help the North by sending in the People's Liberation Army in the guise of 'volunteers'. Once the PLA moved in the North pushed the front down to the original 38th parallel, and with two million dead, the original stalemate was more or less retained. The armistice agreement obliged both sides to withdraw 2000m from the ceasefire line, thus creating the Demilitarized Zone (DMZ), still in existence today.

Rebuilding the Country

Despite the Chinese having alienated Kim by taking control of the war – Chinese commander Peng Dehuai apparently treated Kim as a subordinate, much to the future Great Leader's anger – the Chinese remained in North Korea and helped with the massive task of rebuilding a nation all but razed to the ground by bombing.

Simultaneously, following his ill-fated attempt to reunite the nation, Kim Il-sung began a process of political consolidation and brutal repression. He executed his foreign minister and those he believed threatened him in an attempt to take overall control of the Korean Workers' Party. Following Khrushchev's 1956 denunciation of Stalin's personality cult, Central Committee member Yun Kong-hum stood up at one of its meetings and denounced Kim for similar crimes. Yun was never heard from again, and it was the death knell for North Korean democracy.

Unlike many communist leaders, Kim's outlandish personality cult was generated almost immediately – the sobriquet *suryong* or 'Great Leader' was employed in everyday conversation in the North by the 1960s – and the initial lip service paid to democracy and multiparty elections was soon forgotten.

The first decade under Kim Il-sung saw vast material improvements in the lives of workers and peasants. Literacy and full health care were soon followed by access to higher education and the full militarisation of the state. However, by the 1970s North Korea slipped into recession, from which it has never recovered. During this time, in which Kim Il-sung had been raised to a divine figure in North Korean society, an *éminence grise* referred to only as the 'party centre' in official-speak began to emerge from the nebulous mass of Kim's entourage.

At the 1980 party congress this enigmatic figure, to which all kinds of wondrous deeds had been attributed, was revealed to be none other than the Great Leader's son, Kim Jong-il. He was awarded several important public posts, including a seat in the politburo, and even given the honorific title 'Dear Leader'. Kim Jong-il was designated hereditary successor to the Great Leader and in 1991 made supreme commander of the Korean army, despite never having served a day in it. From 1989 until 1994, Kim father and son were almost always pictured together, praised in tandem and generally shown to be working in close proximity, preparing the North Korean people for a hereditary dynasty far more in keeping with Confucianism than communism.

Beyond Perestroika

It was during the late 1980s, as communism shattered throughout Eastern Europe, that North Korea's development began to differ strongly from that of other socialist nations. Its greatest sponsor, the Soviet Union, disintegrated in 1991, leaving the North at a loss for the subsidies it ironically needed to maintain its facade of self-sufficiency.

North Korea, having always played China and the USSR off against one another, turned to the Chinese, who have acted as the DPRK's greatest ally and benefactor ever since, despite the fact that Chinese 'communism' has produced the fastest-expanding economy in the world and any ideological ties with Maoism remain purely superficial. China's increasingly close relationship to the South and Japan also makes its reluctant support for the Kim regime all the more incongruous. Yet China remains the North's one trusted ally, although several times since the early '90s Beijing has laid down the law to Pyongyang, even withholding oil deliveries to underscore its unhappiness at the North's continuous brinkmanship.

The regime's strategy did pay off in 1994, however, when North Korea negotiated an agreement with the Clinton administration in which it agreed to cancel its controversial nuclear program in return for US energy supplies in the short term. This was to be followed by an international consortium constructing two light-water reactors for North Korean energy needs in the long term.

Midway through negotiations, Kim Il-sung suffered a massive heart attack and died. He had spent the day personally inspecting the accommodation being prepared for the planned visit of South Korean president Kim Young-sam. This summit between the two leaders would have been the first-ever meeting between the heads of state of the two nations, and Kim Il-sung's stance towards the South had noticeably changed in the last year of his life.

Kim's death rendered the North weaker and even less predictable than before. Optimistic Korea-watchers, including many within South Korea's government, expected the collapse of the regime to be imminent without its charismatic leader. In a move that was to further derail the reunification process, Kim Young-sam's government in Seoul did not therefore send condolences for Kim's death to the North – something even then US President Bill Clinton felt obliged to

do. This slight to a man considered to be a living god was a miscalculation that set back any progress another five years.

While the expected collapse did not occur, neither did any visible sign of succession by the Dear Leader. North Korea was more mysterious than ever, and in the three years following Kim Il-sung's death, speculation was rampant that a military faction had taken control in Pyongyang, and that continuing power struggles between them and Kim Jong-il meant that there was no overall leader.

Kim Jong-il finally assumed the mantle of power in October 1997 after a three-year mourning period. Surprisingly, the presidency rested with the late Kim Il-sung, who was declared North Korea's 'eternal' president, making him the world's only dead head of state. However, the backdrop to Kim Jong-il's succession was horrific. While the North Korean economy had been contracting since the collapse of vital Soviet supplies and subsidies to the DPRK's ailing industrial infrastructure in the early 1990s, the terrible floods of 1995 led quickly to disaster. Breaking with a strict tradition of self-reliance (of course, one that had never reflected reality – aid had long been received secretly from both communist allies and even the South two months previously), the North appealed to the UN and world community for urgent food aid.

So desperate was the Kim regime that it even acceded to unprecedented UN demands for access to the whole country for its own field workers, something that would have previously been unthinkable in North Korea's staunchly secretive military climate. Aid workers were horrified by what they saw – malnutrition everywhere, and the beginnings of starvation, which led over the next few years to the deaths estimated anywhere from hundreds of thousands to 3.5 million people.

Axis of Evil

Kim Jong-il's pragmatism and relative openness to change came to the fore in the years following the devastation of the famine, and a series of initiatives to promote reconciliation with both the South and the US were implemented. These reached their height with a swiftly convened Pyongyang summit between the South's Kim Dae-jung and the Dear Leader in June 2000; the first-ever meeting on such a level between the two countries. The two leaders, their countries ready at any second to launch Armageddon against one another, held hands in the limousine from the airport to the guesthouse in an unprecedented gesture of solidarity. The summit paved the way for US Secretary of State Madeleine Albright's visit to Pyongyang later the same year. Kim Jong-il's aim was to have his country legitimised through a visit from the American president himself. However, as Clinton's second term ended and George W Bush assumed power in 2001 the international climate swiftly changed.

In his 2002 State of the Union address, President Bush labelled the North (along with Iran and Iraq) part of an 'Axis of Evil', a phrase that has haunted the DPRK leadership ever since. This speech launched a new era of acrimonious relations between the two countries, exemplified the following year by North Korea resuming its nuclear program, claiming it had no choice due to American oil supplies being stopped and the two promised light-water reactors remaining incomplete. Frustrated at being ignored by the US throughout the Bush presidency, North Korea test-launched several missiles in July 2006, followed by the detonation of a nuclear device on its own soil three months later.

An Uncertain Future

When two US journalists who had been caught illegally entering North Korea were sentenced to 12 years' 'reform through hard labour' in March 2009, the harsh sentences were internationally condemned as unreasonable and wildly disproportionate to the crime. Five months later Laura Ling and Euna Lee were lucky enough to have Bill Clinton fly in and rescue them (providing for the North Koreans a much-gloated-over meeting between the former US President and Kim Jong-il), but this rare display of leniency on Pyongyang's part is definitely not the norm for one of the most repressive nations on earth.

Far more common is for North Korean hostages and kidnap victims to remain forever captive – see p331. An even more unpleasant tale of the North's uncompromising nature is the lesser-known case of a 53-year-old South Korean female tourist shot dead by North Korean soldiers in 2008 after allegedly wandering into a military zone from the holiday resort in Kumgangsan. This incident caused the South Koreans to suspend tourism in the North in protest, and the Hyundai-run South Korean resort in Kumgangsan remains unused to this day.

The Six Party talks (between the North, the South, China, Japan, Russia and the US), which were designed to bring the North in from the cold by tackling its nuclear program, ground to a halt in 2009 after six years of negotiations. They appeared to reopen again briefly in 2012 and then subsequently broke down following a North Korean satellite launch a month later.

Kim Jong-il appeared to have suffered a serious stroke in 2008, following which he lost a great deal of weight and became visibly frail. Shortly afterwards he began promoting his third son, Kim Jong-un, who indeed went on to succeed him following his sudden death in late 2011. Very little is known about Kim Jong-un, including his date of birth (rumoured to be between 1982 and 1984), but since taking over the running of the country he has given long speeches in public, something his reclusive father never did, and has, in a relatively short period of time, established himself as North Korea's third dynastic ruler.

The Culture
The National Psyche

To say that the North Korean national psyche is different to that of its southern cousin is an understatement. While North Korean individuals are generally exceptionally polite people, if rather shy at first, their psyche as a nation is one defined by a state-promulgated obsession with the country's victimisation by the forces of American and Japanese imperialism and one most notable for its refusal to move on in any way from the Korean War. Of course, the Korean War was horrific and its legacy of a divided nation is the source of great sorrow for people on both sides of the DMZ, but the North's constant propaganda about how the war was everyone's fault but North Korea's is quite extraordinary, especially given the true history of the conflict. One of the key ingredients to a pleasant trip here is understanding that this persecution complex is inculcated from birth and that it's borne of ignorance rather than wilful rewriting of history on the part of individuals.

The North Koreans are also a fiercely nationalistic and proud people, again largely due to endless nationalist propaganda fed to the population since birth. Even more significant is the cult of Kim Il-sung (the Great Leader) and Kim Jong-il (the Dear Leader), which pervades everyday life to a degree that most people will find hard to believe.

There are no Kim Il-sung jokes, there is no questioning of the cult and almost no resistance to it. Indeed, all adult members of the population must wear a loyalty badge to Kim Il-sung or Kim Jong-il – submitting to that alone is a psychological step most foreigners would find inconceivable.

While North Koreans will always be polite to foreigners, there remains a large amount of antipathy towards the USA and Japan. Both due to propaganda and the very real international isolation they feel, North Koreans have a sense of being hemmed in on all sides – threatened particularly by the South and the USA, but also by Japan. The changes over the past two decades in China and Russia have also been cause for concern. These two big brothers who guaranteed survival and independence have both sought rapprochement with the South.

On a personal level, Koreans are very good humoured and hospitable, yet remain extremely socially conservative, the combination of centuries of Confucianism and decades of communism. By all means smile and say 'hello' to people you see on the street, as North Koreans have been instructed to give foreigners a warm welcome, but don't take photos of people without their permission, and it may be far more relaxing for both of you to simply leave the camera in its bag. Similarly, giving gifts to ordinary people could result in unpleasant consequences for them, so ask your guide at any point what is appropriate and they will advise.

Far easier is interaction with children, who are remarkably forthcoming and will wave back and smile ecstatically when they see a foreign tour group, and most of them will be able to manage a few phrases in English. Personal relationships with North Koreans who are not your tour guides or business colleagues will be impossible. Men should bear in mind that any physical contact with a Korean woman will be seen as unusual, so while shaking hands is perfectly acceptable, do not greet a Korean female with a kiss in the European manner. Korea is still a patriarchal society and despite the equality of women on an ideological level, this is not the case in day-to-day life.

Lifestyle

Trying to give a sense of day-to-day North Korean life is a challenge indeed. It's difficult to overstate the ramifications of half a century of Stalinism – and it is no overstatement to say that North Korea is the most closed and secretive nation on earth. Facts meld with rumour about the real situation in the country, but certain things are doubtless true; power cuts are regular and food shortages remain facts of everyday life. Outside Pyongyang (and even in the capital after 10pm) you'll notice how few lights there are, with most windows lit only by candlelight, if at all. While at the time of writing famine was no longer an imminent threat in North Korea, most North Koreans will eat meat only a few times a year, the rest of the time living off a diet of rice and gruel that is usually limited to one or two meals a day.

The system of political apartheid that exists in North Korea has effectively created a three-strata society. All people are divided up by *taedo* – a uniquely North Korean caste system whereby people are divided into loyal, neutral or hostile categories in relation to the regime. The hostile are deprived of everything and often end up in forced labour camps in entire family groups, maybe for nothing more than having South Korean relatives or for one family member having been caught crossing into China. The neutral have little or nothing but are not persecuted, while the loyal enjoy everything from Pyongyang residency and desk jobs (at the lower levels) to Party membership and the privileges of the elite. At the top of the tree, the Kim dynasty and its vast array of courtiers, security guards and other staff are rumoured to enjoy great wealth and luxury, although evidence of this is hard to produce – the North Korean elite is also obsessed with secrecy.

North Korea is predictably austere. The six-day week (which even for office workers includes regular stints of backbreaking labour in the rice fields at planting and harvest time) makes for an exhausted populace,

FAUX PAS

» Don't ever take photos of one part of a statue of the Kims; get the whole thing in.

» Don't ever fold, tear or throw away a newspaper with one of the Kims on the cover.

» Don't wander away from your group; this can result in serious consequences for your guides.

» Take it seriously when your guides ask you not to take photographs.

IS NORTH KOREA SAFE?

North Korea isn't a dangerous destination but you'd be foolhardy to openly criticise the regime in general, or any of the Kims in particular. Spare a thought for your guides – despite being official representatives of the regime, it's they who are vulnerable to persecution should you decide to speak your mind, make any form of protest or insult the leadership. Likewise, escaping the group, disobeying photography instructions or otherwise stirring up trouble will be far more dangerous for them than for you.

When meeting North Koreans in the street, take your lead from the guides. Ask before you take photographs, keep conversations nonpolitical and accept that at present you're unable to freely mix with locals – exchanging a few brief pleasantries is normally the furthest you can get with anyone before the guides get nervous.

The obligation to be with your guides at all times outside the hotel is a serious one. It means that individual exploration is totally impossible and often leads to frustration for seasoned travellers unused to the confines of group travel. However, until the rules change, it's important for travellers to accept and conform to them.

but this makes Sundays a real event and Koreans visibly beam as they relax, go on picnics, sing songs and drink in small groups all over the country. A glance at the showcase shops and department stores in Pyongyang confirms that there is only a small number of imported goods available to the general population, highly priced and of variable quality. Testimonies taken from North Korean refugees in China give a particularly grim picture of daily life in the north of the country: malnourishment is a common fact of life for much of the rural population and standards of living are particularly low.

While in the 20 years following the Korean War it could genuinely be claimed that Kim Il-sung's government increased the standard of living in the North, bringing literacy and health care to every part of the country, the regression since the collapse of communism throughout the world has been spectacular; most people are now just as materially poor as their grandparents were in the early 1950s. Outside Pyongyang the standard of living is far worse, and this is visible on the streets, although your carefully planned bus journeys will never fully expose the poverty of the nation to the casual tourist. Still, glimpses of life in rural villages from the bus can be chilling.

Population

A 2008 UN-sponsored census was the first in 15 years and pronounced the population of the country at just over 24 million people, which surprised many DPRK-watchers who expected the population to have declined following a series of famines in the late 1990s during which millions of people starved to death.

North Korea is conspicuous for its ethnic homogeneity, a result of the country's long history of isolation and even xenophobia, dating back to the 'hermit kingdom' days. The number of foreigners living in North Korea is very small, all of them either diplomats or temporary residents working in the aid or construction industries. All of the three million inhabitants of Pyongyang are from backgrounds deemed to be loyal to the Kim regime. With a complete lack of free movement in the country (all citizens need special permission to leave their town of residence), no visitor is likely to see those termed 'hostile' - anyway, most people in this unfortunate category are in hard-labour camps miles from anywhere. All North Korean adults have been obliged to wear a 'loyalty' badge since 1970 featuring Kim Il-sung's portrait (and more recently, that of Kim Jong-il). You can be pretty certain that anyone without one is a foreigner.

Sport

Soccer is the national sport, and seeing an international match in Pyongyang is sometimes a possibility (local fixtures are off-limits to foreigners). Volleyball is the game you're most likely to see locals playing though, as both sexes can play together, making it popular among work groups.

The North's greatest sporting moment came at the 1966 World Cup in England, when they thrashed favourites Italy and stunned the world. They subsequently went out to Portugal in the quarter-finals. The story of the team is told in a strangely touching documentary – one of the few ever to be made by Western crews in the DPRK – called *The Game of Their Lives*.

Weightlifting and martial arts are the other sporting fields in which North Korea has created an international impact, although its bronze and silver medal-winning shooter Kim Jong-su was disqualified from the Beijing Olympics in 2008 when he failed a drugs test.

One homegrown sporting phenomenon (for want of a more accurate term) that visitors should try to see is the Mass Games, held annually from August to October at the May Day Stadium in Pyongyang. These mass gymnastic displays involve over 100,000 soldiers, children and students holding up coloured placards to form enormous murals in praise of North Korea's achievements – truly an amazing sight.

Religion

In North Korea, all traditional religion is regarded, in accordance with Marxist theory, as an expression of a 'feudal mentality' and has been effectively banned since the 1950s. However, as the Kim regime became more and more deified in the 1990s, official propaganda against organised religion accordingly stopped. Indeed, one guide on a recent visit told us that Juche was a religion and that one could not follow both it and Buddhism. A number of Buddhist temples are on show to tourists, although they're always showpieces – you won't see locals or any real Buddhist community. However, in recent years three churches have been built in Pyongyang, catering to the capital's diplomatic community.

TRADITIONAL RELIGIONS

The northern version of Korean shamanism was individualistic and ecstatic, while the southern style was hereditary and based on regularly scheduled community rituals. As far as is known, no shamanist activity is now practised in North Korea. Many northern shamans were transplanted to the South, chased out along with their enemies the Christians, and the popularity of the services they offer (fortune-telling, for instance) has endured there. Together with the near-destruction of southern shamanism by South Korea's relentless modernisation, we have the curious situation where the actual practice of North Korean shamanism can only be witnessed in South Korea.

Northern Korea held many important centres of Korean Buddhism from the 3rd century through the Japanese occupation period. The Kumgangsan and Myohyangsan mountain areas, in particular, hosted large Zen-oriented (Jogye) temple complexes left over from the Goryeo dynasty. Under the communists, Buddhism in the North (along with Confucianism and shamanism) suffered a fate identical to that of Christianity.

Some historically important Buddhist temples and shrines still exist, mostly in rural or mountainous areas. The most prominent among them are Pyohon Temple at Kumgangsan, Pyohon Temple at Myohyangsan and the Confucian Shrine in the Songgyungwan Neo-Confucian College just outside Kaesong.

Arts

North Korean film enjoys something of a cult following with movie buffs, mainly as cinema was a lifelong passion of Kim Jong-il's and the industry was relatively well financed for decades. Perhaps the most famous North Korean film is Shin Sang-ok's *Pulgasari*, a curious socialist version of *Godzilla* made by the kidnapped South Korean director, who escaped back to the South in 1986 (see p331), though since his escape and subsequent 'non-person' status in the DPRK, his involvement in the film is no longer credited by the North Koreans.

Separating truth from myth is particularly hard with the film industry in North Korea; despite claims that scores of films are produced annually, the reality is probably far less impressive. Cinema visits are sometimes included on tours, when local films are shown with English subtitles, and are a fascinating experience. You can also request a visit to the Pyongyang Film Studios when booking your tour – and you may even be lucky enough to see a political-propaganda piece in production.

North Korean literature has not profited from the Kim dynasty, which has done nothing to encourage original writing. Despite an initial artistic debate in the 1950s, all non-party-controlled forms of expression were quickly repressed. Bookshops stock an unimaginably restrictive selection of works, focusing heavily on the works of Kim Il-sung and Kim Jong-il.

Tourists with an interest in traditional arts can request visits to performances of traditional Korean music, singing and dance, though these are rarely available. More feasible is a visit to a (revolutionary) opera or a classical-music concert in Pyongyang (see p313).

TOP FIVE DPRK DOCUMENTARIES

The following documentaries are all highly recommended for a glimpse into the DPRK, and are a great way for prospective visitors to get an idea of what to expect.

» *A State of Mind* (www.astateofmind.co.uk) Unprecedented access to the lives of normal North Koreans is the hallmark of this beautiful documentary about two young Korean girls preparing for the Mass Games in Pyongyang.

» *Friends of Kim* (www.friendsofkim.com) A wry look at the pro-regime Korea Friendship Association's annual pilgrimage to North Korea and a wonderful portrait of the eccentrics who truly believe that the country is paradise on earth.

» *Seoul Train* (www.seoultrain.com) This superb documentary looks at the huge problems facing North Korean refugees, how they escape the North, survive in China and – if they're lucky – make it to South Korea.

» *Crossing the Line* Telling the incredible story of an American soldier who defected to the DPRK in the 1960s and continues to live there today, this bittersweet film provides haunting insight into life in the North.

» *The Red Chapel* (www.theredchapel.com) Mags Brügger's satirical documentary follows two Danish-Korean comedians, one of whom is mentally handicapped, on a very uncomfortable journey to Pyongyang, where North Korean reality grinds up against the European mentality.

Environment

North Korea is spookily litter-free, with streets cleaned daily and no graffiti save that scratched onto the windowpanes of the Pyongyang Metro, explained by the fact that carriages were bought from Berlin after German reunification. However, the country's cities are polluted and there is little or no environmental consciousness.

The varying climatic regions on the northern half of the Korean peninsula have created environments that are home to subarctic, alpine and subtropical plant and tree species. Most of the country's fauna is contained within the limited nature reserves around the mountainous regions, as most of the lower plains have been converted to arable agricultural land. An energetic reforestation program was carried out after the Korean War to replace many of the forests that were destroyed by the incessant bombing campaigns, a notable exception being the area to the north of the DMZ, where defoliants are used to remove vegetation for security purposes. The comparatively low population has resulted in the preservation of most mountainous regions.

Areas of particular biodiversity are the DMZ, the wetlands of the Tumen River and the Paekdusan and Chilbo mountains in the far north. For those interested in tours with a greater emphasis on nature, it is possible to organise an itinerary with your Korean tour company, though any hopes of a truly nature-focused tour are likely to be dashed by the ubiquitous revolutionary sights that always take priority over hikes.

Two particular flora species have attracted enormous attention from the North Koreans, and neither of them are native. In 1965 Indonesia's then President Sukarno named a newly developed orchid after Kim Il-sung – *kimilsungia* – popular acclaim overcoming Kim's modest reluctance to accept such an honour. Kim Jong-il was presented with his namesake, *kimjongilia,* a begonia developed by a Japanese horticulturist, on his 46th birthday. The blooming of either flower is announced annually as a tribute to the two Great Leaders and visitors will notice their omnipresence throughout official tourist sites.

Environmental Issues

The main challenges to the environment in North Korea are from problems that are harder to see. The devastating floods and economic slowdown during the 1990s wreaked havoc not only on property and agricultural land, but also on the environment. Fields were stripped of their topsoil, which, combined with fertiliser shortages, forced authorities to expand the arable land under cultivation. Unsustainable and unstable hillside areas, river banks and road edges were brought under cultivation, further exacerbating erosion, deforestation, fertiliser contamination of the land and rivers and the vulnerability of crops. The countryside is slowly recovering from the devastation of the 1990s, though the threat of floods and famine remains.

Food & Drink
Staples & Specialities

While tour groups eat sumptuously by North Korean standards, the standard fare is usually fairly mediocre. There is no danger of tourists going hungry though, and you'll find you get by very well on a diet of *kimchi*, rice, soups, noodles and fried meat. Vegetarians will be catered for without a problem, but their meals will usually be bland and heavy on the rice, egg and cucumber. One culinary highlight is the barbecues of duck and squid often given to tourists.

Drinks

Taedonggang, a pleasant locally produced lager, is the most commonly found beverage, although imported beers such as Heineken are also common.

Other drinks on offer include a range of North Korean fruit juices and sodas, and Coke and Fanta are also available in some Pyongyang hotels and restaurants.

Soju (the local firewater) is also popular; it's rather strong stuff. Visitors might prefer Korean blueberry wine; the best is apparently made from Mt Paekdu blueberries. Blueberry wine comes in two forms: the gently alcoholic, which tastes like a soft drink, and the reinforced version, which could stun an elephant.

SURVIVAL GUIDE

NORTH KOREA DIRECTORY A–Z
Accommodation

All accommodation in North Korea is in state-run hotels, which are all of a perfectly decent standard – particularly those in Pyongyang. You won't usually have much control over where you stay unless you organise your own private group tour but you can always make requests. All hotels have the basics of life: a restaurant, a shop (although bring everything you need if you're outside Pyongyang) and usually some form of entertainment, from the ubiquitous karaoke to pool tables and a bar.

A homestay scheme in Chilbo opened in 2006, although it's about as far from a homestay as you can imagine, being set in something of a showcase village (see p320). Elsewhere homestays are not possible.

While many hotels may indeed be bugged, there's only a very small chance that anyone's listening, so there's no need to worry about what you say in your room.

Children

While North Koreans love children, a DPRK tour is not suitable for kids. The long, exhausting days and endless sightseeing may tire out even the most diehard Kimophiles, and they are likely to bore a child to tears. Equally, the lack of creature comforts and facilities for foreign children may make prospective foreign residents think twice before bringing their families.

Customs Regulations

North Korean customs procedures vary in severity from general polite inquiries to thorough goings over. This book and other North Korea guides are fine to bring in, although any other books about the country and its politics or history should be left at home. Cameras of almost any size and nonprofessional video recorders are fine, though huge zoom lenses and enormous tripods are not allowed. Mobile phones are also forbidden, though you can bring them to North Korea with you and leave them at customs (they are used to this and it's perfectly safe). Even if you are flying in and taking the train out, your phone will be returned through your guides. Laptops, once not allowed, are now fine to bring with you. Religious materials for personal use are also fine.

Embassies & Consulates

North Korea now enjoys diplomatic relations with most EU countries, although few maintain embassies in Pyongyang. In theory, North Korean embassies can all process visa applications abroad, but in practice the Beijing embassy remains the most useful: **China** (✆10-6532 1186/1189, visa section 6532 4148/6639; fax 6532 6056; Ritan Beilu, Chaoyang District, Beijing) The entrance to the consular section is on the east side of the building at the northern end of the fruit-and-vegetable stalls.

KIDNAP VICTIMS

Nobody could accuse the North Korean government of lacking pragmatism. Need to teach spies Japanese? The obvious solution is to kidnap Japanese civilians and employ them to do the job. By their own sheepish admission in 2002, the DPRK government kidnapped 13 Japanese nationals between 1977 and 1983, including couples enjoying romantic walks on desolate beaches and even tourists who were visiting Europe.

The Japanese government is unlikely to normalise relations with North Korea and pay billions of dollars in compensation for its colonial rule of the peninsula until the DPRK gives a fuller and more truthful account of the fate of its kidnap victims. As well as Japanese citizens, more than 400 South Koreans, mainly fishermen, have been abducted by the North and their fates remain unknown.

The most sensational kidnap of all was orchestrated by Kim Jong-il himself, according to reports from the BBC and the *Guardian*. The keen cineaste, appalled by the state of film production in the North, ordered that South Korean director Shin Sang-ok and his movie-star wife Choi Eun-hee be kidnapped and brought north to make films. After surviving four years in the Gulag for attempting to escape, Shin and Choi were brought before Kim Jong-il who greeted them like old friends, explaining how much he needed them. Given unlimited funds and the elite lifestyle exclusive to the inner circle of Kim Jong-il, Shin made seven films before managing to escape with Choi during a visit to Vienna. His autobiography *Kingdom of Kim* makes for some chilling reading about living among North Korea's elite.

EMBASSIES & CONSULATES IN NORTH KOREA

The few embassies that might be of help to travellers are listed here.

The UK Embassy represents the interests of Australians, New Zealanders and citizens of the Republic of Ireland, while the Swedish legation looks after US and Canadian citizens as well as EU citizens whose own country does not have representation in Pyongyang. Most embassies are in the Mun-sudong diplomatic compound.

China (☑381 3133, 381 3116; fax 381 3425)

Germany (☑381 7385; fax 381 7397)

India (☑381 7215, 381 7274; fax 381 7619)

Russia (☑381 3101/2; fax 381 3427)

Sweden (☑381 7485; fax 381 7663)

UK (☑382 7980, 381 7980; fax 381 7985)

Internet Access

There is no internet access in the DPRK for tourists. You can apparently send an email (though not receive a reply) via the communication centre at the Yanggakdo Hotel in Pyongyang, though we've never actually heard of anyone doing this.

Intranet (ie a closed internet with no connections to the wider web) is being developed in a few places in the country but obviously this remains entirely government controlled. Foreigners working in Pyongyang do have internet access, however.

Legal Matters

It is extremely unlikely that a tourist will experience legal problems with the North Korean authorities but if this does occur, stay calm and ask to speak to your country's diplomatic representative in North Korea. Usually, tourists who break the law in North Korea are deported immediately.

Maps

You do not need maps of anywhere in North Korea, due to the unique hand-holding arrangement with the guides. However, Pyongyang maps are available at most hotels and shops in the capital and can be helpful for getting to grips with the capital's layout. There are few good-quality maps of North Korea available outside the country; the best on offer from travel specialists is the general map of Korea published by Nelles Maps.

Money

The unit of currency is the North Korean won (KPW), which was drastically revalued in 2009 leading to economic chaos, unheard-of public unrest and even suicides as people lost their life savings overnight. Banknotes now come in denominations of five, 10, 50, 100, 200, 500, 1000, 2000 and 5000KPW and coins come in denominations of one, five, 10 and 50 chon, as well as one won. However, visitors do not usually deal with local currency: everything can be paid for with euro or Chinese yuan (but bring small change of both; big notes can be impossible to change). US dollars and Japanese yen can also be exchanged but generally at bad rates. While you are unlikely to use the won, it may be possible to get some from your guides as a souvenir (it's officially illegal to take it out of the country, so hide it deep in your luggage). Pre-revaluation notes are available to buy in some places and they make good souvenirs.

Credit cards are completely useless everywhere in the country, so bring as much cash as you'll need with some leeway for any unexpected expenses. Bring your cash in euros or yuan, though US dollars and Japanese yen can also be exchanged at poor rates. Travellers cheques are not usable in North Korea and there are no ATMs anywhere in the country.

Photography & Video
RESTRICTIONS
Always ask first before taking photos and obey the reply. North Koreans are especially sensitive about foreigners taking photos of them without their permission, acutely aware of the political power of an image in the Western press. Your guides are familiar with the issue of tourists taking photos that end up in a newspaper article that contains anti-DPRK content, and it's normal for customs officers to give your pictures a quick look through at the border, and they will ask you to delete any offending content. Taking photographs from the bus is officially banned as well, though in practice it's not a big deal as long as you are discreet and are not photographing sensitive objects. Avoid taking photos of soldiers or any military facilities, although you're encouraged to do just that at the DMZ.

EQUIPMENT
Memory cards are not easily available in North Korea, so bring as many as you'll need to store pictures on. Visitors nearly always take huge numbers of shots, so come prepared! Having a laptop to download your pictures to gives you double protection if your camera is checked and any photos deleted when you leave the country.

VIDEO
Restrictions are similar to those with a camera. But, as a number of journalists have made video documentaries about the country in the guise of simply filming tourist sights, the guides and customs officers have become far stricter about their use. Note that filming the Mass Games in full is not possible – you will be closely monitored and expected to film only relatively short pieces of the show.

Post
Like all other means of communication, the post is monitored. It is, however, generally reliable and the colourful North Korean stamps, featuring everything from tributes to the Great Leader to Princess Diana commemoratives, make great souvenirs. Some people have suggested that postcards arrive more quickly that letters, as they do not need to be opened by censors. In either medium, keep any negative thoughts about the country to yourself to ensure your letter gets through.

Public Holidays
New Year's Day 1 January

Kim Jong-il's birthday 16 February

Kim Il-sung's birthday 15 April

Armed Forces Day 25 April

May Day 1 May

The Death of Kim Il-sung 8 July

Victory in the Fatherland Liberation War 27 July

National Liberation (from Japan) Day 15 August

National Foundation Day 9 September

Korean Workers' Party Foundation Day 10 October

Constitution Day 27 December

Note that North Korea does not celebrate Christmas or the Lunar New Year, nor many of South Korea's major traditional holidays. National holidays are a good time to visit North Korea – try to be in Pyongyang during May Day or Liberation Day as both are celebrated with huge extravaganzas featuring military parades that rank among North Korea's most memorable sights.

Telephone & Fax
North Korean telephone numbers are divided into 381 numbers (international) and 382 (local). It is not possible to call a 381 number from a 382 number or vice versa. International calls start at €3 per minute to China and €8 to Europe. To dial North Korea, the country code is 850. Nearly all numbers you dial from abroad will be Pyongyang numbers, so dial +850-2-381 and then the local number.

Mobile phones are not used by the vast majority of locals, although a network has been established in Pyongyang and most other large towns, but it's not accessible internationally. You are not allowed to bring mobile phones into the country (and they wouldn't work even if you did), but it's fine to declare your handset and it will be taken away from you and returned when you leave the country.

Faxing can still be useful in a land without email, assuming anyone you know has a fax machine. From Pyongyang hotels it's not exactly cheap – one page to China will cost you €4.50, while a page to Europe will set you back €13! Following pages are slightly less expensive.

Time

The time in Korea is GMT plus nine hours. When it is noon in Korea it is 1pm in Sydney or Melbourne, 3am in London, 10pm the previous day in New York and 7pm the previous day in Los Angeles or San Francisco.

You will also see years such as Juche 8 (1919) or Juche 99 (2011). Three years after the death of Kim Il-sung, the government adopted a new system of recording years, starting from Juche 1 (1912) when Kim No 1 was born. Despite the wide use of these dates internally, they are always clarified with 'normal' years.

Toilets

In Pyongyang and around frequently visited tourist sites, toilet facilities are basic and smelly, usually with squat toilets. There are regular cuts in the water supply outside Pyongyang, and often a bucket of water will be left in your hotel room or a public toilet for this eventuality. Toilet paper is supplied in hotels but it's always a good idea to carry tissues for emergencies, especially as diarrhoea is a common problem for visitors. Hand sanitiser is also a handy thing to bring with you, as soap is nearly as scarce as running water in public toilets.

Travellers with Disabilities

North Korean culture places great emphasis on caring for the disabled, especially as the Korean War left such a brutal legacy among young recruits. Despite this, seeing disabled people on the streets is actually relatively rare. Facilities are basic, but manageable, and even in situations where disabled access is a problem, the guides are likely to find some locals to help out. Most hotels have lifts due to their large size and many floors.

Visas

People of all nationalities need a visa to visit North Korea. Despite what many people think, US and Israeli citizens are perfectly able to visit the DPRK, though at present it was not possible for citizens of South Korea, although this situation is subject to change.

Restrictions have relaxed somewhat for visa applicants. It used to be necessary to provide a full CV listing all your previous employment as well as a letter from your employer detailing the duties of your current job. As this still didn't prevent journalists entering the country in the guise of tourists, this practice seems to have stopped, and now you just have to supply the name of your employer and your job. If you work in the media, human rights or any other potentially controversial professions, then be sure not to put this on the application form.

Each visa needs approval from Pyongyang, so apply at least one month before you travel. Your travel agency will normally handle the application for you, and in most cases the visa is a formality if you travel with a well-known agency.

Tour groups usually have visas issued in Beijing the day before travel, so don't worry about leaving home without one in your passport. It does mean that you need to spend 24 hours in Beijing before going on to Pyongyang, though, but you won't have to go to the embassy yourself in most cases. Individual visas can usually be issued at any North Korean embassy around the world.

The embassy visa charges (€50 in Beijing) are included in some, but not all, packages. North Korean visas are not put into passports, but are separate documents taken from you when you exit the country. If you want a souvenir, make a photocopy. No stamp of any kind will be made in your passport.

Women Travellers

While communist ideology dictates equality of the sexes, this is still far from everyday reality in a traditionally patriarchal society. However, women travellers will have no problems at all in the country, as no North Korean would be foolhardy enough to get themselves in trouble for harassing a foreigner. There are an increasing number of female guides being employed by Ryohaengsa and it is possible to request two of them for individual travel. Normally all tour groups get a male and female guide.

Getting There & Away

Beijing is the only real transport hub for entering North Korea, offering regular trains and flights to Pyongyang. The only other cities with regular air connections to Pyongyang are Vladivostok in Russia and Shenyang in Northern China. As tourists are often obliged to pick up their visas in Beijing anyway, other routes would generally be impossible even if there were more transport options.

Entering the Country

Once you've got your visa you can breeze into North Korea, even if the welcome at immigration is rather frosty. Your guides will take your passport for the duration of your stay in North Korea. This is totally routine, so do not worry about it being lost.

AIR

Only Air Koryo and Air China connect Pyongyang to the outside world. The national airline, Air Koryo, runs a fleet of old Soviet Tupolevs and Ilyushins, as well as a flagship new Airbus, and flies regularly to Beijing, Shanghai, Shenyang and Vladivostok. By far the most commonly used route is the flight from Beijing, operated every day except Sunday on either Air Koryo or Air China. Air Koryo flies from Shanghai to Pyongyang every Tuesday, and from Pyongyang to Shanghai on Friday. On Wednesday and Saturday there's a flight between Pyongyang and Shenyang in both directions as well, and on Thursday there's a return flight between Pyongyang and Vladivostok on Air Koryo. Pyongyang's airport code is FNJ.

The **Air Koryo** (☑10-6501 1557/1559; fax 6501 2591; Swissôtel Bldg, Hong Kong-Macau Center, Dongsi Shitau Lijiao, Beijing 100027) building adjoins the Swissôtel in Beijing but the entrance is around the back. You must have a visa before you can pick up your ticket, though if you're travelling in a group your travel agency will arrange the ticket.

TRAIN

There are four weekly overnight trains in either direction between Beijing and Pyongyang, the journey takes about 23 hours, though delays are not uncommon. Trains run on Monday, Wednesday, Thursday and Saturday. On each day, train No 27 leaves Beijing at 5.30pm and arrives at Pyongyang the next day at 6pm. Going the other way, train No 26 departs from Pyongyang at 10.10am arriving in Beijing at 8.34am the next morning. In contrast to the plane, it's possible to pick up your train tickets to Pyongyang without a DPRK visa.

The North Korean train is actually two carriages attached to the main Beijing–Dandong train, which are detached at Dandong (Chinese side) and then taken across the Yalu River Bridge to Sinuiju (Korean side), where more carriages are added for local people. You'll remain in the same carriage for the entire journey however, and can mingle with locals in the dining car on both legs of the trip. Accommodation is in four-berth compartments, though sometimes two-berth compartments are available.

Trains usually spend about four hours at the border for customs and immigration: two hours at Dandong and two hours at Sinuiju.

If Sinuiju station is your introduction to North Korea, the contrasts with China will be quite marked. Everything is squeaky-clean and there are no vendors plying their goods. A portrait of the Great Leader looks down from the top of the station, as it does at all train stations in North Korea.

Food is available from the restaurant car on both legs of the journey. Make sure you have some small denomination euro or yuan notes to pay for meals (€6) from the North Korean buffet car, as this is not usually included in tours. There are no facilities for changing money at Sinuiju or on the train.

Your guide will meet you on arrival at Pyongyang train station and accompany you to your hotel. Be very careful taking pictures from the train in North Korea. While you'll get some great opportunities to snap everyday DPRK scenes, do not take pictures in stations as these are considered to be military objects.

As well as the service to Beijing there's a weekly train in both directions between Moscow and Pyongyang, which travels via Dandong and through Northern China along the route of the Trans-Manchurian Railway. The trip takes seven days.

Getting Around

All accommodation, guides and transport must be booked through the government-run Ryohaengsa, or via a travel agency (see p303) who will deal with Ryohaengsa themselves.

The main office of **Ryohaengsa** (☑+86-10-8576 9465; fax 8576 9984; kitcbri@gmail.com) is in Beijing but is not open to the public; you can only call or email. There are branches in Dandong, Liaoning Province and in Yanji in Jilin.

Understand
Korea

population per sq km

KOREA UK USA

≈ 30 people

Korea Today

Changes of Guard

Succession issues have dominated the Korean peninsula of late. In October 2011, Park Won-soon, a former human rights lawyer and independent candidate, was elected Seoul's mayor, ending a decade of right-wing political domination of the capital.

North of the border, Kim Jong-un was hailed the 'great successor', following the death of his father Kim Jong-il in December 2011. Little is known about Kim Jnr, the third in the family dynasty that has ruled the repressive single-party state since 1948; even his birthday (1982–1984?) is unclear. North Korea analysts have since scrambled to interpret scraps of news from the secretive country, such as the public appearances of Ri Sol-ju, officially acknowledged as Kim's wife, and Kim's promotion to the rank of marshal, making him supreme commander of the army.

No such dynasties can be forged in the democratic South, where President Lee Myung-bak served out his five-year term of office and was replaced in an election in December 2012.

> In July 2012 President Lee Myung-bak made a nationally televised apology after several members of his family, including his brother, and close friends were arrested on charges of corruption.

New Mayor, New Policies

After the South Korean president, the mayor of Seoul is the second most powerful job in the country, so it was a wake-up call for Korea's major political parties – the governing Saenuri Party (a conservative party formerly known as the Grand National Party) and the liberal opposition Democratic United Party (DUP) – when the previously unelected and politically unaffiliated Park won the election. Known for promoting a chain of thrift shops for the poor, Park portrayed himself as the nation's first 'welfare mayor': South Korea has a minimal social safety net and the gap between rich and poor is widening.

Top Movies

The Host (2006) Seoul-based classic monster movie which juggles humour, poignancy and heart-stopping action.
JSA (2001) Gripping thriller about friendship between soldiers on opposite sides of the DMZ and its tragic outcome.

In Another Country (2012) Hong Sang-soo, director of award winning *Hahaha*, casts Isabelle Huppert as three different women whose stories intersect in the seaside resort of Mohang.

Top Novels

Please Look After Mum (Shin Kyung-sook, 2011) Emotional drama ensues as a family searches for their mother after she goes missing on the Seoul subway.

country of origin
(% of population)

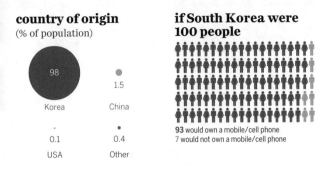

98 Korea

1.5 China

0.1 USA

0.4 Other

if South Korea were 100 people

93 would own a mobile/cell phone
7 would not own a mobile/cell phone

Opinion polls indicated that Park benefited from support from younger voters disillusioned with traditional politics where the needs of the people have come second to those of big business conglomerates (the so-called *chaebol*) such as Samsung and Hyundai. Park has called a halt to the mega construction projects favoured by his predecessors and has started pushing populist ideas such as urban farms.

The Presidential Race

In February 2012, Park affiliated himself with the DUP. However, in the National Assembly elections in April 2012, the beleaguered Saenuri Party, dogged by a series of scandals and corruption cases involving President Lee Myung-bak's aides and relatives, managed to hold on to its majority status in the Korean parliament. Much of that victory was put down to the relentless campaigning of the party's interim leader Park Geun-hye, the daughter of South Korea's former dictator, Park Chung-hee.

Attention subsequently shifted to the presidential poll. In August 2012, Park Geun-hye was nominated as the Saenuri Party candidate. If the 60-year-old wins, she will be South Korea's first female premier although she did serve as the nation's first lady for five years following her mother's assassination in 1974. The DUP's presidential hopeful is Moon Jae-in, former chief of staff of late President Roh Mu-hyun. Also in the running is the unaffiliated Ahn Cheol-soo, a professor and IT businessman who was a major supporter of Park Won-soon to become Seoul mayor; he's popular with young voters but his policies are so similar to those of Moon that he may split the liberal vote and provide a shoe-in for Park.

Korea is the 13th-largest economy in the world with a per-capita GDP of around US$30,000, about the same as the average for the EU.

Top Travel Books

Three Generations (Yom Sangseop, 2005) Originally published in newspaper serialisations in the 1930s, this epic-scale novel focuses on the travails of a family under colonisation.

Meeting Mr Kim (Jennifer Barclay, 2008) Based on Barclay's experiences in 2000, this is an amusing, easy read with fresh insights.

Korea (Simon Winchester, 1988) Winchester travels from Jeju-do to Seoul meeting Korean monks, artists, marriage arrangers, US generals and a barber.

Racial Issues

In monocultural Korea, immigrants continue to be treated with suspicion and even worse. Amnesty International in 2009 reported that that migrant workers are exposed to abusive work conditions including discrimination, verbal and physical abuse. Following the 2012 National Assembly election, Jasmine Lee, born in the Philippines and the country's first elected MP who is also a naturalised citizen, faced a barrage of racial attacks from a small but vocal group of Korean 'netizens'. 'Now there will be illegal immigrants doing what they want and more sham marriages,' wrote one person online. There are nearly 200,000 marriage immigrants in Korea. The attacks on Lee came in the wake of public outrage over the murder of a girl in Suwon by a Chinese immigrant worker.

According to the Korean Immigration Service foreigners accounted for 2.8% of the nation's population in 2012, with most of these being Chinese of Korean ethnicity (known as Joseonjok).

Foes in the North?

In January 2012, Park Jung-geun was arrested under the National Security Law (NSL) for reposting Twitter messages from a North Korean government website. The 23-year-old photographer said he found the North Korean propaganda funny, but the South Korean government isn't laughing; Park could face up to seven years in jail. Under President Lee's conservative administration the NSL has been invoked more frequently; Amnesty International says the law has a 'chilling effect' on freedom of expression.

The nervousness is partially understandable. Events such as the bombing of the island of Yeonpyeongdo in November 2010, the death of Kim Jong-il and the failed launch of a North Korean rocket in April 2012, are inevitably taken very seriously by the South. Not for nothing was Seoul the venue for the 2012 Nuclear Security Summit. US President Barack Obama chose that occasion to make a visit to the DMZ and speak of his country's continued military support for South Korea against aggression from the North.

Top Websites

The Marmot's Hole (www .rjkoehler.com) Eye-opening, entertaining, addictive round-up of Korea-related posts and news. **Ask A Korean** (http://askako rean.blogspot.co.uk) Go on, ask him. You may be surprised by the answer.

Click Korea (www.clickkorea .org) Informative English essays about Korean arts and culture. **Hermit Hideaways** (http:// hermithideaways.com) Beautiful inspirational photos of South Korea by Gregory Curley.

Top Chaebol

Samsung Group Represents 20% of Korean exports. **Hyundai-Kia** Construction firm, also Korea's largest automaker. **SK** Textiles, petrochemicals, telecommunications and leisure. **LG** Plastics manufacturer, now a top electrical goods producer.

History

Koreans are an ancient people, one of the few in the world who can trace a continuous history and presence on the same territory going back thousands of years. This doesn't mean that Koreans have always got along with each other – quite the opposite. The present politically divided peninsula is mirrored by distant eras such as the Three Kingdoms (57 BC–AD 668) period when the kingdoms of Goguryeo, Shilla and Baekje jockeyed for control of territory that stretched deep into Manchuria.

Nor has Korea often got along with its neighbours. Its relationship with Japan, a country that colonised Korea for the first four decades of the 20th century, has been particularly difficult. China has also loomed large in Korea's history; for centuries the country was a vassal state to its larger neighbour, adopting many elements of Chinese culture and statecraft in the process.

Prior to Japanese colonial rule, Korea waxed and waned, first under the 10th-century Goryeo dynasty, and then the 14th-century Joseon dynasty, which lasted for 500 years and bequeathed the country many of its defining cultural elements such as Neo-Confucianism and the writing script *hangeul*. Seoul became the capital, a city of many palaces, surrounded by a fortified wall.

The Korean War (1950–53) cleaved the peninsula into two countries who are technically still at war; for more about North Korean history see p322. Political dictatorship from the 1960s to the 1980s provided the background for South Korea's leap from Third World to First World status. Democracy has seen it flourish even more, with major Korean corporations, such as Samsung and Hyundai, becoming major global economic players and the country ably hosting international event such as the Olympic Games, FIFA World Cup and G20 summit.

Korea's Place in the Sun: A Modern History by Bruce Cumings (2005) offers an overview of Korean history from year one to the 1860s, followed by a close examination of the modern period.

TIMELINE

2333 BC	c 57 BC	AD 372
Dongguk Tonggam, a chronicle of early Korean history compiled in the 15th century, gives this date for the founding of Gojoseon by the mythical leader Dangun.	Start of the Three Kingdoms period in which the ancient kingdoms of Goguryeo, Baekje and Shilla rule over the Korean Peninsula and parts of Manchuria.	Chinese monk Sundo brings Buddhism to Goguryeo where it blends with local Shamanism. It takes two centuries for the religion to spread throughout the peninsula.

The First Korean

The imagined beginning of the Korean nation was the 3rd millennium BC, when a legendary king named Dangun founded old Joseon. Joseon (also spelled Choson) remains the name of the country in North Korea, but South Koreans use the term 'Hanguk', a name dating from the 1890s.

Real or not, Dangun has been a continuous presence from his time down to the present, a kingly vessel filled by different people at different times, who drew their legitimacy from this eternal lineage. Under its first president, for example, South Korea used a calendar in which Dangun's birth constituted year one – setting the date at 2333 BC. If the two Koreas can't agree on many things, including what to call their country, they can agree on Dangun.

Unfortunately there is no written history of Korea until a couple of centuries BC, and that history was chronicled by Chinese scribes. But there is archaeological evidence that human beings inhabited this peninsula half a million years ago, and that an advanced people were there seven or eight thousand years ago in the Neolithic period. These Neolithic people practised agriculture in a settled communal life, and are widely supposed to have had family clans as their basic social grouping. Nationalist historians also trace many Korean social and cultural traits back to these Neolithic people.

Koreans associate their origins with Paekdusan (White-Head Mountain), a 2744m mountain on the border of North Korea and China with a volcanic lake at its summit. North Koreans say that Kim Jong-il was born there, even if most historians think he was born along the Sino–Russian border.

The Three Kingdoms

Around the time of Christ three ancient kingdoms emerged on the Korean Peninsula. The first was Baekje (Paekche), which was a centralised, aristocratic state melding Chinese and indigenous influence. By the 3rd century AD, Baekje was strong enough to demolish its rivals and occupy what today is the core area of Korea, around Seoul.

The common Korean custom of father-to-son royal succession is said to have begun with Baekje king Geun Chugo. His grandson inaugurated another long tradition by adopting Buddhism as the state religion (in AD 384).

The northern kingdom, Goguryeo (Koguryŏ), conquered a large territory by AD 312 and expanded in all directions, especially toward the Taedong River in the south, which runs through Pyongyang. Peninsular geography shaped the political space of Baekje and Goguryeo and a third kingdom called Shilla (Silla), which fills out the trilogy.

Approximately three-quarters of the way down the peninsula, at the 37th parallel, the major mountain range veers to the southwest, dividing the peninsula. This southwest extension of mountains framed Baekje's historic territory, just as it did the Shilla kingdom to the east. Goguryeo, however, ranged over a wild region consisting of northeastern Korea and

Bronze Age (c 10,000 BC) people on the Korean Peninsula built dolmen or stone burial chambers such as those found on the island of Ganghwado.

427

King Jangsu, the 20th monarch of the Goguryeo dynasty, moves his capital southwards from the present-day Chinese–Korean border to Pyongyang on the banks of the Taedong River.

668

Having allied his kingdom with China's Tang dynasty, Munmu of Shilla defeats Goguryeo to become the first ruler of a unified southern Korean peninsula.

721

King Seongdeok orders the construction of a wall along Shilla's northern border to protect against the forces of Balhae, the successor state to Goguryeo.

» King Seongdeok 's Bell (p156)

THE GLORY OF BAEKJE

In its heyday in the 4th century, the Baekje kingdom controlled much of western Korea up to Pyongyang and, if you believe certain controversial records, coastal regions of northeastern China too. By the time it moved its capital to Chungnam, however, its influence was under siege. Its centre of power, Hanseong (in the modern-day Seoul region), had fallen to Goguryeo from the north, and in AD 475 Baekje had to relocate its capital to Gongju (then known as Ungjin), where the mountains offered some protection.

The dynasty thrived anew, nurturing relations with Japan and China, and in AD 538 King Seong moved the capital further south to Buyeo (then known as Sabi). Unfortunately his Shilla allies betrayed him, killing him in battle. Baekje fell into decline and was finally vanquished in AD 660 by a combined army from Shilla and China's Tang dynasty, though pockets of resistance lingered for some years.

In 1971 interest in Baekje got a much-needed shot in the arm when workers at an old tomb in Gongju stumbled across another one, hitherto undiscovered. Inside lay a wealth of funerary objects that had not seen the light of day in 1500 years: the remains of the king and queen's wooden coffins, golden diadem ornaments that would have been set upon their heads, gold jewellery and clothing accessories, the king's sword and much more – all contained in a space about 4m long, 3m wide and 3m high. A stone tablet confirmed that the tomb belonged to King Muryeong, the longest-ruling Baekje king at Gongju, and the royal treasures have taken pride of place in the town ever since.

eastern Manchuria, giving rise to contemporary dreams of a 'greater Korea' in territories that now happen to be part of China and Russia. While South Korea identifies itself with the glories of the Shilla kingdom, which they say unified the peninsula in AD 668, the North identifies with Goguryeo and says the country wasn't truly unified until the founding of the Goguryeo dynasty.

Shilla Ascendancy

Shilla emerged victorious on the peninsula in 668. However, in this process the country had come under the long-term sway of Chinese civilisation. Chinese statecraft, Buddhist and Confucian philosophy, Confucian practices of educating the young, and the Chinese written language were all entrenched. Artists from Goguryeo and Baekje also perfected a mural art found on the walls of tombs, and took it to Japan where it deeply influenced Japan's temple and burial art. But it is the blossoming of Shilla that still astounds contemporary visitors to Korea, and makes its ancient capital at Gyeongju one of the most fascinating tourist destinations in East Asia.

Chihwaseon (2002), which won a prize for director Im Kwon-taek at Cannes, is a visually stunning film based on the true story of a talented, nonconformist painter who lived at the end of the Joseon dynasty.

918	1231	1251	c 1270
The Goryeo dynasty is established by King Taejo; it rules Korea until 1392, during which time the territory under its rule expands to the whole Korean Peninsula.	As part of a general campaign to conquer China, Mongols invade the Korean Peninsula, forcing the Goryeo royal court to regroup on the island of Ganghwado.	Monks at Jeondeung-sa, Ganghwado, complete the second Tripitaka Koreana, 80,000 woodblocks of Buddhist scriptures; the first had been destroyed in the 1232 Mongol invasion.	Although some military leaders in the south refuse to surrender, Goryeo's rulers agree a peace treaty with the Mongols, becoming a vassal state

FLOURISHING LAND IN THE EAST

Shilla had close relations with the great Tang dynasty in China, sent many students to Tang schools, and had a level of civilisation high enough to merit the Chinese designation 'flourishing land in the East'. Its capital at Gyeongju was renowned as the 'city of gold', where the aristocracy pursued a high culture and extravagant pleasures.

Chinese historians wrote that elite officials possessed thousands of slaves, with like numbers of horses, cattle and pigs. Their wives wore solid-gold tiaras and earrings of delicate and intricate filigree. Scholars studied the Confucian and Buddhist classics and developed advanced methods for astronomy and calendrical science. 'Pure Land' Buddhism, a simple doctrine, united the mass of common people, who like today's Hare Krishnas could become adherents through the repetition of simple chants.

Bulguk-sa (Pulguk-sa) temple and the nearby Seokguram Grotto in Gyeongju were originally built around AD 750 and are home to some of the finest Buddhist sculpture in the world. Buddhists came on pilgrimages to Gyeongju from as far away as India, and Arab sojourners sometimes came to the temple to stay.

In spite of Shilla's military strength, broad territories of the old Goguryeo kingdom were not conquered and a section of the Goguryeo elite established a successor state known as Balhae (Parhae), above and below the Amnok and Tuman boundaries that now form the border between China, Russia and Korea. Balhae's continuing strength forced Shilla to build a northern wall in 721 and kept Shilla forces permanently below a line running from present-day Pyongyang in the east to the west coast. As one prominent South Korean historian wrote, 'Shilla and Balhae confronted each other hostilely much like southern and northern halves of a partitioned nation'.

Sourcebook of Korean Civilisation (1993), edited by Peter Lee, has a wide selection of original historical documents and materials, in translation and with commentary.

Like Shilla, Balhae continued to be influenced deeply by the Chinese civilisation of the Tang, sending students to the capital at Ch'angan, on which it modelled its own capital city.

Unification Under Goryeo

A formidable military leader named Wang Geon had defeated Shilla as well as some Baekje remnants by 930, and established a flourishing dynasty, Goryeo, from which came the name Korea. Korea was now fully unified with more or less the boundaries that it retains today. Wang was not just a unifier, however, but a magnanimous one. Regarding himself as the proper lineal king of Goguryeo, he embraced that kingdom's survivors, took a Shilla princess as his wife and treated Shilla aristocracy with unprecedented generosity. His dynasty ruled for nearly half a millennium, and in its heyday was among the most advanced civilisations in the world.

1274	1377	1392	1394
With help from Korea a Mongol army attempts to conquer Japan but is thwarted by a heavy sea storm (*kamikaze*). Similar storms in 1281 scupper a second invasion.	Monks at Cheongju's Heundeok-sa temple beat Johannes Gutenberg by 78 years by creating the *Jikji*, the world's first book printed using moveable metal type.	Having had King Gongyang and his family murdered, General Yi Seong-gye names himself King Taejo and establishes the Joseon dynasty that will rule Korea for the next 500 years.	King Taejo employs geomancy, or *feng shui* (*pungsu* in Korean), to select Hanyang (Seoul) as Joseon's capital. He also adopts Neo-Confucianism as the country's religion.

With its capital at Kaesong, the Goryeo dynasty's composite elite also forged a tradition of aristocratic continuity that lasted down to the modern era. By the 13th century there were two government groupings: civil officials and military officials. At that time the military people were stronger, but thereafter both were known as *yangban* (the two orders), which became the Korean term for aristocracy. Below the hereditary aristocracy were common people like peasants and merchants. Below them were outcaste groups of butchers, tanners and entertainers, who were called *cheonmin* and who lived a caste-like existence, often in separated and ostracised villages, and whose status fell upon their children as well. Likewise, slavery was hereditary (matrilineally), with slaves making up as much as 30% of Goryeo society.

The Rise of the Mongols

The Goryeo aristocracy admired and interacted with the splendid Chinese civilisation that emerged during the contemporaneous Song dynasty (960–1279). Official delegations and ordinary merchants brought Korean gold, silver and ginseng to China in exchange for silks, porcelains and woodblock books. Finely crafted Song porcelains stimulated Korean artisans to produce an even finer type of inlaid celadon pottery – unmatched in the world before or since for the pristine clarity of its blue-green glaze and the delicate art of its inlaid portraits.

Buddhism was the state religion, but it coexisted with Confucianism throughout the Goryeo period. Buddhist priests systematised religious practice by rendering the Korean version of the Buddhist canon into mammoth wood-block print editions, known as the Tripitaka. The first was completed in 1087 after a lifetime of work, but was lost; another, completed in 1251, can still be viewed today at Haein-sa. By 1234, if not earlier, Koreans had also invented movable metal type, two centuries before its inception in Europe.

This high point of Goryeo culture coincided with internal disorder and the rise of the Mongols, whose power swept most of the known world during the 13th century. Korea was no exception, as Kublai Khan's forces invaded and demolished Goryeo's army in 1231, forcing the government to retreat to the island of Ganghwado, a ploy that exploited the Mongol horsemen's fear of water. But after a more devastating invasion in 1254, in which countless people died and some 200,000 people were made captives, Goryeo succumbed to Mongol domination and its kings came to intermarry with Mongol princesses. The Mongols then enlisted thousands of Koreans in ill-fated invasions of Japan in 1274 and 1281, using craft made by Korea's great shipwrights. The Kamakura Shogunate turned back both invasions with help, as legend has it, from opportune typhoons known as the 'divine wind' or *kamikaze*.

The Balhae bequeathed a lasting invention to the Korean people: sleeping on *ondol* floors. This system, that uses flues from a central hearth to heat the floors of each room, is still in wide use in contemporary Korea, with the stone flues covered by waxed and polished rice paper.

ONDOL

1399	1400	1418	1446
As his sons battle to become his successor, Taejo abdicates. His second son Yi Bang-gwa becomes the Joseon monarch Jeongjong but his reign lasts only a year.	Yi Bang-won is crowned King Taejong, and he sets about creating a stronger central government and absolute monarchy. Private armies are banned and many relatives and rivals are killed.	Following King Taejong's abdication his third son becomes King Sejong, later to be known as Sejong the Great. His father continues to wield power until his death in 1422.	Sejong the Great oversees the invention of *hangeul*, Korea's unique script, which is announced to the public in the document known as the *Hunminjeongeum*.

Joseon: The Last Dynasty

The overthrow of the Mongols by the Ming dynasty in China (1316–1644) gave an opportunity to rising groups of Korean military men to contest for power. One of them, Yi Seong-gye, grabbed the bull by the horns and overthrew Goryeo leaders, thus becoming the founder of Korea's longest and last dynasty (1392–1910). The new state was named Joseon, harking back to the old Joseon kingdom 15 centuries earlier, and its capital was built at Seoul.

General Yi announced the new dynasty by mobilising some 200,000 labourers to surround the new capital with a great wall; it was completed in six months in 1394, and remnants of it still stand today, including the Great South Gate (Namdaemun) and the Great East Gate (Dongdaemun).

The deep Buddhist influence on the previous dynasty led the literati to urge the king to uproot Buddhist economic and political influence, which led to exile in the mountains for monks and their disciples. Influential literati in the Joseon dynasty were ideologues who wanted to restore Korean society to its proper path as they saw it, by using the virtues to discipline the passions and the interests. Over many decades the literati thus accomplished a deep Confucianisation of Joseon society. The reforming came in the name of Neo-Confucianism and Chu Hsi, the Chinese progenitor of this doctrine. The result was that much of what we now see as 'Korean culture' or 'tradition' arose from major social reorganisation by self-conscious 15th-century ideologues. Foreign observers declared that Korea was 'more Confucian than China'.

The unquestionable effect of the new reforms and laws was a slow-moving but ultimately radical change in women's social position and an expropriation of women's property, more or less complete by the late 15th century. Where many women were prominent in Goryeo society, they were now relegated to domestic chores of childrearing and housekeeping, as so-called 'inside people'.

From then on, the latticework of Korean society was constituted by patrilineal descent. The nails in the latticework, the proof of its importance and existence over time, were the written genealogies that positioned families in the hierarchy of property and prestige. In succeeding centuries a person's genealogy would be the best predictor of his or her life chances; it became one of Korea's most lasting characteristics. Since only male offspring could prolong the family and clan lines and were the only names registered in the genealogical tables, the birth of a son was greeted with great fanfare.

Such historical influences remain strong in both Koreas today, where first sons and their families often live with the male's parents, and all stops are pulled out to father a boy.

A New History of Korea by Lee Ki-baik (1984) takes a cultural and sociological perspective on the country's history.

Hendrick Hamel's fascinating account of his 13 years in Korea, after he and 36 other sailors were shipwrecked on Jejudo in 1653, is available in Gari Ledyard's *The Dutch Come to Korea*, with full scholarly annotation.

1450s
Following Sejong the Great's death several of his sons take the throne in quick succession. In 1455, Sejo, Sejong's second son, becomes king and reigns until 1468.

1592
Seoul falls to Japan during the Imjin War. Korean forces use metal-covered 'turtle boats' to win several decisive naval battles in the successful quest to expel the invaders.

1666
The Dutchman Hendrick Hamel, held prisoner in the country for 13 years after being shipwrecked off Jejudo, writes the first Western account of the Joseon dynasty.

세 종 대 왕

RICHARD NEBESKY / GETTY IMAGES ©

» Statue of Sejong the Great

DONGHAK DEMANDS

The Donghak Rebellion, which had been building for decades, erupted in 1893 in Jeolla province, attracting large numbers of peasants and lowborn groups of people. The rebels were only armed with primitive, homemade weapons, but they defeated the government army. The rebellion then spread to neighbouring provinces, and when King Gojong called in Chinese troops, Japanese troops took advantage of the uproar to march into Seoul. The rebels were defeated and their leaders (including Jeon Bong-jun, who was known as the 'Green Pea General' because of his small size) were executed by Japanese firing squads.

The demands of the rebels reveal their many grievances against the Joseon social system:

» Slaves should be freed.

» The lowborn should be treated fairly.

» Land should be redistributed.

» Taxes on fish and salt should be scrapped.

» No unauthorised taxes should be levied and any corrupt *yangban* (aristocrat) should be severely punished.

» All debts should be cancelled.

» Regional favouritism and factions should be abolished.

» Widows should be allowed to remarry.

» Traitors who support foreign interference should be punished.

Korea & China: A Special Relationship

General Yi Seong-gye founded his dynasty when he refused to send his troops into battle against a Chinese army, and instead used them to overthrow his own government and make himself king. Not surprisingly, he received the blessing and support of the Chinese emperor, and Korea became a 'tributary' country to China – but more than that, it became the ideal tributary state, modelling itself on Chinese culture and statecraft.

From 1637 until the end of the practice in 1881, Korea sent a total of 435 special embassies and missions to China. The emperor sent gifts in return, however the lavish hospitality provided to the Chinese emissaries when they came to Seoul could take up 15% of the government's revenue.

Most of the time China left Korea alone to run its own affairs, and Korea was content to look up to China as the centre of the only world civilisation that mattered. This policy was known as *sadae* (serving the great). Because of this special relationship, when Japan attacked them in the 1590s, Chinese troops were sent to help repel them. In just one battle as many as 30,000 Chinese soldiers died.

Samurai Invasion by Stephen Turnbull (2002) is a detailed account of the Japanese invasions of Korea in the 1590s.

1767	1776	1796	1800
Confucianism reaches its height under King Yeongjo. He imprisons his possibly mentally disturbed son Sado in a large rice chest, starving him to death in eight days.	Jeongjo, Sado's son, comes to the throne. He establishes a royal library and shakes up the social order by opening government positions to the middle classes.	King Jeongjo moves the royal court to Suwon to be closer to Sado's grave, and builds the Hwaseong fortress (now a World Heritage site) to protect the new palace.	Sunjo succeeds his father as the 23rd king of the Joseon dynasty and reigns for 34 years, during which time Korean Catholics are increasingly persecuted.

KING SEJONG'S GIFT

Hangeul is a phonetic script: concise, elegant and considered one of the most scientific in the world in rendering sounds. It was developed in 1443, during the reign of Korea's greatest king, Sejong, as a way of increasing literacy since it is much simpler and easier to learn than Chinese characters. But the Confucian elite opposed its wide use, hoping to keep the government exams as difficult as possible so that only aristocratic children had the time and money to pass.

Hangeul didn't come into general use until after 1945, and then only in North Korea; South Korea used a Sino-Korean script requiring the mastery of thousands of Chinese characters until the 1990s. Today, though, Chinese characters have mostly disappeared from Korea's public space, to the consternation of Chinese and Japanese travellers who used to be able to read all the street and commercial signs. King Sejong's face, meanwhile, is etched on the ₩10,000 note.

Sadae was in the background during the Korean War as well, when a huge Chinese army intervened in late 1950 and helped rescue the North from certain defeat. Meanwhile, many South Koreans felt that the behaviour of the Chinese troops during the Korean War was superior to that of any other force, including the American troops. Today China is South Korea's largest trading partner, with thousands of Korean students studying there, while China maintains its long-term alliance with North Korea. It can be said that Korea's relationship with China is one of the only foreign entanglements that most Koreans seem happy with, and it's likely to grow ever stronger in the 21st century.

It isn't clear what the common people thought about China until the modern period, nor were they asked; the vast majority were illiterate in a country that marked its elite according to their literacy – in Chinese. The aristocrats were enthusiastic Confucianists, adopting Chinese painting, poetry, music, statecraft and philosophy. The complicated Chinese script was used for virtually all government and cultural activities throughout the Joseon period, even though the native alphabet, *hangeul*, was an outstanding cultural achievement.

War Diary of Admiral Yi Sun-sin, edited by Sohn Pow-key (1977), is a straightforward and fascinating account by Korea's greatest admiral of the battles, floggings and court intrigues that were his daily preoccupations.

Royal Pomp & Ceremony

Many of the premier cultural attractions in Korea today, such as Seoul's palaces, are imperial relics of the long-lived Joseon dynasty. They are windows into a time in Korea's history when absolute monarchs ruled. Pomp and ritual became an essential aspect of royal power, with attention to ritual and protocol developed into an art form. Koreans appeared to break sharply with this royal system in the 20th century, but when

1834	1849	1864	1866
The eight-year-old Heonjong, Sunjo's grandson, is named the 24th Joseon king; during his 15-year reign power resides with his mother's family, the Andong Kim clan.	Following Heonjong's death, the Andong Kims track down the great-grandson of King Yeongjo living in poverty on Ganghwa-do. The illiterate and easily manipulated 18-year-old is crowned King Cheoljong.	The 11-year-old Gojong, son of the shrewd courtier Yi Ha-eung (later called the Daewongun or 'Prince of the Great Court') is crowned Joseon's 26th ruler.	French forces invade Ganghwado, ostensibly in retaliation for the execution of French Catholic priests who had been illicitly proselytising in Korea. They are forced to retreat after six weeks.

you look at the ruling system in North Korea, or the families that run most of South Korea's major corporations, and you can see the family and hereditary principles of the old system continuing in modern form.

In these more democratic times it is difficult to imagine the wealth, power and status of Joseon kings. The main palace, Gyeongbokgung, contained 800 buildings and over 200 gates; in 1900, for example, palace costs accounted for 10% of all government expenditures. In the royal household were 400 eunuchs, 500 ladies-in-waiting, 800 other court ladies and 70 *gisaeng* (female entertainers who were expert singers and dancers). Only women and eunuchs were allowed to live inside the palace – male servants, guards, officials and visitors had to leave at sunset. Most of the women lived like nuns and never left the palace. A *yangban* woman had to be married for years before daring to move in the outer world of society, and then only in a cocoon of clothing inside a cloistered sedan chair, carried by her slaves. In the late 19th century foreigners witnessed these cloistered upper-class women, clothed and swaddled from head to toe, wearing a green mantle like the Middle Eastern *chador* (robe) over their heads and bringing the folds across the face, leaving only the eyes exposed. They would come out after the nightly curfew, after the bells rang and the city gates were closed against tigers, and find a bit of freedom in the darkness.

Korea by Angus Hamilton (1904) is a rare and lively description of life in Korea under the last dynasty.

LIVES OF THE EUNUCHS

The eunuchs were the most extraordinary people. The only 'male' staff allowed to live inside the palaces, they were privy to all the secrets of the state, and had considerable influence because they waited upon the king and were around the royal family 24 hours a day. All access to the king was through them, as they were the royal bodyguards and responsible for the safety of their master. This was an easy way to earn money and they usually exploited it to the full. These bodyguard eunuchs, toughened by a harsh training regime of martial arts, were also personal servants to the king and even nursemaids to the royal children. They played so many roles that life must have been very stressful for them, particularly as any mistake could lead to horrific physical punishments.

Although often illiterate and uneducated, a few became important advisors to the king, attaining high government positions and amassing great wealth. Most were from poor families and their greed for money was a national scandal. Eunuchs were supposed to serve the king with total devotion, like monks serving the Buddha, never thinking about mundane matters like money or status.

Surprisingly, eunuchs were usually married and adopted young eunuch boys who they brought up to follow in their footsteps. The eunuch in charge of the king's health would pass on his medical knowledge to his 'son'. Under the Confucian system eunuchs had to get married. The system continued until 1910 when the country's new Japanese rulers summoned all the eunuchs to Deoksugung and dismissed them from government service.

1871	**1876**	**1882**	**1884**
Ganghwado witnesses another international tussle as a US diplomatic mission is rebuffed, leading to an armed conflict on the island that leaves 243 Koreans and three Americans dead.	The Japanese prevail in getting Korea to sign the Treaty of Ganghwa, formally opening up three of the nation's ports – Busan, Incheon and Wonsan – to international trade.	A military insurrection, supported by the Daewongun, seeks to overthrow King Gojong and reform-minded Queen Min. They escape Seoul in disguise, returning when support arrives from China.	Progressive forces, backed by Japan, attempt a coup at the royal palace. Again Queen Min calls on the Chinese for help and the revolt is suppressed after three days.

Korea & Japan

In 1592, 150,000 well-armed Japanese troops, divided into nine armies, rampaged throughout Korea, looting, raping and killing. Palaces and temples were burned to the ground and priceless cultural treasures were destroyed or stolen. Entire villages of ceramic potters were shipped back to Japan, along with thousands of ears clipped from dead Koreans, which were piled into a mound in Japan, covered over and retained into modern times as a memorial to this war.

A series of brilliant naval victories by Admiral Yi Sun-sin, using ironclad warships, helped to turn the tide against the Japanese. Ming troops also arrived from China, and by 1597 the Japanese were forced to withdraw. Stout resistance on land and sea thwarted Japanese ambitions to dominate Asia, but only at the cost of massive destruction and economic dislocation in Korea.

Japan the Coloniser

Japan's ambitions to seize Korea resurfaced at the end of the 19th century, when Japan suddenly rose up as the first modern great power in Asia. Seizing on the Donghak peasant rebellion in Korea, Japan instigated war with China, defeating it in 1895. After another decade of imperial rivalry over Korea, Japan smashed Russia in lightning naval and land attacks, stunning the world because a 'yellow' country had defeated a 'white' power.

Japan was now in a secure position to realise its territorial ambitions with regard to Korea, which became a Japanese protectorate in 1905 and a colony in 1910, with the acquiescence of all the great powers. It was a strange colony, coming 'late' in world time, after most of the world had been divided up, and after progressive calls had emerged to dismantle the entire colonial system. Furthermore, Korea had most of the prerequisites for nationhood long before most other countries: common ethnicity, language and culture, and well-recognised national boundaries since the 10th century.

Japan tried to destroy the Korean sense of national identity. A Japanese ruling elite replaced the Korean *yangban* scholar-officials; Japanese modern education replaced the Confucian classics; Japanese capital and expertise were built up in place of the Korean versions – Japanese talent for Korean talent; and eventually even the Korean language was replaced with Japanese.

Koreans never thanked the Japanese for these substitutions and did not credit Japan with creations. Instead they saw Japan as snatching away the *ancien regime,* Korea's sovereignty and independence, its indigenous if incipient modernisation and, above all, its national dignity. Most Koreans never saw Japanese rule as anything but illegitimate and

Joseon Royal Court Culture by Shin Myung-ho (2004) details the facts about the unique Confucian royal-court lifestyle. Based on primary sources, the superbly illustrated book gives a human context to the now-empty palaces.

1894	1895
Peasants rise up in the Donghak Rebellion. The rebels are defeated but the Joseon court responds with the Gabo Reform, abolishing slavery among other sweeping changes.	Queen Min is assassinated at Gyeongbokgung palace. Posthumously named Empress Myeongseong, Min is considered a national heroine for her reforms and attempts to maintain Korea's independence.

» Gyeongbokgung Palace (p39)

ADMIRAL YI: KOREA'S NAVAL HERO

Admiral Yi Sun-sin is one of Korea's most celebrated historical figures, a 16th-century naval hero who inflicted a series of defeats on the Japanese before he was killed in battle in 1598. Based in Yeosu, Yi perfected the *geobukseon* (turtle ship), a warship protected with iron sheets and spikes against the Japanese 'grapple and board' naval tactics. Although only a handful were deployed, *geobukseon* replicas can be found on Odongdo and in museums throughout the country, including Seoul's War Memorial of Korea.

The standard Korean warship was the flat-bottomed, double-decked *panokseon*, powered by two sails and hard-working oarsmen. It was stronger and more easily manoeuvrable than the Japanese warships and had more cannons. With these advantages, clever tactics and an intimate knowledge of the complex patterns of tides and currents around the numerous islands and narrow channels off the southern coast, Admiral Yi was able to defeat the Japanese time and time again. His forces sank hundreds of Japanese ships and thwarted Japan's ambition to seize Korea and use it as a base for the conquest of China.

humiliating. The very closeness of the two nations – in geography, in common Chinese civilisational influences, and in levels of development until the 19th century – made Japanese dominance all the more galling to Koreans and gave a peculiar hate/respect dynamic intensity to their relationship.

The result: neither Korea nor Japan has ever gotten over it. In the North countless films and TV programs still focus on atrocities committed by the Japanese during their rule, and for decades the descendants of Koreans deemed by the government to have collaborated with the Japanese occupation authorities were subject to severe discrimination. South Korea, however, punished very few collaborators, partly because the US Occupation (1945–48) reemployed so many of them, and partly because they were needed in the fight against communism.

Collaborating with Japan

A certain amount of Korean collaboration with the Japanese was unavoidable given the ruthless nature of the regime under the Japanese colonialists, and then in the last decade of colonial rule when Japan's expansion across Asia caused a shortage of experts and professionals throughout the empire.

The burst of consumerism that came to the world in the 1920s meant that Koreans shopped in Japanese department stores, banked at Japanese banks, drank Japanese beer, travelled on the Japanese-run railway and often dreamed of attending a Tokyo university.

The Dongnimmun (Independence Gate), built in 1898 in Seoul by the Independence Club, stands where envoys from Chinese emperors used to be officially welcomed to the city.

1897	1900	1905	1907
As an independence movement grows in Korea, King Gojong declares the founding of the Korean Empire, formalising the end of the country's ties to China.	Korea's modernistaion continues with the opening of a railroad between the port of Incheon and Seoul. In the capital an electricity company provides public lighting and a streetcar system.	Treaty of Portsmouth ends the Russo–Japanese war over Manchuria and Korea. Russia recognises Korea as part of Japan's sphere of influence, further imperilling Korea's attempts to become independent.	Having angered Japan by trying to drum up international support for his sovereignty over Korea, Gojong is forced to abdicate in favour of his son Sunjong.

COMMEMORATING THE INDEPENDENCE MOVEMENT

In South Korea, 1 March is a huge national holiday, honouring the day in 1919 when the death of ex-king Gojong and the unveiling of a Korean declaration of independence sparked massive pro-independence demonstrations throughout the country. The protests were ruthlessly suppressed, but still lasted for months. When it was over the Japanese claimed that 500 were killed, 1400 injured and 12,000 arrested, but Korean estimates put the casualties at 10 times these figures.

Ambitious Koreans found new careers opening up to them just at the most oppressive point in this colony's history, as Koreans were commanded to change their names and not speak Korean, and millions of Koreans were used as mobile human fodder by the Japanese. Koreans constituted almost half of the hated National Police, and young Korean officers (including Park Chung-hee, who seized power in 1961), and Kim Jae-gyu (who, as intelligence chief, assassinated Park in 1979) joined the aggressive Japanese army in Manchuria. Pro-Japanese *yangban* were rewarded with special titles, and some of Korea's greatest early nationalists, like Yi Gwang-su, were forced into public support of Japan's empire.

Although collaboration was an inevitable result of the repression of the Japanese occupation, it was never punished or fully and frankly debated in South Korea, leaving the problem to fester until 2004, when the government finally launched an official investigation of collaboration – along with estimates that upwards of 90% of the pre-1990 South Korea elite had ties to collaborationist families or individuals.

The colonial government implemented policies that developed industries and modernised the administration, but always in the interests of Japan. Modern textile, steel and chemical industries emerged along with new railroads, highways and ports. Koreans never thanked Japan for any of this, but it did leave Korea much more developed in 1945 than other countries under colonial rule, such as Vietnam under the French.

The fascinating *Times Past in Korea: An Illustrated Collection of Encounters, Customs and Daily Life Recorded by Foreign Visitors* (2003) was compiled by Martin Uden, former British ambassador to South Korea.

WWII and After

By 1940 the Japanese owned 40% of the land and there were 700,000 Japanese living and working in Korea – an enormous number compared to most other countries. But among large landowners, many were as likely to be Korean as Japanese; most peasants were tenant farmers working their land. Upwards of three million Korean men and women were uprooted from their homes and sent to work as miners, farm labourers, factory workers and soldiers abroad, mainly in Japan and Manchukuo, the Japanese colony in northeast China.

1909	1910	1919	1926
Independence activist An Jung-geun assassinates Hirobumi Ito, Korea's ex-Resident-General, at the train station in Harbin, Manchuria. Japan uses the incident to move towards annexation of the Korean Peninsula.	Emperor Sunjong refuses to sign the Japan–Korea Annexation Treaty, but Japan effectively annexes Korea in August. Terauchi Masatake is the first Japanese Governor-General of Korea.	The March 1st Movement sees millions of Koreans in nonviolent nationwide protests against Japanese rule. A declaration of independence is read out in Seoul's Tapgol Park.	Emperor Sunjong dies. His half-brother Crown Prince Euimin, who had married into a branch of the Japanese royal family, is proclaimed King Ri of Korea by the Japanese.

Over 130,000 Korean miners in Japan – men and women – worked 12-hour days, were paid wages well under what Japanese miners earned, were poorly fed and were subjected to brutal, club-wielding overseers. The worst aspect of this massive mobilisation, however, came in the form of 'comfort women' – the hundreds of thousands of young Korean women who were forced to work as sex slaves for the Japanese armed forces.

It was Korea's darkest hour but Korean guerrilla groups continued to fight Japan in Manchukuo; they were allied with Chinese guerrillas but Koreans still constituted by far the largest ethnic group. This is where we find Kim Il-sung, who began fighting the Japanese around the time they proclaimed the puppet state of Manchukuo in 1932 and continued into the early 1940s. After murderous counter-insurgency campaigns (participated in by many Koreans), the guerrillas numbered only about 200. In 1945 they returned to northern Korea and constituted the ruling elite from that point down to the present.

Japan's surrender to the Allies in 1945 opened a new chapter in the stormy relationship between the two countries. Thanks to munificent American support, Japan began growing rapidly in the early 1950s and South Korea got going in the mid-1960s. Today companies in both countries battle each other to produce the best ships, cars, steel products, computer chips, mobile phones, flat-screen TVs and other electronic equipment. The new rivalry is a never-ending competition for world markets, just as sports became another modern-day battleground to decide who is top dog.

> Isabella Bird Bishop visited Gyeongbokgung in 1895 and noted: 'What with 800 troops, 1500 attendants and officials of all descriptions, courtiers and ministers and their attendants, secretaries, messengers and hangers-on, the vast enclosure of the palace seemed as crowded and populated as the city itself'.

The Korean War

The 38th Parallel

In the immediate aftermath of the obliteration of Nagasaki, three Americans in the War Department (including Dean Rusk, later Secretary of State) drew a fateful line at the 38th parallel in Korea, dividing this nation that had a unitary integrity going back to antiquity. The line was supposed to demarcate the areas in which American and Soviet forces would receive the Japanese surrender, but Rusk later acknowledged that he did not trust the Russians and wanted to get the nerve centre of the country, Seoul, in the American zone. He consulted no Koreans, no allies and not even the president in making this decision. But it followed on from three years of State Department planning in which an American occupation of part or all of Korea was seen as crucial to the postwar security of Japan and the Pacific. The US then set up a three-year military government in southern Korea that deeply shaped postwar Korean history.

> *At the Court of Korea* by William Franklin Sands gives a first-hand account of King Gojong and his government between 1890 and 1910.

1929	1945	1948	25 June 1950
A nationwide student uprising in November leads to the strengthening of Japanese military rule in 1931, after which freedom of the press and of expression are curbed.	With the Allied victory in WWII, Korea is liberated from Japan and divided into two protectorates – the Soviets handling the North and the US the South.	The Republic of Korea is founded in the southern part of the peninsula, with Seoul designated the capital city. The Democratic People's Republic of Korea (DPRK, or North Korea) is also founded.	North Korea stages a surprise invasion of the South over the 38th parallel border, triggering the Korean War. By end of month they occupy Seoul.

HISTORY THE KOREAN WAR

The Soviets came in with fewer concrete plans for Korea and moved more slowly than the Americans in setting up an administration. They thought Kim Il-sung would be good as a defence minister in a new government, but sought to get him and other communists to work together with Christian nationalist figures like Jo Man-sik. Soon, however, the Cold War rivalry overshadowed everything in Korea, as the Americans turned to Rhee Syngman (an elderly patriot who had lived in the US for 35 years) and the Russians to Kim Il-sung.

By 1948 Rhee and Kim had both established separate republics and by the end of the year Soviet troops had withdrawn, never to return again. American combat troops departed in June 1949, leaving behind a 500-man military advisory group. For the first time in its short history since 1945, South Korea now had operational control of its own military forces. Within a year war had broken out and the US took back that control and has never relinquished it, illustrating, according to historian Bruce Cumings, that the US has always had a civil war deterrent in Korea: containing the enemy in the North and constraining the ally in the South.

The War Begins

In 1949 both sides sought external support to mount a war against the other side, and the North succeeded where the South failed. Its greatest strength came from tens of thousands of Koreans who had been sent to fight in China's civil war, and who returned to North Korea in 1949 and 1950. Kim Il-sung also played Stalin off against Mao Zedong to get military aid and a critical independent space for himself, so that when he invaded he could count on one or both powers to bail him out if things went badly. After years of guerrilla war in the South (fought almost entirely by southerners) and much border fighting in 1949, Kim launched a surprise invasion on 25 June 1950, when he peeled several divisions off in the midst of summer war games; many high officers were unaware of the war plan. Seoul fell in three days, and soon North Korea was at war with the US.

The Americans responded by getting the United Nations to condemn the attack and gaining commitments from 16 other countries, although Americans almost always bore the brunt of the fighting, and only British and Turkish combat forces had a substantial role. The war went badly for the UN at first, and its troops were soon pushed far back into a small pocket around Busan (Pusan). But following a daring landing at Incheon (Inchon) under the command of General Douglas MacArthur, North Korean forces were pushed back above the 38th parallel.

Men wearing a topknot was widespread during Korea's peasant relations with the Ming dynasty; later it became a symbol of 'Ming loyalists' in Korea after that dynasty fell. In 1895 King Gojong had his topknot cut off, but conservatives did not follow his example or share his enthusiasm for reforms.

The Dawn of Modern Korea (Andrei Lankov, 2007) is a fascinating, accessible look at Korea in the early 20th century and the cultural and social impacts of Westernisation as King Gojong tried to modernise his tradition-bound hermit kingdom.

September 1950	1953	1960	1963
UN troops led by US General MacArthur mount a daring counterattack in the Battle of Incheon. By 25 September Seoul is recaptured by South Korean forces.	The armistice ending the Korean War is signed by the US and North Korea, but not South Korea. The DMZ is established around the 38th parallel.	Popular protest ousts President Rhee Syngman; attempts at democratic rule fail – a military coup topples the unstable elected government and installs General Park Chung-hee into power in 1961.	Following pressure from the US, civilian rule is restored. However, the Democratic Republican Party, a political vehicle for Park, wins the general election, as it does again in 1967.

Creating the DMZ

The question then became whether the war was over. South Korea's sovereignty had been restored and UN leaders wanted to call it a victory. But for the previous year, high officials in the Truman administration had been debating a more 'positive' strategy than containment, namely 'rollback' or liberation, and so Truman decided to march north to overthrow Kim's regime. Kim's long-time relations with Chinese communists bailed his chestnuts out of the fire when Mao committed a huge number of soldiers, but now the US was at war with China.

By New Year's Eve 1950, US forces were pushed back below the 38th parallel, and the communists were about to launch an offensive that would retake Seoul. This shook America and its allies to the core, Truman declared a national emergency, and WWIII seemed to be at the doorstep. But Mao did not want general war with the US, and did not try to push the UN forces off the peninsula. By spring 1951 the fighting had stabilised roughly along the lines where the war ended. Truce talks began and dragged on for two years, amid massive trench warfare along the lines. These battles created the Demilitarized Zone (DMZ).

At the end of the war, Korea lay in ruins. Seoul had changed hands no less than four times and was badly damaged, but many prewar buildings remained sufficiently intact to rebuild them much as they were. The US Air Force pounded the North for three years until all of its cities were destroyed and some were completely demolished, leaving the urban population to live, work and go to school underground, like cavemen. Millions of Koreans died (probably three million, two-thirds of them in the North), millions more were left homeless, industries were destroyed and the entire country was massively demoralised because the bloodletting had only restored the status quo. Of the UN troops, 37,000 were killed (about 35,000 of them Americans) and 120,000 were wounded.

Postwar Recovery

The 1950s were a time of depressing stagnation for the South but rapid industrial growth for the North. Then, over the next 30 years, both Koreas underwent rapid industrial growth. The North's industrial growth was as fast as any in the world from the mid-1950s into the mid-1970s, and even in the early 1980s its per capita GNP was about the same as the South's. But then the South began to build an enormous lead that soon became insurmountable, and by the 1990s huge economic disparities had emerged. The North experienced depressing stagnation that led finally to famine and massive death, while the South emerged as a major global economic power.

The Korean Sohn Kee-chung won the gold medal for the marathon at the 1936 Berlin Olympics but he was forced to compete as Kitei Son under the flag of Japan, Korea's occupying power.

1968

In January North Korean agents are halted just 800m from the presidential Blue House, foiling a daring assassination attempt on Park Chung-hee.

CHERIE CULLEN / DEPARTMENT OF DEFENSE / HANDOUT / CORBIS ©

1971

The constitution is amended so Park can run for a third term of office. He wins against Kim Dae-jung. The following year Park dissolves parliament and suspends the constitution.

» Blue House

THE HOUSE OF SHARING *SIMON RICHMOND*

An hour's journey south of Seoul, in bucolic countryside, is the **House of Sharing** (http://nanum.org), a very special retirement home. Here live seven women, now in their late 70s or 80s, who were forced to work in Japanese military brothels across Asia before and during WWII. 'Comfort women' is the euphemism coined by the Japanese military for these women, and their existence started to come to international attention in the early 1990s through the courageous testimonies of the victims – 70% of whom were Korean – and their demand for official recognition and compensation from the Japanese government. A study by the UN has put the number of women involved at around 210,000 (the Japanese government claims the figure was only 50,000).

At the House of Sharing they prefer the respectful term *halmoni,* which means grandmother. Described as activists, some *halmoni* still take part in the protests held every Wednesday at noon outside Seoul's Japanese embassy. At the House of Sharing's **museum (adult/student ₩5000/3000; ☉10am-5pm Tue-Sun)** you can learn more about the atrocious conditions and experiences these women were forced to endure. Most of them were aged between 13 and 16, and had to service between 30 and 40 soldiers a day.

'We must record these things that were forced upon us.' These words by Kim Hak Soon, one of the first Korean *halmoni* to testify about her experiences, introduces the museum exhibition which includes a display of the artworks created by the *halmoni* that reflect their feelings and experiences.

The old women do not regularly meet visitors to the House of Sharing to share their stories. Instead, video documentaries about them are screened and discussions are held about their plight and the ongoing sexual trafficking of women around the world. The videos and anecdotes from the guides paint these frail, sometimes crotchety women as pillars of strength who after a lifetime of shame and sorrow have chosen to spend their twilight years as campaigners for social justice.

It's a heavy-going experience but one not without a sense of hope – both at the resilience of the human spirit and the prospect for reconciliation. The greatest number of visitors to the House come from Japan and every year a Peace Road Program brings Korean and Japanese students together to help further understanding of their countries' painfully entwined history and how they might be better neighbours in the future.

This great triumph came at enormous cost, as South Koreans worked the longest hours in the industrial world for decades and suffered under one military dictatorship after another. Corrupt, autocratic rulers censored the media, imprisoned and tortured political opponents, manipulated elections and continually changed the country's constitution to suit themselves; meanwhile Washington backed them up (except for a brief moment in the 1960s) and never did more than issue tepid protests at their authoritarian rule. Student protests and less frequent trade-union

1972	1979	1987	1988
The new constitution, which includes no limits on re-election, turns Park's presidency into a virtual dictatorship. He's re-elected with no opposition in both 1972 and 1978.	After surviving a couple of assassination attempts (one of which had killed his wife), Park is finally shot dead by the trusted head of his own Central Intelligence Agency.	Following sweeping national protests, with the strongest concentration in Seoul, Korea's last military dictatorship under Chun Doo-hwan, steps down to allow democratic elections.	Seoul hosts the Olympic Summer Games, bulldozing and/or concealing slums to build a huge Olympic park and major expressway.

street protests were often violent, as were the police or military forces sent to suppress them. But slowly a democratisation movement built strength across the society.

Dictatorship & Massacre

When the Korean War ended in 1953, Rhee Syngman continued his dictatorial rule until 1961, when he and his wife fled to Hawaii following widespread demonstrations against him that included university professors demonstrating in the streets of Seoul. Ordinary people were finally free to take revenge against hated policemen who had served the Japanese. Following a military coup later in 1961, Park Chung-hee ruled with an iron fist until the Kennedy administration demanded that he hold elections; he narrowly won three of them in 1963, 1967 and 1971, partly by spreading enormous amounts of money around (peasants would get white envelopes full of cash for voting).

In spite of this, the democracy activist Kim Dae-jung nearly beat him in 1971, garnering 46% of the vote. That led Park to declare martial law and make himself president for life. Amid massive demonstrations in 1979 his own intelligence chief, Kim Jae-gyu, shot him dead over dinner one night, in an episode never fully explained. This was followed by five months of democratic discussion until Chun Doo-hwan, a protégé of Park, moved to take full power.

In response the citizens of Gwangju took to the streets on 18 May 1980, in an incident now known as the May 18 Democratic Uprising. The army was ordered to move in, on the pretext of quelling a communist uprising. The soldiers had no bullets, but used bayonets to murder dozens of unarmed protesters and passers-by. Outraged residents broke into armouries and police stations and used seized weapons and ammunition to drive the troops out of their city.

For over a week prodemocracy citizen groups were in control, but the brutal military response came nine days later on 27 May, when soldiers armed with loaded rifles, supported by helicopters and tanks, retook the city. Most of the protest leaders were labelled 'communists' and summarily shot. At least 154 civilians were killed, with another 74 missing and presumed dead. An additional 4141 were wounded and more than 3000 were arrested, many of whom were tortured. For eyewitness accounts of the still-controversial event, read *Memories of May 1980* by Chung Sang-yong (2003) or view www.518.org.

The Return of Democracy

Finally, in 1992, a civilian, Kim Young-sam, won election and began to build a real democracy. Although a charter member of the old ruling groups, Kim had resigned his National Assembly seat in the 1960s when

HISTORY POSTWAR RECOVERY

Eunuch (1968), an artistic film directed by Shin Sang-ok, is about a woman who is forced by her father to become the king's concubine although she loves someone else. The film depicts the inner sanctum in those now-empty and dusty palaces.

US Academic Bruce Cumings' *The Korean War: A Modern History* (2010) and UK journalist Max Hastings' *The Korean War* (1988) are two takes on this pivotal conflict, analysing its causes, progress and repercussions.

1991	**1992**	**1994**	**1997**
Following two years of talks, an Agreement of Reconciliation is signed between Seoul and Pyongyang. One of the aims is to make the Korean Peninsula nuclear free.	The first civilian to hold the office since 1960, Kim Young-sam is elected president. During his five-year term he presides over a massive anti-corruption campaign.	During nuclear program negotiations with the US and prior to what would have been a historic summit with Kim Young-sam, North Korea's Kim Il-sung dies of a heart attack.	Long-time democracy champion Kim Dae-jung is elected president in the midst of a region-wide economic crisis. The International Monetary Fund offers the country a $57 million bailout.

Rhee tried to amend the constitution and had since been a thorn in the side of the military governments along with Kim Dae-jung. Among his first acts as president were to launch an anti-corruption crusade, free thousands of political prisoners and put Chun Doo-hwan on trial.

The former president's conviction of treason and monumental corruption was a great victory for the democratic movement. One of the strongest labour movements in the world soon emerged, and when former dissident Kim Dae-jung was elected at the end of 1997, all the protests and suffering and killing seemed finally to have effected change.

Kim was ideally poised to solve the deep economic downturn that hit Korea in 1997, as part of the Asian financial crisis. The IMF demanded reforms of the conglomerates, or *jaebeol,* as the price for its $57 million bailout, and Kim had long called for restructuring the conglomerates and their cronyism with the banks and the government. By 1999 the economy was growing again.

Sunshine Policy

In 1998 Kim also began to roll out a 'Sunshine Policy' aimed at reconciliation with North Korea, if not reunification. Within a year Pyongyang had responded, various economic and cultural exchanges began, and in June 2000 the two presidents met at a summit for the first time since 1945. Seen by critics as appeasement of the North, this engagement policy was predicated on the realist principles that the North was not going to collapse and so had to be dealt with as it was, and that the North would not object to the continued presence of US troops in the South during the long process of reconciliation if the US normalised relations with the North – something that Kim Jong-il acknowledged in his historic summit meeting with Kim Dae-jung in June 2000.

Between 2000 and 2008, when Lee Myung-bak's administration suspended the policy, tens of thousands of South Koreans were able to visit the North, some for heartbreakingly brief meetings with relations they hadn't seen for half a century. Big southern firms established joint ventures using northern labour in a purpose-built industrial complex at Kaesong. In 2000 Kim Dea-jung was awarded the Nobel Peace Prize for implementing the Sunshine Policy.

After Kim

When President Kim retired after his five-year term his party selected a virtual unknown, Roh Moo-hyun, a self-taught lawyer who had defended many dissidents in the darkest periods of the 1980s. To the surprise of many, including officials in Washington, he narrowly won the 2002 election and represented the rise to power of a generation that had nothing to do with the political system that emerged in 1945 (even Kim Dae-jung

Go to the Korea Society's website (www.koreasoc iety.org) to listen to podcasts about Korean current affairs and the country's recent history.

Korean Foundation (www.kf.or. kr) has video lectures on history and a link to *Koreana,* an excellent quarterly magazine with some history articles.

1998
Kim Jong-il takes full power on the 50th anniversary of the founding of North Korea at the same time as his deceased father is proclaimed the country's 'eternal leader'.

2000
In June Kim Dae-jung and Kim Jong-il meet in Pyongyang at the first ever summit of the two countries. Kim Dae-jung is awarded the Nobel Peace Prize.

» Statues of Kim Il-sung and Kim Jong-il, Pyongyang (p305)

KOREA'S UNRULY GOVERNMENT

Since 1948 South Korea has had a presidential system of government. The president, who is head of state, head of government and commander-in-chief of the armed forces, is elected every five years and can only sit for one term of office.

The president appoints a prime minister and cabinet (on the recommendation of the prime minister) and legislative responsibilities are handled by the 300-seat National Assembly (http://korea.assembly.go.kr). Elections for the assembly are held every four years and result in 246 directly elected members and 54 appointed through proportional representation.

It all sounds pretty orderly and yet *Foreign Policy* magazine in September 2009 cited the National Assembly as one of 'the world's most unruly parliaments' where debates 'are frequently resolved with fists...or whatever heavy object is in the room'. Such were the scenes in 2004 when then President Roh Moo-hyun was being impeached. In 2008 angry opposition lawmakers reached for sledgehammers and electric saws to break into a locked committee room where the governing Grand National Party (now renamed Saenuri or New Frontier Party) was attempting to rush though a free trade bill. This was followed up by a 12-day sit-in before the matter was resolved. Fistfights again broke out during the heated debate in July 2009 over media privatisation.

had been active in the 1940s). That generation was mostly middle-aged, having gone to school in the 1980s with indelible images of conflict on their campuses and American backing for Chun Doo-hwan. The result was a growing estrangement between Seoul and Washington, for the first time in the relationship.

Roh continued Kim's policy of engagement with the North but his mismanagement of the economy and decision to send South Korean troops to Iraq saw his public support plummet. The opposition tried to impeach Roh when, ahead of national parliamentary elections in 2004, he voiced support for the new Uri Party – a technical violation of a constitutional provision for the president to remain impartial. The impeachment failed but Roh's popularity continued to slip and the Uri Party, suffering several defeats by association with the president, chose to distance itself from him by reforming as the Democratic Party.

The end result was a swing to the right that saw Lee Myung-bak of the Grand National Party elected president in 2007, and Roh retire to the village of Bongha, his birthplace in Gyeongsangnam-do. Eighteen months later, as a corruption investigation zeroed in on his family and former aides, Roh committed suicide by jumping off a cliff behind the village. The national shock at this turn of events rebounded on President Lee who was already suffering public rebuke for opening Korea to imports of US beef.

In memory of the prodemocracy martyrs, the Gwangju Prize for Human Rights has been awarded since 2000; recipients have included Aung San Suu Kyi, the prodemocracy politician of Myanmar (Burma).

2002	**2003**	**2005**	**2006**
Human rights lawyer Roh Moo-hyun becomes South Korea's 16th president and continues the 'Sunshine Policy' of engagement with the North. South Korea and Japan co-host soccer's World Cup.	North Korea withdraws from the Nuclear Non-Proliferation Treaty. The first round of the so-called 'six-party talks' between North and South Korea, China, Japan, Russia and the US begin.	The death of King Gojong's 74-year-old grandson Lee Gu in Tokyo ends the Joseon dynasty's bloodline and any possibility of the return of a monarchy in Korea.	In October North Korea claim to have successfully conducted an underground nuclear test explosion. By the end of the month North Korea rejoins the six-party disarmament talks.

The Nuclear Question

After a tumultuous 20th century, South Korea is by any measure one of the star performers of the 21st century. Its top companies, such as Samsung, LG and Hyundai, make products the world wants. Korea is now possibly the most wired nation on earth. The talented younger generation has produced such a dynamic pop culture that *hallyu* (the 'Korean Wave') is a huge phenomenon across Asia and is gaining popularity in the West.

The single anachronism in South Korea's progress, however, remains its fractious relations with North Korea. For decades the North's nuclear ambitions have loomed large on the peninsula. In 2003 China sponsored six-party talks (China, Japan, Russia, the US and both Koreas) to get Washington and Pyongyang talking and negotiating. These intermittent discussions have yet to yield a significant result. On the contrary, the North has successfully tested nuclear bombs, first in October 2006, then again in May 2009. In 2012 it went ahead with a long-range rocket launch, which flew for about one minute before crashing into the ocean.

2007	2009	2010	2011
Former South Korean foreign minister Ban Ki-moon becomes the eighth UN Secretary-General. Lee Myung-bak, ex-CEO of Hyundai Engineering & Construction and Seoul mayor, becomes South Korea's 17th president.	The nation mourns as former president Roh Moo-hyun, under investigation for corruption, commits suicide in May. Another former premier, Kim Dae-jung, succumbs to natural causes in August.	Seoul hosts the G20 Economic Summit and becomes World Design Capital, but its centrepiece – Dongdaemun Design Plaza & Park, by architect Zaha Hadid – remains uncompleted.	Independent candidate and former human rights lawyer Park Won-soon is elected Seoul's mayor; he puts the brakes on major construction projects, focusing instead on welfare spending.

The Korean People

Once divided strictly along nearly inescapable class lines and hierarchical distinctions, South Koreans today are more equal and individual than at any time in their history, while still holding strong loyalties to school, company and church. Nuclear rather than extended families have become the norm, and birth rates are among the lowest in the developed world. Still, there linger strong traces of Korea's particular identity; remnants of its Confucian past coexist alongside 'imported' spiritual beliefs, denting the myth that modernisation necessitates secularisation.

The Main Belief Systems

Confucianism

The state religion of the Joseon dynasty, Confucianism still lives on as a kind of ethical bedrock (at least subconsciously) in the minds of most Koreans, especially the elderly.

The Chinese philosopher Confucius (552–479 BC) devised a system of ethics that emphasised devotion to parents and family, loyalty to friends, justice, peace, education, reform and humanitarianism. He also urged that respect and deference be given to those in positions of authority – a philosophy exploited by the Joseon dynasty's ruling elite. Confucius firmly believed that men were superior to women and that a woman's place was in the home.

These ideas led to the system of civil service examinations (*gwageo*), where one could gain position through ability and merit rather than from noble birth and connections (though it was in fact still an uphill battle for the commonly born). Confucius preached against corruption, war, torture and excessive taxation. He was the first teacher to open his school to all students solely on the basis of their willingness to learn.

As Confucianism trickled into Korea it evolved into Neo-Confucianism, which combined the sage's original ethical and political ideas with the quasireligious practice of ancestor worship and the idea of the eldest male as spiritual head of the family.

Buddhism

When first introduced during the Koguryo dynasty in AD 370, Buddhism coexisted with shamanism. Many Buddhist temples have a *samseionggak* (three-spirit hall) on their grounds, which houses shamanist deities such as the Mountain God.

Buddhism was persecuted during the Joseon period, when temples were tolerated only in remote mountains. The religion suffered another sharp decline after WWII as Koreans pursued worldly goals. But South Korea's success in achieving developed-nation status, coupled with a

NAMES

Koreans give their family name first followed by their birth name, which is typically two syllables, eg Lee Myong-bak. There are less than 300 Korean family names, with Kim, Lee (or Yi) and Park accounting for 45% of the total.

About 90% of Korean Buddhist temples belong to the Jogye order (www.koreanbud dhism.net). The Buddha's birthday is a national holiday, and celebrations includes an extravagant lantern parade in Seoul.

THE CONFUCIAN MINDSET

Not everyone follows the rules but Confucianism does continue to shape the Korean paradigm. Some of the key principles and practices:

» Obedience and respect towards seniors – parents, teachers, the boss, older brothers and sisters – is crucial. Expect a heavy penalty (including physical punishment) if you step out of line.

» Seniors get obedience, but it's not a free ride. Older sisters help out younger siblings with tuition fees, and the boss always pays for lunch.

» Education defines a civilised person. A high-school graduate, despite having built a successful business, still feels shame at the lack of scholastic credentials.

» Men and women have separate roles. A woman's role is service, obedience and management of household affairs. Men don't do housework or look after children.

» Status and dignity are critical. Every action reflects on the family, company and country.

» Everything on and beyond the earth is in a hierarchy. Never forget who is senior and who is junior to you.

» Families are more important than individuals. Everyone's purpose in life is to improve the family's reputation and wealth. No one should choose a career or marry someone against their parents' wishes – a bad choice could bring ruin to a family. Everyone must marry and have a son to continue the family line. (For these reasons homosexuality is considered a grossly unnatural act.)

» Loyalty is important. A loyal liar is a virtuous person.

» Be modest and don't be extravagant. Only immoral women wear revealing clothes. Be frugal with praise.

---

growing interest in spiritual values, is encouraging a Buddhist revival. Temple visits have increased and large sums of money are flowing into temple reconstruction.

Christianity

Korea's first exposure to Christianity was in the late 18th century. It came via the Jesuits from the Chinese Imperial court when a Korean aristocrat was baptised in Beijing in 1784. The Catholic faith took hold and spread so quickly that it was perceived as a threat by the Korean government and was vigorously suppressed, creating the country's first Christian martyrs.

Christianity got a second chance in the 1880s with the arrival of American Protestant missionaries who founded schools and hospitals, and gained many followers – so much so that, today, Christianity is the nation's second most popular religion.

Shamanism

Historically, shamanism influenced Korean spirituality. It's not a religion but it does involve communication with spirits through intermediaries known as *mudang* (female shamans). Although not widely practised today, shamanist ceremonies are held to cure illness, ward off financial problems or guide a deceased family member safely into the spirit world.

Ceremonies involve contacting spirits who are attracted by lavish offerings of food and drink. Drums beat and the *mudang* dances herself into a frenzied state that allows her to communicate with the spirits and be possessed by them. Resentments felt by the dead can plague the living and cause all sorts of misfortune, so their spirits need placating. For shamanists, death does not end relationships. It simply takes another form.

On Inwangsan in northwestern Seoul ceremonies take place in or near the historic Inwangsan Guksadang shrine.

Korean Buddhism operates a Templestay (http://eng.templestay.com) program at facilities across the country. Many Koreans as well as international visitors take part in these programs, regardless of whether they are Buddhist or not, as a chance to escape societal pressures and clear their minds.

Competitive Lives

The country's recovery from the ashes of the Korean War, construction workers on the job seven days a week, or computer-game addicts: they're all strands cut from the same cloth, that of Korea's tenacious, pit-bull spirit. Once Koreans lock onto something, it's difficult to break away. Life is competitive and everything is taken seriously, be it ten-pin bowling, hiking or overseas corporate expansion.

'A person without education is like a beast wearing clothes' is a proverb that nails Korea's obsession with education. Though everyone complains about this manic pursuit, it is a system hard to shake. To get into a top Korean university (nearly all of which are in Seoul), high-school students go through a gruelling examination process, studying 14 hours a day for their one annual shot at the college entrance test.

KOREA'S SPORTING CULTURE

In terms of attendance figures at matches, baseball rules as the most popular spectator sport in Korea. Among the young, soccer is seen as the cool sport, particularly with the success of Park Ji-sung, the most decorated player in Asian history, who currently plays for the English club Queens Park Rangers.

Baseball

There are eight professional teams in the **Korean Baseball Organization** (KBO; www.koreabaseball.com), all sponsored by major *jaebeol* (business conglomerates). Three teams are based in Seoul with the other five playing in Korea's largest cities. The season generally runs from April to October and each team plays 133 games. Teams are allowed to sign two foreign players, a strategy initially designed to increase the calibre of play. Recently, some teams have tended to sign fewer than the limit, suggesting that the US$300,000 salary cap per foreign player is no longer sufficient to attract talent that can excel in the KBO.

Soccer

There are 16 teams in the professional **K-League** (www.kleague.com). Matches are played between March and November. Each team is allowed up to four foreign players. The Korean national team's greatest accomplishment has been to finish fourth in the 2002 World Cup.

Basketball

Ten teams play in the **Korean Basketball League** (KBL; www.kbl.or.kr) from November to March. Two foreign players (usually Americans) are allowed on each team. KBL games tend to be a lot of fun for fans, playing in comparatively small centres.

Taekwondo

By some accounts taekwondo is the world's most popular martial art (measured by number of participants), with benefits related to self-defence, physical strength and mental conditioning. This is despite only having been cobbled together at the end of WWII by fighters who wanted a sport that, on the surface at least, was unrelated to anything Japanese. Bits were taken from (ahem) karate and blended with lesser-known Korean fighting skills such as *taekkyon*, which relies primarily on leg thrusts. By the mid-1950s the name 'taekwondo' was born.

Today, taekwondo thrives as a sport that most boys study as elementary-school students. It is also part of the physical training program that young men must complete as part of their compulsory military service. Taekwondo in Korea is not a popular spectator sport, however: matches are not broadcast on TV and there are few tournaments that draw popular attention outside Olympic contests. The **World Taekwondo Federation** (www.wtf.org) is currently building a major Taekwondo park at Muju in the Deogyusan National Park, which will include a spectator stadium.

FORTUNE-TELLING

These days most people visit street-tent fortune tellers for a bit of fun, but no doubt some take it seriously. For a *saju* (reading of your future), inform the fortune teller of the hour, day, date and year of your birth; another option is *gunhap* (a love-life reading), when a couple give their birth details and the fortune teller pronounces how compatible they are. Expect to pay ₩10,000 for *saju* and double that for *gunhap*. If you don't speak the language, you'll also need someone to translate.

Koreans are also fanatical about health. The millions of hikers who stream into the mountains at weekends are not only enjoying nature but also keeping fit. Thousands of health foods and drinks are sold in markets and pharmacies, which stock traditional as well as Western medicines. Nearly every food claims to be a 'well-being' product or an aphrodisiac – 'good for stamina' is the local phrase.

Contemporary & Traditional Culture

Culture Books

» *Notes on Things Korean* (Suzanne Crowder Han)

» *Understanding Koreans and Their Culture* (Choi Joon-sik)

» *Korea Bug* (J Scott Burgeson)

» *The 48 Keywords That Describe Korea* (Kim Jin-woo & Lee Nam-hoon)

Driven by the latest technology and fast-evolving trends, Korea can sometimes seem like one of the most cutting-edge countries on the planet. People tune into their favourite TV shows via their smart phones and tablet computers. In PC-*bang* (computer game rooms) millions of die-hard fans battle at online computer games, while in *norae-bang* (karaoke rooms) wannabe K-Popsters belt out the latest hit tunes.

General fashions too tend to be international and up to the moment. However, it's not uncommon to see some people wearing *hanbok*, the striking traditional clothing that follows the Confucian principle of unadorned modesty. Women wear a loose-fitting short blouse with long sleeves and a voluminous long skirt, while men wear a jacket and baggy trousers.

Today *hanbok* is worn mostly at weddings or special events, and even then it may be a more comfortable 'updated' version. Everyday *hanbok* is reasonably priced but formal styles, made of colourful silk and intricately embroidered, are objects of wonder and cost a fortune.

Multiculturalism

Korea is a monocultural society with marginal hints of multiculturalism. Foreign residents tend to congregate in pockets, such as Westerners in Seoul's Itaewon or international tradespeople working in the shipbuilding industry on Geojedo, though none qualify as a distinct cultural community.

See p338 for more about racial issues in Korea.

In the Korean Kitchen

Most people think Korean food means *kimchi* and barbecue, which exhibit quintessentially Korean flavours – the ripe tartness of fermented leaves, the delicate marinade of grilled meat. But that's just the starting point. A Korean meal is packed with flavours, unrepentant and full. While the basic building blocks of the cuisine are recognisably Asian (garlic, ginger, green onion, black pepper, vinegar and sesame oil), Korean food strikes out on its own in combining them with three essential sauces: *ganjang* (soy sauce), *doenjang* (fermented soybean paste) and *gochujang* (hot red pepper paste).

The other distinctive feature is that the main course is always served not only with *bap* (boiled rice), soup and *kimchi*, but also a procession of *banchan* (side dishes). Diners eat a bit from one dish, a bite from another, a little rice, a sip of soup, mixing spicy and mild any way they want. Above all, mealtimes are a group affair with family, friends or colleagues – always convivial and rarely, if ever, alone.

Dining options range from casual bites at a market stall to an elaborate *jeongsik* meal at a lavish restaurant. Many places serve a small menu of less than 10 specialities; those at national parks and tourist villages tend to have a wider range. Restaurants outside major cities are unlikely to have menus in English.

Eating out is a social activity, so lone travellers may encounter a quizzical '*Honja?*' ('Alone?'). Occasionally a restaurant may turn away solo diners because they only serve meals in portions for two (especially for *jeongsik* and barbecue).

Restaurant Types & Typical Dishes

Barbecue

Perhaps the most recognisable of Korean restaurants, these are often boisterous establishments where every table has its own small grill and the main selling point is the quality of the meat and the marinade. The menu typically consists of a mind-boggling array of meat cuts. Beef, usually local, is highly prized and more expensive; pork is more affordable. *Bulgogi* describes thin slices of meat, marinated in sweetened soy sauce, while *galbi* are short ribs, similarly flavoured. These terms usually refer to beef but can also be used for pork *(dwaeji)*. Another popular cut is *samgyeopsal* (streaky pork belly).

Diners cook their own meat on the grill, though servers will assist foreign customers. Grilled meats are often eaten wrapped in *ssam* (vegetable leaves) with slices of fresh garlic, green pepper, *kimchi* and a daub of spicy *ssamjang* (soybean and red pepper sauce). The vegetables used for *ssam* are lettuce, perilla (which Koreans call wild sesame), crown

BARBECUE

A helpful guide to deciphering the dizzying range of meat choices at a barbecue restaurant is Kimchimari's Know Your Beef Cut! (http://kimchimari.com/2012/01/28/know-your-beef-cut/).

SAUCY SIDE DISHES

It's not a Korean meal unless there's *kimchi* and *banchan* (side dishes) on the table. *Banchan* is meant to create balance in the meal in terms of saltiness, spiciness, temperature and colour. The number of *banchan* varies greatly, from three in an ordinary meal to 12 in traditional royal cuisine, to an incredible 20 or more in *jeongsik* (set menu or table d'hôte).

Besides the archetypal cabbage *kimchi*, it's common to see radish or cucumber *kimchi*, and dishes with spinach, seaweed, bean sprouts, tofu, *jeon*, *bindaetteok*, small clams, anchovies – just about anything the chefs can concoct. You don't have to eat it all, though if you like a particular dish, you can ask for refills (within reason).

daisy and seaweed. Rounding off the meal – or just to have something to munch on while the meat is cooking – are dishes like *bossam* (steamed pork and *kimchi*), *pajeon* (green-onion pancake) or *jjigae* (stew). Expect to pay ₩15,000 to ₩50,000 per person.

Soups, Stews, Jeongol & Jjim

Many Korean dishes are served as boiling or sizzling hot off the stove as they can get it. Besides the soup that accompanies every meal, there are many hearty, piquant main-course soups called *tang* or *guk*. Soup restaurants usually specialise in just a few dishes.

Samgyetang is a ginseng chicken soup, infused with jujube, ginger and other herbs. It's not spicy and very easy on the palate – the idea is to savour the hint of ginseng and the quality of the chicken. Though it originated as court cuisine, it is now enjoyed as a summer tonic.

A stouter alternative is *gamjatang*, a spicy peasant soup with meaty bones and potatoes. Other meat broths are delicate, even bland, such as *galbitang* or *seolleongtang*. *Haejangguk* or 'hangover soup' (to dispel the night's excesses) is made from a *doenjang* base, with bean sprouts, vegetables and sometimes cow's blood.

Jjigae are stews for everyday eating, often orangey, spicy and served in a stone hotpot. The main ingredient is usually *dubu* (tofu), *doenjang* or *kimchi*, with vegetables and meat or fish. *Budae jjigae* ('army stew') was concocted during the Korean War using leftover hot dogs, Spam and macaroni scrounged from American bases.

Jeongol is a more elaborate stew, often translated as a casserole or hotpot. Raw ingredients are arranged in a shallow pan at the table, then topped off with a spicy broth and brought to a boil. *Jjim* are dishes where the main ingredient is marinated in sauce, then simmered in a broth or steamed until the liquid is reduced. It's a popular (and extremely spicy) serving style for prawns, crab and fish.

Soup and stew meals run from ₩6000 to ₩20,000 per person. Unlike *jjigae*, *jeongol* and *jjim* are rarely served in individual portions.

Fish & Seafood

Hoe (raw fish) is extremely popular in coastal towns, despite the high prices. *Modeumhoe* or *saengseonhoe* is raw fish served with *ssam* or *ganjang* with wasabi, usually with a pot of spicy *maeuntang* (fish soup) to complete the meal. *Chobap* is raw fish served over vinegared rice. Restaurants near the coast also serve squid, barbecued shellfish, octopus and crab. More gung-ho eaters can try *sannakji* (raw octopus, not live but wriggling from post-mortem spasms) or *hongeo* (ray, served raw and fermented, or steamed in *jjim* – neither of which masks its pungent ammonia smell). A seafood meal costs from ₩15,000 per person.

Bosintang (dog-meat soup) is said to make men more virile and it's eaten on the hottest days of the year, although it's less popular with the younger generation and there are growing concerns about animal protection.

Seoul is the best place to take cookery courses in English. A great online resource is Maangchi's recipe archive (www.maangchi.com/recipes), which includes demonstration videos.

Jeongsik

Often translated as a set menu or table d'hôte, this is a spread of banquet dishes all served at once: fish, meat, soup, *dubu jjigae*, rice, noodles, shellfish and a flock of *banchan*. It's a delightful way to sample a wide range of Korean food in one sitting. *Hanjeongsik* (Korean *jeongsik*) may denote a traditional royal banquet spread of 12 dishes, served on *bangjja* (bronze) tableware. Expect to pay from ₩20,000 for a basic *jeongsik* to over ₩100,000 for a high-end version.

Everyday Eats

Not every meal in Korea is a *banchan* or meat extravaganza. For casual dining, look for one-dish rice or noodle dishes. *Bibimbap* is a perennial favourite: a tasty mixture of vegetables, meat and an egg on top of rice. The ingredients are laid out in a deep bowl according to the five primary colours of Korean food – white, yellow, green, red and black – which represent the five elements. Just stir everything up (go easy on the red *gochujang* if you don't want it too spicy) and eat! A variant is *dolsot bibimbap*, served in a stone hotpot; the highlight of this is *nurungji*, the crusty rice at the bottom. Vegetarians can order *bibimbap* without meat or egg.

As in much of East Asia, noodle joints are plentiful. A common dish is *naengmyeon,* buckwheat noodles served in an icy beef broth, garnished with vegetables, Korean pear, cucumber and half a boiled egg. You can add *gochujang*, *sikcho* (vinegar) or *gyeoja* (mustard) to taste. *Naengmyeon* is especially popular in summer. Sometimes it's served with a small bowl of meat broth, piping hot, that you can drink with your meal (but it's not for pouring onto the noodles).

Japchae are clear 'glass' noodles stir-fried in sesame oil with strips of egg, meat and vegetables. A Koreanised Chinese dish is *jajangmyeon,* wheat noodles in a black-bean sauce with meat and vegetables. *Gimbap* joints often serve *ramyeon* (instant noodles) in spicy soup.

Gimbap are colourful rolls of *bap* (rice) flavoured with sesame oil and rolled in *gim* (dried seaweed). Circular *gimbap* contains strips of vegetables, egg and meat. *Samgak* (triangular) *gimbap* is topped with a savoury fish, meat or vegetable mixture. Just don't call it sushi – the rice is not vinegared and not topped with raw fish.

South Koreans eat 1.5 million tonnes of *kimchi* every year and when the country's first astronaut went into space in 2008, he took a specially engineered 'space *kimchi*' with him.

KIMCHI

IN THE KOREAN KITCHEN RESTAURANT TYPES & TYPICAL DISHES

SAY KIMCHI

It appears at every meal (including breakfast) and often as an ingredient in the main course too. What began as a pickling method to preserve vegetables through Korea's harsh winters has become a cornerstone of its cuisine. With its lurid reddish hues and limp texture, *kimchi* doesn't look that appealing, but just one bite packs a wallop of flavours: sour, spicy, with a sharp tang that often lingers through the meal.

The most common type is *baechu kimchi,* made from Chinese cabbage, but there are over 180 varieties, made with radish, cucumber, eggplant, leek, mustard leaf and pumpkin flower, among others. Some are meant to be eaten in tiny morsels while others, such as *bossam kimchi,* are flavour-packed packages containing vegetables, pork or seafood.

To make *kimchi,* vegetables are salted to lock in the original flavour, then seasoned with garlic, red pepper powder, green onions, ginger, fish sauce and other spices, and left in earthenware jars to ferment for hours, days or even years. *Kimchi* can be made all year round using seasonal vegetables, but traditionally it is made in November. Many regions, restaurants and families have their own recipes, jealously guarded and handed down through the generations. High in fibre and low in calories, *kimchi* is said to lower cholesterol, fight cancer and prevent SARS and H1N1 swine flu.

Mandu are dumplings filled with meat, vegetables and herbs. Fried, steamed or served in soup, they make a tasty snack or light meal. Savoury pancakes, often served as a side dish, can also be ordered as a meal. *Bindaetteok* are made with mung-bean flour and heavier on the batter, while *jeon* are made with wheat flour. Common fillings are *kimchi,* spring onion *(pajeon)* and seafood *(haemul pajeon).*

Some eateries specialise in *juk* (rice porridge). Savoury versions are cooked with ginseng chicken, mushroom or seafood, sweet ones with pumpkin and red bean. The thick, black rice porridge is sesame. *Juk* is considered a healthy meal, good for older people, babies or anyone who's ill.

Rice and noodle dishes cost ₩6000 to ₩10,000 each, a meal-sized *jeon* is ₩7000 to ₩10,000, and *gimbap* or *mandu* meals cost ₩3000 to ₩7000.

Street Food

Korean street food runs the gamut from snacks like *tteokbokki* (rice cakes slathered in a spicy sauce) and *hotteok* (brown sugar and cinnamon pancakes) to heavier fare like *dakkochi* (grilled chicken skewers), *sundae* (sausages containing vegetables and noodles) and *odeng* (processed seafood cakes). Look out for *pojangmacha,* the tarp-covered street stalls that sell food and *soju* well into the night. Expect to pay ₩500 to ₩2000 per serving, although some meals at *pojangmacha* cost up to ₩15,000 per dish.

Desserts

While desserts are not traditional in Korean dining, sometimes at the end of a meal you'll be served fruit or *sujeonggwa,* a cold drink made from cinnamon and ginger.

The classic summer dessert is *patbingsu,* a bowl heaped with shaved ice, *tteok* (rice cakes) and sweet red-bean topping with a splash of condensed milk. Modern toppings include strawberries, green-tea powder and fresh or canned fruit. It costs ₩2500 to ₩7000 at cafes.

Bakeries and street vendors sell bite-sized sweets such as *hangwa* and *dasik* (traditional sweets and cookies), and *tteok* flavoured with nuts, seeds and dried fruit.

Drinks

Tea is a staple and the term is also used to describe drinks brewed without tea leaves. The most common leaf tea is *nokcha* (green tea), grown on plantations in Jeju-do (p256) and Jeollanam-do (p216). Black tea is harder to find. Non-leaf teas include the ubiquitous *boricha* (barley tea), *daechucha* (red-date tea), *omijacha* (five-flavour berry tea), *yujacha* (citron tea) and *insamcha* (ginseng tea).

Koreans have taken to coffee, or *keopi,* in a big way in recent decades. Aside from the ubiquitous vending machines which churn out an overly sweet three-in-one (coffee, cream and sugar) instant coffee mix (₩300), the number of gourmet coffee shops in the country has mushroomed by about 10 times since 2006 – from Korean chains like Angel-in-us Coffee and Hollys, to home-grown speciality roasters and slow-brewers, to foreign imports like Starbucks. In Seoul, expect to pay from ₩4000 for coffee at a chain outlet to ₩10,000 for a speciality brew.

Every restaurant serves *mul* (water) or tea. Most serve alcohol, but not usually soft drinks. Some unusual Korean canned soft drinks, readily available from convenience stores, are grape juice with whole grapes inside and *sikhye,* rice punch containing rice grains.

Cooking at Home

» *Growing Up in a Korean Kitchen* by Hisoo Shin Hepinstall

» *Eating Korean* by Cecilia Hae-Jin Lee

» *A Korean Mother's Cooking Notes* by Sun-Young Chang

Alcoholic Drinks

Drinking, and drinking heavily, is the mainstay of Korean socialising, and an evening out can quickly turn into a blur of bar-hopping. The most common poison of choice is *soju,* the mere mention of which tends to elicit looks of dismay from foreigners. The stuff is, to put it bluntly, ethanol mixed with water and flavouring. If you think that it goes down easy, remember it can also leave you with a killer hangover the next day.

The cheaper varieties (which are sold in convenience stores for as little as ₩1500) have all the subtlety of really awful moonshine, while those distilled from grain (₩7000 and up) offer a far more delicate flavour. The cheap stuff has an alcohol content of 20% to 35%, while the good stuff goes up to 45%. The latter includes Andong *soju* and 'white *soju',* available in Gyeongsangbuk-do and Gyeongsangnam-do respectively.

Makgeolli is a traditional farmer's brew made from unrefined, fermented rice wine. Much lower in alcohol content than *soju,* it has a cloudy appearance and a sweetish yogurty flavour. *Dongdongju* is similar, with rice grains floating in it. Both are popular tipples in national parks, where it's practically ritual to swig down a bowl or two after (or during) an arduous hike. They cost ₩1000 to ₩2500 in supermarkets, double that in restaurants.

Easier on the palate are a host of sweetish traditional spirits, brewed or distilled from grains, fruits and roots. *Bokbunjaju* is made from wild raspberries, *meoruju* from wild fruit, *maesilju* from green plums and *insamju* from ginseng.

Beer, or *maekju,* is the least exciting of all Korean alcohol. Local brands, all lagers, are the rather bland Cass, Hite and OB. There are some interesting microbreweries, mainly in Seoul, and imported beers are increasingly available. Local beers cost ₩2000 to ₩5000 in a restaurant or bar.

During an evening of drinking, Koreans usually order *anju* (bar snacks), which traditionally meant *kimchi, dotorimuk* (acorn jelly) or *dubu kimchi.* Nowadays you're more likely to get heaped plates of oil-soaked food – fried chicken, French fries or vegetable *twigim* (fritters). A *hof,* a term inspired by German beer halls, is any watering hole that serves primarily Korean beer, with the requisite plate of fried chicken and other *anju.*

Koreans drink so much *soju* that the brand Jinro Soju has been the top-selling brand of spirits worldwide for the last 11 years.

LOCAL SPECIALITIES

» *jjimdak* (simmered chicken) – Andong
» *ureok* (rockfish) – Busan
» *dakgalbi* (spicy chicken grilled with vegetables and rice cakes) – Chuncheon
» *maneul* (garlic) – Danyang
» *sundubu* (soft or uncurdled tofu) – Gangneung
» *oritang* (duck soup); *tteokgalbi* (grilled patties of ground beef) – Gwangju
» *okdomgui* (grilled, semi-dried fish); *jeonbok-juk* (abalone rice porridge); *heukdwaeji* (black-pig pork) – Jeju-do
» *bibimbap* – Jeonju
» *ojing-eo* (squid) served *sundae* (sausage) style – Sokcho
» *galbi* – Suwon
» *chungmu gimbap* (rice, dried seaweed and kimchi) – Tongyeong
» *gatkimchi* (leafy mustard kimchi) – Yeosu

Vegetarians & Vegans

Although Korean cuisine uses lots of vegetables, much of it is pickled or cooked with meat or seafood. *Dubu jjigae* may be made from beef or seafood stock, and *beoseot deopbap* (mushrooms on rice) may contain a little pork. Even *kimchi* is often made with fish sauce. The only assuredly meat-free meals are those served at Buddhist temples or restaurants. The Seoul Veggie Club on Facebook is a good resource.

The safest approach is to ask about ingredients or order something like *bibimbap* without the ingredients you don't eat. Be as specific about your requirements as you can be – for instance, saying 'no meat' may not suffice to omit seafood.

Dining & Drinking Etiquette

From casual eateries to high-end restaurants, you're as likely to encounter traditional floor seating as Western-style chair seating. If it's the former, remove your shoes at the door and sit on floor cushions (stack a few for more comfort). The menu is often simply posted on the wall. Main courses come with rice, soup, *kimchi* and *banchan* (usually included in the menu price). Don't worry about not finishing the *banchan* as no one is expected to eat everything.

Meals are eaten communally. If the table is not set, there will be an oblong box containing metal chopsticks and long-handled spoons, as well as metal cups and a bottle of water or tea. The spoon is for rice, soup and any dish with liquids; chopsticks are for everything else. Don't touch food with your fingers, except when handling *ssam*. Remember not to let the chopsticks or spoon stick up from your rice bowl – this is taboo, only done with food that is offered to deceased ancestors.

Korean eat out – a lot – and love to sit and sup on a main course for several hours (and over several bottles of *soju*). Seniors or elders begin eating first. Dining companions usually pour drinks for each other – traditionally, never for themselves. It's polite to use both hands when pouring or receiving a drink.

To call a server, say '*Yogiyo*', which if translated seems rude (it means 'here') but is a bona fide way of hailing attention. Tipping is not expected, though high-end restaurants often add a 10% service charge.

Food Sites

» Dictionary of Popular Korean Dishes (www .seouleats. com/2008/01/ dictionary-of -popular-korean -dishes.html)

» Food in Korea (http://english .visitkorea.or.kr/ enu/1051_Food .jsp)

» 100 Korean Foods You Gotta Try (www .zenkimchi .com/Food Journal/korean -food-101/100 -korean-foods -you-gotta-try).

Food Glossary

Fish & Seafood Dishes

chobap	초밥	raw fish on rice
garibi	가리비	scallops
gwang-eohoe	광어회	raw halibut
jangeogui	장어구이	grilled eel
kijogae	키조개	razor clam
kkotgejjim	꽃게찜	steamed blue crab
modeumhoe	모듬회	mixed raw-fish platter
nakji	낙지	octopus
odeng	오뎅	processed seafood cakes
ojingeo	오징어	squid
saengseongui	생선구이	grilled fish
saeugui	새우구이	grilled prawns

Kimchi 김치

baechu kimchi	배추김치	cabbage kimchi; the classic spicy version
kkakdugi	깍두기	cubed radish kimchi
mul kimchi	물김치	cold kimchi soup

Meat Dishes

bossam	보쌈	steamed pork with kimchi, cabbage and lettuce wrap
bulgogi	불고기	barbecued beef slices and lettuce wrap
dakgalbi	닭갈비	spicy chicken pieces grilled with vegetables and rice cakes
dwaeji galbi	돼지갈비	pork ribs
galbi	갈비	beef ribs
heukdwaeji	흑돼지	black pig
jjimdak	찜닭	spicy chicken pieces with noodles
metdwaejigogi	멧돼지고기	wild pig
neobiani/tteokgalbi	너비아니/떡갈비	large minced meat patty
samgyeopsal	삼겹살	barbecued (bacon-like) streaky pork belly
tangsuyuk	탕수육	Chinese-style sweet-and-sour pork
tongdakgui	통닭구이	roasted chicken
yukhoe	육회	seasoned raw beef

Noodles

bibim naengmyeon	비빔냉면	cold buckwheat noodles with vegetables, meat and sauce
bibimguksu	비빔국수	noodles with vegetables, meat and sauce
jajangmyeon	자장면	noodles in Chinese-style black-bean sauce
japchae	잡채	stir-fried 'glass' noodles and vegetables
kalguksu	칼국수	wheat noodles in clam-and-vegetable broth
kongguksu	콩국수	wheat noodles in cold soybean soup
makguksu	막국수	buckwheat noodles with vegetables
naengmyeon	물냉면	buckwheat noodles in cold broth
ramyeon	라면	instant noodles in soup

Rice Dishes

bap	밥	boiled rice
bibimbap	비빔밥	rice topped with egg, meat, vegetables and sauce
bokkeumbap	볶음밥	Chinese-style fried rice
boribap	보리밥	boiled rice with steamed barley
chamchi gimbap	참치김밥	tuna gimbap
chijeu gimbap	치즈김밥	cheese gimbap
daetongbap	대통밥	rice cooked in bamboo stem
dolsot bibimbap	돌솥비빔밥	bibimbap in stone hotpot
dolsotbap	돌솥밥	hotpot rice
dolssambap	돌쌈밥	hotpot rice and lettuce wraps
gimbap	김밥	rice flavoured with sesame oil and rolled in dried seasweed
gulbap	굴밥	oyster rice
hoedeopbap	회덮밥	bibimbap with raw fish
honghapbap	홍합밥	mussel rice
jeonbokjuk	전복죽	rice porridge with abalone
juk	죽	rice porridge
modeum gimbap	모듬김밥	assorted gimbap
pyogo deopbap	표고덮밥	mushroom rice
sanchae bibimbap	산채비빔밥	bibimbap with mountain vegetables
sinseollo	신선로	meat, fish and vegetables cooked in broth
ssambap	쌈밥	assorted ingredients with rice and wraps

Snacks

beondegi	번데기	boiled silkworm larvae
bungeoppang	붕어빵	fish-shaped waffle with red-bean paste
dakkochi	닭꼬치	spicy grilled chicken on skewers
gukhwappang	국화빵	flower-shaped waffle with red-bean paste
hotteok	호떡	wheat pancake with sweet filling
jjinppang	찐빵	giant steamed bun with sweet-bean paste
norang goguma	노랑고구마	sweet potato strips
nurungji	누룽지	crunchy burnt-rice cracker
patbingsu	팥빙수	shaved-iced dessert with tteok and red-bean topping
tteok	떡	rice cake
tteokbokki	떡볶이	pressed rice cakes and vegetables in a spicy sauce

Soups

bosintang	보신탕	dog-meat soup
dakbaeksuk	닭백숙	chicken in medicinal herb soup
dakdoritang	닭도리탕	spicy chicken and potato soup
galbitang	갈비탕	beef-rib soup
gamjatang	감자탕	meaty bones and potato soup
haejangguk	해장국	bean-sprout soup ('hangover soup')
haemultang	해물탕	spicy assorted seafood soup
kkorigomtang	꼬리곰탕	oxtail soup
maeuntang	매운탕	spicy fish soup
manduguk	만두국	soup with meat-filled dumplings
oritang	오리탕	duck soup
samgyetang	삼계탕	ginseng chicken soup
seolleongtang	설렁탕	beef and rice soup

Stews

budae jjigae	부대찌개	'army stew' with hot dogs, Spam and vegetables
dakjjim	닭찜	braised chicken
doenjang jjigae	된장찌개	soybean paste stew
dubu jjigae	두부찌개	tofu stew
galbijjim	갈비찜	braised beef ribs
gopchang jeongol	곱창전골	tripe hotpot
kimchi jjigae	김치찌개	kimchi stew

Other

bindaetteok	빈대떡	mung-bean pancake
donkkaseu	돈까스	pork cutlet with rice and salad
dotorimuk	도토리묵	acorn jelly
gujeolpan	구절판	eight snacks and wraps
hanjeongsik	한정식	Korean-style banquet
jeongsik	정식	set menu or table d'hôte, with lots of side dishes
mandu	만두	filled dumplings
omeuraiseu	오므라이스	omelette filled with rice
pajeon	파전	green-onion pancake
sujebi	수제비	dough flakes in shellfish broth
sundae	순대	noodle and vegetable sausage
sundubu	순두부	uncurdled tofu
twigim	튀김	seafood or vegetables fried in batter

Nonalcoholic Drinks

boricha	보리차	barley tea
cha	차	tea
daechucha	대추차	red-date tea
hongcha	홍차	black tea
juseu	주스	juice
keopi	커피	coffee
mukapein keopi	무카페인 커피	decaffeinated coffee
mul	물	water
nokcha	녹차	green tea
omijacha	오미자차	five-flavour berry tea
saengsu	생수	mineral spring water
seoltang neo-eoseo/ppaego	설탕 넣어서/빼고	with/without sugar
sikhye	식혜	rice punch
sujeonggwa	수정과	cinnamon and ginger punch
uyu	우유	milk
uyu neo-eoseo/ppaego	우유 넣어서/빼고	with/without milk
yujacha	유자차	citron tea

Alcoholic Drinks

bokbunjaju	복분자주	wild berry liquor
dongdongju/makgeolli	동동주/막걸리	fermented rice wine
maekju	맥주	beer
maesilju	매실주	green plum liquor
soju	소주	vodka-like drink

Architecture & Arts

Examples of architecture from all periods of Korea's history can be discovered across the country. Seoul in particular offers a fascinating hodgepodge of the old and the new with ancient fortress walls, grand palaces and decorative temples within walking distance of charming early-20th-century *hanok* (traditional wooden homes) and dramatic contemporary structures such as Dongdaemun Design Plaza. Korea also offers a spectacular range of arts. Rich, colourful costumes set the scene for passionate traditional *pansori* operas. Folk dances such as *samullori*, with its whirling dervish of dancers, seamlessly meld the cacophonous and melodic. Artisans preserve the ancient art of calligraphy with their silken stroke, while contemporary artists push the envelope in exciting and unexpected ways. The country's cinematic output along with Korean pop (K-Pop) and TV operas makes up the *hallyu* (Korean Wave) of popular culture sweeping across the world.

Architecture

Temples & Palaces

Buddhist temples, often re-created after the original work was destroyed or had rotted away, hold some of the country's most impressive ancient architecture. The craftsmanship required to mount wooden beams on stone foundations, often built with notches instead of nails, is technically and aesthetically awe-inspiring. The strikingly bold and colourful painted design under the eaves, called *dancheong*, relies on five colours: blue, white, red, black and yellow.

During the Joseon era, five main palaces were constructed in Seoul. These were cities unto themselves, massive complexes with administrative offices, residences, pleasure pavilions and royal gardens, all hemmed in by imposing walls. Because of centuries of invasion and war, Seoul's palaces have all been painstakingly rebuilt countless times.

Hanok

Traditional houses *(hanok)* are one-storey homes crafted entirely from wood, save for the clay tiled roofs, insulated with mud and straw. The windows are made of a thin translucent paper that allows daylight to stream in. They're heated by the underfloor system called *ondol*.

Unlike the ostentatious manor homes of Europe, even an aristocrat's lavish *hanok* was designed to blend with nature; they are typically left unpainted, their brown and tan earth tones giving off a warm, intimate feel. All of the rooms look onto a courtyard *(madang)*, usually including a simple garden. Life was lived on the floor and people sat and slept on mats rather than chairs and beds.

Architecture Books

» *Hanoak – Traditional Korean Houses* (1999)

» *Joseon Royal Court Culture* (Shin Myung-ho)

» *City as Art: 100 Notable Works of Architecture in Seoul* (Yim Seock-jae)

One of the programs of the National Trust of Korea (www.nationaltrust.or.kr), an NGO charged with helping to protect the country's environment and national relics, focuses on preservation of *hanok*.

SAVING THE HANOK

'Thirty-five years ago there were around 800,000 *hanok* in South Korea, now there are less than 10,000,' says Peter Bartholomew, an American expat in Korea. For over 40 years Bartholomew has been battling the predominant view among Koreans that such traditional houses are an anachronism in their modern country, unworthy of preserving.

Bartholomew has lived in *hanok* since he first came to Korea in 1968 as a Peace Corps volunteer and has owned one in the Dongsomun-dong area of northern Seoul since 1974. He bought an adjacent property in 1991. In 2009 Bartholomew and his neighbours won a two-year legal battle against the city over plans to redevelop the area. 'I deplore the assumption that these old houses are irreparable, dirty and un-sanitary,' he says, pointing out that traditional *hanok* are very easy to modernise in just the same way that centuries-old homes across the West have been adapted to contemporary life.

The proof of this lies in the Bukchon area, where some 900 *hanok* remain, the bulk concentrated in a few streets in Gahoe-dong (also transliterated as Kahoi-dong). 'The preservation program was achieved by the government providing financial incentives to owners for repairs and maintenance,' says Bartholomew. However, according to some local residents, even here, the *hanok* as a private home is under threat. Kahoi-dong 'is being relentless destroyed', says David Kilburn, author of Preservation of Kahoi-dong (www.kahoidong.com), a website that documents the abuses of the preservation sys-tem over the past decade.

Contemporary Seoulites may shun *hanok* as places to live, but tourists clearly love them if the increasing number of *hanok* guesthouses are anything to go by. Ahn Young-hwan, owner of Rak-Ko-Jae, a *hanok* guesthouse in Bukchon, was one of the first people to suggest that *hanok* be used in this way. 'People thought I was crazy,' he says, 'but now many more people are doing it.'

For Ahn, *hanok* are the 'vessels that contain Korean culture' and a way of experiencing the joys of an analogue life in an increasingly digital society. It's a view that Bartholomew underlines when he says that living in his *hanok* has 'filled my life with peace and beauty'.

Social rank dictated the decorations, beam size, roof pitch and number of rooms – rules not relaxed until the 1930s. The traditional home was also divided into two sections, the *sarangchae* for men and the *anchae* for women.

Post WWII & Contemporary Architecture

Post–Korean War urban architecture invariably reflected a keen interest in budget rather than design. Concrete towers that look like shoeboxes define most urban landscapes. As Korea has become a richer country, this uninspiring aesthetic is changing, particularly so in the Seoul-Gyeonggi-do area, where you'll see the greatest concentration of contem-porary architectural imagination.

Spurred on by its winning bid to be the World Design Capital in 2010, Seoul went on a construction spree, hiring world-renowned architects such as Zaha Hadid for the Dongdaemun Design Plaza and Park, and Daniel Libeskind for Archipelago 21, part of the US$28 billion redevelop-ment of the Yongsan International Business District.

The Arts

Cinema

Korea's modern film scene is revered by film buffs worldwide, with the country's movies often winning prizes at major festivals. A government quota ensuring that Hollywood flicks can't push homegrown releases out of theatres has helped the industry flourish.

FILMS

Korean films are occasion-ally shown with English subtitles in cinemas, but the best way to see them is on DVD at one of Korea's numerous DVD-*bang*.

Korean directors haven't shied away from major issues, such as the Korean War (*Taegukgi*, 2004) and its turbulent political aftermath (*The President's Last Bang*, 2005). Pervasive social issues – such as the blistering pace of city life and the shifting notion of family – are tackled in *The Way Home* (2002) and *Family Ties* (2006), both quietly touching. *Marathon* (2005) is the inspiring true tale of a devoted Seoul mother struggling to bring up her autistic son amid societal prejudice.

The horror films *Memento Mori* (1999) and *A Tale of Two Sisters* (2003) provide gruesome shocks, and for an action-revenge flick – something Korea excels at – nothing tops the jaw-dropping *Oldboy* (2003). Other more recent releases to look out for include the murder-mystery drama *Mother* (2009) and Hong Sang-soo's comedy *Hahaha* (2010), an award-winner at Cannes.

Superb films by female directors are receiving greater recognition. These include Jeong Jae-eun's *Take Care of My Cat* (2001), the pitch-perfect story of five girls coming of age in the suburbs outside Seoul, and Yim Soon-rye's *Waikiki Brothers* (2001), a sobering exploration of those left behind by Korea's economic rise. Yim's *Forever the Moment* (2008) follows the Korean women's handball team into the 2004 Olympics, offering a more reflective take than is the genre standard.

Literature

Korean works are increasingly being translated into English and other languages, allowing international readers to discover how rich, reflective and, at times, dark, contemporary writing can be. One of the most recent major hits has been Shin Kyung-sook's *Please Look After Mum* (2011).

Works translated into English that provide a sample of Korean literature include *Toji (1969-1994)*. This serialised novel took Park Kyung-ni 25 years to complete and is considered to be one of the finest literary works in modern Korea. Set in Hadong, South Gyeongsang province, the story follows an aristocratic family during Japanese colonial rule. It's a collection of 16 volumes, some of which have been translated into English.

The Prophet and Other Stories (1999) is a novella by Lee Cheong-jun documenting the life of a social outcast who is the target of group-think mentality. Written by one of Korea's most respected authors, it's an allegory for life under a dictatorship.

The Dwarf (2006) by Cho Sae-hee recounts the daunting social costs of rapid industrialisation on the working poor during the 1970s through the eyes of a midget.

Since being launched in 1996, the Busan International Film Festival (BIFF; www.biff.kr) has grown to become the most respected festival in Asia.

ARCHITECTURE & ARTS THE ARTS

Koreanfilm.org (www.koreanfilm.org) is a top resource covering all aspects of the industry and features numerous reviews. Seoul Selection (www.seoulselection.com) also sells a great selection of Korean DVDs.

EXPAT KOREAN LITERATURE

Several English-language novels deal with Koreans living abroad and their struggles with identity.

» *War Trash* by Ha Jin (2004) – A gritty novel about the life of a POW during the Korean War from the perspective of an English-speaking Chinese soldier.

» *Native Speaker* by Lee Chang-rae (1996) – A political thriller about a second-generation Korean-American man on the outside looking in. Also read Lee's *A Gesture Life* (1999), the story of an older Japanese gentleman who uses grace to mask past mistakes as a soldier in Burma while overseeing Korean comfort women.

» *Appointment With My Brother* by Yi Mun-yol (2002) – A brilliant novella about a man from the South who meets his half-brother from the North. It's an emotional and stressful meeting for both of them, a collision of two worlds.

» *The Descendants of Cain* by Hwang Sun-won (1997) – One of Korea's most celebrated authors writes about life in a North Korean village between the end of WWII and the beginning of the Korean War.

Music

Gugak (traditional music) is played on stringed instruments, most notably the *gayageum* (12-stringed zither) and *haegeum* (two-stringed fiddle), and on chimes, gongs, cymbals, drums, horns and flutes. Traditional music can be subdivided into three categories: *jeongak* is a slow court music often combined with elegant dances; *bulgyo eumak* is played and chanted in Buddhist temples; and *samulnori* is a lively style originally played by travelling entertainers. It died out during Japanese colonial rule but was reinvented in the 1970s by musicians playing four traditional percussion instruments.

K-Pop artists have attracted international attention, though few have attained the level of commercial success of the female singer BoA (www.boaamerica.com) and Rain (www.rain-jihoon.com), one of Korea's most versatile entertainers, who can sing, dance, act and run a company.

Other successful artists include cute boy band Bigbang (www.ygfamily.com), the 13-member group Super Junior (http://superjunior.smtown.com), Wonder Girls (www.wondergirlsworld.com), five bubbly young women, and the nine-piece Girls' Generation (www.girlsgenerationusa.com), currently Korea's top pop group.

In July 2012, Psy (real name Park Jae-sang), a 34-year-old rapper, became the hottest K-Pop export ever when his catchy dance single 'Gangnam Style' went viral on the internet. Two months later the video had 160 million views on YouTube.

Kim Young-ha's *I Have The Right To Destroy Myself* (1996) delves into alienation in Seoul and has been described as both Korean Noir and Kafkaesque.

The Daesan Literary Award (http://daesan.or.kr/eng/business.html?d_code=1618) provides some of the richest prizes (₩30 million) in five categories including poetry, fictional work and translations.

Visual Art

Chinese influence is paramount in traditional Korean painting. The brush line, which varies in thickness and tone, is the most important feature. The painting is meant to surround the viewer and there is no fixed viewpoint. Zen-style Buddhist art can be seen inside and on the outside walls of hundreds of temples around the country. Murals usually depict scenes from the Buddha's life.

K-INDIE SCENE: RAY KANG

US-born singer-songwriter and cafe-bar owner Ray Kang has been in Korea since 1996. He presents Indie Afternoon on TBS 101.3FM.

What is K-Indie? It's a hidden gem – real voices (not manufactured as in K-Pop) and real artists. It covers all genres – rock, jazz, hip-hop etc – and you really see the performers' creative lives. However, it hardly gets any exposure at all. The big record companies are not interested in picking up most artists for wider distribution and apart from our show it's impossible to hear on the radio.

Where can you hear it? Hongdae is the mecca of the K-Indie scene. Check out the live music clubs such as Ta, FF and Freebird. Music festivals are another popular stage for K-Indie artists.

Recommended bands & artists? The Peppertones (http://peppertones.net) are a two-man mod pop rock group. Their music has an electronic rock feel; they've released three CDs and are moving into the mainstream. The Yellow Monsters are a punk group who recently played at music festivals in the US. Energetic electronic rock band The Koxx (www.thekoxx.com) made a lot of waves in 2011. As for singer-songwriters, look out for Park Sae-byul (www.parksaebyul.com) and the acoustic guitarist Choi Go-eun. Big Baby Driver is also excellent – she plays slide guitar and does 1920s and '30s US blues.

Where can I find out more? Read Korean Indie (www.koreanindie.com), which has grown out of a blog Indieful ROK (http://indiefulrok.blogspot.com), kept by a girl in Sweden. Also check CDs and digital tracks put out by the indie labels Beatball (www.beatballrecords.com) and Ruby Salon (www.rubysalon.com). K-Indie CDs are available at Evans Records and Hottracks (www.hottracks.co.kr) in Kyobo bookshops.

KOREAN SOAPS CLEAN UP IN ASIA

Few would pretend they constitute art, but in terms of pop cultural appeal not too many creative products have had as much impact across Asia as Korean soap operas. *Winter Sonata*, a soap opera first screened in Korea in 2002, was the first homegrown TV drama to gain a major international following, demonstrating there was an export market for domestic productions.

Most Korean dramas follow a predictable format: melodramatic soundtrack, sappy romance, parental interference, love triangles and memory loss. *Winter Sonata*'s lead male actor Bae Yong-joon is a superstar in Japan, where middle-aged women fantasise about having a man like Mr Bae: soft, loving and totally into the relationship. The drama is credited with creating a tourism boom to Korea from Japan and has been made into an animated version with voices provided by the original actors.

Subsequent dramas that made a big splash in Asia include *Stairway to Heaven, My Lovely Sam Soon, Princess Hours* and the 2009 hit *Boys over Flowers*.

Stone Buddhist statues and pagodas are the most common examples of ancient sculpture. Cast bronze was also common for Buddhas and some marvellous examples can be seen in the National Museum of Korea. Stone and wooden shamanist guardian posts are common and Jeju-do has its own unique *dolharubang* (grandfather stones).

Korea's best-known modern sculptor is Baek Nam-june (www.paik studios.com), who died in 2006. He was a Korean-American artist who used video monitors to create inspired, sometimes bizarre, work. One of his larger creations, 'The More the Better', is an 18m tower with 1000 monitors on display at the National Museum of Contemporary Art inside Seoul Grand Park. Other modern artists include painter Kim Whanki, mixed-media artist Min Yong-soon, and Kim Tschang-yeul, a painter noted for his dedication to water drops; one of the latter's paintings is at Seoul's Leeum Samsung Museum of Art.

Pottery on the Korean peninsula dates back 10,000 years, but the 12th century is regarded as a special time when skilled artisans turned out celadon earthenware with a green tinge. Today Korean celadon earns thousands of dollars at auction.

Dance & Theatre

Popular folk dances include *samulnori* (drum dance), *talchum* (mask dance) and solo improvisational *salpuri* (shamanist dance). *Samulnori* dancers perform in brightly coloured clothing, twirling a long tassel from a special cap on their heads. Good coordination is required to dance, twirl and play a drum at the same time.

Korea's small, modern theatrical experience is primarily based in Seoul. Nonverbal shows like *Nanta* and *Jump* appeal to an international audience. There's an experimental scene in Daehangno, but it's almost entirely in Korean. *Changgeuk* is an opera that can involve a large cast of characters. Another type of opera is *pansori*, which features a solo storyteller (usually female) singing to the beat of a male drummer. The performer flicks her fan to emphasise dramatic moments.

Pottery fans shouldn't miss out on a visit to Icheon Ceramic Village near Seoul and two pottery villages in Jeollanam-do: the Pottery Culture Centre and the Gangjin Celadon Museum.

The Natural Environment

At 96,920 sq km, South Korea is a similar size to Portugal. Bordered only by North Korea, the country has 2413km of coastline along three seas – the West Sea (also known as the Yellow Sea), the East Sea (Sea of Japan) and the South Sea (East China Sea). Its overall length from north to south (including Jeju-do) is 500km, while the narrowest point is 220km wide.

The largest of some 3400 islands is 1847-sq-m Jeju-do, a volcanic land-mass with spectacular craters and lava tubes. Off the east coast is Ul-leungdo, another scenic volcanic island. Korea is not in an earthquake zone, but there are dozens of mineral-laden *oncheon* (hot springs) that bubble up through the ground, some of which have been developed into health spas.

Forested mountains cover 70% of the land, although they are not very high – Hallasan (1950m) on Jeju-do is the highest peak. Many mountains are granite with dramatic cliffs and pinnacles, but there are also impressive limestone caves to visit. The 521km Nakdong and 514km Han rivers are the country's longest. They, like most other larger rivers, have been dammed, creating scenic artificial lakes.

The plains and shallow valleys are still dominated by irrigated rice fields that are interspersed with small orchards, greenhouses growing vegetables, and barns housing cows, pigs and chickens. In the south are green-tea plantations and on Jeju-do citrus fruit is grown.

The hundreds of sparsely populated islands scattered off the western and southern coasts of the peninsula have relaxed atmospheres; a few have attractive sandy beaches. Here you can go way off the beaten track to islands where the inhabitants have never seen a foreigner.

Caves by Kyung Sik Woo (2005) is a lavishly illustrated book on Korean caves by a geological expert and cave enthusiast.

Animals

Korea's forested mountains used to be crowded with Siberian tigers, Amur leopards, bears, deer, goral antelopes, grey wolves and red foxes. Unfortunately these wild animals are now extinct or extremely rare in Korea.

Small efforts are being made to build up the number of wild animals in the country – goral antelopes have been released into Woraksan National Park and there's an ongoing project to protect the tiny population of Asiatic black bears (known in Korea as moon bears) in Jirisan National Park. In Seoul, small populations of roe deer and elk live on Bukaksan and in Seoul Forest Park.

Jin-do is home to a special breed of Korean hunting dog, Jindogae. Brave, intelligent, loyal and cute as any canine on the planet, the breed can be a challenge to train and control, but they possess an uncanny sense of direction – one dog was taken to Daejeon but somehow made its

International Aid for Korean Animals (www.koreananimals.org/index.htm) promotes animal protection in Korea.

MOONBEARS: A GLIMMER OF HOPE

According to legend the Korean nation was born from a bear – one of the reasons why Asiatic black bears (also called moonbears because of the crescent moon of white fur on their chests) are accorded the status of a national treasure and a protected species. However, by the late 20th century the hunting of bears for their meat and use in traditional medicine had contributed to them being thought extinct in the wild in South Korea.

Then in 2001 video-camera footage proved that up to six wild bears were living in a remote part of Jirisan National Park. Soon after the park established a project with the aim of building up a self-sustaining group of 50 wild bears in Jirisan (as of 2010 it was believed there were 19). However, according to **Moonbears.org** (http://moonbears.org), one of several Korean groups campaigning for protection of the animal, even these few are threatened by poaching. This is despite the fact that well over 1000 bears are bred at farms across the country for the lucrative bear-meat and gall-bladder trade. The conditions that the bears are kept in are often horrific.

Moonbears.org, **Bear Necessity Korea** (bearnecessitykorea.com), Green Korea and other pressure groups have long campaigned for the government to ban such farms. In 2012, the National Assembly voted through a proposal to 'prepare measures to end the practice of bear farming through investigation of the current status of bear farming and its management plan'. A budget of ₩200 million has been set aside for the proposal.

way back to the island, a journey of hundreds of kilometres. Being hunting dogs, they are an active, outdoor breed that is not suited to an urban environment. Any other breed of dog found on Jin-do is immediately deported to the mainland in order to maintain the breed's purity.

Magpies, pigeons and sparrows account for most of the birds in the towns and cities, but egrets, herons and swallows are common in the countryside, and raptors, woodpeckers and pheasants can also be seen. Although many are visiting migrants, over 500 bird species have been sighted, and Korea has a growing reputation among birders keen to see Steller's sea eagles, red-crowned cranes, black-faced spoonbills and other rarities.

Plants

Northern parts of South Korea are the coldest and the flora is alpine: beech, birch, fir, larch and pine. Further south, deciduous trees are more common. The south coast and Jeju-do are the warmest and wettest areas, so the vegetation is lush. Cherry trees blossom in early spring followed by azaleas and camellias.

Korea's mountainsides are a pharmacy and salad bar of health-giving edible leaves, ferns, roots, nuts and fungi. Many of these wild mountain vegetables end up in restaurant side dishes and *sanchae bibimbap* (a meal of rice, egg, meat and mountain vegetables). Wild ginseng is the most expensive and sought-after plant.

National & Provincial Parks

With an abundance of river valleys, waterfalls and rocky outcrops, plus brightly painted wooden Buddhist temples and hermitages gracing many mountains, it's not surprising that many visitors rate Korea's national and provincial parks as its top attractions.

Since the first national park, Jirisan, was established in 1967 it has been joined by 19 others covering 3.7% of the country. For more details see **Korea National Parks** (http://english.knps.or.kr). There are also 22 smaller provincial parks (covering 747 sq km) and 29 county parks (covering 307 sq km). All the parks have well-marked hiking trails that can be so popular that trails have to be closed to protect them from serious erosion.

Field Guide to the Birds of Korea by Lee, Koo & Park (2000) is the standard bird guide, but doesn't include all feathered visitors.

THE NATURAL ENVIRONMENT PLANTS

A DMZ NATIONAL PARK?

The dearth of human intervention in the Demilitarized Zone (DMZ) for over 50 years has made it something of an environmental haven. The zone is home to 2716 wild plants and animals, including 67 endangered species such as the Siberian musk deer, the Amur goral (a mountain goat that resembles an antelope), a third of the world's remaining red-crowned cranes and half the remaining white-naped cranes. Environmentalists hope that the day the two Koreas cease hostilities, the DMZ will be preserved as a nature reserve, a plan that has the support of the Korean government. As a first step towards this goal, trekking and cycling paths are being created within the Civilian Control Zone, a buffer zone that runs along the southern border of the DMZ.

Beautiful Wildflowers in Korea (2002), published by the Korea Plant Conservation Society, has photos of 200 native flowers and will encourage you to stop and ID flowers on your travels.

The parks can be enjoyed in every season. In spring cherry blossoms, azaleas and other flowers are a delight; in summer the hillsides and river valleys provide a cool escape from the heat and humidity of the cities; during the summer monsoon, the waterfalls are particularly impressive; in autumn red-coloured leaves and clear blue skies provide a fantastic sight; and in winter snow and ice turn the parks into a white wonderland, although crampons and proper clothing are needed for any serious hikes at this time of year. Korean winters can be arctic, especially if you're high up in the mountains.

All the parks have tourist villages near the main entrances with restaurants, market stalls, souvenir and food shops, and budget accommodation where big groups can squeeze into a small room. Camping grounds (₩3000 for a three-person tent) and mountain shelters (₩3000 to ₩5000 for a bunk) are cheap, but provide only very basic facilities.

Environmental Issues

South Korea's economic growth since 1960 has transformed the country from an agricultural to an industrial society. Sprawling apartment-block cities and huge industrial complexes have been constructed, rivers have been dammed and freeways have been bulldozed through the countryside. Authoritarian governments stamped on any opposition to development projects and the environmental impacts of the projects were ignored.

Fortunately the 70% of Korea that is mountainous and forested is still largely undeveloped, and the hundreds of offshore islands are also unspoilt. For a developed country Korea is surprisingly green, as 90% of the population is packed into high-rise city apartments.

Nowadays politics is more democratic, politicians win votes by promising green policies and environmental groups are no longer ignored by the media. Unpopular construction projects can face fierce opposition. Among the country's most contentious environmental flashpoints are what to do with nuclear waste and land reclamation.

Nuclear Power & Waste Disposal

South Korea relies on 21 nuclear power plants concentrated in four locations (Gori, Ulchin, Wolseong, Yonggwang) to generate around 40% of its electricity – this compares to a 15.7% average worldwide. As part of its 'low-carbon, green-growth' plan (p382) there are plans to add up to 14 more nuclear facilities by 2030 to boost the level of electricity generation.

However, Korea's nuclear-power industry has long struggled to find a permanent storage site for the radioactive waste that it produces – it's a pressing problem as it's believed by 2025 the current storage sites at each of the plants will be full.

In November 2005 Gyeongju was chosen as the site of the country's first permanent dump for low- and middle-grade nuclear waste. The Korea Hydro & Nuclear Power Corporation would also move its headquarters to the region. Protests naturally followed from this, despite the fact that in a poll close on 90% of the voters had endorsed the plan – a result probably not unconnected to the annual ₩300 billion (US$323 million) in economic subsidies that the central government had promised the region. In 2009 construction of the storage facility was put on hold under pressure from lawmakers and environmental campaign groups, who had uncovered evidence of the site's geological instability.

Land Reclamation

Reclaiming the mud flats off Korea's west coast for farming and construction has become a highly emotive and divisive issue. According to Korean Federation for Environmental Movements (KFEM), since 1990 over 140,000 hectares of coastal wetlands have been reclaimed or are in the process of being reclaimed.

The environmental impact that such projects can have is seen at Saemangeum in Jeollabuk-do where in 2006 a 33km sea wall was built to reclaim 40,000 hectares of mud flats. Opponents, who battled hard against the project during its construction, stressed the importance of the mud flats as a fish and shellfish breeding area and as a vital feeding ground for more than 100,000 migrant birds, including black-faced spoonbills and 12 other threatened species.

In response to the Saemangeum protests, the government declared 60 sq km of wetlands at the Han River estuary in Gyeonggi-do a protected area. Ten smaller wetland areas (covering a total of 45 sq km) had already been protected. The Ministry of Environment has since increased the number of protected wetland areas to 29 and Korea's list of Ramsar Wetlands from 11 to 17. In one of these wetlands – Suncheonman, which is the winter nesting ground of five endangered species of crane – the cancellation of a land-reclamation project in favour of the area's promotion as an ecotourism destination is a positive sign for the future.

With an average of five million visitors a year, Bukhansan National Park, located on Seoul's doorstep, has qualified for a Guinness World Record as the national park with the highest number of visitors per sq ft in the world.

Korea's largest environmental nongovernmental organisation is Korea Federation for Environmental Movements (KFEM; www .kfem.or.kr), which has around 80,000 members and 31 branch offices across the country.

THE NATURAL ENVIRONMENT ENVIRONMENTAL ISSUES

JEJU'S ENVIRONMENTAL INITIATIVES

It's no accident that Jeju was chosen to host the World Conservation Congress in September 2012, a 10-day symposium where experts exchanged ideas for tackling pressing environmental issues including climate change, biodiversity and green growth. South Korea's largest island, recognised by Unesco for its extraordinary ecosystem and natural features, is through various schemes pushing ahead with its aim to be crowned, in the words of Korea's environment minister Yoo Young-sook, as the 'environment capital of the world'.

A trust has been set up to protect *gotjawal* (forests on rocky terrain), which cover around 12% of the island. Considered the 'lungs of Jeju' they are not only an essential part of the island's groundwater supply system but also a species-rich biosphere. Three of Jeju's wetland regions are also listed under the Ramsar Convention as being of 'international importance'.

Along the northeast coast of Jeju, you won't miss the giant windfarms that form part of the island's Smart Grid Testbed (http://smartgrid.jeju.go.kr) – an attempt to use information technology to transmit power and cut down on CO2 emissions. The long-term plan is to make Jeju carbon-free and self-sustainable through renewable energy resources by 2030. Already the island of Gapado off Jeju's southwest coast is carbon free, its power coming from wind farms and solar panels, its cars all replaced with electric vehicles and its water from a desalination plant.

Green Korea?

In August 2008 President Lee announced a 'low-carbon, green-growth' strategy to reduce greenhouse gas emissions and environmental pollution and to create jobs using green technology and clean energy.

Among the 'ecofriendly' projects on the government's green agenda are the clean-up of four major rivers (the Han, Nakdong, Geum and Yeongsan) and their surroundings to reduce flooding by building dams, banks and water-treatment facilities; the construction of more high-speed railway lines and hundreds of kilometres of bicycle tracks; the provision of energy-saving 'green homes' and energy-recycling projects including the production of gas from garbage; and the development of hybrid-vehicle technologies.

Many of these policies have got the thumbs up from the UN Environment Program but local environmental groups have been less enthusiastic, particularly about the four-river project, which they feel is a way for the president to revive a plan for a grand canal between Seoul and Busan. Despite commitments to preserve wetland and coastal areas, Seoul is also pushing ahead with a plan to build four tidal power plants along the west coast, the first of which (at Sihwa Lake in Gyeonggi-do) is now in operation.

What Can You Do?

Responsible travellers can do their bit for Korea's environment by keeping in mind the following:

» Use the country's excellent public transport system or rent a bicycle where you can.

» Place your rubbish in the appropriate recycling bins for paper, cans and plastic.

» Refuse unnecessary packaging in shops – carry your own shopping bag, for example.

» Patronise organic and vegetarian restaurants and businesses that have a seal of approval from LOHAS (Lifestyles of Health & Sustainability; http://korealohas .or.kr).

World Natural Heritage Sites on Jeju-do

» Hallasan National Park

» Seongsan Ilchulbong Peak

» Geomunoreum Lava Tube System

Green Korea (www.greenkorea .org) is a pressure group with practical ideas such as Buy Nothing Day, Car Free Day (22 September in Seoul) and Save Paper Day.

Survival Guide

Directory A–Z

Accommodation

In general you don't need to worry about where to stay in Korea – motels are so numerous that there is usually no need to book ahead. Outside of the big cities and towns – where you'll find regular hotels and hostels – the most common type of accommodation will be *minbak* – private homes with rooms for rent.

Accommodation is normally charged per room, so solo travellers receive little or no discount. Still, it's always worth asking. If you're staying a few days or if it's low season (outside July and August on the coast or outside July, August, October and November in national parks), you can always try for discounts. Some hostels and *hanok* guesthouses include a simple breakfast in their rates; most hotels don't.

Budget and midrange places usually include VAT of 10% in their rates. All top-end hotels will slap a service charge of 10% on the bill as well as VAT (so a total of 21% over the quoted rate); rates listed in this guide include all taxes.

Watch out for internet access charges. This can be as much as ₩35,000 a day. Check whether there's free wi-fi access in the hotel lobby first.

Only staff in Seoul guesthouses and upper midrange and top-end hotels are likely to speak any English. An extra bed or *yo* (mattress or futon on the floor) is usually available. Check-out time is generally noon. Prices can rise on Friday and Saturday and at peak times (July and August near beaches or national parks, and October and November near national parks).

Although some places offer use of a washing machine (and sometimes a dryer) laundry can be a problem – out of Seoul you may find yourself having to wash your clothes in the bathroom and hanging them up in your room to dry, or laying them on the *ondol*-heated floor.

Backpacker Guesthouses & Hostels

The backpacker scene is well established in Seoul, but less common elsewhere in Korea. When you find them, these internationally minded hostels are ideal for budget-oriented tourists, and have staff who are friendly and speak English. They offer dormitories (from ₩15,000 per night) and double rooms (from ₩40,000), some of which have private bathroom. Communal facilities include toilets, showers, satellite TV, a kitchen and washing machine. Free internet and breakfast is also typically provided.

Camping & Mountain & Forest Huts

Camping at beaches and in or near some national and provincial parks is possible. The cost is ₩5000 but facilities are very basic and they are usually only open in July and August.

Only a few major hikes in Seoraksan and Jirisan National Parks require overnighting in a mountain hut. Huts and camping grounds can be fully booked at weekends and during high season.

For more information see http://english.knps.or.kr.

ACCOMMODATION BOOKING SITES

Apart from booking directly with the website listed in our reviews you can also book rooms via the following:

Agoda (www.agoda.com)

Benikea (☎02-1330; www.benikea.com)

Korean Hotel Reservation Center (www.khrc.com)

Lonely Planet (hotels.lonelyplanet.com)

ACCOMMODATION PRICE RANGES

The following price ranges refer to a double room with private bathroom.

PRICE INDICATOR	SEOUL	KOREA
$	up to ₩60,000	up to ₩40,000
$$	₩60,000-250,000	₩40,000-150,000
$$$	over ₩250,000	over ₩150,000

Hanok Guesthouses

Traditional *hanok* are increasingly being turned into guesthouses. Staying in one of these is a unique and memorable experience. Rooms are small and you'll sleep on *yo* (padded quilts and mattresses) on the floor, but underfloor heating systems (*ondol*) keep them snug in winter. At the cheaper *hanok* you'll be sharing the bathroom, but many guesthouses do offer en suite rooms. Rates often include breakfast, and traditional cultural experiences may be offered too.

For more about *hanok* guesthouses across Korea see the KTO site **Hanokstay** (www.hanokstay.or.kr). **Jongno-gu** (http://homestay.jongno.go.kr/homestayEngMain.do) in Seoul also runs a *hanok* homestay program.

Homestays

These are the best way to experience Korean food, customs and family life at close quarters. Most Korean families sign up to such schemes to meet and make friends with foreigners and to practise their English. Some families offer pick-ups and dinner, and rates are greatly reduced if you stay long-term. The charge for bed and breakfast per night can be as low as ₩30,000 per person. See the following sites for more details:

BnB Hero (www.bnbhero.com)

Go Homestay (www.gohomestay.com)

Homestay Korea (www.homestaykorea.com).

Koreastay (www.koreastay.or.kr)

Lex (www.lex.or.kr)

Hotels

Luxury hotels are relatively scarce outside of major cities and Jeju-do. The lobbies, fitness centres, restaurants and other services are often their strong points – when it comes to room design and facilities, motels tend to offer a better deal. We list rack rates (including service and taxes) in this guide, but discounts or packages are nearly always available.

Minbak & Pension

Most *minbak* provide simple accommodation (and usually meals) on islands, near ski resorts, in rural areas and near beaches and national parks. Expect to pay ₩40,000 for a room but double that in peak seasons. You sleep on a *yo* on an *ondol*-heated floor, usually with a TV and a heater or fan in the room. Facilities may not be en suite. Lots of people can squeeze into one room – an extra person usually costs ₩10,000. More upmarket *minbak* cost ₩50,000 or more, and provide smart, stylish rooms with beds and kitchenettes.

Pension are more luxurious than most *minbak* and cost from ₩50,000 upwards with spacious rooms, often with stylish furniture, balconies and kitchens.

Motels & Love Motels

By far the most common form of accommodation across Korea. The rooms are always on the small size but they are packed with facilities – en suite, TV, DVD, telephone, fridge, drinking water, air-con and heating, toiletries and even computers. However, staff rarely speak any English and motels lack communal areas beyond the lobby which is not designed for lingering.

Love motels cater for couples seeking some by-the-hour privacy, but they also accept conventional overnight guests. They're usually easy to spot by the plastic curtains shielding the parked cars from prying eyes. If you can cope with the clandestine trappings (and possibly intrusive noise from neighbouring rooms), they can be an excellent option; some of the extravagantly decorated rooms are a bargain compared what you'd pay for similar facilities at a top-end hotel. Some love motels, however, require a late check-in, around 9pm; earlier check-ins will cost more.

Rental Accommodation

Renting an apartment can be tricky because of the traditional payment system, which involves paying a huge deposit to the landlord and/or having to pay all your rent up front. Browse Seoul websites www.nicerent.com or www.nearsubway.com for

BOOK YOUR STAY ONLINE

For more reviews by Lonely Planet authors, check out http://hotels.lonelyplanet.com. You'll find independent reviews, as well as recommendations on the best places to stay. Best of all, you can book online.

PRACTICALITIES

Daily Newspapers

» **Korea Herald** (www.koreaherald.co.kr)

» **Korea JoongAng Daily** (http://joongangdaily .joins.com)

» **Korea Times** (www.koreatimes.co.kr)

Monthly Magazines

» **10 Magazine** (10mag.com)

» **Bridge** (www.bridgezine.com)

» **Groove Korea** (groovekorea.com)

» **Seoul** (www.seoulselection)

TV, Radio & DVD

» **KBS World** (http://world.kbs.co.kr) News, features.

» **Arirang** (www.arirang.co.kr) English language TV and radio.

» **Radio Gugak** (ww.gugakfm.co.kr) Traditional Korean music.

» **TBS** (http://tbsefm.seoul.kr) Music and news.

» **DVD** Region 3; some with English-language option.

Measurements

Uses the metric system, but real estate is often measured in *pyeong* (3.3 sq m or almost 6ft x 6ft), and some traditional markets still use wooden measuring boxes.

what's on offer. Real estate is measured in *pyeong* (1 *pyeong* is 3.3 sq m). Backpacker guesthouses and motels sometimes offer reduced rates for long-termers.

Korea4Expats.com has useful information on this topic under its Moving To Korea section.

Sauna Dormitories

Saunas and *jjimjil-bang* (luxury saunas) nearly all have a dormitory or napping room. They are not really meant for overnight sleepovers, but they can be used for that purpose. Pay the entry fee (usually under ₩10,000), use the facilities and then head for the dormitory. Don't expect much in the way of bedding, and the pillow may be a block of wood.

Serviced Apartments

Seoul has several serviced apartment complexes, which can be a good alternative to hotel rooms and the hassle of finding and renting an apartment. They're known locally as residences or suites;

prices start at ₩90,000 a day for a studio apartment, with big discounts for month-long stays.

Templestays

From ₩30,000 per night in cluding all meals, around 100 temples across the country provide overnight accommodation in the form of a **Templestay program** (http://eng .templestay.com). No attempt will be made to try to convert you to Buddhism and they provide a chance not only to experience the life of a monk but also to stay in some incredibly beautiful places. Some temples are geared to accepting foreigners, others will also happily let you stay if you bring along a Korean to help translate.

Yeogwan

'Adequate but shabby' sums up most *yeogwan*, which provide old-fashioned budget rooms, but are only ₩5000 to ₩10,000 cheaper than the much better modern motels. Quilts are usually aired rather than washed so you may want to bring sheets with you.

Youth Hostels

Hostelling International Korea (www.kyha.or.kr) runs 70 large modern youth hostels around the country. The dormitories offer a good deal for solo travellers on a budget at around ₩20,000

TAX FREE SHOPPING

Global Refund (☎02-776 2170; www.globalrefund.com) offers a partial refund (between 5% and 7%) of the 10% value added tax (VAT) on some items. Spend more than ₩30,000 in any participating shop and the retailer gives you a special receipt, which you must show to a customs officer at Incheon International Airport. Go to a Customs Declaration Desk (near the check-in counters) *before* checking in your luggage, as the customs officer will want to see the items before stamping your receipt. After you go through immigration, show your stamped receipt at the refund desk to receive your won refund in cash or by cheque.

a night. Private and family rooms cost as much as motel rooms and are unlikely to be as good. They also can be rather institutional and inconveniently located. and are sometimes full of noisy children on a school trip. Sort out a YHA card in your home country as you need to have been a resident in South Korea for over a year before you can apply for a local card (annual membership ₩30,000).

Activities

See p27 for information on outdoor activities such as hiking, diving and winter sports. Martial arts and hot-spring spas are among the other activities available; see the On the Road chapters for other specific suggestions.

Business Hours

Exceptions to the following general hours are listed in reviews.

» **Banks** 9am to 4pm Monday to Friday, ATMs 7am to 11pm

» **Post offices** 9am to 6pm Monday to Friday

» **Shops** 10am to 8pm

» **Cafes** 7am to 10pm

» **Restaurants** 11am to 10pm

» **Bars** 6pm to 1am, longer hours Friday and Saturday

Children

Koreans adore children and make them the centre of attention, so travelling with your offspring here is highly recommended. Expect the locals to be particularly helpful and intrigued. Check out www.travelwithyourkids.com for general advice and a first-hand report on Seoul for kids, which gives the city a thumbs up.

Only luxury hotels are likely to be able to organise a cot, but you could always

ask for a *yo*. Few restaurants have high chairs. Nappy-changing facilities are more common in Seoul toilets than in the provinces. Baby-sitting services are almost nonexistent.

Zoos, funfairs and parks can be found in most cities along with cinemas, DVD rooms, internet rooms, video-game arcades, ten-pin bowling alleys, *norae-bang* (karaoke rooms), pool tables and board-game cafes. Children will rarely be more than 100m away from an ice-cream, cake or fast-food outlet. In winter hit the ski slopes, and in summer head for the water parks or beaches. To keep kids happy in Seoul, see p65. For general advice also pick up a copy of Lonely Planet's *Travel with Children*.

Customs Regulations

Visitors must declare all the plants, fresh fruit, vegetables and dairy products that they bring into South Korea. Meat is not allowed in without a certificate. Log on to www .customs.go.kr for further information.

Antiques of national importance are not allowed to be exported.

Discount Cards

Korea Pass (www.koreapass .or.kr) is a prepaid card, available in denominations from ₩50,000 to ₩500,000 and available at Incheon and Gimpo International Airports, that provides discounts on a range of goods and services.

See p396 for information on the T-money transport card.

Electricity

South Korea is on the 220V standard at 60Hz and uses two round pins with no earth.

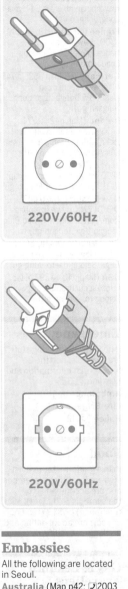

220V/60Hz

220V/60Hz

Embassies

All the following are located in Seoul.

Australia (Map p42; ☑2003 0100; www.south korea.embassy.gov.au; 19th fl, Kyobo Bldg, Jongno 1-ga, Jongno-gu)

Canada (Map p48; ☑3783 6000; www.canadainter national.gc.ca/korea-coree/; 21 Jeong-dong-gil, Jung-gu)

China (Map p42; ☎738 1038; www.chinaemb.or.kr; 54 Hyoja-dong, Jongno-gu)

France (off Map p48; ☎3149 4300; www.amba france-kr.org; 30 Hap-dong, Seodaemun-gu)

Germany (off Map p52; ☎748 4114; www.seoul.diplo .de; 308-5 Dongbinggo-dong, Yongsan-gu)

Ireland (Map p42; ☎774 6455; www.embassyofireland .or.kr; 13th fl, Leema Bldg, 146-1 Susong-dong, Jongno-gu)

Japan (Map p42; ☎2170 5200; www.kr.emb-japan.go.jp; 18-11 Junghak-dong, Jongno-gu)

New Zealand (Map p42; ☎3701 7700; www.nzembassy .com/korea; 15th fl, Kyobo Bldg, Jongno 1-ga, Jongno-gu)

UK (Map p48; ☎3210 5500; http://ukinkorea.fco.gov.uk; 24 19-gil, Sejong-daero, Jongno-gu)

USA (Map p42; ☎397 4114; http://seoul.usembassy.gov; 32 Sejong-ro, Jongno-gu)

Emergency

If no English-speaking staff are available, ring the 24-hour tourist information and help line ☎1330.

Ambulance (☎119)
Fire Brigade (☎119)
Police (☎112)

Food

In this guide, restaurant listings are by author preference and are accompanied by the symbols $ (budget), $$ (midrange) or $$$ (top end).

For more about eating and drinking, see p363.

Gay & Lesbian Travellers

Korea has never passed any laws that mention homosexuality, but this shouldn't be taken as a sign of tolerance or acceptance. Some older Koreans insist that there are no gays in Korea – even though there are at least

several very high profile ones such as the TV personality/Seoul restaurateur Hong Seok-chun and trans-gender celebrity Ha Ri-su.

Attitudes are changing, especially among young people, but virtually all local homosexuals (called *ivan* in Korean) choose to stay firmly in the closet. Gay and lesbian travellers who publicise their sexual orientations should be prepared for less than positive reactions. This said, there are openly gay areas of Seoul where few will blink an eye at your behaviour and other major cities have gay bars too.

Useful resources:

Chungusai (Between Friends; chingusai.net) Korean GLBT human rights group.

iShap (www.ishap.org) Gay HIV/AIDS awareness project; produces a free Korean guidebook to gay bars and clubs across Korea; ask for it at Barcode in Nagwon-dong.

Utopia (www.utopia-asia.com) Check the Korea section.

Health

The quality of medical care in Seoul is high. You need a doctor's prescription to buy most medications and it may be difficult to find the exact medication you use at home, so take extra. A letter from your physician outlining your medical condition and a list of your medications (using generic names) could be useful.

There are no special vaccination requirements for visiting Korea, but you should consider vaccination against hepatitis A and B. Most peo-

ple don't drink the tap water, but those who do seem to come to no harm. Filtered or bottled water is served free in most restaurants. For further information, see **Lonely Planet** (lonelyplanet.com). The **World Health Organization** (WHO; www.who.int/ith) publishes the annually revised booklet *International Travel & Health*, available free online.

Insurance

A policy covering theft, loss, medical expenses and compensation for cancellation or delays in your travel arrangements is highly recommended. If items are lost or stolen, make sure you obtain a police report straight away – otherwise your insurer might not pay up. There is a wide variety of policies available but always check the small print.

Worldwide travel insurance is available at www.lonelyplanet.com/travel_services. You can buy, extend and claim online any time – even if you're already on the road.

Internet Access

With one the highest rates of internet usage in the world, you'll find ubiquitous internet rooms (or PC 방) right across the country, mainly serving youthful computer-game addicts. They charge around ₩2000 per hour. Many places, including tourist information centres, cafes and other establishments provide free internet access, either via a computer or free wi-fi, as do

---

FOOD PRICE RANGES

PRICE INDICATOR	SEOUL	KOREA
$	up to ₩10,000	up to ₩7000
$$	₩10,000-25,000	₩7000-18,000
$$$	over ₩25,000	over ₩18,000

some guesthouses and hotels. Some motels and nearly all hotels provide computers with broadband access.

The major phone companies offer USB dongle devices to rent, in the same way as mobile phones, to connect to the internet anywhere in Korea.

Legal Matters

Most tourists' legal problems involve visa violations or illegal drugs. In the case of visa transgressions, the penalty is normally a fine and possible expulsion from the country. If caught using or selling narcotics, you'll either be deported or spend a few years researching the living conditions in a South Korean prison.

Maps

The Korea Tourism Organization (KTO) and Seoul Metropolitan Government publish numerous free brochures and maps of Seoul, which are fine for most purposes.

Money

The South Korean unit of currency is the won (₩), with ₩10, ₩50, ₩100 and ₩500 coins. Notes come in denominations of ₩1000, ₩5000, ₩10,000 and ₩50,000.

See www.xe.com for up-to-date exchange rates.

ATMs

ATMs that accept foreign cards are common: look for one that has a 'Global' sign or the logo of your credit-card company. ATMs often operate from 7am to 11pm but some are 24-hour. Restrictions on the amount you can withdraw vary. It can be as low as ₩100,000 per day.

Changing Money

Many banks offer a foreign exchange service. In big cities there are also licensed moneychangers, that keep longer hours than the banks and provide a faster service, but may only exchange US dollars cash.

Credit Cards

Increasingly accepted across the board, but plenty of places, including budget accommodation, stalls and small restaurants, still require cash. Always have handy a stash of ₩10,000 notes in case.

Photography & Video

Photographic print shops are not as numerous as they once were, but they can burn your memory-stick photos onto a CD (₩3000). All the major camera and video brands are available including the local ones, such as Samsung. Yongsan Electronics Market and Namdaemun Market in Seoul are the best places to buy the latest camera and video equipment.

Some Koreans are shy, reluctant or even hostile about being photographed, so always ask first. Never take photographs inside Buddhist shrines or of shamanist ceremonies without asking permission first, and don't expect Seoul's riot police to be too happy to be snapped either. In and around the Demilitarized Zone (DMZ) there are very strict rules about what can and can't be photographed.

For professional hints on how to improve your pictures, purchase Lonely Planet's *Travel Photography*.

Post

For postal rates see **Korea Post** (www.koreapost.go.kr); offices are fairly common and have a red/orange sign.

Public Holidays

Eight Korean public holidays are set according to the solar calendar and three according to the lunar calendar, meaning that they fall on different days each year. Restaurants, shops and tourist sights stay open during most holidays, but may close over the three-

FINDING AN ADDRESS

Under an old system of addresses, big cities such as Seoul were divided up into districts (*gu,* eg Jongno-gu) with these districts further divided into subdistricts (*dong,* eg Insa-dong). Buildings were then numbered according to their chronology within the subdistrict. It was all pretty confusing, so Korea has decided to move over to a new address system of logically numbered buildings on named streets (*gil*).

However, until the end of 2013 the old address system will exist alongside the new one. In this guide the practical details for sights, restaurants, hotels etc provide the basic address information that will help you most easily locate a business, typically the *dong* and, if the area in a chapter covers more than one *gu* then also the *gu*. If a place is on a well-known street or on a clearly marked new street address then that information is included too.

If you have the correct full address (either system), or the telephone number, these can be used by satellite navigation in taxi or on phones to locate where you are going. For more information on the address changeover see www.juso.go.kr/openEngPage.do.

day Lunar New Year and Chuseok (Thanksgiving) holidays. School holidays mean that beaches and resort areas are busy in August.

New Year's Day 1 January

Lunar New Year 12 February 2013, 31 January 2014, 19 February 2015

Independence Movement Day 1 March

Children's Day 5 May

Memorial Day 6 June

Constitution Day 17 July

Liberation Day 15 August

Chuseok 19 September 2013, 8 September 2014, 27 September 2015

National Foundation Day 3 October

Christmas Day 25 December

Safe Travel

Drivers routinely jump red lights, so take extra care on pedestrian crossings even if they are protected by lights. Drivers almost never stop for pedestrian crossings that are not protected by traffic lights, so they are useless. Motorcyclists often drive along pavements and pedestrian crossings. Cars also find pavements and pedestrian crossings a convenient place to park.

Visitors to Seoul are often surprised to see police in full riot gear, carrying large shields and long batons, streaming out of blue police buses that have their windows covered in protective wire. Student, trade-union, anti-American, environmental and other protests occasionally turn violent. Keep well out of the way of any confrontations that may occur.

Telephone & Fax

Fax

If you want to send a fax, first ask at your guesthouse, motel or hotel. If they can't help you, try the nearest

stationery store or photocopy shop.

Mobile Phones

Korea uses the CDMA network system, which few other countries use, so you will probably have to rent a mobile (cell) phone while you're in Seoul. The best place to do this is at Incheon International Airport as soon as you arrive, although some top-end hotels will have phones available for guests, and discount electronic stores in Itaewon also sell a range of new and used phones. Mobile-phone hire is available from four companies, which all have counters on Incheon's arrivals floor:

KT (http://roaming.kt.com/eng/index.asp)

LG Telecom (www.uplus.co.kr)

SK Telecom (www.skroaming.com)

S'Roaming (www.sroaming.com)

Each company offers similar (but not identical) schemes; you'll pay more for smartphone rentals. Online discounts can cut daily rental fees. Incoming calls are free and outgoing domestic calls cost around ₩600 a minute, while calls to the US, for example, cost ₩900 a minute. Check that prices quoted include the 10% VAT.

Korean mobile phone numbers have three-digit area codes, always beginning with 01, eg ☎011-1234 5678. When you make a call from your mobile phone you

always input the area code, even if you're in the city you're trying to reach. For example, in Seoul when calling a local Seoul number you would dial '☎02-123 4567'.

Phone Codes

Korea's nine provinces and seven largest cities have their own area codes. It's easy to forget that the major cities have their own codes – thus Gwangju City's code (☎062) is one digit different to the surrounding province of Jeollanam-do (☎061). South Korea's country code is ☎82. Do not dial the first zero of the area codes if you are calling from outside Korea. Phone numbers that begin with a four-figure number starting with 15 do not have an area code. The international access code is ☎001.

Public Phones & Phonecards

With practically everyone having a mobile phone it's increasingly rare to find public pay phones; the best place to look is subway stations. Ones accepting coins (₩50 or ₩100) are even rarer. Telephone cards usually give you a 10% bonus in value and can be bought at convenience stores. There are two types of cards so if your card does not fit in one type of pay phone, try a different-looking one. The more squat pay phones accept the thin cards. A few public phones accept credit cards. Local calls cost ₩70 for three minutes.

Time

South Korea is nine hours ahead of GMT/UCT (London) and does not have daylight saving. When it is noon in Seoul it is 7pm the previous day in San Francisco, 10pm the previous day in New York and 1pm the same day in Sydney.

Toilets

Korea has plenty of clean, modern and well-signed *hwajangsil* (public toilets). Virtually all toilets are free of charge, some are decorated with flowers and artwork, and a few even have music. Toilet paper is usually outside the cubicles. As always, it's wise to carry a stash of toilet tissue around with you just in case. Asian-style squat toilets are losing their battle with European-style ones, but there are still a few around. Face the hooded end when you squat.

Tourist Information

In Seoul the excellent **KTO tourist information centre** (KTO; Map p42; ☑1330; www.visitkorea.or.kr; Gwanghwamun; ◷9am-8pm; Ⓜ Line 1 to Jonggak, Exit 5) has stacks of brochures on every region as well as helpful and well-informed staff. They can book hotels for you and advise you about almost anything. Chat to them also about the nationwide system of **Goodwill Guides** (http://english.visitkorea.or.kr/enu/GK/GK_EN_2_7_3_1.jsp).

Many tourist areas throughout the country have their own tourist information centres, so it's not a problem to locate one – you'll find details in each of the destination chapters.

Travellers with Disabilities

Facilities for travellers with disabilities in Seoul and some other cities are far from perfect but are improving. Most Seoul subway stations have stair lifts, elevators and toilets with wheelchair access and handrails, while buses have ramps to aid wheelchair access. Tourist attractions, especially government-run ones, offer generous discounts or even free entry for people with disabilities and a helper. There are also some hotels with accessible rooms. For more information see http://english.visitkorea.or.kr/enu/GK/GK_EN_2_5_2.jsp.

Before setting off get in touch with your national support organisation (preferably with the travel officer, if there is one). For general travel advice in Australia contact **Nican** (☑02-6241 1220; www.nican.com.au); in the UK contact **Tourism For All** (☑0845-124 9971; www.tourismforall.org.uk); in the USA try **Accessible Journeys** (☑800-846 4537; www.disabilitytravel.com), an agency specialising in travel for the disabled, or **Mobility International USA** (☑541-343 1284; www.miusa.org).

Visas

Tourist Visas

With a confirmed onward ticket, visitors from the USA, nearly all West European countries, New Zealand, Australia and around 30 other countries receive 90-day permits on arrival. Visitors from a handful of countries receive 30-day permits, while 60-day permits are given to citizens of Italy and Portugal. Canadians receive a six-month permit.

About 30 countries – including the Russian Federation, China, India and Nigeria – do not qualify for visa exemptions. Citizens from these countries must apply for a tourist visa, which allows a stay of 90 days.

Visitors cannot extend their stay beyond 90 days except in situations such as a medical emergency. More info is at www.mofat.go.kr and ww.moj.go.kr.

Work Visas

Applications for a work visa can be made inside Korea but you must leave the country to pick up the visa. You can also apply for a one-year work visa before entering Korea but it can take a few weeks to process. Note that the visa authorities will want to see originals (not photocopies) of your educational qualifications. This a safeguard against fake degree certificates.

You don't need to leave Korea to renew a work visa as long as you carry on working for the same employer. But if you change employers you must normally apply for a new visa and pick it up outside Korea.

If you are working or studying in Korea on a long-term visa, it is necessary to apply for an alien registration

---

TRANSLATION & COUNSELLING SERVICES

If you need interpretation help or information on practically any topic, any time of the day or night you can call either of the following:

» **BBB** (☑1588 5644; bbbkorea.org)
» **Tourist Phone Number** In Seoul ☑1330 or ☑02-1330 from a mobile phone; for outside of Seoul dial the provincial or metropolitan code first – so for information on Gangwon-do, dial ☑033-1330

card (ARC) within 90 days of arrival, which costs ₩10,000. This is done at your local immigration office.

The main **Seoul Immigration office** (☑2650 6212; http://seoul.immigration .go.kr; Mok-dong; ☉9am-6pm Mon-Fri; Ⓜ Line 5 to Omokgyo, Exit 7) is always busy, so take something to read. To reach it, carry straight on from the subway exit and walk along the road until it ends, where you'll see a white-tiled building on your left with a big blue sign in English. An Immigration Office at **Seoul Global Centre** (Map p48) can help with issues related to D8 and any C-type visa.

Volunteering

Volunteers are always needed to teach English and entertain children who live in orphanages. Koreans are very reluctant to adopt children, partly because of the huge educational costs and partly because of the traditional emphasis on blood lines. Charities working in this area include US-based **Korean Kids & Orphanage Outreach Mission** (http:// kkoom.org) and **HOPE** (Helping Others Prosper through English; www.alwayshope.or.kr), a Korean-based nonprofit run by foreign English teachers that helps out at orphanages, assists low-income and disadvantaged children with free English lessons and serves food to the homeless.

In Seoul, the Seoul Global Center is a good place to start looking for other volunteer possibilities. More charities and organisations with volunteer opportunities:

Amnesty International (www.amnesty.or.kr/index .htm) Works mainly on raising awareness in Korea about international human rights issues.

Cross-Cultural Awareness Program (CCAP; http:// ccap.Unesco.or.kr/) Volunteer activities for this Unesco-run program include presenting a class about your own

culture to Korean young people, in a Korean public school, or on a weekend trip to a remote area.

Korea Women's Hot Line (KWHL; ☑02-2269 2962; http://eng.hotline.or.kr) Nationwide organisation with 25 branches that also runs a shelter for abused women.

Korean Federation for Environmental Movement (KFEM; ☑735 7000; http:// english.kfem.or.kr) Offers volunteer opportunities on various environmental projects and campaigns.

Korean Unwed Mothers' Families Association (KUMFA; www.facebook.com/ groups/kumfa) Provides support to single mums.

Seoul International Women's Association (www .siwapage.com) Organises fundraising events to help charities across Korea.

Seoul Volunteer Center (http://volunteer.seoul.go.kr) Opportunities to get involved in language and culture teaching, environmental clean ups and helping out at social welfare centres.

World Wide Opportunities on Organic Farms (WWOOF; ☑723 4510; www .wwoofkorea.co.kr) Welcomes volunteer workers to farms across Korea who work five to seven hours a day, five to six days a week in return for free board and lodging.

Women Travellers

Korea is a relatively crime-free country for all tourists, including women, but the usual precautions should be taken. Korea is a very male-dominated society, although it is becoming less so.

Work

Although a few other opportunities are available for work (particularly for those with Korean language skills), the biggest demand is for English teachers.

Native English teachers on a one-year contract can expect to earn around ₩2.5 million or more a month, with a furnished apartment, return flights, 50% of medical insurance, 10 days paid holiday and a one-month completion bonus all included in the package. Income tax is very low (around 4%), although a 4.5% pension contribution (reclaimable by some nationalities) is compulsory.

Most English teachers work in a *hagwon* (private language school) but some are employed by universities or government schools. Company classes, English camps and teaching via the telephone are also possible, as is private tutoring, although this is technically illegal. Teaching hours in a *hagwon* are usually around 30 hours a week and are likely to involve split shifts, and evening and Saturday classes.

A degree in any subject is sufficient as long as English is your native language. However, it's a good idea to obtain some kind of English-teaching qualification before you arrive, as this increases your options and you should be able to find (and do) a better job.

Some *hagwon* owners are less than ideal employers and don't pay all that they promise; do some research before committing yourself. Ask any prospective employer for the email addresses of foreign English teachers working at the *hagwon,* and contact them for their opinion and advice. If you change employers, you will usually need to obtain a new work visa, which requires you to leave the country to pick up your new visa. Your new employer may pick up all or at least part of the tab for this.

The best starting point for finding out more about the English-teaching scene is the **Association for Teachers of English in Korea** (ATEK; www.atek.or.kr).

Transport

GETTING THERE & AWAY

Entering the Country

Most visitors don't need a visa, but if your country is not on the visa-free list, you will need one (see p391).

Air

Airports & Airlines

Most international flights leave from Incheon International Airport (p90), connected to Seoul by road (80 minutes) and train (60 minutes). There are also some international flights (mainly to China and Japan) from Gimpo International Airport (p90), Gimhae International Airport (p192) for Busan, and Jeju International Airport (p238). View www.airport .co.kr for information on all the airports.

Tickets

Good deals can be found online and with discount agencies. Korean airport departure taxes are included in the ticket price.

Prices of flights from Korea can increase 50% in July and August, and special offers are less common during holiday periods. The peak of the peak for outbound flights is early August, when it can be difficult to find a seat.

Sea

International ferries are worth considering if you're travelling around North Asia.

China

Ferries link a dozen Chinese ports with Incheon (p110).

Japan

Regular ferries shuttle between Busan and four Japanese cities: Fukuoka, Shimonoseki, Osaka and Tsushima. Faster services are available on **hydrofoils** (**www.mirejet.co.kr**) from Busan to Fukuoka – see p193 for full details.

Korail (www.korail.com) Korea-Japan Joint Railroad Ticket lasts a week and offers discounts of up to 30% on train fares in Korea and Japan and on ferry tickets between the two countries from Busan.

Russia

DBS Cruise Ferry Co (www .dbsferry.com) runs the ferry 'Eastern Dream' that makes the trip from Donghae in Gangwon-do to Vladivostok on a regular basis; check the company website for fares and the schedule, which varies by season.

GETTING AROUND

South Korea is a public-transport dream come true. Planes, trains and express buses link major cities, intercity buses link cities and towns large and small,

---

CLIMATE CHANGE & TRAVEL

Every form of transport that relies on carbon-based fuel generates CO_2, the main cause of human-induced climate change. Modern travel is dependent on aeroplanes, which might use less fuel per kilometre per person than most cars but travel much greater distances. The altitude at which aircraft emit gases (including CO_2) and particles also contributes to their climate change impact. Many websites offer 'carbon calculators' that allow people to estimate the carbon emissions generated by their journey and, for those who wish to do so, to offset the impact of the greenhouse gases emitted with contributions to portfolios of climate-friendly initiatives throughout the world. Lonely Planet offsets the carbon footprint of all staff and author travel.

while local buses provide a surprisingly good service to national and provincial parks and villages in outlying rural areas. Car ferries ply numerous routes to offshore islands. Local urban buses, subways and taxis make getting around cities and towns easy. All transport works on the Korean *ppalli ppalli* (hurry hurry) system, so buses and trains leave on time, and buses and taxis tend to be driven fast with little regard to road rules.

Air

Korean Air and Asiana, the two major domestic airlines, provide flights to and from a dozen local airports, and charge frequently identical but very reasonable fares – competition is being supplied by a handful of budget airlines. Gimpo International Airport handles nearly all of Seoul's domestic flights, but Incheon International Airport also has a handful of domestic flights to Busan, Daegu and Jeju-do. The longest flight time is just over an hour between Seoul Gimpo and Jeju-do.

Fares are 15% cheaper from Monday to Thursday, when seats are easier to obtain. Flights on public holidays have a surcharge and are often booked out. Students and children receive discounts, and foreigners should always carry their passports on domestic flights for ID purposes.

Airlines in Korea

South Korea's domestic carriers include the following:

Air Busan (☑1666 3060; http://flyairbusan.com)
Asiana Airlines (☑1588 8000; http://flyasiana.com/index.htm)
Eastar Jet (☑1544 0080; www.eastarjet.com)
Jeju Air (☑1599 1500; http://en.jejuair.net)
Korean Air (☑1588 2001; www.koreanair.com)
T'way Air (☑1688 8686; www.twayair.com)

Bicycle

The Korean government has been promoting cycling as a green and healthy means of transport. Seoul's metropolitan government has also expanded cycling infrastructure in the city. However, something will have to be done about poor local driving habits though, because currently these make cycling in Korea a less than pleasurable experience, especially in urban areas.

This said, hiring a bike for short trips in areas with bike paths or little traffic is a good idea. Bicycle hire starts at ₩3000 an hour, with discount available for a day's hire. You'll have to leave your passport or negotiate some other ID or deposit. Helmets are typically not available and you may need your own padlock.

Jan Boonstra's website **Bicycling in Korea** (http://user.chollian.net/~boonstra/korea/cycle.htm) has some useful information.

Boat

Korea has an extensive network of ferries that connects hundreds of offshore islands to each other and to the mainland. Services from Incheon's Yeonan Pier connect to a dozen nearby and more distant islands, while other west-coast islands further south can be reached from Daecheon harbour and Gunsan.

ISLAND	MAIN-LAND PORT(S)	DETAILS
Jeju-do (Jeju-si)	Incheon, Mokpo, Wando, Sam-chunpo	p238
Jeju-do (Seong-san-ri)	Janghe-ung	p243
Ulle-ungdo	Pohang	p172

Bus

Long-distance buses whiz to every nook and cranny of the country, every 15 minutes between major cities and towns, and at least hourly to

SUSTAINABLE TRAVEL

Unless you're already based in Asia a journey to Korea not using a flight is most likely off the cards. When the train link between North and South Korea resumes it will open the way to the development of a Seoul–London train journey. For now though, such a trip remains a distant dream.

The most direct rail route for getting to this side of the world from Europe or Asia is to ride the Trans-Siberian Railway. Lonely Planet's *Trans-Siberian Railway* guide provides the low-down on how to get to Vladivostok, from where it's possible to hop on a ferry to Sokcho. There are also regular ferries to Korea from several ports in China or from Japan.

Once in Korea it's far easier to do your bit for the environment by using the country's excellent public transport system. Seoul's extensive subway and train system is particularly impressive and the city is in the process of moving over to low-polluting natural-gas buses as well as full-hybrid and fuel-cell electric buses.

K-SHUTTLE BUS TOURS

In 2012, the foreigner-only **K-shuttle** (k-shuttle .com) tour bus service was launched. Starting from Seoul, a couple of three days/two nights packages (₩290,000) are available, including accommodation, breakfast, a guide who speaks English, Japanese or Chinese, and admission fees to various tourist sites along the way:

» **Southwest Course** Stops in Buyeo, Jeonju, Yeosu and Busan before returning to Seoul.

» **Southeast Course** Stops in Gangneurig, Pyeonchang, Wonju, Andong, Gyeongju and Busan before returning to Seoul.

It's also possible to use the service to cover one or more sectors of a tour without the package component; for example, the fare from Seoul to Jeonju is ₩42,000 or to Andong ₩70,000.

Reserve your place on the 35-seater coaches at least five days in advance. There is no designated seating.

small towns, villages, temples and national and provincial parks. Only a selection of bus destinations are given in the transport sections of each city, town or tourist site covered. All the bus frequencies given are approximate, as buses don't usually run on a regular timetable and times vary throughout the day. Bus terminals have staff on hand to ensure that everyone boards the right bus, so help is always available. Most buses don't have toilets on board, but on long journeys drivers take a 10-minute rest at a refreshment stop every few hours.

Express buses link major cities, while intercity buses stop more often and serve smaller cities and towns. The buses are similar, but they use separate (often neighbouring) terminals. Expressways have a special bus lane that operates at weekends and reduces delays due to heavy traffic. Buses always leave on time (or even early!) and go to far more places than trains, but are not as comfortable or smooth, so for travelling long distances trains can be the better option.

Udeung (superior-class express buses) have three seats per row instead of four, but cost 50% more than *ilban* (standard buses). Buses that travel after 10pm have a 10% surcharge and are generally superior class.

Expect to pay around ₩4000 for an hour-long journey on a standard bus.

Buses are so frequent that it's not necessary to buy a ticket in advance except on weekends and during holiday periods. Buy tickets at the bus terminals. You can check schedules on www.kobus.co.kr and www.hticket.co.kr.

Car & Motorcycle

Bring Your Own Vehicle

Contact **customs** (http://english.customs.go.kr/) for information on regulations concerning importing your own car. The vast majority of cars running in the country are Korean-made, although a few luxury cars are imported. Repairs and spare parts are not generally available for most imported cars.

Driving Licence

Drivers must have a current (ie issued the year of travel) International Driving Permit, which should be obtained in your home country before arrival in Korea; they are not available in Korea and many car-rental companies will not rent you a vehicle unless you have one.

Car Hire

Not recommended for first-time visitors, but travellers who wish to hire a car must be 21 years or over and must by law have an International Driving Permit (a driving licence from your own country is not acceptable). Rates start at around ₩65,000 per day for a compact car but can be discounted by up to 50%. Insurance costs around ₩10,000 a day, but depends on the level of the excess you choose. Chauffeur service is also an option.

Incheon International Airport has a couple of car-rental agencies. Try **KT Kumho** (www.kumhorent.com) or **Avis** (www.avis.com).

Insurance

Insurance is compulsory for all drivers in Korea. Since the chance of having an accident is higher than in nearly all other developed countries obtain as much cover as you can, with a low excess.

Road Conditions

Korea has an appalling road-accident record, and foreign drivers in large cities are likely to spend most of their time lost, stuck in traffic jams, looking for a parking space or taking evasive action. Impatient and careless drivers are a major hazard and traffic rules are frequently ignored. Driving in rural areas or on islands such as Jeju-do or Ganghwado is more feasible but public transport is so good that there's little incentive to sit down behind a steering wheel.

Road Rules

Vehicles drive on the right side of the road. The driver and front-seat passenger must wear seatbelts, drunk drivers receive heavy fines, and victims of road accidents are often paid a big sum by drivers wanting to avoid a court case.

Hitching

Accepting a lift anywhere always has an element of risk so we don't recommend it. Also hitching is not a local custom and there is no particular signal for it. However, Korea is relatively crime-free, so if you get stuck in a rural area, stick out your thumb and the chances are that some kind person will give you a lift. Drivers often go out of their way to help foreigners. Normally bus services are frequent and cheap enough, even in the countryside, to make hitching unnecessary.

Local Transport

Bus

Local city buses provide a frequent and inexpensive service (around ₩1000 a trip, irrespective of how far you travel), and although rural buses provide a less frequent service, many run on an hourly or half-hourly basis. Put the fare in the glass box next to the driver –

make sure you have plenty of ₩1000 notes because the machines only give coins in change.

The main problem with local buses is finding and getting on the right bus – bus timetables, bus-stop names and destination signs on buses are rarely in English, and bus drivers don't speak English. Writing your destination in big *hangeul* (Korean phonetic alphabet) letters on a piece of paper will be helpful. Local tourist information centres usually have English-speaking staff, and are the best places to find out which local bus number goes where, and where to pick it up.

Subway

Six cities have a subway system: Seoul, Busan, Daejeon, Daegu, Gwangju and Incheon. The subway is a cheap and convenient way of getting around these major cities, and since signs and station names are in English as well as Korean, the systems are foreigner-friendly and easy to use.

Taxi

Taxis are numerous almost everywhere and fares are inexpensive. Every taxi has a meter that works on a distance basis but switches to a time basis when the vehicle is stuck in a traffic jam. Tipping is not a local custom and is not expected or necessary.

Ilban (regular taxis) cost around ₩2400 for the first 2km, while the *mobeom* (deluxe taxis) that exist in some cities cost around ₩4500 for the first 3km.

Any expressway tolls are added to the fare. In the countryside check the fare first as there are local quirks, such as surcharges or a fixed rate to out-of-the-way places with little prospect of a return fare.

Since few taxi drivers speak any English, plan how to communicate with the driver; if you have a mobile phone you can also use the ☏1330 tourist advice line to help with interpretation. Ask to be dropped off at a nearby landmark if the driver doesn't understand what you're saying or doesn't know where it is. It can be useful to write down your destination or a nearby landmark in *hangeul* on a piece of paper.

Train

South Korea has an excellent but not comprehensive train network operated by **Korean National Railroad** (☏1599 7777; www.korail.go.kr). Trains are clean, comfortable and punctual, and just about every station has a sign in Korean and English. Trains are the best option for long-distance travel.

If you plan to travel by train a lot over a short period consider buying a 'KR pass' – see the website for details.

Classes

The fastest train is the Korea Train Express (KTX). A grade down are *Saemaeul* services, which also only stop in major towns. *Mugunghwa* trains are also comfortable and fast but stop more often.

Many trains have a train cafe where you not only buy drinks and snack foods but also surf the internet, play computer games, even sing karaoke. If a train is standing-room only, hanging out in the train cafe for the journey is the best way to go.

T-MONEY CARDS

Bus, subway, taxi and train fares can all be paid using the rechargeable, touch-and-go **T-Money card** (http://eng.t-money.co.kr); the card provides a ₩100 discount per trip. The basic card can be bought for a nonrefundable ₩3000 at any subway station booth, bus kiosks and convenience stores displaying the T-Money logo across the country; reload it with credit at any of the aforementioned places and get money refunded that hasn't been used (up to ₩20,000 minus a processing fee of ₩500) at subway machines and participating convenience stores before you leave.

Costs

The full range of discounts is complicated and confusing. For fares and schedules see the Korail website. KTX trains are 40% more expensive than *Saemaul* trains (and KTX 1st class is another 40%). *Saemaul* 1st class is 22% more than the standard *Saemaul* fare. *Saemaul* standard fares are 50% more than *Mugunghwa* class. KTX tickets are discounted 7% to 20% if you buy them seven to 30 days before departure. Tickets are discounted 15% from Monday to Friday, and *ipseokpyo* (standing tickets) are discounted 15% to 30% depending on the length of the journey; with a standing ticket, you are allowed to sit on any unoccupied seats. Children travel for half price any time; over 65-year-olds receive a 30% discount Monday to Friday.

Reservations

The railway ticketing system is computerised and you can buy tickets up to a month in advance online, at train stations and many travel agencies. Seat reservations are sensible and necessary on weekends, holidays and other busy times.

Train Passes

Foreigners can buy a **KR Pass** (www.korail.com/kr_pass .jsp) at overseas travel agencies or online; it offers unlimited rail travel (including KTX services) for one/three/five/seven/10 consecutive days at a cost of ₩58,200/84,600/127,000/160,000/185,000. Children (four to 12 years) receive a 50% discount, and youths (13 to 25 years old) receive a 20% discount.

However, distances in Korea are not great, and trains don't go everywhere, so the pass is unlikely to save you much, if any, money unless you plan to shuttle even more frequently than a Lonely Planet researcher back and forth across the country.

WANT MORE?

For in-depth language information and handy phrases, check out Lonely Planet's *Korean Phrasebook*. You'll find it at **shop .lonelyplanet.com**, or you can buy Lonely Planet's iPhone phrasebooks at the Apple App Store.

Language

Korean belongs to the Ural-Altaic language family and is spoken by around 80 million people. The standard language of South Korea is based on the dialect of Seoul.

Korean script, *hangeul,* is simple and accessible, as each character represents a sound of its own. There are a number of competing Romanisation systems in use today for *hangeul*. Since 2000, the government has been changing road signs to reflect the most recent Romanisation system, so you may encounter signs, maps and tourist literature with at least two different Romanisation systems.

Korean pronunciation is pretty straightforward for English speakers, as most sounds are also found in English or have a close approximation. If you follow our coloured pronunciation guides, you should be understood just fine. Korean distinguishes between aspirated consonants (formed by making a puff of air as they're pronounced) and unaspirated ones (pronounced without a puff of air). In our pronunciation guides, aspirated consonants (except for s and h) are followed by an apostrophe ('). Syllables are pronounced with fairly even emphasis in Korean.

BASICS

Hello.	안녕하세요.	an·nyŏng ha·se·yo
Goodbye. (if leaving/ staying)	안녕히 계세요/ 가세요.	an·nyŏng·hi kye·se·yo/ ka·se·yo
Yes.	네.	né
No.	아니요.	a·ni·yo
Excuse me.	실례합니다.	shil·lé ham·ni·da
Sorry.	죄송합니다.	choé·song ham·ni·da

| Thank you. | 고맙습니다./ 감사합니다. | ko·map·sŭm·ni·da/ kam·sa·ham·ni·da |
| You're welcome. | 천만에요. | ch'ŏn·ma·ne·yo |

How are you?
안녕하세요? — an·nyŏng ha·se·yo

Fine, thanks. And you?
네. 안녕하세요? — ne an·nyŏng ha·se·yo

What is your name?
성함을 여쭤봐도 될까요? — sŏng·ha·mŭl yŏ·tchŏ·bwa·do doélk·ka·yo

My name is ...
제 이름은 ...입니다. — che i·rŭ·mŭn ...·im·ni·da

Do you speak English?
영어 하실 줄 아시나요? — yŏng·ŏ ha·shil·jul a·shi·na·yo

I don't understand.
못 알아 들었어요. — mot a·ra·dŭ·rŏss·ŏ·yo

ACCOMMODATION

Do you have a ... room?	... 룸 있나요?	... rum in·na·yo
single	싱글	shing·gŭl
double	더블	tŏ·bŭl
twin	트윈	t'ŭ·win

How much per ...?	...에 얼마예요?	...·é ŏl·ma·ye·yo
night	하룻밤	ha·rup·pam
person	한 명	han·myŏng
week	일주일	il·chu·il

air-con	냉방	naeng·bang
bathroom	욕실	yok·shil
internet	인터넷	in·t'ŏ·net
toilet	화장실	hwa·jang·shil
window	창문	ch'ang·mun

Is breakfast included?
아침 포함인가요?   a·ch'im p'o·ha·min·ga·yo

DIRECTIONS

Where's a/the ...?
... 어디 있나요?   ... ŏ·di in·na·yo

What's the address?
주소가 뭐예요?   chu·so·ga mwŏ·ye·yo

Could you please write it down?
적어 주시겠어요?   chŏ·gŏ ju·shi·gess·ŏ·yo

Please show me (on the map).
(지도에서) 어디인지   (chi·do·e·sŏ) ŏ·di·in·ji
가르쳐 주세요.   ka·rŭ·ch'ŏ ju·se·yo

Turn left/right.
좌회전/   chwa·hoé·jŏn/
우회전 하세요.   u·hoé·jŏn ha·se·yo

Turn at the ...	...에서 도세요.	....e·sŏ to·se·yo
corner	모퉁이	mo·t'ung·i
pedestrian crossing	횡단 보도	hoéng·dan· bo·do

It's ...	... 있어요.	... iss·ŏ·yo
behind ...	... 뒤에	... dwi·é
in front of ...	... 앞에	... a·p'é
near ...	... 가까이에	... kak·ka·i·é
next to ...	... 옆에	... yŏ·p'é
on the corner	모퉁이에	mo·t'ung·i·é
opposite ...	... 반대 편에	... pan·dae· p'yŏ·né
straight ahead	정면에	chŏng·myŏ·né

EATING & DRINKING

Can we see the menu?
메뉴 볼 수 있나요?   me·nyu bol·su in·na·yo

What would you recommend?
추천   ch'u·ch'ŏn
해 주시겠어요?   hae·ju·shi·gess·ŏ·yo

Do you have any vegetarian dishes?
채식주의 음식   ch'ae·shik·chu·i ŭm·shik
있나요?   in·na·yo

I'd like ..., please.
... 주세요.   ... ju·se·yo

Cheers!
건배!   kŏn·bae

That was delicious!
맛있었어요!   ma·shiss·ŏss·ŏ·yo

KEY PATTERNS

To get by in Korean, mix and match these simple patterns with words of your choice:

When's (the next bus)?
(다음 버스) 언제   (ta·ŭm bŏ·sŭ) ŏn·jé
있나요?   in·na·yo

Where's (the train/subway station)?
(역) 어디예요?   (yŏk) ŏ·di·ye·yo

I'm looking for (a hotel).
(호텔) 찾고   (ho·t'el) ch'ak·ko
있어요.   iss·ŏ·yo

Do you have (a map)?
(지도) 가지고   (chi·do) ka·ji·go
계신가요?   kye·shin·ga·yo

Is there (a toilet)?
(화장실) 있나요?   (hwa·jang·shil) in·na·yo

I'd like (the menu).
(메뉴) 주세요.   (me·nyu) ju·se·yo

I'd like to (hire a car).
(차 빌리고)   (ch'a pil·li·go)
싶어요.   shi·p'ŏ·yo

Could you please (help me)?
(저를 도와)   (chŏ·rŭl to·wa)
주시겠어요?   ju·shi·gess·ŏ·yo

How much is (a room)?
(방) 얼마예요?   (pang) ŏl·ma·ye·yo

Do I need (a visa)?
(비자) 필요한가요?   (pi·ja) p'i·ryo·han·ga·yo

Please bring the bill.
계산서 가져다   kye·san·sŏ ka·jŏ·da
주세요.   ju·se·yo

I'd like to reserve a table for ...	... 테이블 예약해 주세요.	... t'e·i·bŭl ye·ya·k'ae ju·se·yo
(eight) o'clock	(여덟) 시	(yŏ·dŏl)·shi
(two) people	(두) 명	(tu)·myŏng

Key Words

bar	술집	sul·chip
bottle	병	pyŏng
bowl	사발	sa·bal
breakfast	아침	a·ch'im
chopsticks	젓가락	chŏk·ka·rak
cold	차가운	ch'a·ga·un
dinner	저녁	chŏ·nyŏk
fork	포크	p'o·k'ŭ
glass	잔	chan

Signs

영업 중	Open
휴무	Closed
입구	Entrance
출구	Exit
... 금지	...Prohibited
금연 구역	No Smoking Area
화장실	Toilets
신사용	Men
숙녀용	Women

hot (warm)	뜨거운	ddŭ·gŏ·un
knife	칼	k'al
lunch	점심	chŏm·shim
market	시장	shi·jang
plate	접시	chŏp·shi
restaurant	식당	shik·tang
snack	간식	kan·shik
spicy (hot)	매운	mae·un
spoon	숟가락	suk·ka·rak

Meat & Fish

beef	쇠고기	soé·go·gi
chicken	닭고기	tak·ko·gi
duck	오리	o·ri
fish	생선	saeng·sŏn
herring	청어	ch'ŏng·ŏ
lamb	양고기	yang·go·gi
meat	고기	ko·gi
mussel	홍합	hong·hap
oyster	굴	kul
pork	돼지고기	twae·ji·go·gi
prawn	대하	tae·ha
salmon	연어	yŏ·nŏ
seafood	해물	hae·mul
tuna	참치	ch'am·ch'i
turkey	칠면조	ch'il·myŏn·jo
veal	송아지 고기	song·a·ji·go·gi

Fruit & Vegetables

apple	사과	sa·gwa
apricot	살구	sal·gu
bean	콩	k'ong
capsicum	고추	ko·ch'u
carrot	당근	tang·gŭn
corn	옥수수	ok·su·su
cucumber	오이	o·i
eggplant	가지	ka·ji
fruit	과일	kwa·il
legume	콩류	k'ong·nyu
lentil	렌즈콩	ren·jŭ·k'ong
lettuce	양상추	yang·sang·ch'u
mushroom	버섯	pŏ·sŏt
nut	견과류	kyŏn·gwa·ryu
onion	양파	yang·p'a
orange	오렌지	o·ren·ji
pea	완두콩	wan·du·k'ong
peach	복숭아	pok·sung·a
pear	배	pae
plum	자두	cha·du
potato	감자	kam·ja
pumpkin	늙은 호박	nŭl·gŭn ho·bak
spinach	시금치	shi·gŭm·ch'i
strawberry	딸기	ddal·gi
tomato	토마토	t'o·ma·t'o
vegetable	야채	ya·ch'ae
watermelon	수박	su·bak

Other

bread	빵	bbang
cheese	치즈	ch'i·jŭ
egg	계란	kye·ran
honey	꿀	ggul
noodles	국수	kuk·su
rice (cooked)	밥	pap
salt	소금	so·gŭm
soup	수프	su·p'ŭ
sugar	설탕	sŏl·t'ang

Drinks

beer	맥주	maek·chu
coffee	커피	k'ŏ·p'i
juice	주스	jus·sŭ
milk	우유	u·yu
mineral water	생수	saeng·su
red wine	레드 와인	re·dŭ wa·in
soft drink	탄산 음료	t'an·san ŭm·nyo
tea	차	ch'a
water	물	mul
white wine	화이트 와인	hwa·i·t'ŭ wa·in

EMERGENCIES

Help!	도와주세요!	to·wa·ju·se·yo
Go away!	저리 가세요!	chŏ·ri ka·se·yo

Call ...!	... 불러주세요!	... pul·lŏ·ju·se·yo
a doctor	의사	ŭi·sa
the police	경찰	kyŏng·ch'al

I'm lost.
길을 잃었어요.   ki·rŭl i·rŏss·ŏ·yo

Where's the toilet?
화장실이   hwa·jang·shi·ri
어디예요?   ŏ·di·ye·yo

I'm sick.
전 아파요.   chŏn a·p'a·yo

It hurts here.
여기가 아파요.   yŏ·gi·ga a·p'a·yo

I'm allergic to ...
전 ...에   chŏn ...é
알레르기가 있어요.   al·le·rŭ·gi·ga iss·ŏ·yo

SHOPPING & SERVICES

I'm just looking.
그냥   kŭ·nyang
구경할게요.   ku·gyŏng halk·ke·yo

Do you have (tissues)?
(휴지) 있나요?   (hyu·ji) in·na·yo

How much is it?
얼마예요?   ŏl·ma·ye·yo

Can you write down the price?
가격을 써   ka·gyŏ·gŭl ssŏ
주시겠어요?   ju·shi·gess·ŏ·yo

Can I look at it?
보여 주시겠어요?   po·yŏ ju·shi·gess·ŏ·yo

Do you have any others?
다른 건 없나요?   ta·rŭn·gŏn ŏm·na·yo

That's too expensive.
너무 비싸요.   nŏ·mu piss·a·yo

Please give me a discount.
깎아 주세요.   ggak·ka·ju·se·yo

Question Words

how	어떻게	ŏt·tŏ·k'é
what (object)	무엇을	mu·ŏ·sŭl
what (subject)	뭐가	mwŏ·ga
when	언제	ŏn·jé
where	어디	ŏ·di
which	어느	ŏ·nŭ
who (object)	누구를	nu·gu·rŭl
who (subject)	누가	nu·ga
why	왜	wae

There's a mistake in the bill.
계산서가   kye·san·sŏ
이상해요.   i·sang·hae·yo

ATM	현급인출기	hyŏn·gŭ·min·ch'ul·gi
internet cafe	PC방	p'i·shi·bang
post office	우체국	u·ch'e·guk
tourist office	관광안내소	kwan·gwang an·nae·so

TIME & DATES

What time is it?
몇 시예요?   myŏs·shi·ye·yo

It's (two) o'clock.
(두) 시요.   (tu)·shi·yo

Half past (two).
(두) 시 삼십 분이요.   (tu)·shi sam·ship·pu·ni·yo

At what time ...?
몇 시에 ...?   myŏs·shi·é ...

At (five) o'clock.
(다섯) 시에.   (ta·sŏs)·shi·é

morning	아침	a·ch'im
afternoon	오후	o·hu
evening	저녁	chŏ·nyŏk
yesterday	어제	ŏ·jé
today	오늘	o·nŭl
tomorrow	내일	nae·il

Monday	월요일	wŏ·ryo·il
Tuesday	화요일	hwa·yo·il
Wednesday	수요일	su·yo·il
Thursday	목요일	mo·gyo·il
Friday	금요일	kŭ·myo·il
Saturday	토요일	t'o·yo·il
Sunday	일요일	i·ryo·il

January	일월	i·rwŏl
February	이월	i·wŏl
March	삼월	sa·mwŏl
April	사월	sa·wŏl
May	오월	o·wŏl
June	유월	yu·wŏl
July	칠월	ch'i·rwŏl
August	팔월	p'a·rwŏl
September	구월	ku·wŏl
October	시월	shi·wŏl
November	십일월	shi·bi·rwŏl
December	십이월	shi·bi·wŏl

Numbers

Use pure Korean numbers for hours when telling the time, for counting objects and people, and for expressing your age.

1	하나	ha·na
2	둘	tul
3	셋	set
4	넷	net
5	다섯	ta·sŏt
6	여섯	yŏ·sŏt
7	일곱	il·gop
8	여덟	yŏ·dŏl
9	아홉	a·hop
10	열	yŏl

Use Sino-Korean numbers for minutes when telling the time, for dates and months, and for addresses, phone numbers, money and floors of a building.

1	일	il
2	이	i
3	삼	sam
4	사	sa
5	오	o
6	육	yuk
7	칠	ch'il
8	팔	p'al
9	구	ku
10	십	ship

TRANSPORT

Public Transport

A ... ticket (to Daegu), please.	(대구 가는) ... 표 주세요.	(tae·gu ka·nŭn) ... p'yo chu·se·yo
1st-class	일등석	il·dŭng·sŏk
one-way	편도	p'yŏn·do
return	왕복	wang·bok
standard class	일반석	il·ban·sŏk
standing room	입석	ip·sŏk

When's the ... (bus)?	... (버스) 언제 있나요?	... (bŏ·sŭ) ŏn·jé in·na·yo
first	첫	ch'ŏt
last	마지막	ma·ji·mak

Which ... goes to (Myeongdong)?	어느 ...이/가 (명동)에 가나요?	ŏ·nŭ ...i/·ga (myŏng·dong)·é ka·na·yo
boat	배	pae
bus	버스	bŏ·sŭ
metro line	지하철 노선	chi·ha·ch'ŏl no·sŏn
train	기차	ki·ch'a

platform	타는 곳	t'a·nŭn·got
ticket machine	표 자판기	p'yo cha·pan·gi
timetable display	시간표	shi·gan·p'yo
transportation card	교통카드	kyo·t'ong k'a·dŭ

At what time does it get to (Busan)?
(부산)에 언제 도착하나요? (pu·san)·é ŏn·jé to·ch'a·k'a·na·yo

Does it stop at (Gyeongju)?
(경주) 가나요? (kyŏng·ju) ka·na·yo

Please tell me when we get to (Daejeon).
(대전)에 도착하면 좀 알려주세요. (tae·jŏn)·é to·ch'a·k'a·myŏn chom al·lyŏ·ju·se·yo

Please take me to (Insa-dong).
(인사동)으로 가 주세요. (in·sa·dong)·ŭ·ro ka·ju·se·yo

Driving & Cycling

I'd like to hire a ...	... 빌리고 싶어요.	... pil·li·go shi·p'ŏ·yo
4WD	사륜구동	sa·ryun·gu·dong
car	차	ch'a

I'd like to hire a bicycle.
자전거 빌리려고요. cha·jŏn·gŏ pil·li·ryŏ·go·yo

Do I need a helmet?
헬멧 써야 하나요? hel·met ssŏ·ya ha·na·yo

Is this the road to (Donghae)?
이게 (동해) 가는 길인가요? i·gé (tong·hae) ka·nŭn ki·rin·ga·yo

(How long) Can I park here?
(얼마 동안) 여기 주차해도 되나요? (ŏl·ma·dong·an) yŏ·gi chu·ch'a·hae·do doé·na·yo

Where's a petrol station?
주유소가 어디있나요? chu·yu·so·ga ŏ·di·in·na·yo

I need a mechanic.
자동차정비사가 필요해요. cha·dong·ch'a chŏng·bi·sa·ga p'i·ryo·hae·yo

I'd like my bicycle repaired.
자전거 고치려고요. cha·jŏn·gŏ ko·ch'i·ryŏ·go·yo

GLOSSARY

For more food and drink terms, see the Food Glossary (p368).

ajumma – a married or older woman
~am – hermitage
anju – snacks eaten when drinking alcohol

bang – room
bawi – large rock
~bong – peak
buk~ – north
buncheong – Joseon-era pottery with simple designs

celadon – green-tinged pottery from early 12th century
cha – tea
~cheon – small stream
Chuseok – Thanksgiving Day

dae~ – great, large
dancheong – ornate, multi-coloured eaves that adorn Buddhist temples and other buildings
Dangun – mythical founder of Korea
DEP – Democratic Party
DMZ – the Demilitarized Zone that runs along the 38th parallel of the Korean peninsula, separating North and South
-do – province, also island
-dong – neighbourhood or village
dong~ – east
donggul – cave
DPRK – Democratic People's Republic of Korea (North Korea)
DVD-bang – room for watching DVDs

-eup – town

-ga – section of a long street
~gang – river
geobukseon – 'turtle ships'; iron-clad warships from the late 16th century
gil – small street
-gu – urban district
gugak – traditional Korean music
~gul – cave
-gun – county
~gung – palace
gwageo – Joseon government service exam

hae – sea
haenyeo – traditional female divers of Jeju-do
hagwon – private school where students study after school or work
hallyu – (Korean Wave) increasing global interest in Korean pop culture
hanbok – traditional Korean clothing
hang – harbour
hangul – Korean phonetic alphabet
hanja – Chinese characters
hanji – traditional Korean handmade paper
hanok – traditional Korean one-storey wooden house with a tiled or thatched roof
harubang – lava-rock statues found only on Jeju-do
~ho – lake
hof – local pub

insam – ginseng

jaebeol – huge family-run corporate conglomerate
~jeon – hall of a temple
~jeong – pavilion
jjimjil-bang – upmarket spa and sauna
Juche – North Korean ideology of economic self-reliance

KTO – Korea Tourism Organization
KTX – Korea Train Express; fast 300km/h train service

minbak – private homes with rooms for rent
mudang – female shaman
Mugunghwa – semi-express train
~mun – gate
-myeon – township
~myo – shrine

nam~ – south
~neung – tomb
~no – street
norae-bang – karaoke room
~nyeong – mountain pass

oncheon – hot-spring bath
ondol – underfloor heating system

pansori – traditional Korean solo opera
PC-bang – internet cafe
pension – upmarket accommodation in the countryside or near beaches
pocketball – pool
pokpo – waterfall
pyeong – real-estate measurement equal to 3.3 sq m

~reung – tomb
-ri – village
~ro – street
ROK – Republic of Korea (South Korea)
~ryeong – mountain pass

-sa – temple
Saemaul – luxury express train
samulnori – drum-and-gong dance
~san – mountain
sanjang – mountain hut
sanseong – mountain fortress
seo~ – west
Seon – Korean version of Zen Buddhism
~seong – fortress
seowon – Confucian academy
shamanism – set of traditional beliefs; communication with spirits is done through a *mudang*
~si – city
sijang – market
sijo – short poems about nature and life; popular in the Joseon period
soju – the local firewater; often likened to vodka
ssireum – Korean-style wrestling

taekwondo – Korean martial art
tap – pagoda
tonggeun – commuter-class train

yangban – aristocrat
yeogwan – motel with small en suite
yeoinsuk – small, family-run budget accommodation with shared bathroom
yo – padded quilt that serves as a mattress or futon for sleeping on the floor

behind the scenes

SEND US YOUR FEEDBACK

We love to hear from travellers – your comments keep us on our toes and help make our books better. Our well-travelled team reads every word on what you loved or loathed about this book. Although we cannot reply individually to postal submissions, we always guarantee that your feedback goes straight to the appropriate authors, in time for the next edition. Each person who sends us information is thanked in the next edition – the most useful submissions are rewarded with a selection of digital PDF chapters.

Visit **lonelyplanet.com/contact** to submit your updates and suggestions or to ask for help. Our award-winning website also features inspirational travel stories, news and discussions.

Note: We may edit, reproduce and incorporate your comments in Lonely Planet products such as guidebooks, websites and digital products, so let us know if you don't want your comments reproduced or your name acknowledged. For a copy of our privacy policy visit lonelyplanet.com/privacy.

OUR READERS

Many thanks to the travellers who used the last edition and wrote to us with helpful hints, useful advice and interesting anecdotes:

Trygve Anderson, Martin Arkowitz, William Burnett, Dongkwon Choi, Laura Ciammaruchi, Zillah De Groot, Moritz Eppenstein, Michael Fong, Ashley Gordon, Jane Gray, Khorshid Hakemi, Petros Isaakidis, Bora Kim, Matt Koch, Petr Kuldan, David Lacy, Dana Lamb, Jongkil Lee, Jill Linderwell, Norman Loewenthal, Pál Lővei, Mikael Lypinski, Tony Marshall, Toni Mcnickle, Julie Park, Samuel Park, Sejin Park, Mark Patterson, Stef Russell, Andrea Sacchetti, Florian Sarkar, Karl Scharbert, Pietro Schisler, Colleen Scrocca, Jenn Seva, L Shellenberger, Diego Sommavilla, Amanda Soon, Hal Swindall, Gary Tan, Ursula Theisen, Catherine Threlfall, Kieran Tully, Derek Uram and Jonas Wernli.

AUTHOR THANKS

Simon Richmond

Many thanks to the following: Shin Ok-ja and her team at KTO, Maureen O'Crowley, Kim Heesun, Park Seo-Young, Daniel Gray, Elly Kim, Matt Kelly, Sam Hammington, Aram Kim, Hassan Haider, Shin Haein, Ray Kang, David Kilburn, Zhang Ki Chul, Shin Ok-ja, Jesse Lord, Angela Hong, the great staff at Han Suites, Ko Min-jung, Ivy Lee, Ralf Deutsch, Darryl Coote, Todd Thaker, and Kendra, Jamie and Alistair in Jeju-si. And Neil for his loving support and keeping my creative juices flowing.

Shawn Low

As always thanks to the commissioning editor, Glenn, for believing and, more importantly, hiring! Cheers also to coordinating author Simon (yet another one done and dusted!). Thanks to the LP crew working on this. Cheers also to friends on the ground, both old and new: Esther and Mark (wishing a happy new life to you both in Vietnam), Shin Ok-ja at KTO and my Swiss-utility-knife buddy Hyun Ha. Much love to Wyn-Lyn: can't wait for our future adventures together.

Timothy N Hornyak

A big *kamsamnida* to Simon Richmond and Lonely Planet staff, and especially Eugene Shim and her cousin Seoyeon for their inspiration, help and kindness. I also thank Shin Ok-ja of KTO, MJ Lee of Gangwon Tourism, Ms Park in Sokcho City Hall, Matthew Choi in Gangneung, Raymond Kim of the Busan CVB, Brian Lee from Los Angeles for joining me on my tour of Namhae, and Wendy at the Jinju National Museum for her amazing assistance around Jinju.

ACKNOWLEDGMENTS

Climate map data adapted from Peel MC, Finlayson BL & McMahon TA (2007) 'Updated World Map of the Köppen-Geiger Climate Classification', *Hydrology and Earth System Sciences*, 11, 163344.
Cover photograph: Guryong-sa temple, Chiaksan National Park, Gangwon-do, Topic Photo Agency/Agefotostock.

This Book

This 9th edition of Lonely Planet's *Korea* guidebook was researched and written by Simon Richmond, Timothy N Hornyak and Shawn Low, and Yu-Mei Balasingamchow wrote the In the Korean Kitchen chapter. The previous edition of this book was written by Simon Richmond, Yu-Mei Balasingamchow, César G Soriano and Rob Whyte.

This guidebook was commissioned in Lonely Planet's Melbourne office, and produced by the following:

Commissioning Editor Glenn van der Knijff

Coordinating Editors Kate James, Kristin Odijk
Coordinating Cartographer Jacqueline Nguyen
Coordinating Layout Designer Frank Deim
Managing Editors Barbara Delissen, Brigitte Ellemor
Senior Editors Andi Jones, Catherine Naghten
Managing Cartographers Corey Hutchison, Adrian Persoglia
Managing Layout Designer Chris Girdler
Assisting Editors Jackey Coyle, Pat Kinsella, Erin Richards, Helen Yeates

Assisting Cartographer Enes Basic
Cover Research Naomi Parker
Internal Image Research Louise Beanland, Aude Vauconsant
Language Content Branislava Vladisavljevic

Thanks to David Connolly, Ryan Evans, Larissa Frost, Mark Griffiths, Jane Hart, Jonathan Hilts-Park, Trent Paton, Kirsten Rawlings, Raphael Richards, Suzannah Shwer, Marg Toohey, Di Von Holdt, Gerard Walker

index

how to use this book

These symbols will help you find the listings you want:

- ◉ Sights
- 🏃 Beaches
- 🏃 Activities
- 🐊 Courses
- ☝ Tours
- 🎊 Festivals & Events
- 🛏 Sleeping
- ✕ Eating
- 🍷 Drinking
- ☆ Entertainment
- 🔒 Shopping
- ① Information/ Transport

These symbols give you the vital information for each listing:

- ☑ Telephone Numbers
- ☺ Opening Hours
- Ⓟ Parking
- ⊖ Nonsmoking
- ❆ Air-Conditioning
- @ Internet Access
- ☎ Wi-Fi Access
- ⊠ Swimming Pool
- ✔ Vegetarian Selection
- ⓜ English-Language Menu
- ⓯ Family-Friendly
- 🐾 Pet-Friendly
- ▣ Bus
- ⏚ Ferry
- Ⓜ Metro
- Ⓢ Subway
- ⊖ London Tube
- ▣ Tram
- ▣ Train

Reviews are organised by author preference.

Look out for these icons:

TOP CHOICE Our author's recommendation

FREE No payment required

🌿 A green or sustainable option

Our authors have nominated these places as demonstrating a strong commitment to sustainability – for example by supporting local communities and producers, operating in an environmentally friendly way, or supporting conservation projects.

Map Legend

Sights
- Beach
- Buddhist
- Castle
- Christian
- Hindu
- Islamic
- Jewish
- Monument
- Museum/Gallery
- Ruin
- Winery/Vineyard
- Zoo
- Other Sight

Activities, Courses & Tours
- Diving/Snorkelling
- Canoeing/Kayaking
- Skiing
- Surfing
- Swimming/Pool
- Walking
- Windsurfing
- Other Activity/ Course/Tour

Sleeping
- Sleeping
- Camping

Eating
- Eating

Drinking
- Drinking
- Cafe

Entertainment
- Entertainment

Shopping
- Shopping

Information
- Bank
- Embassy/ Consulate
- Hospital/Medical
- Internet
- Police
- Post Office
- Telephone
- Toilet
- Tourist Information
- Other Information

Transport
- Airport
- Border Crossing
- Bus
- Cable Car/ Funicular
- Cycling
- Ferry
- Monorail
- Parking
- Petrol Station
- Taxi
- Train/Railway
- Tram
- Underground Train Station
- Other Transport

Routes
- Tollway
- Freeway
- Primary
- Secondary
- Tertiary
- Lane
- Unsealed Road
- Plaza/Mall
- Steps
- Tunnel
- Pedestrian Overpass
- Walking Tour
- Walking Tour Detour
- Path

Geographic
- Hut/Shelter
- Lighthouse
- Lookout
- Mountain/Volcano
- Oasis
- Park
- Pass
- Picnic Area
- Waterfall

Population
- Capital (National)
- Capital (State/Province)
- City/Large Town
- Town/Village

Boundaries
- International
- State/Province
- Disputed
- Regional/Suburb
- Marine Park
- Cliff
- Wall

Hydrography
- River, Creek
- Intermittent River
- Swamp/Mangrove
- Reef
- Canal
- Water
- Dry/Salt/ Intermittent Lake
- Glacier

Areas
- Beach/Desert
- Cemetery (Christian)
- Cemetery (Other)
- Park/Forest
- Sportsground
- Sight (Building)
- Top Sight (Building)

OUR STORY

A beat-up old car, a few dollars in the pocket and a sense of adventure. In 1972 that's all Tony and Maureen Wheeler needed for the trip of a lifetime – across Europe and Asia overland to Australia. It took several months, and at the end – broke but inspired – they sat at their kitchen table writing and stapling together their first travel guide, *Across Asia on the Cheap*. Within a week they'd sold 1500 copies. Lonely Planet was born. Today, Lonely Planet has offices in Melbourne, London, Oakland and Delhi, with more than 600 staff and writers. We share Tony's belief that 'a great guidebook should do three things: inform, educate and amuse'.

OUR WRITERS

Simon Richmond
Coordinating Author; Seoul, Gyeonggi-do & Incheon, Jeju-do Long before he became a travel writer and photographer, Simon spent several years living in Japan. It was from here that he first visited Seoul in 2004. He next returned in 2009 to coordinate Lonely Planet's *Korea*, spending six weeks exploring Seoul and the surrounding areas. For this edition he spent two months living in Seoul before heading to Jeju-do and loved pretty much every minute. Simon has written scores of other titles for Lonely Planet and other publishers, and has contributed features to many travel magazines and newspapers around the world.

Read more about Simon at:
lonelyplanet.com/members/simonrichmond

Shawn Low
Jeollanam-do, Jeollabuk-do, Chungcheongnam-do, Chungcheongbuk-do Shawn grew up in hot, humid, food-crazy Singapore but later made his way to less hot, less humid, food-crazy Melbourne (Australia, not Florida). He's spent the last six years working for Lonely Planet: as an editor, commissioning editor, author, TV host and travel editor. Exploring more than half of Korea via car, bus and ferry is a hard job, but someone's gotta do it. So he did. Post-trip hunger pangs have already struck though... Find Shawn on Twitter @shawnlow.

Read more about Shawn at:
lonelyplanet.com/members/shawnlow

Timothy N Hornyak
Gangwon-do, Busan & Gyeongsangnam-do A native of Montreal, Tim wrote his master's thesis on Korean reunification after a research stint in Seoul. He went on to write about Japanese technology for media including CNET News and *Scientific American*, and has contributed to nine other Lonely Planet guidebooks including *Japan* and *Montréal & Québec City*. He firmly believes that his hometown's greatest contribution to life on Earth is the perfection of the bagel.

Read more about Timothy at:
lonelyplanet.com/members/timothyhornyak

Yu-Mei Balasingamchow
In the Korean Kitchen Yu-Mei lives in Singapore and is the co-author of the popular history title *Singapore: A Biography*. She has covered Vietnam and Korea for Lonely Planet, as well as Singapore and Taiwan for other publications. Her favourite Korean comfort food is *dubu jjigae* and her favourite Korean tipple is *makgeolli* (best enjoyed after a bracing hike up the nearest mountain). Follow her at www.toomanythoughts.org. She tweets at @bubblevicious.

Read more about Yu-Mei at:
lonelyplanet.com/members/tym

Published by Lonely Planet Publications Pty Ltd
ABN 36 005 607 983
9th edition – February 2013
ISBN 978 1 74179 918 7
© Lonely Planet 2013   Photographs © as indicated 2013
10 9 8 7 6 5 4 3 2 1
Printed in China